MW01484596

Risk Management Techniques in Perinatal and Neonatal Practice

Edited by

Steven M. Donn, M.D.
Professor of Pediatrics
Section of Neonatal-Perinatal Medicine
Medical Director, Holden Neonatal Intensive Care Unit
University of Michigan Medical Center
Ann Arbor, Michigan

Charles W. Fisher, J.D.
Senior Partner
Kitch, Drutchas, Wagner & Kenney
Detroit, Michigan

Futura Publishing
Company, Inc.
Armonk, NY

Library of Congress Cataloging-in-Publication Data

Risk management techniques in perinatal and neonatal practice/edited by Steven M. Donn, Charles W. Fisher.

p. cm.

Includes bibliographical references and index.

ISBN 0-87993-640-1 (alk. paper)

1. Forensic obstetrics. 2. Obstetricians—Malpractice. 3. Neonatologists—Malpractice. 4. Obstetrics—Quality control. 5. Neonatology—Quality Control. I. Donn, Steven M. II. Fisher, Charles W., J.D.

[DNLM: 1. Perinatology—organization & administration—United States—legislation. 2. Malpractice—United States. 3. Neonatology—organization & administration—United States—legislation. 4. Obstetrics—organization & administration—United States—legislation. 5. Risk Management—methods—legislation. WQ 34 AA1 R5 1996]

RA 1064.R54 1996

614'.—dc20

DNLM/DLC

for library of Congress

96-12740

CIP

Published by

Futura Publishing Company, Inc.

135 Bedford Road

Armonk, New York 10504

LC #: 96-12740

ISBN #: 0-87993-640-1

Contributors

Stanley M. Berry, M.D.
Assistant Professor of Obstetrics and Gynecology, Division of Maternal-Fetal Medicine, Wayne State University/Hutzel Hospital, Detroit, MI

Kurt Benirschke, M.D.
Professor of Pathology and Reproductive Medicine, University of California-San Diego Medical Center, San Diego, CA

Gerald J. Bloch, J.D.
Senior Partner, Warshafsky, Rotter, Tarnoff, Reinhardt & Bloch, S.C., Milwaukee, WI

James A. Brunberg, M.D.
Associate Professor of Radiology, Neurology, and Neurosurgery, Director, Division of Neuroradiology; Co-Director, Division of Magnetic Resonance Imaging, Department of Radiology, University of Michigan Medical Center, Ann Arbor, MI

Michael P. Burke, B.A.
Director of Risk Management, Providence Hospital, Southfield, MI

Ronald T. Burkman, M.D.
C. Paul Hodgkinson Chair, Department of Gynecology-Obstetrics, Henry Ford Hospital, Detroit, MI

Jeffrey Chilton, J.D.
Kitch, Drutchas, Wagner & Kenney, Detroit, MI

Rosemary Cicala, R.N.
Clinical Nurse Manager, Labor and Delivery, Providence Hospital, Southfield, MI

Rita W. Cikanek, B.S., HCA
Associate Coordinator, Patient/Staff Relations, University of Michigan Medical Center, Ann Arbor, MI

Catherine E. Cochell, B.S.N., R.N.C., C.C.E.
Staff Nurse, Labor and Delivery Unit, Hutzel Hospital, Detroit, MI

Barbara A. Colwell, R.N., M.P.H.
Clinical Nurse Specialist, Perinatal Outreach Coordinator, University of Michigan, Medical Center, Ann Arbor, MI

Marvin Cornblath, M.D.
Professor of Pediatrics, University of Maryland School of Medicine, Baltimore, MD

Margaret Copp Dawson, R.N.
Coordinator, Patient/Staff Relations, University of Michigan Medical Center, Ann Arbor, MI

Virginia Delaney-Black, M.D.
Associate Professor of Pediatrics, Wayne State University; Children's Hospital of Michigan, Detroit, MI

Philip C. Dennen, M.D.
Assistant Clinical Professor, Yale University School of Medicine; Attending Obstetrician-Gynecologist, Waterbury Hospital, Waterbury, CT

Mitchell P. Dombrowski, M.D.
Associate Professor of Obstetrics and Gynecology, Division of Maternal/Fetal Medicine, Wayne State University/Hutzel Hospital, Detroit, MI

Steven M. Donn, M.D.
Professor of Pediatrics, Section of Neonatal-Perinatal Medicine; Medical Director, Holden Neonatal Intensive Care Unit, University of Michigan Medical Center, Ann Arbor, MI

Mark I. Evans, M.D.
Professor and Vice-Chief of Obstetrics/Gynecology, Professor of Molecular Biology & Genetics and Pathology, Director, Division of Reproductive Genetics; Director, Center for Fetal Diagnosis and Therapy, Wayne State University/Hutzel Hospital, Detroit, MI

Roger G. Faix, M.D.
Associate Professor of Pediatrics, Director, Section of Neonatal-Perinatal Medicine, University of Michigan Medical Center, Ann Arbor, MI

Charles W. Fisher, J.D.
Senior Partner, Kitch, Drutchas, Wagner & Kenney, Detroit, MI

Peter L. Forster, B.A., M.B.A.
Associate Hospital Administrator, University of Michigan Medical Center, Ann Arbor, MI

Molly R. Gates, M.S., R.N.C.
Clinical Nurse Specialist; Neonatal Outreach Coordinator, University of Michigan Medical Center, Ann Arbor, MI

Sandra Geller, R.N., M.S.N.
Clinical Nurse Specialist; Perinatal Outreach Coordinator, Edward W. Sparrow Hospital, Lansing, MI

Pamela J. Gill, R.N., M.S.N.
Perinatal Clinical Specialist, Assistant Clinical Professor, Department of Family Health Care Nursing, University of California, San Francisco, San Francisco, CA

Edward B. Goldman, J.D.
Medical Center Attorney; Adjunct Lecturer, School of Public Health, University of Michigan Medical Center, Ann Arbor, MI

Leila R. Hajjar, M.D.
Department of Obstetrics and Gynecology, Henry Ford Hospital, Detroit, MI

James H. Harger, M.D.
Professor of Obstetrics/Gynecology, University of Pittsburgh School of Medicine, Pittsburgh, PA

John V. Hartline, M.D.
Assistant Clinical Professor, Department of Pediatrics, Kalamazoo Center for Medical Studies, Michigan State University, Kalamazoo, MI; Attending Neonatologist, Bronson Methodist Hospital, Kalamazoo, MI

Robert B. Hilty, M.D.
Attending Obstetrician-Gynecologist, Kettering Medical Center, Dayton, OH

Roderick F. Hume, Jr., M.D.
Post-doctoral Fellow, Division of Reproductive Genetics, Departments of Obstetrics and Gynecology and Pathology, Wayne State University/Hutzel Hospital, Detroit, MI

Mark P. Johnson, M.D.
Associate Professor, Associate Director, Division of Reproductive Genetics, Departments of Obstetrics and Gynecology, Molecular Biology and Genetics, and Pathology, Wayne State University/Hutzel Hospital, Detroit, MI

Michael V. Johnston, M.D.
Schaller Professor of Neurology and Pediatrics, Vice-President of Medical Affairs, Kennedy-Krieger Institute, Johns Hopkins University, Baltimore, MD

Michael Katz, M.D.
Associate Professor of Obstetrics and Gynecology and Reproductive Sciences, University of California at San Francisco; Chief, Perinatal Services, California Pacific Medical Center, San Francisco, CA

Robert A. Knuppel, M.D., M.P.H.
Professor and Chairman, Department of Obstetrics, Gynecology, and Reproductive Sciences, Robert Wood Johnson Medical School, University of Medicine and Dentistry of New Jersey, New Brunswick, NJ

Denise A. Landis, B.S.N., M.S.A.
Manager, Critical Care Transport, University of Michigan Medical Center, Ann Arbor, MI

Robert P. Lorenz, M.D.
Director, Maternal-Fetal Medicine, Vice-Chief of Obstetrics, William Beaumont Hospital, Royal Oak, MI and Associate Professor of Obstetrics and Gynecology, Wayne State University, Detroit, MI

Trevor Macpherson, M.B., Ch.B., FRCOG (London)
Professor of Pathology, University of Pittsburgh School of Medicine; Chief of Pathology, Magee-Women's Hospital, Pittsburgh, PA

Michael F. McNamara, D.O.
Clinical Instructor, Department of Obstetrics and Gynecology, Division of Maternal/Fetal Medicine, Wayne State University/Hutzel Hospital, Detroit, MI

Michelle L. Murray, Ph.D., R.N.C.
Perinatal Educator and Consultant, Learning Resources International, Albuquerque, NM

Kenneth R. Niswander, M.D.
Professor Emeritus, Department of Obstetrics and Gynecology, University of California, Davis, Sacramento, CA

George Nolan, M.D.
Department Head, High Risk Obstetrics, Henry Ford Hospital, Detroit, MI

Clark E. Nugent, M.D.
Clinical Associate Professor of Obstetrics and Gynecology, Division of Maternal-Fetal Medicine, University of Michigan Medical Center, Ann Arbor, MI

J. Douglas Peters, J.D.
Senior Partner, Charfoos & Christensen, Detroit, MI

Angela C. Ranzini, M.D.
Assistant Professor of Clinical Obstetrics and Gynecology, Division of Maternal-Fetal Medicine, Department of Obstetrics, Gynecology and Reproductive Sciences, Robert Wood Johnson Medical School/St. Peter's Medical Center, University of Medicine and Dentistry of New Jersey, New Brunswick, NJ

Barry S. Schifrin, M.D.
Director, Maternal-Fetal Medicine, Department of Obstetrics and Gynecology, AMI Tarzana Regional Medical Center, Tarzana, CA

Richard L. Schreiner, M.D.
Edwin L. Gresham Professor and Chairman, Department of Pediatrics, Indiana University School of Medicine, James W. Riley Children's Hospital, Indianapolis, IN

Robert E. Schumacher, M.D.
Associate Professor of Pediatrics, Section of Neonatal-Perinatal Medicine, University of Michigan Medical Center, Ann Arbor, MI

Thomas R. Shimmel, J.D.
Kitch, Drutchas, Wagner & Kenney, Detroit, MI

Baha M. Sibai, M.D.
Professor of Obstetrics and Gynecology; Chief, Division of Maternal-Fetal Medicine, University of Tennessee, Memphis, Memphis, TN

C. Giles Smith, Jr., J.D.
Senior Partner, Smith, LaParl and Mequio, P.C., Portage, MI

Carl V. Smith, M.D.
Associate Professor and Vice Chairman, Department of Obstetrics/Gynecology, University of Nebraska Medical Center, Omaha, NE

Michael D. Volk, J.D.
Senior Partner, Volk & Montes, El Paso, TX

Elizabeth L. Workman, R.N.C.
Clinical Nurse II, Holden Neonatal Intensive Care Unit, University of Michigan Medical Center, Ann Arbor, MI

Philip E. Young, M.D.
Clinical Professor of Obstetrics and Gynecology, University of California-San Diego School of Medicine, San Diego, CA

Susan Healy Zitterman, J.D.
Kitch, Drutchas, Wagner & Kenney, Detroit, MI

Foreword

Each day in the United States there are approximately 5.5 million physician-patient interactions. These occur in offices, hospitals, and clinics throughout this country and involve both basic and extremely complex medical conditions that most often result in satisfying and positive outcomes. On occasion, however, these interactions are neither satisfying nor positive, and in many cases lawyers are contacted to evaluate the appropriateness of a medical negligence claim. In 1994, 75,000 such claims were filed nationwide with an estimated cost of $5 billion in settlements or verdicts.

Many of these claims involve obstetric and newborn care and outcome. With four million live births each year in this country, and with some of these pregnancies ending with suboptimal outcomes, obstetricians as well as pediatricians have been plagued with lawsuits. It has been estimated that approximately 80% of obstetrician-gynecologists in this country have been sued once for medical malpractice and 25% have been sued at least four times. Because of all this physicians have had to learn the process of litigation while attorneys have had to learn the nuances of medical care. Unfortunately, there have been few textbooks (from a combined effort by both the medical and legal sectors) to aid both these professions in understanding the important issues involved in medical negligence cases. *Risk Management Techniques in Perinatal and Neonatal Practice* is a text that will help remedy this situation. By choosing some of this country's leading medical and legal experts to educate the reader on important subjects relating to prenatal, intrapartum, and neonatal medicine the editors have provided physicians and attorneys with useful and important information that will help each in their respective professional goals.

The editors have made a special effort to enable the physician to understand the legal consequences that he/she may face as well as helping the attorney involved in medical malpractice cases understand the different schools of thought and methods of approach involved in the medical care of a pregnant woman and her newborn child.

The editors and the authors are to be congratulated in putting together a thoughtful text that addresses an extremely important element of medical care.

Frank H. Boehm, M.D.
Professor of Obstetrics and Gynecology
Director, Division of Maternal-Fetal Medicine
Vanderbilt University Medical Center
Nashville, TN

Preface

The settlement or verdict of a single "bad baby case" can easily exceed $1,000,000. For this reason, the modern day hospital and its health care providers must develop a sound program of risk management to deal with potential medical malpractice litigation. Part of this program should involve a prospective system to include recognition of the "red flags" that signify possible future allegations of malpractice. Early intervention in such cases can often ameliorate a problem with lesser economic and emotional consequences, perhaps even resolve it.

In addition to identifying cases for early risk management and quality assurance review, rapid identification of a potential obstetrical or neonatal lawsuit may also open avenues for further investigation while the patient is still hospitalized, leading to an exploration of alternative etiologies to explain the patient's condition and a more contemporaneous assessment of the specifics of a case while the memory of that case is still fresh in the minds of the health care providers.

Many systems of risk management deal with issues in a retrospective manner, generally after a lawsuit has been filed. Two significant problems arise, including the fact that the patient has already left the hospital and the risk manager loses access to subsequent records that might indicate a poor outcome, and the opportunity is lost for prospective investigation of the case and interaction with the family.

A great number of obstetrical and neonatal sequelae are not manifested until well beyond the initial hospitalization. It is our belief that the most logical system of risk management is one that focuses on the obstetrical and neonatal courses in order to identify those cases that are in need of risk management from either a medical or a legal standpoint.

The text that follows examines the most common situations in perinatal and neonatal practice that lead to claims of malpractice. It was not our intent to create a medical or nursing textbook, and we have assumed that the interested reader already possesses a reasonable fund of knowledge in these areas. We are not suggesting nor implying that there is a single standard of care; rather, the objective of this book is to examine the "red flags" in several high-risk situations to enable the development of a prospective approach to risk management. This may be summarized as a five-step process: recognition, analysis, response, communication, and documentation.

We have been most fortunate in assembling a group of expert authors who have distinguished themselves in their respective areas of interest. We are indebted to them for the efforts they have given to this project. Their recommendations reflect their experiences and personal preferences and should not be perceived as the only acceptable approach to a particular problem. In addition, four distinguished and experienced attorneys have provided commentaries that offer a valuable legal insight. We have interjected their thoughts directly into the text in the hope of emphasizing the point— or counterpoint—of their remarks.

A number of legal terms will appear throughout the text. Four of these are critical to the understanding of the tort systems in the United States. The *standard of care* is defined as "that which the average, prudent physician of like or similar training would do under the same or similar circumstances." *Causation* refers to "the event or events which directly brought about the injury or disability." In order for a jury to determine *medical malpractice*, it must be shown that there was both a breach in the standard of care and that this had a causal relationship to the injury or disability. In a court of law, opinions are expressed to a *reasonable degree of medical certainty or probability*, which is defined as "more likely than not," or in other words, greater than a 50% probability.

The often long delay between the filing of a complaint and the commencement of a medical malpractice trial underscores the need for comprehensive record keeping. Health care providers can do much to protect themselves from the future allegations of negligent care. We also believe that these techniques of risk management will serve to bring about changes in the behavior of health care professionals that ultimately improve the quality of care they give to their patients.

We would also like to acknowledge the efforts of a number of individuals who helped to make this project possible. We are indebted to Paula Donn, Betty Passon, Susan Peterson, and Sharon Reed for invaluable technical and secretarial assistance. We would like to thank Barry Schifrin and Pamela Boland for their editorial contributions. We appreciate the continued support of Futura Publishing Company and especially its Chairman of the Board, Mr. Steven Korn. Finally, we would like to thank our colleagues, without whom we would not have had the time, opportunity, nor motivation to undertake this task.

Steven M. Donn, M.D.
Ann Arbor, Michigan

Charles W. Fisher, J.D.
Detroit, Michigan

Contents

Section III: Intrapartum Obstetrical Issues

Section IV: Pathologic and Laboratory Evaluation

Section V: Neonatal Issues

Section VI: Maternal and Neonatal Transport

Section VII: Communication

Section VIII: Documentation and Risk Management

Section I

Introduction

_____ Chapter 1 _____

Professionalism and the Avoidance of Malpractice

◆◆◆

Richard L. Schreiner, M.D.

Introduction

What are the factors that lead to medical malpractice lawsuits? This book will consider many elements of medical and nursing practice that may affect the risk of litigation, as well as address strategies that may be helpful in avoiding legal entanglements. Obviously, the competency of the physicians, nurses, and other health care providers is of extreme importance in this arena, but certainly not the only—and some would argue, perhaps not the most important—determinant of risk. Even the most expert physician or nurse will make an occasional mistake either in the actual delivery of care or in the documentation of that care. The quality of the medical record, including legibility and completeness, is high on the list of reasons why lawsuits are filed, lost, or settled. In addition to these two major areas (competency and documentation), which will be discussed in great detail throughout this text, the perception of the overall quality of care on the part of the patient or the patient's family may be even more important in determing the risk of litigation. Does the patient perceive a caring attitude, professional integrity, open communication, and standards of excellence in his/her care providers? Is there a sense of trust between the patient/family and the physician? If not, it may not matter whether the care was, in fact, excellent. In other words, the relationship of the physician and the health care team to the patient and the family, the quantity and the quality of communication between them, and the general professional conduct of the care providers may determine more than any other factor whether a medical malpractice lawsuit will be filed.[1]

From: Donn SM, Fisher CW (eds.): *Risk Management Techniques in Perinatal and Neonatal Practice.* © Futura Publishing Co., Inc., Armonk, NY, 1996.

Commentary by Mr. Goldman: The record may be an important reason to question care, but it is not ordered or reviewed until the patient elects to retain an attorney. So, while the record is important in the defense of cases, it is not why patients decide to start the process of making a claim. Patients decide to start because of their perceptions about how they were treated. If communications did not go well, if the physician was rude, if a sense of rapport and trust was not established, there is a predilection for the patient to inquire about a suit should anything go wrong.

Excellence

Somehow, patients and families develop an opinion of the quality of their physicians and other health care providers. As just noted, competence in one's clinical field is certainly a determining factor in this perception of quality. However, the vast majority of patients have no way of accurately assessing the level of a physician's expertise.

Commentary by Mr. Goldman: If patients had a way to assess a physician's expertise through review of articles, comments of other patients, comments of co-workers, or data from the national data bank, they do not take advantage of these avenues. Typically patients rely instead on things like: are the office staff friendly?; is the office clean?; and do people seem professional? Thus, it is important to project a professional appearance in the office and with all of the staff.

Therefore, opinions regarding competency are often based on perceptions established during a visit to the health care provider. If the care provider is perceived as concerned, caring, and compassionate, then it is highly likely that the individual will be perceived as an excellent physician. Of course, all clinicians believe that they are excellent—competent, concerned, caring, and compassionate. However, what the physician believes is not nearly as important as what the patient and the family believe. Each clinician should ask himself/herself, "How do my patients and their families perceive me?" It is incumbent upon all health care providers to obtain honest and, hopefully, accurate opinions regarding these perceptions. Different ways to accomplish this may include soliciting feedback from a sampling of patients, or seeking comments from impartial observers on a regular basis.

Commentary by Mr. Goldman: Physicians can also do chart review with colleagues, putting themselves in the role of expert witnesses. In other words they can, on an informal basis, agree that they will review a random sample of colleagues' charts and vice versa and each will comment about completeness, accuracy, readability, and other items that could result in the chart not being an ally in defensible malpractice case. Physicians can also encourage patients to report back by using surveys or simply telling them they are interested in feedback. Typically, simply asking the patient for feedback can have a positive effect. Of course, if surveys are used, it is important to read and review the results and follow-up. For example, a survey could be returned where the patient says that they still have that pain, and it will then be necessary for the physician to set up an appointment to assess the patient.

First Impressions

The duration and intensity of the relationship between the physician and patient or family will vary. In the Neonatal Intensive Care Unit, the relationship is usually of a short duration; generally there is no meaningful doctor-patient/family relationship before admission to the Neonatal Intensive Care Unit, although there may have been some communication between the parties, either prenatally or just prior to delivery. For the obstetrician, the affiliation with the family is usually of a much longer duration, especially if there were multiple pregnancies. For the patient referred to the high risk maternal-fetal specialist, the relationship may also be of a relatively short duration. When we do not know our patients and their families well, the initial contact with them assumes an even greater importance in establishing their perception of the clinician's level of care and concern. In these situations, first impressions—how the physician looks, speaks, listens, and acts—may be critical in forming a good—or bad—relationship between the care giver and the patient.

What influences the first impression of the patient or family when they meet the physician? Is the physician dressed neatly, even if wearing medical "scrubs?" Does the physician appear to take time with the family, introducing himself/herself, and sitting down with them, if even for just a few minutes? Does the physician address the patient or family as Mr. or Mrs. and refer to their child by first name, rather than "he," "she," or "it?" Is the general demeanor of the physician consistent with the family's perception of an excellent physician? Is the physician serious and pleasant, or is the physician perceived as being cavalier and unimpressed by the gravity of the situation? Does the physician present himself/herself as being primarily concerned for the patient and family, rather than being more interested in getting home quickly to watch the Monday night football game? A few patients and families may not notice or care about the physical appearance of the physician. However, more families have a clear image of what comprises, in their minds, a competent, concerned, caring, and compassionate physician; they do not expect the clinician to be wearing dirty or wrinkled clothes, blood-stained shoes, or soiled tennis shoes. They do not expect the physician to have unkempt and greasy hair, an unshaven face, or offensive body odor. Even if the physician has been up throughout the night caring for sick patients, there is almost always adequate time to shower, put on clean clothes, and shave if necessary.[2,3]

> **Commentary by Mr. Goldman:** What is the physical setting—do you see the family in a hall or in an office? Are your eyes on the same level as the patient, or do you stand over the patient? Your body language says a lot about how open you are to discussion. Do you allow the patient/family to share uncertainty, express fear and anxiety, or do you cut off this conversation? Of course cutting off conversation does not allow a free exchange of information. Are you careful to speak in non-medical terms? Do you avoid patronizing comments, disparaging comments, and criticism of other facilities and physicians? How the family sees the way you treat others— nurses, therapists, etc.—can strongly influence how the family views you either as a tyrant or a team player.

I can personally recall when, as a neonatology fellow, I transported premature twins to our Newborn Intensive Care Unit. After a lengthy hospital stay, the babies were finally ready for discharge. The mother mentioned that when I originally came to the community hospital, she almost refused to allow me to take the infants to the Children's Hospital. She said that at that time she thought that I was one of the hospital maintenance personnel. I had been up for nearly 72 hours caring for sick babies. My physical appearance was inappropriate with wrinkled, dirty hospital scrubs, an unshaven face, and a generally unkempt appearance. Fortunately, this mother communicated this to me and taught me a lesson that I never forgot.

Communication

Patients and parents expect health care professionals to be good communicators. Communication is achieved through our speaking and listening, as well as through our behavior—our eye contact, our posture, our touching, etc. Some simple rules of good communication include the following:

1. Physicians should introduce themselves to the patient or parents. Most patients or parents prefer to be addressed as Mr. or Mrs. or other appropriate titles. Some will, in fact, be insulted if addressed informally by their first names. Very few, if any, patients or parents will be offended if they are addressed more formally by their surnames.

Commentary by Mr. Goldman: The physician should take his/her lead from the patient and if unsure should be formal until being told otherwise.

2. Physicians should speak and act as mature ladies and gentlemen. It is inappropriate to be loud or to use coarse, rough language. Foul language in verbal or written communication in the profession of medicine is never appropriate. Laughing and joking in view of patients or families may frequently be misinterpreted. Families see nothing funny about their child or other children being sick, no matter how minor or routine the problem appears to the clinicians. When families see clinicians joking at a bedside, they will not understand how such a serious issue as a sick child could possibly be humorous. They may misinterpret this behavior and believe that the humor is actually aimed at their child or family. A good sense of humor is an important ingredient of good medical practice; however, we must constantly be aware of how our behavior in public view of patients and families may be interpreted or misinterpreted. Most of us have been guilty at times of making derogatory remarks about patients, but we should learn early in our careers that such comments are always inappropriate and frequently harmful. Comments that may seem benign to clinicians are frequently offensive to the family and indicate to them a lack of sensitivity and compassion. How often have clinicians heard or said "What a great case this is?" From an academic standpoint this sounds like an innocent remark, but to the parents the reference to their child as a "great case" reflects a total lack of caring. It is worthwhile for clinicians to step back occasionally and ask how they would feel if someone spoke about their critically ill child, spouse, parent, or sibling in similar terms.

Commentary by Mr. Goldman: If you are discussing a case you should do so in private, not in front of the patient or other patients. Elevators and cafeterias are public places and not suitable areas to discuss confidential issues with your colleagues.

3. The use of medical jargon and slang is prevalent throughout the health care environment. Medical students and house staff learn this "med speak" culture very early in their education.[4] Of course, they learn it primarily from senior house officers, who, in turn, learned it from seasoned faculty and practitioners. Terms such as "A's and B's" (apnea and bradycardia), "tube the patient" (place an endotracheal tube), and "crumped" or "crashed and burned" impede communication, frustrate and anger families, and tend to give the perception of

poor quality of care. Use of such medical jargon and slang interferes with the development of a trusting relationship between the care giver and the patient. Faculty and practitioners teach medical students, house officers, and young physicians by example—good and bad.[5] Communication skills may be learned and refined with practice—they are not necessarily innate nor intuitive. As faculty and practitioners, we must model excellent communication skills and encourage students and house officers to improve their skills.

4. Avoid the use of technical terms. Why do we speak in such ways that people cannot understand us clearly? Some of this is natural, as it is difficult to communicate medical information without using technical terms. On the other hand, few lay persons will understand terms such as "high frequency ventilation," "exploratory laparotomy," "ECMO," or "amnio-infusion" without an explanation in simple language. Such explanations do take time, of which physicians seem to have too little. Nonetheless, we must explain what we are saying or doing, so that patients and families understand what we are recommending or expecting to happen, and what their choices are. Again, feedback from patients and families on a regular basis may be an important way of evaluating the effectiveness of our communication skills.

   Commentary by Mr. Goldman: When explaining, it is helpful to make it clear to patients what the choice points are and how the patient will be involved in making choices. Remember that the informed consent process should be thought of as an informed choice process where you provide information to a competent patient about the procedure, its risks, benefits, and alternatives and the patient then makes a choice.

5. Another common problem with communication is "scapegoating"— the use of terms that are perceived as demeaning of other health care providers or suggestions that care provided by other clinicians is substandard.[6] The use of the term "LMD" (local medical doctor) is considered by most physicians to be insulting, yet it continues to be used extensively in the teaching environment. Making comments that suggest to the patient or family that the prior care was inappropriate or inadequate, when in fact the clinician had no actual first hand knowledge of what care was provided, introduces doubt regarding the quality of care provided and increases the likelihood of malpractice litigation in the event of a less than optimal outcome. This does not mean that the physician should avoid criticism of inferior care; however, such criticism should be undertaken in a setting appropriate

to the situation, generally privately. Unfortunately, many times when such comments are made, the individual making the remark does so in public, despite having no first hand knowledge of the prior clinical situation. Such remarks are rarely accurate and will almost always be perceived by the family as intimating inappropriate care. Sometimes these comments or notes in the medical record represent defensive posturing to place blame on someone else, such as the note in a medical record that stated, "I gave inappropriate doses of medication because the nurse gave me the wrong weight." Sometimes they reflect anger, such as, "The doctor did not want a blood gas done in 40% oxygen." Most often they reflect immaturity, naivete, and misunderstanding of the actual circumstances. The excellent professional always communicates a positive attitude about his colleagues, other clinical services, other hospitals, and other health care professionals in public. This helps enormously in building a supportive environment for the patients and their families.

Commentary by Mr. Goldman: The medical record is a place for facts that lead to a medical conclusion. It is never the place for disparaging remarks about other services or blaming language.

Sometimes it can be very difficult to be positive about individual patients, families, or others. Nonetheless, the mature professional should be supportive and non-judgmental regarding his/her patients and families, even though he/she may not approve of their lifestyle, their attitude toward the problem, or their perception of their child's problem. It is probably fair to say that in most situations the patient or family has far greater problems than does the physician.

Commentary by Mr. Goldman: Caveat: It may in some cases be necessary to consider reporting abuse or neglect and in those few cases the physician will have an obligation mandated by state law that requires judgment. If the physician has reasonable cause to believe that, for example, child abuse has occurred, the physician must be judgmental and will be obligated by state law to report to the relevant state agency.

The delivery room is an environment in which professional behavior is especially important. This time for the family should be a happy and positive experience, although naturally blended with some degree of fear and anxiety. Health care professionals should be calm and soft spoken in the delivery room. They sould be polite, asking for things rather than demanding them. Discussion should be limited to medical issues of this pregnancy rather than discussing other patients or conducting non-medical discussions about social and personal interests.

Conclusion

Why do health care professionals sometimes act in an immature and unprofessional manner? Often it is because they are insecure, and this is a way of coping with stressful situations. It is easier to put things at a distance, fearing that objectivity will be lost if the physician becomes too "caring" or too "involved." Most health care professionals do not intend to be insensitive, and they certainly do not want to be perceived by the patient or family as uncaring. In fact, if health care providers knew that families interpreted their communication and behavior negatively, it would likely change for the better. If trainees and young professionals saw senior clinicians acting in a mature and caring manner, they would likely do the same; then, the importance of senior clinicians acting as role models for young professionals cannot be overemphasized. Ideally, young professionals in training should seek role models who are competent, concerned, caring, and compassionate physicians, but perhaps, more importantly, they must seek role models who are perceived by others as concerned, caring, and compassionate human beings. Nearly all health care professionals believe that they reflect these traits; however, our own opinion of ourselves is not important in the delivery of care to others. We must be aware that it is the opinion of the patients and families we serve that is critical in establishing the bonds of trust with those for whom we provide care.

Why should physicians care how they act towards the patient? The most important reason is that the physician wants to be a good person as well as a good physician. However, if this is not adequate incentive, other less admirable incentives might be that the physician develops a good reputation, that the physician remains busy, and that the physician avoids medical malpractice litigation.

> **Commentary by Mr. Goldman:** Professional distance is important both for good advice and to avoid burnout, but distance does not equal detachment. It is important to acknowledge a family's feelings and understand their concerns while continuing to be able to render professional advice and care.

It may be a cliché that families do not sue their friends. The Journal of the American Medical Association, in its November 20–30, 1994 issue, reported a survey done in Florida showing that physicians who are most often sued also have the most complaints for rudeness. The article concluded that the high level of patients' interpersonal complaints is a source for malpractice claims.

References

1. Hoekelman RA. A pediatrician's view—a way to avoid malpractice suits. Pediatr Ann 1991;20:60.

2. Taylor PG. Does dress influence how parents first perceive house staff competence? Am J Dis Child 1987;141:426.
3. Dunn JJ, Lee TH, Percelay JM, et al. Patient and house officer attitudes on physician attire and etiquette. JAMA 1987;257:65.
4. Cleveland WW. Physicians' handy guide to medspeak. J Pediatr 1987;111:78.
5. Reitemeier RJ. Teachers as role models. Indiana Med 1988;81:160.
6. Keating JP. Scapegoating. Am J Dis Child 1987;141:948.

Section II

Prenatal Obstetrical Issues

Chapter 2

Genetics and Prenatal Diagnostic Techniques

◆◆◆

Mark I. Evans, M.D., Roderick R. Hume Jr., M.D., Mark P. Johnson, M.D.

Introduction

There has perhaps been no area of medicine that has progressed more rapidly over the past decade than genetics, which has gone from being a pediatric curiosity to one of the principal foundations of emerging therapies. Discoveries in the genomic control of development and molecular techniques for the diagnosis of now literally hundreds of disorders have expanded geometrically the opportunities as well as the exposures for physicians dealing with pregnant patients. The obstetrician should now be aware of the myriad of approaches to diagnosis of genetic disorders. That which was undiagnosable even only a few years ago may be possible today, and every obstetrician needs to know how to find out salient information.[1] In this chapter we will attempt to present relevant, real life examples of pitfalls—some avoidable and some not—that are faced in the practice of obstetrics and genetics in the 1990s.

Real Cases Facing Obstetricians

Case 1

A 34-year-old woman who will be 35 at delivery is offered amniocentesis but declines to have it. Multiple marker screening is performed that confers a low risk for Down syndrome. Nevertheless, a baby with Down syndrome is born. A lawsuit alleges the doctor should have recommended strongly that the

From: Donn SM, Fisher CW (eds.): *Risk Management Techniques in Perinatal and Neonatal Practice.* © Futura Publishing Co., Inc., Armonk, NY, 1996.

patient have the amniocentesis and that components of the multiple marker screening should have been interpreted individually as well as collectively.

Case 2

A 27-year-old woman has an ultrasound examination performed in her doctor's office at 17 weeks gestation, which is interpreted as normal. At 26 weeks, severe ventriculomegaly is documented, and a baby with significant handicaps is born at term. The lawsuit alleges that ventriculomegaly should have been discovered early enough in the gestation to have allowed the patient to have a termination of pregnancy, and that at the very least, once the ventriculomegaly was discovered the patient should have been offered in utero ventriculo-amniotic shunting to relieve the excess cerebrospinal fluid.

Case 3

A 36-year-old woman undergoes a chorionic villus sampling (CVS) procedure at 11 1/7 weeks of gestation. At 38 weeks gestation she delivers a fetus with a transverse limb reduction defect. A lawsuit alleges that the CVS procedure caused the limb reduction defect.

Case 4

A 31-year-old woman undergoes a genetic amniocentesis procedure performed by her obstetrician at 17 weeks of gestation. No fluid is obtained. The procedure is rescheduled for a week later and is performed. Bloody fluid is obtained, and the patient miscarries 2 days later. The lawsuit alleges that the physician was not qualified to perform the procedure, that the procedure was not medically indicated, and that the pregnancy loss is a direct result of incompetence.

Case 5

A 25-year-old becomes pregnant despite taking birth control pills, which are continued until she is approximately 14 weeks pregnant. She has a baby at term who has a ventricular septal defect. The lawsuit alleges that the progesterones in the birth control pills are responsible for the cardiac defect, and both the manufacturer and physician are liable because they should have known the risk.

Analyses

Case 1

Medical Issues

The increasing risk of chromosome abnormalities with advancing maternal age has been known for decades.[2] Statistical compilations of risk figures were originally categorized in 5-year groupings, thus showing an apparent big jump between patients 30-34 and 35-39. In subsequent years, detailed epidemiologic studies mostly by Hook[2] showed that there is a definite gradual increase in risk with each successive maternal age year, with the slope of risk increasing in the 30s.

When amniocenteses first became possible in the late 1960s and early 1970s, and the number of physicians who could perform them and the number of laboratories capable of handling analyses were very few and far between, those services were restricted to those patients considered to be at highest risk.[1] Initially, a maternal age of 40 or greater was the risk threshold. By the late 1970s this had fallen to approximately 38, and has been considered to be 35 at delivery since the early 1980s.

While the percentage of patients considered at high risk has clearly benefited from the availability of prenatal diagnostic services, the fact remains that if amniocentesis, or now CVS, were offered only to women over 35, about 80% of all chromosome abnormalities would be missed, as these occur to women in younger age groups.[3] In the early 1970s, Brock and Sutcliffe[4] first reported on the ability to diagnose neural tube defects in amniotic fluid using alpha-fetoprotein. Shortly thereafter, serum screening for neural tube defects with maternal serum alpha-fetoprotein was developed,[5] and it was 10 years later in 1984 that the first associations with low maternal serum alpha-fetoprotein and chromosome abnormalities, particularly Down syndrome, were published.[6] The use of low maternal serum alpha-fetoprotein increased the potential overall detection of Down syndrome cases from the 20% seen in women over age 35, to approximately 45% of the total, including the 20% from those over 35, and approximately one-third of those under age 35. In 1988, Wald et al.[7] first proposed the inclusion of two additional markers, beta-hCG and unconjugated estriol, and that the use of these three markers plus maternal age in a calculation, would increase the overall detection frequency to approximately 60% of the total (Figure 1).

Current investigations are centering on the use of additional markers, the cost effectiveness of current ones, differing mathematical approaches to calculation of risk, and the cost benefits of differing approaches.[8-11]

Screening for Chromosomal Abnormalities

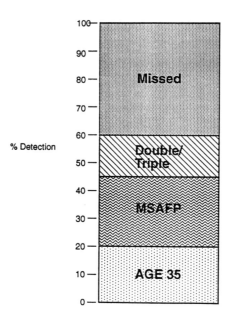

Figure 1. Histogram showing percentage of detectable Down Syndrome. Twenty percent occurs to women over age 35. Low maternal serum alpha-fetoprotein (MSAFP) will detect about one-third of the remaining 80%, which occurs to women under age 35, bringing the total to 45%. Double and triple screening can increase the total to about 60%.

Potential Exposures

The tremendous advances in genetic technology over the past decade have made literally hundreds of metabolic and Mendelian disorders diagnosable via sophisticated laboratory analyses, and the development of screening tests for neural tube defects and chromosome abnormalities have made many, but not all fetuses with chromosome abnormalities, such as Down syndrome, potentially detectable.[1] One of the key elements of understanding necessary for physicians, patients, and the medico-legal system, is that "testing" is not the same as "screening." A test, such as amniocentesis or CVS, and its appropriate laboratory follow-up, can give a definitive answer to specific questions. For example, does the fetus have Down syndrome, cystic fibrosis, Tay-Sachs disease, Sickle cell disease, etc.? While invasive tests such as amniocentesis, CVS, and cordocentesis are appropriate for patients in given "at-risk" categories, the vast majority of patients with chromosome abnormalities are born to patients in the supposedly low risk group, and cannot be generally tested. There is not sufficient manpower or resources to perform amniocentesis or CVS on every single pregnant patient. In fact, for many patients, particularly younger ones for whom the genetic risk is very low, the procedure-related complication rates of the invasive procedures would, in fact, be higher than the detection rates expected. Nevertheless, particularly for biochemical screening, there is occasionally an inherent assumption made by patients, and certainly in claims of malpractice, that screening tests were either: 1. never offered; 2. never done; 3. done improperly; or 4. interpreted improperly. Another area of ambiguity is when did the offering of the various tests move from being experimental to being the standard of care?[12,13] A tremendous number of legal actions have debated this subject with no uniform agreement having been reached.

Maternal serum alpha-fetoprotein (MSAFP) testing became routinely available in America in the early-mid 1980s principally for detection of neural tube defects.[14] When the first papers on chromosomal detection appeared in the mid-1980s, a few pilot programs relatively quickly began offering such screening. It was only towards the end of the 1980s that there was finally an agreement among the academic centers performing these investigations, that such technology was useful and beneficial. It is still not clear exactly when offering low maternal serum alpha-fetoprotein screening for Down syndrome would be considered to have become the standard of care.

In the late 1980s and early 1990s, a number of articles suggested that the addition of hCG, with or without estriol, could significantly increase the detection frequency.[7-11] While early papers were tarnished by aggressive marketing campaigns from certain laboratories, it is now abundantly clear that hCG is the best of the three currently available markers. In 1994, the American College of Obstetricians and Gynecologists finally issued a technical bulletin recommending multiple markers screening, which certainly will be used in court as evidence of standard of care for multiple markers.[15] There is some reason to believe that following an article in 1992 by Haddow et al.,[10] touting an increased detection rate of Down syndrome, an argument could be made that multiple marker screening at that point should have become standard. Nevertheless, certainly in the mid-1990s it would be difficult to defend the offering of only MSAFP in a case where MSAFP alone missed detection of a Down syndrome infant that potentially could have been detected had multiple marker screening been performed.

One confounding problem, however, is what exactly is the best combination? The original proposed cocktail of AFP, hCG, and estriol has been used extensively, although there are now several studies questioning the effectiveness of the third marker. While many have touted the so-called "triple screen," it is abundantly clear that there is no one uniformly accepted protocol today as the best, and all protocols that can detect about 60% of anomalies should be considered acceptable until newer technology makes higher percentages likely.[15]

Biochemical screening continues to be voluntary despite allegations that failure to have the screening performed was evidence of malpractice. Consensus statements from the American College of Obstetricians and Gynecologists, and the American Society of Human Genetics, all state unequivocally that screening should be "offered," not routinely "done." The implications of screening tests are serious and have considerable emotional concern, and they involve patients having to deal with issues that may be uncomfortable or religiously inappropriate for them.

There is no one standard way in which to interpret the risk rates generated from the combination of these tests. No one laboratory has ever had enough experience to verify that a "one in 327.4" risk, in fact, really means that. Clearly, these are various approximations. Published data have suggested considerable variance between actual published risks and those that appear likely from experience. Newer approaches to refine the mathematics will continue to evolve[11] and to improve the sensitivity and specificity of screening. Certainly a program's performance is an area of potential exposure that will come to play an increasing role over the next several years. In a recent case it was alleged that the components of a triple screen result should have been interpreted separately and not collectively, despite the fact that all the relevant literature shows that this is not the way to do it. Nevertheless, there will continue to be neophyte and often ridiculous theories put in front of juries who will not necessarily be in a position to understand that these are fringe interpretations.

Case 2

Medical Issues

The development of increasingly sophisticated sonographic equipment, and the emergence of physicians extremely competent in its use, has allowed for the diagnosis of an ever-increasing percentage of structural fetal abnormalities, very often at gestational ages early enough to allow a patient to decide whether or not to continue the pregnancy.[16] Over the course of the past decade, the increasing resolution of such pictures has also allowed physicians not so well trained to obtain equipment that is not terribly expensive, and to perform scanning even in their own offices.

The components of a basic scan have continued to evolve and increase, and the number of subtle findings that are not diagnosable that have implications for other system abnormalities, has likewise continued to increase.

Certain findings, for example first trimester nuchal membranes, are now known to be associated with a higher than average risk of chromosome abnormalities such as trisomy 21 and trisomy 18.[17] Other findings, such as choroid plexus cysts, have become identifiable only within the past several years, and the implications of these findings and what to do about them in follow-up, is likewise uncertain and highly controversial.[18]

The diagnosis of a significant abnormality, such as ventriculomegaly, needs to be conveyed to the patient with appropriate counseling. The patient's options (including termination of pregnancy) need to be relayed to her, regardless of the physician's own personal beliefs about abortion. If he or she does not feel it morally appropriate, the physician does have an obligation to convey to the patient information about where she can get such services.[19]

For experimental therapy such as in utero shunting, however, the rules are certainly different.[20] No physician is required to even offer or mention an experimental therapy. Certainly, a physician who is aware of such possibilities should as a matter of good practice make his/her patient aware of the availability. In the case of shunting for ventriculomegaly, this procedure was performed for a short time between the late 1970s and early 1980s, and then was abandoned. In fact, a de facto moratorium was declared because the outcomes following such procedures were very poor. In the early 1990s several institutions are considering re-evaluation of the procedure because it is now known that many of the patients who underwent the procedure were poor candidates for it because they had other associated anomalies that rendered their prognosis dismal at best.

Exposures

Lawsuits over missed fetal anomalies will increase exponentially. Such lawsuits have been seen not only in terms of simple and relatively straightforward anomalies missed by physicians performing procedures for which they did not have considerable training or decent equipment, through subtle abnormalities missed in compromised patients, such as the morbidly obese, even with the best equipment and best trained physicians. There is no one blanket answer as to how to address these issues other than to suggest to physicians that sonography is not something that should be done by every single obstetrician, and is a procedure that should be limited to physicians with considerable experience.

The offering of abortion for patients who are near the time of the legal limit of their rights poses a special problem. Patients can be referred to facilities in other jurisdictions where the laws are more liberal and allow for abortions at times not permitted in some states. It is not at all clear, however, whether such would be considered an "obligation" or merely an added service beyond the call of duty.

Case 3

Medical Issues

When a new clinical procedure is introduced, generally a limited number of centers participate in its development and implementation. After there has been sufficient experience to document the primary safety and efficacy, the number of physicians performing the procedure begins to expand, and the technology then diffuses across the land. CVS has been among the most heavily studied procedures ever introduced in medicine, with a National Institutes of Health sponsored randomized trial with outcome being performed from the mid-1980s into the mid-1990s. Data confirming the procedure's safety and accuracy were developed over this period with no suggestion of any particular problems. In 1991, an English group suggested that procedures performed earlier in gestational age than is typically done (at 7-8 weeks instead of 9-12 weeks), found four cases of limb reduction defects among 400 patients.[22] These data were reported in the Lancet, a respected medical journal. No other center could confirm these findings, and the issue was relatively quickly forgotten. In 1992, investigators from Chicago held a press conference long before they published their data, and declared that they too had had a 1% incidence of limb reduction defects in their first 400 cases. They suggested that the procedure must, therefore, be abandoned. It was not for several months later until the actual paper showed their real findings, that an interpretation was possible.[23] Their data revealed that for this group the gestational age was in the usual time frame, but that the pregnancy loss rate of this group was 8% overall, and 20% if two passes were made, which are roughly four and ten times the accepted rates of loss at experienced centers! The general interpretation of those in the field was that when procedures are performed by physicians not terribly competent in their use, many types of damage are possible. The news media however, emphasized the initial press reports without bothering to investigate the overall context, frightened many patients, and gave some physicians an opportunity to talk their patients out of going to genetic centers for the test, and instead to stay with the primary physician for amniocentesis.

Evaluation of the potential teratogenicity of any agent, including a procedure, rests upon the documentation of four principles: 1. secular data; 2. animal models; 3. timing, and; 4. biologic plausibility.[24] Secular data (i.e., has the number of limb reduction defects gone up since the introduction of CVS?), most notably the registry of all births in British Columbia, combined with the outcome data of the International CVS Registry coordinated at

Jefferson Medical College in Philadelphia,[25] show in several large studies, that the incidence of limb reduction defects in patients who have undergone CVS is absolutely identical to the background population. Two of the studies suggesting an association had serious methodologic flaws. Some of the series have, in fact, been known to have counted patients at least twice, and sometimes even three times. Furthermore, a case control study using the Atlanta area (conducted at the Centers for Disease Control) had a principal conclusion that there was no difference in incidence between the two groups.[26] Yet, when the data were analyzed three separate ways and the number of cases reduced from 150 to seven in the sub-group, only then did a difference show up, which was highly publicized.

Analysis of the available data suggests that there is no real increased risk when the procedure is performed at the appropriate time (> 9.5 weeks) and by physicians with experience. Data from reputable centers, such as that in Milan, show that if the procedure is performed extremely early in gestation (6-7 weeks), there may be a slight increase in risk, even when done by experienced physicians.[27] Furthermore, the collaborative data suggest that when the procedure is performed by novices, there can be increased numbers of complications of all sorts.

Exposures

The considerable adverse publicity despite how inappropriate has certainly led to the occurrence of a number of lawsuits in cases in which babies with limb reduction defects were born following CVS. As with any other "bad baby case" there is considerable concern about sympathy for the plaintiff as opposed to a rigorous analysis of medical negligence. Legal interpretation of these cases will depend upon how well a jury can be made to understand the distinction between background rates of malformations, and that the occurrence of a malformation in an exposed group does not automatically mean that the exposure is causal. As has been seen with various teratogens, there likely will be much contention over such occurrences.

Case 4

Medical Issues

Amniocentesis has become a mainstay of prenatal diagnosis the late 1970s and early 1980s. With the use of concomitant sonographic guidance, the procedure has become extremely safe, and in experienced hands a complication rate of about one per 200-300 procedures is considered reasonable. There is considerable debate as to whether or not every obstetrician should perform amniocentesis. The majority opinion is that only those physicians who have special training and expertise, and who perform it on a regular basis are going to have lower complication rates than those who perform the procedure infrequently. Nevertheless, there is no guideline that specifically states that a physician without continuing experience should not perform the procedure. A physician may counsel his patients that he has a nine out of ten chance of being able to obtain a specimen for a given amniocentesis procedure. The problem is that he is telling the truth. The patients, however, do not have any way of knowing that in fact it should have been 99 out of 100, or 999 out of 1000! As with most procedures, a physician with a track record of successful outcomes will be in a far better position to defend against a bad outcome than will someone with less experience or poor history.

Exposures

Damages for loss of pregnancy will also be hotly contested, and there are track records in different jurisdictions as to typically how much such cases are worth. One problem, however, with losses following genetic amniocentesis is that these can and do happen to the best of physicians with the best of intentions and the best of skill. Determining whether or not a procedure loss resulted from negligence or one unfortunate side effect can be very difficult to determine. Certainly, if the procedure were completely uncomplicated, i.e., drawing clear fluid, it would be hard to argue that the procedure was negligently performed. However, as in the case described above, where no fluid was obtained and then there was trouble on a second occasion at a time when the procedure should normally have been relatively straightforward, it will be problematic to defend such a case. Exactly what level of training is appropriate for amniocentesis is also difficult to quantitate. In most large metropolitan areas, in the mid-1990s amniocenteses are generally performed by physicians who sub-specialize in the area, and usually have training in maternal-fetal medicine or genetics. Most obstetrics residents today do not get substantial experience. How such issues apply to a maloccurrence when it occurs to a physician in a rural area where there are minimal alternatives to the patient is somewhat different than when better trained physicians are readily available. This paradigm will be played out legally in many venues over many cases in the next several years.

Indications for amniocentesis and CVS were discussed under case #1. However, an additional point and one for which there is not uniform agreement is the "best" maternal age at which to offer procedures. There is general agreement that 35+ years at delivery is the minimum standard, but what about the 34-year old who requests it?[1] There needs to be discretion and individualization. In our practice we believe that 30 is "old enough" to warrant the offering of procedures, but it is absolutely not the standard to do so. If a patient > 35 has been made aware of her options, any choice is definable. Not being told or being denied because of insurance issues will be a source of continuous litigation over the next several years.

Case 5

Medical Issues

Throughout the early 1970s there was considerable concern about teratogenicity of birth control pills and hormonal pregnancy tests. Applying the same rationale as described earlier, the four criteria of secular data, animal models, timing, and biologic plausibility need to be applied. There is an overwhelming body of literature on allegations of associations of progesterone with birth defects, including limb reduction defects and cardiac defects. The general consensus is that there is no known association.[28,29] Known teratogens, such as alcohol, have defined phenotypic patterns of abnormality that are known to correlate with amount and timing of exposure in animal models. These data therefore, confirm the biologic plausibility of the argument. For hormonal pregnancy tests and birth control pills, such data generally do not exist.

Exposures

There are now famous teratogens such as DES and thalidomide, whose use has generated several lawsuits claiming damaged babies that have characteristic patterns of anomalies. However, in contradistinction to the above, progesterone and Bendectin for example, have *not* shown any specific pattern of malformations, or in fact, even unusual numerical occurrences. Nevertheless, multiple lawsuits have been argued over the years with variable results, although in most instances defendants have prevailed. Accordingly, one must be cautious in the administration of any agent, particularly in early pregnancy when organogenesis is occurring, because of the practical consideration of litigation, and not necessarily secondary to any true risks.

Litigation in areas of birth defects that occur at the same level as background occurrences will continue to be among the most frustrating for physicians and their attorneys to defend. So long as any "expert's" opinion is deemed to be equal to any other, the courts will continue to be plagued by "junk science." Totally incontrovertible top notch science has been kept out of court because plaintiff's counsel convinced a judge that it was "too new," when in fact there was testimony that the techniques were *routine*, daily use methods. Similarly, totally insubstantial drivel can be presented to the jury by professional outcasts who have no credibility in their field, which gets held up and made the equal of mainstream opinion. Until such miscarriages of justice are fixed, there is no hope for equity in the judicial system.

Commentary by Mr. Fisher: The issue of "junk science" as it pertains to first trimester teratogens, whether they be chemical, radiation, or otherwise is well highlighted in this chapter. Numerous so-called "experts" can be found to testify that almost anything in the first trimester will cause a teratogenic effect, resulting in dysmorphism, brain insult, limb deformity, etc. Given the nature of the legal process, regardless of the qualifications of the experts on the defense side, the jury has little understanding of the scientific relationship between a specific teratogen and fetal injury. Thus, the jury system does not really address nor eliminate the problem of "junk science."

However, more recently, several cases have brought to light "junk science" through the application of the Davis-Frye rule and the more recent scientific reliability case of Daubert vs Merrell Dow, 113 S. Ct. 2786 (1993). [Additional cases include (6th Circuit) and Turpin vs Merrell Dow, 9229 Fed 2d 1349 (6th Circuit)]. In those cases the *judge*, not the jury, initially screened the scientific reliability to determine if it was even appropriate for the jurors to hear the evidence. The court pointed out that the judge is the "gatekeeper" and decides whether or not there is sufficient scientific evidence to call a particular expert to testify regarding a cause and effect relationship.

Thus, there was a separate evidentiary hearing in which estimony, medical journals, treatises, and methodology of scientific testing based on scientific method, was evaluated by the judge before a jury would even hear the evidence.

It is in this manner, that defendants can now legally challenge the "professional expert" who opines without a sufficient medical or scientific basis. For further details, one should review the Daubert vs Merrell Dow case, in which the court lists various criteria that are to be evaluated before opinion testimony can be said to be based upon scientifically reliable information, including such things as the method of testing, the ability to repeat the results, peer review articles, showing general acceptance, etc.

References

1. Evans MI (ed). *Reproductive Risks and Prenatal Diagnosis.* Norwalk, CT, Appleton & Lange Publishing Co., 1992.
2. Hook EB. Rates of chromosomal abnormalities at different maternal ages. Obstet Gynecol 1981;58:292.

3. Evans MI, O'Brien JE, Dvorin E, et al. Biochemical screening. Curr Opin Obstet Gynecol 1994;6:453.
4. Brock DJ, Sutcliffe RG. Alpha-fetoprotein in antenatal diagnosis of anencephaly and spina bifida. Lancet 1972;2:197.
5. Brock DJ, Bolton AE, Monaghan JM. Prenatal diagnosis for anencephaly through maternal serum alpha-fetoprotein measurements. Lancet 1973;2:923.
6. Merkatz IR, Nitowski HM, Macri JN, et al. An association between low maternal serum alpha-fetoprotein and fetal chromosome abnormalities. Am J Obstet Gynecol 1984;148:886.
7. Wald NJ, Cuckle HS, Densem JW, et al. Maternal serum screening for Down syndrome in early pregnancy. Br Med J 1988;297:883.
8. Crossley JA, Aitken DA, Connor JM. Prenatal screening for chromosome abnormalities using maternal serum chorionic gonadotrophin, alpha-fetoprotein, and age. Prenat Diag 1991;11:83.
9. Cole LA, Kardana A, Park SY, et al. The deactivation of hCG by nicking and dissociation. J Clin Endocrinol Metab 1993;76:704.
10. Haddow JE, Palomaki GE, Knight GJ, et al. Prenatal screening for Down syndrome with use of maternal serum markers. N Engl J Med 1992;327:588.
11. Evans MI, Chik L, O'Brien JE, et al. MOMs and DADs: Improved specificity and cost effectiveness of biochemical screening for aneuploidy with DADs. Am J Obstet Gynecol 1995;172:1138.
12. Roe WI. Technology assessment and reimbursement implications for fetal diagnosis and therapy. In: Evans MI, Fletcher JC, Dixler AO, et al. (eds). *Fetal Diagnosis and Therapy.* Philadelphia, J.B. Lippincott Co., 1989, pp. 187-191.
13. Rosen FM. Liability and emerging technology. In: Evans MI, Fletcher JC, Dixler AO, et al. (eds). *Fetal Diagnosis and Therapy.* Philadelphia, J.B. Lippincott Co., 1989, pp. 192-198.
14. Evans MI, Dvorin E, O'Brien JE, et al. Alpha-fetoprotein and biochemical screening. In: Evans MI (ed). *Reproductive Risks and Prenatal Diagnosis.* Norwalk, CT, Appleton & Lange Publishing Co., 1992, pp. 223-236.
15. ACOG Committee on Obstetric Practice. Down syndrome screening. ACOG Committee Opinion, 1994, p. 141.
16. Chervenak FA, Isaacson GC, Campbell S (eds). *Ultrasound in Obstetrics and Gynecology.* Boston, Little, Brown and Co., 1993.
17. Johnson MP, Barr M, Treadwell MC, et al. Fetal leg and femur/foot length ratio: A marker for trisomy 21. Am J Obstet Gynecol 1993;169:557.
18. Greb AE, Sepulveda W, Romero R, et al. Isolated fetal choroid plexus cyst: Karyotyping is indicated. Am J Hum Genet (abstract 96) 1993.
19. Fletcher JC. Ethics issues. In: Evans MI, Fletcher JC, Dixler AO, et al. (eds). *Fetal Diagnosis and Therapy.* Philadelphia, J.B. Lippincott Co., 1989, pp. 4-7.
20. Fletcher JC. Ethics in experimental fetal therapy: Is there an early consensus? In: Evans MI, Fletcher JC, Dixler AO, et al. (eds). *Fetal Diagnosis and Therapy.* Philadelphia, J.B. Lippincott Co., 1989, pp. 438-448.
21. Jackson LG, Zachary JM, Fowler SE, et al. A randomized comparison or transcervical and transabdominal chorionic villus sampling. N Engl J Med 1992;327:594.
22. Firth HV, Boyd PA, Chamberlain P, et al. Severe limb abnormalities after chorionic villus sampling at 56-66 days gestation. Lancet 1991;1:762.
23. Burton BK, Schulz CJ, Burd LI. Limb anomalies associated with chorionic villus sampling. Obstet Gynecol 1992;79:726.

24. Brent RL, Beckman DA. Principles of teratology. In: Evans MI (ed). *Reproductive Risks and Prenatal Diagnosis.* Norwalk, CT, Appleton & Lange Publishing Co., 1992, pp. 43-68.
25. Froster UG, Baird PA. Upper limb deficiencies and associated malformations: A population-based study. Am J Med Genet 1992;44:767.
26. Olney RS, Khoury MJ, Alo CJ, et al. Increased risk of transverse digital deficiency after chorionic villus sampling: Results of the United States multistate case-control study, 1988-1992. Teratology 1995;51:20.
27. Brambati B. Early CVS and limb reduction defects. Sixth International Conference on Early Prenatal Diagnosis of Genetic Disorders, Milan, Italy, May, 1992.
28. Katz Z, Lancet M, Knornik J, et al. Teratogenicity of progestins given during the first trimester of pregnancy. Obstet Gynecol 1985;67:775.
29. Resseguie LJ, Hick JF, Bruen JA, et al. Congenital malformations among offspring exposed in utero to progestins, Olmsted County, Minnesota, 1936-1974. Fertil Steril 1985;43:514.

Chapter 3

Multiple Pregnancy Losses

◆◆◆

James H. Harger, M.D.

Introduction

Multiple pregnancy losses may encompass a wide variety of abnormal reproductive histories. Different authors have used a variety of criteria to define the population they are discussing when referring to women having more than one unintended loss of a pregnancy. Some authors have used the term "habitual abortion" to describe women losing their pregnancies prior to the gestational age of 20 weeks in order to conform with the standard definition of the word "abortion." While this relatively circumscribed term does limit the scope of the problem, its flaw lies in restricting the potential causes of the problem and arbitrarily limits the range of pregnancy losses that can be attributed to a specific cause. In this chapter, a more inclusive definition that allows consideration of women with previous ectopic pregnancies, spontaneous abortions, induced or voluntary abortions, fetal deaths (stillbirths), and neonatal deaths will be used. Neonatal deaths following previable pregnancies, that is, prior to a gestational age of 24 weeks as well as those occurring after viability has been attained but before full term (37 weeks) has been attained will also be included.

Finally, not only will women who have met the classic definition of recurrent pregnancy losses (three or more pregnancy losses, whether or not they are successive) be considered, but also the diagnosis and management of women with only two pregnancy losses will be discussed. Of necessity, risk management problems associated with women who have had only one prior pregnancy loss, or indeed, those with no previous pregnancy losses, but

---

From: Donn SM, Fisher CW (eds.): *Risk Management Techniques in Perinatal and Neonatal Practice.* © Futura Publishing Co., Inc., Armonk, NY, 1996.

who present with evidence of incipient pregnancy loss in the index pregnancy will be addressed.

Illustrations of Typical Cases

Some of the most difficult medico-legal cases regarding the prevention of pregnancy loss involve the woman without any precedent or history of pregnancy losses. In large part because most women currently expect pregnancies to reach a normal conclusion with minimal morbidity to mother or baby, medico-legal cases do arise from pregnancy losses in which the patient has never before lost a pregnancy. Most of these cases, however, result from the patient's grief and anger over the loss of a pregnancy in the second trimester. Although most women could not articulate the 15% risk of losing any recognized pregnancy in the first trimester, most realize that first-trimester spontaneous abortion does occur in a substantial number of pregnancies. As a consequence, very few medico-legal actions initiate from the loss of a pregnancy prior to a gestational age of 14 weeks.

The main exception to this general rule occurs in women who suffer a fall, motor vehicle accident, or a physical assault. In these cases, the plaintiffs argue that the trauma increased the chance of spontaneous abortion, an allegation that is completely unsubstantiated in the medical literature. In such cases, it is essential to ascertain the point of impact, since the pregnant uterus is extremely well protected in the first trimester. For this reason, falls and motor vehicle accidents rarely cause direct trauma to the uterus itself; and the uterus is, of course, suspended safely within the center of the pelvis by the cardinal ligaments, round ligaments, and protected by the bony pelvis around it.

At the other end of the gestational age spectrum, medico-legal action may be taken when the patient, her husband, or her family concludes that the diagnosis of preterm labor was not made sufficiently early to prevent and/or treat the problem (see Chapter 7).

Most of the medico-legal cases arising from the loss of a first pregnancy stem from adverse events in the second trimester. Many of these patients have had previous, successful, full-term pregnancies and then develop signs of pregnancy loss in the second trimester of the index pregnancy. In a few cases, primigravida women developed signs of pregnancy loss in the second trimester and alleged that the signs and symptoms of cervical insufficiency (often termed "cervical incompetence") were not considered or detected early enough to permit cervical cerclage.

The typical scenario in such patients includes very subtle and nonspecific complaints, such as pelvic pressure, backache, increased amounts of vaginal discharge, spotting, or symptoms of urinary tract infection which, after the pregnancy is lost in the second trimester, are then attributed to cervical insufficiency. The allegation made is usually one of failure to diagnose the condition soon enough for intervention to be effective in preventing the pregnancy loss.

A much more common situation leading to medico-legal action, however, is in the patient with one or more prior pregnancy losses in which similar symptoms have developed but have not been considered significant enough to warrant repeated cervical examinations by palpation or ultrasound. The assumption usually made by the plaintiff is that the previous history of pregnancy losses should have led to a diagnostic evaluation of cervical length, softness, or dilation. Typically, the patient arrives at a physician's office or hospital with the cervix dilated 1-3 cm. Since the cervix is beginning to dilate, then, the plaintiff reaches the conclusions that the cervix must have been "incompetent" to retain the products of conception within the uterine cavity until full term is reached. The theory developed by the plaintiff is almost always that the patient has cervical insufficiency rather than preterm labor, and that the attending has failed in any number of preventive actions.

The plaintiffs may theorize that the physician should have counseled the patient to observe for the presence of such symptoms and to report their occurrence immediately. Another allegation is that the patient was falsely reassured by the physician or an agent of the physician that the symptoms were unimportant and not indicative of an impending pregnancy loss, so timely action was not taken. Currently some plaintiffs even use cause-and-effect arguments based on very new and unsubstantiated hypotheses about the causes of preterm delivery, such as the presence of bacterial vaginosis or vaginal trichomoniasis. While there are preliminary data suggesting an increased risk of preterm delivery and preterm rupture of membranes associated with both of these conditions, the current data are epidemiologic and have not been substantiated in randomized, prospective clinical trials. Further, even if a cause-and-effect relationship could be established between bacterial vaginosis or vaginal trichomoniasis, there are no conclusive data demonstrating that the treatment of either condition would result in a lower rate of pregnancy loss or preterm delivery.

In some circumstances, medico-legal action has been undertaken on the theory that a diagnosis of cervical insufficiency was established in a prior pregnancy or by a diagnostic test on the current pregnancy. In some cases, the patient may have presented to a hospital with some degree of cervical dilation and with the membranes either bulging or completely protruding through the cervix in an "hourglass" fashion. The admitting resident or attending physician may then theorize or jump to the conclusion that the patient has cervical insufficiency, even though the diagnosis is not substantiated by prior history or by exclusion of other causes of preterm labor.

These patients then present to another physician for a subsequent pregnancy after recovering from the earlier loss. The patient assumes that they have cervical insufficiency and that the diagnosis will be accepted without further consideration. In other circumstances, the patient may be found to have cervical dilation of 1-3 cm during the current pregnancy and may be told that she has cervical insufficiency by the examining physician, by a radiologist performing an ultrasound scan that includes her cervix, or by physicians in training who lack sufficient experience and perspective to exclude other causes of the change in cervical dilation and effacement. Although the diagnosis of cervical insufficiency in a previous pregnancy may have been incorrect, patients often disregard the uncertainty or ambiguity of the diagnosis and reach the simplistic conclusion that therapy would involve nothing more complicated or risky than a cervical cerclage performed on an emergency basis.

Many of these simplistic assumptions about the causes of premature cervical dilation and effacement are based upon myths and outmoded beliefs about factors that may cause significant cervical injury and cervical insufficiency. Some of the factors that are assumed to be important predictors of an increased risk of cervical insufficiency include: diethylstilbestrol (DES) exposure in utero[1]; previous cervical biopsies, and/or cone biopsy of the cervix[2-5]; and previous induced abortions resulting in "damage" to the structural elements of the internal cervical os.[6-9] While many of these erroneous assumptions are deeply embedded within the belief systems of obstetricians and other physicians as well as those of the general public, there is little scientific support for them. In fact, in many instances, there are scientific studies that fail to show such associations to be significant or, indeed, to exist at all.

Ironically, the majority of medical actions regarding pregnancy losses are not really directed at a failure to prevent an immature or premature delivery. Most medico-legal actions in this area find fault with the physician for not acting quickly enough to perform a cervical cerclage, to initiate therapy for preterm labor with tocolytic agents, or to do some other intervention. The claims made about the nature of the loss involve the failure to salvage a live baby from the pregnancy. Unfortunately, the most serious cases and certainly those associated with the largest damages result from the birth of a very preterm infant with multiple complications of prematurity, and the allegation used by the plaintiff is usually that, had the physician intervened earlier, the severity of the prematurity would not be so great and the neurologic morbidity would be less severe. Only rarely does the plaintiff allege that the physician acted without a complete evaluation of the causes of pregnancy loss.

Medical Aspects of Recurrent Pregnancy Loss

Several studies of populations of women with recurrent pregnancy losses at varied gestational ages disclose five broad etiologic categories.[10-12] In couples with recurrent pregnancy losses, slightly over half can be found to have an abnormality in the morphology of the uterus, a genetic abnormality, an immunologic problem, endocrine causes, or a recurring infectious disease as the reason for the pregnancy losses. Each of these categories should be considered in a couple with recurrent pregnancy losses, and some of the causes may be observed in those women having their first or second pregnancy loss.

Congenital Uterine Abnormalities

Congenital uterine abnormalities may be found in as many as 20%-25% of couples with recurrent pregnancy losses. These abnormalities include a bicornuate uterus, a subseptate uterus, or a unicornis uterus. These congenital anomalies are best diagnosed with a hysterosalpingogram (HSG) performed in the second week of the menstrual cycle, although abnormal findings on the HSG usually must be confirmed by hysteroscopy. Both procedures do involve some risk to the patient, since an HSG carries a 1%-2% chance of endometritis or salpingitis. Rare patients can have an allergic reaction to the contrast material used for the HSG. Patients undergoing hysteroscopy may have unexpected complications of the general anesthetic, and other patients undergoing hysteroscopy may suffer from fluid overload and pulmonary edema secondary to excessive absorption from the fluid used to distend the uterus. Recent preliminary findings suggest that transvaginal sonography may be nearly as sensitive at detecting significant uterine abnormalities as the HSG and hysteroscopy, although the sensitivity and ability of the sonography to portray uterine morphology accurately remains to be established. Many uterine abnormalities can be corrected surgically at the time of hysteroscopic diagnosis, making this procedure an appealing one-step process in the evaluation of couples with recurrent pregnancy loss. The cost of hysteroscopy, the need for a skilled operator, and the risks of general anesthesia, however, remain the major concerns with this modality.

Genetic Abnormalities

Genetic abnormalities usually involving a balanced translocation in either parent are important causes to be excluded because of their implications for potential genetic abnormalities in future offspring. A thorough, complete family history is an essential element of detection of genetic abnormalities. In addition, parental peripheral lymphocyte karyotyping should be considered, although it is fairly expensive, averaging $300-$400 per person. The process of karyotyping an adult has minimal risk involving only a venous blood sample. Other than the cost of the test, the only significant hazard is the psychological effect on the involved parent of knowing that they have a cytogenetic abnormality and the subsequent guilt and shame that may be caused by this knowledge. Most couples with recurrent pregnancy loss, however, remain anxious to find a cause for their problem and feel relieved once they have a concrete reason for their pregnancy losses.

Immunologic Problems

Fewer than 5% of women with recurrent pregnancy losses may be found to have an immunologic reason for the pregnancy complications. Such complications are termed "primary antiphospholipid antibody syndrome," and they refer to an autoimmune condition in which the woman's immune system produces antibodies against such phospholipids as the blood clotting factors (so-called "lupus anticoagulants" [LACs]). Since patients with the primary antiphospholipid antibody syndrome typically have other medical manifestations such as stroke, pulmonary embolus, deep venous thrombosis, and other symptoms of autoimmune disease, a careful medical history is essential. At present, unfortunately, the diagnosis of LAC is very difficult, since laboratory tests for this syndrome are not standardized. In addition, there is confusion between the primary antiphospholipid antibody syndrome and those patients who merely have a low-positive test for anticardiolipin antibodies of the IgG isotype or any IgM anticardiolipin antibodies. The significance of such antibodies is unclear. Determination of the presence of these conditions requires a very specialized, experienced laboratory and may require consultation with other physicians who are familiar with the diagnosis and management of these unusual patients.

Endocrine Causes

Endocrine causes of recurrent pregnancy loss have long been considered an important category. Unfortunately, it is very difficult to define these endocrine causes precisely. These causes may include hyperthyroidism, hypothyroidism, and the so-called "luteal phase defect" (LPD). The diagnosis of LPD requires a disparity between the date of an endometrial biopsy sample and the calculated day of the menstrual cycle. This disparity must be present in at least two different menstrual cycles. While this diagnosis is rare, it may account for some causes of early first-trimester spontaneous abortions.[10] Hyperthyroidism and hypothyroidism are very uncommonly found in populations with recurrent pregnancy losses, although testing for them only requires a simple and inexpensive blood test. The question of whether women with type I diabetes mellitus are more likely to suffer spontaneous abortion is controversial.

Recurrent Infections

Past studies have indicated that women with recurrent pregnancy losses are more likely to harbor *Mycoplasma hominis* or *Ureaplasma urealyticum* in the cervix. Hypothetically, these organisms might gain entrance into the uterine cavity and cause an infection within the embryo or amniotic sac. The recent literature has failed to support a significant link between *U. urealyticum* colonization of the cervix and recurrent pregnancy losses, nor is there any evidence that eradication of *U. urealyticum* has a beneficial outcome on the pregnancy. With the increasing quality of culture techniques of these two organisms, so many patients are found to be colonized in the cervix and vagina with *U. realyticum* or *M. Hominis* that it is difficult to attribute any pregnancy losses to these organisms.

The Special Problem of Cervical Insufficiency

Cervical insufficiency has been blamed for many cases of pregnancy loss, both recurrent and initial. As originally defined, cervical insufficiency was a condition in which the cervix softened, shortened, and dilated painlessly in the second trimester, resulting in prolapse of the membranes and loss of an otherwise normal live fetus. Classically, the subsequent pregnancy losses occur earlier and earlier in gestation because of recurring damage to the collagen stroma of the cervix. Cervical insufficiency has been assumed to be related to DES exposure in utero,[1] previous cone biopsy of the cervix,[2-5] previous obstetrical cervical lacerations, previous Duhrssen's incisions to facilitate breech delivery, and previous induced abortion by forcible dilation of the cervix in the first trimester.[6-9] Since most studies of cervical cerclage do not find any of these risk factors present in the majority of patients who carry the diagnosis, the contribution of these risk factors is small. Further, a recent study concludes that cervical insufficiency is not an all-or-none phenomenon.[13] Rather, it points to defects of varying severity in the collagenous structure of the cervix and a relative deficiency of elastin in the cervix. These subtle defects would theoretically lead to a diminished ability of the cervical stroma to resist either the gravitational force applied to the uterine contents (fetus and amniotic fluid) or to very mild uterine contractions that would ordinarily not cause cervical dilation and effacement. While the hypothesis is interesting and somewhat plausible, it is nearly impossible to establish the diagnosis of cervical insufficiency in the presence of active uterine contractions because a normal cervix (i.e., one that is not weak or insufficient in any way) will dilate and efface in the presence of uterine contractions.

Since many patients who develop preterm labor in the second or early third trimester do not report specific sensations of painful uterine contractions in the early phase, uterine contractions in the second trimester may not produce the typical painful sensations of labor. Rather, such patients have only the vague symptoms of pelvic pressure, backache, and abdominal pain so often found early in women with preterm labor. The exact relationship between palpable uterine contraction in the second and early third trimester and the progressive cervical dilation and effacement that occurs with cervical insufficiency remains to be clarified. The most important distinction to be made by the physician attempting to diagnose the cause of second-trimester pregnancy losses is whether the patient had evidence of preterm labor. *If evidence of preterm labor can be established, it is virtually impossible to conclude that the cause of pregnancy loss was cervical insufficiency.* Rather, cervical insufficiency is a diagnosis by exclusion, since there are no diagnostic tests that have been proven to define the presence of cervical insufficiency.

The diagnosis of preterm labor in second trimester patients depends on the presence or absence of important but subtle clues. Patients presenting with a current pregnancy should be questioned carefully about abdominal pain, pelvic pain, pelvic cramps similar to those experienced during menstrual periods, increased vaginal discharge (which may be watery or mucoid in character), and the presence of any vaginal bleeding. Evidence of fever or leukocytosis should be sought. Abdominal and uterine palpation may detect contractions that are not perceived by the patient, and the palpation may also detect uterine tenderness indicative of abruptio placentae. A pelvic examination should evaluate cervical length, cervical softness, cervical position, and cervical dilation. Since it is impossible to palpate the entire length of the cervix, transabdominal or transvaginal ultrasonography provides an objective and non-invasive method of determining cervical length.[13] During ultrasound examination of the cervix, however, over-filling of the bladder may cause spurious readings of cervical length that are too long. If the patient has had previous pregnancies, similar information about the uterine contractions and cervical condition at the time of presentation should be sought. Prior evidence of fever or leukocytosis, along with a pathologic diagnosis of chorioamnionitis in the placenta and funisitis in the fetus, would help to confirm infection as the cause of labor. Conversely, the presence of uterine tenderness, vaginal bleeding, coagulation abnormalities, and a retro-placental clot are more suggestive of abruptio placentae as the cause of preterm labor. Since preterm labor may occur with congenital malformation of the uterus, an HSG or hysteroscopy should be performed 1-2 months after the pregnancy loss to ascertain the presence of bicornuate, subseptate, or unicornis uterus. Often careful reading of the initial history and physical examination performed by the admitting physician will disclose evidence of infection or abruption that was not mentioned in the discharge summary. Similarly, physician progress notes and nursing notes often provide useful information about the etiology of the pregnancy loss.

Management Problems

Once the differential diagnosis of the recurrent or imminent pregnancy loss has been resolved as fully as possible, management should be instituted on the basis of randomized prospective clinical trials whenever possible. Unfortunately, in a sensitive area such as recurrent pregnancy losses, many forms of therapy have not been validated by appropriate clinical trials. In this situation, it is essential to balance the known risks of the proposed therapy against the unknown effectiveness of that therapy. For example, some physicians advise patients with an unknown cause for recurrent pregnancy losses to undergo routine antenatal genetic testing. While such a strategy may a priori seem rational, there are no data to suggest that invasive diagnostic genetic tests are useful. If parental karyotypes have ruled out balanced translocations and the family history is not compatible with a genetic disorder, the risk of pregnancy loss from chorionic villus sampling, early amniocentesis, or conventional amniocentesis at a gestational age of 16 weeks is not warranted. Many patients with recurrent pregnancy losses are, of course, over 30-35 years of age, so they are at risk for the age-related trisomies. Counseling and testing of these patients, then, depends on other factors than the simple presence of recurrent pregnancy losses.

Couples in whom one partner has a balanced translocation should be informed about the possibility of an unbalanced translocation in their fetus and should be offered prenatal diagnostic studies if they so desire. They should, however, be instructed that, depending on the size of the involved chromosomal segment, the chance of a phenotypically-normal child ranges from 70%-80%.

In women with a proven uterine abnormality, the potential benefits of metroplasty should be compared with the potential surgical complications of repair of the defect. In women with intrauterine synechiae or with a subseptate uterus, operative hysteroscopy may be used by experienced specialists to resect the synechiae or the septum under direct vision. In either event, there is the possibility of uterine perforation by incising too deeply into the uterine wall. This complication, however, may be avoided by laparoscopic monitoring of the hysteroscopy.[14] Unfortunately, randomized studies of hysteroscopic metroplasty have not been conducted on a large scale, so it is difficult to know the benefits of such surgery. In the case of the bicornuate uterus, a laparotomy with Thompkins or Strassman metroplasty poses a greater risk. In addition, one study demonstrated that 15 of 840 women with a bicornuate uterus had a normal reproductive history.[15] For that reason, it is not clear that the metroplasty will substantially improve the outcome of the patient's pregnancy. In addition, the metroplasty causes a through-and-through scar in the myometrium that may not heal well and that may, therefore, rupture during a subsequent pregnancy, even prior to the onset of labor.

In patients whose pregnancy losses are attributed to luteal phase deficiency, the best documented treatment is progesterone vaginal suppositories twice daily during the first 12 weeks of pregnancy.[10] There are virtually no complications from this treatment and, therefore, practically no medico-legal risks. The progesterone provided is the same hormone that normally circulates in the patient during a normal pregnancy.

Similarly, patients whose recurrent pregnancy losses are attributed to chronic infection with *U. urealyticum* cervical colonization are treated with oral tetracycline for 10-14 days before the pregnancy. Tetracycline is, of course, contraindicated during the first trimester because of adverse effect on fetal bone growth and because third trimester treatment has been proven to cause developmental damage to bones and teeth in the newborn. As long as the tetracycline is not used during pregnancy, however, treatment for these cervical "infections" carries virtually no medico-legal risks.

Patients in whom the diagnosis of an autoimmune disease is made, especially those with so-called LAC, may be offered treatment, but which is potentially quite hazardous. These patients may be categorized into two groups: the primary antiphospholipid antibody syndrome, in which the LAC appears with high-level anticardiolipin antibody titers but no diagnosis of an autoimmune disease, such as systemic lupus erythematosus; and the secondary antiphospholipid antibody syndrome, in which the patient has both the diagnosis of an autoimmune disease and an LAC with or without high-titer anticardiolipin antibodies. In the secondary syndrome, patients may be continued on therapy for the autoimmune disease. While the therapy may be fairly benign, some patients are treated with anti-malarial drugs such as Plaquenil. This class of drugs has been linked to disorders of eye development and retinal damage in animals, but the incidence of such complications in human pregnancies treated with anti-malarial drugs is very low.

The more common therapy in pregnancy for patients with secondary or primary antiphospholipid antibody syndrome has been oral prednisone with or without low-dose aspirin (LDA). The alternative treatment for either the primary or secondary syndrome, especially with a previous history of maternal venous thrombosis or a pulmonary embolus, has been subcutaneous heparin in full anticoagulant doses. This therapy is often accompanied by LDA administration.

Patients treated with prednisone and LDA are at risk for a variety of complications, almost all attributed to the prednisone. These complications include hypertension, striae, excessive weight gain, peptic ulcer disease, osteoporosis, idiosyncratic aseptic necrosis of the femoral head, cataracts, immunosuppression, slow wound healing, and suppression of the maternal adrenal gland. In the latter situation, suppression of the maternal adrenal gland leads to an inability to adapt to physical stress situations, requiring a "stress dose" of steroids whenever major illness or surgery occurs during the prednisone regimen. In addition, 1%-2% of women treated with a 7- to 8-month course of oral prednisone will not recover adrenal function and will require chronic steroid replacement for the remainder of their lives. Clearly, it is imperative to caution patients about these potential hazards before choosing this alternative.

Subcutaneous heparin has some serious complications as well. Subcutaneous heparin given in a dose that produces full anticoagulation may lead to: 1. increased bleeding after trauma; 2. the risk of spontaneous intracranial, gastrointestinal, or bladder hemorrhage; and 3. significant blood loss. Patients anticoagulated with subcutaneous heparin have a risk of both a dose-related and an idiosyncratic thrombocytopenia, and are also at risk for osteoporosis and hip fractures. While it is difficult to compare the magnitude and severity of subcutaneous heparin with oral prednisone, each one used with LDA, there are no randomized, prospective studies demonstrating that one approach is better than the other, nor indeed, that either of these treatments is more effective than placebo. It can be difficult to justify the use of either therapy for these rather exotic conditions, but most patients with recurrent pregnancy losses and the diagnosis of LAC would insist on being treated with one or the other.

Finally, the use of cervical cerclage does carry some significant risks. First, there is the risk of inappropriate use of cerclage in women for whom other causes of recurrent losses have not been excluded. It is, therefore, imperative that the other causes be excluded before a cerclage is placed electively. The direct hazards of cervical cerclage seem infrequent, but about 1 woman in 50 with an elective cervical cerclage will lose her pregnancy within 4 weeks of the surgery.[16-19] The reason for the loss is not always clear and could be unrelated to the cerclage, but any complication following a surgical procedure is likely to be attributed to the surgery itself. Further clinical studies demonstrate that women with an elective cerclage in place are much more likely (130%) to have a cervical laceration requiring suturing at the time of delivery.[16] The laceration probably occurs because the artificial suture material elicits a fibrous scarring reaction in the cervix, which prevents it from dilating and effacing smoothly during labor. Rather, the fibrotic tissue in the cervix tears suddenly once its tensile strength has been exceeded. There are more serious reports of women with rupture of the uterus when they begin labor with a cerclage in place,[20,21] and there are reports of maternal death from overwhelming chorioamnionitis in a woman with a cerclage in place.[22] Finally, there are several reports of urinary tract fistulas opening into the vagina following cerclage procedures.[23-25]

Against the background of these complications, it would be important to determine whether cervical cerclage has any benefits. Unfortunately, most clinical publications in the last 40 years have failed to include a control group, so the efficacy of cervical cerclage has not been documented. There are only four prospective, randomized studies within the English language medical literature of cervical cerclage.[25,26] Three of the studies failed to show any improvement in outcome in women randomized to the cerclage group compared to the women randomized to a no-cerclage group.[26-28] In fact, women randomized to the cerclage group spent significantly more time in the hospital before delivery compared to women in the control group.[28] The fourth study, a very large international trial organized and analyzed in England, demonstrated no benefit of cerclage in the treated population with respect to birth weight, length of gestation, or rate of spontaneous abortion in either the first or the second trimester.[29] On the other hand, this most recent study indicates that women with two or three second trimester abortions did have a reduced frequency of second trimester spontaneous abortion and of preterm delivery before 33 weeks gestational age. This international study may, then, have demonstrated that there is a subtle advantage to using a cervical cerclage in women with a carefully selected reproductive history.

Documentation

In both preventing and defending a medico-legal action for recurrent pregnancy losses, there are several documentation issues that must be considered. First, the medical history must be carefully chronicled to provide a substantial basis for the diagnosis. Second, the results of each diagnostic test must be carefully documented on the patient's antepartum chart. Third, the physician must carefully document the reasons for choosing one therapeutic approach over the alternatives. Fourth, the results of formal and informal consultations with other physicians about the appropriate management plan should be documented by the attending physician. Fifth, the continuing evaluation of the patient throughout the antepartum visits must be documented to account for any changes in the management. Finally, and perhaps most importantly, the attending physician must document instructions and advice given to the patient by all health care providers. We shall examine each of these issues with respect to ways to reduce the medico-legal risk and to improve the quality of the available documentation.

Documentation of the Patient's Past and Recent Obstetric History

In the vast majority of medico-legal claims for recurrent pregnancy losses, chart review discloses very little attention to detail about the previous pregnancies. The history of the patient's previous pregnancies has often been limited to a single line on the standard prenatal record. This limited information often includes no more than the year in which the pregnancy loss occurred and the gestational age assumed for that pregnancy loss. In many instances, no fetal weight or details are available; rather, the prenatal record merely notes the sex of the infant and the fact that it is no longer surviving. On occasion, simple conclusions are stated in the "comments" section of the form, but statements such as "preterm labor" or "questionable cervical incompetence" are rarely helpful or sufficient. Not only is this information inadequate to defend against a medico-legal action, it is woefully inadequate to permit thorough chart review for quality assurance. While the conclusion may be plausible, valid, or proven, it is essential to have a legible record of those details available for review.

Documentation of each previous pregnancy should include a complete description of salient details and should include copies of relevant prior medical records whenever possible. When the patient has had a previous cone biopsy, the technique for the cone biopsy and the size of the cervical specimen should be described, especially through copies of the medical record, the operative note, and the pathology report. There may be significant differences in the risk of subsequent pregnancy losses if the patient had a "cold knife" cone biopsy compared to a "laser cone" or simple laser ablation of low-grade cervical intraepithelial neoplasia. Copies of ultrasound examinations may help to confirm the gestational age at which the pregnancy loss occurred.

Circumstances surrounding the pregnancy loss should be described in detail. The presence of uterine contractions, vaginal bleeding, pelvic pressure, increased vaginal discharge, or cervical dilation and effacement upon presentation to the health care provider should be obtained from medical records and recorded on the patient's chart. Often it is helpful to scrutinize the handwritten admission note as well as the nurse's notes on admission for a description of symptoms, cervical changes, amount of bleeding, and the reports of laboratory studies. The presence of fever, leukocytosis, or cultures of the products of conception may help to distinguish chorioamnionitis from other causes of pregnancy loss.

The pathology report of the placenta is a very important piece of evidence about the cause of the pregnancy loss (see Chapter 19). The presence of acute chorioamnionitis in the placenta can be very significant. Further, the presence of funisitis may indicate an actual fetal response to infection with consequent inflammation of the umbilical arteries and the umbilical vein. Further, the presence of significant autopsy findings (see Chapter 21), and/ or cytogenetic studies on the fetus may reveal significant congenital anomalies incompatible with life and probably responsible for the pregnancy loss.

Such information should be collected for each of the prior pregnancy losses, and it often requires obtaining copies of medical records from different hospitals. Although tedious, the practice of collecting the information satisfies two objectives. First, it provides accurate information that may have been erroneously interpreted and misstated by the patient. Patients are often not conversant with medical terminology, may have forgotten or confused details from several previous pregnancies, and may have misunderstood colloquial explanations by the attending physician at that time. Second, a careful evaluation of all previous records is an indication of a prudent and thorough physician who is not jumping to a conclusion or reaching a diagnosis based on insufficient information.

Documentation of Diagnostic Studies

Depending on the exact medical history of the pregnancy losses, the patient may have undergone a variety of diagnostic tests in order to complete a comprehensive evaluation for any previous pregnancy losses. Results of parental karyotypes and fetal karyotypes should be on the chart along with a careful assessment of HSG results. The prudent physician will review the HSG films personally rather than relying on a written report from a radiologist, who may not have sufficient experience in interpreting some subtle HSG findings. The results of cervical cultures for *U. urealyticum, M. hominis,* and urine cultures should be included. The results of endometrial biopsies and the timing of associated menstrual periods should be clearly written in the chart to exclude or include a diagnosis of luteal phase deficiency. Blood tests for autoimmune diseases, antiphospholipid antibody syndrome, and LACs should be available in the chart. If the family history has included recurrent pregnancy losses, congenital anomalies, or mental retardation in other family members, the results of any cytogenetic studies on the family members should also be included in this section of the chart. A simple way to accomplish these aims is to dictate a letter summarizing all of the details of the obstetrical history, medical history, and family history as well as a summary of all of the laboratory studies in logical sequence. Often, a consultant will provide such a letter, and a copy of such a summary should be included in the present antepartum chart for completeness and clarity. If the consultant or specialist is primarily caring for the patient during the index pregnancy, the consultant should summarize all the salient features that led to the final opinion. If other consultations were obtained with any other medical specialists about concomitant diseases or other conditions, i.e., a coagulation specialist or a rheumatologist, copies of those consultations should also be included in the current chart.

The Management Plan

Each prenatal record must include a summary of the preceding information along with the conclusions. Once a diagnostic impression has been formed, it is essential that the attending physician write a statement, however brief or lengthy as necessary, describing the alternatives that were considered and that were presented to the patient. This summary should include the potential risks of each therapy and the likely benefits and the prognosis for a successful live birth. This written statement of the conclusions and prospective management plan is usually the crux of any successful medico-legal defense. If the appropriate alternatives have been considered, and the reasons for the choice of one alternative over the other is clearly articulated, most malpractice cases dissolve into a quarrel over which approach is correct. Since there are few prospective studies to guide the choice of one therapy over another, it is usually relatively easy to defend any chosen course of action. If, on the other hand, no statement of reasoning has been made in the prenatal chart, all parties are left to assume what facts were known and what issues were considered in the final decision.

It is also essential to include a statement that the attending physician has shared these alternatives, risks, and prognoses with the affected couple and has at least sought their agreement in the chosen plan of management. For example, in a patient with a history of second trimester fetal death associated with early pre-eclampsia and small-for-gestational age fetuses, the diagnosis of LACs would be quite plausible. Appropriate management plans would include prednisone and LDA, heparin and LDA, or some more exotic experimental therapy. If the patient had a history of peptic ulcer disease, however, the prednisone and LDA combination should be rejected because of the known proclivity of patients on prednisone therapy to develop peptic ulcer disease. Such a mitigating circumstance should be clearly listed in the management plan to explain the reason for choosing the alternatives of subcutaneous heparin and LDA. In a patient with a significant hemorrhagic complication of heparin, then, the reason for choosing this therapy would be clear and much more difficult to criticize successfully.

As another example, in a patient with a history of a single second trimester live birth with neonatal death and normal cytogenetic results, the choice of an expectant management plan could be documented by explaining that cerclage had been considered but rejected because of a lack of prospective, controlled scientific studies supporting the use in women with only one previous second-trimester pregnancy loss. On the other hand, the documentation must include a plan to monitor the course of the patient's pregnancy and to alter the management should additional evidence of a specific cause for pregnancy loss become apparent.

Documentation of Antepartum Care

Although the initial diagnosis and management plan may seem reasonable in light of the available information, frequent reassessment of the patient's condition must be conducted and documented throughout the antepartum course.

Equally important is documentation of the instructions given to the patient about signs or symptoms that should be reported immediately to the health care provider. Patients should be instructed about the signs of preterm labor such as pelvic pressure, backache, increased watery discharge, and abdominal pain. The health care provider must document that the patient has been informed of the significance of these findings and of the need to report them immediately. Similarly, the health care provider(s) needs to document that they told the patient to call them if any of the above symptoms were to appear.

As new information becomes available during the antepartum course, the physician must document it carefully and continually reassess the original diagnosis in light of the new information. If a patient, for example, is undergoing weekly cervical examinations to determine the presence of cervical dilatation and effacement, the development of abdominal pain or rhythmic uterine contractions should be grounds for immediate assessment for labor contractions. The assessment may involve either manual palpation of the uterus or electronic fetal monitoring, but the results of the assessment should be recorded along with an interpretation of their influence on the original diagnosis. In another example, a patient with an uncertain diagnosis of "lupus anticoagulants" may develop a superficial venous thrombosis in one leg. Comprehensive assessment of coagulation tests should be undertaken immediately, and the appearance of a prolonged activated partial thromboplastin time or a prolonged dilute Russell viper venom time should be considered additional evidence of the LACs. At that time, then, the attending physician must discuss the treatment alternatives with the patient and write a revised management plan based on the new information.

Progressive cervical shortening, softness, and dilation during the second trimester should prompt consideration of a cerclage if no uterine contractions can be detected. Similarly, a sonographic finding of a very short (< 2.0 cm long) cervix with widening of the cervical canal should raise the possibility of cervical insufficiency. These incidental findings should not, however, be assumed to indicate cervical insufficiency, since there simply may be a substantial amount of mucus in the cervical canal. At that point, it would be essential to determine the presence of contractions and to document the relevance of the new information on the previous diagnosis and on the original management plan.

Documentation of Advice and Instructions

Many malpractice actions are complicated by allegations of inappropriate statements, cavalier treatment, and a failure to understand the gravity of the patient's complaint. The physician must develop a method for documentation of all telephone contacts with the patient, with an emergency room, or with a colleague asking for suggestions. If the physician provides advice to the patient via telephone, it is imperative that the physician document the substance of this telephone conversation in the patient's antepartum record on the very next day. For example, the patient may claim that she notified her physician about increased vaginal discharge, pelvic pressure, and backache, but was reassured that such symptoms were "typical in pregnancy." In the high-risk patient with multiple pregnancy losses or a concern about an imminent pregnancy loss, such complaints must be taken seriously, evaluated promptly, and documented extensively. In one recent instance, a radiologist jumped to the conclusion of cervical insufficiency from an ultrasound examination performed for fetal biometry at a gestational age of 18 weeks. The radiologist indicated that a given nurse had been notified of these findings, but there was no documentation that the nurse received the information, nor that she understood it. Rather, the alarming information should have been provided to the attending physician promptly, and his decision about the significance of the information documented on the chart. Thus, the physician-patient interaction must be prudent and interpreted in view of the patient's risk status, and it must be written on the antepartum record.

Further complicating this important issue is the presence of additional health care providers in the system. In physician group practices it is important to discuss new findings in patients on a frequent and regular basis, documenting the discussions in the chart. Even more important, however, is the need to have all personnel having contact with the patient document their interactions. A receptionist, medical secretary, or office nurse may erroneously reassure the patient about the insignificance of her complaints, only to find later that the patient was truly describing typical signs of preterm labor, chorioamnionitis, abruption, or medical complications of the pregnancy. Again, each health care provider and health care system is responsible for developing a plan to document the symptoms reported by the patient, the physical findings during the antepartum course, and the necessary revisions in the management plan based on the new information. Often the weakest link in the chain is the relatively unsophisticated telephone receptionist or answering service that is not aware of the significance of the complaints reported by the patient. Patients will, however, feel very angry and justifiably distraught that they were not allowed to speak directly with their own physician. To avoid such a problem, the physician should develop protocols for patient contact that document the time and nature of the incoming complaint as well as the character and identity of the individual responsible for the action taken.

Finally, although it seems almost too obvious to mention, the patient's reported complaints and her questions should never be treated with condescension or scorn. No matter how fatigued and harassed the health care providers may feel, patients are most likely to react negatively and initiate medico-legal action if they feel their complaints have not been taken seriously. Patients should be treated with courtesy and respect, and the health care provider must listen to the patient very carefully. If the patient's concern or complaint is not clear, the physician should ask the patient to re-state the concern until it has been clarified. It is incumbent upon the health care provider, further, to interpret the way in which the questions and report are phrased in order to detect any subliminal meaning. If the patient's questions and anxiety are greeted with concern and a serious regard for the welfare of the patient and her pregnancy, most medico-legal actions can be forestalled. Such conversations must, obviously, be documented in antepartum records for two purposes. First, it permits adequate quality assessment of the medical care. Second, it enables a successful defense of unwarranted medico-legal action.

In summary, careful documentation of the entire process of history taking, physical examination, laboratory studies, and previous medical records is a vital aspect of the care of these complex and high-risk patients. Even if the health care provider has chosen a controversial management option, careful documentation of the decision-making process will demonstrate that considerable thought went into making the choice. Since most of the management choices are controversial to some degree, it is critical that the chart demonstrate prudent consideration about the options. Even if a poor outcome results from the pregnancy, it may have happened anyway; the compelling evidence of a thoughtful approach to the diagnosis and management of the patient will virtually preclude a successful legal challenge.

> **Commentary by Mr. Fisher:** Most medico-legal problems transpiring from a claim of incompetent cervix involve one or more of four basic features:
>
> 1. Failure to accurately determine and document the history of prior pregnancy losses.
> 2. Failure to obtain or order medical records from prior pregnancy losses.
> 3. Failure to recognize the potential for an incompetent cervix and to document an appropriate treatment plan accompanied with patient informed consent.
> 4. Failure to adequately assess and determine the reason for the actual pregnancy loss that becomes the basis of the current lawsuit.
>
> Historical information regarding prior pregnancy losses is critical and should be maintained in the chart. If it is determined that the prior pregnancy losses are not attributable to incompetent cervix or are unlikely

to be attributable to incompetent cervix, the physician should make a specific statement in the medical record, such as "the patient does not have a history of incompetent cervix because...." This will provide a much stronger basis to later argue that there was a rational approach with documented historical facts that led to the physician's conclusion at the time of the incident. Explanations after the lawsuit has been filed often bring a claim of fabrication.

Ordering and/or obtaining prior medical records is important to challenge the claim that many patients give unreliable historical information, especially in the context of a questionable incompetent cervix. The physician should maintain any correspondence requesting such medical records from other physicians or institutions to prove that such a request was made.

Often the medical records will not be made available prior to the 24th week, or even during pregnancy, given the usually slow process of obtaining medical records. Retaining a copy of a letter requesting the same, however, is critical to show that the physician did all that could be done to address the prior pregnancy loss or losses.

Documented knowledge regarding the history, medical records, and plan of treatment is quite important. This, again, shows a thoughtful process on the part of the physician that is more defensible than an empty record. Discussions with the patient are important to avoid potential claims of lack of informed consent. There are those physicians who advocate cerclage, but others feel that it has not been shown to be beneficial, and perhaps even potentially dangerous. There are expert witnesses who will not acknowledge the conservative, non-cerclage treatment plan. Those expert witnesses will contend that only cerclage should be used as a treatment for suspected incompetent cervix. It should not be wrong to advocate as a physician, your personal preference, for or against cerclage, for or against conservative treatment with weekly examinations, but at the same time, because of the medico-legal environment, the physician should recognize that there are those experts who will challenge the conservative method. Because of this, it is suggested that when the conservative method is recommended by the physician, a discussion with the patient should be undertaken with that recommendation in mind, and documentation of the patient's informed consent should be placed in the medical record. This will assist the physician in not only defending the case from a conservative method standpoint, but it will prove that there are two schools of thought. Methods, recommendations, patient understanding, and choice need to be documented.

Finally, when the pregnancy at issue leads to an early second trimester loss, the reason for the second trimester loss is often not adequately investigated or documented from patient history and patient evaluation.

As Dr. Harger's chapter points out, there are so many potential explanations for multiple pregnancy losses, it would be hard to assign an early second trimester pregnancy loss simply to incompetent cervix without an adequate investigation of many potential factors. Even in cases where historically there has been good evidence of an incompetent cervix, this would not mean or prove that a current loss is related to the same thing. Current pregnancy loss should be investigated with an intense history, vaginal and cervical cultures prior to delivery if possible, placental pathology with culture, and postmortem examinations with cultures, as well. It would seem that these would be minimum investigational parameters along with possible genetic testing as well.

References

1. Nunley WC, Kitchin JD. Successful management of incompetent cervix in a primigravida exposed to diethel stilbesterol in utero. Fertil Steril 1979;31:217.
2. Dristensen J, Langhoff-Ross J, Fristensen FB. Increased risk of preterm birth in women with cervical conization. Obstet Gynecol 1993;81:1005.
3. Jones JM, Sweetnam P, Hibbard BM. The outcome of pregnancy after cone biopsy of the cervix: A case-controlled study. Br J Obstet Gynaecol 1979;86:913.
4. Buller RE, Jones HW. Pregnancy following cervical conization. Am J Obstet Gynecol 1982;142:506.
5. Moinian M, Andersch B. Does cervical conization increase the risk of complications in subsequent pregnancies? Acta Obstet Gynecol Scand 1982;61:101.
6. Schoenbaum SC, Monson RR, Stubblefield PG, et al. Outcome of the delivery following an induced or spontaneous abortion. Am J Obstet Gynecol 1980;136:19.
7. Madore C, Hawes WE, Many F, et al. A study of the effects of induced abortion on subsequent pregnancy outcome. Am J Obstet Gynecol 1981;139:516.
8. Harlap S, Shiono PH, Rancharan S, et al. A prospective study of spontaneous fetal loss after induced abortions. N Engl J Med 1979;301:677.
9. Daling JR, Emanuel I. Induced abortion in subsequent outcome of pregnancy in a series of American women. N Engl J Med 1977;297:124.
10. Tho PT, Byrd JR, McDonough PG. Etiology and subsequent reproductive performance of 100 couples with recurrent abortion. Fertil Steril 1979;32:389.
11. Harger JH, Archer DF, Marcheses SG, et al. Etiology of recurrent pregnancy losses and outcome subsequent pregnancies. Obstet Gynecol 1983;62:574.
12. Stray-Pedersen B, Stray-Pedersen S. Etiologic factors in subsequent reproductive performance in 195 couples with a prior history of habitual abortion. Am J Obstet Gynecol 1984;148:140.
13. Iams JD, Johnson FF, Sonek J, et al. Cervical competence as a continuum: A study of ultrasonographic cervical length and obstetric performance. Am J Obstet Gynecol 1995;172:1097.
14. Daly DC, Maier D, Soto-Albors C. Hysteroscopic metroplasty: Six years' experience. Obstet Gynecol 1989;73:201.
15. Ashton D, Amin HK, Richart RM, et al. The incidence of asymptomatic uterine anomalies in women undergoing transcervical tubal sterilization. Obstet Gynecol 1988;72:28.

16. Harger JH. Comparison of success and morbidity in cervical cerclage procedures. Obstet Gynecol 1980;56:543.
17. Golan R, Barnan R, Wexler S, et al. Incompetence of the uterine cervix. Obstet Gynecol Surv 1989;44:96.
18. Harger JH. Cervical insufficiency and recurrent pregnancy loss. In: Cetrulo CL, Sbarra AJ (eds). *The Problem-Oriented Medical Record for High-Risk Obstetrics.* New York, NY, Plenum Publishing Corp, 1984.
19. Harger JH. Cervical cerclage: Patient selection, morbidity, and success rates. Clin Perinatol 1983;10:321.
20. Lindberg BS. Maternal sepsis, uterine rupture, and coagulopathy complicating cervical cerclage. Acta Obstet Gynecol Scand 1979;58:317.
21. Thurston JG. Rupture of uterus following Shirodkar suture. Br Med J 1963;2:1392.
22. Dunn LJ, Robinson JC, Steer CM. Maternal death following suture of incompetent cervix during pregnancy. Am J Obstet Gynecol 1959;78:335.
23. Bates JL, Cropley I. Complication of cervical cerclage. Lancet 1977;2:1035.
24. Ulmsten U. Complication of cervical cerclage. Lancet 1977;2:1350.
25. Ben-Baruch G, Rabinovitch O, Madjar I, et al. Ureterovaginal fistula—a rare complication of cerclage. Isr J Med Sci 1980;16:400.
26. Dor J, Shaley J, Mashiach S, et al. Elective cervical cerclage of twin pregnancies diagnosed ultrasonically in the first trimester following induced ovulation. Gynecol Obstet Invest 1982;13:155.
27. Lazar P, Gueguen S, Dreyfus J, et al. Multicentered controlled trial of cervical cerclage in women with moderate risk of preterm delivery. Br J Obstet Gynaecol 1984;91:731.
28. Rush RW, Isaacs S, McPherson K, et al. A randomized controlled trial of cervical cerclage in women of high-risk of spontaneous preterm delivery. Br J Obstet Gynaecol 1984;91:724.
29. MRC/RCOG—Working party on cervical cerclage. Final report of the Medical Research Council/Royal College of Obstetricians and Gynaecologist multicentre randomised trial of cervical cerclage. Br J Obstet Gynaecol 1993;100:516.

Chapter 4

Diagnosis and Management of Ectopic Pregnancy

◆◆◆

Philip E. Young, M.D.

Introduction

The 1992 American College of Obstetricians and Gynecologists (ACOG) Professional Liability Survey examined malpractice claims brought against ACOG members in 1990 and 1991. Of gynecologic claims opened or closed in that time period, 8.7% involved ectopic pregnancy. Of the closed claims, one-third involved settlement or adverse judgment, with awarded amounts up to $100,000.[1] Considering that this study was conducted among gynecologists, who, as a whole, can be presumed to make fewer, or certainly no more, errors in the diagnosis and management of this entity than do family practitioners, internists, emergency room physicians, and other care providers, the subject of ectopic pregnancy clearly represents an area in which our diagnostic and management skills, as practiced, need improvement. Furthermore, based on 25 years' experience as a consultant to the legal system, it is clear to this author that the majority of ectopic-related lawsuits are based on failure to diagnose the entity in a timely fashion, leading to delay and the consequences therefrom. On the one hand, this fact may not be surprising; St. Paul Fire and Marine Insurance Company has reported that of the ten "most costly" malpractice verdicts in their experience, "failure to diagnose" a condition was the underlying liability in six of the ten verdicts.[2] On the other hand, the consistent occurrence of "failure to diagnose" lawsuits involving ectopic pregnancies should be surprising; modern technology makes the diagnosis of this entity, except perhaps where it is too early to matter, virtually always possible within 5 days or less of the presentation of the patient, and most

From: Donn SM, Fisher CW (eds.): *Risk Management Techniques in Perinatal and Neonatal Practice.* © Futura Publishing Co., Inc., Armonk, NY, 1996.

failures to diagnose this entity arise solely from the lack of consideration of the diagnosis or from the improper use, or the nonuse, of simple available technologies.

> **Commentary by Mr. Volk:** I would agree with Dr. Young that failure to timely diagnose is a major component of the complaints that women with ectopics have when they decide to visit an attorney's office. However, in the last several years, the women that I have seen often have a further complaint: that the surgeon failed to attempt to surgically save the affected tube. The first time I was presented with this argument, it was the second ectopic this patient had. Her physician, an obstetrician-gynecologist, had cared for her for years. Her first ectopic was treated by this physician by removal of the tube. When she presented with the second ectopic, there was no attempt to save her last tube and she consulted me. Since that time, I have been consulted on two further occasions by women with essentially the same history. Even with women who have one tube left, having had only one ectopic, they routinely complain about the failure to attempt to save the affected tube if it was removed.

Diagnosis

The most important tools of diagnosis of ectopic pregnancy are:

1. A high index of suspicion on the part of the clinician.
2. The use of the quantitative beta subunit hCG (qβhCG).
3. The vaginal ultrasound examination.

Some clinicians also rely on the serum progesterone, but this is not required to meet the standard of care.

Index of Suspicion

Every woman of reproductive age who presents to her physician or to the emergency room with irregular bleeding and/or pelvic pain must be considered to potentially have an ectopic pregnancy, regardless of additional history obtained. A frequent cause of lawsuits is the cavalier assignation of a lesser diagnosis to the complex of symptoms consisting of abdominal pain and/or vaginal bleeding, simply because the patient denies recent coitus, is known to be sterilized, or has some other readily identified explanation for her bleeding, such as missed birth control pills. *At the minimum*, a urine pregnancy test must be obtained in all such situations. Previously, urine pregnancy tests were felt to be quite unreliable in the diagnosis of this entity and were said to be negative in up to 50% of cases; however, modern pregnancy tests will detect levels of qβhCG in the urine as low as 25 mIU/mL, which means the test really is quite sensitive and is at least moderately reliable as a quick screening test. However, it does not replace the qβhCG, and if the clinical suspicion of pregnancy is at all high, a negative urine pregnancy test cannot be relied upon and the qβhCG must be obtained. There seems to be little indication in modern gynecology for the use of the qualitative serum βhCG in most situations, as any ambiguity in the diagnosis will require a follow-up qβhCG and in that case comparison of the quantitative values of the two studies will be essential in making the diagnosis.

With respect to index of suspicion, it is especially important to be suspicious in persons who have predisposing factors to this diagnosis. These include, but are not limited to, prior known pelvic infections, prior use of the intrauterine device, prior corrective tubal surgery of any sort, long-term prior infertility, and history of multiple sexual partners. These considerations will be especially important in the patient who presents in the nonemergent situation to her obstetrician for prenatal care. In these situations, where there are no symptoms to alert the clinician, it is especially critical that the predisposing factors be borne in mind and that appropriate diagnostic studies, as described below, be undertaken.

The Quantitative βhCG

Whether or not a screening urine test is used, the mainstay of diagnosis for this entity, and hence the standard of care requirement, is the use of the qβhCG. In most institutions, results of this test can be available within a few hours, and if not, the results should certainly be available by the next morning, when those results will serve as a backup to a negative urine test or, if the urine test was positive but no immediate intervention was undertaken, can begin the process of definitive evaluation.

Every laboratory has its own baseline level of qβhCG below which the test can definitively be taken to be negative. In most laboratories, this is < 5 mIU/mL. Such a result allows the clinician to safely pursue some other diagnosis and to consider ectopic pregnancy ruled out. This negative qβhCG should not be confused with a negative qualitative βhCG. The qualitative test is reported negative at somewhat higher values of qβhCG, usually 25-50 mIU/mL, and is not "negative" in the diagnostic sense that a qβhCG < 5 mIU is negative. This is another reason why the qualitative βhCG is of little value in the situation where ectopic pregnancy is a diagnostic concern.

A qβhCG that is not clearly negative requires follow-up. The basic requirement for following a qβhCG is based on the fact that in a normal pregnancy the value should double approximately every 2 days. Patients who are suspect for ectopic pregnancy must have this value determined at least every 3 days, and if doubling does not occur, other definitive diagnostic and/ or therapeutic intervention must be undertaken. As long as the qβhCG continues to double along the assigned curve, no further action is required until a level of ± 1800 is reached, at which time diagnostic sonography is used to rule in or rule out ectopic pregnancy based on the presence of an intrauterine sac (see ultrasound below).

Quantitative βhCGs that fail to double every 2 days represent abnormal pregnancies, either pending spontaneous abortions or ectopics. A common solution to making the differential diagnosis between these two entities at the time that the qβhCG is found to be abnormal is to perform endometrial sampling. This is usually best done as a dilatation and curettage (D&C), since if the abnormal pregnancy is in utero, the D&C will be therapeutic as well as diagnostic. Failure to obtain products of conception at the time of endometrial sampling is highly suspicious of ectopic pregnancy, while obtaining products of conception rules out ectopic pregnancy except in the very rare case where the two situations, intrauterine and extrauterine pregnancy, exist simultaneously. In the first situation, where no products of conception are obtained, a next step in diagnosis/treatment is required. In the latter case, where products of conception have been obtained at D&C, follow-up qβhCGs are required at 3- to 7-day intervals until the level has become negative.

The Ultrasound Examination

Vaginal sonography, when a normally doubling qβhCG reaches the ± 1800 mIU/mL level, is essential to management because the mere fact that the qβhCG is following the normal doubling curve does not exclude the diagnosis of ectopic pregnancy. Presence of a sac in utero is diagnostic of an intrauterine pregnancy, as opposed to an ectopic pregnancy. Care must be taken in interpreting these sonographically seen early intrauterine sacs. Decidual reaction in early ectopics can, on occasion, mimic a normal intrauterine sac; hence, the appearance of an intrauterine sac at ± 1800 mIU/mL is not of itself always sufficient, and if there is any doubt, the sonogram should be repeated in 1 week, at which time the situation should be clear.

Although it is not required in most protocols, vaginal sonography is often performed even in the face of nondoubling qβhCGs, partly in the mistaken hope that there will be an intrauterine sac, but also for the intention of seeing and measuring adnexal masses. However, it must be emphasized that failure to see an adnexal mass, or even the equivocal presence of what is believed to be possibly an intrauterine sac, in the presence of abnormal qβhCGs, does not rule out the need for following a definitive diagnostic protocol as outlined above.

The Serum Progesterone

Several investigators have demonstrated that serum progesterone of < 5 ng/mL in the presence of a positive qβhCG is not compatible with normal pregnancy.[3] Clinicians who depend on this measurement will immediately proceed to endometrial sampling (usually D&C) when a progesterone < 5 ng/mL is found in the presence of a positive qβhCG, without following the qβhCGs, waiting for doubling. In our experience, this is a very reliable way of accelerating the diagnostic process. The major inhibiting factor to the more widespread use of this test is that, unlike the qβhCG, the serum progesterone is not generally available on a stat basis and in many situations will not be available for up to 48-72 hours, by which time the second determination of qβhCG will already have been obtained. Failure to utilize the serum progesterone test does not render ectopic management below the standard of care. Nevertheless, physicians should be aware of its value and use it more often as it can be very helpful if the second qβhCG is in any way equivocal. It can, for example, be ordered as an afterthought on blood already in the laboratory when the first qβhCG is reported positive and the patient is being prepared for discharge in the case where no definite diagnosis of ectopic is being made. The result will then be available to assist in the interpretation of the second qβhCG determination if, as sometimes happens, the "doubling" is marginal at the second qβhCG determination.

Culdocentesis

Culdocentesis, previously a mainstay in the diagnosis of ectopic pregnancy, has no application in the diagnosis of early (unruptured) ectopics. It may occasionally still be useful in the emergency room situation to define the presence of blood in the cul de sac, but largely it has been replaced by the use of ultrasound techniques.

Management

The dictum of most of our residencies—that "the sun should never set on a suspected ectopic pregnancy"—is no longer true. Most ectopics today will be diagnosed long before they rupture; management, whether medical or surgical, can be carried out in these cases in a nonemergent situation. In particular, planned surgical management may be scheduled for the following day in most cases, when the patient is NPO and the full resources of the hospital are available.

Commentary by Mr. Volk: Obviously, the claim that is made for the patient that has significant morbidity, or for the family in the case of mortality, is the most costly—both in terms of money and emotion.

When you have a medical condition that can be alleviated in a fairly efficient and routine manner when the standard of care is met as Dr. Young has outlined, but is not, and the outcome is a disaster, the defense has serious problems.

Surgical Management

The mainstay of management of ectopic pregnancies remains surgical. It has become possible to make the diagnosis earlier and earlier, and as laparoscopic techniques have improved, the strong trend is the use of laparoscopy as opposed to the use of laparotomy for surgical treatment. Further, because of the availability of in vitro fertilization (IVF), conservation of the ipsilateral ovary has become an important consideration. Additionally, the tendency is toward performing the least surgery appropriate to the clinical condition, emphasizing conservation of the tube when possible. Laparotomy is the treatment of choice in patients who have large amounts of intra-abdominal fluid (presumably blood) seen on sonography and who are hemodynamically unstable, or who have large and/or complex masses encountered at diagnostic laparoscopy, or for any suspected ectopic where the physician is more comfortable with this open procedure.

> **Commentary by Mr. Volk:** Patients are becoming much more sophisticated about surgical and medical choices. When reading this section, I could envision a claim wherein the patient was unhappy because an open procedure was performed instead of a laproscopic one. Physicians and hospitals are advertising heavily about their new technologies. The potential exists for a claim that there was a failure to offer a laproscopic procedure and the patient was caused to be in the hospital rather than outpatient surgery, had a longer healing time, unsightly scars, etc.

As indicated above, however, these advanced states of ectopic pregnancy are becoming increasingly rare with modern diagnostic tools, and hence *laparoscopy* can often be used instead of laparotomy. Salpingectomy, where necessary, can be done with either of these approaches, or if preferable, linear salpingostomy and/or segmental resection can be used, always following the dictum to do the least surgery appropriate to the situation. Those patients who are treated laparoscopically can often leave the hospital within hours of the procedure, providing adequate follow-up is made available.

Follow-up after surgery is absolutely essential, especially after any conservative treatment. Incomplete removal of the ectopic is relatively common after conservative treatment, probably on the order of 10% of cases, although reported by some to be higher.[4] Following surgical treatment, patients must have periodic qβhCGs, probably about weekly, until the results are negative. Clearance of a positive qβhCG from the serum may sometimes take surprisingly and painfully long, over 3 weeks, but as long as the level is falling, further treatment is not required. If the qβhCG does not fall, definitive intervention is required. Some patients may require re-operation, but methotrexate therapy (see below) is a reasonable first alternative for the persistent qβhCG.

Medical Management

Single-dose methotrexate treatment in women with an unruptured ectopic pregnancy of 3.5 cm or less in greatest dimension on sonography has been described by Stovall and co-worker,[5] as well as others, and is being increasingly used in the United States. These patients do not require admission or any form of surgery. In 120 patients treated by Stovall and co-worker,[5] all pregnancies resolved successfully without a single one requiring surgical intervention. Eighty-two percent of the patients so treated who subsequently had hysterosalpingograms showed patency on the ipsilateral side. A few histologic studies have been performed on the affected tube in patients treated with methotrexate who had subsequent pelvic surgery for one reason or another at a later date, and these tubes have shown no residual effect from the methotrexate therapy when examined microscopically.[6] An unanswered question has to do with what is the physical appearance of the tubes in which patency is not achieved postoperatively. It is possible that in these pregnancies, methotrexate treatment results in a segmental defect in the tube similar to that seen after segmental resection, which would explain the occasional spontaneous finding of such a defect in a patient with no known surgical intervention. In that case, we may assume that the defect results from the spontaneous resolution of an ectopic pregnancy.

Single-dose methotrexate therapy, then, remains a viable alternative to surgery for management of the ectopic pregnancy, but, if used, it is essential that the patient be completely reliable for follow-up purposes, that careful attention be paid to the details of a protocol (which usually includes pretreatment curettage), and that a very fully documented informed consent be obtained from the patient to this less well-established therapy. The latter is essential if one is to avoid potential liability in the event of an unsatisfactory outcome. It is to be emphasized that in the Stovall protocol not a single patient required additional surgery and there were no serious maternal sequelae. The clinician who chooses this modality, especially in a noninstitutional setting, and suffers a maternal consequence, may expect to be exposed to liability.

Commentary by Mr. Volk: I would definitely agree with Dr. Young that the physician who utilizes methotrexate for ectopics has exposed himself/herself to liability unless all the parameters for experimentation of human subjects is covered. The potential toxicity of this drug would make a claim of injury to the mother utterly indefensible outside of a controlled setting with exquisite informed consent, especially where there are other avenues of treatment available that are effective.

Other Treatments

Expectant management, defined as the deliberate following of a known or suspected ectopic pregnancy without intervention of any kind in anticipation of spontaneous resolution, based on the fact that these conditions do resolve spontaneously in as many as 50% of cases,[7] is rarely, if ever, defensible.

> **Commentary by Mr. Volk:** I again agree with Dr. Young that failing to act, in the face of knowing (the standard legal words are "knew or should have known") that an ectopic pregnancy exists in your patient, is indefensible. There is no ability to advance the position that the standard of care allows one to utilize expectant management. In this circumstance, expectant management is no management. When you factor in the downside of "doing nothing," the potential exists for a very unhappy jury in the case of serious maternal injury.

Surgical management using local injection of the ectopic with substances such as methotrexate, prostaglandin, potassium chloride, or hyperosmolar glucose has recently been described; these are not standard techniques and should not be undertaken without the thoroughly documented consent of the patient, and, in my judgment, should not be undertaken outside of a carefully controlled institutional protocol. Utilization of any of these "other treatments" is not usual in the United States, and may well be considered below the standard of care in the event of an untoward outcome.

Common Mistakes Seen in Cases Coming to Lawsuit

Essentially, virtually all cases of ectopic pregnancy that come to lawsuit contend that there was a delay in diagnosis by the caretaker that resulted either in the death of the patient, which is unusual but not unheard of today, or, most commonly, in blood transfusion and/or extensive surgery that would not otherwise have been indicated.

> **Commentary by Mr. Volk:** As I noted earlier, I have evaluated several cases where the allegation was made that the surgeon failed to attempt to save the tube by performing a procedure less destructive.

As is implied by the remarks in the preceding paragraphs, these delays are virtually always the result of failure to order a qβhCG when it should have been ordered at the first visit, or failure to follow-up on it adequately.

This author has personally reviewed a case in recent years in which a legal secretary presented to the emergency room four times in 3 days complaining of nausea, vomiting, abdominal pain, cramps, and vaginal spotting. In addition to this, she reported on each occasion, and it was recorded by the nurses on the emergency room sheet, that she believed she could be pregnant. At the first visit a complete blood count was obtained, and it was normal. She was signed out with the diagnosis of gastroenteritis. She made three subsequent visits in the next 72 hours. No blood work was repeated. The same diagnosis was assigned at each visit. No pregnancy test was ever obtained. At her last visit she was brought in by the paramedics and pronounced dead. Postmortem examination confirmed the obvious: She had exsanguinated from an ectopic pregnancy. The case clearly was indefensible.

There are really only two major scenarios in which this "delayed diagnosis" problem typically evolves:

1. *The Emergent Visit*: The patient presents to the emergency room with some symptomatology. It is rare, in my experience, for delay problems to arise if the pregnancy test is obtained in this situation. The difficulty comes from persons repeatedly failing to order the test during the visit, for reasons outlined in the introductory paragraphs. To reiterate, the rule is to consider that any woman of reproductive age who has any lower abdominal complaints may well have a complication of pregnancy and a pregnancy test should be obtained. It is never a defense in retrospect when the patient has had a significant delay in diagnosis of an ectopic pregnancy to look at the ER sheet and say that the signs and symptoms did not indicate this test.

The other, related difficulty in the emergency room is the situation where the test is done automatically, but the emergency room physician is not highly suspicious of an ectopic pregnancy and discharges the patient with routine follow-up instructions before the test has been returned. Then, when the test is returned, it is somehow not brought to the physician's attention. Pregnancy tests, unlike many laboratory tests, when viewed in the abstract on a report, do not declare themselves to be normal or abnormal, since a positive is just as able to be normal as a negative. Hence, these laboratory tests are often unconsciously signed off later by personnel as "normal," simply because the connection is not made between that positive test and the patient who was seen the night before.

Several simple precautions can help to avoid this latter problem. One is to be sure to inform the patient, if she is being discharged without the pregnancy result coming back, that it is her obligation to call the next day for the result of the tests and to record this in the chart. A second (better) solution is simply not to discharge the patient until the test is back, although this may not always be possible in practice, especially in smaller hospitals. In that case, however, at least a urine pregnancy test result should have been obtained. A third precaution is that no pregnancy test ordered in an emergency room and returned to an emergency room should be filed without examination of the result by a physician and without a signature of the physician on same.

> **Commentary by Mr. Volk:** I agree completely with Dr. Young's analysis of the emergency department visit of a woman of childbearing age with lower abdominal complaints. In the situation wherein a female patient is discharged without the pregnancy test results back to the physician for interpretation, there has got to be a procedure in place for evaluation of the test results by the physician who evaluated the patient and notification of the patient of the analysis of the test results in light of the patient's evaluation. All this must be documented. It is entirely correct that too often non-physician personnel review the laboratory results and make decisions what to do with those results. I have seen many cases where this has occurred and imposed liability. In addition to that situation, in emergency departments, often the physician who sees the patient does not review the returned laboratory data because he/she is off-shift. The physician on shift at the time the data are returned reviews it, but does not have the benefit of having seen the patient. This also happens frequently and can lead to liability.

2. *The Nonemergent Visit*: The other source of difficulty arises with the patient who presents to the obstetrician with what appears to be a normal pregnancy and it is not appreciated by either patient or physician that she is at high risk for ectopic. "High-risk" situations include all the conditions listed above ("index of suspicion"). A patient meeting any of these high-risk criteria requires the following of qβhCGs until the ± 1800 mIU/mL level is reached and a definitive ultrasonographic diagnosis of intrauterine pregnancy can be made. Failure to do so will frequently be found to be below the standard of care.

In both the emergent and the nonemergent situations, inadequate follow-up instructions are frequently a problem. Since the qβhCG is the cornerstone of early diagnosis and it must be obtained at 3-day intervals, it is clear that follow-up not to exceed 3 days must be scheduled. Patients must be told of the importance of this and, if they are referred from an emergency room to a private physician, they must be clearly informed that they cannot accept appointment delays from the physician's front desk when seeking to make a follow-up appointment. It is often difficult—if not impossible—for physicians' offices to correctly screen these calls if the caller does not identify the urgency of the follow-up appointment. Unfortunately, at this time, the medical system in the United States does not permit fully computerized control of this situation, even though this is theoretically achievable in any kind of national health insurance environment. At this time, therefore, heavy reliance must be placed upon the patient to properly arrange follow-up; for this, she must be properly informed.

> **Commentary by Mr. Volk:** I would suggest an additional procedure that should be utilized. The persons responsible for making return appointments, either when the patient is leaving the office, taking appointments over the telephone, or *canceling and rescheduling because the physician will not be available*, should be required to determine the reason for return visit. (It is my experience that these mistakes may occur when the office staff has to cancel patient appointments for whatever reasons.) The office staff must have a list of situations that require urgent appointments and how they are to be scheduled. Too often, grievous mistakes are made by poorly trained, or worse, non-trained personnel, which may cause serious morbidity, or even mortality because of a failure to appreciate the urgency of follow-up. Further, it is dangerous to rely on patients to understand the medical need for follow-up. In 99.9% of the cases, reliance on the patient will be sufficient, but in that rare case it will not be. This must not be left to chance.

Consequences of Delay in Diagnosis

Significant delays in diagnosis that result in either the death of the patient or in transfusion and/or extensive surgery that would otherwise not have been necessary, are clearly substantial sources of liability. Where delays of more than a few hours have been involved and a patient has either died or required a blood transfusion, it will often be correctly found that there has been an error in management.

Even where the delays have not resulted in death or transfusion, however, if the delay is significant (on the order of days), the result is that the ectopic is given time to enlarge and, because of the enlargement, the ultimate operation requires the loss of a tube or at least more extensive loss of a portion of a tube than otherwise would have been necessary. If the affected tube happens to be the patient's only remaining tube, the damage to her as a result of the delay is often claimed to be substantial, since in any "natural" sense she is no longer able to bear children.

Commentary by Mr. Volk: As previously discussed, I had just such a case. This type of case is a serious one.

It is also possible to argue with some merit that even if the lost tube is not the last tube, it may well have been the best tube, and hence the same argument of "substantial damage" from the delay applies. With delays of several days' duration, these are very valid arguments.

The more intriguing question in the matter of delay in these situations, however, is the question of the significance of delay of hours or even 1 or 2 days. I have seen it argued in court that delay of a few hours was the difference between saving and not saving a tube. Such an argument is, in my opinion, largely preposterous. As a general rule, it is clear that the tube that ruptures was in most cases greatly dilated and distended and already virtually destroyed in the few hours immediately prior to rupture, and I doubt that the diagnostic delay of a few hours or even 1-2 days greatly affects the extent of the surgery required in most cases.

Commentary by Mr. Volk: The testimony that would support the party's position would have to use the standard of medical probability. The opinion of an expert must be to a "reasonable degree of medical probability." The test is whether or not medical science can answer this question to that standard. If the state of medical science cannot determine that a delay of a few hours, etc. resulted in not being able to save the tube, the plaintiff patient has not met her burden. An essential element of the patient's case has not been proven and that element is causation. The patient must prove that the delay in diagnosis directly and proximately caused the harm.

On the subject of the consequence of delayed diagnosis, it is my opinion that delays of < 24-48 hours cannot reasonably be assumed to have changed the overall magnitude of tubal conservation that was possible. Delays greater than that, however, as indicated above, may significantly damage the tube beyond that which was present at the earlier diagnostic opportunity, resulting in either less residual tube for future re-anastomosis or more likelihood of nonpatency of the operated tube, or even the removal of the tube as a whole.

Calculating the Damages of Mismanagement

The logical potential for monetary damages claimable by the patient who has lost a tube because of what she perceives to be mismanagement has been greatly reduced in recent years by the existence of IVF. It has been shown that patients who have a single ectopic pregnancy have approximately a 60%-80% chance of conceiving again, and of those subsequent conceptions, 10%-20% will be ectopic. After two ectopics, the subsequent conception rate goes down even more and the repeat ectopic rate goes up. Generally speaking, the pregnancy rate for IVF can be taken to be 30% for one try, approximately 45%-50% for two tries, and as much as 60% over three tries. For most patients who have had a prior ectopic, that 60% figure approximates the intrauterine pregnancy rate that they could have expected even with the most expeditious surgical or medical management. There exists, therefore, some number of IVF attempts that statistically would render the patient with a "lost" tube just as likely to be pregnant as if she had not lost her tube. Therefore, in a patient who has, in fact, lost either her only remaining or her best tube as a result of delay in diagnosis, even if she is considered to be rendered infertile thereby, so long as she has both ovaries remaining, she can be regarded to have a chance of getting pregnant by IVF. Accordingly, the calculation of monetary value of lost fertility should currently be sharply limited, not exceeding the cost of three or four IVF attempts, all certainly well below a total cost of $50,000.

> **Commentary by Mr. Volk:** I applaud Dr. Young in attempting to determine a system for evaluating the damages in the type of claims that we are discussing. However, there are several types of damages that he does not discuss. For instance, an element of damage exists because the patient cannot conceive in a more natural manner than IVF. Surely, loss of the natural ability to conceive is a significant one! The psychological dysfunction, loss of time, inconvenience, embarrassment, and other circumstances surrounding the requirement to attempt pregnancy through IVF, rather than coitus, are other examples of damages that readily come to mind. There are certainly others.

Of course, delays that result in more serious problems, such as the loss of one or more ovaries, or even of both tubes, ovaries and/or the uterus, or blood transfusions, present entirely different problems. Lawsuits over the total loss of reproductive organs (beyond those which can be overcome with IVF), and the resulting hormonal and psychological deficiencies, over and above any infertility considerations, present potentially very substantial monetary liabilities. Also, I have seen several lawsuits in which the only damage was the fact that the patient had had a blood transfusion that could have been avoided with earlier diagnosis, and was now concerned about contracting AIDS, even though subsequent testing failed to show HIV III positivity. It is apparently very difficult to put a price on "concern."

> **Commentary by Mr. Volk:** The HIV "concern" claims are very interesting ones. On the one hand, you have a patient who has no evidence of any physical harm from the transfusion who alleges that

the transfusion was made necessary as a result of the malpractice of a health care provider. The patient has "HIV-phobia." In law school remedies class, one is taught that every wrong has a remedy. Following that axiom, the patient with an unnecessary transfusion has some remedy for the damages of HIV-phobia. On the other hand, the law requires proof of causation between the malpractice and damages. Does an unnecessary transfusion directly cause the damages that a patient alleges result from HIV-phobia? Or should the law require proof of the reasonable person standard—that is, would a reasonable person have HIV-phobia from an unnecessary transfusion, and therefore liability only attaches if the reasonable person standard is met? This is a difficult question.

Documentation Matters

It follows from the statements above that it is critically important that the emergency room physician document his/her pregnancy tests and follow-up instructions to the patient; that these follow-up instructions be adequate; that obstetricians' offices be acutely aware of the necessity of providing timely follow-up when patients call on the telephone for emergency room follow-up, instruct their staffs accordingly, and retain scheduling information (to show availability) for several years; and that obstetricians follow closely, and document their follow-up of those patients who have apparently normal pregnancies but fall into high-risk groups. It is also critically important at the time of any ectopic surgery that the rationale and thinking behind the extent of surgery that was performed be explained in the operative note. This will be particularly important if the operating surgeon knows that there have been prior visits to health care providers. The operating physician has an obligation to both the previous provider and to the patient to document the most accurate assessment possible of the anatomy encountered and of the circumstances under which this operation took place; and to render, where possible, an opinion as to what difference, if any, any delays in diagnosis made. A carefully recorded operative note that notes the findings and makes an honest attempt to postulate how these are related to the preceding diagnostic interventions or lack thereof is a very powerful tool in the defense of the case, where that is appropriate, or is a powerful tool on behalf of the plaintiff in seeking deserved redress in the case where the patient has been badly served by the providers. Also, careful documentation of the rationale for whatever form of surgical treatment is chosen will provide a defense against subsequent claims of too much or too little surgery for the presenting situation. This advice to give detailed and explicit information in the operative note is contrary to usual physician practice, but is, I believe, more consistent with good patient care and good risk management. The vaguely worded operative note that is intended to shield prior caretakers (or oneself) from subsequent legal criticism is a transparent sham anyway and only impugns the writer's integrity in any liability dispute.

Final Comments

It cannot be emphasized strongly enough that the emergency room physician must order a pregnancy test in any woman of reproductive age group who does not clearly and obviously have some other problem. Obviously, a pregnancy test may be inappropriate in a person who presents with a gunshot wound to the head, but for anything less obvious, the surest way to provide definitive diagnosis for the patient and definitive protection for the emergency room physician is a serum qβhCG. It is equally important to re-emphasize that the obstetrician must not overlook the importance of careful scrutiny of the qβhCG in asymptomatic patients who fall into high-risk groups, and to follow a logical and aggressive protocol in the case of abnormal qβhCGs. It has been my unfortunate experience to have reviewed a number of cases in which obstetrician-gynecologists started out properly by ordering the qβhCGs and then made improper assumptions about falling qβhCGs without adequate endometrial sampling and/or laparoscopic follow-up, as required by protocol, to ascertain that this falling qβhCG resulted from an intrauterine pregnancy and not an ectopic. The subsequent delay led to unnecessary additional and complex procedures at a later date that would not have been necessary earlier.

Attorneys and patients alike tend to feel that when multiple visits have been made prior to the diagnosis of ectopic that the health care provider has not provided the best possible care and that the patient has sustained substantial damages. Where multiple visits are concerned, especially visits that do not move the caretaker closer to a diagnosis, this assumption may often be correct. Again, it is critically important that the care provider have a high index of suspicion and once the qβhCGs are under way, that a logical, aggressive, directed plan of management be followed until a definitive resolution is obtained. It is only in this way that the patients will get maximum care and that the physicians will reduce their liability for this significant problem to a minimum.

Commentary by Mr. Volk: Dr. Young has written an interesting and informative chapter and I believe has tried to fairly evaluate both sides in this type of claim. In this day and age, claims involving the ability to reproduce are being seen and evaluated on a more frequent basis as medical science has the ability to preserve the reproductive capacities of patients by timely intervention.

References

1. Heland K. ACOG Professional Liability Department, personal communication.
2. Fasburg RG. Chief of Staff Newsletter, Scripps Memorial Hospitals, San Diego, California, January 1994.
3. Carson SA, Buster JE. Current concepts: Ectopic pregnancy. N Engl J Med 1993;329:1174.
4. DiMarchi JM, Kosasa TS, Kobara TY, et al. Persistent ectopic pregnancy. Obstet Gynecol 1987;70:55.
5. Stovall TG, Ling FW. Single-dose methotrexate: An expanded clinical trial. Am J Obstet Gynecol 1993;168:1759.
6. Kooi S, Van Etten FHPM, Kock HCLV. Histopathology of 5 tubes after treatment with methotrexate for a tubal pregnancy. Fertil Steril 1992;57:341.
7. Lund JJ. Early ectopic pregnancy: Comments on conservative treatment. J Obstet Gynecol Brit Emp 1955;62:70.

Chapter 5

Hypertensive Disorders in Pregnancy

◆◆◆

Baha M. Sibai, M.D.

Introduction

Hypertensive disorders are the most common medical complications of pregnancy, with a reported incidence of about 10%.[1] The incidence may reach 20% in nulliparous women, women with multifetal gestation, women with pre-existing chronic hypertension-renal disease, and in those with previous pregnancies complicated by hypertension and/or pre-eclampsia.[2] In addition, these disorders are a major cause of maternal and perinatal mortality and morbidity.[1,2] As a result, the presence of these disorders is a major cause of litigation against physicians and hospitals involving cases of alleged misdiagnosis and/or treatment. In this discussion, opinions are given regarding definitions, diagnosis, management, and pregnancy outcome of these disorders that have been derived from the literature and from personal experience of reviewing such claims.

Definitions and Classification

The term "hypertension in pregnancy" is usually used to describe a wide spectrum of patients who may have only mild elevations in blood pressure or severe hypertension with various organ dysfunction. Hypertension may be present before pregnancy or it may become evident for the first time early in pregnancy, in the second trimester, at term, intrapartum, or postpartum. The terminology used to describe these disorders has been confusing and inconsistent. "Pregnancy-induced hypertension" (PIH) is a term that is used

From: Donn SM, Fisher CW (eds.): *Risk Management Techniques in Perinatal and Neonatal Practice.* © Futura Publishing Co., Inc., Armonk, NY, 1996.

in the American College of Obstetricians and Gynecologists (ACOG) technical bulletin[3] and is vague and broad—thus, it should not be used in clinical practice. A better term to use in the medical record is to describe exactly what the findings are, for example: hypertension, generalized edema, proteinuria, or a combination of the above. The term "pre-eclampsia" should be used only to describe patients who have persistent hypertension and new onset proteinuria. In addition, the physician should document the presence or absence of associated symptoms such as persistent headache, blurred vision, epigastric or right upper quadrant pain, and vaginal bleeding.

Hypertension

Hypertension is the hallmark for the diagnosis of these disorders. The diagnosis of hypertension is based on blood pressure criteria that could be relative (a threshold value from an earlier recording prior to pregnancy or early in the first trimester), or absolute (at least 140 mmHg systolic and/or at least 90 mmHg diastolic). The hypertensive recordings must be present on two occasions at least 6 hours apart. Therefore, it is important to comment about or obtain (if possible) all recorded blood pressures prior to pregnancy. This recording should serve as the baseline blood pressure. If this blood pressure is not available, then the first trimester blood pressure should serve as the baseline. In the absence of either of these readings, absolute blood pressure elevations should be used. It is important to emphasize that the threshold increase criteria are inadequate to diagnose gestational hypertension or pre-eclampsia, since a gradual increase in blood pressure from first-to-third trimester is seen in a large number of normotensive pregnancies (67%-75%).[4,5] However, these criteria should be used as a red flag for close observation of the patient, particularly in association with the presence of generalized edema, proteinuria, and other symptoms such as headaches, blurred vision, or epigastric pain. Indeed, the presence of these symptoms is more important than the absolute level of blood pressure regarding pregnancy outcome.

Edema

The so-called classic triad of pre-eclampsia includes hypertension, proteinuria, and edema. Edema is diagnosed as a clinically evident swelling or as rapid increase in weight; however, there are no standardized methods used in reporting these findings. In addition, edema occurs in about 80% of all pregnancies, and generalized edema with excessive weight gain has been reported in 30%-60% of normotensive pregnancies.[6] Moreover, 35% of patients with eclampsia at the University of Tennessee, Memphis had no edema before the onset of convulsions. Hence, the presence of edema should not be used in the diagnosis of pre-eclampsia. Nonetheless, the presence of pathologic edema such as facial puffiness, periorbital edema, ascites, or weight gain 5 pounds or greater per week during the third trimester should be documented in the records. These women should be seen more frequently (at least every week) because they are at risk for impending pre-eclampsia. The presence of proteinuria and/or associated symptoms of pre-eclampsia with generalized edema should lead to immediate hospitalization and maternal evaluation to rule out the presence of HELLP syndrome.[7]

Proteinuria

The presence of proteinuria is usually detected by either urine dipstick evaluation or the sulfosalicylic acid cold test on random urine samples. The concentration of protein in random samples is highly variable and is influenced by several factors, particularly vaginal secretions, urinary tract infection, and activity. Several clinical studies define abnormal proteinuria as at least 1+ on dipstick upon two occasions at least 6 hours apart. A common problem encountered in medico-legal claims is the assumption by health care providers that the presence of proteinuria resulted from contamination or urinary tract infection. To avoid this problem, dipstick proteinuria should be confirmed by obtaining a catheterized urine sample, urine culture, and (if necessary) by 24-hour urine collection.[8]

The presence of abnormal proteinuria (2+ on dipstick or > 300 mg/24-hour collection) in association with hypertension establishes the diagnosis of pre-eclampsia. It is important to document and explain to the patient that this combination increases the likelihood for convulsions, abruptio placentae, fetal growth retardation, and preterm delivery.[9] The risks for these complications will depend on gestational age at onset as well as the severity of the abnormalities. A simple clinical classification for hypertensive disorders of pregnancy is listed in Table 1.

Antepartum Management

The ultimate goals of therapy of these disorders must always be safety of the mother first, and then delivery of a live, mature newborn who will not require intensive and prolonged neonatal care. The decision between outpatient management or hospitalization and between expectant management or consideration for delivery is usually dependent on one or more of the factors listed in Table 2. As a result, it is important to document these findings as well as to discuss these options with the patient.

Patients with Hypertension Only

In clinical practice, the majority of women with hypertensive disorders of pregnancy will have only hypertension. The hypertension could be chronic

Table 1
Classification

I. Gestational Hypertension
    Mild hypertension
        systolic < 160 mmHg or
        diastolic < 110 mmHg
    Severe hypertension
        systolic ≥ 160 mmHg or
        diastolic ≥ 110 mmHg

II. Gestational Proteinuria
    Mild (≥ 1+ on dipstick and < 5 g/24 hour)
    Severe (≥ 5 g/24 hour)

III. Pre-eclampsia (Hypertension + Proteinuria)
    Onset > 20 weeks gestation
    Mild pre-eclampsia
        mild hypertension and mild proteinuria
    Severe pre-eclampsia
        severe hypertension and proteinuria
        mild hypertension and severe proteinuria
        persistently severe cerebral symptoms

IV. Chronic Hypertension
    Hypertension before pregnancy
    Hypertension before 20 weeks gestation

V. Superimposed Pre-eclampsia
    Hypertension and new-onset proteinuria or new-onset
    Uric acid > 6 mg/dL

Table 2
Clinical Factors to be Considered in Management

Diagnosis of the condition
Severity of the disease process
Fetal gestational age
Fetal growth and well-being
Maternal condition
    results of blood tests
    presence of symptoms
Presence of labor
Bishop cervical score

or gestational and the degree could be mild or severe. For women with chronic hypertension, the risks include exacerbated hypertension (10%-15%), superimposed pre-eclampsia (15%-25%), abruptio placentae (1%-3%), and fetal growth retardation (8%-20%).[9,10] It is important to note that most complications are related to the development of superimposed pre-eclampsia. Moreover, lowering maternal blood pressure with antihypertensive drugs will not reduce these complications—with the exception of exacerbated hypertension. Therefore, these women should be observed very carefully during the initial stages of pregnancy. Early detection of superimposed pre-eclampsia is best accomplished by means of serial testing of uric acid and 24-hour urine protein if they develop ≥ 1+ proteinuria on dipstick evaluation. These patients should have careful fundal height measurements and serial ultrasonographic examination for fetal growth starting in the third trimester. Repeat testing should be performed every 3-4 weeks (or more often) if clinically indicated. Nonstress testing should start at time of diagnosis of superimposed pre-eclampsia and/or if abnormal fetal growth is suspected. Otherwise, nonstress testing should be started at about 34- to 36-weeks gestation and should be repeated at weekly intervals. Antihypertensive therapy with methyldopa or labetalol may be used if systolic blood pressure exceeds 160 mmHg or diastolic pressure exceeds 100 mmHg. This therapy may reduce exacerbated hypertension and the subsequent need for hospitalization.[11] However, the use of methyldopa or labetalol may obscure the diagnosis of superimposed pre-eclampsia, which should then be made based on elevated uric acid, proteinuria, or low platelet counts (< 100,000/mm^3). The patient should be instructed to report the onset of abdominal pain and/or vaginal bleeding. If such symptoms are present, the physician should immediately evaluate the patient for early detection of abruptio placentae. It is important to emphasize that the development of superimposed pre-eclampsia dictates frequent observation, which is best accomplished in the hospital.[1,10]

Mild Gestational Hypertension

In general, pregnancy outcome in these patients is invariably good. However, some of these pregnancies may be associated with reduced uteroplacental blood flow. In addition, about 20% of these patients may progress to pre-eclampsia and be at slightly increased risk for development of fetal growth retardation (5%-10%), abruptio placentae (0.6%-0.8%), HELLP syndrome (1%), and eclampsia (0.1%). Thus, those who have a Bishop's cervical score of more than 5 at (or near) term should undergo induction of labor for delivery. Even if conditions for induction are unfavorable, the pregnancy should not continue past term. In addition, delivery should be considered at < 37-weeks gestation in patients who have associated symptoms, in those who are unreliable (would not comply with home bedrest), and in those with suspected fetal growth retardation. For those who are remote from term (< 37 weeks), management should include home bedrest, close observation of maternal blood pressure and urine protein (preferably daily), instructions regarding symptoms of pre-eclampsia, checking platelet count and liver enzymes twice weekly, plus evaluation of fetal status with sonography and nonstress testing. Ultrasound assessment of fetal growth should be performed at the time of diagnosis and then repeated every 3 weeks. Nonstress testing should be performed at the same time and repeated on at least weekly intervals. The frequency of subsequent office visits, as well as the need for fetal testing, will depend on initial clinical findings and the ensuing clinical progression. If the maternal condition remains stable (i.e., no significant change in blood pressure, weight gain, absent proteinuria, appropriate fundal height growth, or stable fetal kick count), then weekly visits are appropriate. Onset of maternal symptoms, a sudden increase in blood pressure, or development of proteinuria requires more frequent evaluation, preferably in-hospital. In my experience, most medico-legal claims encountered in these patients have dealt with issues of patient selection for outpatient management, documentation of instructions and patient options, and failure to appreciate the clinical significance of patient complaints during telephone calls. It is important to consider outpatient or home management only in those who are considered highly reliable. Patients should be instructed to rest at home and to avoid operating a car when returning to the physician's office. In addition, the patient should be instructed to report immediately symptoms such as headache, blurred vision, epigastric pain, nausea or vomiting, abdominal pain, contractions, or vaginal bleeding. One way to avoid communication problems during patient management is to instruct the patient to mention that she was diagnosed with gestational hypertension when talking with either the office or hospital nursing or clerical staff, another doctor in the same group practice who may not be familiar with her case, or with personnel at the answering service. A policy should be available where such calls should be communicated to the physician as soon as possible. Presence of the aforementioned symptoms (particularly if persistent) is an indication for immediate evaluation either at the office or hospital.

Mild Pre-Eclampsia

Pregnancies with mild pre-eclampsia, particularly those < 36-weeks gestation, are associated with increased rates of fetal growth retardation (10%-15%), preterm delivery (50%), abruptio placentae (1%-2%), and eclampsia (0.2%).[12-14] The first step in the management of these patients is prompt evaluation of maternal and fetal conditions, usually in the hospital. Based on

Table 3

Indications for Delivery in Mild Pre-eclampsia

Gestational age ≥ 37 weeks with ripe cervix
Onset of labor and/or membrane rupture
Onset of persistent headaches or visual symptoms
Epigastric or right upper quadrant pain
Abdominal tenderness or vaginal bleeding
Thrombocytopenia (platelets < 100 × 10^3/mm^3)
Severe oligohydramnios or IUGR by ultrasound
Abnormal fetal heart rate testing*

*Non-reactive nonstress test confirmed by biophysical profile or contraction test.

Table 4

Characteristics of Patients Eligible for Outpatient Management

Systolic pressure < 150 or diastolic pressure < 100 mmHg
Proteinuria ≤ 1000 mg/24 or < 2+ on dipstick
Highly reliable
Absent cerebral signs and symptoms
Absent epigastric or upper quadrant pain
Absent fetal growth retardation by ultrasound
Normal antepartum fetal testing
Normal liver enzymes and platelet count

the results of this evaluation, a decision is then made regarding the need for delivery, expectant management, or prolonged hospitalization. Maternal evaluation should include serial measurements of blood pressure, urine dipstick evaluation for proteinuria, 24-hour urine protein measurements, platelet count, liver enzymes, and presence of symptoms. Fetal evaluation should include ultrasound examination of the amount of amniotic fluid and estimated fetal weight, and nonstress test. Table 3 lists some of the indications for delivery in these patients. For patients who remain undelivered, subsequent management will depend on maternal findings and response during hospitalization. Some of these women may be eligible for outpatient management with rest at home if they satisfy the criteria listed in Table 4. Subsequent management plans for these patients (in-hospital or outpatient) are outlined in Table 5. For those being managed as outpatients, prompt hospitalization is indicated if there is any evidence of disease progression (hypertension, proteinuria, excessive weight gain, new onset of symptoms) or if there is abnormal fetal growth.

Table 5
Antepartum Management of Mild Pre-eclampsia

Relative bedrest (hospital or home)
Blood pressure measurement (4×/day)
Dipstick for urine protein (daily)
Evaluate symptoms of pre-eclampsia (daily)
Platelet count and liver enzymes (2×/week)
Fetal movement counts (daily)
Antepartum fetal testing (2×/week)
Ultrasound for fetal growth every 3 weeks

Severe Pre-Eclampsia

These pregnancies are usually associated with marked reduction in utero-placental and fetoplacental blood flow. This reduction is particularly severe in those who develop it at < 32 weeks gestation. As a result, these pregnancies are associated with high rates of perinatal mortality and morbidity mainly because of severe fetal growth retardation and preterm delivery. In addition, they may be associated with increased rates of maternal morbidity such as HELLP syndrome, disseminated intravascular coagulopathy (from severe abruptio placentae), pulmonary edema, eclampsia, or acute renal failure. Consequently, the onset of severe pre-eclampsia requires immediate hospitalization to an area for intensive monitoring of maternal and fetal conditions. The first step in management is to administer magnesium sulfate for the prevention of convulsions, to use antihypertensive drugs for the control of extreme levels of hypertension, evaluation of maternal condition for the presence of symptoms as well as the presence of hemolysis, elevated liver enzymes, elevated serum creatinine, and thrombocytopenia.

In general, delivery is considered the appropriate therapy for the mother regardless of gestational age. However, such therapy may not be appropriate for the fetus, particularly when the gestational age is < 33 weeks. As a result, expectant management in an attempt to prolong pregnancy for fetal reasons may be appropriate for gestations between 24 and 32 weeks.[15-18] It is important to emphasize that this therapy is appropriate only in a select group of patients and should be practiced only in a tertiary care center with adequate maternal and neonatal care facilities. These patients should be informed of the risks and benefits of such management. They also require close monitoring of maternal-fetal conditions on a daily basis.[18,19] It is recommended that such patients be managed in consultation with a perinatologist. Antepartum fetal testing and maternal liver enzymes and platelet counts should be performed

---

Table 6
Indications for Delivery During Expectant
Management of Severe Pre-eclampsia

Fetal Indications
> 34 weeks gestation
33–34 weeks with documented lung maturity
Estimated fetal weight < fifth percentile by ultrasound
Evidence of severe oligohydramnios
Abnormal fetal testing
Rupture of membranes

Maternal Indications
Preterm labor or vaginal bleeding
Eclampsia or encephalopathy
Pulmonary edema or renal failure
Persistent oliguria despite therapy
Persistent thrombocytopenia
Severe epigastric pain or cerebral symptoms
Maternal desire
Severe hypertension unresponsive to maximum drugs therapy

---

daily. Indications for delivery during expectant management are listed in Table 6.

HELLP Syndrome

Hemolysis (H), elevated liver enzymes (EL), and low platelets (LP)—or a combination of these (HELLP)—are well recognized complications of pre-eclampsia-eclampsia. Several of the signs, symptoms, and laboratory abnormalities that constitute the HELLP syndrome may be confused with similar findings that are usually present in a number of distinct medical and surgical disorders. This is particularly true when the manifestations develop remote from term. Diagnosis is often delayed and management is usually complicated by inappropriate medical and surgical treatments that may be dangerous for both mother and fetus.[7,20] As a result, complications related to this syndrome are currently a major cause of litigation claiming failure to diagnose pre-eclampsia. It is therefore critical that physicians be alert to the many facets of this syndrome and its presentation.

The typical patient is usually white and complains of epigastric or right upper quadrant pain at < 36-weeks gestation. Some will have nausea and vomiting (40%-50%) or diarrhea (5%-10%), and others will have nonspecific viral syndrome-like symptoms. The majority of patients will give a history of malaise for the past few hours or days before presentation. Some of these patients may complain of flank or shoulder pain, hematuria, bleeding from the gums, or jaundice. Hypertension or proteinuria may be slight or absent. Physical examination will show right upper quadrant tenderness, significant weight gain (ascites, generalized edema), petechiae, or purpura. Thus, some of these patients may have a variety of signs and symptoms—none of which are diagnostic of classic pre-eclampsia. Consequently, it is recommended that all pregnant women with gestations beyond 20 weeks and having any of these symptoms should have a platelet count and liver enzyme determinations irrespective of maternal blood pressure level. Since 30% of cases of HELLP syndrome develop postpartum, similar evaluation should be performed in all women having these complaints within 1 week of delivery.[20]

Intrapartum Management

Some of the medico-legal claims typically encountered during this time are failure to give magnesium sulfate to prevent convulsions, failure to distinguish bleeding of a "bloody show" from abruptio placentae, failure to use antihypertensive drugs to treat a certain blood pressure level, mode of delivery, and the association of abnormal fetal heart rate tracing with subsequent neonatal outcome.

Prevention of Convulsions

Patients with diagnosed pre-eclampsia are at increased risk for convulsions during labor and for the first 12- to 24-hours postpartum. The risks are slight in those with mild disease (1%), but may reach 3%-10% in those with severe disease at < 32 weeks gestation and those with HELLP syndrome. Therefore, all patients with diagnosed pre-eclampsia should receive parenteral magnesium sulfate during labor and for at least 12-hours postpartum. In patients with severe pre-eclampsia, or HELLP syndrome, magnesium sulfate should be continued for at least 24-hours postpartum. A typical regimen to use may be a loading dose of 6 g to be given over 20 minutes followed by a maintenance dose of 2 g/hour as a continuous intravenous solution (5% Dextrose in lactated Ringer's solution).

Diagnosis of Abruptio Placentae

As stated previously, the rate of abruptio placentae is slightly increased in patients with hypertensive disorders. The risk of abruptio placentae is not related to hypertension, but rather to the presence of pre-eclampsia. The highest risk is usually seen in patients during or immediately after convulsions or in those with HELLP syndrome. Therefore, it is important to document that patients were informed about reporting the onset of abdominal tenderness or vaginal bleeding. It is also important that nursing personnel be informed that they should report this finding to the physician once it occurs. The physician should evaluate the patient immediately once this finding is reported. Early in labor the bleeding may signify a "bloody show," particularly when it is minimal, not persistent, and is not associated with uterine contractions or fetal heart rate changes. Generally, the onset of vaginal bleeding in such patients requires frequent and continuous evaluation of uterine activity and fetal heart rate patterns. Abruptio placentae should be suspected if there are tetanic contractions, if uterine contractions occur more than five times in 10 minutes, or if there are repetitive late decelerations and/or fetal bradycardia. Additionally, abruptio placentae should be suspected if bleeding is persistent in the absence of placenta previa (see Chapter 13).

Antihypertensive Therapy

The objective of treating severe hypertension is to prevent cerebrovascular accidents without compromising uteroplacental blood flow, which is already reduced in severe pre-eclampsia-eclampsia. There is considerable confusion regarding what blood pressure level to treat and the level to achieve and maintain during treatment. Most studies and textbooks recommend treatment if the diastolic blood pressure exceeds 110 mmHg. Some require this elevation to be persistent for at least 6 hours, some for 1 hour, and others for 30 minutes.[17,21,22] In addition, the recommendation is to lower the diastolic level to below 100 mmHg and then keep it between 90 and 100 mmHg.[2] Moreover, a recent consensus report recommended treating lower levels of diastolic blood pressures for young primigravidas; however, no specific level was described.[1] A review of all such recommendations indicates considerable inconsistencies and none of these recommendations is based on scientific data. Nonetheless, because of these recommendations, several expert witnesses have testified that diastolic blood pressure as low as 100 mmHg should be treated.

Pre-eclampsia is characterized by endothelial cell injury as well as vasospasm.[1] These vascular pathologic changes have been described in cerebral blood vessels using Doppler velocimetry, angiography, computerized tomography scanning, magnetic resonance imaging, and autopsy.[23-25] Some of these patients are predisposed to cerebral ischemic changes and stroke as a result of the disease process itself. Also, some patients with severe pre-eclampsia-eclampsia will have thrombocytopenia and DIC because of the progression of the illness or because of abruptio placentae. These patients are also predisposed to intracerebral hemorrhage at normal or mildly elevated blood pressures. Finally, some patients with pre-eclampsia have a propensity to develop cerebral complications because of the above abnormalities. In these patients, the presence of hypertension (usually fluctuating with wide pulse pressure) is the result of intracerebral hemorrhage rather than the cause. Consequently, any aggressive or rapid reduction in maternal blood pressure may consequently result in reduced cerebral blood flow—producing cerebral ischemia to normal brain tissue.[26]

Cerebral tissue perfusion is directly related to mean arterial blood pressure (MAP). MAP is calculated from both systolic and diastolic pressures:

$$\text{MAP} = \frac{1 \text{ systolic} + 2 \text{ diastolic}}{3}$$

In the nonpregnant state, there is loss of cerebral autoregulation when MAP exceeds 150 mmHg.[27] This loss of autoregulation will result in cerebral vascular injury leading to hypertensive encephalopathy or hemorrhage. The upper limit of cerebral autoregulation in pregnancy is unknown and most recommendations for treating blood pressures have focused on diastolic blood pressure values. In addition, the duration of sustained hypertension before starting therapy is unknown.

Recently, Patterson-Brown et al.[27] recommended a threshold level for treatment during pregnancy as a sustained MAP > 125 mmHg. This level was chosen to allow a reasonable safety margin. The authors recommended treatment if MAP > 125 mmHg was sustained for > 45 minutes or if MAP > 140 mmHg was sustained for > 15 minutes. Control of blood pressure was achieved using intravenous bolus doses of hydralazine.

In view of the above inconsistencies (and in order to avoid potential medico-legal claims), the following steps are recommended. Antihypertensive treatment should be started if the MAP is persistently > 125 mmHg for at least 1 hour or if the diastolic blood pressure is persistently > 105 mmHg for at least 1 hour. The aim of therapy is to keep MAP below 125 mmHg (but not < 105 mmHg) and diastolic pressure below 105 mmHg (but not < 90 mmHg). This therapy can be achieved with the use of 5 mg bolus doses of hydralazine to be repeated as needed every 15-20 minutes for a maximum total dose of 20 mg/hour. Blood pressure should be recorded every 15 minutes during therapy and then every 1 hour once the desired blood pressure values are achieved. If hydralazine does not lower blood pressure as needed and/or if maternal side effects such as tachycardia or headache develop, another drug such as labetalol (20 mg intravenous bolus doses) or nifedipine (10 mg oral tablets) can be used. If recurrent hypertension as defined above develops, then antihypertensive drugs should be repeated as needed. Therefore, it is important to document serial measurements of blood pressure during labor and postpartum in all patients with severe pre-eclampsia-eclampsia. It is important to emphasize that these threshold values are empiric and that there is no evidence to suggest any correlation between maternal blood pressure values and the likelihood of stroke in women with pre-eclampsia. Indeed, in the absence of cerebrovascular disease (aneurysms, malformations, or cerebral venous thrombosis) or severe thrombocytopenia, the likelihood of stroke in patients with severe hypertensive disorders of pregnancy is < 0.1%. The majority of these women were not treated despite having a diastolic blood pressure exceeding 110 mmHg for at least 3 hours. These data do not seem to indicate that a 5-10 mmHg difference in diastolic pressure is going to make a difference regarding the development of stroke. In addition, it is important to obtain arteriography or autopsy in all patients with cerebral hemorrhage in pregnancy or postpartum to rule out the presence of anatomic cerebral vascular malformations.

Fetal Distress and Mode of Delivery

Some of the typical medico-legal claims in this case deal with the issue of performing Cesarean section to prevent maternal and neonatal complications in patients with pre-eclampsia, HELLP syndrome, and eclampsia. It is important to emphasize that vaginal delivery is the best method for delivery in these patients. Cesarean section should be reserved for obstetric reasons only. There should be no limit on duration of labor in these patients in the presence of normal progress of labor. As stated previously, pre-eclamptic pregnancies may be associated with reduced uteroplacental blood flow and higher than normal rates of fetal growth retardation, oligohydramnios, abruptio, or preterm birth. As a result, these pregnancies are more likely to have abnormal fetal heart rate patterns than normotensive pregnancies.[28] In addition, some of these infants will be delivered with low Apgar scores and acidotic blood gases secondary to their antenatal complications, rather than labor itself. It is, therefore, important to document the presence of these complications before the onset of labor, and to utilize continuous fetal heart rate monitoring during labor in all such patients.

In some patients, the presence of severe abnormal fetal heart rate patterns (absent beat-to-beat variability with repetitive late or severe variable decelerations) during labor is evidence of an already compromised fetus that has suffered cerebral injury during the prenatal period and/or prior to monitoring. This is particularly true when the pregnancy is complicated by severe fetal growth retardation, oligohydramnios, or abruptio placentae. Therefore, delivery of such fetuses by emergency Cesarean section will not guarantee that the infant will escape neurologic deficits later in life.

Occasionally, severe fetal heart rate abnormalities or "ominous patterns" can be found in patients who are either unconscious after eclamptic convulsions, in shock from ruptured liver hematoma, or because of severe abruptio placentae and possible coagulopathy. In such cases, emergency Cesarean section for fetal reasons may lead to catastrophic outcome for both mother and infants. In patients with eclampsia, fetal bradycardia and late decelerations are common findings during (and immediately after) a convulsion. These abnormalities are reversible following correction of maternal hypoxia and acidosis. Additionally, these patients should be oriented to name, place, and time before being subjected to anesthesia and surgery.

> **Commentary by Mr. Fisher:** Physicians often face the claim that the fetus was simply "more susceptible to intrapartum fetal distress" as a result of PIH, placental insufficiency, intrauterine growth retardation (IUGR), etc. In most cases, it is virtually impossible to know if there was neurologic compromise before labor. Therefore, it is very important to avoid intrapartum fetal distress in the PIH mother.

Outcomes

Neonatal Outcome

Hypertensive disorders during pregnancy as a group are reportedly associated with preterm delivery, fetal growth retardation, increased fetal distress during labor, and increased perinatal mortality and neonatal morbidity.[2] However, the published reports included a heterogeneous group of patients with various etiologies for hypertension—including women with severe pre-eclampsia, renal disease, various forms of hypertension, and various times of pre-eclampsia onset (as well as various modalities of management). In addition, the published data are based on studies that do not distinguish infants with IUGR from those without this complication, or extremely premature infants from term infants.[29] Moreover, some of these studies do not differentiate between women who had severe hypertension early in pregnancy from those who had mild uncomplicated hypertension during pregnancy.[10] Therefore, in evaluating immediate as well as long-term infant complications, it is important to take the above variables into consideration.

There are several studies describing neonatal complications in pregnancies complicated by severe pre-eclampsia or hypertensive disorders of pregnancy. Brazy et al.[30] compared neonatal complications between one group of 28 infants of severely hypertensive women who delivered 36-weeks gestation to another group of 28 infants of normotensive women matched by gestational age. Infants of hypertensive mothers had significantly higher incidences of growth retardation, microcephaly, thrombocytopenia, leukopenia, neutropenia, and low Apgar scores (Table 7). Additionally, Koenig and Roberts[31] reported that 49% of newborns of hypertensive mothers had neutropenia that was more prevalent among preterm and growth retarded newborns. Moreover, Sibai and associates[32,33] reported a high incidence of neonatal

Table 7
Neonatal Complications in Hypertensive and Normotensive Pregnancies*

	Hypertensive Group (n = 28)	Control Group (n = 28)
Gestational age (week)	31.6 ± 2.3	31.6 ± 2.3
weight (g)	1311 ± 353	1606 ± 400
< tenth percentile (%)	43	0
microcephaly (%)	29	0
Platelets < 150,000/mm³ (%)	36	11
Neutrophils < 2000/mm³ (%)	43	11
Disseminated coagulopathy (%)	11	0

*Brazy JE, et al. J Pediatr 1982;100:265.

complications (such as respiratory distress syndrome, infection, pulmonary and cerebral hemorrhage) among preterm infants delivered of women with severe pre-eclampsia prior to 34-weeks gestation. However, the authors found similar complications in infants matched by gestational age and growth status.[32,33] These findings suggest that most of these complications were related to extreme prematurity and severe growth retardation.

Martinkainen et al.[29] compared neonatal complications among 241 babies born to hypertensive mothers and 303 babies born to normotensive mothers. The groups were further subdivided according to whether they were preterm or small-for-gestational age. The authors found that infants of hypertensive mothers were more likely to be born after Cesarean section than the control infants (whether term or preterm). The authors also found that full-term growth retarded babies from the hypertension group exhibited a higher frequency of abnormal fetal heart rate tracings (46%) than those from the control group (11%). There was also a higher frequency of neonatal seizures in the hypertensive group (4%) versus the control group (1%). The preterm infants in both groups had similar neonatal complications, but morbidity in the two preterm SGA groups was greater than in the two preterm AGA groups. The authors concluded that maternal hypertension affects both full-term and preterm babies, but that morbidity seems related to the presence of fetal growth retardation.

Recently, Spinillo and associates[34] compared early neonatal complications between one group of 117 low-birth infants born to mothers with pre-eclampsia and a second group of 234 control infants matched for gestational age. Using univariate analysis, they found that infants of hypertensive mothers had higher rates of acidosis, abnormal fetal heart rate tracings, delivery after Cesarean section, hypoglycemia, intraventricular hemorrhage, and periventricular leukomalacia. However, analysis by conditional logistic regression demonstrated that the increased neonatal morbidity in the pre-eclampsia group was mainly the result of perinatal complications associated with pre-eclampsia (low birthweight, severe fetal growth retardation, and perinatal distress).

It is important to emphasize that all matched case-control studies reported higher incidences of Cesarean section in the hypertensive group compared to the normotensive group. However, delivery by Cesarean section did not reduce the frequency of neonatal complications such as low Apgar scores, acidosis, or neonatal cerebral hemorrhage in these infants.[29,31-34]

Long-Term Neurologic Outcome

Determining the effects of hypertension in pregnancy as well as labor on an infant's subsequent growth and neurologic development is often difficult. This is because a number of confounding perinatal factors usually exist, such as prematurity, severe growth retardation, neonatal infection, thrombocytopenia, and respiratory complications. In general, neurologic morbidity is a result of a cluster of antenatal, intrapartum, and neonatal complications rather than a single etiologic factor.[35] For example, an infant who is born preterm with severe growth retardation is very likely to have antenatal and intrapartum fetal distress, hypoglycemia, sepsis, and abnormal hematologic findings. As a result, this infant may have neonatal seizures, intracerebral hemorrhage, or periventricular leukomalacia. This infant also may have long-term neurologic deficit because of these complications irrespective of hypertension or delivery by Cesarean section.[33,35]

There are few studies describing the growth and development of children born to hypertensive pregnant women. In two of these studies, Ounsted et al.[36,37] evaluated the intellectual abilities of 242 children at the age of 7.5 years. Associations among 15 maternal, fetal, perinatal, postnatal, and environmental factors and test scores were studied. The authors found that children whose mothers had developed superimposed pre-eclampsia had higher scores than those whose mothers had not suffered pre-eclampsia. In addition, children delivered by elective Cesarean section had lower scores than those delivered spontaneously.

Martinkainen[35] studied the growth and development of 58 preterm and 143 preterm children of hypertensive mothers at 1.5 years (corrected age). The results were compared with 128 preterm and 175 term children of normotensive mothers. The mean of weight, height, and head circumference at 1.5 years of age did not differ among the four pairs of groups. The frequency of neurologically suspect or abnormal children was similar between the groups matched according to being preterm or term, and being AGA or SGA (Table

Table 8
Frequency of Abnormal or Suspect Neurologic Findings at 1.5 Years of
Age between Infants of Hypertensive and Normotensive Mothers*

	Hypertensive Group	Control Group
Preterm SGA (%)	36	41
Preterm AGA (%)	21	22
Term SGA (%)	27	19
Term AGA (%)	15	17

SGA = small for gestational age; AGA = appropriate for gestational age.
*Martikainen A. J Perinatal Med 1989;17:259.

Table 9
Handicap Rates of Infants Born to Mothers
with and without Hypertensive Disorders*

Handicap	Hypertensive Group (n = 260) # (%)	Control Group (n = 684) # (%)
Major	15 (5.8)	44 (6.4)
Minor	27 (10.4)	84 (12.3)
Total	42 (16.2)	128 (18.7)

*Van Zeben-Van der Aa. Eur J Obstet Gynecol Raprod Biol 1991;39:87.

8). Nevertheless, the frequency of definite neurologically abnormal children in the hypertensive group was < 5%.

Van Zeben-Van der Aa and associates[38] compared handicap rates of preterm infants born to mothers with and without hypertensive disorders at a corrected age of 2 years. The study group included 260 children born to hypertensive mothers and 684 children born to normotensive mothers. The frequency of handicap in these children is summarized in Table 9.

Some epidemiologic studies report increased frequencies of maternal pre-eclampsia in cases of children with cerebral palsy. However, all longitudinal case-control studies do not demonstrate such an association. In my experience, the frequency of this complication in term AGA infants is < 1%.[32,38] In the majority of cases the neurologic abnormality will be bilateral, reflecting chronic reduction in uteroplacental blood flow, particularly in infants born with severe growth retardation. In addition, it is extremely rare to find an infant having hemiplegia as a result of this disorder. In general, a one-sided injury is an in utero event that appears invariably unrelated to hypertensive disorders of pregnancy.

Commentary by Mr. Peters: Dr. Sibai's coverage of "Hypertensive Disorders in Pregnancy" is comprehensive and practical in its application. His seeming expectation and possible acceptance of neurologic sequelae in these patients, however, may explain his reluctance to intervene with Cesarean section where varying degrees of fetal distress are present. From a medico-legal point of view, this conservative non-interventionist approach may expose the practitioner to liability. For a variety of reasons, including cost containment, non-intervention is the emerging trend. Non-intervention, however, where intervention is indicated, will lead to physician and institutional jeopardy.

It is also important to recognize the obstetrician's obligation to anticipate the fetal/neonatal consequences of hypertensive pregnancies and assure the presence of a pediatrician or neonatologist at delivery. The timely diagnosis and treatment of cerebral hemorrhages and other complications foreseeable in such pregnancies is important to patient care and the avoidance of obstetrical and hospital liability.

References

1. National High Blood Pressure Education Program Working Group. Report on high blood pressure in pregnancy. Am J Obstet Gynecol 1990;163:1689.
2. Sibai BM, Anderson GD. Hypertension. In: Gabbe SG, Niebyl JR, Simpson JL (eds). *Obstetrics: Normal and Problem Pregnancies*, Second Edition. New York, Churchill Livingstone, 1991, p. 373.
3. American College of Obstetricians and Gynecologists. Technical Bulletin No. 91. Washington, DC, February, 1986.
4. MacGillivray I, Rose GA, Rowe D. Blood pressure survey in pregnancy. Clin Sci 1969;37:395.
5. Villar MA, Sibai BM. Clinical significance of elevated mean arterial blood pressure in second trimester and threshold increase in systolic or diastolic blood pressure during third trimester. Am J Obstet Gynecol 1989;160:419.
6. Sibai BM. Pitfalls in the diagnosis and management of preeclampsia. Am J Obstet Gynecol 1988;159:1.
7. Sibai BM. The HELLP syndrome (hemolysis, elevated liver enzymes, and low platelets): Much ado about nothing? Am J Obstet Gynecol 1990;160:311.
8. Meyer NL, Mercer BM, Friedman SA, et al. Urinary dipstick protein: A poor predictor of absent or severe proteinuria? Am J Obstet Gynecol 1994;170:137.
9. Sibai BM, Mabie WC, Shamsa F, et al. A comparison of no medication versus methyldopa or labetalol in chronic hypertension during pregnancy. Am J Obstet Gynecol 1990;160:960.
10. Sibai BM. Diagnosis and management of chronic hypertension in pregnancy. Obstet Gynecol 1991;78:451.

11. Plouin PF, Breart E, Llado J, et al. A randomized comparison of early with conservative use of antihypertensive drugs in the management of pregnancy-induced hypertension. Br J Obstet Gynaecol 1990;97:124.
12. Sibai BM, Barton JR, Aki S. A randomized prospective comparison of nifedipine and bedrest versus bedrest alone in the management of preeclampsia remote from term. Am J Obstet Gynecol 1992;166:280.
13. Barton JR, Stanziano GJ, Sibai BM. Monitored outpatient management of mild gestational hypertension remote from term. Am J Obstet Gynecol 1994;170:765.
14. Sibai BM. Management of preeclampsia. Clin Perinatol 1991;18:793.
15. Fenakel K, Fenakel G, Appleman Z, et al. Nifedipine in the treatment of severe preeclampsia. Obstet Gynecol 1991;77:331.
16. Sibai BM, Akl S, Fairlie F, et al. A protocol for managing severe preeclampsia in the second trimester. Am J Obstet Gynecol 1990;163:733.
17. Odendaal HG, Pattinson RC, Rant R, et al. Aggressive or expectant management for patients with severe preeclampsia between 28-34 weeks gestation: A randomized trial. Obstet Gynecol 1991;76:1070.
18. Sibai BM, Mercer BM, Schiff E, et al. Aggressive versus expectant management of severe preeclampsia at 28-32 weeks gestation: A randomized controlled trial. Am J Obstet Gynecol 1994;170:409.
19. Schiff E, Friedman SA, Sibai BM. Conservative management of severe preeclampsia remote from term. Clinical Commentary. Obstet Gynecol 1994;84:626.
20. Sibai BM, Ramadan MK, Usta I, et al. Maternal morbidity and mortality in 442 pregnancies with hemolysis, elevated liver enzymes, and low platelets. Am J Obstet Gynecol 1993;169:1000.
21. Mabie WC, Gonzalez AR, Sibai BM, et al. A comparative trial of labetalol and hydralazine in the acute management of severe hypertension complicating pregnancy. Obstet Gynecol 1987;70:328.
22. Cunningham FG, MacDonald PC, Gant NF. Hypertensive disorders in pregnancy. In: Cunningham FG, MacDonald PC, Gant NF (eds). *Williams Obstetrics,* Eighteenth Edition. Norwalk, CT, Appleton & Lange, 1989, p. 653.
23. Royburt M, Seidman DS, Serr DM, et al. Neurologic involvement in hypertensive disease of pregnancy. Obstet Gynecol Surv 1991;46:656.
24. Belfort MA, Moise KJ Jr. Effect of magnesium sulfate on maternal brain blood flow in preeclampsia: A randomized, placebo-controlled study. Am J Obstet Gynecol 1992;167:661.
25. Richards A, Graham D, Bullock R. Clinicopathological study of neurological complications due to hypertensive disorders of pregnancy. J Neurol Neurosurg Psychiatry 1988;51:416.
26. Richards AM, Moodley J, Bullock MRR, et al. Maternal deaths from neurological complications of hypertensive crisis in pregnancy. S Afr Med J 1987;71:487.
27. Patterson-Brown S, Robson SC, Redfern N, et al. Hydralazine boluses for the treatment of severe hypertension in preeclampsia. Br J Obstet Gynaecol 1994;101:409.
28. Montan S, Ingemarsson I. Intrapartum fetal heart rate patterns in pregnancies complicated by hypertension. A cohort study. Am J Obstet Gynecol 1989;160:283.
29. Martinkainen AM, Heinonen KM, Saarikoski SV. The effect of hypertension in pregnancy on fetal and neonatal condition. Int J Gynecol Obstet 1989;30:213.
30. Brazy JE, Grimm JK, Little VA. Neonatal manifestations of severe maternal hypertension occurring before the thirty-sixth week of pregnancy. J Pediatr 1982;100:265.

31. Koenig JM, Roberts DC. Incidence, neutrophil kinetics, and natural history of neonatal neutropenia associated with maternal hypertension. N Engl J Med 1989;321:557.
32. Sibai BM, Anderson GD, Abdella TN, et al. Eclampsia III. Neonatal outcome, growth and development. Am J Obstet Gynecol 1983;146:307.
33. Sibai BM, Taslimi M, Abdella TN, et al. Maternal and perinatal outcome of conservative management of severe preeclampsia in mid-trimester. Am J Obstet Gynecol 1985;152:32.
34. Spinillo A, Iasci A, Capuzzo E, et al. Early neonatal prognosis in preeclampsia. A matched case-control study in low birthweight infants. Hypertension in Pregnancy 1993;12:507.
35. Martinkainen A. Growth and development at the age of 1.5 years in children with maternal hypertension. J Perinatal Med 1989;17:259.
36. Ounsted M, Cockburn J, Moar VA, et al. Maternal hypertension with superimposed preeclampsia: Effects on child development at 7-1/2 years. Br J Obstet Gynaecol 1983;90:644.
37. Ounsted M, Moar VA, Cockburn J, et al. Factors associated with the intellectual ability of children born to women with high risk pregnancies. Br Med J 1984;288:1038.
38. Van Zeben-Van der Aa DM, Verwy RA, Verloove-Vanhorick P, et al. Maternal hypertension and very preterm infants' mortality and handicaps. Eur J Obstet Gynecol Reprod Biol 1991;39:87.

_____ Chapter 6 _____

Gestational Diabetes Mellitus

Robert P. Lorenz, M.D.

_____

Introduction

Litigation claiming malpractice related to gestational diabetes mellitus (GDM) commonly includes the delivery of a large baby that is either stillborn or has suffered birth injury with the allegation of failure to diagnose GDM or failure to treat GDM properly. Two important aspects of care of GDM from a medico-legal viewpoint are the issues of documentation and patient noncompliance. The purpose of this chapter is to provide an approach to care and risk management of GDM.

Risk management has been defined as "an effort to identify, prevent, and evaluate risk and to reduce or eliminate financial loss."[1] To be most effective, a program for risk management in the office and the hospital should be integrated with the broader approach of quality assessment and improvement, which is defined as "an effort to improve patient care through the ongoing, objective assessment of important aspects of patient care and the correction of problems identified."[1] The latter should be part of practices and hospital departments and is based on organizational policies and professional guidelines (e.g., *Technical Bulletins of the American College of Obstetricians and Gynecologists* [ACOG][2]; and *Guidelines for Perinatal Care*, a joint publication of American Academy of Pediatrics and ACOG).[3] An approach to quality assessment and improvement for obstetrics is available from ACOG.[1] The reader is encouraged to review the above documents in planning risk management for GDM. In addition, the reader is directed to more extended material on GDM available in textbooks.[4-10]

_____

From: Donn SM, Fisher CW (eds.): *Risk Management Techniques in Perinatal and Neonatal Practice.* © Futura Publishing Co., Inc., Armonk, NY, 1996.

There are few areas in obstetrics with more confusion, controversy, and conundrums than GDM. There are disagreements regarding the definition, clinical importance, methods of diagnosis, choice of management, and implications for pregnancy, delivery, and beyond. Given this wide array of opinions, it is possible to find some justification for apparently divergent approaches to clinical care and risk management. This diversity is based on the multiplicity of opinions regarding the clinical significance of the problem. Terms like "conservative," "expectant," and "aggressive" can be confusing. For purposes of this discussion the range of options will be listed as "most active" on one extreme and "least active" on the other. The "most active" approach will be the one described in some literature involving the most intense testing and therapy. The "least active" approach will be one of minimal intervention. Some typical approaches between the two extremes will also be presented. The author's suggestion for a recommended approach will be identified. The reader is encouraged to review the original data before formulating his/her own approach.

The term "standard of care" is often used in medical discussions. It is actually not a medical term and is not something doctors should define. It is a legal term that applies to the conclusion of a jury after reviewing a specific medical malpractice allegation. It tends to mean whatever the jury wants it to mean, nothing more and nothing less. All a doctor can offer as an expert witness is his/her opinion on what the jury should conclude is the standard of care. This term will not be used in this chapter.

> **Commentary by Mr. Volk:** The standard of care is formulated by publications in the various fields, such as journals, standards, and textbooks and by the methods of practice in the various specialties. A physician is not required to practice to the highest standard, only to the minimal acceptable standard. The standard, for instance, may call for screening for GDM during pregnancy. This is not mandated by a jury finding, but by the methods of practice of the physicians who care for these patients. Any medico-legal case tried to a jury has to involve physicians who are testifying, and being cross-examined about the standard of care. A physician cannot formulate his/her own standard, the applicable standard is explained to the jury based on the knowledge and methods of treatment that existed at the time of the medical care.

Definition

The most commonly used definition of GDM in the United States is "carbohydrate intolerance of variable severity with onset or first recognition during pregnancy. The definition applies regardless of whether insulin is used for treatment or the condition persists after pregnancy."[11] The clinical and laboratory criteria to establish the diagnosis will be reviewed below.

Screening for and Diagnosis of Gestational Diabetes Mellitus

Screening is defined an "examination of a group of usually asymptomatic individuals to detect those with a high probability of having a given disease, typically by means of an inexpensive test."[12] Screening may be by history, physical examination, or laboratory tests. This definition relates to GDM in two ways. First, the importance of screening is directly related to the importance of finding and then managing the disease itself at the time of the testing. Second, a method for screening is only the first step in establishing a diagnosis and must be followed by further testing to prove a diagnosis in most cases. These two issues will be discussed in order.

The advocates of screening for GDM argue that the diagnosis is associated with an increased risk of fetal macrosomia and associated birth trauma, neonatal hypoglycemia, and other metabolic disorders, perinatal mortality,[13] and subsequent development of Type II diabetes mellitus in the mother. Because there is no universal agreement on laboratory criteria for the diagnosis of GDM, the actual risks of GDM may vary among different populations with GDM. Thus, the objectives of screening and diagnosis relate to the clinical outcomes of concern.[14-16] Fetal surveillance during the pregnancy and treatment of persistent elevations of blood glucose in GDM with dietary management and, when appropriate, insulin will lower the perinatal risks described above.[17]

The "least active" extreme position on screening and treatment is that derived from a meta-analysis of four randomized clinical trials of 508 patients.[18] Walkinshaw[18] found a significant reduction in the rate of macrosomia (odds ratio 0.35, 95% confidence intervals [CI] 0.24-0.52) and neonatal polycythemia (odds ratio 0.18, CI 0.06-0.052) with insulin therapy, but no other demonstrable effect. He concluded, "There is nothing from these studies to substantiate the wide recommendation that all pregnant women should be screened for gestational diabetes, let alone that they should be treated with insulin."[18]

A "minimally active" position on screening is that of the Canadian Task Force on the Periodic Health Examination.[19] It opined that there was poor evidence to justify screening as part of the periodic health examination of pregnant women by any of the following methods: 1. historic risk factors or office glycosuria as a basis for a glucose tolerance test (GTT); 2. a 50-g 1-hour glucose measurement at 28 weeks gestation; or 3. measurement of fasting and random blood glucose levels. However, the group also hedged this position. "The Task Force recognizes that women have various degrees of glucose intolerance during pregnancy and that a certain proportion will have adverse outcomes and could benefit from screening...Pending the results of ongoing studies...factors such as clinical judgement (assessment of risk factors and pregnancy evolution) and available resources should be taken into account in choosing a screening strategy."[19] Thus, even a "least active" position on screening must include some assessment of each patient for degree of risk for GDM with laboratory testing for some cases.

If resources are limited, screening by a single operator performing capillary glucose by reflectance photometry is not widely advocated but has been reported. Murphy et al.,[20] using a single operator and a single AccuChek III® (Boehringer Mannheim Diagnostics, Inc., Indianapolis, IN, USA), with a cutoff of 155 mg/dL, claimed a higher sensitivity and the same specificity as laboratory measurements in a small sample of patients who underwent GTT and multiple screening methods.

A "less active" approach to screening is that proposed by the ACOG in a 1986 Technical Bulletin, which is presently under revision.[21] It advocates laboratory screening by the method described above at 24 to 28 weeks gestation for women with any of the following: age 30 or older; a family history of diabetes; previous delivery or a macrosomic, malformed, or stillborn infant; obesity; hypertension; or glycosuria.

A "more active" position on screening would be to use the post 50-g glucose load screen at the first visit for women at risk, at 24-28 weeks for low risk women, and to do a GTT for a screen value ≥ 130 mg/dL. A "more active" approach to the diagnostic test (i.e., to increase sensitivity and lower specificity) would be to use Sack's conversion of O'Sullivan's data for the 100-g 3-hour GTT: fasting 96 mg/dL; 1 hour 172 mg/dL; 2 hour 152 mg/dL; and 3 hour 131 mg/dL.[22]

An "intermediate" approach to screening commonly used in the United States and advocated by the National Diabetes Data Group, the Third International Workshop of Gestational Diabetes Mellitus, and the American Diabetes Association (ADA) is to do laboratory screening of all pregnant women for GDM at 24 to 28 weeks gestation by a random 50-g 1-hour glucose challenge.[11] If the result of a laboratory plasma glucose level measured by enzymatic assay techniques (not test strips or reflectance meters) is ≥ 140 mg/dL (> 7.8 mM), then further testing by administration of a 100 g 3-hour GTT after an 8- to 14-hour overnight fast and 3 days of carbohydrate loading. A diagnosis of GDM is established if at least two of the measurements of laboratory plasma glucose level measured by enzymatic assay techniques (not test strips or reflectance meters) exceed the following:

fasting: ≥105 mg/dL (5.8 mM)
one hour: ≥190 mg/dL (10.6mM)

two hour: ≥165 mg/dL (9.2 mM)
three hour: ≥145 mg/dL (8.1 mM)

The above screening method has a sensitivity of 79%, a specificity of 87%, and a positive predictive value of 14%. A sensitivity of 79% implies that in some very high risk patients, there may be a role for avoiding the screening test and doing the 3-hour GTT directly. Remember that six out of seven women with a positive 1-hour glucose screen will not have the diagnosis of GDM by the 3-hour GTT criteria, and therefore should not be managed on the basis of the screen alone. The screen is not diagnostic!

The above criteria for the 3-hour GTT are a modification of the original population studies by O'Sullivan and Mahan,[23] which utilized the now obsolete whole blood glucose measurement by the Somogyi-Nelson method and identified the limit of two standard deviations above the mean. Carpenter and Coustan[24] and Sacks et al.[22] compared the two methods and believe that the above criteria are set too high and do not represent an accurate conversion from O'Sullivan and Mahan's to current plasma measurements. Using a lower threshold that changed the frequency of GDM from 3.2% to 5% of all pregnancies, Magee et al.[25] identified a group of patients with increased perinatal morbidities.

The "most active" extreme position theoretically would be to do a diagnostic GTT in all pregnant women. This position provides 100% sensitivity but is not supported by the literature and has been used only in research.

Other laboratory screening methods and other diagnostic methods, including intravenous testing,[15] a 75-g 2-hour GTT advocated by the World Health Organization,[26] and a "mixed nutrient" meal GTT[27] are discussed by others and will not be reviewed here. Whether these diagnostic methods are "more" or "less" active than the 100-g 3-hour GTT is uncertain. A "more active" approach to diagnostic criteria is based on the information that adverse outcomes such as macrosomia, pre-eclampsia, and Cesarean section rates are higher among women with "normal" GTT, but higher 2-hour values.[28] Similarly, a single elevated value on the 3-hour GTT may be associated with worse outcome and has been suggested as a basis to begin intervention.[29] Screening by random blood glucose or 1- or 2-hour postprandial blood glucose measurements have been described, but the sensitivities are unknown.[16] Both the glycosylated hemoglobin or hemoglobin A1C are poor screening methods because of low sensitivity.

The advantage of the 50-g 1-hour test is that its sensitivity and specificity were established for a population of pregnant women using the diagnostic GTT in the whole population. Other screening tests have not been as thoroughly assessed.[15]

Screening by Risk Factors

What is the role of screening by physical examination or by history? Physical examination screening is basically identification of obesity. Studies vary in the definition for obesity. Defining it as 120%-150% of ideal pre-pregnancy body weight by Metropolitan Life Insurance Company tables, with morbid obesity defined as > 150% and normal defined as 85%-120%, Garbaciak et al.[30] demonstrated that the frequency of diabetes in pregnancy was 1.4% for normal weight, 3.9% for obese women, and 10.4% for morbidly obese women. Gross, et al.[31] found the incidence of GDM to be 6.5% among obese women compared to 0.8% for nonobese patients. In a review of the literature, Ruge and Anderson[32] found the frequency of GDM in obese patients to be a median of 7% (range 0%-20%) with 60% of studies showing an increased risk. Obesity has other associated complications in pregnancy including fetal macrosomia, hypertensive disease, increased rates of labor abnormalities, and operative delivery. In summary, obesity increases the relative risk of having GDM, but most obese patients do not have GDM.

Historical risk factors are related to risk of GDM but may miss up to 50% of patients with GDM.[33] GDM occurs in 3.8% of women age 35-39 compared to 0.7% of women younger than age 20.[33]

A "more active" approach to screening by history and prepregnancy weight would be to identify patients at risk by historic factors or obesity at the first prenatal visit and do the laboratory work-up then; if it is negative, then repeat the laboratory screening at 24 to 28 weeks gestation. This approach fits with the work of Super et al.,[34] who demonstrated that 66% of the patients at risk for GDM based on history can be found by laboratory testing in the first half of gestation.

In summary, there is a range of accepted approaches to screening methods and a commonly accepted (in the United States) laboratory method for definitive diagnosis. All practices should use some internally consistent method for screening. Risk factors should be used to determine laboratory screening by 1-hour 50-g glucose testing at the first prenatal visit with follow-up by a 3 hour GTT if positive. Patients without risk factors and those with an initial negative screen can have the laboratory screening at 24-28 weeks using the same algorithm.

Antepartum Care in Gestational Diabetes Mellitus

Litigation involving antepartum management of identified GDM is less common than in other areas but may include allegations of failure to identify macrosomia or impending fetal death or failure to treat GDM adequately to prevent stillbirth or macrosomia associated with birth trauma.

In addition to providing routine obstetric care, the obstetrician should provide additional support in diagnostics (blood glucose surveillance, fetal assessment, sonography), and therapy (diet, exercise, selected use of insulin, timing and mode of delivery).[3]

Blood Glucose Surveillance

Because morbidity and mortality are directly related to the degree of hyperglycemia, adequate surveillance of maternal blood glucose is necessary to demonstrate therapeutic efficacy. The role of self-monitored blood glucose (SMBG) versus intermittent laboratory measurements is controversial. If insulin therapy is instituted, especially at levels exceeding "prophylactic" doses (see below), then SMBG is usually performed.

Theoretically, the "least active" approach to blood sugar surveillance would be to not do any. This approach is the logical extension of the position of Walkinshaw.[18] His meta-analysis of randomized trials was unable to demonstrate any benefit from either diet therapy and/or insulin therapy in affecting any outcomes other than neonatal hyperbilirubinemia and macrosomia.

A "less active" approach to blood sugar monitoring in the GDM not on insulin is that of ACOG: laboratory measurement of fasting and 2-hour postprandial glucose at 2 weekly intervals.[21] This approach may miss the chronically hyperglycemic patient who fasts and decreases her diet once every 2 weeks in preparation for the laboratory measurement.

An "intermediate" approach to such patients is that recommended by the ADA.[35] They recommend SMBG four times a day, fasting, and 1-2 hours after meals.

A "most active" approach to the same patient would be self-monitored blood sugar performed at least seven times per day (fasting, before lunch and dinner, 2 hours after each meal, and bedtime) with a reflectance meter that has electronic memory to verify the reported data.[17] Langer et al.[17] have shown that neonatal morbidities, birthweights, and operative delivery rates are improved with this approach as compared to less intense surveillance. They believe the overall cost is lower with intense surveillance.

Fetal Assessment

Fetal testing includes identification of birth defects, fetal size, and biophysical assessment of well being, or fetal surveillance. The purpose of fetal surveillance is to reduce the risk of antepartum asphyxia and fetal death. In a recent review of 23 studies published since 1979, the overall stillbirth rate for GDM ranged from 5-45/1000 births.[17] There are no controlled studies addressing the role of fetal surveillance in GDM. The actual risk of stillbirth probably varies between close to that of the nondiabetic in the well controlled young GDM with no other risk factors to the other extreme of the stillbirth risk for women with pre-existing diabetes mellitus.

The intensity of surveillance should be individualized and should be increased compared to normal pregnancy if other risks are identified: poor metabolic control; poor compliance; maternal age above 25; macrosomia; and polyhydramnios.

A "less active" approach was suggested by Landon and Gabbe[36] and includes no biophysical testing until 40 weeks in the diet controlled patient with normal fasting and postprandial glucose levels. In patients requiring insulin or those with fetal growth retardation, chronic hypertension, pre-eclampsia, or a previous stillbirth, twice weekly nonstress tests (NSTs) were begun at 32 weeks gestation.

A "less active" approach in the uncomplicated GDM is weekly testing beginning at 36 weeks as advocated by Coustan.[37] He suggested using the testing methods commonly used locally.

A "more active" approach is to do weekly fetal testing beginning at 34 weeks gestation.[38]

A "most active" approach is that of Moore[39] who varies the intensity of surveillance with the severity of the disease. He uses fetal movement counts beginning at 28 weeks gestation and NSTs from 36 to 40 weeks gestation in "most" patients with GDM. Diet controlled GDM with occasional post-prandial blood glucose concentrations above 120 mg/dL have weekly NSTs. Patients receiving insulin are managed the same as women with pre-existing DM: fetal movement counts beginning at 28 weeks and twice weekly NSTs beginning at 32 weeks gestation.

Fetal Sonography

Fetal sonography can be used for identification of anomalies, assessment of well being by biophysical profiles and/or Doppler, or assessment of growth. Most studies have not demonstrated an increased rate of congenital anomalies in GDM, so additional fetal sonography for this purpose is not required. Regarding biophysical profiles, some centers use them rather than NSTs and/or contraction stress tests (CSTs) in weekly surveillance (see above). Doppler studies have not been shown to add additional benefit to other standard methods of fetal surveillance in GDM or otherwise.

The assessment of fetal growth in GDM is important in principle but frustrating and limited in its application. Clinical assessment of fetal growth should be done in all obstetric patients during the antepartum period and on admission in labor, but its accuracy is limited. In fact, Chauhan et al.[40] demonstrated that the fetal weight estimated by the multiparous patient in labor was as accurate as either clinical or sonography estimates. For large babies, the accuracy is even less than other circumstances. Sabbagha et al.[41] developed a specific formula for large for gestational age (LGA) fetuses. LGA is usually defined as an estimated fetal weight (EFW) above the 90th percentile for the gestational age. They found that when the abdominal circumference was above the 90th percentile and they used the LGA formula, the random error was less (two standard deviations were ± 22.4%) than for LGA fetuses whose EFW was done by the formula of Hadlock et al.[42] However, a two standard deviation range of results of 22% makes utilization of this tool impractical because of its inaccuracy.

There is a risk in using sonographically derived EFW for management. Levine et al.[43] found that for normal size fetuses incorrectly labeled as LGA by ultrasound, there were more Cesarean sections and diagnoses of abnormal labor compared to same weight controls.

Thus, a "least active" approach to assessing fetal weight would be to do it clinically only, or by asking the multiparous patient her estimate of the baby's weight, as suggested by Sandmire.[44] His provocative position is that the adverse outcome that we should try to prevent is permanent brachial plexus palsy, an event that is estimated to occur once in 7403 to once in 39,840 births. For vaginal births over 4500 g, the incidence was estimated as once in 1140 to once in 2480. Evidence based decision making would dictate use of sonography if it could be demonstrated that it affects these frequencies. Because of the above limitations, he concludes for large babies, "clinicians must avoid making delivery decisions based on inaccurate EFW. Until reliable methods of estimation are available, clinicians should declare a moratorium on ultrasonic EFW...."[44]

> **Commentary by Mr. Volk:** The prevention of permanent brachial plexus injury would indeed be a worthy goal, both from a humanitarian and societal standpoint. There are approximately 12,500 labors complicated by shoulder dystocia in the United States each year (In 1991 there were 4.14 million live births and the incidence is approximately 0.3). The reduction of disability and increase in functioning of these children and the savings to society by prevention is potentially enormous.

Diet

When GDM is diagnosed, the "least active" approach is to place the patient on a diet. Dietary therapy is addressed in detail by others.[45,46] It is advisable to document that dietary instruction has occurred. If blood glucose levels or weight gain are not consistent with the expected response to the diet, dietary indiscretion should be considered and having the patient do a formal diet diary may be worthwhile.

The purpose of diet therapy is to maintain normoglycemia, provide adequate nutrient intake for mother and fetus, avoid ketosis, and allow adequate weight gain. There is considerable debate regarding the total calories as well as ideal weight gain. There is agreement that total calories and weight gain targets vary by body weight. Mulford et al.[47] suggested the following daily caloric intake (kcal/kg of current weight) by ratio of current to ideal body weight (IBW): < 80% IBW, 35-40 kcal/kg; 80%-120% IBW, 30 kcal/kg; 120%-150% IBW, 24 kcal/kg; > 150% IBW, 12-15 kcal/kg. Many authors suggest fewer calories in the first trimester. The ADA recommends that the distribution of calories be 40%-50% carbohydrate, 20%-25% protein, and 30%-40% fat.[35] The ADA recommends: avoiding sugar, concentrated sweets, and convenience foods; eating small frequent meals; eating a small breakfast; and choosing high fiber foods. Caloric restriction for the obese patient with GDM has been suggested; however, enthusiasm for severe restriction is tempered by the work of Rizzo et al.[48] who demonstrated that there were adverse neurodevelopmental effects on children after diabetic pregnancies complicated by maternal circulating ketone bodies. Obese patients with GDM not taking insulin can meet their caloric needs with three meals a day without snacks in contrast to the lean patient who should eat two to three snacks per day.

Exercise

Exercise along with diet can improve blood sugar control compared to diet alone.[49] Jovanovic-Peterson et al.[49] studied the use of an arm ergometer three times a week for 20 minutes each time in seated pregnant women who were previously inactive. Fasting, postprandial, and glycohemoglobin levels were improved compared to controls. This approach could be labeled the "most active" approach to exercise therapy for GDM. Exercise should be carefully chosen during pregnancy, especially in the previously inactive patient. The intensity should be less than outside of pregnancy. The maternal musculoskeletal system is more prone to injury, and balance is affected by the asymmetric weight gain and distribution as pregnancy advances. Weight bearing exercise is restricted by some.[35] Intense levels of exercise have been related to decreased uterine blood flow and fetal heart rate changes. Minute ventilation and oxygen consumption are higher in the resting pregnant versus nonpregnant state, and total exercise capacity is reduced by pregnancy in the fit athlete.

Insulin

Few areas of GDM generate more controversy than the role of insulin therapy.[50] Insulin therapy has been used in a wide range of applications with GDM, from "prophylactic" treatment in all patients with GDM at one extreme to therapeutic use only in the persistently hyperglycemic patient after an unsuccessful trial of diet therapy.

The "most active" approach to insulin use is the administration of low dose insulin in the morning to all patients with GDM. Patients who have persistent hyperglycemia would then need additional therapy. Randomized trials by O'Sullivan et al.[51,52] and Coustan and Lewis[53] of insulin prophylaxis demonstrated a lower average birthweight and a lower rate of large babies in the treated group compared to controls given dietary management alone. O'Sullivan et al.[51,52] administered 10 units of NPH insulin every morning; Coustan and Lewis[53] utilized 20 units of NPH insulin and 10 units of regular insulin every morning. O'Sullivan et al.[51,52] also noted a lower perinatal mortality for the mother over age 25. In another randomized study of daily use of 8-12 units of insulin, Persson et al.[54] was unable to demonstrate any beneficial impact. In a retrospective non-randomized study of 445 pregnancies given prophylactic insulin or diet, Coustan and Imarah[55] found that the treated group had lower rates of large babies, birth trauma, operative vaginal deliveries, and Cesarean births.

Critics of prophylactic insulin include the Canadian Task Force on the Periodic Health Examination[15] and Walkinshaw.[18] Both noted the addition of assigned to randomized patients in Coustan's study. In his meta-analysis (which excluded Coustan's study), Walkinshaw found a significant reduction in the rate of macrosomia (odds ratio 0.35, 95% CI 0.24-0.52) and neonatal polycythemia (odds ratio 0.18, CI 0.06-0.052) with insulin therapy, but no other demonstrable effect. He concluded, "There is nothing from these studies to substantiate the wide recommendation that all pregnant women should be screened for gestational diabetes, let alone that they should be treated with insulin."[18]

A "more active" approach to insulin would be to utilize historic risk factors and blood sugar determinations to identify a subset for therapy.

An "intermediate" approach that is commonly used is to follow fasting and postprandial blood glucose levels and institute insulin if a trial of diet for 1-2 weeks is ineffective. Criteria for insulin therapy in this approach varies. ACOG recommends insulin if the fasting glucose is $\geq$ 105 mg/dL or the 2-hour postprandial glucose is $\geq$ 120 mg/dL.[21] Most clinicians would not begin insulin unless an abnormal value occurred more than once. Langer advocates instituting insulin for a fasting glucose $\geq$ 95 mg/dL, based on the belief that this approach will lower the rate of macrosomia.

This reviewer uses the ACOG guidelines for instituting insulin therapy but also considers insulin use in women with GDM who have additional risk factors for a large baby, i.e., previous large baby, previous birth trauma, morbid obesity.

Timing and Mode of Delivery: Primary Cesarean Birth?

If the risks of traumatic delivery are significant, then is there a basis for primary Cesarean birth for GDM? Given the prevalence of GDM varying from 2%-11% of populations studied, and the fact that most patients deliver vaginally safely with GDM, this diagnosis alone is not justification for Cesarean birth. This is especially true because the maternal risks of surgical compared to vaginal delivery increase with other problems that often accompany GDM: maternal obesity; advanced maternal age; etc. There is no justification for primary Cesarean birth simply for GDM.

In planning delivery, an option is induction of labor to reduce the risk of birth trauma or fetal loss. A gestational diabetic who has required insulin for documented failed dietary control should be managed as a patient with pre-existing diabetes mellitus. For such a patient, timing delivery should be individualized based on metabolic control, other risk factors (i.e., prior loss, hypertension, etc.), fetal size (arguably, see discussion elsewhere), cervical "ripeness," etc. Such patients are frequently delivered by their due date. For other patients who are at less risk with GDM, induction as a specific intervention has not been well studied. Langer (personal communication) performs sonography at 37 weeks and considers induction for EFW near 4000 g. He induces labor in 25% of GDM with conventional therapy and 22% of those with intensified therapy.[17] Amniocentesis for fetal pulmonary maturity is probably appropriate for induction at < 39 weeks for this indication. Induction for GDM at term if the fetal weight percentiles are high (≥ 75%) is an approach that reflects Langer's data but has not been specifically reported.

A reasonable "less active" approach is simply to await spontaneous labor and integrate fetal weight estimates into the management of labor.

A "more active" approach would be to consider primary Cesarean section in GDM based on an EFW or some other measurement by sonography. Elliot et al.[56] observed that a predictor of dystocia in maternal diabetes is a fetal transthoracic diameter 1.4 cm greater than the biparietal diameter.

Primary Cesarean birth for large fetuses and GDM has been suggested as a method to reduce the risk of traumatic vaginal delivery. Most studies addressing the relationship of the size of the baby and birth trauma are retrospective and are based on actual birth weight. In general, the larger the actual birthweight, the higher the frequency of birth trauma, but developing guidelines based on actual birthweight begs the question. When it is time to decide mode of delivery if all we have is EFW, which is not the same. To be certain of delivering all infants of X-g birthweight by Cesarean section, then the operation should be performed on all patients with fetal weight estimates of X minus ?? g.

A decision should not be based on EFW alone. An obstetric history of a prior safe vaginal delivery of a large baby (especially if it can be verified by review of the delivery record) would be as important as any other consideration. Clinical pelvimetry again is important.

In planning mode of delivery, an absolute rule for primary Cesarean section in GDM based on EFW cannot reasonably be provided because the data do not provide justification, nor do authors agree. The frequency of large babies and the frequency of shoulder dystocia varies considerably with the population, so approaches should vary. For instance, Sandmire[57] reports that although the distribution of birthweights is significantly higher in Green Bay than in Cleveland, the frequency of serious sequelae from shoulder dystocia in Green Bay is low. Using the fetal weight estimate of 4500 g (diabetics and nondiabetics combined), he concluded that 978 Cesarean births would have to be performed to eliminate one case of permanent mild arm weakness.

Spellacy et al.[58] suggested that because of the limitations of sonography in determining fetal weight, that to reduce the morbidity and mortality for babies with actual birthweights $\geq$ 4500 g (diabetics and nondiabetics combined), one should consider primary Cesarean birth only for sonographically EFW $\geq$ 5000 g.

Certainly one should individualize based on prior obstetric history, clinical pelvimetry, and a thorough discussion with the patient. Primary Cesarean birth for a large fetus and GDM has been suggested at an EFW of: 1. not at all based on sonography[44]; 2. 4000 g[59]; 3. 4250 g[60]; and 4. 4500 g[6]; and 5. 5000 m (diabetics and nondiabetics combined).[58]

Intrapartum Care

Litigation in this area most frequently involves issues of traumatic delivery, i.e., failure to identify a large fetus, failure to diagnose or properly manage a labor abnormality, inappropriate method of delivery, and management of shoulder dystocia. Shoulder dystocia will be addressed separately in the last section and in Chapter 18.

Intrapartum care of the patient with GDM is similar to that of the normal patient in many ways, and those aspects should not be overlooked: assessment of fetal size and pelvic adequacy is especially important; true labor abnormalities should be identified on a timely basis; re-evaluation for the possibility of fetopelvic disproportion is necessary[61]; and operative vaginal delivery should be undertaken selectively and carefully.

On admission in spontaneous labor or with an induction, the patient should be assessed clinically for EFW. If an ultrasound study has been performed recently, those data should be available, including the EFW. Clinical pelvimetry should be done to assess the adequacy and type of pelvis. Maternal weight by prenatal records or direct measurement should be on the admission record for use with medications and because of the increased risk for shoulder dystocia with obesity.

If a labor abnormality (e.g., an arrest disorder by Friedman's criteria) develops, then it is reasonable to reassess the clinical estimate of fetal weight as well as the clinical pelvimetry. The causes of an arrest disorder are numerous and can include analgesia or conduction anesthesia, fetal position (i.e., occiput posterior), and uterine dysfunction. These factors may be treatable or reversible. Of more concern is the possibility of fetopelvic disproportion secondary to a problem pelvis, and/or a large baby. If one can be certain an arrest disorder results from cephalopelvic disproportion (CPD), then abdominal delivery rather than use of oxytocin or operative vaginal delivery is advised. Being certain of CPD is rare. When one is uncertain of the likelihood of CPD as the case of an arrest disorder, then clinical judgment must weigh the relative risks and benefits of continuing to vaginal delivery. As risk factors for traumatic delivery rise in number, there is less reason to anticipate a safe vaginal delivery.

The risks of instituting oxytocin for an arrest disorder of unknown etiology at 5-cm cervical dilation in an uncomplicated gestational diabetic with a normal size baby and adequate pelvimetry are certainly much less than the risks of attempting a midforceps delivery for a second stage arrest in an obese patient with GDM and a macrosomic fetus. The question is not whether the fetal head can be safely delivered under the latter conditions, but rather the risks of shoulder dystocia and attendant injury. Under most circumstances, the combination of a presumably large baby, GDM, and a labor abnormality without other explanation is a contraindication to midpelvic operative vaginal delivery.

The major risk of operative vaginal delivery in the patient with GDM is the increased risk of shoulder dystocia that this clinical combination represents. These will be discussed below.

Intrapartum care of GDM also includes assessment of fetal well being and management of diabetes. Assessment of fetal well being in labor can be either by intermittent auscultation every 15 minutes for 30 seconds at a time in the first stage of labor and every 5 minutes in the second stage of labor, or electronic fetal monitoring. There is no convincing evidence that outcome is better in low or high risk women with either method.[62] Electronic fetal monitoring should be considered "more active" because the rate of subsequent intervention by operative delivery is higher for the method compared to auscultation in controlled comparisons.

Control of blood glucose concentration in labor is relatively easy in most patients with GDM. The purpose of glucose control is to provide the fetus with an euglycemic environment during labor to: 1. reduce the chance of fetal acidosis; 2. avoid the adverse interaction of asphyxia and hyperglycemia; and 3. reduce the chance of neonatal hypoglycemia.

For spontaneous labor in the diet controlled patient, food is usually withheld, and if admission blood sugar is normal there may be no need for further surveillance. If labor is long or urinary ketones develop, then some fuel (e.g., intravenous 5% dextrose) may be added. Large boluses of glucose in the normoglycemic patient in labor (diabetic or otherwise) should be avoided because of the increased rate of neonatal hypoglycemia that follows. Patients with GDM on insulin therapy may have intermittent glucose measurements throughout labor, the frequency depends on the severity of the pre-existing disease and the levels found. It is rare that a GDM patient needs hourly glucose determinations and an insulin infusion, as is done with pre-existing DM patients in labor.

Induction of labor can be managed in much the same way as spontaneous labor. Patients on insulin are asked to take their regular meals and snacks and insulin the evening before the induction, whether or not cervical ripening agents are being used that night. If bedtime intermediate acting insulin was given the night before, the frequency of surveillance of blood sugar in labor is increased.

Shoulder Dystocia

Shoulder dystocia is presented in detail elsewhere in the text (see Chapter 18). Important aspects related to GDM will be reviewed here. One important consideration is that the presence of brachial plexus injury is not proof that shoulder dystocia occurred, or that the delivery was mismanaged. Brachial plexus injury has been described with Cesarean birth[63] and with a spontaneous birth without medical intervention.

> **Commentary by Mr. Volk:** The incidence of observed brachial plexus injury following Cesarean section or after a spontaneous birth without medical intervention is so rare as to be almost non-existent. Every physician who delivers and every experienced ob-gyn litigator realizes that. The fact that an article describes this occurrence does not mean that there are not clear cases when the permanent injury to a child is the result of the failure to meet the standard of care. Clearly, any attorney's duty to the judicial system is to litigate only meritorious cases, and if there is adequate evidence to prove that the child's injury was not proximately caused by the failure to meet the standard, then the case should not be litigated.

In a review of 39 cases of brachial plexus injury among 57,597 births from 1977-1990 in Phoenix, Jennet et al.[64] found that only 43% had an identified shoulder dystocia described in the medical record. They concluded that "brachial plexus impairment should not be taken as prima facie evidence of birth process injury."

> **Commentary by Mr. Volk:** This report has to be analyzed further. It is my experience that nearly all of the medical records of brachial plexus injuries that I have reviewed have documentation of shoulder dystocia and/or a "difficult delivery." If, in fact, there were so few reported in this study, then there clearly had to be a lack of adequate documentation by the health care providers in the medical records that were reviewed.

In commenting upon Jennet et al.'s findings, Young[65] described a rapid and uncontrolled delivery of an obese patient who spontaneously delivered the head, which then retracted. Because the attendants were busy trying to gown and glove, no manipulation of the patient occurred before she had a strong urge to push and spontaneously delivered the remainder of the baby. The baby had a brachial plexus palsy after spontaneous resolution of a shoulder dystocia.[65]

> **Commentary by Mr. Volk:** The fact that the delivering doctor did not apply improper traction of fundal pressure, etc., does not mean that the standard of care was met. There may have been a failure to adequately determine the EFW or a failure to adequately manage the prenatal period, etc. Obviously, it is difficult to determine this based on the information available. The point is that there are many areas of potential medico-legal difficulty that a physician may encounter, starting with the initial visit with the patient.

A precipitate delivery may be a risk factor for shoulder dystocia. Acker et al.[59] found that three of four diabetics with precipitate labors and birthweights over 4000 g had shoulder dystocias. They retrospectively reviewed vaginal deliveries of > 2500-g infants of 144 diabetic (GDM and pre-existing DM were combined) women from 1975-1982 in Boston.[59] Diabetes increased the risk of shoulder dystocia five fold (10.2% versus 2.0% in nondiabetics). When grouped by 500-g intervals for birthweight, diabetics had a relative risk of shoulder dystocia of 4.23 versus nondiabetics for the birthweight group 3500-3900 g; 2.31 relative risk for 4000-4499 g; and 2.21 for > 4500 g. Diabetics delivered 67 babies > 4000 g, 46.3% by Cesarean birth. Shoulder dystocia occurred in 30.6% of those delivered vaginally at > 4000 gm with diabetes. Thirty-one diabetics in this weight group delivered spontaneously with a shoulder dystocia rate of 29%. Acker et al.[59] concluded that these risk factors cannot be relied upon for anticipating the condition. They suggested that because 11 of 15 cases of shoulder dystocia in diabetics occurred with birthweights > 4000 g, that those be delivered abdominally.[59]

Again there is the problem of recommendations from a retrospective study that used birthweights applying to prospective management based on the limited accuracy of EFW.

Gross and co-workers[66] reviewed the prediction of shoulder dystocia among pregnancies in Cleveland with birthweights of > 4000 g (nondiabetics and diabetics were combined). Shoulder dystocia occurred in 17%. A three way discriminant analysis assessed antepartum and intrapartum factors to predict birth without shoulder dystocia, shoulder dystocia without trauma, and shoulder dystocia with trauma. Three factors contributed significantly to the prediction of outcome: birthweight; prolonged deceleration phase; and length of second stage of labor. However, the predictive value was poor. Although 94% of cases without shoulder dystocia were correctly predicted, only 16% of cases of shoulder dystocia with trauma were predicted by this model. They concluded for this birthweight group, "the occurrence of shoulder dystocia cannot be predicted from clinical characteristics or labor abnormalities, and that the occurrence of shoulder dystocia is not evident of medical malpractice."[66]

> **Commentary by Mr. Volk:** This illustrates a point that all attorneys and physicians must remember: Each and every claim must be evaluated on a case-by-case basis. There are obviously certain patterns that occur over and over, but a reviewer must always individualize the evaluation.

Nocon et al.[67] also reviewed risk factors for shoulder dystocia in 12,532 vaginal deliveries from 1986-1990 in Indiana. Diabetes and midforceps delivery became significant risk factors only in the presence of a large fetus. They concluded "shoulder dystocia itself is an unpredictable event, and infants at risk for permanent injury are virtually impossible to predict." They could not demonstrate that any particular maneuver to manage shoulder dystocia was more effective than another.

A Toronto study reviewed risk factors for shoulder dystocia in 91 cases among 10,662 births between 1980-1985. "Fundal pressure, in the absence of other maneuvers, resulted in a 77% complication rate and was strongly associated with orthopedic and neurologic damage. Delivery of the posterior shoulder and the corkscrew maneuver were associated with good fetal outcome."[68] The McRoberts maneuver[69] was not mentioned.

Keller et al.[70] reviewed 210 patients with GDM who delivered babies ≥ 3500 g in Chicago. Of 121 (71% of GDM) vaginal deliveries, there were 15 shoulder dystocias (12% incidence) with one permanent injury. Seven of the 15 occurred in deliveries of babies > 4000 g. Only the use of forceps was clearly associated with an increased risk of shoulder dystocia (odds ratio 5:1). They concluded, "forceps should be used with caution in pregnancies complicated by gestational diabetes mellitus when the birth of a large infant is anticipated." They disagreed with the suggestion that Cesarean section should be recommended for patients with GDM and an EFW of > 4000 g.

Langer et al.[60] reviewed 75,979 vaginal deliveries between 1970-1985 in San Antonio to address the role of primary Cesarean section to reduce the risk of shoulder dystocia. Logistic regression identified birthweight, diabetes (all types), and labor abnormalities as principal contributors to shoulder dystocia. Adverse pregnancy outcome (perinatal mortality, birth trauma, low Apgar score) was more common with shoulder dystocia than without it, and more common among diabetics (an 81% incidence) with shoulder dystocia than among nondiabetics with shoulder dystocia. When grouped by 250-g birthweight intervals, shoulder dystocia was significantly more common with diabetes at each interval at or above 4250 g. When grouped by actual birthweight percentile for gestational age, the infants of diabetics had a higher risk of shoulder dystocia than nondiabetics at all birthweight percentiles above 75% (relative risk 6.4) (i.e., 97th percentile has a relative risk of 13.9 for shoulder dystocia). They concluded that Cesarean birth for GDM with an EFW of 4250 g would reduce shoulder dystocia by 76% in this population and that that weight group had a risk of shoulder dystocia of 24%.

In order to prevent the risks of shoulder dystocia and its attendant complications in GDM, the obstetrician can take steps during pregnancy, in planning mode of delivery, during labor, and at the time shoulder dystocia occurs.

During pregnancy a "most active" approach to prevention would be to aggressively screen by laboratory testing women at risk for GDM and do intense blood sugar surveillance and institute insulin for failure of diet therapy early in pregnancy and for fasting blood sugar concentrations $\geq$ 95 mg/dL, a 2-hour postprandial value $\geq$ 120 mg/dL, or a mean glucose concentration $\geq$ 100 mg/dL.[17] Alternatively, use of insulin for all GDM probably would also lower birthweight and reduce risk. Other "less active" approaches to screening, diagnosis, and treatment during pregnancy are discussed in those sections of this chapter.

In planning the timing and mode of delivery to reduce the risks of shoulder dystocia, the role of induction of labor and primary Cesarean section based on EFW are discussed above ("Timing and Mode of Delivery: Primary Cesarean Birth?").

During labor, a "most active" approach to reduce shoulder dystocia would be to consider abdominal delivery whenever a major labor abnormality develops that cannot easily be explained otherwise, especially with a large baby. For example, at our institution 60% of all births (diabetic and nondiabetic) have epidural analgesia in labor, an intervention that clearly affects the frequency of labor abnormalities. In such a setting, is the critical factor CPD or is it the epidural agent? Clinical assessment and judgment are necessary, and management may include continuing the labor while stopping the conduction anesthetic.

An intermediate approach with which virtually all authors agree is to avoid operative vaginal delivery if there is GDM, a large baby, and a labor abnormality (without other cause for the labor abnormality).

If there are multiple risk factors for shoulder dystocia during labor, it is also reasonable to alert the support team to be ready to assist in management. A sufficient number of assistants should be nearby and available. Delivery should be planned on a bed and in a setting where maneuvers can easily be performed in the dorsal lithotomy position with leg supports and access to the posterior perineum.

During delivery, it may be possible to reduce the frequency of shoulder dystocia by how the delivery is managed after the head delivers. Iffy[71] believes that routine management of delivery after the head is delivered affects the frequency of shoulder dystocia. He advocates the technique in use in Great Britain described by Bottoms and Sokol.[72] "Apart from releasing the cord if wrapped around the neck, the obstetrician waits for the next uterine contraction and extracts the shoulders at the peak of the same."[71] Iffy reports few cases of shoulder dystocia with this method in 10 years.

When shoulder dystocia is identified, additional excess traction of or attempts at rotation of the delivered head and fundal pressure should be avoided.[68] Additional assistance should be called for if not already present.

As discussed elsewhere (see Chapter 18), a methodical controlled sequence of steps should be properly performed. Often suprapubic pressure (it helps to have a step stool already in place for an assistant to have adequate height above the symphysis to work) and the McRoberts maneuver (extreme flexion of the hips by bringing the knees up to the maternal chest) are effective. If those are unsuccessful, the obstetrician should use those next steps with which he/she has experience and success. They may include rotation of the trunk (Wood's corkscrew maneuver), and delivery of the posterior arm. Cephalic replacement with abdominal delivery has been advocated, but others have noted mixed success. O'Leary[73] reported the results of a registry that described 59 reported cases of attempted cephalic replacement, with successful replacement in all but six.

Documentation

As in any area of medicine, the medical record should reflect all major aspects of the care of the patient, either directly or indirectly by reference to other documents. Risk management techniques include documentation of receipt by date and person of all laboratory results, correspondence, patient communications, etc. Similarly all planned interventions such as diet, patient education, insulin institution, diagnostic studies, etc., should be clearly stated in the chart, as well as the fact that the patient was informed. These principles of documentation obviously also apply to the inpatient stay. A delivery note should clearly describe the findings and methods used. At major decision points the record should reflect that "the patient (and anyone with her) was (were) informed of the diagnoses, recommendations, risks, alternatives, and extreme uncertainty, and in my professional opinion they understand and agree." (Personal communication, with thanks, to Eric Knox.) It is much harder to subsequently demonstrate that an event happened if it is not recorded in the medical record.

> **Commentary by Mr. Volk:** It would also be useful to have the patient, and anyone with her, sign the note also. I have even advised one physician to utilize a rubber stamp that states: "I have been informed of the risks and alternative treatment/treatments for my condition by my doctor, and I agree with the proposed plan." The patient then signs at the appropriate place under the stamp. This has helped remind the physician to give informed consent and to document it. Obviously, a note detailing risks and benefits by the physician and signed by the patient would be even better.

Given a complex management plan, what happens with the non-compliant patient? Obviously any plan to affect maternal metabolism and to do fetal surveillance requires a large measure of cooperation from the patient. It has been said that "it is more important what patient has the disease, than what disease the patient has." Patients are noncompliant for a large number of reasons. These include, but are not limited to: lack of appreciation of the risks of noncompliance; lack of resources to travel to care and/or pay for medications or materials; substance abuse; other responsibilities considered a higher priority such as a job, childcare, care of another relative; communication barriers such as language; and an inadequate or hostile family support system. A first step with a noncompliant patient is to identify the problem directly and to try to determine the cause. In many cases simple specific interventions can transform patient noncompliance to compliance. Resources such as public agencies, social workers, and Medicaid may be effective. The medical record should reflect all missed appointments and other episodes of noncompliance (failed to follow diet, would not measure blood sugars, etc.). The introductions of the reflectance meters with built in memory has been a tremendous tool to verify blood sugar records and to help motivate patients to comply.

When other methods have failed, a formal conference with the patient and other health care members/witnesses about the possible adverse outcome that may result from inadequate compliance should occur. Additional means of demonstrating the importance of compliance include sending the patient a letter expressing the concerns and the potential risks. Having the patient sign an acknowledgment of receipt of such correspondence may be effective. Ultimately, such discussions and correspondence may include a recommendation that a patient reconsider care with you and provide options for alternative care. Under such circumstances, legal advice regarding local law is recommended so that adequate interval care occurs, emergency care is provided, and charges of abandonment are avoided. On a practical level, noncompliant patients will often remain loosely attached to the original team until they present in labor, even though contact throughout pregnancy is sporadic. Management should be primarily directed toward trying to fully inform the patient of the risks, work with her and others to improve compliance, document the problem extensively, and then do the best one can given the difficult situation. If a patient leaves hospital care against medical advice, this should also be well documented.

Conclusion

Although considerable controversy exists regarding the screening, diagnosis, and management of GDM, there is consensus on broad issues of medico-legal relevance.

GDM is associated with an increase in perinatal morbidity predominantly related to large babies and birth trauma. It is also probably associated with an increased risk of perinatal mortality if it is severe and inadequately managed. There is no agreement regarding the choice of steps to intervene to reduce these risks or their effectiveness.

The clinician should establish a consistent plan for screening for GDM that will apply to all patients, and a plan for timely follow-up diagnostic testing, and then management of diet, blood sugar, and other therapy during the pregnancy. Labor should be managed with an understanding of the increased risks of shoulder dystocia and associated birth trauma in the larger babies. Selected primary Cesarean section in some women with very large babies and GDM is advocated by many authors; however, the ability to properly identify these babies by any means is so limited that absolute rules are inappropriate.

References

1. Quality Assessment and Improvement in Obstetrics and Gynecology, 1994 edition, American College of Obstetricians and Gynecologists, Washington, D.C., 1994, p. 41.
2. ACOG Technical Bulletins, American College of Obstetricians and Gynecologists, Washington, D.C., 1983-1994.

3. Guidelines for Perinatal Care, American Academy of Pediatrics and American College of Obstetricians and Gynecologists, Third Edition, Washington, D.C., 1992.
4. Hare JW. Gestational diabetes. In: Hare JW (ed). *Diabetes Complicating Pregnancy, the Joslin Clinic Method*. New York, Alan R. Liss, 1989, p. 15.
5. Jowanovic L, Peterson CM, Fuhrmann K (eds). *Diabetes in Pregnancy*. Conneticut, Praeger Publishers, 1986.
6. Reece EA, Coustan DR (eds). *Diabetes Mellitus in Pregnancy: Principles and Practice*. New York, Churchill Livingstone, 1988.
7. Moore TR. Diabetes in pregnancy. In: Creasey RK, Resnik R (eds). *Maternal Fetal Medicine*, Third Edition. Philadelphia, WB Saunders, 1994, p. 934.
8. Landon MB. Diabetes mellitus and other endocrine diseases. In: Gabbe SG, Niebyl JR, Simpson JL (eds). *Obstetrics: Normal and Problem Pregnancies*, Second Edition. New York, Churchill Livingstone, 1991, p. 1097.
9. Hollingsworth DR. *Pregnancy, Diabetes, and Birth*, Second Edition. Baltimore, Williams & Wilkins, 1992.
10. Landon MB. Diabetes in Pregnancy. Clin Perinatol 1993;20:507.
11. Metzger BE. Summary and recommendations of the Third International Workshop-Conference on gestational diabetes mellitus. Diabetes 1991;40(Suppl 2):197.
12. *Stedman's Medical Dictionary*, Twenty-fifth Edition. Baltimore, Williams & Wilkins, 1990, p. 1396.
13. O'Sullivan JB, Charles D, Mahan CM, et al. Gestational diabetes and perinatal mortality rate. Am J Obstet Gynecol 1973;116:901.
14. Coustan DR. Diagnosis of gestational diabetes, what are our objectives? Diabetes 1991;40(Suppl 2):14.
15. Carpenter MW. Rational and performance of tests for gestational diabetes. Clin Obstet Gynecol 1991;34:544.
16. Coustan DR. Screening and diagnosis of gestational diabetes. Isr J Med Sci 1991;27:503.
17. Langer O, Rodriquez DA, Xenakis EMJ, et al. Intensified versus conventional management of gestational diabetes. Clin Perinatol 1993;20:557.
18. Walkinshaw SA. Diet + insulin vs diet alone for gestational diabetes. In: Enkin MW, Keirse MJNC, Renfrew MJ, et al. (eds). *Pregnancy and Childbirth Module, Cochrane Database of Systematic Reviews; Review No. 06550*, 20 April 1993, Cochrane Updates on Disk, Oxford, Update Software, Spring 1993.
19. Canadian Task Force on the Periodic Health Examination. Periodic health examination, 1992 update: 1. Screening for gestational diabetes mellitus. Can Med Assoc J 1992;147:435.
20. Murphy NJ, Meyer BA, O'Kell RT, et al. Screening for gestational diabetes mellitus with a reflectance photometer: Accuracy and precision of the single-operator model. Obstet Gynecol 1994;83:1038.
21. Management of Diabetes Mellitus in Pregnancy, Technical Bulletin #92, American College of Obstetricians and Gynecologists, Washington DC, 1986.
22. Sacks DA, Abu-Fadil S, Greenspoon JS, et al. Do the current standards for glucose tolerance testing in pregnancy represent a valid conversion of O'Sullivan's original criteria? Am J Obstet Gynecol 1989;161:638.
23. O'Sullivan JB, Mahan CM. Criteria for the oral glucose tolerance test in pregnancy. Diabetes 1964;13:278.
24. Carpenter MW, Coustan DR. Criteria for screening tests for gestational diabetes. Am J Obstet Gynecol 1982;144:768.

25. Magee MS, Walden CE, Benedetti TJ, et al. Influence of diagnostic criteria on the incidence of gestational diabetes and perinatal morbidity. JAMA 1993;269:609.
26. World Health Organization Expert Committee on Diabetes Mellitus. Technical Report Series 646. Geneva:WHO 1980:9.
27. Sutherland HW, Pearson DWM, Lean MEJ, et al. Breakfast tolerance test in pregnancy. In: Sutherland HW, Stowers JM, Pearson DWM (eds). *Carbohydrate Metabolism in Pregnancy and the Newborn IV*. London, Springer Verlag, 1989, p. 267.
28. Tallarigo L, Giampietro O, Penno G, et al. Relation of glucose tolerance to complications of pregnancy in nondiabetic women. N Engl J Med 1986;315:989.
29. Langer O, Anyaegbunam A, Brustman L, et al. Management of women with one abnormal oral glucose tolerance test value reduces adverse outcome in pregnancy. Am J Obstet Gynecol 1989;161:593.
30. Garbaciak JA, Richter M, Miller S, et al. Maternal weight and pregnancy complications. Am J Obstet Gynecol 1985;152:238.
31. Gross T, Sokol RJ, King KC. Obesity in pregnancy: Risk and outcome. Obstet Gynecol 1980;5:446.
32. Ruge S, Andersen T. Obstetric risks in obesity. An analysis of the literature. Obstet Gynecol Survey 1985;40:57.
33. Coustan DR, Nelson C, Carpenter MW, et al. Maternal age and screening for gestational diabetes: A population-based study. Obstet Gynecol 1989;73:557.
34. Super DM, Edelberg SC, Philison EH, et al. Diagnosis of gestational diabetes in early pregnancy. Diabetes Care 1991;14:288.
35. American Diabetes Association. Medical Management of Pregnancy Complicated by Diabetes, ADA. Alexandria, VA, 1993, p. 86.
36. Landon MF, Gabbe SG. Fetal surveillance in the pregnancy complicated by diabetes mellitus. Clin Perinatol 1993;20:557.
37. Coustan DR. Management of gestational diabetes. In: Reece EA Coustan DR (eds). *Diabetes Mellitus in Pregnancy: Principles and Practice*. New York, Churchill Livingstone, 1988, p.450.
38. Girz BA, Divon MY, Merkatz IR. Sudden fetal death in women with well-controlled, intensively monitored gestational diabetes. J Perinatol 1992;12:229.
39. Moore TR. Fetal Surveillance. In: Hollingsworth DR (ed). *Pregnancy, Diabetes, and Birth*, Second Edition. Baltimore, Williams & Wilkins, 1992, p.217.
40. Chauhan SP, Lutton TC, Bailey KJ, et al. Intrapartum clinical, sonographic, and parous patients' estimates of newborn birth weight. Obstet Gynecol 1992;79:956.
41. Sabbagha RE, Minogue J, Tamura R, et al. Estimation of birth weight by use of ultrasonographic formulas targeted to large-, appropriate-, and small-for-gestational-age fetuses. Am J Obstet Gynecol 1989;160:854.
42. Hadlock F, Harris RB, Sharman RS, et al. Estimation of fetal weight with the use of head, body, and femur measurements—a prospective study. Am J Obstet Gynecol 1985;151:333.
43. Levine AB, Lockwood CJ, Brown B, et al. Sonographic diagnosis of the large for gestational age fetus: Does it make a difference? Obstet Gynecol 1992;79:55.
44. Sandmire HF. Whither ultrasonic prediction of fetal macrosomia. Obstet Gynecol 1993;82:860.
45. Ney DM. Maternal nutrition and diet. In: Hollingsworth DR (ed). *Pregnancy, Diabetes, and Birth*, Second Edition. Baltimore, Williams & Wilkins, 1992, p.103.

46. Hollingsworth DR, Ney DM. Dietary management of diabetes during pregnancy. In: Coustan DR, Reece EA, *Diabetes Mellitus in Pregnancy: Principles and Practice.* New York, Churchill Livingstone, 1988, p.285.
47. Mulford MI, Jovanovic-Peterson L, Peterson CM. Alternative therapies for the management of gestational diabetes, Clin Perinatol 1993;20:630.
48. Rizzo T, Metzger BE, Burns WJ, et al. Correlations between antepartum maternal metabolism and intelligence of offspring. N Engl J Med 1991;325:911.
49. Jovanovic-Peterson L, Durak EP, Peterson CM. Randomized trial of diet versus diet plus cardiovascular conditioning on glucose levels in gestational diabetes. Am J Obstet Gynecol 1989; 161:415.
50. Coustan DR. Maternal insulin to lower the risk of fetal macrosomia in diabetic pregnancy. Clin Obstet Gynecol 1991; 34:288.
51. O'Sullivan JB, Mahan CM, Charles D, et al. Medical treatment of the gestational diabetic. Obstet Gynecol 1974;43:817.
52. O'Sullivan JB, Gellis SS, Dandrow RV, et al. The potential diabetic and her treatment in pregnancy. Obstet Gynecol 1966; 27:683.
53. Coustan DR, Lewis SB. Insulin therapy for gestational diabetes. Obstet Gynecol 1978;51:306.
54. Persson B, Stangenberg M, Hansson U, et al. Gestational diabetes mellitus; comparative evaluation of two treatment regimens, diet vs insulin and diet. Diabetes 1985;34(Suppl 2):101.
55. Coustan DR, Imarah J. Prophylactic insulin treatment of gestational diabetes reduces the incidence of macrosomia, operative delivery, and birth trauma. Am J Obstet Gynecol 1984; 150:836.
56. Elliott JP, Garite TJ, Freeman RK. Ultrasonic prediction of fetal macrosomia in diabetic patients. Obstet Gynecol 1982; 60:159.
57. Sandmire HF. Comment. Am J Obstet Gynecol 1987;156:1414.
58. Spellacy WN, Miller S, Winegar A, et al. Macrosomia-maternal characteristics and infant complications. Obstet Gynecol 1985; 66:158.
59. Acker DB, Sachs BP, Friedman EA. Risk factors for shoulder dystocia. Obstet Gynecol 1985;66:762.
60. Langer O, Berkus MD, Huff RW, et al. Shoulder dystocia: Should the fetus weighing ≥ 4000 gm be delivered by cesarean section? Am J Obstet Gynecol 1991;165(#4, part 1):831.
61. Friedman EA (ed). *Labor: Clinical Evaluation & Management,* Second Edition. New York, Appleton-Century-Crofts, 1978.
62. Intrapartum fetal heart rate monitoring. ACOG technical bulletin #132, Washington, D.C., ADOG, 1989.
63. Morrison JC, Sanders JR, Magann EF, et al. The diagnosis and management of dystocia of the shoulder. Surg Gynecol Obstet 1992;75:515.
64. Jennet RJ, Tarby TH, Kreinick CJ. Brachial plexus palsy: An old problem revisited. Am J Obstet Gynecol 1992;166(#6, part 1):1673.
65. Young PE. Comment. Am J Obstet Gynecol 1992;166(#6, part 1):1677.
66. Gross TL, Sokol RJ, William T. Shoulder dystocia: A fetal-physician risk. Am J Obstet Gynecol 1987;156:1408.
67. Nocon JJ, McKenzier DK, Thomas LJM, et al. Shoulder dystocia: An analysis of risks and obstetric maneuvers. Am J Obstet Gynecol 1993;168(#6, part 1):1732.
68. Gross SJ, Shime J, Farine D. Shoulder dystocia: Predictors and outcome. Am J Obstet Gynecol 1987;156:334.

69. Gonik B, Stringer CA, Held B. An alternate maneuver for management of shoulder dystocia. Am J Obstet Gynecol 1983;145:182.
70. Keller JD, Lopez-Zeno JA, Dooley SL, et al. Shoulder dystocia and birth trauma in gestational diabetes; a five year experience. Am J Obstet Gynecol 1991;165(#4, part 1):928.
71. Iffy L. Comment. Am J Obstet Gynecol 1987;156:1416.
72. Bottoms SF, Sokol RJ. Mechanisms and conduct of labor. In: Iffy L, Kaminetzky HA (eds). *Principles and Practice of Obstetrics and Perinatology*. New York, John Wiley & Sons, 1981, p. 875.
73. O'Leary JA. Cephalic replacement for shoulder dystocia: Present status and future role of the Zavanelli maneuver. Obstet Gynecol 1993;82:847.

Chapter 7

Preterm Labor: Diagnosis and Treatment

◆◆◆

Michael Katz, M.D., Pamela J. Gill, R.N., M.S.N.

Introduction

Over the last several decades, thousand of publications on the subjects of preterm birth, preterm labor, their etiology, and their therapy, have appeared in the literature. However, in spite of this massive effort by the medical profession, both on the research and the clinical sides, very little progress has been made in effectively reducing prematurity rates in this country. The lack of a significant improvement should by no means lead to the conclusion that nothing can be done to help an individual pregnancy, but rather point out that we are dealing with complex multi-factorial pathologic events that may ultimately result in an early delivery. This early delivery occurs sometimes in spite of providing the best available care and sometimes, unfortunately because of suboptimal care. The purpose of the following chapter is to provide a very brief review of current issues that concern the obstetric aspects of preterm birth prevention with emphasis on medico-legal risk management issues. For readers who wish a more thorough review of the topic, please see the reference section at the end of the chapter.

Definitions

Term Birth: Delivery after 37 completed gestational weeks (269 days after last menstrual period).
Preterm Birth: Delivery anytime before 37 completed gestational weeks.

From: Donn SM, Fisher CW (eds.): *Risk Management Techniques in Perinatal and Neonatal Practice.* © Futura Publishing Co., Inc., Armonk, NY, 1996.

113

Labor: Such uterine activity that will ultimately lead to progressive cervical dilation, which will permit passage of the uterine contents, and delivery.

Preterm Labor: Onset of labor before 37 completed gestational weeks.

Spontaneous Labor: Labor that starts and progresses without interference to stimulate and bring about contractions.

Induced Labor: The bringing about of labor through external stimulation by medical means such as medications, artificial rupture of the membranes, cervical stimulation devices, etc.

Intentional Preterm Birth: Accomplishing preterm birth by terminating the pregnancy for medical indications. This termination can be accomplished via induction of labor, to be followed by vaginal delivery, Cesarean section, or by discontinuation or avoidance of tocolytic therapy to permit spontaneous preterm labor to proceed and become preterm birth.

Spontaneous Preterm Birth: Preterm birth that results from spontaneous preterm labor.

Preterm Premature Rupture of the Membranes: Rupture of the fetal membranes before the onset of labor and before 37 completed gestational weeks. The membranes may rupture spontaneously or may be ruptured artificially.

Tocolysis: (Toco = birth, labor, contractions. Lysis = gradual abatement, dissolution). The medical act of treating labor to decrease the frequency and intensity of contractions.

High-Risk Patient: A woman whose risk of developing preterm labor is significantly increased over her peers in the same community. In this context, the following are important:

1. *Positive predictive value:* The proportion of known high-risk patients who ultimately develop preterm labor. For instance, a predictive value of 50% means one-half of patients thought to be high risk for preterm labor did indeed develop preterm labor.

2. *Negative predictive value:* The proportion of patients thought to be not high-risk for preterm labor who nevertheless develop preterm labor in the index pregnancy.

3. *Sensitivity:* The proportion of patients known to be high-risk among all those who developed preterm labor. For instance, in San Francisco, only 35%-40% of patients who develop preterm labor are high-risk. The rest were thought to be low-risk up to that point.

4. *Specificity:* The proportion of patients not known to be high-risk (e.g., low-risk) among the group of patients who do not develop preterm labor.

Home Uterine Activity Monitoring (HUAM): Utilizing ambulatory devices that record uterine activity at home and transmit the data to a center where they are evaluated. Usually if a certain threshold has been reached, patients are instructed to be evaluated for a possibility of preterm labor, or if they have already been treated, treatment may be adjusted. The usage of this modality for preterm birth preventions, while FDA approved, is still controversial in the obstetric community.

Terbutaline Pump: Usage of a small, portable, programmable pump to give parenteral tocolytic therapy at home. This method is mostly reserved for patients in whom oral tocolysis has proven ineffective.

Risk Assessment

The first step in dealing with prematurity prevention is dealing with the issue of risk.[1-8] Ideally, a risk scoring system should have a high positive predictive value and a high sensitivity (see definitions). While it is not clear to what extent one can deal with each and every risk factor in terms of prevention, the consensus is that such risk screening is an integral part of acceptable prenatal care. It is amazing how often obstetricians focus on their patient's age, blood pressure, nutrition, or weight gain, yet fall short when it comes to screening for the single most important perinatal killer, namely, prematurity. Numerous statistical studies with multitudes of conditions have shown that a number of conditions are associated with a significantly increased risk of preterm birth. When using the term "increased risk" one needs to be careful in defining the exact meaning of that (see definitions). At this point, the obstetrician may benefit from knowing the overall preterm birth rate in his/her community and relate the risk of a particular patient as multitudes of risk. For example, a woman's risk for preterm labor in San Francisco is 5%, and for a woman carrying twins is 50%, a risk increased by tenfold. Speaking to the patient in these terms of increased risk is also quite often easier for them to comprehend. In terms of commonly considered risk factors (Table 1), it should be noticed that the risk factors for preterm birth in general as opposed to spontaneous preterm birth (see definitions) may not be identical. For instance, hypertension is a risk factor for intentional preterm birth, but not for spontaneous preterm labor. However, this chapter deals mostly with spontaneous preterm birth because there are almost no preventive measures to deal with intentional (or indicated) preterm deliveries. A specific example where a risk may be mitigated is the known association between smoking, drugs, and preterm birth. Both of the above are clearly preventable and proper counseling may help. Needless to say, the documentation of such counseling and its outcome are all part of prenatal records.

One important aspect of dealing with the patient who is determined to be at risk for preterm labor and delivery is setting proper expectations. The care giver must make it very clear from the outset, that even with proper diagnosis and treatment, term birth will not and cannot always be reached. In addition, it is advisable to make the patient aware that even if most high-

---

Table 1
Risk Factors Associated with Preterm Labor

Major Factors

Previous preterm labor or delivery
Misshapen uterus
DES daughter
Abdominal surgery and/or cerclage
More than two second-trimester abortions (spontaneous or therapeutic)
Cone biopsy
Multiple pregnancy: twins, triplets, etc.
Cervical change and/or excessive uterine contractions at < 33 weeks of
    pregnancy
Serious infection during this pregnancy
Excessive amount of amniotic fluid
Unexplained vaginal bleeding after 20 weeks of pregnancy

Minor Factors

More than two first-trimester abortions (spontaneous or therapeutic)
Bleeding after the first 12 weeks of pregnancy
Urinary tract infection during this pregnancy
Smoking more than ten cigarettes per day
Extreme mental or physical stress

---

risk pregnancies reach term (50%-70%), others end up not only preterm (30%-50%), but at such gestational ages that some difficult medical and ethical decisions may have to be made. When these discussions take place early in gestation as soon as risk factors are identified, the expectations are set appropriately, and the risks of disappointment, anger, misunderstanding, and even litigation are greatly diminished. All such discussions need to be recorded. Since most patients who deliver preterm do not have identifiable risk factors, up until they developed preterm labor, discussions about outcome have to take place as soon as the diagnosis is made.

Even though at present there is no conclusive scientific evidence that population-based screening and education of patients at risk will help prevent preterm birth, it might be advisable to provide at least some brief education to these patients. Educational material can be obtained at many university medical centers, the March of Dimes, American College of Obstetricians and Gynecologists (ACOG), etc. It is recommended that patients review this material as it may help them feel more in control of their pregnancy, may set proper expectations, and on occasion, may help prevent preterm birth.

At present, there is no evidence to show that the prophylactic administration of tocolytics, bed rest, cerclage, or most other interventions that are

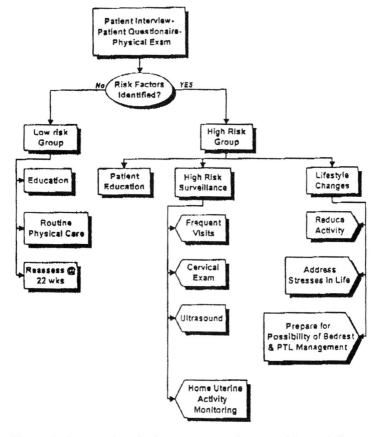

Figure 1. Suggested medical management of preterm labor risk factors.

used after preterm labor has been diagnosed will also be effective in preventing onset of preterm labor. It is thus recommended that utilizing the above measures be reserved for those patients in whom the diagnosis has been confirmed. On the other hand, certain interventions may yield some benefits in terms of helping the patients cope with preterm labor if and when it may occur, and on occasion may even help establish the diagnosis of preterm labor at an earlier stage. The flow diagram in Figure 1 delineates these measures. Again it should be clear that measures such as frequent visits for either digital or sonographic assessment of cervical status, as well as HUAM are *not* universally accepted as part of the current management of patients at risk, and not using them does not mean that one is providing substandard care. They are mentioned here only as suggestions and for the sake of completeness.

Table 2
Symptoms and Signs of Preterm Labor
Regular contractions or painless tightening of the uterus at > 4/hour
Menstrual-like cramps
Low back ache
Abdominal cramps
Pelvic pressure
Increase or change in character of vaginal discharge (amount, consistency, or color)

Making an Early Diagnosis

Failure to make an early diagnosis is one of the most troubling aspects of preterm labor.[9-26] In spite of having tocolytics available for almost 4 decades, most patients who develop preterm labor are not suitable candidates for therapy by the time preterm labor is diagnosed. Most of the patients are either too far dilated, are infected, or have ruptured membranes, when treatment is considered.

A good example is the Canadian study of Ritodrine, where a very significant proportion of participants had their treatment started after rupture of the fetal membranes, or when the cervix was dilated 2 or more cm. On many occasions, preterm labor develops in a more subtle fashion and in spite of the most dedicated surveillance, the patient has her diagnosis established at a stage too late for effective long-term treatments. However, it is the cases in which management is suboptimal and the diagnosis is made at a stage too advanced for therapy that provide cause for many of the lawsuits in obstetrics. Since prematurity can often have such a devastating outcome, the apparent unwillingness of care givers to promptly respond to patients' complaints of symptoms and signs of preterm labor can be regarded very unfavorably by patients, peers, experts, and ultimately the courts. Here again one must emphasize that although studies looking into using symptoms or signs to prevent preterm birth have not resulted in a uniform endorsement, the prudent care giver should use common sense and exercise a liberal policy of prompt patient evaluation whenever one of the symptoms or signs of preterm labor (Table 2) appears. The suggested evaluation in response to these complaints should probably include an assessment of contractility and if not contraindicated, an assessment of cervical status.

Because of the inability to clearly demonstrate that following symptoms and signs will consistently enhance the making of an earlier diagnosis of preterm labor, alternative methods have been examined. One of these methods is the daily HUAM (see definitions) system. This system includes an ambulatory tocodynamometer that usually is used by high-risk patients for 1 hour twice a day, to record and transmit uterine activity data. The data are then interpreted by a nurse or technician who advises the patient, according to the frequency of contractions, whether or not an evaluation to rule out preterm labor is required. The rationale behind HUAM is that preterm labor contractions are often subtle and a sensitive objective monitor may help an earlier detection. In addition, daily contact with a care giver could in and of itself elicit additional symptoms and signs that, once again, will assist in bringing in the patients at risk for evaluation at an earlier stage of preterm labor. In spite of the fact that HUAM was introduced to the obstetric community more than a decade ago, its utilization is still controversial and studies both for and against HUAM are being added to the literature on a regular basis. At this point, the prescribing of HUAM for patients at risk of preterm birth is not considered a standard practice. The failure, therefore, to prescribe HUAM should not be associated with any liability. However, just like with fetal heart rate monitoring in labor, one must not prescribe HUAM and then ignore the data because HUAM is not a universally accepted modality. The same goes for educational material. If practitioners distribute books, booklets, tapes, or videos about preterm labor symptoms to their patients, they are expected to respond and evaluate later if their patients follow instructions and call them with possible preterm labor.

Over the past few years, the role on oncofetal fibronectin as a possible predictor of preterm labor, preterm birth, or premature rupture of the membranes has been studied. Oncofetal fibronectin is a protein first described in 1985, which is restricted in the second half of normal pregnancy to the fetal compartment. Most of this newly discovered form of fibronectin is found at the choriodecidual junction and is thought to play a role in establishing the extracellular interface between mother and fetus. So far, studies have shown that leakage of this substance into the cervicovaginal secretions of pregnant women, where it can be picked up by a cotton swab (like a Pap smear), often precedes the onset of preterm labor, or if a patient is symptomatic, often predicts the subsequent occurrence of preterm delivery. The usage of fetal fibronectin as a clinical test to evaluate the risk that a symptomatic patient with symptoms and signs of preterm labor will indeed end up with preterm birth, has been approved by the FDA. While the positive predictive value in most studies ranges between 45%-75% (depending on whether or not other high-risk factors are present), the negative predictive value is between 90%-98%. At present, exact guidelines for using fetal fibronectin in clinical practice are not available, but it seems likely that patients who are evaluated with symptoms of possible preterm labor will have their vaginal secretions tested. A negative test (< 50 mg/mL) will be just like a reactive nonstress test, namely, it will provide reassurance that the risk of preterm birth is almost negligible for the following 2-3 weeks. The test may have to be repeated after 2-3 weeks if the symptoms persist. On the other hand, a positive test serves as an indicator of increased risk of preterm birth, and will alert the practitioner to step up pregnancy surveillance. Fetal fibronectin could, on the one hand, reduce the incidence of unnecessary administration of tocolytics, while on the other, provide objective information to substantiate subjective complaints by patients.

In summary, the confirmation or the ruling out of preterm labor as soon as the symptoms and/or signs appear, is critical in avoiding possible litigation exposure in the future. The above actions need to be documented carefully on each and every occasion. When education, technology, or chemical tests are used, their input and results must be incorporated into the management scheme. Using a modality and then ignoring its input because it is controversial or not the standard of care is a bad and risky idea.

Providing Effective Therapy

Once the diagnosis of preterm labor has been confirmed, namely documented uterine activity that leads to significant cervical change, the next step is how to respond.[27-31] It is important to understand that there is no fixed, agreed upon frequency of contractions or agreed upon cervical change that is universally defined as preterm labor. Practitioners thus have a latitude that can be used in accordance with either protocols in their institution or the accepted practice in their communities. Nevertheless, while this is a so called "medical judgment" issue, proper documentation is mandatory. As far as treatment protocols are concerned, every unit that provides tocolytic therapy needs to have established protocols for the administration, follow-up, nursing surveillance, and documentation of tocolytic drugs. Because these medications have very significant cardiovascular, metabolic, neurologic, gastro-intestinal, and fetal side effects, the risks and benefits must be considered for each individual case. There is very little doubt that most tocolytics are effective in achieving a significant short-term delay 2-3 days in delivery. This short-term delay is quite important in allowing the effects of corticosteroids to take place and also permit the carrying out of a maternal transport to a higher level facility, should that be required. In lower level hospitals, protocols for referral to higher level facilities, protocols for perinatal consultations, and one way and two way transports can be helpful in managing preterm labor patients. These protocols, in addition to reducing the incidence of complications and improving the level of care, will help reduce liability in cases where preterm delivery is unavoidable. The referral criteria to another institution should be clearly defined and be adjusted periodically to the level of care available in the referring institution. Particular caution is advised when the gestational age is in the "gray zone" of borderline viability or uncertain dates. These pregnancies at 23 to 28 weeks gestation are disproportionately represented in very sick intensive care nursery populations as well as lawsuits involving premature births.

Since treatment is almost universally accepted to be effective at least for the short-term, it is expected that the practitioner document if he/she elects not to treat. It may also be a good idea to document that the patient was informed in regard to the risks, benefits, and alternatives of treatment, especially when long-term therapy or unconventional therapy (higher than usual dose, combination of several drugs, non-approved drugs, etc.) are used. There is no unanimous agreement as to how long to treat parenterally, and whether to follow parenteral therapy with oral medication. It is suggested that protocols be created and followed along with proper documentation. For example, in the authors' institution, treatment for preterm labor starts parenterally with magnesium sulfate or β-mimetics as soon as the diagnosis is made after 20 weeks gestation and no later than 36 weeks gestation when dates are uncertain. Once a patient has been stable for approximately 24 hours (i.e., no increase in contractions with accompanying additional cervical change), the parenteral treatment is tapered and replaced by oral maintenance medication. Patients are then observed for another 12-24 hours while on bed rest with bathroom privileges, and if stable, are sent home with the same maintenance oral dose and documented instructions as to activity restrictions at home, diet, when to come back for follow-up, what to watch for in terms of symptoms and signs, whom to contact in an emergency, and which side effects to report. A great source of medico-legal problems is the alleged premature discharge of patients from the hospital either before treatment was started or after an initial successful arrest of preterm labor. In either case, practitioners should try to document that a patient is indeed stable enough to go home, that preterm labor is no longer present, and that information was given in regard to the appearance of symptoms and signs in the future. Those who do not consider long-term oral tocolysis as helpful and who practice in communities where this treatment is not part of standard treatment need not use it or worry about it. However, those practitioners who do not want to use it in communities where oral medications are commonly used or where long-term parenteral tocolysis is used commonly, may want to document their considerations and even discuss this issue with their patient who might have certain expectations. While most practitioners agree that tocolytic treatment may offer benefit to pregnancies at < 34 weeks gestation and probably no benefit at ≥ 36 weeks gestation, the gray zone between 34 and 36 weeks remains an issue of personal judgment. In our institution, parenteral treatment is offered up until 35 to 36 weeks gestation and oral treatment is usually discontinued at 37 weeks gestation. If one is practicing in an environment where a consensus in regard to the issues of long-term tocolysis, oral tocolysis, etc., cannot be developed, consideration should be given to obtaining informed consent from the patient. The latter, however, is rarely necessary.

In regard to the usage of corticosteroids, there is very little controversy as to whether or not they should be used if preterm birth is a real possibility between 26 and 34 weeks gestation. Since the data are quite convincing in regard to their effectiveness, one needs to document the reasons for not administering them in a particular case. For instance, if delivery is imminent within a few hours, or if preterm labor is easily arrested, one can avoid giving steroids. Needless to say, if lung maturity is likely to be present, or if the membranes have ruptured, the considerations are altogether different.

From a medico-legal perspective, claims usually arise because of the fact that several key issues were not attended to by the practitioner. A great number of these cases have very little to do with providing poor care. Practitioners can avoid or mitigate the impact of claims by adhering to the following principles (Table 3):

1. The records should provide a clear description of when the first symptoms appeared, the progression of symptoms, and when they were first reported. It is important to have these data so that a year or two later, when questions arise, one does not rely only on recall by the patient and her relatives.
2. The time of response by the office personnel, the practitioner, etc., as well as the exact instructions must be documented.
3. If preterm labor has been diagnosed, using the standard criteria for the community, this fact should be mentioned. Cervical status, uterine activity, and the likely prognosis also need to be mentioned.
4. It is always recommended that one also mention the prognosis to the patient so that her expectations remain reasonable. An explanation like, "Ms. Johnson, you are 2- to 3-cm dilated and the baby's head is very low. I will try to stop your labor, but I doubt if we are likely to delay delivery by more than 24 hours," can go a long way towards preventing later problems.
5. Do not ever get into the "blaming game." As long as the etiology of preterm labor is unknown, no particular action by the patient or other stressors should be pointed out as causes. Phrases like, "Didn't we tell you to avoid intercourse, Ms. Jones?" or "You should have listened to me when I said complete bed rest" are to be avoided at all costs. Once one gets on the track of accusations, there is no knowing where it will end.
6. Discuss treatment, side effects, options, etc. and be clear about *your* philosophy in regard to therapy. There is nothing wrong about men-

Table 3
Preterm Labor Risk Management

Event	Comment	Document
Pregnancy	If no risk present: re-evaluate later If risk present: give instructions Discussion in office Evaluate re: symptoms and signs of preterm labor Literature More frequent office visits: Fibronectin? HUAM?	Screening done
Initial symptoms and signs or risk factors	Give literature Education class Discuss in office Give instructions	Risk factors Risk screening Time when started TIme when reported Your response
Evaluation of symptoms and signs	Confirm or rule out preterm labor Fibronectin?	Uterine activity Cervical status
Preterm labor	Send home Protocols	Instructions re: life style, what to watch for, when to return to office, self-monitoring HUAM?
Preterm labor present	Tocolysis Hospital protocols Perinatal consult? Neonatal consult? Steroids	Risk/benefits Long-term vs. short-term Prognosis
Tocolysis successful	Oral therapy? Activity, bed rest? Diet Work HUAM? Intercourse Stop at 36–37 weeks' gestation Steroids	Instructions Stable cervical status Contacts in case of recurrence Side effects of therapy
Tocolysis only short-term	Tocolysis Steroids Perinatal consult Neonatal consult Prepare for safe delivery Transport	Prognosis Status pretransport
Recurrent preterm labor	See Preterm labor present Consider change of medications Rule out precipitating factors: infection, non-compliance with medications, etc.	See Preterm labor present

tioning that there are oral tocolytics available, but that you do not believe their usage has been proven effective. Or, there are devices to monitor contractions at home, but their efficacy is controversial and you happen not to be using them for this particular condition. Most patients appreciate having the information and do not feel deprived later if they find out about other treatment modalities.

7. In dealing with high-risk patients, and especially when practicing in a lower level facility, the issue of transport, maternal versus neonatal, needs to be discussed and recorded.

8. Call in your consultants early. Whenever you feel that a patient might be difficult, not necessarily medically, but rather medico-legally, call in the specialists early. Sharing the responsibility, setting the expectations straight, and demonstrating that the condition is serious and that you are truly concerned, are all of advantage.

9. Avoid, at any point, implications that you have given up on the fetus, especially when dealing with babies in the gray zone of 23 to 26 weeks gestation. Having the "wrong" attitude along with a surviving and severely damaged 25 week newborn often ends up with unnecessary and avoidable litigation. Should a decision be made not to interfere on fetal behalf, a very careful description of all considerations must be made. If the decision is made by the patient against the practitioner advice, this fact should also be mentioned, along with the means used to explain and inform the patient about the known consequences of her decision. Factual objective description is always preferred over an emotional and defensive one.

10. Having a neonatal or pediatric consultation on every patient who is treated for preterm labor at ≤ 36 weeks gestation is routine in our institution, and contributes significantly towards appropriate post-partum expectations.

11. If transporting to a higher level facility, it is suggested that the following be mentioned: a. time and contact person at the receiving institution; b. condition of patient and time when patient leaves your facility; and c. instructions for action during transport if no hospital protocol is in place.

12. When sending a patient home, document as mentioned earlier in the section.

Conclusion

In spite of a great body of research, there is no unanimous agreement among care givers as to most of the basic aspects associated with preterm labor.[32-36] There is no uniform way of assessing the risk, using subjective symptoms and signs, making the diagnosis, or providing therapy. Nevertheless, in order to be able to cope with the significant medico-legal risk that accompanies premature labor and birth, it is important that an approach and strategy be developed to deal with this particular complication of pregnancy. This approach can be individual, institutional, or regional, and should be based on established protocols and supported by current interpretation of available medical science. The presence of controversy will never justify ignoring complaints by patients, ignoring objective findings, or providing substandard care. Prematurity is not always preventable but a poor attitude and sometimes the wrong approach to its management can and should be avoided.

> **Commentary by Mr. Bloch:** The attorney reviewing a case involving damages related to prematurity must attempt to answer a myriad of questions, all of which are alleged to have controversial answers, and at times must deal with defenses that suggest prematurity is always idiopathic, unpreventable, and untreatable. In the real world, when the membrane remains intact, we know that many cases of premature labor are successfully stopped, that delivery is handled in a non-traumatic method, and appropriate treatment can sometimes increase survivability without major morbidity. To translate that real world thinking into negligence and legal cause presents a formidable task to anyone handling cases involving prematurity. The questions addressed will almost always include the following:
>
> 1. Were risk factors properly identified and incorporated into a treatment plan?
> 2. Was premature labor appropriately identified?
> 3. Was appropriate treatment given to stop premature labor? Do tocolytic agents work?
> 4. Would sufficient delay have been accomplished to affect outcome? Would there have been an opportunity to use steroids to promote fetal lung maturation?
> 5. Was the appropriate route of delivery utilized?
> 6. Was the given facility capable of handling prematurity, both in terms of arresting labor and treating the premature newborn when delivery is unavoidable?

Every obstetric author is quick to point out that despite advances in education and treatment, no noticeable progress has been made in preventing preterm labor and delivery. Indeed, many argue that the incidence of preterm birth is rising in this country. While these general statements are true, they are based on multiple social and economic factors (i.e., poverty, absence of prenatal care, teenage pregnancies, etc.). Such conclusions are to a large extent inapplicable to the question of whether or not opportunity existed *in a given case* to identify the patient at risk to prevent preterm labor or to successfully intervene once preterm labor commences.

The single most important factor in high risk identification is a history of prior preterm labor. *ACOG Technical Bulletin*, #133 (The American College of Obstetricians and Gynecologists, "Preterm Labor," Washington, D.C. (1989), lists the following as risk factors associated with preterm labor:

Prior preterm delivery
Multiple gestation
Three or more first-trimester abortions
Previous second-trimester abortion
Cervical incompetence
Abdominal surgery during current pregnancy
Uterine or cervical anomalies (DES exposure, etc.)
Placenta previa
Premature placental separation (spontaneous or drug induced, such as resulting from cocaine use)
Fetal abnormality
Hydramnios
Serious maternal infection
Second-trimester bleeding
Cervical effacement or dilatation (> 50% or > 1 cm)
Pre-pregnancy weight < 45 kg (100 lbs)
Single parent
No prenatal care

The extent to which any one or a combination of these factors is present is crucial in determining when a treatment plan should be altered to assist in the prevention of preterm birth. The defense position often centers around the definition of preterm labor, insisting that preterm labor is not present until there is both evidence of regular contraction and cervical change. Much of the obstetric literature, in defining premature labor as requiring cervical dilation of 2 cm or greater, essentially defeats the possibility of arresting preterm labor, especially in the very low birth weight infant (under 1500 g).

In the real world, where high risk mothers have been identified and are under the care of perinatologists or other high risk specialists, tocolysis is often started when there is a clear pattern of contraction and *before* cervical change is noted. There are those in the obstetrical community who advocate that the only way to detect and treat preterm labor earlier would be to change the definition of preterm labor. The following statement appeared in *OB GYN News*, January 15, 1992, citing presentations made at the District V ACOG Annual Meeting: "The definition of preterm labor is undergoing a change that will lead to earlier identification of patients at risk of premature delivery. Preterm labor is usually defined as regular uterine contractions 7-8 minutes apart at 20-36 weeks gestation."

The traditional definition of preterm labor requiring cervical change is, in many respects, related to preventing overtreatment with tocolytics, especially in a non-high risk setting where adverse reactions are less likely to be properly managed. The likelihood of damage from overtreatment in a high risk setting is negligible. In an era where HMOs and their family practitioners are reluctant to refer even identified high risk patients to outside specialists, many opportunities for preventing preterm labor are going to be missed, simply because of the insistence that preterm labor does not exist until it is too late to stop it.

It becomes extremely important to thoroughly search the record for evidence of cervical change. Descriptions of effacement are often subjective, such as closed, thick, hard, soft, etc. Two examiners making the same observation may describe them differently. Two examiners may attribute different dimensions to the exact same degree of effacement.

Despite the conventional definition, most perinatologists will agree that at least in very low birth weight infants, tocolytics should be administered before cervical change, if possible, when presented with a high risk mother having regular contractions. The key to successful treatment requires that the high risk mother is identified and is in a facility where practitioners recognize what they are feeling and seeing, and are comfortable in the use of medication.

Most cases of injury related to prematurity will not give rise to legal action, especially when accompanied by premature rupture of membranes and the onset of infection (chorioamnionitis/fetal sepsis). These and other conditions may be contraindications to attempts to extend gestation. Nevertheless, some cases of morbidity resulting from preterm birth are clearly avoidable. To identify these cases requires a thorough history, a complete understanding of the medical records, and a working knowledge of the multiple factors surrounding preterm labor and birth. The focus will always be on whether risk factors were properly identified and handled, and whether intervention was timely and appropriate.

Commentary by Mr. Fisher: This chapter rather eloquently details the issues, care patterns, and controversies of preterm labor. Clearly, the issues of prematurity and its prevention are under significant scrutiny, research, and discussion as we speak, with not just multiple viewpoints, but quite diverse viewpoints in the literature.

The most significant *medico-legal* issue is whether or not tocolytics can effectuate a long-term delay in delivery. Having found no real efficacy in their ability to do that, Cunningham and Leveno, as well as *Williams Obstetrics* (18th Edition), indicate that essentially tocolytics at Parkland Hospital are not the standard of care. Unfortunately, many physicians feel compelled to use tocolytics even when they feel they are not efficacious, simply because they are afraid of being sued. This is, of course, a wise choice given the medico-legal environment in which it is very easy to obtain experts to criticize the failure to use tocolytics or the timeliness of the administration of the same, as well as the fact that those experts will testify that "in their experience" one can expect anywhere from 4 to 6 weeks delay in delivery by use of such medication. Given the present state of scientific knowledge, such testimony is not just unfair to the physician defendant, but is unwarranted in a court of law where "more probably than not" is the test.

Although the medical consciousness was raised with the Canadian study regarding tocolytics in 1992, and perhaps slightly earlier by the British study of King et al. in 1989, the question of efficacy of the tocolytics was probably raised as early as 1984. In the *Journal of Reproductive Medicine*, Volume 29, No. 2, February, 1984, a comparison of placebo, magnesium sulfate, and terbutaline was undertaken by Cotton et al. In that study it was found not only that the placebo was as effective as the medication, but perhaps more importantly, 24-48 hours was used as the test time for effectiveness. There was no indication in that article that any of the medications or intravenous fluid extended delivery "more probably than not" beyond the 48-hour mark.

Thus, in looking back, it would seem that shortly after the initial push for the use of tocolytics in the late 1970s and early 1980s, clearly by 1984 information began to surface that raised the question as to the efficacy of the so-called tocolytic medication. Following Cotton's article, of course, the "great debate" began regarding the efficacy of tocolytics for long-term purposes with eventual culmination in proof that they worked for 24-48 hours in most instances. However, there is no scientific proof that they are predictably able to produce a long-term delay in delivery. In other words, scientifically no one has been able to show that "more probably than not" one can arrest labor for several weeks.

Shortly following the Canadian study, in November of 1992, an often overlooked study regarding ritodrine by Lye et al. appeared in the November, 1992, *American Journal of Obstetrics and Gynecology,* Volume 167, No. 5, page 1399. This article, entitled "Failure of Ritodrine to Prevent Preterm Labor in the Sheep," incidated that although labor contractions could be inhibited initially for approximately 16 hours, the amplitude and frequency of the contractions returned thereafter.

The animal model, in essence, reflected the clinical data in humans, noting that essentially labor generally recommenced within 24-48 hours. Additionally, the study pointed out that the "receptors" to the tocolytic medication became desensitized after a period of time of exposure to the medication, and that was the suspected reason as to why there was a tocolytic failure to prevent preterm labor for more than 48 hours.

It is this attorney's impression that although short-term delays of 24-48 hours can definitely be achieved by the use of tocolytics, it would be improper to say that medical science has proven "more probably than not," that one can expect delays of several weeks after the administration of tocolytic therapy. As in most studies, there are points of criticism, variables that may not have been taken into account, and of course, the often asked question, "Was she in labor or not when the tocolytics were administered?" However, it should be pointed out that these questions simply address the accuracy of a particular study and its conclusions *but by no means prove that the converse of the study result is true.*

References

1. Creasy RK, Gummar BA, Liggins GC. System for predicting spontaneous preterm birth. Obstet Gynecol 1980;55:692.
2. Papiernik E, Kaminski M. Multifactorial study of the risk of prematurity at 32 weeks' gestation. J Perinat Med 1978;2:30.
3. Main DM, Gabbe SG. Risk scoring for preterm labor: Where do we go from here? Am J Obstet Gynecol 1987;157:789.
4. Fedrick J, Anderson AB. Factors associated with spontaneous preterm birth. Br J Obstet Gynaecol 1976;83:342.
5. Hobel CJ. Premature birth: Spotting the risks. Contemp Obstet Gynecol 1982;19:209.
6. Guzik DS, Daikoku NH, Kaltreider DF. Predictability of pregnancy outcome in preterm delivery. Obstet Gynecol 1984;63:645.
7. Holbrook RH, Laros RK, Creasy RK. Evaluation of a risk scoring system for prediction of preterm labor. Am J Perinatol 1989;6:62.

8. Shiono PH, Klebanoff MA. A review of risk scoring for preterm birth. Clin Perinatol 1993;20:107.
9. Katz M, Goodyear K, Creasy RK. Early signs and symptoms of preterm labor. Am J Obstet Gynecol 1990;162:1150.
10. Iams JD, Stilson R, Johnson FF, et al. Symptoms that precede preterm labor and preterm premature rupture of the membranes. Am J Obstet Gynecol 1990;162:486.
11. Herron MA, Katz M, Creasy RK. Evaluation of a preterm birth prevention program: Preliminary report. Obstet Gynecol 1982;59:452.
12. Mueller-Henboch E, Reddick D, Psorrett D, et al. Preterm birth prevention: Evaluations of a prospective controlled randomized trial. Am J Obstet Gynecol 1989;160:1172.
13. Meis PJ, Ernest JM, Moore ML, et al. Regional program for prevention of premature birth in northwestern North Carolina. Am J Obstet Gynecol 1987;157:550.
14. Collaborative Group on Preterm Birth Prevention. Multicenter randomized controlled trial of a preterm birth prevention program. Am J Obstet Gynecol 1993;169:3552.
15. Katz M, Gill PJ, Newman RB. Detection of preterm labor by ambulatory monitoring of uterine activity: A preliminary report. Obstet Gynecol 1986;68:773.
16. Scheerer LJ, Belluomini J, Katz M. Uterine activity monitoring to detect preterm labor. In: Fuchs AR, Fuchs F, Stubblefield PG (eds). *Preterm Birth: Causes, Prevention, and Management*, Second Edition. New York, McGraw Hill, 1993, pp. 229-242.
17. Morrison JC, Martin JN, Martin RW, et al. Prevention of preterm birth by ambulatory assessment of uterine activity: A randomized study. Am J Obstet Gynecol 1987;156:536.
18. Iams JD, Johnson FF, O'Shaughnessy RW, et al. A prospective random trial of home uterine activity monitoring in pregnancies at increased risk of preterm labor. Am J Obstet Gynecol 1987;157:638.
19. Iams JD, Johnson FF, O'Shaughnessy RW. A prospective random trial of home uterine activity monitoring in pregnancies at increased risk fo preterm labor. Part II. Am J Obstet Gynecol 1988;159:595.
20. Mou SM, Sanderji SG, Gall S, et al. Multicenter randomized trial of home uterine activity monitoring for detection of preterm labor. Am J Obstet Gynecol 1991;165:858.
21. Grimes DA, Schulz KF. Randomized controlled trials of home uterine activity monitoring: A review and critique. Obstet Gynecol 1992;79:137.
22. Wapner RJ, Cotton DB, Artal R, et al. A randomized multicenter trial assessing a home uterine monitoring device used in the absence of daily nursing contact. Am J Obstet Gynecol 1995;172:1026.
23. Newman RB, Gill PJ, Katz M. Maternal perception of prelabor uterine activity. Obstet Gynecol 1986;68:765.
24. Lockwood CJ, Senyei AE, Dische MR, et al. Fetal fibronectin in cervical and vaginal secretions as a predictor for preterm delivery. N Engl J Med 1991;352:669.
25. Morrison JC, Allbert JR, McLaughlin BN, et al. Oncofetal fibronectin in patients with false labor as a predictor of preterm delivery. Am J Obstet Gynecol 1993;168:538.
26. Mageotte MP, Casal D, Senyei AE. Fetal fibronectin in patients at increased risk for premature birth. Am J Obstet Gynecol 1994;170:20.

27. Caritis SN, Darby MJ, Chan L. Pharmacologic treatment of preterm labor. Clin Obstet Gynecol 1988;31:635.
28. Fuchs F, Niebyl J. Principles of tocolysis: An overview. In: Fuchs AR, Fuchs F, Stubblefield PG (eds). *Preterm Birth: Causes, Prevention and Management*, Second Edition. New York, McGraw Hill, 1993, pp. 217-227.
29. Creasy RK, Katz M. Basic research and clinical experience with β-adrenergic tocolytics in the United States. In: Fuchs AR, Fuchs F, Stubblefield PG (eds). *Preterm Birth: Causes, Prevention and Management*, Second Edition. New York, McGraw Hill, 1993, pp. 243-277.
30. Amon E, Petrie RH. Magnesium sulfate, nifedipine and other calcium antagonists. In: Fuchs AR, Fuchs F, Stubblefield PG (eds). *Preterm Birth: Causes, Prevention and Management*, Second Edition. New York, McGraw Hill, 1993, pp. 333-366.
31. The Canadian preterm labor investigators group. Treatment of preterm labor with the beta-adrenergic agonist ritodrine. N Engl J Med 1992;327:308.
32. Fuchs AR, Fuchs F, Stubblefield PG (eds). *Preterm Birth: Causes, Prevention, and Management*, Second Edition. New York, McGraw Hill, 1993.
33. Witter FR, Keith LG (eds). *Textbook of Prematurity: Antecedents, Treatments, and Outcome*. Boston, Little Brown and Co., 1993.
34. Gonik B, Creasy RK. Preterm labor: Its diagnosis and management. Am J Obstet Gynecol 1986;154:3.
35. Iams JD. Obstetric inertia: An obstacle to the prevention of prematurity. Am J Obstet Gynecol 1988;796.
36. Katz M, Gill PJ, Turiel J (eds). *Preventing Preterm Birth: A Parents' Guide*. San Francisco, Health Publishing Co., 1988.

Chapter 8

Antepartum Fetal Assessment

Carl V. Smith, M.D.

Introduction

When antepartum fetal surveillance was first introduced, its goal was to accurately and reliably predict fetal survival or death in high risk pregnancies. While death is the most easily definable endpoint, refinements of antepartum surveillance techniques have given clinicians the opportunity to reduce perinatal morbidity as well as mortality. Numerous techniques are available to assure fetal well-being, ranging from daily fetal movement counting in the low risk population to multi-parameter tests of fetuses at high risk for intrauterine fetal death.

Maternal perception of gross body movement has long been recognized as associated with a low likelihood of fetal compromise. However, the mother's perception of diminished movement may result from sleep states rather than impending fetal compromise. Hon and Quilligan[1] in the 1960s reported a relationship between certain fetal heart rate (FHR) patterns and perinatal outcome. A pattern of repetitive late decelerations was associated with an increased need for neonatal resuscitation. Fetuses that demonstrated no clear pattern of decelerations associated with uterine contractions were likely to be vigorous. These intrapartum observations were extended into the antepartum period, as investigators questioned whether the FHR patterns could reliably predict fetal health.

The first described FHR test of well-being was the contraction stress test (CST); originally called the oxytocin challenge test (OCT). Ray and colleagues[2] published their initial observations in 1976, correlating a pattern of repetitive late decelerations with an increased likelihood of fetal death.

From: Donn SM, Fisher CW (eds.): *Risk Management Techniques in Perinatal and Neonatal Practice.* © Futura Publishing Co., Inc., Armonk, NY, 1996.

Simultaneous with this discovery, investigators observed that when fetal movements and accompanying accelerations of the FHR were noted in association with the OCT, the likelihood of fetal compromise was remote. Lee and colleagues[3] reported on their experience with the fetal activity determination (FAD) test. This test, subsequently named the nonstress test (NST), has remained the most commonly used FHR test of well-being for several years.

All tests of fetal well-being are reliable when results are normal. In up to 50% of cases, abnormal FHR tests do not indicate fetal compromise, but merely reflect changes in fetal behavior. Manning and colleagues[4] developed a multi-parameter test called the biophysical profile (BPP). This ultrasound-guided test assessed fetal movement, fetal tone, fetal breathing movements, amniotic fluid volume, and the NST. The BPP appeared to be as reliable as the NST and reduced the rate of falsely abnormal results.

The most recent fetal surveillance technique is Doppler umbilical artery velocimetry.[5] This test, most helpful in pregnancies complicated by intrauterine growth retardation or hypertension, is being used in many centers. Its precise role is screening populations at risk for these disorders and its value as a primary method of surveillance remains to be determined.

By identifying fetuses at risk for fetal compromise and by appropriately applying the testing technologies, practitioners can reduce the risk of fetal death and neonatal morbidity. What follows is a discussion of these technologies.

> **Commentary by Mr. Volk:** From the medico-legal perspective, it is vitally important to have the medical record accurately reflect the evaluation of the abnormal FHR by the examiner, setting out the steps taken to further evaluate the well-being of the fetus. If the outcome is poor, and the efforts to differentiate the compromised fetus from the uncompromised are either not accurately reflected in the chart or were not undertaken, the case will be difficult to defend. Health care providers constantly complain about the amount of documentation that is necessary, but spending years preparing for trial and trying a case takes a lot more time. From my observation of reviewing thousands of medical records and practicing primarily plaintiffs medico-legal litigation, documentation is generally poor in the cases I accept. Poor documentation makes it extremely difficult to recall, and more importantly, to convince a jury that you can recall. You must convince a jury you are not merely supplying information years later that is in your best interests.

Fetal Movement Counting

Functional maturation of the fetal central nervous system has been demonstrated by a variety of investigative techniques. None has provided more insight into the process than the assessment of fetal body movements. Fetal gross body movements require coordination of the central nervous system and peripheral neuromuscular control. The degree of control is similar to that seen in the newborn infant.

Many techniques are available for observing fetal movement.[6] Sophisticated behavioral studies using continuous real-time ultrasound guidance and Doppler ultrasound have permitted long-term monitoring. Although this is of little use in the clinical management of patients at risk for fetal compromise, such studies have allowed us to appreciate maturation of the central nervous system and its effects on gross fetal body movements throughout gestation.

Fetal movement counting can be used as a primary testing method in the low risk obstetrical patient and adjunctively in the high risk patient. In the former situation, it frequently is a "stand alone test." Fetuses at higher risk for fetal compromise, such as those complicated by postdates or medical complications of pregnancy, benefit from a combined approach using daily fetal movement counting along with more sophisticated techniques. At a minimum, all obstetrical patients should be informed about normal patterns of fetal activity in the third trimester. Maternal observations are the oldest method of assessing fetal well-being but perhaps the least utilized. Numerous approaches have been reported, ranging from complex techniques requiring 30-60 minutes two or three times a day to the more simple "count to 10" method. Regardless of the method chosen, patients should be instructed to contact their health care provider when decreased fetal movement is noted. More sophisticated tests, commonly the NST, should then be used to determine fetal condition more precisely.

> **Commentary by Mr. Volk:** In addition to informing the patients of these matters, it is necessary to document the instructions. One method is to document in the chart and have the patient sign the note. There are several other methods and all are sufficient so long as they get the job done. The key is to inform and document that the patient was instructed and warned. The record must reflect the patient acknowledgment that she received the warnings and information.

The most attractive method of fetal movement counting is the "count to 10" method. Originally described as used in Cardiff, Wales, this technique was applied to a low risk American population by Piacquadio and Moore.[7] Many investigators have reported accurate correlations between maternally perceived body movements and those demonstrated on ultrasound. Approximately 85% of movements visualized ultrasonographically are perceived by the patient. These movements take many forms including movements of the fetal trunk, extremities, whole body, and even diaphragmatic movements or hiccups.

Changes in gross body movements frequently precede fetal death. Most of the reports demonstrating the significance of abrupt cessation of fetal body movements have been in high risk populations. Nonetheless, patients who complain of decreased fetal movement require additional evaluation. In otherwise low risk patients not requiring regular fetal assessment, a reactive NST and normal volume of amniotic fluid should be reassuring. If fetal activity returns to normal, additional surveillance is *generally* not required.

> **Commentary by Mr. Volk:** It has been my experience that a health care provider does not always order additional evaluations. I have represented several women for the death or damage to her child that reported to me that she informed her doctor of decreased fetal movement and the physician told her not to worry. Invariably, the reason given to the mother for the decreased movement was that the fetus has "dropped" and, therefore, not as much fetal movement is expected. On most occasions, the report of the mother to the physician was not documented in the records, but in three cases there was a third party at the conversation with the doctor that corroborated the mother's testimony.

Clinical Methods

Numerous techniques have been reported as useful in clinical evaluation of fetal activity. Perhaps the best is the so-called "count to 10" method. It presents the fewest time restrictions, is easily understood by patients, and can be applied to a low risk population. Other methods are more complex, reducing patient compliance without improving the predictive reliability of the test.

In our practice, patients are instructed to count fetal movements daily. Most prefer counting in the evening hours, which usually corresponds with the time when the fetus is most active. We instruct the patient to lie in a quiet room on her left side and to pay particular attention to fetal activity. The time for the fetus to move ten discrete times is then recorded. The average patient will require monitoring for < 20 minutes. Patients are instructed to notify the clinic or their physician if the fetus requires longer than 60 minutes to move ten times.

We have found written instructions to be helpful, along with telephone numbers for the woman's physician and labor and delivery. Requiring a record written by the patient does not improve the accuracy of tests, but it does serve as a reminder to the patient that she should perform this task daily.

Piacquadio and Moore[7] have demonstrated the usefulness of this technique in a low risk population. It resulted in a modest increase in the number of NSTs performed, but lowered perinatal mortality.

For high risk patients we encourage daily fetal movement counting and add more sophisticated techniques, usually the NST and amniotic fluid volume assessment. Both low and high risk patients are then instructed to call if there is an abrupt decrease in fetal movement.

Nonstress Testing

The NST has become the primary method of surveillance in most institutions, replacing the technically more difficult and time-consuming CST.[8] Because of controversy as to the precise frequency of testing and criteria for a reactive NST, comparison between institutions is sometimes difficult. The interpretation of the NST is based on a coupling of fetal movement and accelerations of the FHR. Ultrasound visualization has demonstrated that most, if not all, accelerations of the FHR are associated with fetal body movements. Abrupt onset of hypoxemia reduces fetal motor activity and secondarily the accompanying FHR accelerations. The length of time required to observe these reductions is variable and depends on fetal reserve. Typically, as hypoxemia persists there is an initial reduction in amplitude and frequency of FHR accelerations associated with fetal movements. Next, an uncoupling of fetal movements and heart rate accelerations occurs such that the majority of movements are not associated with accelerations. As fetal condition deteriorates, gross fetal body movements decrease and spontaneous decelerations of the fetal heart rate may occur.

The goal of NST is to identify a fetus at risk for hypoxemia by identifying reduced frequency and duration of accelerations. A nonreactive test may result from many conditions other than fetal problems. Factors such as gestational age, maternal dietary status, and drug administration may affect the results of the NST.

Clinical Methods

Table 1 lists commonly accepted indications for antepartum fetal surveillance and the approximate gestational age at which testing is recommended. Patients with complicated medical or obstetrical problems should undergo earlier testing. For example, a mother suffering from mild pre-eclampsia at 34 weeks gestation would be a candidate for antepartum testing. A chronic hypertensive requiring multiple medications for blood pressure control should begin surveillance as early as 26 weeks. Testing should not be performed earlier than the physician is prepared to act on behalf of the fetus if results are abnormal.

Commentary by Mr. Volk: It would also be important to document that the testing is not offered *later than the parents* would be prepared

Table 1

Indications for Fetal Surveillance

Indication	Gestational Age at First Test
Postdates	41 weeks
Diabetes mellitus	
Gestational	36 weeks
*Insulin	32 weeks
*Chronic hypertension	32 weeks
Prior stillbirth	32 weeks
Fetal growth restriction	At Diagnosis
Decreased fetal movement	At Diagnosis

*Complicated patients with severe disease may require surveillance as early as 26 weeks.

to act on behalf of the fetus. The parents are not in the same position as the physician to understand the timing that must be considered and may want the physician to intervene earlier than is medically possible. If it is documented that the parents were informed of the options available and why it is not possible to intervene sooner, the requirement for informed consent is met and documentation exists to refute the allegation that earlier intervention was not considered.

In most cases, surveillance should not be instituted until an estimated gestational age of 26 weeks or, if gestational age is uncertain, before the fetus reaches a weight of 750 g. Survival rates vary between institutions, and practitioners should consider survival statistics for their own institutions to guide decisions about intervention for the markedly preterm fetus.

Prematurity can have profound influences on fetal biophysical parameters.[9,10] The most commonly observed association is an increased frequency of nonreactive NST. This *usually* is caused not by worsening fetal condition, but by immaturity of the central nervous system. Delivery of a preterm fetus is usually not appropriate for a nonreactive NST alone. Fetal condition should be confirmed by additional methods such as a BPP.

Testing Protocol

Patients are attached to a fetal monitor and placed in either a left lateral recumbent or semi-Fowler's position to avoid aortocaval compression. The absence of supine hypotension is confirmed by recording the maternal blood pressure. The majority of our patients undergo fetal surveillance in recliners, which avoids the need for cumbersome hospital beds. Some institutions require a minimum 30-40 minutes of observation. Other institutions, including the author's, monitor the patient only until a reactive NST is obtained.

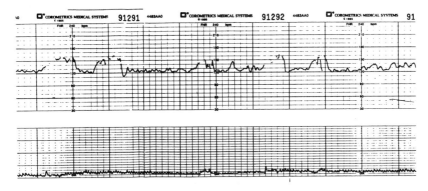

Figure 1. Electronic fetal heart rate monitor tracing demonstrates reactive non-stress test. Baseline ranges from 120-130 bpm with normal variability and multiple qualifying accelerations.

In our institution, a test is termed reactive if there are two, 15 bpm, 15-second accelerations of the FHR in a 10-minute window (Figure 1). Another commonly used criterion for reactivity is the presence of two accelerations in a 20-minute window.

Some authors have advocated liberalizing the criteria for a reactive NST, particularly in the preterm fetus. The preterm fetus is often unable to achieve a 15 bpm, 15-second acceleration. It has been suggested that 10 bpm, 10-second accelerations should qualify as reactive for preterm fetuses. Insufficient data exist at present to recommend this approach.

After a specified period of observation, usually 40-60 minutes, a test is termed nonreactive if criteria for reactivity are not met (Figure 2). Depending on the indication for testing, additional surveillance is recommended. Fetal sleep states commonly cause nonreactivity. However, Brown and Patrick[11] found a high probability of fetal compromise for tracings that remained nonreactive for 2 hours or more.

The optimal frequency of antepartum testing is uncertain. A minimum of 7 days between tests is recommended. In general, the greater the risk of fetal compromise, the more frequent the testing. In our institution, twice weekly testing is used for well-dated postdate pregnancies, diabetic mothers who require insulin, and fetal growth restriction evident on sonography.

Variable decelerations on NST require additional evaluation (Figure 3).[12] These variable decelerations may be associated with oligohydramnios, abnormal cord position, and fetal anemia. Their presence requires a real-time ultrasound evaluation to assure normal cord position and normal amounts of amniotic fluid. In the postdate fetus, variable decelerations may be associated with increased likelihood of compromise, and the fetus should be evaluated

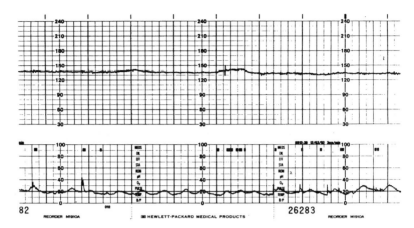

Figure 2. This is a non-reactive non-stress test with a marked reduction in variability, strongly suggestive of fetal compromise.

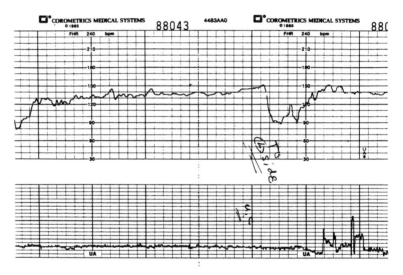

Figure 3. A prolonged deceleration of the fetal heart rate is noted from a normal baseline. A search for abnormal umbilical cord position and oligohydramnios is warranted.

for delivery. In the non-postdate fetus with variable decelerations and a normal amount of amniotic fluid, a negative CST may provide additional reassurance. Continuation of the pregnancy may be reasonable, particularly if the cervix is unfavorable.

Predictive Reliability

A reactive NST is associated with an extremely low probability of fetal death. The false negative rate, or the fetal mortality rate, within 7 days of reactive NST varies between 2 and 4 per 1000.[13,14] In contrast, the mortality rate in the general obstetrical population may be as high as 10 per 1000. Falsely reassuring tests can occur and may be associated with sudden unexpected changes in maternal condition, such as diabetic ketoacidosis, hypertensive crisis, and placental abruption.

> **Commentary by Mr. Volk:** Here we have a potential example of the difference in perspective between law and medicine. Many physicians would be of the opinion that the difference between a mortality rate of between 2 and 4 and as high as 10 may not be statistically significant. Many attorneys would be of the opinion that the difference is extremely significant and that all pregnancies should utilize NST as a screening tool because of the potential for fetal safety. What must be evaluated is the morbidity/mortality to the fetus and parents, the cost to society of an injured newborn with possible lifelong care requirements, and the medico-legal consequences to the health care provider. Should a screening NST be performed on all pregnancies?

Of equal concern clinically is a nonreactive NST that is not associated with an increased chance of fetal compromise. In most cases, a nonreactive test is associated with a healthy fetus. Faced with a nonreactive NST, the clinician has two alternatives: either utilize additional surveillance techniques or attempt some alteration of fetal arousal. Vibroacoustic stimulation has been extremely useful in improving the efficiency of antenatal testing.[15-17] Studies have shown that vibroacoustic stimulation with a Model 5C electronic artificial larynx (Western Electric, Glenshaw, PA, USA), or the Model 146 fetal acoustic stimulator (Corometrics Medical Systems, Wallingford, CT, USA), reduced the frequency of nonreactive tests by approximately 50%.[16] These devices have a fundamental frequency of about 85 Hertz with a sound pressure level of 85 decibels measured at one meter in air.[16] They produce prompt, vigorous fetal movement and frequently result in a change in fetal behavioral state (Figure 4).

On occasion, more common in the preterm fetus and pregnancies complicated with oligohydramnios, the sudden nonphysiologic stimulus may be associated with bizarre FHR patterns that may make it difficult to interpret the FHR tracing.[18] Finally, longitudinal studies have shown there would appear to be no adverse effects on hearing when infants are exposed to vibroacoustic stimulation.[19,20]

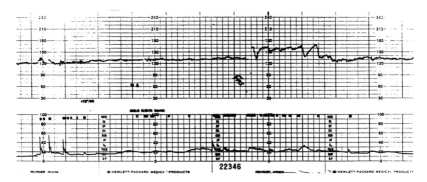

Figure 4. A non-reactive pattern is altered by the application of fetal acoustic stimulation.

Contraction Stress Testing

The presence of repetitive late decelerations is presumptive evidence for fetal hypoxia. The most common cause of fetal hypoxia is uteroplacental insufficiency in high risk pregnancies. A normal fetus will tolerate the brief reduction in uteroplacental blood flow that occurs during contractions. When placental reserve is exceeded, recurrent late decelerations appear as an early indicator of compromise. Fetuses with a positive CST are at increased risk for perinatal asphyxia, intrauterine death, and neonatal death. Conversely, a negative CST is associated with a low rate of fetal compromise similar to that observed following a reactive NST.[21]

Testing Methodology

Patients should be positioned in a manner similar to the NST. Avoidance of aortocaval compression and supine hypotension syndrome are keys to the successful interpretation of a CST.

The FHR monitor is attached, and if spontaneous uterine activity is present, test interpretation may be possible. For the interpretation uterine activity should include three palpable uterine contractions lasting 40-60 seconds in a 10-minute window.

If spontaneous uterine activity is not present, uterine contractions may be stimulated by unilateral or bilateral nipple stimulation. Uterine activity evoked by nipple stimulation is just as predictive as that evoked by intravenous oxytocin.[22] In most instances, the need for establishing an intravenous line and administration of oxytocin is obviated by nipple stimulation. Our approach is to use unilateral nipple stimulation, over the clothing, with one finger or the palm of the hand. Stimulation is continued for 2 minutes with a 2-minute rest period for up to four cycles. If contractions remain inadequate, bilateral nipple stimulation is used.

If uterine activity is not sufficient at this point, a dilute solution of oxytocin is begun at a continuous infusion rate of 0.5 mU/min. This rate is then increased by 1-2 mU/min every 30 minutes until the desired uterine activity is achieved. Usually the infusion rate will be < 10 mU/min.

Test Interpretation

A test result is negative when there are no late or significant variable decelerations (Figure 5). The patient may be tested again in 3-7 days. In a positive CST, late decelerations occur after > 50% of the uterine contractions. A test is considered suspicious if late decelerations are present, but after fewer than half of the uterine contractions. If adequate uterine contractions cannot be evoked by oxytocin, or the fetal heart rate tracing is not of sufficient quality for interpretation, the test is termed unsatisfactory and repeated the following day. On rare occasions, uterine hyperstimulation can occur. Even the most normal of fetuses may exhibit late decelerations when uterine hypertonus is encountered.

A negative CST requires three contractions in a 10-minute window. If uterine activity is less than desired, but the majority of contractions are followed by late decelerations, the test can accurately be termed positive and further evaluation undertaken. In this situation, giving additional oxytocin may increase the chance of fetal hypoxemia and precipitate acute fetal distress and a need for emergent delivery.

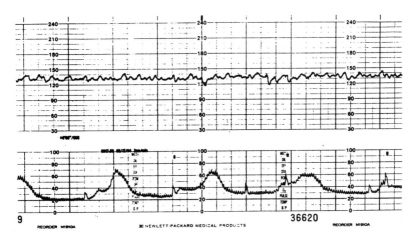

Figure 5. A negative contraction stress test is shown. The baseline is normal, and late decelerations are absent.

In general, CST is not begun until near term. Contraindications to performance of the CST include a prior classic Cesarean section, placenta previa, and risk for preterm labor, including history of preterm birth or premature rupture of the membranes. In such situations, noninvasive fetal monitoring utilizing the NST or BPP is appropriate. If the CST is interpreted as nonreactive or suspicious, additional surveillance techniques are helpful, usually the BPP.

Patients who have a positive CST require that delivery be considered. If fetal pulmonary maturity can be assured, delivery should be accomplished. The optimal route of delivery depends on the clinical indication for testing, the state of the cervix, and the presence of persistent late decelerations. The false positive rate for CST has been estimated at 50%. Therefore, many patients can safely deliver vaginally. If oxygen administration and placing the patient in the left lateral position restore a normal FHR pattern, induction of labor is reasonable. If the patient has an unfavorable cervix or persistent FHR decelerations, Cesarean delivery should be considered.

Reactivity is another important parameter during performance of a CST.[23] Reactive FHR patterns are rarely associated with a positive CST, and may be associated with a normal outcome. The most ominous situation is one in which the FHR tracing is nonreactive and the CST is positive, a pattern associated with fetal compromise. Cesarean delivery for fetal distress during subsequent induction of labor is common.

As with the NST, a positive CST, particularly in a preterm fetus, requires assurances of pulmonary maturity prior to delivery. A positive CST in a preterm fetus should require confirmation of fetal condition by NST, amniotic fluid determination, or BPP prior to delivery.

Fetal Biophysical Profile

Multi-parameter fetal testing has been proposed as an alternative to the more traditional NST. As first described by Manning and colleagues,[4] assessing multiple variables gives higher predictive accuracy than assessing each individual variable alone. Table 2 indicates a commonly used scoring system for biophysical profiles.

A maximum 30-minute observation period is most commonly utilized. Imaging along the longitudinal axis of the fetus permits simultaneous observation of gross fetal body movements, tone, and fetal breathing. The majority of infants will meet criteria for a normal test within a few minutes. A score of 0 for an individual parameter requires observation for the full 30-minute period.

According to the scoring system originally described by Manning,[4] total scores of 0, 2, and 4 are considered abnormal and require evaluation for delivery (Table 3). If the fetal lungs are mature, delivery is recommended.

Table 2
Scoring System for Biophysical Profile

	2 Points	0 Points
Nonstress test	Reactive	Nonreactive
Amniotic fluid index	AFI ≥ 5	AFI < 5
Fetal breathing	≥ 30 seconds of sustained breathing	< 30 seconds of sustained breathing
Fetal body movements	≥ 3 Discrete movements	< 3 Discrete movements
Fetal tone	Flexion/Extension of an extremity	No Flexion/Extension of an extremity

AFI = amniotic fluid index.

Table 3
Management Using the Biophysical Profile

Biophysical Profile	Management
0–4	Evaluate for delivery
5–7	Retest in 12 hours
8–10	Retest in 3–7 days

Scores of 8 and 10 are considered normal. In many institutions, the NST is not considered an integral part of the BPP. This "modified" BPP, often used by radiologists, yields a maximum score of 8 when the NST is excluded.

Assessment of Amniotic Fluid Volume

Amniotic fluid volume (AFV) may be an important indicator of fetal condition. Numerous maternal and obstetrical disease states are associated with abnormalities of AFV.[24] With oligohydramnios fetal conditions most commonly seen are intrauterine growth retardation, postdates, and genitourinary abnormalities. Premature rupture of the membranes may also result in an abnormally low AFV. Pregnancies complicated by polyhydramnios may have an increased incidence of maternal diabetes and fetal central nervous system or gastrointestinal malformations.

Amniotic Fluid Production

In the first trimester of pregnancy, accumulation of AFV is likely the result of free water flowing down an osmotic gradient. The semipermeable amnion permits the passage of free water into the amniotic cavity. In later pregnancy, the principal source of amniotic fluid is fetal urination. Fetal urine production, which begins at 8 weeks, averages 500-600 mL/day near the end of pregnancy. About 400 mL/day of additional amniotic fluid accumulates from output of the fetal lung.

Amniotic fluid is removed from the amniotic cavity by fetal swallowing and subsequent absorption from the fetal gastrointestinal tract. The overall AFV depends upon a balance between fetal swallowing and fetal urination. In a near term pregnancy, nearly all of the amniotic fluid is turned over in the course of a 24-hour period.

Obstetricians have long recognized the significance of AFV and its association with fetal health. In infants at risk for uteroplacental insufficiency, increased resistance to blood flow is felt to result in decreased fetal renal blood flow and subsequent decreases in urine output. Therefore, oligohydramnios is likely to be an important marker for fetal hypoxemia. Amniotic fluid volume reaches a maximum at 38-40 weeks and thereafter begins to decline until 42 weeks of pregnancy. Oligohydramnios in pregnancies complicated by postdates is particularly worrisome and is seen in fetuses with dysmaturity. This group of high risk fetuses is more likely to experience meconium staining and aspiration, fetal distress, and Cesarean delivery.

Ultrasound Imaging Techniques

The optimal method of AFV assessment remains controversial. Early articulated arm B-mode ultrasound machines were used to measure total intrauterine volume and thus to estimate AFV. These older machines gave way to real-time ultrasound evaluation and different techniques of amniotic fluid assessment were required.

Criteria to define oligohydramnios were then developed. With the BPP, oligohydramnios was defined as the absence of a single pocket of amniotic fluid whose maximum vertical depth was at least 1.0 cm.[4] As investigators examined the relationship between AFV and fetal outcome, it became apparent that this definition represented "end-stage" oligohydramnios.[25] More liberal criteria for defining oligohydramnios emerged; a single pocket with maximum vertical depth of at least 2.0 cm was suggested as being an adequate amount of amniotic fluid. No prospective comparison of these definitions has been made. Most investigators have recommended discarding the 1.0-cm rule as too restrictive.

Phelan and colleagues[26] reported on a new method of amniotic fluid assessment called the four quadrant technique. A linear or phased array ultrasound transducer was placed perpendicular to the floor and parallel to the sagittal plane of the uterus. The uterus was divided into four quadrants, using the umbilicus as the horizontal axis and the linea nigra as the vertical axis.

The maximum vertical depth pocket of amniotic fluid was measured in each of these four quadrants, and the mathematical sum of the four quadrant measurements yielded the amniotic fluid index (AFI). This semiquantitative technique has been used in multiple investigations, and has been found superior to the single vertical pocket depth. With this method, oligohydramnios is defined as an AFI of < 5. In a prospective investigation by Rutherford,[27] the combination of AFI with an NST was helpful in the management of high-risk pregnancies. Patients with oligohydramnios (AFI < 5) had an increased incidence of depressed 5 minute Apgar scores, fetal compromise, and meconium staining at delivery.

Some authors have suggested that each institution develop normative data for its populations at each gestational age. Moore and Cayles[28] described this method of assessing normal AFV, which is more precise but more cumbersome. Additional investigation is required to determine the optimal criteria for defining oligohydramnios.

Clinical Usefulness

Possibly, all fetuses requiring antenatal assessment would benefit from AFV determinations. Indeed, in the author's antenatal testing unit, this approach is used. A recent investigation by Clark and colleagues[29] revealed an astonishingly low perinatal mortality rate among infants tested with a combination of NST and AFI. They reported no unexpected fetal deaths in their at-risk population.

Even if AFV assessments are not routinely performed in all clinical situations requiring fetal surveillance, certain patients would appear to benefit from this technique. One such group is postdate pregnancies, where the clinical goal is to identify the dysmature fetus. Oligohydramnios is highly associated with dysmaturity. Postdate pregnancies complicated by oligohydramnios have an increased incidence of fetal distress, meconium staining, and meconium aspiration syndrome. When oligohydramnios is found during antepartum fetal surveillance for this indication, delivery is recommended. Concerns have been raised about unnecessary intervention. Small and colleagues,[12] utilizing an active management strategy for postdate pregnancies, delivered patients because of oligohydramnios or variable decelerations and they did not find an increased incidence of Cesarean deliveries.

A second group of fetuses that benefit from AFV assessment are patients with suspected intrauterine growth retardation. Initially, abnormal amounts of amniotic fluid were used to screen for intrauterine growth retardation. If oligohydramnios is uncovered during a routine ultrasound examination for other indications, intrauterine growth retardation should be suspected. When oligohydramnios is noted in the term patient, additional fetal surveillance by utilizing the NST, CST, or BPP should be considered. Fetuses with intrauterine growth retardation and oligohydramnios may require amniocentesis to document lung maturity prior to delivery.

Real-time ultrasound evaluation of patients experiencing premature rupture of the membranes is another clinical situation in which amniotic fluid assessment is important. Pregnancies complicated by oligohydramnios are at increased risk for intra-amniotic infection, preterm delivery, and fetal distress. In instances of oligohydramnios, prolonged fetal monitoring may disclose repetitive severe variable decelerations that may merit at least close observation on labor and delivery, if not delivery itself.

Last, when ultrasound assessment of AFV reveals polyhydramnios, consideration should be given to detailed ultrasound evaluation. Abnormalities of the central nervous system or gastrointestinal tract and diabetes mellitus may cause hydramnios. Up to 20% of infants with polyhydramnios may have karyotypic abnormalities.[30] Polyhydramnios was initially defined as an AFI of > 25. However, Smith and colleagues did not find an increased incidence of significant malformations but did report an increase in infant birthweight.[31] The higher the AFI, the more likely the polyhydramnios is to be pathologic and be associated with adverse perinatal outcome.

Many clinicians have adopted AFV assessment as part of their routine for antepartum fetal surveillance. In some institutions, this test has been called the "modified BPP." Insufficient perinatal resources exist at present to recommend this approach strongly for all patients. Real-time ultrasound, when available, appears to be beneficial and its use should be considered.

Doppler Umbilical Artery Velocimetry

Doppler ultrasound has been used for many years to assist the obstetrician in auscultating the FHR.[5] The technique can be also used to assess blood flow through the umbilical artery and other fetal vessels. Three types of Doppler ultrasound are available for use during pregnancy: pulsed wave Doppler; continuous wave Doppler; and two-dimensional color flow mapping. Pulsed wave Doppler is frequently used during duplex ultrasonography. First, real-time ultrasound imaging is used to identify a fetal vessel and place a Doppler gate over the vessel of interest. Doppler waveforms are then evaluated. This technique may also be used to measure blood flow within the fetal heart. Continuous wave Doppler principles are used to auscultate the FHR. In this situation, the ultrasound crystal continuously emits and receives ultrasound data. This technique has also been used to measure umbilical artery blood flow, but unlike pulsed wave Doppler, is not directed by real-time ultrasound. Last, color flow mapping may be used during fetal echocardiography to aid in the detection of complex cardiac malformations.

Umbilical Arterial Waveform Analysis

The most common use of Doppler velocimetry is for assessment of umbilical artery blood flow. If the frequency and angle of incidence of the ultrasound beam are known, then the velocity of blood flowing through a vessel can be calculated. Use of the Doppler principle allows quantification of blood flow, but many problems are encountered with this technique. Small errors in the measurement of the diameter of the vessel and angle of incidence may produce large errors in the calculation of blood flow. Normative data in the human fetus are lacking and much of what we understand about Doppler umbilical artery blood flow is based on flow probes attached to fetal sheep.

Umbilical artery blood flow is best evaluated using mathematical calculations, the most common of which is the systolic/diastolic (S/D) ratio.[32,33] The S/D ratio is a ratio of peak systolic to end diastolic flow. The human placenta is a high flow, low resistance system such that, during diastole, forward blood flow to the fetus continues. As gestational age increases, the S/D ratio falls, demonstrating a reduction in placental resistance.

Pathologic studies of the human placenta have revealed that reduced vascularity of the placenta results in altered S/D ratio. Doppler blood flow through the umbilical cord is believed to be a direct reflection of the resistance to blood flowing through the placenta. As resistance increases, the S/D ratio also increases. In very high resistance states, forward flow to the fetus during diastole stops.[34,35] Reverse diastolic flow, in which blood flows towards the placenta during diastole, represents a marked elevation of resistance to fetal blood flow.

Umbilical artery Doppler can be performed with either commercially available continuous wave ultrasound machines, most commonly, during real-time ultrasound evaluation using duplex sonography. Authors have failed to identify benefit to the routine incorporation of umbilical artery velocimetry in high risk obstetrical patients.[36] It may be of value in cases of fetal growth restriction.

In the normal term pregnancy, the S/D ratio is < 3.0. Values > 3.0 are more likely to be associated with intrauterine growth retardation. Fifty percent of growth restricted infants with an S/D ratio > 3.0 will require admission to the intensive care unit, and the perinatal mortality rate approaches 10%. Doppler ultrasound may be used to screen fetuses at risk for intrauterine growth retardation and may detect 50%-75% of such fetuses. Increases in the S/D ratio and resistance to blood flow result in an increased incidence of perinatal morbidity and mortality. The stillbirth rate approaches 33% among infants who have reverse diastolic flow. Similarly, the incidence of congenital malformations is also increased in this population. Additional prospective investigations are required to evaluate the clinical utility of Doppler umbilical artery velocimetry in screening an unselected population for intrauterine growth retardation.

Doppler technology may also be used to assess absolute and relative blood flow through other structures in the fetus. Doppler blood flow assessment of the middle cerebral artery, fetal renal arteries, and heart have all been used but remain largely experimental. Their role in routine antepartum fetal surveillance remains to be determined.

Summary

Assessment of fetal well being is integral to the management of both low and high risk pregnancies. Low risk pregnancies benefit from daily fetal movement counting with additional surveillance when fetal movement is felt to be diminished. The NST and AFI appear to be the most reasonable method for screening an "unselected" high risk obstetrical population. Because the positive predictive value of an abnormal test is so low, confirmation of fetal compromise is necessary prior to delivery. In the case of a preterm fetus, lung maturity should be documented prior to delivery for fetal compromise. The earliest gestational age at which testing should begin is variable and depends upon the indications for testing and survival statistics. In no case should fetal surveillance be initiated before the clinician is ready to consider delivery for fetal indications.

Knowledge of the surveillance techniques available and their limitations will aid the clinician in deciding the optimal time for delivery of the high risk obstetrical patient.

> **Commentary by Mr. Volk:** Dr. Smith has written an informative and excellent chapter on this very important time in the life of the fetus—the time that the fetus cannot consciously protect its own well being. It is hoped that medical science will strive to utilize the old and new technologies discussed in this chapter to further guard the fetal existence.

References

1. Hon EH, Quilligan EJ. Electronic evaluation of the fetal heart rate. Clin Obstet Gynecol 1968;11:145.
2. Ray M, Freeman R, Pine S, et al. Clinical experience with the oxytocin challenge test. Am J Obstet Gynecol 1972;114:1.
3. Lee CY, DiLoreto PC, O'Lame JM. A study of fetal heart rate acceleration patterns. Obstet Gynecol 1975;45:142.
4. Manning FA, Platt LD, Sipos L. Antepartum fetal evaluation: Development of a fetal biophysical profile. Am J Obstet Gynecol 1980;136:787.

5. Trudinger B, Giles W, Cook C, et al. Fetal umbilical artery flow velocity wave-forms and placental resistance: Clinical significance. Am J Obstet Gynecol 1985;92:23.
6. Rayburn WE. Fetal body movement monitoring. Clin Obstet Gynecol 1990;17:95.
7. Piacquadio K, Moore T. A prospective evaluation of fetal movement screening to reduce the incidence of antepartum fetal death. Am J Obstet Gynecol 1989;160:1075.
8. Phelan JP. The nonstress test: A review of 3000 tests. Am J Obstet Gynecol 1981;139:7.
9. Castillo RA, Devoe LD, Searle N, et al. The pre-term nonstress test: Effects of gestational age and length of study. Am J Obstet Gynecol 1989;160:172.
10. Smith CV. Antepartum fetal surveillance in the preterm fetus. Clin Perinatol 1992;19:437.
11. Brown R, Patrick J. The nonstress test: How long is enough? Am J Obstet 1981;141:646.
12. Small ML, Phelan JP, Smith CV, et al. An active management approach to the postdate fetus with a nonstress test and fetal heart rate decelerations. Obstet Gynecol 1987;70:636.
13. Druzin ML, Gratacos J, Paul RH. Antepartum fetal heart rate testing. VI. Predictive reliability of "normal" tests in the prevention of antepartum death. Am J Obstet Gynecol 1980;137:746.
14. Phelan JP, Cromartie AD, Smith CV. The nonstress test: The false negative test. Am J Obstet Gynecol 1982;142:293.
15. Read JA, Miller FC. Fetal heart rate acceleration in response to acoustic stimulation as a measure of fetal well being. Am J Obstet Gynecol 1977;129:512.
16. Smith CV, Phelan JP, Broussard PM, et al. Fetal acoustic stimulation testing: A retrospective experience with the fetal acoustic stimulation test. Am J Obstet Gynecol 1985;153:562.
17. Smith CV, Phelan JP, Platt LD, et al. Fetal acoustic stimulation. II. A randomized clinical comparison with the nonstress test. Am J Obstet Gynecol 1986;155:131.
18. Thomas RL, Johnson TRB, Bersinger RE, et al. Preterm and term fetal cardiac and movement responses to vibratory acoustic stimulation. Am J Obstet Gynecol 1989;161:141.
19. Ohel G, Horowitz E, Lindes M, et al. Neonatal auditory acuity following in utero vibroacoustic stimulation. Am J Obstet Gynecol 1987;157:440.
20. Nyman M, Barr M, Westgren M. A four-year follow-up of hearing and development in children exposed in utero to vibroacoustic stimulation. Br J Obstet Gynaecol 1992;99:685.
21. Pircon R, Freeman R. The contraction stress test. Clin Obstet Gynecol 1990;17:129.
22. Huddleston JF, Sutliff G, Robinson D. Contraction stress test by intermittent nipple stimulation. Obstet Gynecol 1984;63:669.
23. Grundy H, Freeman RK, Letterman S, et al. Nonreactive contraction stress test: Clinical significance. Obstet Gynecol 1984;64:337.
24. Seeds AE. Current concepts of amniotic fluid dynamics. Am J Obstet Gynecol 1980;138:575.
25. Hoddick WK, Callen PW, Filly RA, et al. Ultrasonographic determination of qualitative amniotic fluid volume in intrauterine growth retardation: Reassessment of the 1 cm rule. Am J Obstet Gynecol 1984;149:758.

26. Phelan JP, Smith CV, Broussard P, et al. Amniotic fluid volume assessment with the four-quadrant technique at 36-42 weeks' gestation. J Reprod Med 1987;32:540.
27. Rutherford SE, Phelan JP, Smith CV, et al. The four-quadrant assessment of amniotic fluid volume: An adjunct to antepartum fetal heart rate testing. Obstet Gynecol 1987;70:353.
28. Moore TR, Cayle JE. The amniotic fluid index in normal human pregnancy. Am J Obstet Gynecol 1990;162:1168.
29. Clark SL, Sabey P, Jolley P. Nonstress testing with acoustic stimulation and amniotic fluid assessment: 5973 tests without unexpected fetal death. Am J Obstet Gynecol 1989;160:694.
30. Carlson DE, Platt LD, Medearis AL, et al. Quantifiable polyhydramnios: diagnosis and management. Obstet Gynecol 1990;75:989.
31. Smith CV, Plambeck RD, Rayburn WF, et al. Relation of mild idiopathic polyhydramnios to perinatal outcome. Obstet Gynecol 1991;72:387.
32. Fleischer A, Schulman H, Farmakides G, et al. Umbilical artery velocity waveforms and intrauterine growth retardation. Am J Obstet Gynecol 1985;151:502.
33. Schulman H, Fleischer A, Stern W, et al. Umbilical velocity wave ratios in human pregnancy. Am J Obstet Gynecol 1984;148:985.
34. Rochelson B, Schulman H, Farmakides G, et al. The significance of absent end-diastolic velocity in umbilical artery velocity waveforms. Am J Obstet Gynecol 1987;156:1213.
35. Brar HS, Platt L, Paul R. Fetal umbilical blood flow velocity waveforms using Doppler ultrasonography in patients with late decelerations. Obstet Gynecol 1989;73:363.
36. Newnham JP, Paterson LU, James IR, et al. An evaluation of the efficacy of Doppler flow velocity waveform analysis as a screening test in pregnancy. Am J Obstet Gynecol 1990;162:403.

Chapter 9

Postdates Pregnancy: Diagnosis and Management

◆◆◆

Angela C. Ranzini, M.D.,
Robert Knuppel, M.D., M.P.H.

Introduction

For centuries, the duration of pregnancy has been recognized to be variable. The majority of women deliver at term. A smaller but significant group delivers in the post-term period. Postdates, post-term, and prolonged pregnancy are all synonyms for pregnancies that have gone past their due date by 2 weeks, or 294 days from the first day of the last menstrual period (LMP). Most studies used this definition for postdates; however, some authors chose to begin their postdate period at 287 days past LMP or 41 weeks of gestation. Postdate pregnancies are a problem separate from the postmature or dysmature infant who is identified as having signs of intrauterine nutritional deprivation. While there may be overlap in the two problems, it is clear that not all postdate pregnancies result in postmature infants.

While the vast majority of babies delivered postdates are in good condition, some may have problems recognized in the immediate neonatal period or in early infancy. Some of these children are the subject of litigation alleging negligence or deviation from standards of care by their obstetricians. In this chapter, we discuss the medico-legal issues that obstetricians face when dealing with the postdate pregnancy, define a group of patients at risk for problems in the postdate period, and offer management strategies to decrease the risk of perinatal morbidity and mortality. However, no current management plan will eliminate fetal or maternal risk.

From: Donn SM, Fisher CW (eds.): *Risk Management Techniques in Perinatal and Neonatal Practice.* © Futura Publishing Co., Inc., Armonk, NY, 1996.

Historical Background

In 1902, Ballantyne,[1] a Scottish midwife, wrote a paper describing the current problems of some infants. "The post-mature infant . . . has stayed too long in intrauterine surroundings; he has remained so long in utero that his difficulty is to be born with safety to himself and his mother." These difficulties were subsequently found to arise from both fetal growth restriction as a result of placental dysfunction, and fetal overgrowth with continuing normal placental function. The physical characteristics of the postmature infant were first recognized in the modern literature in 1954 by Clifford.[2] He recognized that some infants born after prolonged pregnancy exhibited signs of dry, cracked skin, loss of subcutaneous fat, meconium staining, absent vernix caseosa, and lanugo hair, and he described three stages of dysmaturity with increasing morbidity and mortality. He attributed these signs to nutritional deprivation as a result of placental dysfunction. The incidence of dysmaturity increases from about 3% at term to 10%-20% in the postdates period.[3,4] McClure-Browne[5] observed the natural history of postdate pregnancies, and concluded in 1963, that the incidence of placental dysfunction rose after term and was linked to a doubling of the perinatal mortality rate at 43 weeks, a tripling at 44 weeks, and a quintupling at 45 weeks.

In contrast, fetuses born after postdate pregnancies who have normally functioning placentas continue to grow normally. This results in an increased incidence of macrosomia when compared to term babies. Some of these infants experience birth trauma during the deliver process. In addition, there is an increased incidence of meconium-stained amniotic fluid, intrapartum non-reassuring fetal heart rate patterns, and oligohydramnios, which result in increased incidence of Cesarean delivery and induction of labor when compared to term infants. Despite these risks, the vast majority of fetuses delivered in the postdate period are healthy and delivered in good condition.

Incidence

The incidence of postdate pregnancy ranges from 3%-12% based on the dating criteria used to establish the pregnancy.[6-8] Many patients do not have accurate dates. Accurate dating of pregnancies will decrease the incidence of postdate pregnancy by at least 40%.[8] Dombrowski, et al.[9] developed gestational age-based charts of neonatal measurements (birth weight, length, and head circumference) recorded at birth based on gestational age derived from LMP alone and compared them to those based on best obstetric estimate (LMP plus sonographic examination) and found that dating only by LMP significantly overestimated the prevalence of postdates pregnancy five-fold. A large postdates trial study group screened 4566 pregnant women for inclusion in their study and found that 2428 patients (59%) were ineligible because of uncertain gestational age.[10]

It is important to accurately assess each patient's gestational age as early in pregnancy as possible in order to generate the most accurate assessment of gestational age. This will avoid confusion as the patient nears term. At the patient's first prenatal visit, it is important to assess gestational age from her history and physical examination. It is much more difficult to determine accurate dating from the patient's history the longer the patient is from her LMP. Helpful information to assess gestational age from the patient's history includes: the first day of her last normal menstrual period; the interval between periods; her certainty of these dates; unusual vaginal bleeding; and immediate prior use of oral contraceptives. Additional useful information may include use of ovulation predictor kits, basal body temperature charts, previous pregnancy tests (including home pregnancy tests), and previous ultrasound examinations. Some patients have gestational age established by infertility procedures such as in vitro fertilization, gamete intrafallopian transfer, or zygote intrafallopian transfer, and should be dated based on conception date rather than LMP. A history of fibroid uterus is also important, as uterine size may be larger than expected for gestational age. Although the patient may be absolutely sure of these dates, there still may be variability in these estimates. An estimated date of confinement or delivery (EDC or EDD) can then be calculated according to pregnancy "wheels," or based on Nagele's rule (subtract 3 months from the LMP and add 7 days). The LMP should be confirmed at the first visit by correlation with uterine size.

Additional clinical data should be recorded and checked for correlation with the patient's gestational age[11]:

1. Fetal movement felt first between 16-20 weeks.
2. Fetal heart tones heard with a non-electronic stethoscope between 18-20 weeks.
3. First trimester uterine size.
4. Uterine fundal height should be about 20 cm above the symphysis pubis, which generally corresponds to the umbilicus at 20-weeks gestation.

Any inconsistencies, uncertainty of LMP, or concern about the accuracy of the gestational age should be further evaluated through ultrasound examination preferably between 7- and 12-weeks gestation by crown-rump length (CRL). Some have suggested that LMP dating should be confirmed by ultrasound examination in all patients,[12] however this recommendation is not followed routinely in the United States.

Determining gestational age based on ultrasound information has been shown to be accurate when the fetus is < 20-weeks gestation. A CRL measured between 7- and 12-weeks gestation is accurate to within 3-7 days.[13,14] Between 14 and 20 weeks, a biparietal diameter (BPD) or femur length (FL) should be accurate to within 1 week.[14-16] Fetal measurements of the BPD, head circumference, abdominal circumference, and FL, and the mean gestational age corresponding to each measurement can be averaged to derive a composite fetal age. This composite age is then compared to the patient's actual gestational age by LMP.[17] When the gestational age based on LMP differs from the ultrasound-derived dates by more than a week in the first trimester or 10-12 days from 13-20 weeks, the patient should be re-dated, unless early intrauterine growth retardation is suspected.

Unfortunately, after the second trimester, there is too much variation in the size of normally grown fetuses to reliably assign a due date by sonography. Our policy in these cases is to assign an EDC based on the best ultrasound estimate of gestational age using fetal cerebellum and fetal foot length and to begin fetal surveillance at term (40 to 41 weeks gestation).

Complications Associated with Postdate Pregnancy

The most common complications of pregnancy in the postdate period are those associated with macrosomic fetuses, oligohydramnios, meconium passage, and antepartum death (Table 1). Management of the postdate pregnancy should focus on attempting to identify and prevent complications associated with these problems. Unfortunately, many fetuses with these complications are not able to be prospectively identified as "at risk," and therefore, policies of routine induction have been proposed in an attempt to improve neonatal outcome without adversely affecting the mother. A distinctive benefit to both mother and fetus has yet to be scientifically proven.

Macrosomia

Macrosomia is generally defined by fetal weight > the 90th percentile for gestational age. In the postdate pregnancy, however, we are particularly concerned with the macrosomic fetus, which is large in absolute values. At term, approximately 10% of infants will weigh more than 4000 g.[18] The number increases to 25% in the postdate patient.[19] Birth weights of > 4500 g have been reported in 2.8%-5.4% of postdate infants compared with 0.8% at term.[20,21] When compared to the normally grown infant, the macrosomic infant is at an increased risk for Cesarean delivery, birth trauma, and shoulder dystocia; however, most infants who are macrosomic deliver without any complications.

The problem is compounded by the inaccuracy of sonographic examinations in estimating fetal weight at term. In general, estimates of fetal weight at term can be in error by up to 15%,[22] because of technical factors and the variabil-

Table 1

Perinatal Outcome in Uncomplicated Postdates Pregnancies*

	Term (%)	Postdates (%)	Odds Ratio (CI)
Meconium	19.4	26.5	1.50 (1.36–1.64)
Breech	2.1	2.1	1.01 (0.77–1.33)
Cord prolapse	0.2	0.2	4.12 (1.21–14.10)
Delivery method:			
Forceps	14.0	17.0	1.26 (1.13–1.40)
Cesarean	8.3	17.6	2.36 (2.10–2.65)
Shoulder dystocia	0.7	1.3	1.87 (1.26–2.77)
Macrosomia (> 4,500 gm)	0.8	2.8	3.58 (2.61–4.92)
IUGR (< 2500 gm)	0.6	0.2	0.33 (0.15–0.74)
Apgar Score:			
1 min < 7	6.7	10.2	1.58 (1.37–1.82)
5 min < 7	0.8	1.7	2.16 (1.51–3.07)
Meconium aspiration			
syndrome	0.6	1.6	2.67 (1.81–3.93)
Congenital malformations	2.0	2.8	1.41 (1.09–1.82)
Corrected perinatal mortality:			
(per 1,000 births)	21	14	1.57 (0.80–3.09)
antepartum	6	7	2.75 (0.92–8.19)
intrapartum	0	0	—
neonatal	15	7	1.10 (0.45–2.70)

IUGR = intrauterine growth retardation.
*Derived from data presented in Eden RD, Seifert LS, Winegar A, Spellacy WN. Perinatal characteristics of uncomplicated postdate pregnancies. Obstet Gynecol 69;296:1987.

ity of fetal proportions. Fetuses who are macrosomic often cannot be visualized on the ultrasound screen, so measurements are estimated from that portion of the baby that can be seen. In addition, large babies often have substantial amounts of subcutaneous fat, which is less dense than muscle. Fetal measurements, which must take into account subcutaneous fat, will routinely overestimate fetal weight by approximately 4%.[23] This will lead to unnecessary Cesarean deliveries if one relies on sonographic estimates of fetal weight.

Pollack et al.[24] compared sonographic estimates of fetal weight within 1 week of delivery in 519 pregnancies at more than 41-weeks gestation with fetal weight at birth and found that 23% of infants had birth weights > 4000 g and 4% had birth weights > 4500 g. The sensitivity and specificity of a diagnosis of fetal macrosomia were only 56% and 91%, respectively. When the baby had a birth weight of > 3700 g, sonographic estimation of fetal weight routinely overestimated the baby's actual weight.

For these reasons and the fact that many women can safely deliver large fetuses vaginally, there is no consensus about the estimated fetal weight at which vaginal delivery is no longer advisable. In general when the baby approaches 4500 g and the head circumference to abdominal circumference ratio is abnormally low, abdominal delivery may be considered. These estimates are suggested primarily in an effort to decrease the number of cases of shoulder dystocia, which occurs in approximately 1.7% of infants with weights over 4500 g.[25] In the absence of maternal diabetes, we consider careful trial of labor for vaginal delivery in those fetuses with estimated weights < 4500 g.

Others have evaluated fetal proportions in an attempt to predict fetal macrosomia and increased risk for shoulder dystocia. BPD to chest diameter measurements,[26] fetal growth rates,[27] shoulder soft tissue thickness,[28] shoulder to head,[29] and FL to abdominal circumference[22] measurements have all been suggested as predictors of macrosomia. Unfortunately, none of these measurements has sufficient sensitivity and specificity to be clinically useful in the prediction of fetal macrosomia, much less shoulder dystocia.

Meconium-Stained Amniotic Fluid

Meconium-stained amniotic fluid is present in approximately 11%-13% of all deliveries at term,[30] but it is far more common in the postdate pregnancy. The incidence of meconium-stained fluid increases to 27% at 41 completed weeks of gestation and is present in 30% of deliveries at 42 completed weeks of gestation.[31] In pregnancies associated with oligohydramnios, the incidence of meconium-stained fluid may be as high as 50%.[32] In addition, the presence of meconium must be suspected when there is little or no fluid upon amniotomy.[32] In the antepartum period, prior to rupture of fetal membranes, the presence of meconium should be suspected when sonography shows severe oligohydramnios in a postdate pregnancy, or when layering of particulate matter in the amniotic fluid is observed. Approximately 5% of all babies experiencing in utero passage of meconium develop meconium aspiration syndrome (MAS), and approximately 5% of those with MAS die as a result.[33] Many investigators have tried to identify those fetuses who are at increased risk for MAS, and have focused on Apgar scores, cord and scalp pH, fetal heart rate tracings, "thick" or "thin" meconium and "fetal distress." It is increasingly clear that meconium passage in utero by itself is not a risk factor for adverse perinatal outcome, as most fetuses with meconium passage in utero are born in good condition.

It is now known that the fetus may pass meconium in the antepartum period, during labor, or at delivery, and also may aspirate meconium in any of these periods. Apgar scores and cord blood gases, which reflect the condition of the fetus at delivery and the need for resuscitation, are not useful in determining the status of the fetus when meconium passage occurred.

Many studies have focused on "thick" versus "thin" meconium. Most investigators define "thick" meconium as meconium that contains visible particulate matter, whereas "thin" meconium contains no particulate matter. When patients with "thin" meconium are compared to those with clear amniotic fluid, there are no significant differences in Apgar scores,[34,35] MAS, intrapartum or neonatal deaths,[35] or intrapartum scalp pHs.[34] "Thick" meconium, when combined with abnormal heart rate tracings, places the fetus at higher risk for low Apgar scores, MAS, neonatal death, and intrapartum acidemia.[34,35] Thick meconium associated with fetal tachycardia and the absence of heart rate accelerations can correctly identify half of the infants who will develop MAS.[36] Figure 1 shows the heart rate tracing of a fetus in labor with meconium at 42-weeks gestation, who later died as a result of MAS. The fetal heart rate shows tachycardia and absent accelerations.

Since the 1970s, the "combined approach" of oropharyngeal suctioning on the perineum followed by suctioning of the neonatal trachea after direct visualization of the vocal cords by the pediatrician has been in general use in an effort to decrease the incidence of MAS.[37] Oropharyngeal suctioning should be done with a flexible 8 or 10 Fr catheter and gentle wall suction with pressures of < -100 mmHg. Up to 74% of physicians using the older DeLee device, which used mouth suction provided by the delivering physician, experienced ingestion of neonatal secretions, and transmission of *Neisseria gonorrhea*, herpes simplex, varicella, and *Staphylococcus* from infant to physician has been documented.[38] Two studies have questioned the need for flexible catheter suctioning, as there was no difference in the incidence of meconium below the vocal cords in newborns who were bulb suctioned compared to those who were catheter suctioned.[39,40] In our institution, we recommend suctioning of the nares and mouth of all newborns by either bulb or flexible catheter after delivery of the head.

There has been considerable debate about which infants should receive intubation and tracheal suctioning as suggested by Carson et al.[37] In a prospective study, intubation was associated with an increased morbidity, including MAS, hoarseness, and stridor in 2% of infants versus none in the control group of infants with 1-minute Apgar scores > 8.[41] Intubation has also been associated with cardiac arrhythmias, even in experienced hands.[42] As a result, it has been proposed that only those infants who are depressed at birth receive direct tracheal suctioning.[43] Other investigators disagree with a policy of selective intubation and propose that all newborns delivered through meconium receive direct laryngoscopy and suctioning.[44] Despite the "combined approach," the expected decrease in MAS has not occurred. Thus, we can conclude that much of the clinically significant MAS may occur in utero prior to birth and is not detectable by antenatal or intrapartum testing and not preventable with the "combined approach."[45,46]

Recommendations on meconium suctioning issued jointly by the American Academy of Pediatrics and the American College of Obstetricians and Gynecologists (ACOG) state that the mouth and hypopharynx should be thoroughly suctioned after delivery of the head. If thick meconium is present and the infant is depressed, the trachea should be intubated and suctioned to remove meconium or other aspirated material.[47]

Amnioinfusion of normal saline has been proposed as a means of decreasing MAS. The theory behind this technique is that "thick" or "thin" meconium is simply a reflection of the amount of amniotic fluid in the uterine cavity. Diluting the meconium thus decreases the volume of particulate matter the fetus can potentially aspirate and cushions the umbilical cord, reducing the incidence of umbilical cord compression and variable decelerations. Amnioinfusion involves placing an intrauterine catheter into the amniotic cavity and infusing normal saline. It is possible only after the amniotic sac is ruptured during labor. Amnioinfusion studies have noted a decrease in the incidence of "thick" meconium,[48] improved umbilical cord arterial blood pH at delivery,[48] fewer infants with more than trace meconium below the vocal cords at delivery,[48-51] decreased need for positive pressure ventilation at birth,[48] improved 1-minute Apgar scores,[50] lowered Cesarean section rate for fetal distress,[49,50] and decreased incidence of MAS.[49] The most recent study suggests benefit in only those patients with meconium-stained amniotic fluid as well as variable decelerations.[52] These studies show a trend toward improvement of neonatal outcome, but they have not been large enough to warrant routine use of amnioinfusion in all patients with meconium-stained amniotic fluid. In addition, it will not impact the fetus who has already aspirated meconium prior to placing the infusion.

Oligohydramnios

An adequate amount of amniotic fluid is now considered to be one of the most important measures of fetal well being in the postdate pregnancy.[53,54] Conversely, decreased amniotic fluid volume has been associated with an increased incidence of adverse perinatal outcome.[55,56] In 5 of the 11 randomized, prospective, controlled studies of expectant management versus induction of postdate pregnancies (discussed later), amniotic fluid volume was routinely assessed and decreased fluid was an indication for delivery.

Amniotic fluid is produced by the fetus and is composed primarily of fluid from fetal urination, although fetal lung fluid, transport of fluid across fetal membranes, and skin transudate contribute to amniotic fluid production.[57,58] Amniotic fluid volume increases to a maximum at 34-36 weeks, and decreases

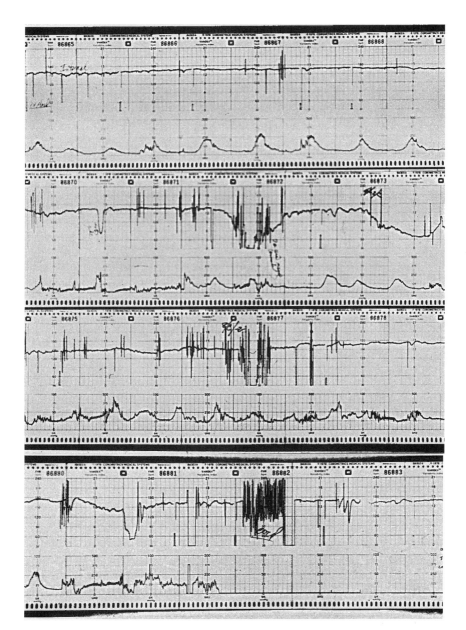

Figure 1. Fetal heart rate tracing of fetus with meconium aspiration syndrome.

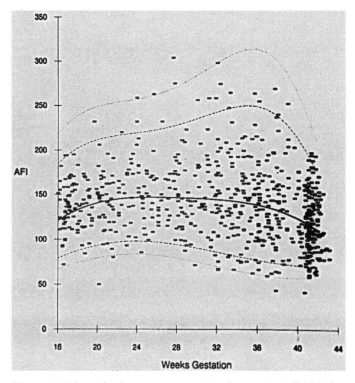

Figure 2. Normal values across gestation for amniotic fluid index.

thereafter (Figure 2).[59] In the postdate pregnancy, oligohydramnios is found in 11.5% of all patients.[60] The amniotic fluid index (AFI) decreases by 12%-33% per week beyond 41 weeks.[59-62] Trimmer et al.[63] measured fetal bladder volumes in normal and postdate pregnancies and found that the oligohydramnios in these pregnancies resulted from decreased fetal urine production. They specu-late that placental dysfunction and decreased amounts of amniotic fluid already present in the uterine cavity result in decreased fetal swallowing.

There are many ways to assess amniotic fluid volume. Some investigators routinely report "normal," "increased," or "decreased" amniotic fluid vol-ume. The earliest attempts to estimate amniotic fluid volume were made by assessment of total intrauterine volume measurements with "B-scanners."[64] Subsequent investigators, using real-time ultrasound, evaluated the largest pocket of amniotic fluid found in the uterine cavity. Initially, fetuses were considered at increased risk for abnormal outcome when < a 1.0-cm pocket of amniotic fluid was present.[65] This was subsequently found to be too restric-tive, and 2.0-cm pockets[66] and 3.0-cm pockets[67] have been suggested as the lower limits of normal. Fischer et al.[68] recently evaluated 190 women with well-dated postdate pregnancies undergoing twice weekly nonstress tests and amniotic fluid volumes and concluded that a largest vertical pocket of < 2.7 cm had a sensitivity of 50% and specificity of 88% for abnormal perinatal outcome, which was superior to an AFI of 5 and a single 2.0-cm largest vertical pocket measurement. Some authors have found that AFI assessment is better than single pocket techniques in predicting oligohydramnios, with an AFI < 5 used as the abnormal cut-off value.[61,69] Others have found that pocket width and height is a better predictor of oligohydramnios than AFI.[70]

Most recently, the AFI has been used to quantify amniotic fluid volume and to allow serial comparisons between different observers.[71] The AFI is useful for quantification of amniotic fluid volume in the postdates pregnancy, as it is simple, easy to perform, and reproducible.[56,72-74] It provides a semi-quantifiable method of following amniotic fluid volume changes over time.[73] Figure 2 shows the normal values for AFI across gestation in well-dated pregnancies, illustrating the cut-off values for oligohydramnios (< 5th percentile).[73]

While these percentiles show the lower limits of the normal AFI, they are higher than the values used in clinical practice and in most studies. There is no consensus about how to measure clinically relevant amounts of oligohydramnios. The most common methods used for determination of oligohydramnios include an AFI of < 5 or a single pocket < 2.0 cm by 2.0 cm. In our practice, fluid volumes less than these cut-offs are an indication for delivery in the postdate patient.

Labor Induction of Conservative Management?

The management of the postdate pregnancy has generated considerable debate about appropriate methods of antepartum testing, timing of induction, and maternal versus fetal risks. Studies that involve induction at 40 weeks gestation evaluate the policy of post-dates prevention, while those dealing with management schemes at 42 weeks report the effects of postdates pregnancy on the fetus after it has occurred.[75]

A recent meta-analysis of 11 randomized trials of expectant management versus induction of labor suggests that the induction group is slightly less likely than the expectant management group to have fetal distress, Cesarean section, and neonatal death.[76] These trials, however, involve a variety of management schemes, some of which are suboptimal or outdated. In addition, some of the studies included in the meta-analysis have not been published in their entirety. In this section, we will evaluate the existing prospective trials, pointing out their strengths and weaknesses. Since the incidence of adverse perinatal events in the postdate pregnancies is low, studies with very large numbers of patients are necessary to show a significant difference in these events. Most of the trials have not enrolled sufficient numbers of patients to demonstrate significant differences in outcomes.

The earliest report of a randomized trial of expectant management versus induction for postdates pregnancy involved identification of meconium-stained fluid and amniotic fluid volume by amnioscopy.[77] Patients were recruited at 42 weeks gestation and randomized to amnioscopy or surgical induction with amniotomy and oxytocin induction. Amnioscopy, which is no longer used for surveillance of amniotic fluid volume, was performed three times weekly until labor was induced for indications, or the patient spontaneously went into labor. Induction was performed in 21% of patients in the amnioscopy group. There were two perinatal deaths in the amnioscopy group, one associated with MAS after meconium was diagnosed and the patient refused labor induction, and one associated with abnormal glucose control. Operative delivery was higher in the amnioscopy group, although this did not reach statistical significance. The study concluded that surgical induction of labor was superior to amnioscopy in managing postdate patients.

Twenty-four hour urinary estriol-creatinine ratio determinations were proposed by Witter and Weitz[78] as a primary screening measure to evaluate patients at 42 completed weeks gestation. Patients with certain dating were randomized to expectant management or serial estriol determinations. The study found that the urinary estriol ratios correctly predicted fetal distress in labor, but they failed to identify small-for-gestational age or postmature infants. In addition, the Cesarean section rate in both groups was high (27% in the expectant management versus 29% in the induction group), with an excess of Cesarean deliveries in prolonged latent phase in the induction group. The study concluded that induction was preferable although it was slightly more expensive, as there was no decrease in the Cesarean delivery rate with expectant management, and estriol determinations failed to identify potentially compromised fetuses.

Bergsjo et al.[79] reported observations on 188 post-date patients at 42 weeks gestation randomized to induction versus hospitalization for fetal movement, atropine and estriol testing, and an unspecified form of ultrasound testing. There were significantly more operative deliveries in the expectant management group than in the induction group. Unfortunately, this study suffers from problems with enrollment. The distribution of the length of pregnancy was similar in the two groups, suggesting that a policy of expectant management was carried out for all patients. In addition, urinary estriol testing is no longer used for fetal surveillance.

There have been six prospective, randomized, controlled studies published in their entirety that have compared patients randomized to immediate induction versus expectant management with current methods of fetal surveillance. Patients in all these studies were managed with 2-3 times weekly fetal surveillance (nonstress tests and/or contraction stress tests, as well as amniotic fluid monitoring).[10,80-84] A seventh, very small study, included well-dated patients at 41 weeks gestation monitored on a weekly basis with sonographic evaluation of amniotic fluid volume and nonstress tests or contraction stress tests.[85] Overall, 5138 patients have been randomized in these studies, with 2617 in the immediate induction group and 2521 in the expectant management group. There was a slightly increased incidence of Cesarean delivery (24%) in the expectant management group, compared with 19% in the immediate induction group (OR = 0.74, CI = 0.65-0.85). Interestingly, some of the studies restricted their study populations to those women with unfavorable cervical examinations.

The earliest of these studies was reported by Katz et al.[82] In that study, 156 well-dated patients at 42 weeks gestation were evaluated with amnioscopy, nonstress test, and vaginal examination for pelvic score of 4 or less, and subsequently randomized. The control group underwent immediate induction. The expectant management group was followed with amnioscopy, oxytocin challenge testing, and pelvic score evaluation every 3 days. Induction was performed with amniotomy and oxytocin in both groups. Patients randomized to the expectant management group were induced when the pelvic score rose above 4, or if the testing became abnormal. Katz et al.[82] noted a significant decrease in the duration of labor (6.7 ± 4.1 hours vs 9.4 ± 5.9 hours), a decrease in the Cesarean delivery rate (9% vs 20.5%), no difference in the incidence of meconium-stained amniotic fluid (15.3% vs 14%), and no difference in the incidence of intrapartum fetal heart rate changes (6.4% vs 11.5%) with expectant management. The expectant management babies were significantly larger, with 29.4% of babies > 4000 g versus only 7.9% in the immediate induction group. This study did not report the incidence of shoulder dystocia or other complications of large babies. There was one neonatal death in the induction group attributed to "asphyxia" and one in the expectant management group from an unspecified congenital cardiac defect. The study concluded that expectant management was justified because of the low incidence of Cesarean delivery and the absence of serious neonatal morbidity in this group of patients.

Cardozo et al.[81] studied 402 uncomplicated prolonged pregnancies and randomized patients at 41.5 weeks gestation to expectant management or induction of labor at 42 weeks gestation. The conservative management group was evaluated with fetal sonographic scanning for head-to-abdominal circumference ratio, nonstress tests on alternate days, and daily kick counts, with induction for abnormal antepartum testing, intrauterine growth delay, or obstetrical or maternal complications. The induction group had labor initiated with a 3 mg prostaglandin E2 pessary followed 3 hours later by oxytocin and amniotomy. The study found no significant difference in the prevalence of fetal distress during labor, the incidence of Cesarean delivery, or neonatal complications between the two groups. A greater number of babies from the immediate induction group required intubation, but admission to the special baby nursery did not differ between groups. The authors concluded that routine induction of labor at 42 weeks gestation was unnecessary.

Dyson et al.[84] managed low risk patients with unfavorable cervical examinations and well-dated pregnancies of at least 287-days gestation by randomizing them into an expectant management (150 patients) or routine induction (152 patients) group. The expectant management group was followed with nonstress tests once per week until 42 weeks gestation and twice per week thereafter, and the induction group received prostaglandin ripening of the cervix. Amniotic fluid volume was routinely assessed at each visit. An amniotic fluid volume of < 1.0 cm was defined as oligohydramnios and required induction. The routine induction group had a statistically significant decrease in the incidence of MAS, fetal distress requiring immediate delivery, and postmaturity syndrome. The Cesarean section rate in the immediate induction group was also lower (14.5% vs 27.3%, P < 0.01). However, this difference was confined to nulliparous patients. The authors concluded that earlier delivery in the patient with an unfavorable cervix by prostaglandin ripening resulted in improved neonatal outcome and a lower Cesarean delivery rate. Unfortunately, an amniotic fluid volume of 1.0 cm has subsequently been found to be too small a volume to safely consider continuing the pregnancy. Using this very restrictive definition for oligohydramnios may have contributed to the increased Cesarean section rate, the incidence of meconium aspiration, fetal distress, and postmaturity syndrome seen in the expectant management group.

In 1987, Augensen et al.[83] randomized postdate gravidas with uncomplicated pregnancies to induction at 42 weeks gestation (214 patients) or to further testing for 1 week and induction at 43 weeks gestation (195 patients). Patients did not undergo Cesarean delivery for failed induction, but were managed expectantly for 1 more week and induction was again attempted. Induction of labor was performed with oxytocin and amniotomy after labor was initiated. There were four patients in the early induction group and one patient in the later induction group who required three induction attempts before delivery was accomplished. All patients managed expectantly had nonstress testing twice per week. Fluid volume was not assessed. There was no significant difference in the incidence of operative delivery or perinatal asphyxia, but there was a high incidence of failed induction in the induction group (23%), and a higher rate of spontaneous labor in the expectant management group when compared to the immediate induction group (68% vs 18%). The authors concluded that either management scheme was safe.

The largest study to date was published in 1992 by the Canadian Multicenter Post-term Pregnancy Trial Group.[10] It included 3407 women with uncomplicated pregnancies > 41 weeks gestation. They were randomized to either immediate induction of labor with intracervical prostaglandin E2, or to expectant management with subsequent nonstress tests 3 times per week, amniotic fluid volume measurements 2-3 times per week (normal > 3.0-cm pocket), and fetal kick counts. There were 1701 women in the induction group, of whom 360 (21.2%) underwent Cesarean delivery compared to 418 (24.5%) of the 1706 women assigned to the expectant management group (P = 0.03). Patients were slightly less likely to undergo Cesarean delivery (OR = 0.83, CI = 0.70-0.97) with induction of labor with prostaglandin pessaries. This resulted from a statistically lower incidence of fetal distress requiring delivery in the induction group. There were no significant differences in the incidence of perinatal morbidity and neonatal mortality between the two groups. The authors concluded that routine induction of labor should be performed.

The most recent prospective randomized trial compared expectant management to immediate induction of labor with either intracervical prostaglandin E2 gel or placebo.[80] Only patients with an unfavorable cervix (Bishop's score < 7) and uncomplicated, well-dated, non-macrosomic (< 4500 grams) pregnancies were enrolled. Patients randomized to the expectant management group were evaluated twice weekly with a nonstress test and sonographic estimation of amniotic fluid volume, and a weekly cervical examination. The immediate induction group included 265 patients, and the expectant management group included 175 patients. Of the induction patients, 91 received placebo gel and 174 received intracervical prostaglandin E2 gel. The incidence of Cesarean delivery did not differ between groups. The incidence of adverse fetal-neonatal complications, including meconium-stained amniotic fluid, neonatal meconium aspiration syndrome, late decelerations during labor, and low 5-minute Apgar scores was similar between all groups. Because the incidence of adverse perinatal outcome is uncommon, the authors commented that a study enrolling more than 5600 patients would be necessary to show a statistically significant difference between the groups if one were to exist. They concluded that either expectant management with fetal electronic surveillance and sonographic estimation of amniotic fluid volume or induction of labor is acceptable.

Based on the above studies, we feel that either induction of labor or expectant management with fetal surveillance in the postdate period are acceptable options. Although there may be a small overall decrease in the Cesarean delivery rate with induction of labor, not all studies have reached the same conclusion, suggesting that other factors not analyzed may account for this difference.

Induction of Labor

When the cervix is inducible in the postdate patient, there is usually little difficulty in achieving active labor in a patient undergoing induction. When the cervix is "unfavorable" and induction is necessary, there have historically been multiple methods, both mechanical and biochemical, which obstetricians have used to attempt to "ripen" the cervix, or make it more favorable for induction.

There are several scoring systems for determining if the cervix is "favorable" or "unfavorable" for induction. The most frequently used scoring system was proposed by Bishop,[86] which was developed to determine the likelihood of successful induction. It evaluates five characteristics of the cervix: dilatation; effacement; station of the presenting part of the fetus; consistency; and position of the cervix within the pelvis, and it assigns a score of 0-3 to each component, with a total possible score of 13. In his original paper, Bishop found that multiparous patients with a score of 9 or greater had no failed inductions and had labors of 4 hours or less when induced with oxytocin and amniotomy. There is no generally accepted score that defines an "unfavorable" cervix, although scores of < 5 or 6 were arbitrarily defined as unfavorable in the prospective randomized controlled studies discussed above.[80,84,85]

Historically, there have been a number of methods used to ripen an unfavorable cervix, including amniotomy, oxytocin, breast stimulation, hydrostatic dilation, relaxin, and oral, vaginal, endocervical, and extra-amniotic prostaglandins. Currently the only FDA approved agent available for labor induction is the intracervical prostaglandin PGE_2 (Prepidil, The Upjohn Company, Kalamazoo, Michigan, USA). Prostaglandin preparations have been shown to improve Bishop scores by three points after a single dose,[87] and have been shown to decrease the induction to delivery time.[88] Others have shown an increase in spontaneous labor in patients receiving intracervical PGE_2.[80,89] Unfortunately, these preparations are not without some risk, as patients have developed hyperstimulation after instillation, and some have required Cesarean delivery during the cervical ripening period.[87,90,91] In addition, some patients do not go into labor after instillation of cervical ripening agents, oxytocin, or amniotomy and require Cesarean delivery.

At present, there does not appear to be a statistically significant reduction in the incidence of Cesarean delivery directly attributable to prostaglandins. The primary benefit of prostaglandin preparation of the cervix appears to be in the reduction of induction to delivery time.

Long-Term Outcome of Pregnancies Progressing to 42 Weeks Gestation

Several studies have evaluated the long-term outcome of postdate pregnancies. In general, they have concluded that there are good long-term outcomes for these children. The most frequent outcomes evaluated have been illnesses requiring hospitalization, growth, and intellectual function. Most studies have concluded that there are few or no differences between those children born in the post- dates period when compared to those born at term.

Zwerdling[92] first evaluated long-term mortality and morbidity of newborns delivered after 43 weeks gestation within the Kaiser Foundation Health Plan from 1959-1964. He found that these children experienced a slightly increased incidence of illness and hospitalization during the first 3 years of life when compared to term infants. He did not find any differences in the rates of growth in these children. When the Kaiser data were combined with data from the New York City birth and death records for the same period, he found that post-term children had twice the incidence of fetal or neonatal death compared to term infants. The death rate for post-term infants was slightly higher up to the age of 2 compared to term infants. In the small number of children who had reached age 5, there was no difference in the height, weight, or intelligence of these children when compared to children delivered at term. Similar observations were made by Wagner and Arndt,[93] who evaluated children in the School for Cerebral Palsied Children of Southern California, and Drillien,[94] who evaluated children with low IQ test scores during the same period. Unfortunately, all of these studies suffer from a retrospective design, imprecise gestational age dating, and a lack of appropriate control groups.

Several authors have evaluated dysmature infants, presumably the infants most adversely affected by prolonged intrauterine life.[95-99] In 1962, Engleston et al.[96] suggested that infants who experienced more signs of dysmaturity had a higher incidence of slower weight gain, repeated infections, and delayed speech. Overall, however, dysmaturity was not felt to be a serious disadvantage for these children. Lovell[97] evaluated dysmature infants over the first year of life and found lower social quotients and a greater frequency of sleep disorders and hospital admissions compared to control infants. The long-term consequences of these findings are unclear.

Field et al.[95] evaluated 40 post-term, dysmature infants and compared them to 40 normal control infants during the first year of life. Although the two groups did not differ in the incidence of postnatal complications, there were significant differences between the two groups at 4 and 8 months. At 4 months, the infants in the postdate group were more "difficult" and scored lower on the Denver developmental screening test, while at 8 months, they had a higher incidence of hospitalizations, feeding and sleep disturbances, and lower Bayley mental and motor scores. They extended their study to 57 dysmature infants and found minor evidence of delayed social skills and mental abilities when these children were studied through age 5. Whether these findings were significant for long-term outcomes is unknown. As these babies exhibited signs of dysmaturity, they do not represent the typical post-term newborn. In addition, the examiner may not have been blinded to the group assignment.

In what is probably the best prospective study of dysmature infants, Ting et al.[99] followed 210 African-American dysmature infants from birth through age 7 as part of the National Collaborative Perinatal Project. The authors found no differences in IQ, neurologic examination, and growth between normal controls and dysmature infants. In addition, they found no prenatal or environmental differences that could identify mothers of dysmature or non-dysmature infants.

The first prospective longitudinal study to involve all postdates (294 days) patients, studied 184 control and 129 patients with certain dating. The patients were followed through the labor and delivery process[3] and the infants subsequently were followed through age 2.[100] Each patient was followed with weekly monitoring, primarily with a biophysical profile (which includes a nonstress test), although some patients underwent only nonstress testing. There were no fetal deaths. The combination of a suboptimal nonstress test, oligohydramnios, and a low biophysical score was predictive of dysmaturity. In general, the incidence of advanced dysmaturity rose significantly after 44 weeks, and those fetuses were at a greater risk for fetal distress, low Apgar scores, and need for emergency Cesarean delivery. Follow-up testing in 89 of the postdate infants and 130 control infants was performed at 1 year of age and in 76 postdate and 111 control infants at 2 years of age. The authors found no difference between the intelligence quotient, physical milestones, and general health of the postdate infants, whether dysmature or not, compared to term control infants.

Based on the above studies, we feel comfortable advising pregnant women that prolonged pregnancy should have little effect, if any, on the long-term physical and intellectual development of their children.

Suggested Management Protocols

We currently favor beginning our postdate protocol with accurate gestational age determination based on dating criteria and early sonographic examinations, if necessary. This will eliminate over half of the patients who become potentially "postdate." Patients with significant medical or obstetric complications during pregnancy should be evaluated on an individual basis for delivery at term and induced for maternal or fetal indications. Usually these patients are already undergoing intensive surveillance of their pregnancies with nonstress testing or modified biophysical profiles during the last trimester of pregnancy. Other relevant data to be considered prior to and during induction are listed in Table 2.

Table 2

Considerations in Informed Judgment

Prior to Induction:
Clinical or ultrasound estimation of fetal weight
Clinical pelvimetry
Inducibility of cervix (Bishop score)
Previous obstetrical history
Previous Cesarean delivery
Reassuring fetal heart rate tracing
Maternal medical problems
Gestational diabetes

Intrapartum:
Fetal heart rate tracing
Progress of labor
Meconium-stained amniotic fluid
Need for midpelvic delivery
Estimated fetal weight
Availability of experienced personnel for newborn resuscitation

In our center, well-dated patients with postdate pregnancies are evaluated twice weekly with biophysical assessment, with either nonstress testing or biophysical profiles and once weekly with amniotic fluid assessment, as shown in the flow diagram in Figure 3 and the summary in Table 3. Patients have cervical assessment on a weekly basis. If the cervix is favorable and the dates are certain, induction is allowed at 41 weeks gestation. If induction is not performed, a nonstress test is performed at approximately 41 weeks gestation. The patient is scheduled for a biophysical profile at 41 weeks gestation. An estimated fetal weight is also scheduled at 41 weeks if one was not done for some other reason within the past 3 weeks. The cervical examination is repeated weekly, and the nonstress test and biophysical profiles are repeated alternately every 3-4 days until 42 weeks gestation when the patient is scheduled for induction. Cesarean delivery is considered in the presence of fetal macrosomia (estimated fetal weight > 4500 grams), especially if there is a low head circumference-to-abdominal circumference ratio, an unengaged vertex, and the patient has not previously delivered a baby vaginally. Patients are also delivered for non-reassuring fetal heart rate tracings confirmed by abnormal biophysical testing, or oligohydramnios. Oligohydramnios is diagnosed if the AFI is < 5 or the largest pocket of fluid measures < 2.0 by 2.0 cm.

Management of the patient who has uncertain dates is less straight forward. We favor erring on the side of beginning fetal surveillance earlier rather than later, and we begin nonstress testing and amniotic fluid evaluations

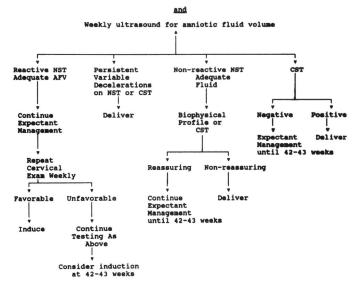

Figure 3. Management of prolonged pregnancy: protocol for care.

Table 3
Management of Prolonged Pregnancy

At 41 weeks, if the cervix if favorable and dates certain, you may induce labor.

If induction is not performed, you may begin antepartum fetal surveillance at 41 weeks gestation. This consists of nonstress tests (NST) and/or biophysical profiles twice weekly or contraction stress tests (CST) weekly and a sonogram for assessment of amniotic fluid weekly.

Pregnancy may be allowed to continue only if amniotic fluid volume is deemed adequate (largest pocket greater than 2 × 2 cm or amniotic fluid index greater than 5 cm) and the remaining testing is reassuring.

Persistent, significant variable decelerations on a reactive NST or negative CST are an indication for delivery.

Induction of labor at 42 weeks may be considered regardless of testing results or cervical condition.

Do not allow pregnancy to continue beyond 43 weeks if dating is absolutely certain.

around term, recognizing that some fetuses may already be postdate when surveillance begins.

Medico-Legal Issues

Scarcely a physician exists who is not concerned about malpractice cases. Obstetricians, in particular have a high rate of malpractice cases. As of 1992, 79.4% of obstetrician-gynecologists had at least one case filed against them, with 20.5% having one claim, 19.9% with two claims, 13.8% with three claims, and 24.8% with four or more claims. On average each obstetrician-gynecologist has had 2.5 claims filed against him/her.[101] The proliferation of malpractice cases has led to many physicians practicing defensive medicine by ordering more testing than is necessary. This adds unnecessary costs to health care.

It has been shown that obstetricians who have been sued frequently are perceived to have more difficulty in communicating with their patients in an unhurried, interested manner.[102] Malpractice attorneys report that more than 80% of malpractice suits arise from problems in communicating with the patient.[103] Thus, the first step in preventing malpractice cases is to establish a good rapport with patients and to involve them in their own care. The risks and benefits associated with each proposed treatment should be discussed, and the patient should be encouraged to participate in the decision-making process. All of the patient's questions should be answered. When dealing with a pregnancy approaching term, the patient should be advised well in advance of plans for her pregnancy if she goes beyond her EDC. Many patients have concerns and fears based on previous experience and anecdotes from friends that may or may not be accurate. Unfortunately, there is only one published study that addresses women's attitudes toward postdate pregnancy. The authors found that satisfaction with postdate care was dependent, in large part, on the final route of delivery, with vaginally delivering women more satisfied than those who underwent Cesarean delivery.[81]

Postdate pregnancy presents several areas of risk for the physician. The ACOG began a survey of its Fellows in 1983, seeking information about the areas of obstetrics that were especially risky for physicians. Unfortunately, the design of the 1983 survey is not very useful as it included all claims prior to 1983; the results of the 1990 and 1992 surveys are informative. In the years 1988-1989 and 1990-1991, ACOG reported that 7.8% and 8.0% of claims respectively were for problems with pregnancies that went beyond term.[104]

To recover in a malpractice case, the plaintiff must prove that the physician had a duty to the patient, failed to provide care consistent with reasonable standard of care in the community, that breach of this duty caused damages, and that those damages warrant compensation. It is important to document all plans and conversations adequately in the chart, and to instruct office staff in procedures for handling phone calls and results of abnormal testing. In the event of a malpractice case, accurate chart documentation is invaluable for defense.

Summary

Pregnancies that pass their due date are recognized by both patients and physicians alike to pose potential problems for the mother and fetus. Most authorities consider these pregnancies to be "at risk." Our goal as obstetricians is to identify those pregnancies that pose unacceptable risks for the mother and/or fetus and to deliver the baby at an optimal time for both. Unfortunately, as we have discussed, there are several problems involved in assessing those fetuses at risk for adverse outcome, and we are not always able to deliver the baby in a timely fashion in a way that is cost effective and does not expose the mother to the risk of Cesarean delivery. Macrosomic fetuses at increased risk for traumatic delivery have been difficult to identify. Oftentimes, meconium-stained amniotic fluid cannot be detected prior to ruptured membranes. Moreover, fetuses at risk for MAS prior to or during labor cannot be identified, and fetuses who will develop oligohydramnios while waiting for labor to begin may not always be predicted.

Induction of labor for all patients at 41 to 42 weeks gestation has been suggested to decrease the potential for complications in some newborns. There remains considerable debate about the usefulness of this strategy. There may possibly be a small decrease in the Cesarean delivery rate with elective induction of labor; however, there is no improvement in neonatal outcome, which has been demonstrated with routine induction. Expectant management with careful fetal surveillance in the patient with an unfavorable cervix may not be unreasonable.

We strongly urge accurate gestational age assessment, as it may decrease the incidence of "postdate" pregnancies by half. It is clear that when a pregnancy is postdate, some form of fetal monitoring (generally with twice weekly nonstress tests or biophysical profiles, or weekly contraction stress tests) should be performed. Fetal size should be reassessed, either clinically or by ultrasound. Amniotic fluid assessment should be performed at least weekly. Fetuses with non-reassuring testing or oligohydramnios should undergo induction. Induction may be performed at 42 weeks gestation even with an unfavorable cervix.

Current methods of fetal surveillance have acceptable levels of fetal and maternal risk. Unfortunately, they may not prevent the occasional fetus from experiencing adverse outcome secondary to postdates pregnancy. We will probably never be able to prevent all suboptimal outcomes related to postdate pregnancies but we can try to identify some fetuses who will possibly benefit from timely delivery.

Commentary by Mr. Peters: This chapter, "Postdates Pregnancy: Diagnosis and Management" by Drs. Ranzini and Knuppel, should be read in conjunction with Dr. Schumacher's Chapter 28. Drs. Ranzini and Knuppel offer the reader a great array of research data. Dr. Schumacher's approach to neonatal diagnosis, management, and complications is more focused and helpful from a risk management point of view.

The emphasis and importance of patient education and participation in the decision-making process is effectively presented by Drs. Ranzini and Knuppel. These authors stress that failures of communication and malpractice litigation are correlated in a direct fashion. Practitioners will be wise to heed their advice.

Drs. Ranzini and Knuppel appropriately advise the readers of the importance of making clear record notations of the information given to the patient as well as the patient's decisions made in response to this information. If it is not written or noted in the record, it is not likely to be believed later that it actually occurred.

References

1. Ballantyne JW. The problem of postmature infant. J Obstet Gynaecol Br Emp 1902;2:36.
2. Clifford SH. Postmaturity with placental dysfunction. J Pediatr 1954;44:1.
3. Shime J, Gare DJ, Andrews J, et al. Prolonged pregnancy: Surveillance of the fetus and neonate and the course of labor and delivery. Am J Obstet Gynecol 1984;148:547.
4. Vorherr H. Placental insufficiency in relation to postterm pregnancy and fetal postmaturity. Evaluation of fetoplacental function; management of the postterm gravida. Am J Obstet Gynecol 1975;123:67.
5. McClure-Browne JC. Postmaturity. Am J Obstet Gynecol 1963;85:573.
6. Beisher NA, Evans JH, Townsend L. Studies in prolonged pregnancy. I. The incidence of prolonged pregnancy. Am J Obstet Gynecol 1969;103:476.
7. Lagrew DC, Freeman RK. Management of postdate pregnancy. Am J Obstet Gynecol 1986;154:8.
8. Saito M, Yazawa K, Hashiguchi A, et al. Time of ovulation and prolonged pregnancy. Am J Obstet Gynecol 1972;112:31.
9. Dombrowski MP, Wolfe HM, Brans YW, et al. Neonatal morphometry. Relation to obstetric, pediatric and menstrual estimates of gestational age. Am J Dis Child 1992;146:852.
10. Hannah ME, Hannah WJ, Hellman J, et al. Induction of labor as compared with serial antenatal monitoring in post-term pregnancy: A randomized controlled trial. N Engl J Med 1992;326:1587.

11. American College of Obstetricians and Gynecologists. Diagnosis and management of post-term pregnancy. ACOG Technical Bulletin 130, Washington, DC, 1987.
12. Campbell S, Warsof SL, Little D, et al. Routine ultrasound screening for the prediction of gestational age. Obstet Gynecol 1985;65:613.
13. Robinson HP, Flemming JEE. A critical evaluation of sonar "crown-rump length" measurements. Br J Obstet Gynaecol 1975;82:702.
14. Kopta MM, May RR, Crane JP. A comparison of the reliability of the estimated date of confinement predicted by crown-rump length and biparietal diameter. Am J Obstet Gynecol 1983;145:562.
15. Kurtz AB, Wapner RJ, Kurtz RJ, et al. Analysis of biparietal diameter as a accurate indicator of gestational age. J Clin Ultrasound 1980;8:319.
16. Jeanty P, Rodesch F, Delbeke D, et al. Estimation of gestational age from measurements of fetal long bones. J Ultrasound Med 1984;4:75.
17. Hadlock FP, Harrist RB, Shah YP, et al. Estimating fetal age using multiple parameters: A prospective evaluation in a racially mixed population. Am J Obstet Gynecol 1987;156:955.
18. Boyd ME, Usher RH, McLean FH: Fetal macrosomia: Prediction, risks, proposed management. Obstet Gynecol 1983;61:715.
19. Freeman RK. Postdates pregnancy. Am J Obstet Gynecol 1981;140:128.
20. Eden RD, Seifert LS, Winegar A, et al. Perinatal characteristics of uncomplicated postdates pregnancies. Obstet Gynecol 1987;69:296.
21. Yeh S, Bruce SL, Thorton YS. Intrapartum monitoring and management of the postdate fetus. Clin Perinatol 1982;9:381.
22. Hadlock FP, Harrist RB, Fearneyhough TC, et al. Use of femur length/abdominal circumference ratio in detecting the macrosomic fetus. Radiology 1988;54:503.
23. Hadlock FP. Ultrasound evaluation of fetal growth. In: Callen PW (ed). *Ultrasonography in Obstetrics and Gynecology*, Third Edition. Philadelphia, WB Saunders Company, 1994, p. 129.
24. Pollack RN, Hauer-Pollack G, Divon MY. Macrosomia in postdates pregnancies: The accuracy of routine ultrasonographic screening. Am J Obstet Gynecol 1992;167:7.
25. Sack RA. The large infant: A study of maternal, obstetric, fetal and newborn characteristics including a long-term pediatric follow-up. Am J Obstet Gynecol 1969;104:195.
26. Elliott JP, Garite TJ, Freeman RK, et al. Ultrasonic prediction of fetal macrosomia in diabetic patients. Obstet Gynecol 1982;60:159.
27. Ogata ES, Sabbagha R, Metzger BE, et al. Serial ultrasonography to assess evolving fetal macrosomia: Studies in 23 pregnant diabetic women. JAMA 1980;243:2405.
28. Mintz MC, Landon MB, Gabbe SG, et al. Shoulder soft tissue width as a predictor of macrosomia in diabetic pregnancies. Am J Perinatol 1989;6:240.
29. Modanlou HD, Komatsu G, Dorchester W, et al. Large for gestational age neonates: Anthropometric reasons for shoulder dystocia. Obstet Gynecol 1982;60:417.
30. Eden RD, Seifert LS, Winegar A, et al. Perinatal characteristics of uncomplicated postdate pregnancies. Obstet Gynecol 1987;69:296.
31. Usher RJ, Boyd ME, McLean FH, et al. Assessment of fetal risk in postdate pregnancies. Am J Obstet Gynecol 1988;158:259.

32. Druzin ML, Adams DM. Significance of observing no fluid at amniotomy. Am J Obstet Gynecol 1990;162:1006.
33. Wiswell TE, Tuggle JM, Turner BS. Meconium aspiration syndrome; have we made a difference? Pediatrics 1990;85:715.
34. Starks GC. Correlation of meconium-stained amniotic fluid, early intrapartum fetal pH and Apgar scores as preditors of perinatal outcome. Obstet Gynecol 1980;56:604.
35. Meis PJ, Hall M, Marshall JR, et al. Meconium passage: A new classification for risk during labor. Am J Obstet Gynecol 1978;131:509.
36. Rossi EM, Philipson EH, Williams TG, et al. Meconium aspiration syndrome: Intrapartum and neonatal attributes. Am J Obstet Gynecol 1989;161:1106.
37. Carson BS, Losey RW, Bowes WA Jr, et al. Combined obstetric and pediatric approach to prevent meconium aspiration syndrome. Am J Obstet Gynecol 1976;126:712.
38. Ballard JL, Musial MJ, Myers MG. Hazards of delivery room resuscitation using oral methods of endotracheal suctioning. Pediatr Infect Dis 1986;5:198.
39. Locus P, Yeomans E, Crosby U. Efficacy of bulb vs. DeLee suction at deliveries complicated by meconium stained amniotic fluid. Am J Perinatol 1990;7:87.
40. Cohen-Addad N, Chatterjee M, Bautista A, et al. Intrapartum suctioning of meconium: Comparative efficacy of bulb syringe and DeLee catheter. J Perinatol 1987;7:111.
41. Linder N, Aranda JV, Tsur M, et al. Need for endotracheal intubation and suction in meconium-stained neonates. J Pediatr 1988;112:613.
42. Cordero L, Hon EH. Neonatal bradycardia following nasopharyngeal stimulation. J Pediatr 1971;78:441.
43. Cunningham AS. Tracheal suction and meconium, a proposed standard of care. J Pediatr 1990;116:153.
44. Wiswell TE, Henley ME. Management of the meconium-stained neonate. J Pediatr 1990;117:341.
45. Sunoo C, Kosasa TS, Hale RS. Meconium aspiration syndrome without evidence of fetal distress in early labor before elective cesarian delivery. Obstet Gynecol 1989;73:707.
46. Falciglia HS, Henderschott C, Potter P, et al. Does DeLee suction at the perineum prevent meconium aspiration syndrome? Am J Obstet Gynecol 1992;167:1243.
47. Frigoletto FD, Little GA (eds). *Guidelines for Perinatal Care*, Second Edition. Elk Grove Village, Illinois, American Academy of Pediatrics, and Washington, DC, American College of Obstetricians and Gynecologists, 1988.
48. Sadovsky Y, Amon EA, Bade ME, et al. Prophylactic amnioinfusion during labor complicated by meconium: A preliminary report. Am J Obstet Gynecol 1989;161:613.
49. Macri CJ, Schrimmer DB, Leung A, et al. Prophylactic amnioinfusion improves outcome of pregnancy complicated by thick meconium and oligohydramnios. Am J Obstet Gynecol 1992;73:647.
50. Wenstrom KD, Parsons MT. The prevention of meconium aspiration in labor using meconium amnioinfusion. Obstet Gynecol 1989;73:647.
51. Eriksen NL, Hostetter M, Parisi VM. Prophylactic amnioinfusion in pregnancies complicated by thick meconium. Am J Obstet Gynecol 1994;171:1026.
52. Spong CY, Ogundipe OA, Ross MG. Prophylactic amnioinfusion for meconium-stained amniotic fluid. Am J Obstet Gynecol 1994;171:931.

53. Johnson JM, Harman CR, Lange IR, et al. Biophysical profile scoring the management of the post-term pregnancy: An analysis of 307 patients. Am J Obstet Gynecol 1986;154:269.

54. Clement D, Schifrin BS, Kates RB. Acute oligohydramnios in postdate pregnancy. Am J Obstet Gynecol 1986;154:884.

55. Phelan JP, Platt LD, Yeh SY, et al. The role of ultrasound assessment of amniotic fluid volumes in the management of the postdate pregnancy. Am J Obstet Gynecol 1985;151:304.

56. Rutherford SE, Phelan JP, Smith CV, et al. The four quadrant assessment of amniotic fluid volume: An adjunct to antepartum fetal heart rate testing. Obstet Gynecol 1987;70:353.

57. Seeds AE. Current concepts of amniotic fluid dynamics. Am J Obstet Gynecol 1980;138:575.

58. Brace RA. Amniotic fluid dynamics. In: Creasy RK, Resnick R (eds). *Maternal-Fetal Medicine*, Second Edition. Philadelphia, WB Saunders Company, 1989, p. 130.

59. Queenan JT, Thompson W, Whitefield CR, et al. Amniotic fluid volumes in normal pregnancy. Am J Obstet Gynecol 1972;114:34.

60. Marks AD, Divon MY. Longitudinal study of the amniotic fluid index in postdates pregnancy. Obstet Gynecol 1992;79:229.

61. Moore TR: Superiority of the four-quadrant sum over the single-deepest-pocket technique in ultrasonographic identification of abnormal amniotic fluid volumes. Am J Obstet Gynecol 1990;163:762.

62. Beisher NA, Brown JB, Townsend L. Studies in prolonged pregnancy III: Amniocentesis in prolonged pregnancy. Am J Obstet Gynecol 1969;193:496.

63. Trimmer KJ, Leveno KJ, Peters MT, et al. Observations on the cause of oligohydramnios in prolonged pregnancy. Am J Obstet Gynecol 1990;163:1900.

64. Gohari P, Berkowitz RL, Hobbins JC, et al. Prediction of intrauterine growth restriction by total intrauterine volume. Am J Obstet Gynecol 1977;127:255.

65. Manning FA, Hill LM, Platt LD. Quantitative amniotic fluid volume determination by ultrasound: Antepartum detection of intrauterine growth retardation. Am J Obstet Gynecol 1981;139:254.

66. Chamberlain PF, Manning FA, Morrison I, et al. Ultrasound evaluation of amniotic fluid volume. I. The relationship of marginal and decreased amniotic fluid volumes to perinatal outcome. Am J Obstet Gynecol 1984;150:245.

67. Crowley P, O'Herlihy C, Boylan P. The value of ultrasound measurement of amniotic fluid volume on the management of prolonged pregnancies. Br J Obstet Gynaecol 1984;91:444.

68. Fisher RL, McDonnell M, Bianculli KW, et al. Amniotic fluid volume estimation in the postdate pregnancy: A comparison of techniques. Obstet Gynecol 1993;81:698.

69. Hoskins IA, McGovern PG, Ordorica SA, et al. Amniotic fluid index: Correlation with amniotic fluid volume. Am J Perinatol 1992;9:315.

70. Magann EF, Nolan TE, Hess W, et al. Measurement of amniotic fluid volume: Accuracy of ultrasonography techniques. Am J Obstet Gynecol 1992;167:1533.

71. Phelan JP, Smith CV, Broussard P, et al. Amniotic fluid volume assessment using the four quadrant technique in the pregnancy between 36 and 42 weeks. J Reprod Med 1987;32:540.

72. Rutherford SE, Phelan JP, Smith CV, et al. The four quadrant assessment of amniotic fluid volume: Interobserver and intraobserver variation. J Reprod Med 1987;32:597.
73. Moore TR, Cayle FE. The amniotic fluid index in normal human pregnancy. Am J Obstet Gynecol 1990;162:1168.
74. Peedicayil A, Mathai M, Regi A, et al. Inter- and intra-observer variation in the amniotic fluid index. Obstet Gynecol 1994;84:848.
75. Enkin M, Keirse MJNC, Chalmers I a (eds). *A Guide to Effective Care in Pregnancy and Childbirth.* New York, Oxford University Press, 1989, p. 154.
76. Hannah ME. Post-term pregnancy: Should all women have labor induced? A review of the literature. Fetal Matern Med Rev 1993;5:3.
77. Henry GR. A controlled trial of surgical induction of labour and amnioscopy in the management of prolonged pregnancy. J Obstet Gynaec Br Commonw 1969;76:795.
78. Witter FR, Weitz CM. A randomized trial of induction at 42 weeks gestation versus expectant management for postdates pregnancies. Am J Perinatol 1987;4:206.
79. Bergsjo P, Huang GD, Yu SQ, et al. Comparison of induced versus non-induced labor in post-term pregnancy. Acta Obstet Gynecol Scand 1989;68:683.
80. The National Institute of Child Health and Human Development Network of Maternal-Fetal Medicine Units. A clinical trial of induction of labor versus expectant management in post-term pregnancy. Am J Obstet Gynecol 1994;170:716.
81. Cardozo L, Fysh J, Pearce JM. Prolonged pregnancy: The management debate. Br Med J 1986;293:1059.
82. Katz Z, Yemini M, Lancet M, et al. Non-aggressive management of post-date pregnancies. Eur J Obstet Gynecol Reprod Biol 1983;15:71.
83. Augensen K, Bergsio P, Eideland T, et al. Randomised comparison of early versus late induction of labor in post-term pregnancy. Br Med J 1987;294:1192.
84. Dyson DC, Miller PD, Armstrong MA. Management of prolonged pregnancy: Induction of labor versus antepartum fetal testing. Am J Obstet Gynecol 1987;156:928.
85. Martin JN, Sessums JK, Howard P, et al. Alternative approaches to the management of gravidas with prolonged-post-term-postdate pregnancies. J Miss State Med Assoc 1989;30:105.
86. Bishop EH. Pelvic scoring for elective induction. Obstet Gynecol 1964;24:266.
87. Trofatter KF Jr. Effect of preinduction cervical softening with dinoprostone gel on outcome of oxytocin-induced labor. Clin Ther 1993;15:838.
88. Hutchon DJR, Geirsson R, Patal NB. A double blind controlled trial of PGE$_2$ gel in cervical ripening. Int J Gynaecol Obstet 1980;17:604.
89. Nimrod C, Currie J, Yee J, et al. Cervical ripening and labor induction with intracervical triacetin base prostaglandin E$_2$ gel: A placebo-controlled study. Obstet Gynecol 1984;64:476.
90. Laube DW, Zlatnik FJ, Pitkin RM. Preinduction cervical ripening with prostaglandin E$_2$ intracervical gel. Obstet Gynecol 1986;68:54.
91. Graves GR, Baskett TF, Gray JH, et al. The effect of vaginal administration of various doses of PGE$_2$ gel on cervical ripening and induction of labor. Am J Obstet Gynecol 1985;151:178.
92. Zwerdling MA. Factors pertaining to prolonged pregnancy and its outcome. Pediatr 1967;40:202.

93. Wagner MG, Arndt R. Postmaturity as an aetiological factor in 124 cases of neurologically handicapped children. In: Keith RM, Bax M (eds). *Clinics in Developmental Medicine, No. 27. Studies in Infancy.* London, William Heinemann Medical Books, 1968, p. 89.
94. Drillien CM. Studies in mental handicap. II. Some obstetric factors of possible aetiological significance. Arch Dis Child 1968;42:283.
95. Field TF, Dabiri C, Hallock N, et al. Developmental effects of prolonged pregnancy and the postmaturity syndrome. J Pediatr 1977;90:836.
96. Engleson G, Rooth G, Tornblom M. Follow-up study of dysmature infants. Arch Dis Child 1963;38:62.
97. Lovell KE. The effect of postmaturity on the developing child. Med J Aust 1973;1:13.
98. Callenbach JC, Hall RT. Morbidity and mortality of advanced gestational age: Post-term or postmature. Obstet Gynecol 1979;53:721.
99. Ting RY, Wang MH, Scott TFM. The dysmature infant: Associated factors and outcome at 7 years. J Pediatr 1977;90:943.
100. Shime J, Librach CL, Gare DJ, et al. The influence of prolonged pregnancy on infant development at one and two years of age: A prospective controlled study. Am J Obstet Gynecol 1986;154:341.
101. Opinion Research Corporation, Professional liability and its effects: Report of a 1992 survey of ACOG's Membership, prepared for The American College of Obstetricians and Gynecologists. Washington DC, October 1992.
102. Hickson GB, Clayton EW, Entman SS, et al. Obstetricians' prior malpractice experience and patients satisfaction with care. JAMA 1994;272:1583.
103. Avery JK. Lawyers tell what turns some patients litigious. Med Malpract Rev 1985;2:35.
104. Personal communication, American College of Obstetricians and Gynecologists.

Chapter 10

Prevention of Neonatal Group B Streptococcal Infection

◆◆◆

Mitchell P. Dombrowski, M.D.,
Michael F. McNamara, D.O.

Introduction

Streptococcus agalactiae (GBS) is a gram positive coccobacillus that commonly colonizes the female genitourinary tract. GBS is a facultative bacillus that shows complete hemolysis on blood agar plates. It is Lancefield classification B with serotypes Ia, Ib, Ic, II, and III. GBS is a leading cause of neonatal sepsis and meningitis, with 12,000-15,000 cases reported annually.[1]

Neonatal GBS early onset disease, which includes all GBS serotypes, occurs before 7 days of birth with most cases caused by vertical transmission at delivery. Early onset disease has a frequency of 1.3-3.7 cases per 1000 and accounts for two-thirds of neonatal infections.[2] Fifty percent of newborns are symptomatic at birth, and most manifest infection within 48 hours.[3] The onset of disease is often rapid; neonatal death may occur within hours of onset of symptoms. The overall mortality rate for early onset GBS disease is 26%, with rates of 3% among infants weighing > 2500 g, 50% among those weighing < 2500 g, and 90% among those weighing ≤ 1000 g.[4] The most frequent complications of early onset disease include septicemia, pneumonia, and meningitis, with common clinical symptoms of hypotension, apnea, tachypnea, lethargy, poor feeding, fever, and hypothermia.[4-6]

Late onset disease, which manifests 7 or more days after delivery, occurs in 0.7-1.0 cases per 1000 births.[2] Late onset disease accounts for approximately one-third of cases and presents as meningitis in 85% of cases. The mortality is

From: Donn SM, Fisher CW (eds.): *Risk Management Techniques in Perinatal and Neonatal Practice.* © Futura Publishing Co., Inc., Armonk, NY, 1996.

20%; however, 20%-50% of survivors have permanent neurologic sequelae.[4,5] Late onset disease is primarily caused by Group B, type III serotype.

Epidemiology and Risk Factors

While the frequency of colonization of the female genital tract is not affected by pregnancy, it is affected by other factors. In a 1991 study by Regan et al.,[7] the rates of GBS colonization was for African-Americans 21.2%, Hispanics 20.8%, and whites 13.7%. GBS colonization was increased with age, sexual activity and number of partners, and diabetes, but was decreased with ethanol and tobacco use, and higher levels of education. Colonization rates also differed geographically, with prevalence rates of 26.4% in New York, 20.8% in Louisiana, 17.5% in Washington, 13.6% in Oklahoma, and 9.2% in Texas.

GBS carriage does not change throughout pregnancy, and colonization may be chronic, transient, or intermittent.[8] Cultures performed at or beyond 26 weeks gestation appear to be reflective of carrier status at delivery; only 4%-7% of women who are apparently culture negative in the late second trimester are subsequently GBS positive at delivery.[8,9] It has been recommended that routine antenatal GBS cultures be obtained at 26 to 28 weeks gestation.[10,11]

Neonatal colonization of GBS occurs in 40%-73% of culture positive women, but only 1%-2% of their newborns develop early onset disease.[2] Risks for vertical transmission include heavy maternal colonization, prematurity, prolonged preterm rupture of membranes, and intrapartum maternal fever > 37.5°C.[4,12-15] Premature neonatal colonization rates are similar to those of term infants, but the attack (disease) rate is higher. In 1983, Boyer et al.[4] reported attack rates per 1000 newborns: term = 1.1, infants weighing 2001-2500 g = 4.3; 1001-2000 g = 8.5; and 501-1000 g = 26.2. Maternal antibodies to type III GBS may be protective with lower infection rates and higher survival rates.[16]

Carrier State Identification

GBS carriers are identified primarily by culture. While GBS can be isolated from the cervix, urine, and urethra, the optimal technique is to culture the distal one-third of the vagina and the rectum. It should be noted that culture limited to the cervix may have a 50% false negative rate.[2] Todd Hewitt broth has replaced blood agar plates as the media of choice. This media includes Polymyxin B, gentamicin, and nalidixic acid, which allows selective growth of GBS. Properly performed culture of the female genital tract is considered the standard to which other methodologies are compared. Cultures typically require 24-48 hours to become positive, thus obviating intrapartum clinical utility in most cases.

Eriksen and Blanco[17] summarized the literature for rapid testing methodologies. A number of experimental and commercially available rapid diagnostic tests have been developed and evaluated. Gram stain has been shown to have a sensitivity of 34%-100%, specificity of 61%-72%, and a positive predictive value of 13%-33%. In order to improve upon the positive predictive values, newer rapid (30-45 minute) techniques have been developed that rely on direct antigen detection. Coagglutination tests have reported sensitivities of 4%-88%. Latex particle agglutination testing has reported sensitivities of 15%-88%, and specificities of 92%-100%. Enzyme immunoassays have reported sensitivities of 11%-74%, and specificities of 95%-100%. All of these techniques have improved accuracy with growth amplification and heavy colonization. A promising technique is the DNA chemiluminescence probe. Unfortunately, Gram stain and direct antigen testing techniques do not presently have sufficient accuracy to replace properly performed cultures (of the distal vagina and anorectum with selective medium performed beyond 26 weeks).

Management and Prevention Protocols

Antenatal, intrapartum, and neonatal antibiotic prophylaxis protocols have been proposed in an attempt to reduce the incidence of early onset GBS disease. Unfortunately, antenatal treatment has not been found to reliably prevent GBS carrier status at delivery. In 1976, Hall et al.[18] showed that 7% of gravida had GBS in the third trimester by cervical and urethral cultures. Treatment with ampicillin decreased the colonization rates for only 3 weeks, with a return to baseline rates, and no change in the frequency of neonatal colonization. In 1979, Gardner et al.[19] treated pregnant carriers and their partners with penicillin, however, 70% remained positive for GBS, with 67% of these colonized at delivery. Klebanoff et al.[20] recently reported their results of a trial of 938 carriers of GBS. Subjects were cultured at 23 to 26 weeks gestation; they were then randomized to receive either erythromycin or placebo for 10 weeks duration, or until 36 weeks gestation. There were no significant differences among the two groups in regard to birth weight, gestational age at delivery, or frequency of preterm premature rupture of the membranes. It is believed that failure of antepartum prophylaxis results from re-colonization from the rectum, which is a normal reservoir for GBS. Inactivation of penicillin class antibiotics by other enteric organisms may increase the failure rates of antepartum prophylaxis.

In 1983, Pyati et al.[21] performed a prospective study of newborns weighing < 2000 g, who were randomized to be controls or receive intramuscular penicillin. Of the 589 infants receiving intramuscular penicillin, 10 had

Table 1
Recommendations of the American College of Obstetricians and Gynecologists

Routine prenatal screening cultures are not recommended.
Intrapartum chemoprophylaxis is recommended for colonization with GBS, or unknown GBS status plus:
    labor < 37 weeks, or
    rupture of membranes < 37 weeks, or
    rupture of membranes > 18 hours
Regardless of maternal carrier status, chemoprophylaxis is indicated for:
    previous child affected by GBS disease, or
    intrapartum fever (not defined)

GBS disease, a rate not different than the 11 of 598 control infants. The fatality rates were also similar in both groups, six who received penicillin versus eight controls. This and other studies suggest that neonatal prophylaxis is not an efficacious modality. To overcome the failure of antepartum and neonatal prophylaxis, intrapartum prophylaxis was advocated by a number of investigators. However, giving chemoprophylaxis to all women who carry GBS is not without considerable risk and cost. Such a strategy would require intrapartum treatment of up to one million women per year. This could result in ten maternal deaths from anaphylaxis, and tens of thousands of less severe antibiotic reactions per year.[11] Emergence of antimicrobial resistance is also a known risk from widespread antimicrobial use.

To reduce the rate of antibiotic usage, strategies using intrapartum risk factors were developed. In 1986, Boyer and Gotoff[22] conducted the first randomized controlled study of intrapartum chemoprophylaxis. GBS carriers with labor prior to 37 weeks gestation, or rupture of membranes > 12 hours, were randomized to receive either ampicillin (N = 85) or nothing (N = 79). Twenty-four subjects in the control group who developed an intrapartum temperature > 37.5°C were removed from the randomization protocol and were treated with ampicillin. The group receiving ampicillin prophylaxis had a 9% incidence of neonatal colonization and 0% bacteremia. The group receiving no prophylaxis had a significantly increased incidence of colonization (51%) and bacteremia (6%). None of the 24 newborns receiving ampicillin for maternal fever had early onset GBS disease.

Based upon these and other studies, the American College of Obstetricians and Gynecologists (ACOG), the American Academy of Pediatrics (AAP), and the Centers for Disease Control and Prevention (CDC) all released recommendations in the past several years. Table 1 represents the position of the ACOG according to a 1992 Technical Bulletin, with clarifications in

Table 2
Guidelines of the American Academy of Pediatrics

Screen all gravida at 26–28 weeks gestation
Single swab of lower vagina and anorectum in selective medium
Antepartum treatment of asymptomatic women not recommended except
    those with GBS bacteriuria
Women without prior GBS cultures may have cultures or antigen testing
    when admitted for preterm labor or premature rupture of membranes
Intrapartum chemoprophylaxis is recommended when positive maternal
    colonization with GBS or unknown status plus:
        labor < 37 weeks, or
        rupture of membranes < 37 weeks, or
        rupture of membranes > 18 hours, or
        intrapartum fever (not defined)
        multiple gestation
Previous child with GBS disease warrants chemoprophylaxis

Table 3
Recommendation of the Centers for Disease Control and Prevention

Screen all gravida at 26–28 weeks gestation, or when possible thereafter
Culture lower vagina and anorectum in selective medium
Do not antenatally treat colonized women
Previous child with GBS diseases warrants chemoprophylaxis
Antepartum treatment of asymptomatic women not recommended except
    those with GBS bacteriuria
Intrapartum chemoprophylaxis for known maternal colonization or
    unknown GBS status plus
        labor < 37 weeks, or
        rupture of membranes < 37 weeks, or
        rupture of membranes < 12 hours, or
        intrapartum fever ≥ 37.5°C not attributable to extrauterine source

ACOG Newsletters in 1993 and 1994.[23-25] The 1992 AAP guidelines are presented in Table 2,[10] and 1994 CDC strategies are listed in Table 3.[11] It should be noted that the CDC guidelines define intrapartum fever as being ≥ 37.5°C. While the ACOG and AAP guidelines do not specifically define fever, the standard definition of maternal intrapartum fever has been an oral temperature ≥ 38°C.[26]

There continues to be significant controversy regarding the optimal management and prevention of GBS neonatal infection. In 1994, Rouse et al.[27] used decision analysis to determine the likely outcomes of 19 GBS screening and treatment strategies. They focused on three main outcomes: the expected num-

Table 4
Intrapartum GBS Chemoprophylaxis

Ampicillin 2 g then 1 g every 4–6 hours IVPB
Penicillin 5 million units every 6 hours IVPB
For Penicillin Sensitive Patients
Erythromycin 500 mg every 6 hours IVPB
Clindamycin 900 mg every 8 hours IVPB

ber of cases of early onset disease; the percent of gravidas who would receive intrapartum antibiotics; and the total cost. They concluded that universal intrapartum therapy would be the most effective strategy in reducing early onset GBS sepsis (6% of expected), and it was also the least costly. However, as previously discussed this strategy could result in unacceptably high risks of the development of antibiotic resistance and maternal morbidity and mortality because of antibiotic sensitivity. The second most effective modality was intrapartum chemoprophylaxis based upon known risk factors. This paradigm, endorsed by ACOG (Table 1), lowers the theoretical rate of neonatal sepsis to 31% of expected, with an 18% rate of intrapartum treatment. The third most effective strategy was universal culturing at 36 weeks. Treatment of all colonized patients and all having preterm birth would lower neonatal sepsis to 14% of expected with a 27% rate of antibiotic prophylaxis.

Although there is controversy as to the best criteria for deciding to use GBS prophylaxis, there is a general consensus in regard to acceptable intrapartum antibiotic prophylaxis (Table 4). While appropriate intrapartum prophylaxis significantly decreases early onset GBS in the newborn, it does not entirely prevent it. In a study of 96 newborns with blood cultures positive for GBS, 16 had mothers who received intrapartum antibiotics; 2 infants died from sepsis.[28]

Maternal Complications

Women colonized with GBS have a higher incidence of postpartum complications. In a study of gravida delivered by Cesarean section, GBS carriers were found to have significantly increased fever (67% vs 30%), clinical endomyometritis (61% vs 12.5%), and antibiotic requirement (61% vs 26%) than non-colonized women.[26] Endometritis caused by GBS is characterized by a distended abdomen, and exquisite tenderness of the uterus, parametrium, and adnexae.[29] The incidence of postpartum fever > 37.5°C was significantly decreased by intrapartum prophylaxis of ampicillin (8%) compared to controls (21%) among carriers of GBS.[22]

Medico-Legal Issues

The ideal GBS prophylaxis strategy would maximize maternal and neonatal health while minimizing cost. From the preceding discussion, it is clear that there is no national consensus as to the optimal strategy for the prevention of early onset GBS neonatal infection. Because of the lack of a national consensus, treatment regimens vary by region, institution, department, and by individual practitioners within an institution. Adherence to either the AAP, ACOG, or CDC recommendations should be construed as meeting the standard of care. While there are significant differences among these regimens, important points of consensus include chemoprophylaxis for intrapartum risk factors, as well as for a previously affected child. A standard of care can be based upon a synopsis of the elements common to the recommendations of ACOG, CDC, and AAP protocols. These guidelines (Table 5) represent acceptable expectations for appropriate care. Breach of the recommendations presented in Table 5, with sequelae of onset neonatal disease, would be difficult to defend. Failure to offer chemoprophylaxis under these conditions would violate ACOG, AAP, and CDC recommendations.

Medical malpractice litigation cases involving neonatal GBS disease typically have several recurrent alleged breaches of care. These have included: 1. failure to appropriately communicate (or document communication) positive GBS status to obstetric and pediatric care givers; 2. failure to treat the newborn when the mother was not a carrier but had a risk factor such as intrapartum fever; and 3. alleged failure to treat with positive urinary or anogenital cultures. However, it should be noted that antibiotic prophylaxis is only indicated when a positive carrier state is complicated by the risk factors previously

---

Table 5
Acceptable Standards of Care

Intrapartum chemoprophylaxis for previous child with GBS disease regardless of culture status.

Intrapartum chemoprophylaxis is not required when antenatal cultures are negative and properly conducted (cultures of the distal vagina and anorectum with selective medium performed beyond 26 weeks).

Intrapartum chemoprophylaxis is required in the case of a positive anogenitourinary culture, of a properly conducted antenatal culture was not performed, or is of unknown status, with one or more risk factors:
    labor < 37 weeks
    rupture of membranes < 37 weeks
    rupture of membranes > 18 hours
    intrapartum fever ≥ 38°C not attributable to an extrauterine source

outlined. Other related sources of litigation have involved maternal chorioamnionitis and endometritis, and failure to timely treat potentially infected (febrile, tachypneic, etc.) newborns without known risk factors or a positive GBS carrier history.

Conclusion

Early onset GBS disease continues to be a significant cause of neonatal morbidity and mortality. Intrapartum chemoprophylaxis can reduce—but not eliminate—this entity. There is currently no national consensus as to the optimal regimen for deciding when to offer chemoprophylaxis. This controversy is based ultimately upon differing methods of balancing and mitigating the risks of neonatal disease, maternal complications, the development of antibiotic resistance, and cumulative national cost. Nonetheless, a careful review of the literature and recommendations of ACOG, AAP, and the CDC reveals that reasonable and prudent strategies for guiding intrapartum antibiotic prophylaxis can be based upon historical and/or antenatal GBS culture results.

Commentary by Mr. Bloch: While cases arising from the failure to diagnose and/or treat neonatal GBS have been essentially non-existent, there is a growing public perception that this perinatal infection can be prevented. Since GBS infections are more common than illnesses such as rubella and spina bifida, for which all pregnant women are presently screened, a strong argument can be made that GBS screening should be routine.

The obvious difficulty in the litigation of a successful medical negligence case involving GBS is the lack of consensus regarding both prevention and treatment. While it is always an option to perform routine antepartum cervical cultures for GBS, this has not reached the level of a required standard. Likewise, there does not seem to be any consensus on what to do with asymptomatic pregnant women who have been incidentally identified to carry GBS, although such information can be critical in the face of prematurity or premature rupture of membranes.

In December 1992, the Association of Trial Lawyers of America issued an alert urging universal screening of pregnant women for the GBS bacteria, calling it a "wake up call for expectant parents, an effort to avert tragedy." Two weeks after the alert, the Academy of Pediatrics called for GBS testing for all pregnant women at 26 to 28 weeks gestation. While it is extremely unusual to see a non-medical organization advocating standards for patient care, it is nevertheless a recognition that much more can be done than is being done.

In the recently released fourth edition of *Infectious Diseases of the Fetus and Newborn Infant*, edited by Remington and Klein, the authors state on p. 1028:

"The impressive measure to which our understanding of group B streptococcal infections has progressed in more than two decades has not been accompanied by universal implementation of an effective method for their prevention. Similarly, development of new antimicrobial agents and improved modalities of intensive care has not negated the morbidity and mortality associated with these infections. Their sustained incidence and the too-frequent failure of therapeutic intervention to result in a favorable outcome, however, suggest that intense effort should continue to be focused on development of prevention methods."

Ultimately there will be a reduction in the mortality and morbidity caused by this pathogen. Unfortunately, there may continue to be a high fatality rate, and a high incidence of CNS sequelae among survivors. While it is difficult to understand how it took ACOG so long to issue a position paper or technical bulletin on GBS, the fact that they have done so should hasten the creation of a standard of care that some day will both save lives and prevent injury, especially in high risk patients.

References

1. Baker CJ. Summary of the workshop on perinatal infections due to group B streptococcus. J Infect Dis 1977;136:137.
2. Baker CJ, Edwards MS. Group B streptococcal infections: Perinatal impact and prevention methods. Ann N Y Acad Sci 1988;549:193.
3. Stewardson-Krieger PB, Gotoff SP. Risk factors in early onset neonatal group B streptococcal infections. Infection 1978;6:50.
4. Boyer KM, Gadzala CA, Burd LI, et al. Selective intrapartum chemoprophylaxis of neonatal group B streptococcal early-onset disease. I. Epidemiologic rationale. J Infect Dis 1983;148:795.
5. Baker CJ. Immunization to prevent group B streptococcal disease: Victories and vexations. J Infect Dis 1990;161:917.
6. Sweet FL, Gibbs RS (eds). *Group B Streptococci, Infectious Diseases of the Female Genital Tract*, Second Edition. Baltimore, Williams and Wilkins, 1990, pp. 22-37.
7. Regan JA, Klebanoff MA, Nugent RP. The epidemiology of Group B Streptococcal colonization in pregnancy. Obstet Gynecol 1991;77:604.
8. Anthony BF, Eisenstadt R, Carter J, et al. Genital and intestinal carriage of group B streptococci during pregnancy. J Infect Dis 1981;143:761.
9. Thomsen AC, Morup L, Hansen KB. Antibiotic elimination of group B streptococci in urine in prevention of preterm labor. Lancet 1987;1:59.
10. American Academy of Pediatrics. Guidelines for prevention of group B streptococcal (GBS) infection by chemoprophylaxis. Pediatrics 1992;90:775.

11. Prevention of Group B Streptococcal diseases: A public health perspective: Notice. Centers for Disease Control and Prevention. Federal Register 1994;59:64764.
12. Dillon HC, Khare S, Gray BM. Group B streptococcal carriage and disease: A 6 year prospective study. J Pediatr 1987;110:31.
13. Evaldson GR, Melmborg A, Nord CE. Premature rupture of the membranes and ascending infection. Br J Obstet Gynaecol 1982;89:793.
14. Schuchat A, Deaver-Robinson K, Plikaytis BD, et al. Multistate case-control study of maternal risk factors for neonatal group B streptococcal disease. Pediatr Infect Dis J 1994;13:623.
15. Pass MA, Khare S, Dillon HC. Twin pregnancies: Incidence of group B streptococcal colonization and disease. J Pediatr 1980;97:635.
16. Baker CJ, Kasper DL. Correlation of maternal antibody deficiency with susceptibility to neonatal group B streptococcal infection. N Engl J Med 1976;294:753.
17. Eriksen NL, Blanco JD. Group B streptococcal infection in pregnancy. Semin Perinatol 1993;17:432.
18. Hall TD, Barnes W, Krishnan L, et al. Antibiotic treatment of parturient women colonized with group B streptococci. Am J Obstet Gynecol 1976;124:630.
19. Gardner Se, Yow MD, Leeds LJ, et al. Failure of penicillin to eradicate group B streptococcal colonization in the pregnant woman. Am J Obstet Gynecol 1979;135:106.
20. Klebanoff MA, Regan JA, Rao B, et al. Outcome of the vaginal infections and prematurity study: Results of a clinical trial of erythromycin among pregnant women colonized with group B streptococci. Am J Obstet Gynecol 1995;172:1540.
21. Pyati SP, Pildes RS, Jacobs NM, et al. Penicillin in infants weighing two kilograms or less with early onset group B streptococcal disease. N Engl J Med 1983;308:1282.
22. Boyer KM, Gotoff SP. Prevention of early onset group B streptococcal disease with selective intrapartum chemoprophylaxis. N Engl J Med 1986;314:1665.
23. Group B streptococcal infections in pregnancy. ACOG Technical Bulletin #170, July, 1993.
24. Hankins GB, Chalas E. Group B streptococcal infections in pregnancy: ACOG's recommendations. ACOG Newsletter 1993;37:1.
25. American College of Obstetricians and Gynecologists. Survey shows continued confusion over management of GBS in pregnancy. ACOG Newsletter 1994;38:1.
26. Minkoff HL, Sierra MF, Pringle GF, et al. Vaginal colonization with Group B beta-hemolytic streptococcus as a risk factor for post-cesarean section febrile morbidity. Am J Obstet Gynecol 1982;142:992.
27. Rouse DJ, Goldenberg R, Cliver SP, et al. Strategies for the prevention of early onset neonatal group B streptococcal sepsis: A decision analysis. Obstet Gynecol 1994;83:483.
28. Ascher DP, Becker JA, Yoder BA, et al. Failure of intrapartum antibiotics to prevent culture proved group B streptococcal sepsis. J Perinatol 1993;13:212.
29. Faro S. Group B beta hemolytic streptococci and puerperal infections. Am J Obstet Gynecol 1981;139:686.

Section III

Intrapartum Obstetrical Issues

Chapter 11

Electronic Fetal Monitoring: Role of the Physician

◆◆◆

Barry S. Schifrin, M.D.

Introduction

Electronic fetal monitoring (EFM) has had a broad impact on obstetrical care and has come to play a pivotal role in lawsuits, especially in the "bad baby" case. In this chapter, I will discuss the utilization of EFM in the detection of fetal hypoxia and injury. I will also attempt to provide an overview of its role in obstetrical risk management and medico-legal confrontations.

By the timely detection of fetal asphyxia, EFM was expected to reduce the intrapartum stillbirth rates as well as enhance the condition of the newborn and ultimately reduce the risk of long-term disability, including cerebral palsy. On a practical level, it would reduce the Cesarean section rate for fetal distress, as most fetal distress determined by auscultation did not correlate with objective neonatal distress. While the stillbirth rate during labor has essentially fallen to zero and the neonatal mortality has fallen dramatically,[1] the risk of neurologic handicap, however, seems to be rising.[2,3]

> **Commentary by Mr. Volk:** Clearly at least some of this is the result of the survival of very small, high-risk, premature babies.

The Cesarean section rate has also shown no tendency to fall. Such statistics have fueled controversy about the value of EFM and prompted a number of studies both randomized and non-randomized.

Virtually all the non-randomized trials suggest a benefit of monitoring; none suggests a benefit of auscultation. Of the ten randomized controlled trials (RCTs) of EFM during labor, three suggest a benefit; the remainder

From: Donn SM, Fisher CW (eds.): *Risk Management Techniques in Perinatal and Neonatal Practice.* © Futura Publishing Co., Inc., Armonk, NY, 1996.

are either neutral or imply detriment as a function of increasing the Cesarean section rate or increasing the risk of cerebral palsy.[4] Too much attention has been paid to the conclusions of these studies and too little attention has been paid to their methodology.[5] Ultimately, the RCTs prove unsatisfying as definitive answers to the benefits of monitoring. Paneth et al.[6] have even suggested that the RCTs were undertaken prematurely. No study of auscultation alone suggests any clinical benefit of auscultation. Table 1 defines diagnostic criteria and nomenclature for individual features of the fetal heart rate pattern (FHR). Table 2 represents an attempt to condense these features into a clinically meaningful evaluation of the fetal condition. It further delineates a range of reasonable responses to these assessments.

The presumed benefits of EFM are obvious. EFM predicts the absence of asphyxia with greater accuracy than any other known technique or combination of techniques. It has a lower false normal rate than fetal blood sampling (FBS) or auscultation with a stethoscope. EFM provides insights into the mechanism of asphyxia and the likelihood with which such problems can be ameliorated with conservative management. The sudden, unexpected death of a fetus with a normal pattern has not been reported. Furthermore, EFM appears beneficial in both high and low risk patients. Compared to auscultation, the electronic recording of heart rate makes a permanent record available for review and analysis. Auscultation, furthermore, is unreliable, not reproducible, and will often fail to detect important prognostic features clearly present in FHR patterns.[7-9]

> **Commentary by Mr. Volk:** I have learned from numerous cases that nursing personnel do not utilize and document monitoring of the FHR by auscultation very well. What I mean by that is when they are required to testify under oath, the nurse often cannot explain the mechanism of how the FHR is monitored by auscultation. In addition, the documentation is often very poor.

Unfortunately, we have yet to determine how many babies are injured during labor, how many are injured before, and what role, if any, EFM plays in the detection and prevention of injury.

Quantifying Fetal Hypoxia

Hypoxia, an acknowledged mechanism of injury in the fetus, is quantifiable. For this purpose, numerous indicators have been applied including: the Apgar score; umbilical cord acid-base balance; FHR patterns; and many others. Although there is a strong correlation between very prolonged low Apgar scores and adverse outcome including neurologic injury, the Apgar scores per se are relatively insensitive indicators or either asphyxia or subse-

Table 1
Features of Fetal Heart Rate Patterns

Baseline Heart Rate
A. Normal range 110–150 bpm.
B. Tachycardia:
    1. Mild   151–180 bpm.
    2. Moderate   181–200 bpm.
    3. Severe   > 200 bpm.
C. Bradycardia:
    1. Mild   109–100 bpm.
    2. Moderate   99–80 bpm.
    3. Severe   < 80 bpm.

Baseline Variability Long-Term
A. Fluctuations in heart rate measured over many seconds.
B. Characteristics:
    1. Amplitude: 2. Frequency:
      a. Increased   > 15 bpm   a. 2–6 cycles per minute
      b. Average   5–15 bpm   b. Occasionally sinusoidal
      c. Decreased   < 5 bpm
      d. Absent   < 2 bpm

Baseline Variability Short-Term
A. Interval (or rate) differences between successive heart beats.
B. Characteristics: Not well defined:
    1. Amplitude range: 0–40 bpm
    2. Frequency: Probably in range of 60 cycles per minute average
    3. Avg. interval difference: About 5 msec
    4. Changes are unpredictable

Early Decelerations
Characteristics:
A. Shape: Uniform
B. Onset: Coincident with onset of UC
C. Lag time: < 20 seconds
D. Duration: Proportional to duration of UC
E. Amplitude: Proportional to amplitude of UC
F. Repetitive

Proposed Mechanism:
A. Head (fontanel) compression
B. Increased intracranial pressure
C. Increased peripheral resistance
D. Increased blood pressure
E. Reflex (vagal) deceleration

Late Decelerations
Characteristics:
A. Shape: Uniform
B. Onset: Late in UC cycle
C. Lag time: > 20 seconds
D. Duration: Proportional to duration of UC
E. Amplitude: Proportional to UC amplitude
F. Repetitive

Table continues on next page

Table 1
Features of Fetal Heart Rate Patterns *(continued)*

Proposed Mechanism:
A. Diminished uterine blood flow with UC
B. Critical reduction of pO_2 following peak of UC

C. Reflex slowing (vagal) of heart rate
D. Hypoxic slowing (local) of heart rate

Variable Decelerations
Characteristics:
A. Shape: Variable
B. Onset: Variable
C. Lag time: Variable
D. Amplitude: Variable; usually unrelated to amplitude and duration of UC

E. Need not be repetitive
F. Frequently preceded or followed by brief variable accelerations (shoulders)

Proposed Mechanisms:
A. Umbilical cord occlusion (spasm):
   1. Increased peripheral resistance
   2. Stimulation of baro-/chemoreceptors
   3. Reflex (vagal) deceleration— (initial)

   4. Hypoxia
   5. Bradycardia (late)

B. Head compression:
   1. Sustained/profound head compression
   2. Increased intracranial pressure
   3. Responses as above

Prolonged Decelerations
Characteristics:
A. Onset: Abrupt
B. Amplitude: At least 30 bpm
C. Duration: At least 2 minutes
D. Not homogeneous group of patterns—vary in:
   1. Rapidity of onset
   2. Relationship to uterine UCs
   3. Rapidity of recovery
   4. Patterns during recovery
E. Most distinguish from baseline bradycardia

Proposed Mechanism:
A. Uncertain
B. Most probably reflex (vagal) in origin—at least initial part of deceleration
C. Potential for developing hypoxia if prolonged
D. Predisposing causes—not always obvious:
   1. Cord compression
   2. Sustained head compression
   3. Uterine hypertonus
   4. Vaginal examination
   5. Scalp sampling
   6. Position change
   7. Drugs—especially with oxytocin, PCB
   8. Convulsions, shock in mother

Table continues on next page

Table 1
Features of Fetal Heart Rate Patterns *(continued)*

Spontaneous Accelerations
Characteristics:
Uniform, symmetrical accelerations unassociated with UCs or periodic decelerations
Mechanism:
A. See with fetal movement or stimulation:
  1. Represent integrated response of fetal CNS
  2. Basis of reactive NST
B. Apparently benign response

Uniform Accelerations
Characteristics:
Uniform, symmetrical acceleration:
Mechanism:
  1. Coincident with uterine UCs
  2. Reflects shape of UC

Variable Accelerations
Characteristics:
Variably-shaped accelerations, which do not reflect shape of uterine UC:
Mechanism:
  1. "Shoulders" on variable decelerations
  2. As feature of "increased variability" with UC
  3. Usually associated with good baseline variability

Rebound Accelerations (Overshoot)
Uniform accelerations following variable decelerations.
Characteristics:
  1. Smooth baseline
  2. Follows variable deceleration regardless of amplitude
  3. Usual duration—longer than 12 seconds
  4. May also be seen following administration of atropine, or with immature fetus
  5. Do not confuse with exaggerated variable acceleration following moderate-severe variable deceleration
Mechanism:
Ominous commentary on variable deceleration

quent neurologic handicap.[10-12] In addition to hypoxia, other factors including drugs, trauma, anomaly, maladroit resuscitation, and most obviously, gestational age, may all interfere with neonatal adaptation. Despite an increased risk of adverse outcome with newborn acidosis, it is nevertheless a poor predictor of long-term disability.[11,12] The range of values in normal infants is wide, and the majority of acidosis is respiratory, rapidly correctable, and unlikely to be associated with significant handicap. Metabolic acidosis may also reflect maternal not fetal acidosis.[13] Furthermore, acidosis and depression at birth cannot measure how long the fetus has been asphyxiated nor the mechanism. Neonatal seizures are clearly related to risk factors such as long labors and FHR patterns as well as the quality of obstetrical care.[14-16] The combination of low Apgar scores and neonatal seizures have emerged as important indicators of subsequent neurologic handicap—irrespective of the pH. Infants with neonatal seizures are ten times as likely to have severe cerebral palsy and 18 times more likely to have epilepsy.[17]

Current guidelines suggest clinical cerebral palsy may be related to intra-partum asphyxia *only* when asphyxia is severe and prolonged and *only* when the newborn exhibits signs of moderate or severe hypoxic-ischemic encephalopathy and only when other causes have been excluded.[15] These guidelines, however, fail to deal with the most common causes of neurologic injury associated with subsequent handicap.

> **Commentary by Mr. Volk:** Many attorneys who deal in medico-legal matters, myself included, are very cautious when confronted with "current" guidelines concerning cerebral palsy (I am not disagreeing with Dr. Schifrin—he did not formulate the guidelines discussed). There almost seems to be a movement to protect the obstetrical brothers and sisters from adverse medico-legal outcomes. For instance, Apgar scores are used to defend a case if they are "normal." If they are low, the testimony is that Apgar scores are very crude indicators and do not tell us whether or not the newborn will be disabled. The bottom line is that each individual outcome must be analyzed relative to the facts of each case. If there is evidence of factors other than obstetrical events, those must be considered. Please, do not tell us that the failure to adequately respond to a bad labor, managed by incompetent, poorly trained or absent doctors, with a nasty FHR monitor strip, low Apgar scores, and a newborn who needs to be vigorously resuscitated, has cerebral palsy and will be permanently handicapped does not have a cause of action against the health care providers. I am not advocating suing anyone until the facts are known to the attorney and they have been thoroughly investigated. I am advocating a careful analysis of the facts and representation of children who have not been adequately taken care of by their health care providers.

Such severe asphyxia results in persistently low Apgar scores, severe neonatal acidosis (pH < 7.0), neonatal depression, and multisystem organ involvement.[18] Central to this theory is the assumption that during acute asphyxia, redistribution of blood flow (the diving reflex) spares the brain. Thus, if the brain is injured, then other organs must be also impaired (see Chapter 25).[19]

If injury were a linear function of the fall in pH, then all babies born with severely low pH values would either reveal later injury or die. However, neither death nor disability is the usual consequence of severe asphyxia, irrespective of the pH.[20]

> **Commentary by Mr. Volk:** This may very well result from the hardiness of the human body. It is amazing how much insult a fetus or newborn can withstand. This does not mean that the standard of care was met by the health care providers, only that the fetus or newborn withstood the assault of negligent treatment without permanent injury.

Nor does there appear to be evidence that brain injury causes fetal asphyxia. Brain injury indeed affects the FHR pattern, but such changes are related to impaired neurologic control over heart rate—not hypoxia (see below).

While the diagnosis of fetal asphyxia (at the time of delivery) requires a blood gas and an acid-base assessment with evidence of a significant metabolic acidosis, no consensus has been established as to what constitutes a significant degree of metabolic acidosis. A more rational definition will ultimately require a measure of the duration as well as the degree of the asphyxia, plus an expression of the biologic response of the fetus to the asphyxial insult. Using biochemically determined fetal asphyxia (base deficit > 12 mmol/L or an extracellular base deficit of 8 mmol/L), Low[11] found that in term infants a significant relationship exists between the degree of metabolic acidosis at delivery and the incidence of an abnormal outcome. The incidence of deficits at 1 year increased with an umbilical artery buffer base < 34 mmol/L. The majority of depressed newborns, and those with subsequent neurologic handicap, however, are not acidemic at birth. Visser et al.[21] found that the fetus with low Apgar scores and normal pH values at birth were far more likely to have subsequent neurologic deficit than were those with significant acidosis. Dennis et al.[22] confirmed these data and even suggested that acidosis was protective of the fetus. Avoiding these apparent paradoxes requires that more attention be paid to other models of injury.

Fetal oxygen deprivation may be acute, subacute, or chronic; within each category the deprivation may be intermittent or continuous. Uterine contractions and bearing down efforts of the mother may add additional *intermittent* stresses by temporarily impeding uterine, umbilical, or even cerebral blood flow—the latter from mechanical compression of the fetal head.[23] Even when catastrophe strikes (prolapsed cord, abruption), the asphyxial episode is rarely complete. Except in rare instances, the distribution of lesions and survivability of the human fetus does not appear consistent with experimental models of total fetal asphyxia. On the other hand, experimental lesions in lambs, monkeys, and rabbits mimicking those of cerebral palsy can be produced with intermittent ischemia without either chronic hypoxia or severe systemic acidosis.[24-26] Thus, there is reason to endorse the notion, as stated by Vannucci,[24] that *ischemia* of the brain is the critical factor in the etiology of fetal neurologic injury. Systemic asphyxia with acidosis at the time of birth seems incidental.[24]

Intrauterine growth retardation (IUGR) significantly increases the risk of fetal/neonatal death, fetal distress during labor, acidosis at birth, and low Apgar score, as well as adverse neurologic outcome.[27] IUGR is often associated with meconium staining and oligohydramnios. While this constellation is often ascribed to chronic fetal hypoxia, there appears to be little clinical or experimental support for hypoxia as the etiologic factor in this model. Acute hypoxia indeed diminishes fetal urinary output, but chronic hypoxia without acidosis finds urine output at normal levels and amniotic fluid volume replenished.

As originally described, EFM was predicated on the search for fetal hypoxia "revealed" by the presence of abnormalities such as tachycardia, bradycardia, decreased variability, increased variability (early distress), sinusoidal patterns, late decelerations, "severe" variable decelerations, and prolonged decelerations. The normal term fetus is capable of producing decelerations, accelerations, and decreased variability along with discernible, epochal patterns of sleep (rest), wakefulness (activity), breathing, sucking, mouthing movements, and responses to intrinsic stimulation—unrelated to hypoxia.[28] FHR patterns associated with fetal breathing movements may stimulate late decelerations, and fetal sucking may simulate sinusoidal patterns.[28] These responses, which may be less obvious in the premature fetus, represent fetal neurologic behavior—not hypoxia.[28-30]

During labor, fetal hypoxia of any severity produces decelerations (late, variable, prolonged) *before* any other change in baseline rate, accelerations, or pH. These decelerations, which persist as long as the fetus is hypoxic, will invariably induce a rise in baseline rate and diminution in baseline variability (if both were previously normal). If hypoxia is relieved by appropriate measures, the decelerations disappear first, then the baseline returns to its previous level. The time taken for the fetus to recover to its preceding normal baseline rate and variability appears to be the best measure of the severity of the insult. If the hypoxia continues, both decelerations and abnormalities of the baseline will persist. Before the fetus dies, the pattern may reveal an unstable baseline and persistently absent variability but may show few decelerations. Decelerations that do not impact on the previously normal baseline rate and variability cannot reasonably represent meaningful fetal hypoxia and cannot be used to infer ongoing fetal hypoxia or injury therefrom. Similarly, tachycardia and/or decreased variability during labor can only represent hypoxia if decelerations are also present.[31-33]

Recent intelligence suggests that one can simplify the approach to the analysis of FHR patterns by focusing separately on the features of hypoxia (decelerations and the responses thereto) and the features of behavior (variability and cyclicity). This approach is summarized in Table 2. Part A defines the behavioral and asphyxial heart rate features for the various combinations. Part B describes the clinical circumstances under which these patterns may be found. Part C defines the responses to these classes of patterns.

The correlation between FHR patterns of hypoxia and subsequent neurologic handicap is poor—expectedly so. Unfortunately, most authors have sought to relate subsequent injury to FHR markers of hypoxia and not markers of neurologic integrity. Abnormal heart rate patterns, *separate from asphyxia*, are found in fetuses with neurological malformations, especially anencephaly; those treated with neurotropic drugs, including cocaine, atropine, barbituates, tranquilizers, and local and general anesthetics; and those destined to have neonatal seizures, hypoxic-ischemic encephalopathy, or later cerebral palsy.[33-39]

> **Commentary by Mr. Volk:** An attorney investigating a potential claim with an abnormal FHR pattern obviously must attempt to rule out causes other than hypoxia for the neurologic injury to the child. That is the obligation of any attorney practicing in this area. When those other causes are ruled out, the correlation is no longer poor. The legal test is to a reasonable degree of medical probability, not to a scientific certainty. The inquiry is, "What do we know about this fetus, this newborn? Are there any knowable causes for the neurologic dysfunction other than the labor events?"

Persistently absent baseline variability has been found in several cases of fetal decerebration after catastrophic collapse followed by recovery in the mother.[40,41] At delivery these infants were markedly hypotonic and functionally decerebrate but had normal acid-base values in cord blood.

Several authors have reported persistently absent variability without acidosis in many infants subsequently found to have cerebral palsy.[33,34] Of interest, about one-third of these ultimately developed acidosis during labor but only in association with severe decelerations. Unexpectedly, those with acidosis superimposed upon the flat heart rate pattern fared no worse than those without acidosis. These findings appear consistent with the notion that EFM may reveal fetal injury antedating the onset of labor. In a follow-up study of 44 cerebral palsy patients with absent variability in early labor, Schifrin et al.[34] found that the majority had normal patterns on antepartum testing in the week preceding delivery. These data suggest that the injury developed late in pregnancy in the time period of the conversion. Recently, Asakura et al.[42] have reported on the sudden conversion of a previously normal pattern into one of tachycardia and persistently absent variability in a fetus with

Table 2
Analysis of Fetal Heart Rate Patterns

A. Classification According to Interpretation

| Asphyxia | Electronic Fetal Monitoring Fetal Behavioral Patterns | |
	Normal	Abnormal
Absent	Reassuring	Suspicious Drugs, prematurity, anomaly, injury
Present	Threatening Recoverable Fetal distress Epidural, Oxytocin, etc.	Pathological Uncompensated Fetal distress

B. Classification According to Feature

| Asphyxia | Electronic Fetal Monitoring Fetal Behavioral Patterns | |
	Normal	Abnormal
Absent	Reassuring Variability present Accelerations present Rest-activity cycles	Suspicious Variability absent Accelerations absent Decelerations absent OR Normal variability Baseline tachycardia Baseline bradycardia

Present	
	
	Threatening
	Variability present
	Decelerations present
		Pathological
		Ominous
		  Variability absent
		  Decelerations present
		  High or Rising baseline
		Agonal
		  Unstable/sinusoidal baseline
		  Decelerations absent
		  Sinusoidal

C. Classification According to Responses

| Asphyxia | Electronic Fetal Monitoring Fetal Behavioral Patterns | |
	Normal	Abnormal
Absent	Reassuring Repeat as indicated	Suspicious Attempt to define cause Intervention may be necessary Usually normal outcome Sometimes anomaly, injury

Present	Threatening
	Attempt to correct
	  problem
	Intervene if pattern
	  deteriorates
		Pathological
		Consider immediate intervention

massive intracranial hemorrhage. This pattern appeared during the second stage of labor with the fetus in occiput posterior position and was not associated with acidosis at birth. Despite these trends, EFM cannot reliably predict outcome of problems unrelated to oxygen deprivation or those in which behavior is unaffected. These potential benefits and insights from EFM, notwithstanding, are secondary to the reassurance provided by the normal FHR pattern.

The combination of low Apgar scores, severe acidosis, and the need for prolonged resuscitation, by themselves, seem overly stringent criteria for the diagnosis of neurologic injury during labor. The absence of one or more of these signs cannot be used to exclude perinatal asphyxia (ischemia) as the cause of injury. Since ischemia to the brain and other organs (i.e., localized asphyxia), not systemic global asphyxia, appears to be the major precursor of human fetal injury it seems unreasonable to insist on systemic fetal asphyxia at any time to validate the timing or mechanism of fetal injury.[24] Most hypoxic newborns are not injured and most injured newborns are not hypoxic. Furthermore, that a baby is injured as a result of hypoxia during labor does not mean that it was preventable.

> **Commentary by Mr. Volk:** The overwhelming majority of inquiries that I receive from potential clients turn out, after investigation, to not involve any failure to meet the standard of care, nor is there a proximate cause linking the care to injury of the patient. However, if a baby is injured as a result of hypoxia during labor, the health care provider's conduct must be scrutinized very closely. In these circumstances, there is at least a strong possibility that a cause of action exists.

Deterioration of the FHR may be rapid or slow, influenced by the frequency and intensity of uterine contractions and the intensity of pushing during the second stage of labor. Lateral position, hydration, careful titration of oxytocin, and restricting potentially compromising techniques to the demonstrably normal fetus can do much to forestall the appearance of fetal distress. In addition, careful attention to the timing and ancillary support of the patient receiving epidural anesthesia especially in the second stage of labor is prudent. Fetal decelerations related to fetal head compression and occasionally cord compression, may begin with the onset of pushing. Decelerations are especially common when the head is occiput posterior and/or significantly molded. The amplitude and duration of the deceleration are often proportional to the expulsive effort. Cessation of pushing, at least temporarily, may have a salutary effect on severity of the deceleration (Table 3).

It is obvious that the fetus may be injured so rapidly during labor that no interval of time, short of immediate, will suffice if the fetus is to be rescued

---

Table 3
Impact of Maternal Pushing

Maternal expulsive efforts in the second stage of labor should be governed by
proper utilization of FHR pattern information as follows:

    Pushing should never be implemented before full dilatation.
    When the patient pushes involuntarily before full dilatation she should be
        encouraged to refrain from pushing. Properly timed analgesia may
        reduce the desire to push prematurely.

    Pushing should never be extended beyond the uterine contractions.

    The following features of decelerations require no modification of expulsive
        efforts:
    Stable baseline heart rate
    Normal short-term *baseline* variability
    The deceleration returns to the previously normal baseline rate and variability
        immediately after cessation of pushing
    Within these parameters the frequency and amplitude of decelerations are
        probably unimportant

Decelerations that require modification of expulsive efforts:
Prolonged decelerations:
    Fetal heart rate returns to the previously normal baseline rate and variability
        more than 20 seconds after the cessation of pushing—"slow return to
        baseline" or prolonged deceleration

Rising or undefinable baseline:
    Decelerations which return promptly but where the baseline rate is rising or
        undefinable

Sustained low heart rates (90–110 bpm)
    Fetal heart rate drops to 90–110 bpm
    Variability is average to increased
    Decelerations are absent—"second stage bradycardia"
    This pattern represents increased intracranial pressure—*not fetal hypoxia*
    Despite the lack of acidosis the pattern should not be regarded as benign

In response to these pattern:
    Have gravida moderate or curtail her expulsive efforts with subsequent
        contractions
    Turn patient to lateral position, administer oxygen
    Notify the physician
    Consider tocolytic (e.g., terbutaline 0.25 mg SQ)
    Consider elevation of the presenting part (decelerations may represent cord
        compression).
    If there is still no recovery then consider prompt intervention
    Recovery endpoint: Fetal heart rate returns to its *previously normal baseline*
        rate and variability

---

intact. Usually, however deterioration develops relatively slowly and can be anticipated by decelerations, and rising heart rate—usually in association with the administration of oxytocin or epidural anesthesia or pushing during the second stage. A sudden drop in FHR from 140 to 60 bpm, which does not respond to conservative measures (including cessation of pushing) within several minutes requires immediate intervention.

Electronic Fetal Monitoring and the Standard of Care

Today we monitor with EFM most obstetrical patients during labor and almost all high-risk patients before labor. While the practice or custom of a majority of obstetricians does not necessarily define the standard of care, the use of EFM for fetal surveillance during labor represents, I believe, the prevailing medical and legal standards of care. Nevertheless, the American College of Obstetricians and Gynecologists guidelines nominally permit auscultation under any circumstances. Thus, given the current climate, a doctor must demonstrate that he has based a decision not to apply EFM on a thorough understanding of the facts of the case (i.e., the indications, limitations, complications, and alternatives to EFM). A physician who decides against EFM may also be sued for failing to inform his or her patient of the benefits and hazards of EFM, and seeking her participation in the decision. The issue of informed consent is independent of the determination of malpractice and will be discussed elsewhere.

In any medical malpractice case, an expert is necessary both to explain the medical details to the judge and jury, and to compare the care rendered the patient to the prevailing standard. In judging the reasonability of a physician's actions, experts are duty-bound to apply a minimal standard of care. They must use those principles of interpretation that represent a broadly understood, minimal standard at that particular time.

> **Commentary by Mr. Volk:** The standard is a minimal, fundamental national standard. It is no longer a local one, partly because of the ability to distribute teaching materials throughout the United States.

Under these circumstances the most sophisticated analysis may not be used against the physician but may be used in his or her defense. For example, research carried out after the fact may reveal that a particular FHR pattern defines pre-existing fetal injury, although the pattern was appropriately not recognized at the time care was provided. The physician is entitled to use information currently available but not available at the time of care to show that his care was unrelated to the injury, and also, that it was not below the standard of care to fail to recognize the pattern.

Commentary by Mr. Volk: The *standard* is set at the time the medical care is rendered. An elevation in the standard at a later time cannot be utilized to prove that there was a failure to comply with the applicable standard. You cannot utilize later medical knowledge to prove that the standard was met in an earlier time. Therefore, you do not use information currently available to show that it was not below the standard to fail to recognize a pattern. What the author is discussing concerning showing that the care was unrelated to the injury simply means that you can utilize knowledge developed after care is rendered to attempt to show that the conduct of the health-care provider did not proximately *cause* any injury to the patient.

The fetal monitor produces a continuous record that must be interpreted and retained. To utilize the monitor without the capacity to interpret the tracing is negligent. Not only do the nomenclature of the various patterns and the techniques of monitoring vary, no authoritative body has defined the minimal standard of interpretation. This lack of standardization has resulted in a proliferation of interpretations of fetal monitoring records by the medical expert and confounded many a judge and jury.

Provided the physician/nurse exhibits certain minimal knowledge about the physiology of heart rate patterns and the mechanics of fetal monitoring devices, offers a reasonable interpretation and a plan of action, the individual cannot reasonably be held liable for an inaccurate interpretation of a monitor strip. Nor can they be held to the interpretation of widely published authors.

Commentary by Mr. Volk: A health care provider can be held responsible for an inaccurate interpretation, if the standard of care tells us that a reasonably prudent person would have interpreted the strip to include other reasonable interpretations. You must be able to differentiate between alternate choices and recognize the potential for disaster in one or more of the choices. This is done all the time by physicians in setting out a differential diagnosis. For instance, if there are two interpretations of a set of facts, one that is benign to the patient, but one that is disastrous, the standard requires that the health care provider rule out the disastrous one. You cannot practice by what I call the "99%" rule. This simply means that even though 99% of the time the patient will do fine, you must be alert to the possibility that you are dealing on this occasion with the 1% and act accordingly. So, therefore, if your interpretation is "reasonable" but wrong, and there are other reasonable interpretations that you should have considered and ruled out, you have not met the standard.

The knowledge necessary to meet these interpretive standards of care is of two sorts. First, some technical points must be understood. The responsible health care provider must recognize the limits of both internal and external monitoring. He/she must know, for example, that an external monitor tends to exaggerate the variability of the heart rate and must be wary of overinterpreting a "noisy signal," that is, one which contains a great deal of artifact ("all that wiggles is not variability"). He/she must also be aware that external devices (applied to the abdomen) may half-count a FHR > 160 bpm and double count a fetal rate < 80 bpm. He/she must understand the potential of these devices to count the maternal heart rate. When the tracing is not understood or potentially inaccurate, the nurse or physician must also utilize other techniques of surveillance, such as auscultation and/or FBS, and obtain consultation.

> **Commentary by Mr. Volk:** What bothers me is the use of the word "minimal." It seems as if Dr. Schifrin is saying that only minimal knowledge is needed to monitor a labor by EFM. I do not believe that is true and I believe the standard requires much more. The person monitoring the labor must be able to demonstrate that he/she is competent to undertake the monitoring of a labor because there is so much at stake for the fetus and parents.

Given this minimal understanding about the pathophysiology of FHR patterns and the technical quality of the tracing, the health care provider must formulate a plan of action. What the physician decides to do is less important than how he or she goes about making that decision. A physician or nurse who commits his or her interpretation and plan to the medical record is much less likely to be sued successfully, regardless of the accuracy of assessment of the fetal monitor tracing. It is the reasonable—but not necessarily accurate—interpretation of the tracing, combined with a reasonable—but not necessarily correct—plan of action that is crucial both for successful patient care and for successful legal defense.

> **Commentary by Mr. Volk:** The fact that a person documents an interpretation in the medical record only tells us that he/she did so. It is obviously proper to document, and fails to meet the standard if it is not done, but documentation of an incorrect interpretation does not tell us that the standard was met. As discussed above, a reasonable interpretation that excludes another interpretation that is disastrous to the patient does not meet the standard and is negligent.

Consistency of action provides an added dimension to the physician's defense. If intervention is decided upon, the urgency of the action must be consistent with the perceived seriousness of the pattern. When the patient is moved into the delivery room for other than a normal delivery, or if complications develop within the delivery room, the fetus should be monitored there, and the physician's note must account for all of the intervening time between the move to the delivery room and the delivery. The operative note, required on all operative deliveries, forceps or Cesarean section, must include the details of the operation, the indication for the operative delivery, the station and position of the presenting part, and any unusual findings or difficulties encountered.

> **Commentary by Mr. Volk:** It is amazing how many times this basic information is not documented in the medical record. I have litigated multiple cases where something as basic as station of the fetus prior to the application of forceps or vacuum is not documented anywhere. This is a disaster for the defense.

The obstetrician should obtain an umbilical cord blood sample for acid-base studies from any fetus delivered where difficulties have been encountered or anticipated. Cord blood gases (see Chapter 20) assist in eliminating the asphyxia just prior to delivery (not earlier) as a cause of neonatal depression or confirm acidosis as an indication for intervention. They should not be done routinely!

An expert who is asked to review FHR pattern in connection with a malpractice action is limited in the conclusions he or she may reach. With rare exceptions, there are no recognized FHR patterns that are pathognomonic of infection, traumatic injury, drugs, or congenital anomaly. These non-asphyxial conditions account for about one-half of babies depressed at birth. On the other hand, the normal FHR tracing is conclusive evidence of the absence of significant fetal asphyxia during labor. However, abnormal tracings often do not correlate with bad outcome and, except at extremes, must not be used to infer fetal asphyxia (distress) or inevitable brain damage. Similarly, when the pattern reveals persistently absent variability without decelerations from the onset of labor, the expert may conclude with reasonable medical probability, that the period of labor did not cause the ominous outcome. Even when the tracing reveals acute asphyxia, for example, it does not mean that the expert can declare with certainty that this pattern indeed reflects injury. Certain very unusual patterns permit the reasonably definitive diagnosis of acute neurologic injury. Even here, however, the patterns do not permit any quantification of the severity of injury, only that the fetus has "crossed the threshold of injury." Irrespective of the FHR pattern and the obstetrical events, other experts in pediatrics or neurology must determine the extent of the baby's handicap and the likely etiology thereof.

Current recommendations about FBS now range from "you must do it," to "you should do it," to "it is almost never indicated." The theory behind sampling the fall in pH (which is the same as a rise in the hydrogen ion or acid concentration of the blood) is a measure of the oxygen availability to the baby. In fact, it is a better indicator of oxygenation than is the oxygen tension itself. Even the most optimistic statistics about FBS are inadequate justification for the procedure. Simply stated, if you were 50% wrong in your diagnosis of fetal distress, then presumably scalp sampling would prevent 50% of Cesarean deliveries in these cases. Yet, because we do so many sections for risks < 50%, this justification seems dubious.

It is axiomatic that the standard of interpretation and the standard of care with regard to surveillance today is not the same as it was 10 or 20 years ago. Keeping abreast of current developments, providing forthright communication with the patient, manifesting compassion, and maintaining comprehensive records are always within the standard of care, and when practiced assiduously can do much to forestall any medico-legal encounter.

> **Commentary by Mr. Volk:** The standard for testimony of an expert is whether or not he/she can formulate an opinion based upon his/ her education, training, experience, and reasonable medical proba- bility. If the expert is able to give an opinion based upon all the data and the above standard, a jury will be entitled to agree with the expert. The conclusions reached in any case are based on the facts and the body of medical knowledge.

> **Rebuttal by Dr. Schifrin:** I would like to respond to a number of Mr. Volk's commentaries, and I will do so chronologically.

1. Auscultation is inaccurate, not reproducible, insensitive to variability, and misleading with respect to type and extent of decelerations. Other than the frequency of auscultation, there are no published standards on the duration of counting, the establishment of a baseline, or the re- sponse to auscultated deviations. Except for the so-called "RCT of EFM" where auscultation is used for the control group, there are no scientific studies of auscultation per se that suggest it relates to outcome in any way. Indeed, much paradoxical data exist to show that ausculta- tory evidence of fetal distress is not a risk factor for adverse outcome!

2. If you use conventional interpretations of fetal monitoring (i.e., all decelerations and all injury is related to severe fetal asphyxia), the correlation with subsequent handicap is VERY POOR. On the other hand, if you begin to use the FHR pattern intelligently, you can begin to make neurologic diagnoses, and determine the timing and mechanism of injury.

> There are many knowable causes for fetal neurologic dysfunction other than labor. The majority of babies who come to malpractice, in my experience, are injured by ischemic events prior to labor. Some of these

do result from negligent care. The fetal monitor pattern can easily exclude the time of monitoring as the time of insult if certain criteria are met. Babies with anomalies, inborn errors of metabolism, and numerous other disorders may have neurologic dysfunction unrelated to labor or obstetrical events.

3. I agree that if a baby is injured as a result of hypoxia during labor, the conduct must be scrutinized very closely. I do not agree that there is necessarily a "strong possibility that a cause of action exists." For example, ruptured uterus, prolapsed cord, ruptured vasa previa, or fetal stroke may occur so quickly that no reasonable response time would prevent the injury. On the other hand, in the absence of such catastrophic events, the likelihood of cause of action clearly increases considerably.

4. I agree that the standard of care is set at the time care is rendered and must be assessed PROSPECTIVELY. Later intelligence can be brought to bear on causation that can be assessed RETROSPECTIVELY. I hope we are all in agreement here.

5. Inaccurate interpretation of FHR monitor tracings is a fundamental issue. The health care provider is held responsible for providing a differential diagnosis for most conditions. Having provided that differential, he/she is obliged to make a reasonable response to the information that was or should have been known. In the example given, the physician must weigh the impact of each diagnosis. It is below the standard of care to choose a plan of action arbitrarily, one that fails to deal with the risks involved in each differential. In my experience this situation arises frequently when a test result is abnormal. When repeated, the test is normal. I believe that it is below the standard of care to accept the results of the second test—a third test or other means of confirmation must be obtained. The provider cannot resolve issues of significance arbitrarily when the technical means of resolution are at hand. The word "reasonable" as I mean it includes the notion of considering all the options and the consequences of those options.

6. The documentation of an incorrect interpretation is below the standard of care. As an example, with the fetal monitor in place, the nurse records "FHR 140 and strong." This is negligence even though it is recorded and the FHR is indeed 140. This is insufficient interpretation of the strip and is negligent. The reference to "strong" means that the volume of the machine was turned up.

References

1. Erkkola R, Gronroos M, Punnonen R, et al. Analysis of intrapartum fetal deaths: Their decline with increasing electronic fetal monitoring. Acta Obstet Gynecol Scand 1984;63:459.
2. Hagberg BG, Hagberg G, Zetterstrom R. Decreasing perinatal mortality—increase in cerebral palsy morbidity. Acta Paediatr Scand 1989;78:664.
3. Bhushan V, Paneth N, Kiley JL. Impact of improved survival of very low birth weight infants on recent secular trends in the prevelance of cerebral palsy. Pediatrics 1993;91:1094.
4. Vintzileos AM, Guzman E, Knuppel R, et al. Intrapartum electronic fetal heart rate monitoring versus intermittent ausculation. A meta-analysis. Obstet Gynecol (In Press).
5. Schifrin BS, Meyers S. Letter to the Editor. N Engl J Med 1990;323:346.
6. Paneth N, Bommarito M, Stricker J. Electronic fetal monitoring and later outcome. Clin Invest Med 1993;16:159.
7. Schifrin BS, Amsel J, Burdorf G. The accuracy of auscultatory detection of fetal cardiac decelerations: A computer simulation. Am J Obstet Gynecol 1992;166:566.
8. Morrison JC, Chez BF, Davis ID, et al. Intrapartum fetal heart rate assessment: Monitoring by auscultation or electronic means. Am J Obstet Gynecol 1993;168:63.
9. Miler F, Pearse K, Paul RF. Fetal heart rate pattern recognition by the method of auscultation. Obstet Gynecol 1984;64:332.
10. Nelson KB, Elenberg JH. Antecedents of cerebral palsy. Multivariate analysis of risk. N Engl J Med 1986;315:81.
11. Low JA. The role of blood gas and acidbase assessment in the diagnosis of intrapartum fetal asphyxia. Am J Obstet Gynecol 1987;159:1235.
12. De Souza SW, Richards B. Neurological sequelae in newborn babies after perinatal asphyxia. Arch Dis Child 1978;53:564.
13. Roversi GD, Cannussio V, Spennacchio M. Recognition and significance of maternogenic fetal acidosis during intensive monitoring of labor. J Perinat Med 1975;3:53.
14. Spellacy WN, Peterson PQ, Winegar A, et al. Neonatal seizures after cesarean delivery: Higher risk with labor. Am J Obstet Gynecol 1989;157:377.
15. Freeman JM, Nelson KB. Intrapartum asphyxia and cerebral palsy. Pediatrics 1988;82:240.
16. Dennis J, Chalmers I. Very early neonatal seizure rates: A possible epidemiological indicator of the quality of perinatal care. Br J Obstet Gynaecol 1982;89:418.
17. Editorial. Cerebral palsy, intrapartum care and a shot in the foot. Lancet 1989;2:1251.
18. Fee SC, Malee K, Deddish R, et al. Severe acidosis and subsequent neurologic status. Am J Obstet Gynecol 1990;162:802.
19. American College of Obstetricians and Gynecologists. ACOG Technical Bulletin, number 132, September 1989, Washington DC.
20. Bax M, Nelson KB. Birth asphyxia: A statement. Dev Med Child Neurol 1993;35:1015.
21. Visser GHA, Bekedam DJ, Ribbert LSM. Changes in antepartum heart rate patterns with progressive deterioration of the fetal condition. Int J Biomed Comput 1990;25:239.

22. Dennis J, Johnson A, Mutch L, et al. Acid-based status at birth and neurodevelopmental outcome at four and one-half years. Am J Obstet Gynecol 1989;161:213.
23. O'Brien WF, Davis SE, Grisson MP, et al. Effect of cephalic pressure on fetal cerebral blood flow. Am J Perinatol 1984;1:223.
24. Vannucci R. Mechanisms of perinatal hypoxic-ischemic brain damage. Sem Perinatol 1993;17:330.
25. Clapp JF, Peress NS, Wesley M, et al. Brain damage after intermittent partial cord occlusion in the chronically instrumented fetal lamb. Am J Obstet Gynecol 1988;159:504.
26. Brann AW, Myers RE. Central nervous system findings in the newborn monkey following severe in utero partial asphyxia. Neurology 1975;25:327.
27. Dijxhoorn MJ, Visser GH, Touwen BC, et al. Apgar score, meconium and acidaemia at birth in small-for-gestational age infants born at term, and their relation to neonatal neurological morbidity. Br J Obstet Gynaecol 1987;94:873.
28. Visser GH, Mulder EJ, Stevens H, et al. Heart rate variation during fetal behavioural states 1 and 2. Early Hum Dev 1993;34:21.
29. Smith CV, Phelan JP, Paul RA. A prospective analysis of the influence of gestational age on the baseline fetal heart rate and reactivity in a low risk population. Am J Obstet Gynecol 1984;153:780.
30. Vintzileos AM, Campbell W, Dreiss RJ, et al. Intrapartum fetal heart rate monitoring of the extremely premature fetus. Am J Obstet Gynecol 1985;151:744.
31. Zalar RW Jr, Quilligan EJ. The influence of scalp sampling on the cesarean section rate for fetal distress. Am J Obstet Gynecol 1979;135:239.
32. Paul RH, Suidan AK, Yeh S, et al. Clinical fetal monitoring. VII. The evaluation and significance of intrapartum baseline FHR variability. Am J Obstet Gynecol 1975;123:206.
33. Phelan JP, Ahn MO. Perinatal observations in forty-eight neurologically impaired term infants. Am J Obstet Gynecol 1994;171:424.
34. Schifrin BS, Rubenstein B, Shields JR. Fetal heart rate patterns and the timing of fetal injury. J Perinatol 1994;14:174.
35. Horimoto N, Koyanagi T, Maeda H, et al. Can brain impairment be detected by in utero behavioural patterns? Arch Dis Child 1993;69:3.
36. Gray PH, Tudehope DI, Masel JP, et al. Perinatal hypoxic-ischemic brain injury: Prediction of outcome. Dev Med Child Neurol 1993;35:965.
37. Shields JR, Schifrin BS. Perinatal antecedents of cerebral palsy. Obstet Gynecol 1988;71:899.
38. Keegan KA, Waffarn F, Quilligan EJ. Obstetric characteristics and fetal heart rate patterns of infants who convulse during the newborn period. Am J Obstet Gynecol 1985;153:732.
39. Bekedam DJ, Visser GH, Mulder EJ, et al. Heart rate variation and movement incidence in growth-retarded fetuses: The significance of antenatal late heart rate decelerations. Am J Obstet Gynecol 1987;157:126.
40. Adams RD, Prod'hom LS, Rabinowicz TH. Intrauterine brain death. Acta Neuropathol 1977;40:41.
41. Nijhuis JG, Crevels AJ, van Dongen PW. Fetal brain death: The definition of a fetal heart rate pattern and its clinical consequences. Obstet Gynecol Surv 1990;45:229.
42. Asakura H, Schifrin BS, Myers, S. Intrapartum, atraumatic, non-asphyxial intracranial hemorrhage in a full term infant. Obstet Gynecol 1994;84:680.

Chapter 12

Electronic Fetal Monitoring: Role of the Nurse

◆◆◆

Michelle L. Murray, Ph.D., R.N.C.

Introduction

During labor, electronic fetal monitoring (EFM) has become a standard part of the overall supervision of labor. Fetal monitoring is used to establish fetal well being and to identify the fetus at risk for asphyxia and other abnormalities including death.[1,2] Fetal monitoring also provides an objective measure of uterine activity and the fetal response thereto.

By custom and regulation, obstetrical nurses function as "care givers of superior knowledge and skill." They are required to do more than just inform physicians and follow orders[3]; they are not the physician's handmaidens. They are expected to perform in a prudent, reasonable manner as a collaborative member of the obstetrical health care team. Because they are frequently the first health care provider to see the obstetrical patient in labor, often in the absence of the physician or certified nurse midwife, the care and understanding they provide may play a crucial role in the outcome.

EFM responsibility is only one part of the manifold roles nurses play in patient care, including education, evaluation, etc. Nurses collaborate with health care colleagues, assess human responses to health and illness, formulate nursing diagnoses, explicate nursing interventions, and direct and evaluate nursing practice. Those who evaluate the tracing share the responsibility to appropriately gather additional data.

This chapter examines general and specific roles and responsibilities of nurses who use fetal monitors. It emphasizes the critical role of communication between nurses and other health care professionals and with the medical

From: Donn SM, Fisher CW (eds.): *Risk Management Techniques in Perinatal and Neonatal Practice.* © Futura Publishing Co., Inc., Armonk, NY, 1996.

record. It further focuses on the role of timely monitoring, proper assessment, and interventions in the promotion of proper health care and in the avoidance of lawsuits.

The Nurse's Role in General

Fetal monitors began to appear in medical facilities across the country in the early 1970s. To apply these devices it was necessary for nurses and physicians to obtain specialized knowledge and skills based on newly understood physiologic principles. It was also necessary to define standards of practice for both physicians and nurses to describe responsibilities that reflected values and priorities. In addition, it was necessary to promulgate a framework for the evaluation of these standard practices.[4] There has been a proliferation of "standards" or "guidelines," both local and national, that are sometimes incompatible. It is important, nevertheless, that these policies, procedures, and protocols be written to delineate the roles and responsibilities of nurses and other health care providers. Policies should set limits, expectations for consultation, documentation requirements, and outline conflict resolution procedures.[5] Where controversies are known to exist they should be addressed. The purpose of the guidelines are to help establish the "standard of care."

> **Commentary by Mr. Volk:** It has been my experience, practicing mainly in the southwestern part of the United States, that *written* policies, protocols, and guidelines are few and far between to delineate the responsibilities, etc., between nursing staff and the physicians. The lack of written guidelines, policies, and the like do much to retard the defense of a nurse in a case. There is often testimony about what is usually done, but it is somewhat vague. The failure to set out written policies clearly causes confusion among the health care providers, usually to the detriment of the defense of the nursing staff. It is unclear why a hospital would not have written policies— it may be from a desire to keep the practice at the hospital between the nursing staff and physicians vague out of a perception that doing so will assist in the defense of a case.

The Standard of Care

Both the Association of Women's Health, Obstetric, and Neonatal Nursing (AWHONN) and the American College of Obstetricians and Gynecologists (ACOG) recognize the nurses' and physicians' responsibilities in relation to fetal monitoring: "Nurses and physicians who perform fetal monitoring are responsible for their actions and will be held to the established standards of care as defined by their professional organization, the standards of practice in their hospitals, and the laws governing practice in their respective states."[6]

In order to demonstrate that the standard of practice was met in relation to assessment of the fetal heart rate (FHR), ACOG has identified the following assessment and documentation guidelines when risk factors are present during labor or when intensified monitoring is elected:

1. Intermittent auscultation, performed at least every 15 minutes (and recorded at least every 15 minutes). Auscultation is best done immediately following a uterine contraction.
2. Continuous electronic fetal heart rate monitoring, with or without external or internal uterine contraction monitoring. Heart rate patterns should be evaluated at least every 15 minutes.[7]

Since there were no data to demonstrate optimal time intervals for intermittent auscultation in low-risk patients, the ACOG standard is to evaluate and record the FHR following a contraction at least every 30 minutes.

The failure to apply the fetal monitor does not contradict current preaching on the standard of care, but recognition must be paid to the pitfalls of failing to monitor, nonetheless. According to the *Guidelines for Perinatal Care*, Third edition:

> When electronic fetal heart monitoring is selected as the mode of fetal assessment, the physician and obstetric personnel attending the patient should be qualified to identify and interpret abnormalities. It is appropriate for physicians and nurses to use the descriptive terms that have been given to fetal monitoring patterns (e.g., accelerations and early, late, or variable decelerations) in chart documentation and verbal communication.[8]

The nurse must communicate information on EFM tracings, either antepartal or intrapartum, to the primary health care provider in a timely manner in accordance with institutional policy.[6] "The physician who is responsible for the patient's care should be kept informed of her progress and notified immediately of any abnormality. He or she should be readily available when the patient is in the active phase of labor." In other words, when the nurse calls the physician it is expected that the physician will be on the unit within a very short period of time.[8]

Commentary by Mr. Volk: There is much testimony about this precise issue in an obstetrical malpractice case. The crucial questions in the claim against the hospital are often whether or not the nursing staff timely and properly informed the physician of the progress of labor and timely and properly advised of any abnormalities, including an abnormal labor pattern, lack of progression, length of second stage, failure of the fetus to descend, and the like. On countless occasions in my practice, the delivering doctor has testified that the nurse in charge of the patient failed to do so and squarely put liability on the hospital.

Communication

Problems of communication abound in regard to EFM. In obstetrics, a feeling of urgency (sometimes expressed as anger or panic) about the pattern may arise, while at the same time there may lack a common terminology to describe it further. Afraid of calling in the physician unnecessarily further limits communication. When a nurse perceives impending or imminent danger to the patient, it might be difficult to communicate clearly or completely, especially if help is not readily available. As computers become an integral part of the hospital setting, protocols will need to reflect computer-mediated communication, e.g., the exchange of information via electronic mail, computer conferencing, and bulletin board systems.

For nurses to feel safe communicating in a timely manner, they must be empowered, encouraged, and supported by their hospital administrators and physicians to promptly notify physicians when abnormal patterns, abnormal findings, or meconium are noted, even during the wee hours of the morning. Once the nurse determines that the physician is needed on the unit and calls, it is important to ascertain how long it will take the physician to appear.

If the physician refuses to come to the hospital, the nurse should discuss the reasons for the refusal. If the nurse still feels the physician should be present on the unit, and the physician again refuses, it is the nurse's duty to safeguard the health and safety of the client. In order to safeguard the health and safety of the fetus and mother, the nurse may again ask the physician to come to the hospital or ask which physician should be called to come in his place.

The physician should be sensitive to the extraordinary role played by the nurse's unique circumstances and should ask the nurse to briefly describe the situation and determine what measures are currently being undertaken. Then, an appropriate plan of care should be determined until the physician arrives at the hospital. The oncoming nurse should review the tracing with the reporting nurse.

Reports to other nurses or the physician should also include observations and events that precipitated interventions, actions taken, and the maternal and fetal responses to those actions. Response to epidural anesthesia, vaginal examination, pushing, loss of variability with pushing, etc., must all be elucidated. The quality of communication and documentation will determine how much of the responsibility of patient care, and thus the liability for that care, will be shared by the nurse and other health care providers. In addition, the patient and her family should be taught about the fetal monitor and its use.[9]

Communication of the FHR pattern is hindered when the communication is only verbal and the message transmitter and receiver use different terminology to describe the same image. For example, type 1 and type 2 decelerations are now called early and late decelerations. If the physician's or the nurse's terminology is antiquated, a barrier to conveying meaning exists. Modern communications resources can immediately transmit the tracing in question to any location. Thus, if a facsimile machine or computer modem is available, the physician or consultant may view the monitor strip simultaneously with the nurse.

> **Commentary by Mr. Volk:** The advice as to what the standard should be in this section is clearly correct. However, many nurses do not utilize these practices to safeguard fetus and mother. So many nurses do not do so because they perceive that the hospital does not want them to antagonize the physician. For instance, many hospitals I have litigated against have an unwritten policy that the nurse not document the actual conversation with a physician, although the nursing standards require that proper documentation of all significant events be recorded in the chart. The physicians complain when the nursing staff document those late night or less than pleasant conversations. The physicians are the ones with the power because they bring revenue into the hospital. Nurses are often intimidated by the physician and hospital administration and fail to do what is right for the patient. To allow oneself to be intimidated to the detriment of the patient is clearly below the standard. Nurses are equal care givers, and although they may not be as highly trained as the physician, they must give their best for the patient. So many cases I have litigated result from the failure of the nurse to put the patient's best interests first.

Pitfalls in Interpretation of Fetal Heart Rate Patterns

Utilization of EFM for patient care, as well as the defense of malpractice cases, is plagued by questions of agreement on interpretation and the value of monitoring. Judgments vary within and among interpreters of FHR patterns—even so-called "experts." Each interpreter has a different educational background and different learning experiences related to fetal monitoring. As a result, there has been wide variation in interpretation between experienced obstetricians and experienced nurses.[10-15] When five perinatologists reviewed the same 50 tracings from nonstress tests (NSTs) on two occasions, they only classified 11 tracings the same on both readings. Overall, they agreed between themselves (interobserver agreement) 41% of the time and agreed with themselves (intraobserver agreement) 55% of the time.[16] Problems of reproducibility plague not only the NST but the contraction stress test (CST) and intrapartum interpretation as well. Even uterine activity is subject to considerable variation, especially if the external tocodynamometer is used.

The implementation of scoring systems in the 1970s and 1980s for analyzing fetal monitor tracings did not greatly enhance consistency. For example, Trimbos and Keirse[15] found that using a scoring system had advantages over subjective assessments, especially in the interpretation of the baseline FHR. Yet, the assessment of accelerations was very unreliable. In addition, the greater the number of people reviewing a tracing and the greater the number of endpoints being evaluated, the greater was the disagreement. Lotgering et al.[14] tested three rating systems to evaluate tracings and found a low level of agreement between observers for all three systems. Beaulieu et al.[10] found that five physicians agreed on only 29% of the classification of the tracings.

The NST is the most widely used screening test of fetal well being.[17] In one large study, 16% of nurses labeled one NST tracing as reactive, indicating fetal well being, when it was not.[11] The number of features in the classification also plays a role. The interobserver agreement of nurses was as high as 98% when a two-point scale (reactive or nonreactive was used). This rate of agreement dropped when a three-point or a five-point scale was used.[13] Additionally, whether one's title is physician or nurse does not confer any greater accuracy. Murray[18] has shown that both nurses and physicians have difficulty in reaching consensus when reading the same fetal monitor tracings.

Cohen et al.[12] concluded that the uniformity of opinion may be neither reasonable nor attainable. Redman[19] concluded that intrapartum FHR records cannot be interpreted reliably by the human eye and suggested that fetal monitoring during labor was of uncertain clinical value. There is universal agreement that interpretation ability requires adequate training, along with a consideration of gestational age, maternal condition, and medications. There is considerable debate about the value of pH analysis in assessments of the fetal condition,[20] and its use seems to be declining.

To reduce this lack of agreement, several researchers have developed and tested computer software interpretation systems for antepartal test analyses.[21-25] Computer software programs such as the Porto system[®] (University of Porto, Porto, Portugal),[26] the Sonicaid 8000[®] (Oxford Sonicaid, Chichester, UK),[27] and Foetos[®] exist to provide objective evaluation of antepartal or intrapartal FHR tracings. Devoe[28] identified benefits and limitations of these computerized systems. On the positive side, the algorithm used for baseline determination is objective and consistent; serial tracings can be compared and archived, and an online record of approximately 1 year's worth of testing data can be maintained in a compact, economical format. On the limitation side, computerized systems are still experimental. Sometimes, the computer finds the tracing to be abnormal when the visual analysis was normal; false positives have been found 13% of the time.[29] In addition, there has yet to be a final determination of the legal status of computer-archived FHR records.

> **Commentary by Mr. Volk:** What we are really talking about when we talk about the legal status of computer-archived FHR records is whether or not a particular archive has been given the stamp of standard of care approval. If the utilization of a certain archive is approved by an organization such as ACOG, then you would have an argument that the interpretation sets the standard for interpretation of a certain pattern.

The analysis of FHR recordings has been limited to numeric analysis with limited suggestions for actions. Some feel the visual and automated methods of assessment should be used as complementary rather than alternative techniques,[30] but until the obstetric community as a whole has reached consensus on the parameters selected for analysis, computer analysis will remain experimental.

From a medico-legal standpoint, the considerable intra- and interobserver variation and even the discussions about the value of EFM (and the pitfalls in interpreting these statistics) have little impact on the individual case. Simply stated, if the device has merit and can be interpreted reasonably and logically (if not infallibly), then it should be used. If it cannot meet these criteria it must be abandoned. There is no logical premise in using something that cannot be interpreted and is potentially harmful. Accordingly, in malpractice cases, differences in opinion about the tracing rarely achieve major significance. Being appropriate and manifesting concern for the patient override the need for sophisticated interpretation.

> **Commentary by Mr. Volk:** I agree with the following caveat: there may be differences in opinion about the interpretation during the litigation; however, often the positions taken by defendant doctors and nurses are not reasonable. In other words, the testimony attempts to retrospectively analyze a pattern as benign but the interpretation is not reasonable and everyone knows it. Therefore, in the final analysis any differences are not of major significance. If there is a question as to the health of the fetus, timely and proper evaluations must be performed.

Education to Minimize Misinterpretation

In 1986, NAACOG (now AWHONN) recommended that "competency in electronic fetal monitoring should be documented in writing before the nurse functions independently on the intrapartum unit."[31] It was also written that "maintaining the quality of individual practice...remains inherent in the responsibilities of the professional nurse.'[31] Thus, both the institution and nurse share the responsibility for the quality of fetal monitoring interpretation ability and practice. One area of competency rarely dealt with is the ongoing review of critical cases in the hospital. Under these circumstances, where most training is obtained from outside the institution, there may be no readily available sources to review a case even after the outcome is known.

McRae[32] feels that "the lack of attention paid to proficiency in EFM is alarming" and in inexperienced or uneducated hands, EFM becomes a liability. She also believes that hospitals must have the following in place: documentation of orientation programs for newly-hired staff; documentation of competencies and how these are taught, measured, and maintained; a policy regarding the nurse's role in intrapartum care; and criteria for documentation in the medical record and on the EFM tracing.[32]

> **Commentary by Mr. Volk:** In my experience in the Southwest, it is very unusual for a hospital to have these programs in place. I do not know the reason for this since they obviously would help in maintaining the nursing staff at the standard of care.

Educators of nurses and physicians have a responsibility to "maintain optimal standards of nursing practice and education" and to uphold and support the current standards of practice and to teach these in their classes.[33] Their personal beliefs should not be conveyed to students if they contradict standards, as this could confuse the learner, create misconceptions, and compromise patient care. There is also the need to overcome the misperceptions that abound about monitoring—not only among health care providers—but among patients as well. It is not uncommon to find negative attitudes towards EFM among childbirth educators.

Educational program designers and certification examination writers can identify content areas from standards. For many nurses and physicians, there may be a lack of knowledge of fetal monitoring concepts, partly stemming from a lack of educational opportunities or evaluation of learning. According to Lavoir,[34] traditional teaching methods do not effectively change misconceptions. In order to "unteach" the misconception, a think-aloud interview should be used to identify erroneous problem solving misconceptions. Then, instruction should include a simple to complex approach and provide opportunities for systematic review of tracings or interpretation practice. Even if educational opportunities are offered, learning conditions, such as poor visual media, may prevent the learner from learning. Course content may be limited or the instructor may have misconceptions that are conveyed to the learner.

Instructors of fetal monitoring vary in their qualifications to teach and their ability to interpret FHR patterns. Many physicians and nurses teach fetal monitoring but have received no graduate education or teaching credentials to do so. As a result, basic fetal monitoring classes vary from institution to institution in their content and quality.

Basic fetal monitoring courses should include the rules of recognition for the concepts of baseline, accelerations, and decelerations. For example, to recognize the baseline, one must be taught the concepts of range, stability, and variability (short-term and long-term). To recognize accelerations and decelerations, one must be taught shape of configuration of the two types of accelerations (spontaneous and uniform), and shape or configuration and timing in relation to contractions of the four basic types of decelerations (early, late, variable, and prolonged). These features, however, must be put into a physiologic context.

AWHONN documents provide topics for course content.[6,35] In addition, to enhance prototype development, matched examples and non-examples should be presented to learners. Learners should be shown more than five examples of each concept and should be asked questions when shown examples and non-examples of concepts.[36] Ultimately, copies of the tracings reviewed in the class should be distributed to the students.

Basic classes should be standardized for all nurses and physicians who interpret FHR tracings. Utilization of computer-assisted instructional programs such as Fetal Monitor Interpretation Version 2.0[R] by Catanzarite and Murray (Williams and Wilkins, Baltimore, MD, USA) can be used to standardize instruction. If all health care providers at the institution who interpret tracings attend the same basic EFM education program, they should develop similar prototypes of FHR images and use similar terminology in their daily communications. Improved communication of FHR images should ultimately improve interpretation agreement and patient care as well as rapprochement between nurses and physicians.

Because there are various schools of thought regarding the significance of certain FHR patterns, controversial topics should be taught and discussed with the experienced nurse or physician who has mastered the basic concepts in order to avoid the development of misconceptions. Examples of controversies include: the assessment of short-term variability with an external monitor; the definition of an acceleration and reactivity; typical versus atypical variable decelerations; periodic versus non-periodic as adjectives that describe patterns of accelerations and decelerations; and the use of the terminology mild, moderate, and severe variable decelerations. Other controversies include using the labels variable deceleration with a "late component" and "late/variable" decelerations.

Misconceptions abound concerning late decelerations. For example, many nurses report that they have been told that late decelerations do not exist if there are accelerations on the tracing, or that late decelerations do not fall below 100 bpm. Late decelerations do indeed appear in the presence of accelerations (the fetus is not yet metabolically acidotic), and late decelerations can be very deep, even falling below 70 bpm.[37] By teaching the critical characteristics of accelerations and decelerations, and emphasizing signs of fetal well being and compromise, confusion and controversy can be diminished.

Documentation

The primary purpose of the medical record is to disseminate information between personnel. Blackwell states "one of the most important tasks of a nurse is providing an accurate account of all events related to the care and hospitalization of the patient."[38] Documentation promotes continuity of care and should be concise yet comprehensive as well as impartial. It is also a defense tool and a legal instrument.[38,39] While some feel that the saying "not documented, not done" is a legal standard[40] (it is not!), the absence of documentation requires greater explanation and places greater burdens on the defense.

> **Commentary by Mr. Volk:** The problem the defense has when there is a failure to document is three-fold: 1. there is always testimony that the standard requires, and the health care providers are taught, that all significant events must be properly documented in the chart; 2. without documentation, the argument can be made, and it is a logical one, that the witness is now "supplying" testimony that is favorable to the doctor or hospital—there is no independent support for the testimony; and 3. where the medical care necessarily occurred in the past (months or even years before the testimony) and there is no documentation, how can these events be accurately recalled? If there is no documentation, how can the witness accurately recall these events? If they were not important enough to document, or if the witness did not realize their importance at the time, how can they accurately remember what occurred now?

It has been recommended that nurses treat flow sheets seriously. Flow sheets must be consistent with narrative notes. Yet, nurses should not depend too heavily on flow sheets, as they also need to record the patient's response to care, so that a progressive picture of the patient's status is evident.[41] The most thoughtful way to deal with departure from the flow sheet (for either nurse or physician) is to document that in this particular respect, the flow sheet, guideline, etc., does not apply, and medical reasons justify the modification in care.

Those who write in the medical record are responsible for what information they put in the record and for the care with which the record is maintained, safe-guarded, and disclosed. Specifically, health care providers are liable for complete records, the loss of records, improper disclosure on the record, and illegibility.[42]

The American Nurses' Association has identified requisites for documentation in *Standards of Clinical Nursing Practice*.[43] The following should be documented: relevant health data; diagnoses; the plan of care; interventions; and any subsequent revisions in diagnoses, outcomes, and the plan of care. Each and every significant event, each major task, information essential to the treatment of the patient, patient reactions and responses to care, and the nurse's actions that have occurred during the time the nurse was caring for the patient should be accounted for in the notes.[38]

> **Commentary by Mr. Volk:** What is set out as the requirements for documentation by the American Nurses' Association proves the point in my above comment. A nurse who does not document in this manner has not met the standard and is subject to the argument that "not documented, not done."

Verbal and telephone orders should be clearly written. Late entries are acceptable, and should be dated and timed, but it is far better to document contemporaneously rather than to wait and document later.

> **Commentary by Mr. Volk:** Late entries made after a catastrophe are subject to intensive cross-examination. A health care provider who waits to document crucial events well after the fact is in trouble. I have litigated cases where the late entries are hours or even 1-2 days after the events. I have even examined nurses at trial or deposition who testified that the late entries were made at the risk manager's office and at his/her suggestion! We are not talking about an entry that is made shortly after an event, although the much better practice is to document contemporaneously.

Documenting the nurses' notes reflects the care provided and will be judged against the standards of practice at the time. The medical record reflects the nurse's observations, assessments, and specific actions taken when changes in the FHR pattern or uterine activity are observed. To promote clear written communication between health care providers, documentation should be neat, orderly, legible, well organized, and thorough. Notes should be factual and objective, specific with the times that assessments or observations were made, as well as actions. Words should be spelled correctly. Only acceptable abbreviations should be used. Failure to document may be criticized by the Joint Commission on the Accreditation of Healthcare Organizations, as its standards require that nursing assessments, patient needs, interventions, outcomes of care, and discharge planning are in the patient's record.

Documentation Specific to Fetal Monitoring

The FHR tracing is a legal document that sometimes represents the most crucial evidence in an obstetrical malpractice case.[44] ACOG suggested that during delivery, notations could be made on the tracing at least every 15 minutes.[7] However, sometimes the tracing is lost.[32] If notations are not duplicated in the record as well, these will also be lost. Documenting in the nurses' notes is more important than documenting on the tracing, as tracings are more likely to be lost than the hospital record.

> **Commentary by Mr. Volk:** It is just as inexcusable to have lost the FHR tracing as it is to lose any part of the medical record. A case where the record, or part of it, is "lost" is extremely difficult to defend. When a record is "lost" the patient and the family may be the only persons to remember the events, because the health care providers do not usually have recall of the specific events.

Nurses should, therefore, be discouraged from charting entirely on the fetal monitor tracing during labor, then transferring these notations to the nurses' notes after delivery. Initialing the monitor tracing to "prove you were in the room" merely reflects the health care provider's initials. Initials do not reflect appropriate interpretation of the tracing nor that the standard of care was met. Therefore, if one initials the tracing, there should also be evidence in the notes that the tracing was interpreted and that appropriate actions were taken in response to the FHR pattern and/or uterine activity.

It is essential that the nurse record assessments, actions, patient responses, and communications at or near the time they occur. This reflects the quality of care rendered to the patient and must appear in the medical record or chart.

Because tracings are lost, a systematic review of the FHR pattern should be documented so that the tracing could be reproduced at a future date. In some cases, the tracing can be archived on a disk so that the likelihood of its disappearance diminishes. In those instances it is important to continue to annotate the medical record with reasonable interpretations of the EFM strip. "Regardless of which antepartum surveillance test is used, a documented, official interpretation should be placed in the patient's chart" and the FHR tracing and recommended plan for subsequent action should be noted and maintained.[8] This interpretation may be made by nurses or physicians, but the hospital policy or procedure should specify who makes the official interpretation.

Typical Claims Related to Fetal Monitoring

There are too few data on the role of EFM in malpractice suits. The role they play is probably significant. Although technology (durable precautions) increases the number of negligence claims, most of the claims in obstetrics continue to focus on nondurable precautions (actions of health care providers).[45] In 1986 and 1987, erroneous interpretation or a delay or failure to diagnose "fetal distress" during labor were alleged in 17%-24% of obstetric claims.[46,47] One ACOG study in 1988 found that EFM played a significant role in 45.8% of medical malpractice cases.[48]

> **Commentary by Mr. Volk:** There is no question that EFM plays a significant role in claims in my practice. It is impossible to exactly quantify the number of claims nationwide that EFM plays a part in because no study includes all claims for a given period. There is no way to prove that technology per se increases the number of claims.

Failure to Apply the Fetal Monitor

Numerous cases have alleged this failure but the track record of the various courts in this regard is inconsistent and rarely depends solely on the failure to monitor.

> **Commentary by Mr. Volk:** It is impossible to state that courts are inconsistent on this matter because it is impossible to know what all the courts are doing on a given matter at any one time. We can say that 1, or 2, or 12, etc., verdicts are inconsistent with each other, but there are so many factors peculiar to a case that make this inquiry truly impossible. There are cases in my practice wherein I have alleged that there was a failure to apply the monitor. There may have been broken monitors where the hospital did not have them timely repaired, or just a lack of utilizing the monitor on a high-risk pregnancy, etc.

As an example of a violation of a durable precaution, failure to monitor the FHR during a 1977 delivery was blamed for the child's brain damage (Kings County Supreme Court, Index No. 23944/87 Michael DeJesus vs Brooklyn Jewish Hospital and Kasturi Chawla, M.D.). A defense verdict was returned. In another case, the plaintiff claimed failure to perform a Cesarean section led to her child's mental retardation and cerebral palsy. She also claimed emotional distress. The obstetrician settled for $956,000 prior to trial. The verdict award was $49.2 million with a present value of $10.2 million. This included $100,000 for emotional distress.[49]

Failure to Recognize Abnormal Patterns

It is expected that physicians and nurses who use fetal monitors have the ability to recognize FHR components and categorize the pattern on a continuum from normal to abnormal. Failure to recognize abnormal patterns is most likely a result of inadequate training, inadequate learning, and a lack of FHR pattern exposure or experiences. Although it receives inadequate attention, the problem of too hasty intervention because of overinterpretation of the tracing can be linked to improper use of forceps, etc. EFM seminars and on the job training, inservices, and case reviews with a process of performance evaluation and feedback should increase the knowledge of health care providers who use fetal monitors, decrease erroneous interpretations, and potentially reduce obstetric claims.

When patient injury has occurred, there may be an attempt by the plaintiff attorney to attribute the lack of appropriate medical or nursing actions on the institution's failure to provide training and to assure nurse competence. Plaintiff attorneys continue to attribute their client's brain damage to the lack of nursing or medical care or the lack of fetal monitoring interpretation ability. For example, in Case No. 90L-20183 from Cook County (IL) Circuit Court, it was alleged that there was a failure to recognize placental abruption from either the change in uterine activity, the change in the FHR pattern, or the patient's complaints of pain.[49] In another case No. GCG 90-261 filed in Polk County (FL) Circuit Court, it was alleged that there was a failure to monitor and promptly diagnose fetal distress, and that was blamed for the child's cerebral palsy. In that case, a defense verdict was returned.[49]

The responsibility of nurses to interpret the FHR pattern correctly might be the focus of questions in a deposition. Such questions might include:

1. "What training have you had for the reading of monitor strips?"
2. "How many hours of training was it?"
3. "How many hours a day?"
4. "What year did you take this training?"
5. "After that time did you have any additional training in monitor reading?"
6. "Do you know whether or not you attended one of these workshops before the time of plaintiff's delivery?"
7. "What requirements were there at your hospital as far as being certified for monitors?"

8. "Did you have a requirement for a review course every 2 years on monitoring?"
9. "What resources do you have for reviewing FHR patterns, even after the case is over?"

Failure to Appropriately Respond to Abnormal Patterns

Beyond the recognition of normal and abnormal FHR patterns or nonreassuring characteristics and normal and abnormal uterine activity, nurses must also be able to promptly initiate appropriate interventions.[31] Even if the nurse recognizes the abnormal pattern, she may fail to respond properly to that pattern. In addition, if the nurse responds, she may still be questioned regarding the response in order to determine her knowledge base, level of concern, or if the fetal status and follow-up actions were reported in a timely manner. For example, it might be asked in deposition:

1. "What, if anything, do accelerations indicate on the monitor strip?"
2. "Did you consider the late decelerations to be worrisome for this patient?"
3. "Once the nurse midwife is alerted to a change in the monitoring strip, what do you understand to be your responsibility with regard to patient management?"

Each aspect of the nursing response could be examined to determine if indeed the nurse met the standards of practice and what barriers, if any, prevented the nurse from meeting those standards. For example, if inadequate staffing is suspected, the nurse might be asked by the plaintiff attorney, "What was the process as far as nurse assignments on your shift on that night?" Another question that might be asked to determine who should be told regarding the abnormal pattern is, "Are you able to explain to me the procedure by which a patient is assigned a nurse midwife as opposed to a staff physician?"

Figure 1 is a decision and action process flow chart that indicates the knowledge required to identify basic pattern components that must be identified (novice level) to interpret the FHR pattern and intervene appropriately (expert level).

Failure to Activate the Chain of Command

If the physician does not respond to a call to come to the hospital and cannot send a physician in his place, the nurse must escalate her concerns over the midwife or physician to her immediate nursing supervisor, i.e., the nurse must activate the chain of command so that the patient receives timely

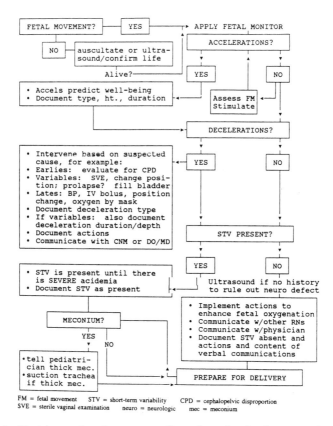

Figure 1. Decision and action process flow chart for the interpretation of FHR patterns and the appropriate intervention.

medical attention.[32] Similarly, if the nurse is asked to comply with an order that she considers inappropriate, she must invoke the chain of command. In the case of a 26-year-old women in her 30th week of pregnancy who reported nausea, vomiting, and abdominal pain, who was not in labor, the nurse called the obstetrician. Antibiotics were ordered for a suspected urinary tract infection, and the nurse was told to discharge the patient. The nurse expressed her concern about the patient's pain, but the doctor ordered morphine and re-stated the order to discharge the patient. The nursing supervisor was notified, but even after requested to do so, the resident and attending physician would not examine the patient. The nurse then discharged the patient. The patient died. The case went to trial. The jury found that giving morphine and discharging the patient, without a physician's evaluation, was below the standard of care. The hospital attorney claimed the nurses had followed the chain of command. The $1.6 million verdict was 65% against the physician and 35% against the hospital. The appeals court upheld the jury verdict and said the nurse and her supervisor had an independent duty to ensure that the patient was properly assessed and to prevent her discharge. Since they had not followed through (such as taking their concerns to the chief of medical services or the president of the hospital), they were still found negligent in their duty.[50]

Therefore, it is very important that nurses be reminded of their duty and supported to act as advocates to safeguard their clients when health care and safety are affected by the lack of medical attention or the incompetent, unethical, or illegal practice of any person.[33,43] The bedside nurse's chain of command is multi-pronged and includes the charge nurse, supervisor, department manager, vice president of nursing, chief executive officer of the hospital, the CNM, resident(s), attending physician, chief of obstetrics, and the chief of medicine. Notification of personnel to obtain appropriate patient care could delay a timely and necessary intervention and even precede patient injury. By empowering and trusting the bedside nurse to make appropriate patient care decisions, the need to activate the chain of command should diminish. All such actions should be accompanied by a complete and factual occurrence report that should be sent to the risk management department. Vague statements should be avoided and a step-by-step account with relevant events and explanations should be included.[51]

Nurses may be asked questions in deposition to determine how well they understood or utilized their chain of command. One such question is, "If you had a concern or a disagreement with the management of the patient, to whom would you go?" Once determining to whom the nurse would "go," the follow-up question might be, "At any time on that shift did you consult (that person) with regard to the management of the patient's care?"

It is natural and commonplace for nurses to attempt to protect the non-responsive physician by either failing to record the notification or the lack of expected appearance. These understandable interactions are unfortunately counterproductive in the long run for the hospital, the nurse, and the physician. Ultimately, it will be the nurse's competence that will receive the greatest scrutiny. For example, the nurse calls a physician at home to tell him about her concern about the late decelerations on the fetal monitor and her desire to have the physician attend the patient directly. The physician dismisses the information and the request with the comment to "call if the pattern gets worse." The nurse records none of this exchange or even the fact of the call. Assuming an adverse outcome and a lawsuit, the opposing lawyer may ask, "Nurse, did you interpret the monitor strip as abnormal?" If she interpreted the strip as abnormal, then there is universal agreement that failure to call the physician is below the standard of care. If she did not interpret the strip as abnormal, then she is negligent in her interpretation of the strip and, therefore, primarily responsible for the injury to the fetus. Furthermore, the hospital will be at risk for failing to insist that its nurses be competently trained. The physician may be questioned on why he did not report the nurse to the hospital administration for the manifest failure to interpret the record properly. The jury may get the notion that nobody cared about the patient, and the size of the award escalates. Attempting to protect the absent physician is counterproductive.

> **Commentary by Mr. Volk:** The author of this chapter has made important comments dealing with the nursing staff of the hospital doing the right thing for the patient. As an aside, it is also the right thing for the defense of a case and is clearly in the hospital's best interests. A nurse has an obligation to properly document the events of a patient's care, including the failure of a physician to respond. A nurse should use the chain of command to make known the failure to respond. The important thing is that these actions are the best thing for the patient. A nurse who does not properly document, advise the physician that the patient needs to be seen and failing that, use the chain of command, has exposed herself/himself and the hospital to liability. Too often, a nurse does not do what needs to be done out of a sense of loyalty to or intimidation by the physician and the hospital and worry over personal consequences. Hospitals should commend nurses for being advocates for the patients.

Additional Nursing Issues

ACOG standards seem to require that only the FHR be recorded. Nevertheless, with a monitor in place, a more thorough assessment would seem to be needed. This should include:

1. baseline—range, stability, variability (long- and short-term);
2. acceleration types, including amplitude and duration of the largest acceleration;
3. deceleration types, including depth, duration, time to recovery, completeness of recovery (e.g., resumption of previously normal rate and variability);
4. contractions—frequency, duration, intensity (peak pressure), tone (resting pressure between contractions);
5. actions taken;
6. maternal and fetal response to actions, and;

7. communication(s).[7]

Signs of fetal well being should be assessed and documented if they are present, i.e., accelerations, short-term variability, fetal movements, and the presence of clear, non-foul smelling amniotic fluid. If accelerations are not present, an attempt to elicit an acceleration could be made, for example, by stimulating the fetal scalp (scalp stimulation) or by use of an acoustic stimulator. Or, the physician may elect to evaluate the fetal scalp pH.

The FHR should also be evaluated immediately after spontaneous or artificial rupture of membranes. In addition, the amount, color, and odor of the amniotic fluid should be recorded.[7] If meconium is present in the amniotic fluid, "careful" monitoring should be initiated. This could be interpreted to suggest that in the presence of meconium, the FHR should be recorded at least every 15 minutes but not necessarily with a spiral electrode.

If signs of hypoxia or fetal compromise exist, such as late decelerations, the nurse should identify, document, and communicate the FHR pattern. The nurse's label or categorization of the deceleration should be based on specific criteria for onset, offset, and nadir (lowest point) of the deceleration in relation to the peak of the contraction. For example, late decelerations always begin after the contraction begins, their nadir is past the peak of the contraction, and they recover after the contraction ends. Late decelerations tend to have similar shapes from one to another. However, late decelerations may not appear to reach baseline after the contraction ends when a tocotransducer (external monitor) is in place. This is because a patient may push out her abdomen in response to pain, even when the contraction has ceased. The critical attributes, therefore, that assist the reviewer in distinguishing late decelerations from variable decelerations are the gradual onset versus abrupt onset, the nadir after the contraction peak versus over the peak of the contraction, and the similar versus varying appearance of one late deceleration to the next.

The nurse's designation of the deceleration pattern may conflict with the interpretation of others, who may see variable decelerations, and vice versa. If the deceleration(s) reflect a fetal hypoxic stress response, the patient care goal is the same: improve oxygen delivery to the fetus. Therefore, it is inappropriate to delay intervention in order to argue over the name of the deceleration or the deceleration pattern.

When there is less than a 60-second interval between the end of a contraction and the beginning of the next contraction, the uterus is hyperstimulated. This can take the form of single contractions that occur in rapid succession, or multiple contractions that occur together, such as with doubling, tripling, or quadrupling. Hyperstimulation patterns evident on the fetal monitor tracing require the nurse to palpate and confirm uterine activity and to consider possible causes of the hyperstimulation. The nurse's response will depend on the maternal and fetal responses to hyperstimulation. For example, if oxytocin appears to be the cause of uterine hyperstimulation, the infusion may be decreased or discontinued until at least 1 minute exists between the end of one contraction until the beginning of another. Causes of hyperstimulation, such as placental abruption, must be considered, and the nurse's additional assessment and actions should be communicated to the patient's midwife or physician in a timely manner.

Additional measures include placing the patient in a position to improve cardiac output, such as sitting semi-Fowler's or lying on her side. An intravenous bolus of a non-glucose-containing solution may be administered if there are no contraindications to the fluid bolus. Oxygen may be given via a tight fitting face mask at 8-10 L/min. These measures are done to increase blood flow and oxygen delivery to the placenta and fetus.

Conclusion

The goal of nursing is that patients be unharmed and regain or maintain their optimal level of well being. To avoid injury, communication with other health care providers must be clear, concise, and complete. Nurses should demonstrate caring behaviors towards patients. To do so, the nurse-to-patient ratio must be adequate to meet the standards of care. Policies and procedures must be in place to guide nurses in their care. While the nurse has a specific role in fetal monitoring, the nurse's role goes far beyond the fetal monitor.

Nurses are responsible for their nursing process, i.e., the collection of data, the assessment of patient needs, the planning of care, collaboration with other health care providers, implementation of their plan, evaluation of patient responses to actions, and patient education and counseling.[52] Each nurse is accountable for maintaining competence in her practice in order to render quality care.[53] Her behavior will be a reflection of her level of education and expertise, the complexity of tasks she is expected to complete, and the resources available within the environment in which she works.

Nursing departments have a primary responsibility for determining required staffing patterns to ensure quality patient care. In fact, NAACOG felt it was essential that orientation, inservice education, and well-defined job descriptions be provided to nurses who work in obstetric, gynecologic, and neonatal settings.[53]

What nurses and physicians do matters. Institutions that provide care to patients must have administrators who support education of nurses to increase expertise. They must provide adequate staffing so that patient care needs can be met. Protocols and policies must be multidisciplinary and current.[53] Hospitals must provide state-of-the-art equipment and create an environment of caring, cooperation, and collaboration between physicians or nurses. Anything less may precede patient injury.

Commentary by Dr. Schifrin: A multiparous patient with chronic hypertension had been monitored weekly with NST. The previous test was reactive with a baseline rate in the 130-140 bpm range. At term, the patient presented to the antepartal testing room. The attending physician was not called until more than 2 hours of testing had transpired and the FHR pattern was both nonreassuring and non-reactive (Figure 2). When the nurse telephoned the physician, it was communicated that there were occasional variable decelerations, but the nurse failed to report the absence of accelerations, the tachycardia baseline, the absence of long-term variability, and the late deceleration and prolonged deceleration that occurred in the first 20 minutes of monitoring. The physician never asked the nurse to describe the entire tracing. Based on hearing only that there were occasional variable decelerations, and assuming the baseline and variability were within normal limits, a biophysical profile was ordered. The patient was transported to the ultrasound department and waited > 1 hour. When the ultrasound technician scanned her fetus, the biophysical profile score was 2, suggesting fetal asphyxia. The patient was transported to labor and delivery where the admitting nurse noted fetal movement. A nonreassuring checkmark (seizure) FHR pattern was clearly evident. However, neither the physician nor the labor and delivery nurses recognized the checkmark pattern. Although an emergency Cesarean section was eventually performed for terminal bradycardia, the fetus was stillborn. Appropriate initial communication would have probably led to an earlier delivery and the avoidance of legal exposure (although not necessarily a live or intact baby).

This case illustrates numerous areas of misunderstanding and controversy among physicians and nurses. Did reasonable care require the nurse to fully appreciate the abnormal pattern and communicate it to the physician? Did the pattern require immediate intervention? Would the intervention have resulted in a live fetus? An intact fetus? Was the failure to understand the "check mark" pattern below the standard of care?

Commentary by Mr. Volk: In the manner that this case is presented, there is potential liability on the part of the nurses, hospital, radiologist, ultrasound technologist, and physician. The analysis could be based on the facts presented, that the various violations are following:

1. There may be a failure on the part of the nurses to immediately recognize the obvious abnormalities of the EFM. There was an obvious failure to timely notify the physician and properly advise

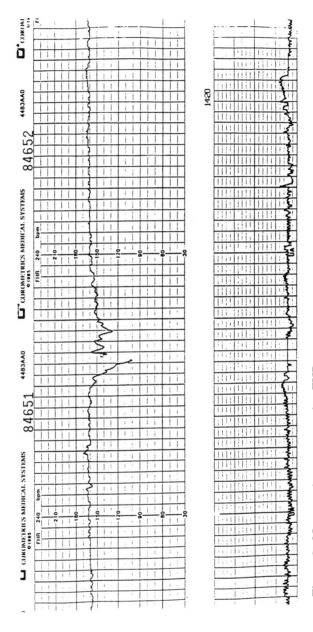

Figure 2. Non-reactive, nonreassuring FHR pattern.

as to the abnormalities at a time that the fetus was alive. When the physician was finally contacted, the data relayed were inadequate and erroneous. There was no attempt to have the biophysical profile done on a "stat" basis. There was a further failure, once mother and fetus were returned to labor and delivery, to again recognize and act on an abnormal pattern. There would also be liability for failing to recognize that a score of 2 must be acted upon immediately.

2. The hospital may be exposed by having an inadequately trained nursing staff. The hospital either allowed this situation to exist and/or did not require the nurses to be evaluated and trained. The hospital should have had a procedure to perform biophysical profiles sooner than 1 hour. The best procedure would be to have them performed on a "stat" basis (the argument would be that they are ordered to evaluate the status of a fetus who could well be compromised, they are not ordered for routine cases, and therefore, they should be performed immediately). The hospital may be liable if the ultrasound technologist failed to immediately notify the nursing staff, radiologist, or attending physician of the results of the BPP.

3. The radiologist may be liable for failure to "triage" the patient in his/her department. A radiologist must be aware of, and responsible for, the patients while in his or her area. It could certainly be argued that a delay of 1 hour was in part caused by the failure to triage. Further, the technologist is supervised by the radiologist and it could be alleged a failure to properly supervise, if the technologist was negligent.

4. The technologist would most likely be an employee of the hospital. There could be alleged a failure to timely perform the BPP, a failure to immediately report the score to the supervising radiologist, the nurse in labor and delivery, and the attending physician.

5. The physician may be liable for having his/her patients in a hospital with incompetent nursing staff who cannot recognize abnormal EFM patterns. There is a failure by the physician not requiring the nurse to report on the entire tracing. A further failure would be not instructing the nurse to telecopy the tracing to the physician either at the office or home. There is a failure to timely come to the hospital to check the patient. There is a failure to order a stat BPP and a failure to recognize abnormal patterns when the physician finally does see the patient.

The answer to the question about whether immediate intervention is required is easy. If the data exist as set out in the hypothetical (abnormal patterns from the beginning, etc.) then intervention, or at least a proper evaluation, is mandated when fetal jeopardy possibly exists. The questions concerning whether or not intervention would have resulted in a live or intact fetus may be academic in one sense. The fact is that there was not timely intervention and without that timely intervention the probable result would be what in fact occurred—a dead fetus. The proximate cause question as to whether or not the fetus would be intact or alive is answered by expert testimony as to what was probable. However, it is difficult to defend the position that the fetus was going to die anyway, so it is permissible to have a > 3 hour delay in recognizing that the fetus is in trouble. The question as to whether the "check mark" pattern was below the standard of care is a two-fold, one—was it below the standard for a nurse, was it below standard for a physician? This is the subject of expert testimony. Another inquiry is the question as to when the pattern was there in relation to when the physician arrived. The proximate cause question is more important here because at least 3 hours elapsed since the patient was admitted and the probability of survival may be diminishing.

References

1. Boylan P. Intrapartum fetal monitoring. Baillieres Clin Obstet Gynaecol 1987;1:73.
2. Daddario JB. Fetal surveillance in the intensive care unit: Understanding electronic fetal monitoring. Crit Care Nurs Clin North Am 1992;4:711.
3. Headlines. Am J Nurs 1993;93:9.
4. Chaska NL (ed). *The Nursing Profession: Views Through the Mist.* New York, McGraw-Hill, 1978.
5. *Didactic Content and Clinical Skills Verification for Professional Nurse Providers of Basic, High-Risk, and Critical-Care Intrapartal Nursing.* Association of Women's Health, Obstetric and Neonatal Nurses. Washington, D.C., 1993.
6. *Electronic Fetal Monitoring Nursing Practice Competencies and Educational Guidelines.* National Association of the American College of Obstetricians and Gynecologists, Washington, D.C., 1986.
7. *Standards for Obstetric-Gynecologic Services.* American College of Obstetricians and Gynecologists, Washington, D.C., 1989.
8. *Guidelines for Perinatal Care,* Third edition. Elk Grove Village, Illinois; American Academy of Pediatrics and American College of Obstetricians and Gynecologists, 1992.
9. *Fetal heart monitoring principle and practices.* Association of Women's Health, Obstetric and Neonatal Nurses. Washington, D.C., 1993.
10. Beaulieu M, Fabia J, Leduc B, et al. The reproducibility of intrapartum cardiotocogram assessments. Can Med Assoc J 1982;127:214.
11. Chez BF, Skurnick JH, Chez RA, et al. Interpretations of nonstress tests by obstetric nurses. J Obstet Gynecol Nurs 1990;19:227.

12. Cohen AB, Klapholz H, Thompson ML. Electronic fetal monitoring and clinical practice. A survey of obstetric opinion. Med Decis Making 1982;2:79.
13. Hage ML. Interpretation of nonstress tests. Am J Obstet Gynecol 1985;153:490-495.
14. Lotgering FK, Wallenburg HCS, Schouten HJA. Interobserver and intraobserver variation in the assessment of antepartum cardiotocograms. Am J Obstet Gynecol 1982;144:701.
15. Trimbos JB, Keirse MJNC. Observer variability in assessment of antepartum cardiotocograms. Br J Obstet Gynaecol 1978;85:900.
16. Borgatta L, Shrout PE, Divon MY. Reliability and reproducibility of nonstress test readings. Am J Obstet Gynecol 1988;159:554.
17. Schifrin BS, Clement D. Why fetal monitoring remains a good idea. Contemp Ob/Gyn 1990;35:70.
18. Murray ML, Higgins P. Computer versus lecture: Strategies for teaching fetal monitoring. J Perinatol 1996;16:15.
19. Redman CW. Communicating the significance of the fetal heart rate record to the user. Br J Obstet Gynaecol 1993;100:24.
20. Gimovsky ML, Bruce SL. Aspects of FHR tracings as warning signals. Clin Obstet Gynecol 1986;29:51.
21. Murray ML. A comparison of fetal monitoring concept learning from a learner-controlled versus teacher-controlled instructional strategy. Unpublished doctoral dissertation, University of New Mexico, Albuquerque, 1992.
22. Mantel F, vanGeijn, HP, Caron FJM, et al. Computer analysis of antepartum fetal heart rate: I. Baseline determination. Int J Biomed Comput 1990;25:261.
23. Arduini D, Rizzo G. Quantitative analysis of fetal rate: Its application in antepartum clinical monitoring and behavioral pattern recognition. Int J Biomed Comput 1990;25:247.
24. Alonso-Betanzos A, Moret-Bonillo V, Hernandez-Sande C. Foetos: An expert system for fetal assessment. Trans Biomed Eng 1991;38:199.
25. Guzman ER, Conley M, Stewart R, et al. Phenytoin and magnesium sulfate effects on fetal heart rate tracings assessed by computer analysis. Am J Obstet Gynecol 1993;82:375.
26. Bernardes J, Moura C, DeSa JP, et al. The Porto system for automated cardiotocographic signal analysis. J Perinatal Med 1991;19:61.
27. Bartnicki J, Ratanasiri T, Meyenburg M, et al. Computer analysis of the antepartum fetal heart rate patterns in the intrauterine growth-retarded human fetus using Sonicaid System 8000. Gynecol Obstet Invest 1991;31:196.
28. Devoe LD. Computerized analysis of fetal heart rate. The Female Patient 1985;15:41.
29. Cheng LC, Gibb DM, Ajayi RA, et al. A comparison between computerised (mean range) and clinical visual cardiotocographic assessment. Br J Obstet Gynaecol 1992;99:817.
30. Bernardes J. Automated methods of analyzing fetal heart rate tests: Already a good alternative to visual analysis? Am J Obstet Gynecol 1994;170:1207.
31. *NAACOG Standards for the Nursing Care of Women and Newborns*, Fourth Edition. NAACOG, Washington, D.C., 1991.
32. McRae MJ. Litigation, electronic fetal monitoring, and the obstetric nurse. J Obstet Gynecol Neonatal Nurs 1993;22:410.
33. *Code for Nurses with Interpretative Statements*. American Nurses' Association, Washington, D.C., 1985.

34. Lavoir DR. The relationship between the process skill of prediction and students' misconceptions in biology. ERIC Document Reproduction Service No. ED 310 943, 1989.
35. *Nursing Practice Competencies and Education Guidelines Antepartum Fetal for Surveillance and Intrapartum Fetal Heart Monitoring.* National Association of the American College of Obstetricians and Gynecologists, Washington, D.C., 1991.
36. Dunn CS. The influence of instructional methods on concept learning. Science Education 1983;67:647.
37. Parer JT. Fetal hemodynamic responses to reduced uterine blood flow in the sheep fetus. In: Kunzel WW (ed). *Fetal Heart Rate Monitoring. Clinical Practice and Pathophysiology.* New York, Springer-Verlag, 1985, pp. 82-93.
38. Blackwell MK. Documentation serves as invaluable defense tool. Am Nurse 1993;25:40.
39. Farrell E. Communication: A critical part of nursing. Am Nurse 1993;25:40.
40. Learn to communicate effectively with patients and each other. NSO Risk Advisor, 1994;4.
41. Avoiding flow sheet headaches. NSO Risk Advisor 1994;2.
42. Brill JM. Handle medical record with care. Am Nurse 1990;22:47.
43. *Standards of Clinical Nursing Practice.* American Nurses' Association, Washington, D.C., 1991.
44. Janulis DM. Primer on electronic fetal monitoring. Pers Inj Rev 1989;175.
45. Grady MF. Why are people negligent? Technology, nondurable precautions and the medical malpractice explosion. Northwest University Law Review 1988;82(note 6):300.
46. Risk Management Foundation. Fetal monitoring problems during labor associated with most serious OB claims. Forum 1986;7:19.
47. General Accounting Office (GAO). Medical malpractice characteristics of claims closed in 1984. GAO/HRD-87-55. U.S. Government Printing Office, Washington, D.C. 1987.
48. American College of Obstetricians and Gynecologists. Professional liability and its effects: Report of a 1987 survey of ACOG's membership. ACOG, Washington, D.C. 1988.
49. Medical malpractice verdicts, settlements and experts. 1994;10:
50. Chain of command. Should these nurses have tried harder to prevent a patient's discharge? NSO Risk Advisor 1994;3.
51. Ballard D. Stretched too think. Am J Nurs 1993;25:21.
52. Weiler K, Rhodes AM. Legal methodology as nursing problem solving. IMAGE: Journal of Nursing Scholarship. 1991;23:241.
53. *Model for utilization of NAACOG standards.* National Association of the American College of Obstetricians and Gynecologists, Washington, D.C., 1977.

Chapter 13

Abruptio Placentae

◆◆◆

Kenneth R. Niswander, M.D.

Introduction

Abruptio placentae (also called placental abruption or separation of the placenta) is a common complication of the later part of pregnancy with a reported incidence of about 1 per 75-100 deliveries; although the incidence is probably decreasing because of the marked reduction in the number of patients of high parity currently being delivered in the United States. The reported perinatal mortality rates vary between 20%-35%, about equally divided between stillbirths and neonatal deaths.[1,2] Whether infants who survive abruption are at higher risk of developing neurologic deficit is currently in dispute.[3,4]

It is likely that the higher incidence of neurologic deficit reported by some investigators can at least be partially explained by the high incidence of prematurity, so common in cases of abruption, in itself a well-recognized "cause" of subsequent neurologic problems.

> **Commentary by Mr. Volk:** From a medico-legal standpoint, it would be difficult to sort out the dysfunction relative to prematurity and that relative to hypoxia from abruption. If the abruption is severe and long, the testimony may very well be that the failure to intervene with delivery, etc., caused or contributed to the dysfunction or death of mother and/or fetus. Obviously an attorney investigating a potential claim would need to analyze the severity and length of the abruption. Each case, for the attorney reviewing it, must stand or fall on its own merit.

From: Donn SM, Fisher CW (eds.): *Risk Management Techniques in Perinatal and Neonatal Practice.* © Futura Publishing Co., Inc., Armonk, NY, 1996.

It is also noteworthy that about a third of the current overall maternal mortality rate is associated with obstetric bleeding, and many of these deaths result from placental abruption. The frequency of the pathology, the high perinatal death risk, the possibility of neurologic deficit in surviving children, and the significant maternal mortality risk clearly establish this disease entity as worthy of "risk management."

In considering risk management of abruption, an attempt will be made to answer certain questions that affect recommendations:

1. What causes placental abruption and can these causes be identified, prevented, or their effects minimized?
2. How is abruption diagnosed?
3. How does placental separation cause fetal jeopardy? Can fetal jeopardy be recognized? How can its effects be minimized?
4. Should labor be allowed when the diagnosis of abruption is established or should Cesarean section always be the preferred method of delivery?
5. What maternal risks result from abruption? Can their effects be minimized?

It should be stated at the outset that the obstetric goal of preventing *all* bad outcomes from the effects of abruption is not achievable given the present state of medical knowledge. Rather, a goal of preventing as many of the deleterious effects of abruption as possible is more realistic and is itself worthy of consideration.

> **Commentary by Mr. Volk:** The standard of care requires a physician to accurately and adequately assess mother and fetus for risks and offer treatment that will best minimize or eliminate these risks. The "standard of care" does not require medical care to the "highest standard." The requisite standard is often characterized as the minimal fundamental standard of care that must be met for treating a patient in the same or similar circumstances. In evaluating an abruptio placentae case, the physician has to be able to prove that he or she did meet the standard of care by adequately and accurately accessing the patient for the risks and to offer the treatment that would best minimize or eliminate these risks. A physician also has to be able to prove that the failure to deliver early did not cause fetal/maternal injury. If mother and fetus are probably healthy when first evaluated and there is subsequent serious morbidity or mortality, the defendant physician is in a difficult medico-legal position.

Causes of Placental Abruption

The cause of placental abruption remains unknown, although a number of theories have been advanced. Certain possible etiologic factors should be mentioned, since it can be argued that these conditions do precede and may possibly cause placental separation in a small percentage of total cases. Their presence should alert the physician to the possibility of subsequent abruption.

Maternal Hypertension

Pritchard et al.[5] have reported that of 201 cases of placental abruption leading to fetal death, nearly half were accompanied by maternal hypertension, half of these from chronic vascular disease and the other half from pregnancy-induced hypertension (PIH). Some authors have confirmed this finding,[3] but others have not identified the relationship.[2] It is important to note there has been no relationship reported between lesser degrees of maternal hypertension and abruption.

Substance Abuse

Placental abruption has been reported to be associated with substance abuse. Cigarette smoking, cocaine, and to a lesser extent, methamphetamines have been the drugs most frequently identified in women with abruption. These drugs all produce maternal vasoconstriction and hypertension. The first report of cocaine use in pregnancy involved placental abruption.[6] Many of the early studies of substance abuse during pregnancy supported such a relationship.[7-10] However, these were usually based on selective toxicology testing. Larger studies, using non-selective or universal screening, have not upheld this association.[11,12] It is probable that merely detecting the presence of a drug is too simplistic an approach. The effect of a drug on uterine and placental circulation and function is related to the actual blood level of the drug. This will depend on the type of drug, dose, route of administration, and gestational age. To date, there have been no studies that have carefully evaluated all of these parameters during pregnancy. An additional consideration is that substance abuse almost always involves multiple drugs (including smoking and alcohol) rather than a single drug. This further confounds attempts to identify the association of a specific drug, such as cocaine, with a specific complication, such as abruption. Thus, the findings of an association between cocaine use and placental abruption may be valid when the dose and route of administration produces a blood level that results in maternal vasoconstriction and hypertension sufficient to interfere with placental function. Pregnant patients presenting with symptoms of abruption should be screened by urine toxicology for the presence of cocaine and amphetamines, particularly if there is unexplained hypertension or no overt explanation for abruption.

Maternal Trauma

The idea that trauma to the maternal abdomen might "shake the placenta loose" and thus cause abruption is appealing but not often true. Some investigators, however, have noted that even relatively minor trauma, and even without apparent involvement of the maternal abdomen, may be followed by placental separation, not always associated with clinical signs.[13-15] The implications for the management of gravida who are involved in, for example, a motor vehicle accident are apparent. The fetus should be monitored with electronic fetal monitoring (EFM) to be certain that there is no fetal jeopardy from the trauma.

> **Commentary by Mr. Volk:** This brings up an interesting and important point. Is it, or should it be, the standard of care to hospitalize and to closely observe a gravida and her fetus that had trauma? Obviously, there are two patients who can be injured, and the potential for catastrophe exists.

Decompression of Uterine Contents

It has been observed that sudden decompression of the uterus (drainage of hydramnios, delivery of the first twin) has on rare occasions been followed by abruption.[5] While it is not certain that there is a cause and effect relationship between these events, the wise obstetrician will keep this possibility in mind.

Previous History of Placental Separation

The risk for recurrence of placental separation is much greater than the risk for its occurrence in a non-selected population. The recurrence rate has varied in the experience of clinicians from 1 in 18 (5%) to 1 in 6 (17%), a 5 to 17-fold increase. These findings clearly suggest that a patient who has previously experienced an abruption in a prior pregnancy should be closely observed for a recurrence with a view to rendering medical care as early as possible. As described below, the practical value of such special care is severely limited.

Risk Management of the Patient with Certain Pre-Existing Conditions

1. Be aware that when abnormal bleeding is seen in a patient with severe PIH or a history of trauma or in a patient who has just delivered the

first of twins, she may be more likely to develop abruption than other patients.

2. Be aware that a history of abruption in a previous pregnancy puts the gravida at higher risk of another abruption in subsequent pregnancies.
3. If a gravida presents with any one of these conditions, react aggressively if abnormal vaginal bleeding or other indications of abruption develop.
4. Apply EFM as emergency care to patients who suffer abdominal or decelerative trauma, even in the absence of vaginal bleeding.

Diagnosis of Placental Abruption

For many reasons, the signs and symptoms associated with placental abruption vary widely. For example, if a large portion of the placenta is separated, the clinical manifestations are likely to be obvious. If the placental separation occurs on the posterior wall of the uterus, uterine tenderness may be absent. Lesser degrees of separation may be associated only with a small amount of vaginal bleeding, without other symptoms. To avoid an argument that a "bloody show" was a sign of abruptio, the nurse should clearly document the amount of "bloody show" (see Chapter 14 regarding the nurse's role in abruptio).

When the placental abruption is large or, in some cases, total, the clinical picture is usually classic. The onset of the symptoms has usually been "abrupt." Abdominal pain, or sometimes back pain, is severe and unremitting. The uterus demonstrates sustained or regular uterine contractions. There is usually significant vaginal bleeding, although bleeding may be retroplacental and, therefore, not clinically evident. The fetus is usually dead upon admission to the hospital. The primary concern for risk management is to minimize the major maternal hazards that accompany this catastrophe since the fetus usually cannot be saved.

Unfortunately, the classic clinical expressions of placental separation are frequently not present with partial or minimal abruption. Vaginal bleeding is present in most cases as is uterine tenderness. In many cases, the symptoms and findings suggest premature labor rather than placental separation. Hypertonus of the uterus and frequent contractions are usually seen only when the separation is moderate or worse in grade. It should be pointed out, however, that the correlation between severity of symptoms and degree of separation is not very precise. Patients with a relatively small separation may experience fairly severe symptoms while, on occasion, a patient with a large separation will present with vaginal bleeding only, at least early in the course of the disease.

Many patients with lesser degrees of abruption may have no symptoms at all other than vaginal bleeding. Such patients should be investigated with sonographic evaluation unless the bleeding can be explained in some other way.

> **Commentary by Mr. Volk:** To meet the standard of care, the bleeding would have to be *reasonably* explained. Anytime a sign or symptom can be explained in some way that is benign and the catastrophic explanation is not considered, reasonably ruled out and documented, the potential for adverse medico-legal consequences exists. On many occasions, physicians opt for testifying as to their evaluation of the patient's condition as a benign one and then catastrophe occurred. This is what I call the "99% rule." Ninety-nine percent of the time the patient's condition will turn out to be a benign one, but 1% of the time serious morbidity or mortality occurs because the condition is not, in fact, a benign one but is catastrophic. From the medico-legal standpoint, the physician that embraces the 99% rule in treating the patients, without ruling out the 1% catastrophic condition, may very well suffer medico-legal consequences.

Sonography can recognize placental separation only in a minority of cases and is, therefore, of limited usefulness in this regard. The importance of sonography is that it can accurately rule out placenta previa. Although abruption can frequently be clinically differentiated from placenta previa by the presence of pain and uterine tenderness, these symptoms are sometimes absent and sonographic examination is of great value in differential diagnosis.

Risk Management Considerations of Diagnosis

1. Investigate any abnormal vaginal bleeding in the latter half of pregnancy, or document that it is trivial in amount or is unaccompanied by other symptoms.
2. Rule out placenta previa by sonography. Is there a more benign cause of the bleeding, such as erosion of the cervix or hemorrhoids?
3. Evaluate any abdominal or back pain. Is it labor-like (less likely to result from an abruption)? Is it continuous?
4. Is the uterus tender or tetanic?
5. Is there any evidence of cardiovascular compromise or shock?
6. Document *all* findings, assessments, and management plans.

The development of a consumptive coagulopathy, disseminated intravascular coagulation (DIC), in the patient with separation of the placenta must be kept constantly in mind. The primary mechanism for its development is apparently an activation of coagulation caused by thromboplastin release from the site of the abruption with consequent intravascular and retroplacental consumption of clotting factors and platelets. Fibrin is deposited in small vessels throughout the body inciting the activation of plasminogen to plasmin, which causes lysis of fibrin and fibrinogen. Defective hemostasis is the ultimate effect. Pritchard has reported that the coagulation defects develop within the first few hours after the onset of pain or bleeding and usually do not worsen with the passage of time.[5] Clinical evidence of a coagulopathy includes bleeding from venipuncture or trauma sites, or spontaneously from the mucous membranes.

The diagnosis of DIC begins with the realization that the disease will be present in many patients with abruption severe enough to cause fetal death. About 30% of such patients will experience the coagulopathy. DIC is much less frequent in patients with lesser degrees of abruption, but it should be suspected if abnormal bleeding occurs, or when the treatment plan for a patient with abruption includes a period of several hours observation without immediate delivery. A quick beside aid in the diagnosis is the whole blood clotting test. If recently drawn blood does not clot in a tube within 4-8 minutes, or if lysis of a clot, especially a soft clot, occurs within an hour or 2, DIC is an extremely likely diagnosis. All patients with an abruption should have blood drawn for Antithrombin III (ATIII), fibrinogen, and fibrin split products (FSP) levels, plus platelet count and determination of prothrombin time. A serum fibrinogen level < 150 mg/dL or a low ATIII level is diagnostic of DIC in a pregnant patient with abruption. If the initial level is normal in a patient in whom DIC is suspected, serial determinations should be ordered, although a serious coagulopathy usually develops very early in the course of the disease. Since the intravascular clotting, which characterizes the disease, invariably activates the fibrinolytic system, high levels of FSP are usually present. FSP then further contribute to defective coagulation.

Many laboratory tests are abnormal with DIC. Few, however, are needed to make the diagnosis. If a patient with abruption bleeds abnormally or if the abruption is severe, the diagnosis can be confirmed with low plasma fibrinogen or ATIII levels. Serial thrombin levels, which reflect fibrinogen levels, are almost as accurate and are more readily available in most laboratories. Little clinical information is added by determining levels of FSP, since they are almost invariably elevated with extensive abruption. While the platelet count may not be initially low, it usually falls within a short period of time as a result of consumption of platelets by intravascular clotting.

Risk Management in Making the Diagnosis of DIC

1. Expect any patient with moderate or severe abruption to develop DIC.
2. Watch for clinical evidence of DIC, i.e., abnormal bleeding from unexpected sites (nose, gums), or failure of blood to clot.

3. Draw a tube of blood at the bedside for observation of clot.
4. Obtain serum fibrinogen and ATIII levels and a platelet count.
5. Perform repeated fibrinogen levels and platelet counts.
6. Document all management, especially if any of these tests are not done.

Fetal Jeopardy

Fetal compromise, and the risk of fetal asphyxia, can be suspected when the EFM presents certain abnormal patterns. In some cases, the abnormal pattern is obvious and may warrant the term "probable fetal distress." Some abnormal patterns of the EFM are less diagnostically obvious. Although EFM is known to overcall the diagnosis of fetal asphyxia in a certain percentage of cases (false positive readings), the experienced clinician faced with a patient with probable placental separation and worrisome changes on the EFM tape will choose to err on the side of overdiagnosis of "fetal distress" rather than underdiagnosis. The worrisome EFM patterns are well known to clinicians: a persistent pattern of late decelerations (the most common abnormal pattern in patients with placental separation), severe variable decelerations pattern (not commonly seen with abruption), or a prolonged decelerative pattern (with falling baseline or frank bradycardia). All of these patterns are made more ominous by the presence of decreased beat-to-beat variability. Readers should consult texts on EFM for more detailed descriptions of abnormal patterns.

Treatment of Placental Abruption

The treatment appropriate for a patient with placental abruption will depend on a number of variables:

1. Whether the diagnosis is certain or just suspected.
2. The severity of the disease as measured in various ways.
3. The severity of the maternal hemodynamic changes.
4. The presence or absence of possible fetal compromise or fetal death.

The initial therapy in all patients seriously suspected of having placental abruption is fluid and blood replacement after the initial laboratory tests have been drawn (CBC, electrolytes, blood for type and cross-match), and after the gravida's vital signs have been taken. An intravenous line is established with a large bore needle (two lines if the bleeding is severe or if there is evidence of impending shock). Lactated Ringer's solution is infused, followed by packed red blood cells as soon as they are available. It is frequently difficult to estimate the amount of fluid and blood that is required. The initial hematocrit may be falsely high because of the recentness of blood loss; much of the bleeding may not be externally evident; maternal shock, suggesting marked blood loss, may not be immediately apparent.

The amount of fluid and blood replacement needed must be judged initially by changes in hemoglobin or hematocrit and changes in the state of shock. Over the longer term, a better gauge of how much blood is needed is urinary output, with at least 30 mL/hour by catheter as a required minimum. More errors are made in underestimating rather than in overestimating fluid requirements. Two to four units of packed red blood cells should be cross-matched whenever the degree of abruption is anything more than mild.

Treatment of Maternal Hypovolemia

Since bleeding from abruption is not always external, the usual estimates of the amount of blood loss and thus the amount needed for replacement are frequently inaccurate. The initial hematocrit at admission of the patient may be falsely high, since the bleeding is usually of very recent occurrence. Evidence of shock (hypotension and tachycardia especially) reflects significant blood loss, but absence of these signs of shock should not always be interpreted as reassuring. A patient with severe PIH and a large hemorrhage may falsely appear to be in stable condition with a lowered, but normal blood pressure. A good rule of thumb is to administer blood and lactated Ringer's solution in amounts that correct shock and maintain the hematocrit at 30%. Hourly urine output should be maintained at 30-60 mL measured with a catheter in the bladder. If urine output is inadequate after apparently adequate volume expansion, invasive hemodynamic (Swan-Ganz catheter) monitoring should be considered. Inadequate treatment of hypoperfusion and shock may lead to such complications as ischemic necrosis of the kidneys.

Risk Management of Treatment of Hemodynamic Changes

In judging the amount of fluid and blood replacement needed, it should be remembered that both the gravida and her fetus are put at risk by inadequate perfusion.

1. Is shock present? Remember the rare exceptional circumstance such as a "normal" blood pressure in a patient who was severely hypertensive before the abruption.
2. Measure the hemoglobin or hematocrit level immediately. Is it low or lower than a prenatal measurement? Repeat the test at frequent intervals if immediate delivery is not indicated.
3. Establish intravenous access with a large bore needle.
4. Cross-match two or more units of packed red blood cells.

5. Coagulant component replacement is rarely necessary.
6. Measurement of hourly urine output should be made if immediate delivery is not indicated.

Labor and Delivery with Placental Abruption

How labor and delivery are conducted will depend on the condition of the mother and the fetus. It should be remembered that a small abruption can extend and jeopardize both mother and fetus. Many patients will go into spontaneous labor and if the condition of the gravida is stable and if surveillance of the fetus shows no compromise, labor can be allowed to continue. Indeed, if circumstances dictate early delivery and if labor has not begun, oxytocin can be used to initiate labor. Due care must be exercised in the use of oxytocin to avoid fetal compromise or excessive uterine contractions with the potential for uterine rupture. Amniotomy is recommended by some authorities not only to help initiate labor, but also to decrease the amount of thromboplastic material entering the maternal circulation. Others have not substantiated these presumed advantages of amniotomy.

Fetal compromise or distress can be caused in several ways. The actual placental separation may reduce the amount of oxygen coming from the mother. Maternal shock will reduce uterine blood flow. Uterine hypertonus may reduce intervillous exchange of oxygen. On rare occasions, a fetal-maternal bleed may occur. Little can be done to change most of these mechanisms for fetal compromise, but rapid correction of maternal hypovolemia, even in the absence of maternal shock, is extremely important to prevent both maternal and fetal complications.

When Should Delivery be Accomplished?

Rapid delivery, almost always by Cesarean section, should be accomplished when:

1. Fetal compromise is present.
2. Blood loss or hypoperfusion cannot be adequately treated and maternal risk exists.

An abnormality on the EFM tracing may sometimes be improved by the correction of maternal hypoperfusion, by maternal oxygen administration, and by a lateral positioning of the mother. If the EFM tracing is ominous, however, use of these means to correct the pattern should be limited to a short time frame.

Risk Management of Labor and Delivery

1. Allow labor to occur (or even initiate labor) unless there is: a. maternal shock; b. excessive bleeding; or c. fetal jeopardy.
2. Initiate continuous EFM as soon as a diagnosis of abruption is suspected.
3. Review the fetal heart rate tracing at frequent intervals.
4. Use the intrauterine pressure catheter only after placenta previa is excluded.
5. A "worrisome" EFM tracing (questionable late decelerations, a "confusing" pattern) requires close observation.
6. An ominous tracing (persistent late decelerations, severe variable decelerations, prolonged deceleration, or bradycardia) requires immediate delivery.
7. Depending on local practice, summon an experienced person to provide infant resuscitation. Remember: prematurity is frequent with abruption and may also require expert resuscitation.
8. *Document* why you have decided against or for early delivery.

Commentary by Mr. Volk: The standard of care is not local but a national one. The standard of care is now routinely testified to as a national standard for anyone delivering children, or practicing any specialty. Obstetricians in even the smallest communities have access to meetings, published materials, tapes, and videos. The knowledge required by a physician delivering babies is not based upon what is known or required in his/her own community any longer. However, the question of whether or not it is malpractice in a small community not having an experienced individual who can resuscitate and stabilize is determined by many factors. Two of them are:

1. Whether or not there were impending signs of a problem pregnancy that could be characterized as high-risk, necessitating referral to a high-risk center, thus affording mother and fetus the opportunity to avoid morbidity and/or mortality.
2. Whether or not the opportunity existed to transfer mother and fetus on a "stat" basis and whether or not it was safe to do so once the possibility of complications occurred.

Treatment of Coagulopathy

The definitive treatment for DIC is delivery of the placenta. Fibrinogen levels begin to rise, and clinically evident DIC is almost unknown beyond 12 hours of delivery. The use of procoagulants to correct the clotting mechanism is no longer thought to be necessary in the vast majority of cases. The elimination of hypovolemia by adequate blood and fluid replacement is of major importance. If vital organs are adequately perfused, activated coagulation factors and FSP are promptly removed by the reticulo-endothelial system.

If bleeding is not controlled by more conservative measures, or if bleeding at Cesarean section cannot be controlled by careful hemostasis, fibrinogen infusion may be needed. The dose recommended is 4 g of fibrinogen, which can be given in the form of cryoprecipitate (15-20 bags). Note that cryoprecipitate does not contain ATIII. In cases where the platelet count is very low (< 20,000/mm³), platelet concentrates may be needed. The use of procoagulants in other circumstances may "fuel the fire" of DIC by increasing the amounts of FSP and are not recommended. The use of heparin and agents that were formerly thought to be useful in decreasing fibrinolysis is no longer recommended. On rare occasions, when bleeding at Cesarean section cannot be controlled by hemostasis or when the uterus will not adequately contract, supracervical hysterectomy may be necessary.

Risk Management of Treatment of DIC

1. If bleeding cannot be controlled by conservative measures, give fibrinogen.
2. Avoid procoagulants unless an exceptional circumstance justifies this treatment.
3. Platelet concentrates may be required for very low platelet counts.

Summary

Abruptio placentae has the potential for causing the deaths of both mother and fetus. Yet, happier outcomes are common. It is important that the clinician caring for a patient with this disease or with a suspicion of the disease carefully document his/her clinical management. A poor outcome cannot always be avoided. If documentation establishes good judgment in the care of the patient, the principles of risk management will have been used successfully.

Commentary by Mr. Volk: The manner in which an attorney may plead a cause of action for abruptio placentae could include the following:

1. Failure to treat the patient as high risk (for instance if there is a previous abruption or, significant high blood pressure, etc.)
2. Failure to recognize early signs and symptoms of abruption.
3. Failure to hospitalize for observation.
4. Failure to timely deliver prior to serious morbidity or mortality.
5. Failure to rule out abruption.

6. Failure to rule out resulting catastrophic conditions (such as DIC).
7. Failure to timely and properly treat resulting catastrophic medical conditions (for instance, DIC).
8. Negligently utilized oxytocin by failing to properly monitor and timely deliver.
9. Failure to personally come to the bedside and monitor the progress of labor.
10. Failure to transfer the patient on a stat basis to a medical facility that was more able to timely and properly care for the patients.
11. Failure to consult a high risk obstetrician to manage the delivery.
12. Failure to consult a hematologist or other specialist to manage the medical complications.
13. Failure to prepare for a newborn in need of experienced resuscitation.

References

1. Karegaard M, Gennser G. Incidence and recurrence rate of abruptio placentae in Sweden. Obstet Gynecol 1986;67:523.
2. Patterson MEL. The aetiology and outcome of abruptio placentae. Acta Obstet Gynecol Scand 1979;58:31.
3. Abdella TN, Sibai BM, Hays JM Jr, et al. Perinatal outcome in abruptio placentae. Obstet Gynecol 1984;63:365.
4. Niswander KR, Friedman EA, Hoover DB, et al. Fetal morbidity following potentially anoxigenic obstetric conditions. I. Abruptio placentae. Am J Obstet Gynecol 1966;95:838.
5. Pritchard JA, Mason R, Corley M, et al. Genesis of severe placental abruptions. Am J Obstet Gynecol 1970;103:33.
6. Acker D, Sachs BP, Tracey KJ, et al. Abrupto placentae associated with cocaine use. Am J Obstet Gynecol 1983;146:220.
7. Chasnoff IJ, Burns WJ, Schnoll SH, et al. Cocaine use in pregnancy. N Engl J Med 1985;313:666.
8. Dombrowski MP, Wolfe HM, Welch RA, et al. Cocaine does not shorten labor but decreases birthweight and increases the incidence of abruptio placentae. Tenth Annual Meeting of the Society of Perinatal Obstetricians, Houston, Texas, 1990.
9. Keith LG, MacGregor S, Friedell S, et al. Substance abuse in pregnant women: Recent experience at the Perinatal Center for Chemical Dependence of Northwestern Memorial Hospital. Obstet Gynecol 1989;73:715.
10. Naeye RL, Harkness WL, Utts J. Abruptio placentae and perinatal death: A prospective case study. Am J Obstet Gynecol 1977;128:740.
11. Gillogley KM, Evans AT, Hansen R, et al. The perinatal impact of maternal substance abuse detected by universal intrapartum screening. Am J Obstet Gynecol 1990;163:1535.
12. Neerhof MG, MacGregor SN, Retzky SS, et al. Cocaine abuse during pregnancy: Peripartum prevalence and perinatal outcome. Am J Obstet Gynecol 1989;161:688.

13. Kettel LM, Branch DW, Scott JR. Occult placental abruption after maternal trauma. Obstet Gynecol 1988;71:449.
14. Stafford PA, Biddinger PW, Zumwalt RE. Lethal intrauterine fetal trauma. Am J Obstet Gynecol 1988;159:485.
15. Barbis SD. Delayed fetal death following accidental trauma: A report of six cases. Trans Pacific Coast Obstet Gynecol Soc 1981;49:120.

Chapter 14

Nursing Identification of Abruptio Placentae

◆◆◆

Catherine E. Cochell, B.S.N., R.N.C., C.C.E., Charles W. Fisher, J.D.

Introduction

Various medico-legal cases have been brought addressing claims against obstetrical nurses for the failure to consider or identify a placental abruption and notify an attending physician of signs and symptoms of abruptio placentae. As most individuals know, medical legal cases, especially with respect to this particular type of claim, become dependent upon two major issues: 1. the medical record that has been created by the nurse; and 2. testimony by the patient.

Medico-legal claims typically faced by the nurse in lawsuits contending the failure to identify abruptio usually are formed around three theories:

1. The nurse failed to take into account high-risk conditions of the mother that would have led her to a higher awareness of the potential for abruptio placentae.
2. The nurse failed to recognize clinical signs and symptoms of the patient indicating abruptio placentae.
3. The nurse failed to notify the attending physician of the abruption and immediately start fetal heart monitoring surveillance.

Interestingly, as will be seen in the discussion below, it is virtually impossible to predict which patient will have an abruption even though there are some associated factors that increase the incidence. Additionally, the failure to notify

From: Donn SM, Fisher CW (eds.): *Risk Management Techniques in Perinatal and Neonatal Practice.* © Futura Publishing Co., Inc., Armonk, NY, 1996.

the attending physician and to start fetal monitoring expeditiously is *entirely* dependent upon whether or not the nurse identifies a potential abruption. In other words, the only real issue that deserves extended discussion is whether or not a particular nurse in a particular situation had information available that should have led her to suspect the possibility of abruptio placentae.

Because of the medico-legal climate, the "unknown factor" that is often overlooked by the medical personnel is the perception and later testimony that is likely to be garnered from the mother and/or family members. Cases involving placental abruption often include statements at deposition or trial such as the following:

1. "I was bleeding so much that on the way to the hospital I had to use towels to absorb the blood."
2. "I told the nurse I had been bleeding, and when I arrived at the hospital, the bleeding continued very fast and it was bright red."
3. "I was bleeding so much at home into the toilet that I bled out enough to fill approximately five inches in the bottom of a five-gallon pail."
4. "At the hospital I was changing my own peripads due to the fact that blood was accumulating and filling up those pads."
   (Statements by plaintiffs were taken from actual cases and paraphrased to protect the parties involved.)

Many cases involve a medical record in which there is no abruption documented until just before delivery and no signs and symptoms documented on the intrapartum flow sheet other than "bloody show." From this single piece of documentation, however, it is easy to fashion a claim that the diagnosis of abruptio placentae was overlooked, the severity of the bleeding was not perceived (as will be testified to by family members), and that the proof that there was an earlier abruption lies in the fact that the doctor diagnosed it at the time that the baby was being delivered. What this tells us is that *the documentation of "bloody show" is insufficient to address and respond to claims of abruption.*

High-Risk Factors

In reviewing various medical textbooks there are so many possible high-risk factors that can be listed that increase the *incidence* of abruptio placentae it is hard to know where to start. However, Friedman's[1] book, *Obstetrical Decision Making*, lists the following:

1. High parity;
2. Chronic hypertension;
3. Pregnancy-induced hypertension;
4. Inferior vena cava compression;

5. Uterine trauma;
6. Short umbilical cord;
7. Sudden uterine decompression;
8. Uterine anomaly;
9. Possible folic acid deficiency;
10. Substance abuse.

Williams'[2] textbook also lists similar types of factors that may increase the incidence. *However, the mere fact that an increased incidence exists does not mean the same thing as a "red flag" that would raise abruption to a level of predictability.* Candidly, abruptio placentae is an unpredictable event, and there really are no such things as "risk factors" that can be used to predict abruptio placentae. In fact, in *Williams Obstetrics*[2] the authors list the frequency as being in a range from 1 in 75 to 1 in 225 and averaging 1 in 150 deliveries. The most important criteria cited is the last one from Parkland Memorial Hospital that reported the frequency of abruption severe enough to be fatal to the fetus as about 1 in 830 deliveries.[3]

Obviously, in terms of serious, dangerous, placental abruptions the actual incidence has to be quite rare, and even less predictable than the general statistics including all placental abruptions. Therefore, what can be said about placental abruption risk factors is that they really do not exist in terms of predictability, red flagging, or heightened expectancy. If there are clinical factors present to suggest placental abruption, then the fact that someone is at increased risk may heighten the concern of the health care providers, *but only after the clinical factors of abruption have surfaced.* Pregnant women are not simply put on an "abruptio watch" on the basis of a maternal condition that increases incidence but which does not actually increase "risk" in the true sense of the word. The obstetrical nurse, therefore, is not required to perform any special investigative techniques, tests, or other, when a patient comes to labor and delivery merely because of an increased incidence factor. Essentially, the standard assessment of any patient coming into labor and delivery would and should cover those things that ordinarily would bring to light an abruption (other than an occult abruption), and this should be sufficient to fall within the standard of care regardless of "so-called" increased incidence factors.

Clinical Signs and Symptoms

Although clinical signs and symptoms vary from being totally absent to severe bleeding, hypovolemia, shock, and fetal demise, there are definitely certain criteria that should raise the index of suspicion and lead to further investigation regarding potential abruptio placentae.

The criteria that are often cited for clinical diagnosis include the following:

1. Vaginal bleeding;
2. Increased uterine tone;
3. Uterine tenderness (localized or general);
4. Non-reassuring or absent fetal heart tones;
5. Hypovolemia and maternal shock;
6. Bright red frank bleeding;
7. Patient history of significant vaginal bleeding prior to arrival.

From a nursing standpoint, very few cases are missed where abruptio placentae is severe on arrival, i.e., significant bleeding, severe pain and tenderness, and a hard abdomen. The severe case on arrival almost never ends up as a lawsuit for several reasons. First, such a case is easily recognized and treated almost immediately. Second, any damage to the fetus in such severe cases has probably already occurred, and intervention, even with a Cesarean section on a timely basis, will not prevent fetal injury or death.

The usual cases of abruptio placentae resulting in litigation are those instances where there are marginal to mild signs present. Some of these signs, as indicated above, will come "after the fact" from the mother and other family members' testimony.

From a medical standpoint, in cases of mild findings, the most important issues to address include the following:

1. With respect to "bloody show," is it consistent with labor, or is it consistent with abruptio placentae?
2. With respect to complaints of uterine contractions, are they consistent with uterine hypercontractility or simply labor?
3. With respect to any complaints of pain, is it simply the pain of contractions or the pain related to a hypersensitive and tender uterus from placental abruption?

When one views the medical record retrospectively, there is often very little differentiation, clarification, or even documentation of these issues. Frequently, there is simply a note regarding bloody show, no physical examination of the patient documented relative to uterine activity or resting phase between contractions, and no evaluation of the patient's status and how she is handling the contractions. A good history and physical examination that is well documented (regardless of the uterine activity), and evaluation by fetal monitoring is not only an appropriate nursing evaluation on a routine basis for an intrapartum patient, but will tell whether or not, retrospectively, there was or was not an abruptio placentae that was clinically evident.

Therefore, the following items should be part of the routine intake procedures on a patient who enters labor and delivery triage:

1. A good history, which includes the chief complaint (obviously, if the chief complaint is simply labor, not bleeding, this serves to impeach any subsequent testimony by the patient that her real problem was significant bleeding such that on the way to the hospital she had to use towels to absorb the same).

2. Evaluation of the uterus, including a note that describes the contraction activity, the uterus as resting well between contractions, being non-tender, etc.

3. A statement regarding the patient's subjective condition (i.e., tolerance of labor). This serves to show that the contractions are not hypertonic, that there is an adequate resting phase, and that the patient does not have a tetanic uterus.

4. Documentation of a normal fetal heart rate pattern as soon as possible, which should also include reference to the fetal heart rates on the monitor, as well as the contraction pattern.

Documentation

There are certain items that need to be documented to assist in either establishing or ruling out the presence of an abruptio placentae. Methods of documentation vary from institution to institution; however, simple "shorthand" notes contained in the admitting record such as the following are most helpful: "Minimal bloody show, no uterine tenderness, contractions q 5 min, patient in early labor, minimal discomfort."

Although the above note does not address everything, it indicates that there was an evaluation of the patient, palpation of the abdomen occurred, a significant bleed was ruled out, and significant pain or a hard abdomen did not exist. Simple notes such as these, especially if there is no chief complaint of active vaginal bleeding, are easy to write and clearly show the lack of clinical suspicion of abruptio placentae.

During labor, documentation does not have to address each one of these factors in each progress note. In fact, unless there is a major change from the initial admitting condition, the nurse ordinarily would not address the positive or negatives of each of those factors. However, many flow charts contain a section for 'bloody show" during labor. Descriptive words such as "small," "moderate," or "large" are often placed in those boxes. Unfortunately, what is a small, moderate, or large bloody show in the context of a "bloody show" means something different to a nurse than what it may mean to a jury. When one hears that there is a "large bloody show" occurring during labor, and then the doctor diagnoses an abruption at delivery, one can see how an argument of misdiagnosis by the nurse can be easily fashioned by plaintiffs and plaintiffs' experts (see Chapter 34).

Therefore, it is suggested that a more *quantitative* approach be made with respect to the documentation of bloody show. First and foremost, if a form is used, the designations of small, moderate, and large could be used to describe bloody show, but *only* if on the same form they are described in terms of approximate amounts. In other words, if one were to designate small as being dime-sized, moderate as being quarter-sized, and large being a fifty-cent piece-sized spot on a peripad, then the significance of otherwise subjective terms would be quantified and less arguable. Subjective terminology is probably best left out of a clinical flow chart. Simply describing the size of the bloody spot on the peripad as "quarter-sized" creates an immediate mental picture. Thus, if between two visits, 30 minutes to an hour apart, there is only the appearance of a quarter-sized spot of blood on the peripad, this would be totally acceptable with normal labor and not clinical evidence of an abruption.

Finally, with respect to the actual identification of abruptio placentae by a nurse, the most important element that should follow that recognition is contact of the physician, and if not already started, immediate electronic monitoring of both the fetal activity and the contraction activity. Considering the fact that Parkland Hospital reported only 1 in 830 deaths from placental abruption this would suggest that most cases of abruptio placentae are neither severe nor apparently of acute impact on the fetus. Thus, in cases where one assumes a potential delay in nursing identification of abruptio placentae, a normal fetal heart monitor tracing and normal uterine contraction pattern would suggest that there still was time to save the fetus, and therefore whatever so-called "neglect" on the part of the nurse that may have occurred initially was not the cause of a potential, later occurring fetal demise or injury.

Conclusion

Dr. Niswander's preceding chapter (Chapter 13) addresses the physician's involvement in abruptio placentae, as well as the statistics of morbidity and mortality regarding the same. It is to be suggested that most cases of abruptio placentae are not of a harmful nature, but in a few cases where there is severe abruption, the question remains as to whether or not medical intervention can be done timely enough to change the outcome. It is difficult to answer this question, since not much is written in the literature regarding progressive abruptio, whether or not it can initially cause injury and then possibly improve, whether or not one can predict a small separation that will extend to a larger separation, or whether progression at all is a salvageable situation.

We were unable to find in *any* fetal monitoring book a specific typical pattern that occurs on the fetal heart rate monitor when abruptio placentae is in progress, or how that pattern changes with time. Since it is not clear as to what pattern might be expected or how it may progress (other than fetal death), it seems as though it would be difficult to indicate at what point intervention becomes necessary, and whether or not that intervention could have changed the outcome. From a nursing perspective, this is not a requirement of knowledge. It is the nursing role simply to *identify abnormal patterns* and conditions that might be consistent with any fetal hypoxia and *contact the physician* for further instructions relative to the same.

Because the nurse is the first line of observation on the admitted patient, and because abruptio placentae of a severe enough nature to threaten the fetus is actually quite unusual, it is easy for the nurse to be "trapped" by the document she creates and be subjected to retrospective "20/20" hindsight, even in those cases where there were no signs and symptoms of abruptio placentae on admission, only an absence of an entry into the record. Therefore, in terms of addressing the documentation of what might be considered significant negatives suggesting the absence of an abruption, information should document examinations beginning when the patient is admitted. Following a habit of such routine documentation, physical findings, etc., will automatically address issues of alleged misdiagnosis, even though the nurse is not specifically thinking in terms of abruptio placentae.

Abruptio placentae is a premature separation of the placenta from the uterine wall resulting in retro-placental bleeding—either concealed or external. The separation may be either sudden or gradual, marginal or complete. The signs and symptoms can range from grade 0 (no signs or symptoms, diagnosis made upon delivery of the placenta, and no sequelae) to grade 3 (numerous signs and symptoms, usually resulting in fetal demise). Bleeding may or may not be present and may not be proportional to the severity of the abruption. The causes are unknown, although associated factors have been identified. Abruptio placentae remains an unpredictable event. The literature shows a wide range of incidence. This is attributable to diagnostic difficulties.

Medico-legal claims against obstetrical nurses involving abruptio placentae usually can be narrowed to one question: whether or not a particular nurse in a particular situation had information available that should have led her to suspect the possibility of an abruptio. Two sources of information are available for answering this question: the medical record created by the nurse and the patient's testimony.

Review of cases reveals that sometimes only "bloody show" is documented in the flow chart. From this, it is easy to claim the diagnosis was overlooked or the severity was not perceived. This documentation is insufficient to address and respond to claims involving abruptio. Documentation methods may vary but common characteristics should include:

1. A good history including the patient's chief complaint;
2. An assessment of the uterus;
3. A description of the patient's emotional condition/demeanor;
4. An evaluation of fetal status;
5. Quantitative data versus subjective description.

The "unknown factor" often overlooked by medical personnel is the perceptions and testimony from the patient and family members. Because of the emotional nature of childbirth and lack of understanding of the process, patients and their families may have misperceptions. Their concerns/chief complaints should be addressed in the record so that the objective data of the history and physical can either support or refute their claim.

References

1. Friedman EA (ed). *Obstetrical Decision Making.* Trenton, NJ, B.C. Decker, 1982.
2. Cunningham FG, MacDonald PC, Leveno KJ, et al. (eds). *Williams Obstetrics,* Nineteenth Edition. Norwalk, CT, Appleton & Lange Publishing, 1993, p. 827.
3. Pritchard JA, Cunningham FG, Pritchard SA, et al. On reducing the frequency of severe abruptio placentae. Am J Obstet Gynecol 1991;165:1345.

Oxytocin and Litigation in Obstetrics

◆◆◆

George H. Nolan, M.D., Leila R. Hajjar, M.D.

Oxytocin Lawsuits

In an effort to assign blame for a less than optimum pregnancy outcome when oxytocin has been used, a variety of allegations are usually made. Each of these complaints almost universally begins with a claim of uterine hyperstimulation. The more common allegations associated with the use of oxytocin are:

1. There has been fetal injury as a result of direct trauma associated with intense uterine contractions.
2. There has been fetal injury because of hypoxic states created by uterine hyperstimulation.
3. There has been maternal injury because of the uncontrolled use of oxytocin.
4. There has been fetal or maternal injury resulting from the use of oxytocin in situations where it is contraindicated.

One needs to fully understand the medical pharmacology, usage, and risk of oxytocin before addressing potential legal liability.

Medical Pharmacology of Oxytocin

Oxytocin's role in obstetrics reflects its ability to stimulate myometrial contractions during labor and to initiate labor, as well as its ability to assist in hemostasis at the placental site. It acts at the myometrium by stimulating

From: Donn SM, Fisher CW (eds.): *Risk Management Techniques in Perinatal and Neonatal Practice.* © Futura Publishing Co., Inc., Armonk, NY, 1996.

its specific receptor. Plasma oxytocin concentration remains stable during pregnancy until the expulsive phase of labor when it increases, presumably as a result of vaginal distension or the Ferguson reflex. The effect of oxytocin on uterine contractility may be direct through receptor stimulation, indirect through prostaglandin synthesis stimulation, or both.

During the initial 30 weeks of pregnancy, uterine contractions are demonstrated to be of two basic types: very low intensity localized contractions, which occur at a frequency of one per minute; and "Braxton-Hicks" contractions, which have a higher intensity, a frequency of approximately one per hour at 30-weeks gestation, and which spread across a larger area of the uterus. Uterine activity has been defined by a number of methods, but the following are generally accepted and will be used in this discussion. Uterine *tone* is that state of the uterine muscle between *contractions*, that is, the lowest muscle tension as measured by the lowest intra-amniotic pressure. Uterine contractions are generally defined in terms of their *intensity* and their *frequency*. Frequency is the number of contractions in an arbitrary period of time, most often identified as 10 minutes. Intensity (or amplitude) is the increase in pressure generated by a uterine contraction during the rise from the baseline uterine tone to its return. The measure of uterine activity most often used is the *Montevideo Unit* (MVDU), defined as the product of the frequency of uterine contractions and the intensity of contractions measured during a 10 minute period of time.

Clinical labor is usually thought to exist when the activity of the uterus reaches 80-120 MVDUs despite the fact that there is no clearly identifiable point between pre-labor and labor. Under most circumstances, uterine intensity during labor increases in a progressive manner from approximately 23 mmHg to approximately 50 mmHg until childbirth.[1] Similarly, uterine contraction frequency increases to approximately five contractions per 10 minute period while the uterine baseline tone rises from 8 to 12 mmHg.[2] This results in MVDU in the range of 250. It is also important to note that the intensity of uterine contractions is generally greater in primiparas than in multiparas.[3] An increase in the frequency of uterine contractions and a decrease in their intensity is also noted to occur when a patient labors on her back; this is ameliorated when a patient assumes a lateral position.[4] Uterine contraction intensity during the second stage of labor often exceeds 60 mmHg without maternal effort and exceeds 80 mmHg with maternal "pushing." Clearly, a number of factors associated with normal labor influence uterine tone, contraction frequency, and intensity, and thus MVDU.

Uterine contractions in the pregnant patient can be palpated when their intensity exceeds 10 mmHg, but this fact is influenced by the tone and thickness of the abdominal wall as well as the experience of the examiner. Generally, the onset and end of the contraction cannot be appreciated by palpation. These limitations in manual assessment of uterine contractions extend to indirect maternal-fetal monitoring. Until the intensity of the contraction reaches 40 mmHg, the uterus can be readily indented by a finger; thereafter, it resists depression. A uterine contraction is typically described as bell-shaped with crescent, acme, and descent phases. The steep crescent slope, until it reaches its acme, represents the actual contraction power phase of the uterus. The intensity of the uterine contraction depends upon the total myometrial mass and the number of myometrial cells stimulated.

The purposes of uterine contractions during labor are to efface and dilate the cervix so as to assist in the expulsion of the fetus by maternal effort. Accordingly, the upper uterine segment thickens and shortens during progressing labor, while the lower uterine segment thins or effaces and dilates.[5,6]

Oxytocin can be used to improve the quality of uterine contractions during labor and in some instances to initiate labor. Its ability to accomplish the above depends upon numerous factors such as the stage of gestation, the hormonal milieu, the maternal physiologic and psychologic state, factors affecting uterine contractions (such as multiple gestation and hydramnios), and numerous other factors, including the use of analgesics. There is abundant recent evidence of the value of oxytocin in augmenting labor, much of which has originated from the National Maternity Hospital of Dublin.[7-10] Information corroborating O'Driscoll's[10] reports has been recently published in the United States.[11]

The use of intravenous oxytocin for the induction of labor, initially reported in 1948, continues to be a recognized valuable tool in obstetrics.[12] The preparation of synthetic oxytocin has enhanced the safety of the drug as has the replacement of oral tablets by intravenous medication. The use of prostaglandin "ripening" of the cervix, Bishop scoring, and amniotomy have improved the efficacy and predictability of induction, but the essential ingredient for success remains oxytocin. There are two methods of oxytocin induction most often used in the United States, the low dose continuous infusion method and the incremental infusion method. Common to both methods is the controlled intravenous administration of diluted amounts of oxytocin and the use of continuous electronic maternal-fetal monitoring to assess its direct and indirect effects. A third method, a more aggressive incremental infusion method proposed by O'Driscoll,[10] has been associated with excellent results and represents a divergent approach to the more common methods of oxytocin use.

Hyperstimulation

Hyperstimulation is a term used frequently in obstetrics when the subject of oxytocin is under discussion. Medical malpractice litigation based on oxytocin use invariably requires that the plaintiff prove hyperstimulation. There is universal approbation of the existence of hyperstimulation of the uterine muscle, but at the same time there is no eclairissement or delineation of the meaning of the term "uterine hyperstimulation."

A review of the literature reveals numerous articles that focus on the assessment of the effects of oxytocin and an assignment of a diagnosis of hyperstimulation. Amazingly, > 50% of those research articles, published in peer review journals, failed to define the term hyperstimulation or to provide criteria used to document its existence. Equally surprising was the finding that over 50% of the articles that did define the term hyperstimulation used different criteria for its definition. There is a consistent inconsistency in the obstetric literature regarding the definition of uterine hyperstimulation.

A number of major, excellent, obstetric textbooks address this issue but fail to clarify it, and some of the major organizations dealing with obstetric issues have proffered statements that allow for variable interpretations of the term uterine hyperstimulation. Consider the American College of Obstetrics and Gynecology Technical Bulletin No. 157, which states, "a maximum of five contractions in a 10 minute period, with resultant cervical dilation is considered adequate." This statement, intended to provide a framework from which physicians and institutions can develop appropriate practices regarding oxytocin induction/augmentation has been misquoted by many, and used, in the legal arena, to set five contractions per 10 minute period of time as the upper limit of normal for oxytocin use. More important is the interpretation that exceeding this number of contractions during the stated interval must be, in and of itself, evidence of hyperstimulation. Presumably, the five contraction per 10 minute period is derived from the research of Caldeyro-Barcia and Poiserio.[13] It must be noted that the investigators themselves were more expansive in their description of normal labor activity. They also made reference to the fact that the frequency of contractions increases as labor progresses, and that uterine contraction frequency can be increased during non-oxytocin-stimulated labors by the laboring patient's assumption of a supine position and by anxiety states.

The issue of concern, relative to the use of oxytocin, is that the stimulation of uterine muscle activity, if excessive, may result in biochemical and physiologic changes that alter placental intervillous space blood exchange dynamics and in so doing may cause fetal hypoxia, acidosis, and eventually fetal injury. Any definition of "hyperstimulation" must include statements relative to uterine muscle contraction frequency, duration, intensity, and resting tone, all with time references. There is no definition at present that meets these criteria. Consider that if uterine contractions do not exceed a 90-second duration, occur with regular and equal spacing, and number five per 10-minute period of time, there will be approximately 30 seconds between each contraction. Assuming a baseline tone of < 12 mmHg, this can be considered a normal pattern.

It is also possible to have uterine contractions occurring at a rate of five per 10 minute period, but with irregular intervals between them and still have no contraction exceed 90 seconds in duration. All of the contractions may be associated with a baseline < 12 mmHg. Does this represent normal, hypo-, or hyperstimulation if oxytocin is being used? Similarly, if there are five contractions within a 10 minute period in an oxytocin-stimulated labor, each lasting 105 seconds, and associated with 15 second intervals between the contractions, and a uterine baseline tone < 12 mmHg, does this represent normal uterine activity, or hyperactivity? If the presence of a reactive fetal heart rate pattern and the absence of any fetal heart rate decelerations are added to each of the scenarios, do any of them now reflect hyperstimulation? If an absence of fetal heart rate variability is added to all of the scenarios and coupled with repetitive late decelerations is a diagnosis of hyperstimulation established in a patient receiving oxytocin? What is the diagnosis if the patient is not receiving oxytocin in any of the scenarios? It can hardly be considered hyperstimulation if there is no stimulation!

The point made here is not simply one of academic curiosity. Seitchek and Castillo[2] demonstrated that hyperstimulation, defined as six or more contractions per 10 minutes for two 10 minute periods, or a baseline resting tone exceeding 15 mmHg for more than 15 minutes, occurred "frequently" during oxytocin-stimulated labors as well as during non-oxytocin-stimulated labors. Equally important was their report of an absence of any adverse fetal-neonatal effects associated with the periods of "hyperstimulation." While not ideal, this observation represents a reasonable description of hypercontractility, whether induced or spontaneous, that incorporates and expands the definitions and statements suggested to guide clinical practice.

There are some indisputable conclusions that can be drawn about oxytocin-induced "hyperstimulation." First, it is a poorly defined concept. Second, the usual definition, more than five contractions per 10 minute period, ignores other studies that expand the limits of this definition. It is apparent that hyperstimulation is neither an isolated nor intermittently occurring event, and once induced, continues unless and until amelioration of the effect is undertaken. If persistent, hyperstimulation may be associated with fetal and/or maternal evidence of stress and/or injury. Nevertheless, little quarrel can be found with any health care personnel who, acting out of concern for fetal and/or maternal well being, disrupts an oxytocin infusion in any instance he/she finds troublesome. It must be stated with emphasis, however, that such action is not confirmation that a problem exists. Finally, the mere fact of the existence of uterine hyperstimulation is not indicative of a cause and effect relationship when the outcome is suboptimum.

Medical Management

Practical Dosage Protocols

The continuous infusion method of oxytocin involves the intravenous administration of a low dose of oxytocin, 2.0 mu/min. Its proponents report success rates in inductions and augmentations equivalent to those of the incremental dose methods. The incremental dose methods use the administration of low doses of oxytocin, 0.5-1.0 mu/min as the initial infusion with changes in the rate of infusion that vary from increases by 1-2 mu/min, plateauing at 8-10 mu/min. The frequency of the infusion rate change varies from 15-60 minutes, with most protocols using a 30 second to 4 minute dosing interval.

During oxytocin infusion for induction and/or augmentation of labor, continuous monitoring of maternal-fetal status, urine output, and cardiovascular stability is considered obligatory. Direct maternal-fetal monitoring is superior to indirect monitoring as it provides more specific information about uterine contractions and the fetus. There is wide individual variation with regard to sensitivity to various oxytocin doses, and it is difficult to predict individual responses. Indeed, oxytocin response depends more upon preexisting uterine activity and sensitivity than it does on dose. Finally, current concepts regarding the use of oxytocin for the induction and/or augmentation of labor reflect a belief that the action achieved reflects oxytocin-receptor stimulation. Unfortunately, the duration of oxytocin-receptor coupling is unknown. Using the incremental oxytocin dose protocols, adequate contractions are usually achieved at doses < 8 mu/min in successful induction/augmentations.

Documentation

Regardless of the approach used for labor induction or augmentation, there are obligatory assessments that must be made and documented in the medical record prior to proceeding with these obstetrical procedures. First, the indication for the intervention must be documented as well as the alternatives to induction and potential side effects of oxytocin. Second, the record should reflect that there has been an assessment to exclude the presence of contraindications to the induction/augmentation. After achieving the above, a physician's order must be recorded with specific information as to the procedure, monitoring, preparation of solutions, and initiating dose all documented. A statement to proceed with the induction in accordance with a written protocol is an acceptable alternative.

Oxytocin-related litigation is likely to be with us for some time. Many of the cases involving oxytocin are resolved because of the use of loose definitions and misquotes of medical literature and teaching tools. The following represents one protocol approach that may reduce the vulnerability of health care personnel and institutions to oxytocin-related litigation:

1. Clearly state the indication for the use of oxytocin.
2. Document the presence and content of a discussion with the patient regarding the planned use of the drug. The documentation should include reference to side effects, alternative approaches, benefits, and risks. Some reference to the patient's acceptance and understanding of the plan should be included.
3. Document the obstetric history and physical findings, such as presentation, gestational age, state of the uterus, and current fetal status at the time the oxytocin infusion is initiated.
4. Initiate induction/augmentation by written medical order.
5. Have in place a departmental/hospital protocol that has been reviewed and accepted by the medical staff. Such a protocol should be reasonably specific in regard to the following:
   a. Preparation of the oxytocin solution;
   b. Initiation dose;
   c. Rate of dose change;
   d. Patient monitoring (maternal and fetal);
   e. Maximum infusion dose;
   f. Actions to be taken in the event of an undesired effect;
   g. Some examples of undesired effects.
6. Clear and thorough documentation of the status of the mother and the fetus in the event of an undesired effect.
7. A working definition of the term hyperstimulation.
8. If the drug is being used contrary to the established protocol, the reason should be explicitly stated in the medical record.

Care should be taken to write a protocol that acknowledges the fact that there are different, albeit legitimate and medically acceptable, approaches to the use of oxytocin, and one that allows for individual practice variation. Similarly, protocols should not be written and structured so rigidly that reasonable obstetric practice will be impeded. Finally, a review of such a protocol should occur at regular intervals so as to ensure that updated information is incorporated.

Commentary

Fetal injury associated with oxytocin use and allegedly resulting from the trauma caused by oxytocin-induced "hard contractions" is a complaint an obstetrician may face. Such a complaint should be a difficult one to prove provided the following can be established:

1. *The absence of malpresentation.* A pre-infusion statement documenting the presenting part is of primary importance, since this is the most likely area of vulnerability. The medical literature, for example, does not provide data to support the conclusion that breech presentations are contraindications to the use of oxytocin for augmentation, even though it contains statements to that effect.
2. *The absence of fetal heart responses consistent with hypoxia and/or acidosis.* The availability of the maternal-fetal monitor tracings and/or documentation in the record of fetal well being is of major significance in this regard.
3. *A description of the newborn at birth as well as at the time of hospital discharge will do much to address injuries that occur after the hospital discharge.*

The treating physician and the medical expert must be alert and prepared to respond appropriately to the "land mines" placed by the plaintiff attorney. Often the important questioning begins with seemingly innocuous questions such as, "isn't it true one of the purposes of using oxytocin is to make uterine contractions harder?" This question should never be answered affirmatively because that is not the purpose of using oxytocin! An appropriate response would be to indicate that, "the purpose of oxytocin use during labor is to stimulate normal uterine contractions." If the question is phrased so as to allow only a yes or no answer, the appropriate response is obvious—it is "no"!

Finally, if there has been fetal injury associated with the birth process, there may have been mitigating circumstances. The record should reflect all other factors, such as the emergency nature of a delivery by forceps or vacuum extraction in any instance where rapid birth was necessitated. One such example might be the need for a rapid birth in a situation where there are fetal heart rate decelerations associated with a terminal abruption. The medical record should clearly reflect the clinical opinion that even a short delay for Cesarean preparation and birth would likely result in major injury or worse, fetal death.

Maternal soft tissue injury allegedly resulting from the use of oxytocin is the claim most often used when there has been a uterine rupture. This is almost an inevitable complaint when oxytocin is used in a patient who has a uterine scar separation. Part of the problem lies in the fact that the literature contains articles in which a prior uterine scar is considered a contraindication to oxytocin use during labor. It is imperative to point out that the obstetric literature also considered oxytocin use appropriate in those situations where labor is considered safe. The abundant recent information regarding vaginal birth following prior Cesarean section as well as the older literature revealing *rare* uterine ruptures associated with oxytocin use will be quite supportive. Clearly, most rupture or dehiscence of uterine scar occurs in instances where there has been no oxytocin used and in many instances where there has been no labor. The defense of such an allegation will have been initiated when the record reflects a discussion of the potential adverse effects of oxytocin use. The second line of defense is established with documentation that the patient has experienced a labor pattern consistent with a normal labor, and that she has been appropriately monitored. Finally, testimony must reflect the fact that the use of oxytocin is not intended to make contractions harder— it is intended to stimulate contraction to simulate normal labor.

Allegations of malpractice based on the contention that fetal-neonatal and maternal injury occurred because oxytocin was used in situations where it is contraindicated, reflect the use of literature that has been developed to *guide* decision making rather than to *make* decisions. Again, the medical record may represent the best defense tool. The indication for the use of oxytocin and an indication that the obstetric plan has been thoroughly discussed is of major import. A thorough discussion of such a case must be held between the defendant and defense counsel prior to making legal decisions. The following example is intended to illustrate such a point:

> A legal action is brought purporting the abusive administration of oxytocin. The allegation is that a patient had had her labor stimulated with oxytocin in the face of a transverse lie. Her position is supported by the postmortem finding of a transected cervical spinal cord in the baby, associated with considerable bruising of the back and occiput, and a conclusion that respiratory paralysis was associated with the neonatal demise. The medical record reflects a sonographic diagnosis of an oblique/transverse lie noted prior to the stimulation of the maternal labor.

This scenario, on the surface, is as bad as they come. It involves the use of oxytocin in the management of a labor problem in the face of a malpresentation, which many have stated to be a contraindication to its use. In this example, it is associated with a very bad outcome.

The case becomes defensible when it is recognized that the estimated gestational age of the fetus was 20 weeks, that there was a nursing and physician record of a lengthy discussion regarding the expected outcome and the options for management. Additionally, the record reflected the recognition of an oblique lie and the family's acceptance of the anticipated fetal demise and agreement that the small risk of her oxytocin augmentation was less than that of a surgical procedure. In this instance, what is generally stated in the medical literature, without qualification, does not represent management that would be recommended by reasonable physicians and experts. It is an example where a generally agreed upon contraindication to the use of oxytocin represents a very appropriate use of the drug. The point being made here is that the medical literature provides broad guidelines that may be superseded in certain situations. The medical record remains the best forum to document the reason for an action, and to document that the patient has been informed and involved in the decision-making process. A defense could have been constructed on the basis of the estimated fetal age, in the absence of the documentation discussed, but it would certainly be a weaker defense than one that adds to it the documentation available in this instance.

Another allegation is that *fetal-neonatal injury* results from hypoxia-asphyxia occurring during oxytocin-induced hyperstimulation of uterine contractions. The allegation of hyperstimulation with oxytocin is found in many legal actions stating that adverse outcomes result from the improper use of this drug. The problem posed here, hyperstimulation, is common to many of the "profitable" lawsuits that have been resolved when there has been an adverse neonatal outcome associated with the oxytocin augmentation or induction of labor. When one allows for the relatively uncommon situation when the allegation is that of a fetal-neonatal injury resulting from strictly "physical" trauma, all other allegations compound the issue. First is the allegation of fetal-neonatal injury. Second, there is an allegation of "fetal distress" (most often in the form of hypoxia-asphyxia). Third, there is an allegation of the "hyperstimulation" of uterine contractions. Fourth, there is an attempted integration of some or all of the preceding issues in a manner to show cause and effect and thus to prove malpractice. Proving malpractice is not usually accomplished, but assigning blame and awarding large judgments in these cases is common.

The one indisputable fact that exists is that there is a child with a permanent injury. The injury is most often manifest in neurologic or cognitive dysfunction. It is frequently labeled as some form of "cerebral palsy." In analyzing the case, it is important to separate the induction of labor from the augmentation of dysfunctional labor. In the latter instance, the situation generally involves a pregnancy that has been considered non-problematic prior to the development of dysfunctional labor and the necessity to use oxytocin. The former situation differs considerably because of the fact that there has been a decision to use oxytocin for the induction of labor. This is a statement that suggests the existence of a prenatal pregnancy problem prior to the onset of labor. The best current information indicates most of the factors involved with the etiology of cerebral palsy are thought to have exerted their effects during the prenatal period, and that at best only a small percentage of cases of cerebral palsy can be explained on the basis of events occurring during labor and childbirth (see Chapters 25 and 26). It is thus improper to view such fetal-neonatal outcomes, in instances when oxytocin has been used, differently from those where it has not been used unless there is clear, consistent, documentable evidence to link an abusive use of oxytocin with the neonatal outcome.

The dysfunctional status of the child, which is often classified as cerebral palsy, is usually explained on the basis of fetal hypoxia-ischemia. Such contentions are often neither supported by fetal monitor evidence (repetitive late decelerations and/or loss of fetal heart rate variability, suggesting hypoxia and/or acidosis), nor by fetal scalp and/or umbilical cord blood gas findings indicative of hypoxia or acidosis. In many oxytocin cases a standard is introduced defining fetal stress that is far below that used in obstetrics, and it is often accepted and unchallenged. In other words, when oxytocin is used, the presence of an isolated fetal heart rate deceleration (late, variable, or otherwise), that may or may not be explainable replaces the accepted standard for considering fetal stress (repetitive late decelerations, and a period of reduced fetal heart rate variability that can be explained and that resolves) is used as the basis for concluding that hypoxia/acidosis existed and caused injury. It is of paramount importance that the criteria for assigning a clinical diagnosis/impression in all other obstetric situations be maintained in oxytocin cases.

Every issue regarding the use of oxytocin to stimulate uterine contractions ultimately involves allegations of excessive oxytocin stimulation of the uterine muscle. In cases of alleged fetal injury from trauma, the allegations suggest that the "hard" contractions produced, forced the fetal head against the pelvic bones resulting in fetal injury. In cases of uterine rupture, allegedly from improper oxytocin use, the claim is that the "hard" contractions resulted in the uterus eventually giving way under the stress of stimulated contractions. These allegations are often made in the face of information about a given labor that reveals uterine contractions that are identical to those of a normal non-stimulated labor. The perception portrayed is that oxytocin-stimulated uterine contractions increase directly and proportionally with increasing doses of oxytocin, indefinitely. This view is clearly inconsistent with our knowledge of effects mediated through receptor stimulation.

Commentary by Mr. Fisher: Through the years, oxytocin augmentation, prolonged labor, arrested labor, prolonged active phase, prolonged second stage, and hyperstimulation have frequently been held responsible for almost any type of subsequent adverse neurologic outcome. This is often done without any real scientific discussions of how the mechanics of such labor events could feasibly cause poor outcomes such as mental retardation and/or cerebral palsy.

In Friedman EA, et al., "Dysfunctional Labor: XII. Long Term Effects on Infant," American Journal of Obstetrics and Gynecology

1977;127:779, and Cohen WR, "Influence of the Duration of Second State Labor or Perinatal Outcome and Puerperal Morbidity," Obstetrics and Gynecology 1977;49:266, it was noted that extended labor *without* instrument delivery was not shown to increase the risk of reduced I.Q. or cerebral palsy.

In cases where there was extended labor, without evidence of hypoxic-ischemic encephalopathy from asphyxial events, there did not seem to be proof that mechanical events of protracted active phase or protracted descent caused some type of global brain damage leading to mental retardation or cerebral palsy. Yet, oxytocin augmentation for protracted labor with alleged claims of hyperstimulation are pervasive in the obstetrical medico-legal arena, and stimulate the rather vivid and excitable imagination of the lay juror. The testimony of experts regarding this theory often includes verbiage such as "flogging the baby down the birth canal," "hammer blows from the contractions driving the baby into the pelvis," "slamming the baby against the pelvis." It is not too difficult to understand why a jury would, without thinking scientifically, accept this theory to explain brain damage.

The idea that a baby moves back and forth substantially during labor contractions, causing a "slamming" or "flogging" event is patently absurd. One need only review *Williams Obstetrics*, Sixteenth Edition, page 376 regarding labor, to find out that the uterus physiologically prevents the baby from moving back and forth at all. The idea that a baby smashes its head back and forth in utero against the pelvis is patently wrong.

The second idea, that is, that compression of the fetal head against the pelvis could cause a global and diffuse, bilateral insult to the brain is scientifically unsupportable. Contact, or compression injuries "do not cause diffuse brain injury" (see Wilkins and Rengachary's *Neurosurgery*, page 1532 in which Dr. Thomas A. Generalli explains mechanisms of head injuries).

Thus, in a compression or contact injury, the most that one would expect would be some type of focal injury to the brain, such as possibly a subdural or a subarachnoid hemorrhage, if the event was severe enough.

A theory that has appeared in obstetrical litigation is the claim that the baby moves so fast in utero back and forth (like a piston) that it suffers an acceleration/deceleration injury that leads to axonal disruption and injury on a diffuse basis bilaterally. The claim is essentially that the injurious event would be analogized to the "whiplash" event in a car accident. Although this preposterous theory, which has no scientific basis whatsoever (nor could it, given the minimal acceleration effects that uterine contraction would have on a baby's head that is laying against a cervix or a pelvis) seems to be beyond all credibility, it has resulted in multimillion dollar verdicts in various jurisdictions.

In fact, mathematical models of head acceleration injuries have been computed using monkeys, to provide minimal angular acceleration formulas that would be required for a threshold before such an injury can occur. (See Bycrot GN. "Mathematical Model of a Head Subjected to an Angular Acceleration," Journal of Biomechanics 1973;6:487-495, and Gennarelli TA. "Biomechanics of Acute Subdural Hematoma," J Trauma 1982;22:680-686.)

Working examples of threshold events causing diffuse axonal shearing injury are likened to a person who falls 25 feet, strikes his head on concrete, stops in 0.1 cm and experiences 200 g's of deceleration, or a car striking a rigid barrier at 40 miles an hour dropping to 0 miles an hour in 35 milliseconds. This is hardly the same as childbirth.

To even remotely suggest that this can occur during labor contractions is not just "junk science" but is probably outright nonsense. Yet, there are those experts who will testify to this issue. It would seem the only method of recourse is to attack such an expert on the scientific principle, requiring him to produce recognized peer review literature to support his position. More often than not, however, such experts are allowed to testify by unsuspecting and unknowing courts of law who are easily deceived and "smoke-screened" by such theories that have no scientific validity whatsoever.

As a final important note to this discussion, it should be clear from Doctors Nolan and Hajjars' chapter that hyperstimulation is a poorly defined, but easily findable event on any monitor strip by a skilled professional testifier. This is an area that should be of major concern to the obstetrical profession, and hopefully, focused efforts will be directed toward defining more clearly what hyperstimulation means in terms of not simply a technical finding on a monitor strip, but a physiologic event and how it affects the fetus.

References

1. Caldeyro-Barcia R, Alvarex H. Abnormal uterine action in labor. J Obstet Gynecol Br Emp 1952;59:5.
2. Seitchik J, Castillo M. Oxytocin augmentation of dysfunctional labor I. Clinical date. Am J Obstet Gynecol 1982;144:899.

3. Turnbull AC. Uterine contractions in normal and abnormal labor. J Obstet Gynecol Br Emp 1957;64:321.
4. Caldeyro-Barcia R, Noreigo G, Cibils LA. Effect of position changes on the intensity and frequency of uterine contractions during labor. Am J Obstet Gynecol 1960 or 1961.
5. Danforth DN, Graham FJ, Ivy AC. The functional anatomy of labor as revealed by frozen sagittal sections in the macacus Rhesus monkey. Surg Obstet Gynecol 1941;74:188.
6. Danforth DN, Ivy AC. The lower uterine segment: Its derivation and physiologic behavior. Am J Obstet Gynecol 1949;57:831.
7. O'Driscoll K, Jackson RJ, Gallagher JT. Prevention of prolonged labour. Br Med J 1969;2:477.
8. O'Driscoll K, Jackson RJ, Gallagher JT. Prevention of prolonged labour. Br Med J 1973;3:135.
9. O'Driscoll K, Foley M. Correlation of decrease in perinatal mortality and increase in cesarean rates. Obstet Gynecol 1983;61:1.
10. O'Driscoll K. Active management of labour as an alternative to cesarean section for dystocia. Obstet Gynecol 1984;63:485.
11. Lopez-Zeno JA, Peaceman AM, Adashek JA, et al. A controlled trial of a program for the active management of labor. N Engl J Med 1992;326-450.
12. Theobald GW, Graham A, Campbell J, et al. Br Med J 1948;2:123.
13. Caldeyro-Barcia R, Posiero JJ. Oxytocin and contractility of the pregnant human uterus. Ann NY Acad Sci 1959;75:813.

Chapter 16

Operative Vaginal Delivery

◆◆◆

Philip C. Dennen, M.D.

Introduction

Operative vaginal delivery pertains to delivery assisted by obstetrical forceps or the vacuum extractor (VE). Both methods have often been involved in complaints that have gone to litigation. Among the common allegations are the following:

1. Use without appropriate indication.
2. Failure to rule out cephalopelvic disproportion prior to attempting vaginal delivery.
3. Improper instrument application resulting from bad technique, high station, or incorrect diagnosis of position.
4. Fetal injury because of the use of excessive force.

Forceps have survived controversy and swings in popularity since introduced to obstetrics in the 17th century. Their use is taught in all obstetrics residency training programs surveyed.[1,2] The incidence of forceps use can vary with the geographic area, physician attitude and training, variation in obstetrical analgesia and anesthesia, and to some extent, patient involvement. Forceps deliveries are reported in percentages that range from near 0%-20%. Descriptions of the many various instruments, and details of their specific applications and use may be found in several texts.[3-5]

The VE, called the ventouse in Europe, was first proposed in the 19th century but gained popularity from the Malmstrom instrument, introduced in 1952. More recently, several plastic soft cup extractors have been developed in response to reports of fetal damage from metal cups. In some areas,

From: Donn SM, Fisher CW (eds.): *Risk Management Techniques in Perinatal and Neonatal Practice.* © Futura Publishing Co., Inc., Armonk, NY, 1996.

particularly in Europe, the VE has replaced forceps. While it was originally proposed and used for higher stations of the fetal head, it is now taught that the indications, contraindications, preparation of the patient, definitions, and prerequisites are the same as those for forceps delivery. The notable exception is that less anesthesia may be required for VE use. The various instruments and their use are described in several texts.[4,6-8] As with forceps, these specifics are beyond the scope of this chapter.

Indications and Contraindications

Indications for operative vaginal delivery may be maternal or fetal. Maternal cardiopulmonary, vascular, or neuromuscular conditions in which voluntary effort is either inadequate or contraindicated are obvious indications. These are encountered relatively infrequently. More commonly the maternal factors of exhaustion, lack of cooperation, intrapartum infection, and anesthesia effect are involved.[2,5]

> **Commentary by Mr. Volk:** Doctor convenience is sometimes, hopefully rarely, involved also. I have litigated several cases wherein this was the only indication. In one case, the mother was admitted to the hospital at 7:45 A.M., was making progress, although slow. The doctor was in the office seeing patients. On his lunch hour, without ever examining the patient during labor, he came to the hospital and attempted delivery with high forceps. Shoulder dystocia occurred with a resulting permanent brachial plexus palsy.

Fetal indications include presumed fetal jeopardy based on non-reassuring heart rate patterns or scalp pH readings. Umbilical cord prolapse or placental separation can be indications. Malposition of the fetal head leading to an arrest of descent occurs more frequently with regional anesthesia.[10,11] Forceps may be indicated after an unsuccessful VE attempt at delivery.[12]

The indication of prolongation of the second stage of labor has been redefined by the American College of Obstetricians and Gynecologists (ACOG).[2] Operative delivery should be considered when a nullipara fails to progress after 2 hours of second stage (1 hour for the multipara). One hour is added in the presence of an effective regional anesthetic.

The prophylactic forceps concept advanced by DeLee in the 1920s became extremely popular in mid-century and still has adherents. Currently, should an operative delivery terminate a short, uncomplicated second stage of labor, the operator would be criticized for inadequate indications should a fetal injury result.

Vaginal delivery of a breech is considered by some authors[3,13,14] to constitute a routine indication for forceps to the aftercoming head. This becomes essential if the body has delivered and the standard maneuvers fail to deliver the head.

The very low birthweight infant, below 1500 g, may not be protected by forceps and may in fact be harmed.[5,15] Spontaneous delivery with liberal episiotomy may be preferable. Most feel that the protective concept is of value in the 1500- to 2500-g preterm infant.[5,16,17]

Contraindications to an operative vaginal delivery include the high or unengaged fetal head, known cephalopelvic disproportion, and severe fetal malposition (such as most brow presentations, and face presentations that are other than chin anterior). Any fetal anomaly or pelvic abnormality that contraindicates vaginal delivery, per se, will obviously contraindicate intervention other than abdominal delivery. Inability to diagnose position of the fetal head or inability to apply the instrument should negate instrumental delivery. Lack of training or experience of the operator is a relative problem to which the solution may be documented supervision.

> **Commentary by Mr. Volk:** The cases I have reviewed fall generally into two categories. The first is the physician who may be a general or family practitioner who has been practicing for many years. This physician has minimal or no formal obstetrical training, has been getting by but has not even made minimal efforts to keep current or be trained in modern obstetrics. This doctor does not realize that he/she should be referring deliveries to a trained obstetrician. What this physician does with forceps is just not acceptable now. The second category breaks down into two subparts: the first is the intern or resident who is just learning and causes injury because of a lack of knowledge, judgment, and experience; and the second is the physician who has completed training but has never really been adept at utilizing forceps or the VE for multiple reasons—lack of practice, liberal use of Cesarean sections, lack of judgment, and the like. It goes without saying that doctors in these categories are either unaware of their shortcomings, or more importantly, have a tremendous lack of judgment. In the cases I have litigated, lack of judgment is nearly always a crucial factor.

The VE is subject to the same indications and contraindications. Reports of cup application to the high head[18] are disturbing. Additional contraindications to VE use include the low birthweight preterm infant, non-vertex presentations, known bleeding problems in the fetus, and previous scalp blood sampling.

Prerequisites

Prerequisites to operative vaginal delivery are as follows: 1. the membranes should be ruptured with the cervix fully dilated and retracted; 2. the bladder should be empty, with the possible exception of simple outlet procedures; 3. the absence of a bony abnormality by clinical pelvimetry should be noted (parenthetically, it is considered unfortunate that the teaching of clinical pelvimetry is frequently inadequate for proper evaluation of the obstetrical pelvis and the feto-pelvic relationship); 4. the position and station of the presenting part should be known (example: Vertex, well-flexed, LOT at +2 to +3 station, hollow of the sacrum filled. This constitutes good justification of a "low" classification); and 5. adequate anesthesia should be used, usually a minimum of pudendal block for forceps. Regional anesthesia is almost mandatory for a rotation and delivery.

> **Commentary by Mr. Volk:** It is absolutely amazing how often the cases that I litigate have no adequate documentation for the applications of forceps or vacuum. It would seem to be elementary that the prerequisites be there and documented, but they often are not.

There should be adequate facilities, equipment, and personnel for support of the patient and her infant, particularly in the situation of a trial of forceps or VE with a reasonable possibility of moving to an abdominal delivery. The physician should have a working knowledge of the various instruments and the mechanical forces involved in their proper use. Since complications tend to increase in inverse ratio to the technical skill and experience of the operator, supervision or other assistance may be indicated. The "learning curve" is not an excuse, since the patient is entitled to the standard of care.

> **Commentary by Mr. Volk:** The law clearly requires the standard to be met, whether or not the operator is fully trained.

The patient and significant others in attendance should be counseled and prepared for the procedure. It should be noted that the absence of an informed consent is often claimed.

> **Commentary by Mr. Volk:** In the multiple cases I have litigated involving forceps or vacuum, I have never seen a written informed consent signed by the patient for the procedure. There is no logical reason for the failure to obtain written consent. Since these procedures are operative and involve known risks, the standard should require written consent. This could be accomplished in three ways:
> 1. A consent signed at the time the operative delivery becomes reality;

Table 1

Criteria of Forceps Deliveries According to Station and Rotation

Types of Procedure	Criteria
Outlet forceps	1. Scalp is visible at the introitus without separating labia 2. Fetal skull has reached pelvic floor 3. Sagittal suture is in anteroposterior diameter or right or left occiput anterior or posterior position 4. Fetal head is at or on perineum 5. Rotation does not exceed 45°
Low forceps	Leading point of fetal skull is at station ≥ +2 cm and not on the pelvic floor a. Rotation ≤ 45° (left or right occiput anterior to occiput anterior, or left or right occiput posterior to occiput posterior) b. Rotation > 45°
Midforceps	Station above +2 cm but head engaged
High	Not included in classification

2. A consent signed when the patient is admitted and signs other consent forms;

3. During the prenatal course when forceps, vacuum, and Cesarean section can be explained. This could be done in the doctor's office and sent over to the hospital with the prenatal records.

Forceps should be checked prior to use to avoid using unmatched blades from different forgings, which can apply asymmetrical force to the fetal head.[19] Similarly, the VE system should be examined for defects and air leakage prior to use of the equipment.[6]

Station is almost routinely a critical factor in litigation related to operative vaginal delivery. This demonstrates its importance in risk management and justifies further comments. Station is estimated by palpating the level of the leading bony point of the presenting part in centimeters above or below the level of the ischial spines. Caput should not be considered.

The 1989 ACOG standardization of forceps classification (Table 1) was a needed clarification of earlier systems. Some confusion has arisen in that the ACOG specifies division of the lower pelvis in 0-5 cm below the spines, rather than into thirds, as in an older system.[1,2] The ACOG guidelines have proven to be effective in clinical practice.[20,21] They deserve to be universally utilized to improve standardization of statistics and to avoid confusion in description.

The anticipated difficulty of any operative procedure is directly related to the station of the fetal head (the lower, the easier). The widest point of that head is the biparietal diameter, which entity must be moved through the birth canal along the curve of Carus. Engagement of the head, or passage of the biparietal diameter through the pelvic inlet, is assumed when the leading bony point is at zero station. The biparietal diameter cannot be palpated; its level in the pelvis must be estimated. With the conditions of marked molding, macrosomia, extension (deflexion) of the head, and occiput posterior position, the biparietal diameter is relatively higher in relation to the leading bony point.[22] The potential for a more difficult delivery must be considered in these cases. The Cesarean section finding of an unengaged extremely molded head, which vaginally was at +1 to +2 station is not uncommon.

Many authors agree that fetal results comparable to spontaneous vaginal delivery are to be expected with operative vaginal delivery from low as well as outlet stations.[20,21,23-27] Mid-station procedures have been associated with an increased risk of both short- and long-term neonatal morbidity when compared to spontaneous vaginal delivery.[28] In the decade of the 1980s many articles presented data attesting to the favorable results of mid-station delivery in relation to Cesarean delivery—a far more realistic comparison.[25,29-31] The operator must consider the risk potentials involved.

> **Commentary by Mr. Volk:** I would add that the patient must be informed of the risks so that adequate consent can be given or another method of delivery discussed between doctor and patient.

Under appropriate circumstances, attempted mid-station operative vaginal delivery (vertex above +2 but engaged) is acceptable while simultaneous preparations are being made for Cesarean delivery.[2]

> **Commentary by Mr. Volk:** I assume that Dr. Dennen is discussing a trial of forceps or vacuum. Probably some physicians are able to complete a mid-station delivery without injury to the fetus or mother, but I wonder how many are really that adept at it. There would seem to be several medico-legal implications that would have to be analyzed:
>
> 1. Did the prerequisites exist and are they documented, preferably by more than one health care provider?
>
> 2. Was the patient informed of the risks of mid-station delivery and the alternatives and is there a written consent?
>
> 3. Is there a need for mid-station delivery that is based on fact, not conjecture? That is, is there danger to the mother and/or fetus that requires mid-station delivery?

4. Is there documentation that preparation is being made for section?

5. Is there documentation that a trial of forceps or vacuum is contemplated?

6. Can the physician demonstrate that on other occasions the trial was ended and other means utilized to deliver?

If the above do not exist, the physician is at great risk for an adverse outcome in any suit that results from a mid-station forceps or vacuum.

Technique: Application and Traction

The technique of forceps and VE use are described in appropriate texts, but certain factors are of greater risk management significance and deserve special comment. The importance of correct application technique and verification of application cannot be overstated. A symmetrical bimalar biparietal forceps application, because of the instrument design, will transmit the required tractive force symmetrically to non-vital areas of the skull. An asymmetrical (i.e., brow-mastoid) application can result in asymmetrical intracranial stress with possible subsequent damage from traction. This is particularly true in the preterm infant.[8] Improper application is associated with an increased incidence of slippage of the forceps, a significant factor in fetal injury. Should the operator be unable to diagnose position from fontanelle and suture landmarks, forceps should not be used. Palpation of an ear can sometimes resolve a problem in diagnosis, but is not routine since undesirable loss of station is unavoidable.

Proper cup placement is critical for VE success. As with forceps, control of flexion and synclitism of the fetal head keeps the long axis of the head in the pelvic axis thus offering the least resistance to descent. Similarly, proper application may be difficult when failure to descend has been caused by malposition of the fetal head.[2,6] Improper placement of the vacuum cup will result in an increased rate of detachment and failure of descent. With either modality the obstetrician should examine the newborn for skin marking, which can validate the accuracy of the instrument application.

Traction involves two elements that must be considered, namely "how and how much." If clinically appropriate, tractive effort is timed to coincide with uterine contractions and voluntary expulsive effort. The number of pulls usually does not exceed three to five using either forceps or the VE. With forceps, special considerations should be observed. Head compression is minimized by using the finger guards rather than squeezing the handles. Since the mechanical advantage of the instrument's pelvic curve is decreased with greater rotation away from occiput anterior (OA), a correcting rotation to

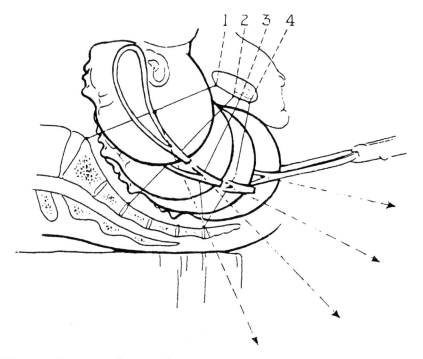

Figure 1. Direction of tractive force according to level of biparietal diameter.

OA is performed before traction is applied. With either instrument, the direction of tractive force is in the axis of the birth canal (curve of Carus) depending on the level of the biparietal diameter (Figure 1). The axis traction principle always applies since proper traction must be perpendicular to the plane of the pelvis where the biparietal diameter is located. Thus, the higher the station, the lower the pull is directed.

The tractive force required will vary but should be the least possible to accomplish reasonable descent. Despite a paucity of hard evidence, it is felt that the maximum permissible force is 45 lbs (20 kg) of traction in the primipara or 30 lbs (13 kg) in the multipara.[32-34] The operator must realize that greater force is not the appropriate solution to unsuccessful traction. With forceps, traction is usually easier with the use of an axis traction aid (either the Bill handle on a classic forceps or a forceps designed to provide axis traction). The operator is best advised to avoid the appearance of a too strenuous tractive effort.

The VE can usually be expected to detach before being able to cause significant fetal injury from traction. As much as 20 kg of traction force can be applied before "popoff" occurs in some cases.[35] It is recognized that increases in negative pressure and prolonged time of contact with the vacuum on the scalp are associated with an increased risk of scalp trauma. The vacuum level and timing should be recorded. Prior to traction the operator should digitally ascertain that there is no maternal tissue between the cup and scalp. Manual torque should not be applied to the cup to decrease the risk of scalp injury.[2] Opinions vary concerning the maximum tolerable number of cup detachments.[2]

> **Commentary by Mr. Volk:** It is important to fully document the delivery maneuvers in the medical record. Writing in the records, "forceps used," or "VE applied" is not adequate for medico-legal purposes.

Complications and Causation

Complications of operative vaginal delivery can be maternal or fetal. Most of the problems have also been seen following spontaneous vertex delivery (and even following abdominal delivery). The onus is on the obstetrician, however, since the incidence of complication is greater with intervention, while the results of non-intervention can only be speculative. Since the need for operative assistance is often accompanied by fetal and labor factors that are associated with traumatic and/or hypoxic-ischemic birth injury, assessment of causation is frequently difficult (see Chapter 25).

Maternal complications are usually related to soft tissue trauma. Uterine, cervical, vaginal, bladder, urethral, or rectal injuries have been recorded with increased blood loss, hematomas, late fistula formation, or other symptomatic anatomic distortion. The incidence of maternal trauma is reported to be less with the VE than with forceps.

Fetal complications include forceps marks, scalp trauma, bruising, laceration, cephalhematoma, subgaleal bleeding, intracranial hemorrhage, skull fracture, and other fractures, particularly clavicular. The incidence of brachial plexus palsy related to shoulder dystocia is increased. Corneal injury can occur following force applied to an incorrect forceps application, if the blade is over the brow and orbit. An increase in facial nerve palsy has been both reported and disputed. Neonatal morbidity is higher overall when using the VE over forceps[6] particularly following higher station VE procedures, which may have replaced some forceps operations.[18] With the VE there is a higher reported incidence of scalp injury, cephalhematoma, retinal hemorrhage, and neonatal jaundice, but severe intracranial damage is uncommon. Traumatic injuries tend to be decreased with the newer soft cup devices. Many studies contrasting delivery by forceps or VE have shown no significant difference in neonatal outcome.[5]

Speculation and controversy continue to arise concerning the possibility of intellectual or neurologic damage related to operative vaginal delivery. Many investigators have found no difference in intelligence scoring of children delivered by forceps or VE versus spontaneous delivery.[36,37] In fact, slight advantage to the operative vaginal deliveries has been given by some authors when scores were compared with those of Cesarean deliveries.[25,30,31,38]

Attempts to link serious neurologic problems (cerebral palsy [CP], epilepsy, and mental retardation) with operative vaginal delivery are not uncommon. Established facts minimize the role of the mode of delivery in causation. It has been observed that the incidence of these handicapping conditions has not decreased despite the decrease in operative vaginal delivery and the increase in abdominal delivery. Cases of CP have shown a definite positive relationship with prematurity, oligohydramnios, postmaturity, increased maternal age and relative infertility, poor obstetrical history, bleeding during pregnancy, genetic influences, mercury poisoning, and possibly other environmental factors. It is estimated that events at delivery may have significance in < 5% of CP cases. Most cases have no history of an obstetrical lapse of care and most cases complicated by hypoxia have no sequelae.[39]

> **Commentary by Mr. Volk:** There clearly are circumstances where the failure of a physician or other health care provider caused significant injury to a fetus, either by acts of commission or omission during the prenatal course or delivery. What percentage of cases of CP are caused by lapses of care resulting in injury is truly unknown. There have been attempts to quantify the percentage. The attorney evaluating a potential claim must have just cause to bring a claim. When that just cause exists, litigation should be pursued to secure benefits for the newborn.

Superficial thinking ignores growing evidence that the causes are far more complex with the contribution of many interrelated damaging factors.[39-42] Newer findings are favoring the unjustly accused obstetrician.

Conclusions

The outcome of the vast majority of operative vaginal delivery cases is normal and there is no reason for complaint or litigation. In the instance of any poor outcome the obstetrician is forced into a defensive posture attempting to prove that the outcome resulted from factors other than his or her intervention. A defense can be extremely difficult unless the chart documents adequate indications, observance of prerequisites, and appropriate performance of the operative vaginal delivery. An expert reviewing a case tends to look for meticulous care and meticulous documentation. Obstetricians are often nonchalant about obstetrical charting. As a defendant, they belatedly realize the importance of the written note. "If it isn't there, it didn't happen." After-the-fact verbal explanations have the appearance of an effort to escape consequences.

Dictation should treat an operative vaginal delivery with the same care as a potentially complicated major gynecologic operation. The notes should include the indications for the procedure, the station, position and attitude of the fetal head, evaluation of clinical pelvimetry, and an estimation of fetal size, molding, and caput, if appropriate. The instrument used, with details of application, verification of an appropriate application, then rotational and tractive maneuvers used should be recorded. The degree of force required to effect rotation and/or descent is most important, regardless of its seeming insignificance in an easy case. Should the chart later be subject to expert scrutiny for any reason, information is protective while its absence is pejorative.

Progress notes written or dictated during the patient's labor should display the cognitive process involved in the decision to intervene, as well as when and how to intervene with operative vaginal delivery. This is potentially a convenient place to note that the procedure was discussed, particularly if an emergency or semi-emergency situation should make an informed consent impractical.

"Failed forceps" is a prejudicial term that the operator should always avoid. It has always carried a suggestion of possible judgmental error, even negligence, in that a disproportion may not have been recognized. A trial of forceps, the preferable term, implies a cautious, tentative attempt at vaginal delivery with discontinuation in favor of an alternative action in case of difficulty. Actually, all forceps and VE deliveries may be considered as trial procedures. A gentle negative trial should not alter outcome.

Choice of instrument is a variable that partially depends on the specifics of the clinical situation. The design of different forceps and VE instruments makes them more effective for certain purposes (i.e., rotation, correction of attitude, traction). The advantages for one purpose may comprise the disadvantages for another purpose. The most important determining factor in choice of instrument should naturally be the preference of the operator. This is related to what works best in his or her hands based on skill and experience.

Fetal trauma is difficult to predict. One can only speculate about the anticipated fetal response to a given amount of trauma. Injury is the result of force applied to tissues that resist that force. Such resistance can be felt by the operator who must resist the temptation to apply force of greater and injurious magnitude.[3] When faced with a failure of descent, the operator should reassess the clinical situation, change traction direction, even reapply the instrument rather than resort to the use of greater force, which invites injury.

Laboratory support is a subject that is frequently overlooked in perinatal risk management. The placenta has the potential of containing a history of antenatal life that may exonerate a physician in the case of a "bad baby." Similarly, a cord pH can give valuable evidence as to the status of the infant at the time of delivery. In many institutions this has been routine following operative vaginal delivery. As a minimum procedure, a segment of cord should be clamped and preserved until there is clear evidence that the infant is free of acidosis, hypoxia, or depression.

It has been stated that whether one does good obstetrics or poor obstetrics, a bad outcome can result in a lawsuit. So why not do good obstetrics? The threat of litigation must not dictate good obstetrical practice and operative vaginal delivery *is* good obstetrical practice. When contemplating operative vaginal delivery, the observance of contemporary guidelines, consideration of the areas of potential risk, cautious performance of the procedure, and meticulous documentation should reduce the chance of medico-legal problems.

References

1. American College of Obstetricians and Gynecologists. Obstetric forceps; Committee Opinion 71, Washington, DC, 1989.
2. American College of Obstetricians and Gynecologists. Operative vaginal delivery. Technical Bulletin 152; 1991. Replaced by Technical Bulletin 196, Washington, DC, 1994.
3. Dennen PC (ed). *Dennen's Forceps Deliveries*. Philadelphia, F.A. Davis Co, 1989.
4. O'Grady JP (ed). *Modern Instrumental Delivery*. Baltimore, Williams and Wilkins, 1988.
5. *Williams Obstetrics*. Eighteenth Edition. Supplement 16: Operative Vaginal Delivery. Appleton-Century-Crofts, 1992.
6. Hayashi RH (ed). *High Risk Pregnancy Management Options. Ventouse Delivery*. London, W.B. Saunders, 1994.
7. Lucas MJ. The role of vacuum extraction in modern obstetrics. Clin Obstet Gynecol 1994;37:794-805.
8. Bowes WA, Katz VL. Operative vaginal delivery: Forceps and vacuum extractor. Curr Prob Obstet Gynecol Fertil 1994;7.
9. Dennen PC (ed). *High Risk Pregnancy Management Options. Forceps Delivery*. London, W.B. Saunders, 1994.
10. Hoult IJ, MacLennan AH, Carrie LES. Lumbar epidural analgesia in labour: Relation to fetal malposition and instrumental delivery. Br Med J 1977;1:14.
11. Kaminski HM, Stafl A, Aiman J. The effect of epidural analgesia on the frequency of instrumental obstetric delivery. Obstet Gynecol 1987;69:770.
12. Williams MC, Knuppel RA, O'Brien WF, et al. A randomized comparison of assisted vaginal delivery by obstetric forceps and polyethylene vacuum cup. Br J Obstet Gynaecol 1991;82:783.
13. Milner RDG. Neonatal mortalities of breech deliveries with and without forceps to the aftercoming head. Br J Obstet Gynaecol 1975;82:783.

14. Myers SA, Gleicher N. Breech delivery: Why the dilemma? Am J Obstet Gynecol 1987;156:6.
15. O'Driscoll K, Meagher D, Mac Donald D, et al. Traumatic intracranial hemorrhage in firstborn infants and delivery with obstetric forceps. Br J Obstet Gynaecol 1981;88:577.
16. Schwartz DB, Miodovnik M, Lavin JP. Neonatal outcome among low birth weight infants delivered spontaneously or by low forceps. Obstet Gynecol 1983;62:283.
17. Laube DW. Forceps delivery. Clin Obstet Gynecol 1986;29:286.
18. Broekhuizen FF, Washington JM, Johnson F, et al. Vacuum extraction vs. forceps delivery: Indications and complications, 1979 to 1984. Obstet Gynecol 1987;69:338.
19. Hibbard BM, McKenna DM. The obstetric forceps—are we using the appropriate tools? Br J Obstet Gynaecol 1987;97:374.
20. Robertson PA, Laros RK, Zhao RL. Neonatal and maternal outcome in low-pelvic and mid-pelvic operative deliveries. Am J Obstet Gynecol 1990;162:1436.
21. Hagadorn-Freathy AS, Yeomans ER, Hankins GDV. Validation of the 1988 ACOG forceps classification system. Obstet Gynecol 1991;77:356.
22. Dennen EH. A classification of forceps operations according to station of head in pelvis. Am J Obstet Gynecol 1952;63:272.
23. Niswander KR, Gordon M. Safety of the low forcep operation. Am J Obstet Gynecol 1973;117:619.
24. Friedman EA, Sachtleben-Murray MS, Dahrouge D, et al. Long term effects of labor and delivery on offspring: A matched pair analysis. Am J Obstet Gynecol 1984;150:941.
25. Gilstrap LC, Hauth JC, Schiano S, et al. Neonatal acidosis and method of delivery. Obstet Gynecol 1984;63:681.
26. Seidman DS, Laor A, Gale R, et al. Long-term effects of vacuum and forceps deliveries. Lancet 1991;337:1583.
27. Yancey MK, Herpolsheimer A, Jordan GD, et al. Maternal and neonatal effects of outlet forceps delivery compared with spontaneous vaginal delivery in term pregnancies. Obstet Gynecol 1992;178:646.
28. Bowes WS, Bowes C. Current role of midforceps operation. Clin Obstet Gynecol 1980;23:549.
29. Richardson SA, Evans MI, Cibils LA. Mid-forceps delivery: A critical review. Am J Obstet Gynecol 1983;145:621.
30. Dierker LJ Jr, Rosen MG, Thompson K, et al. The mid-forceps: Maternal and neonatal outcomes. Am J Obstet Gynecol 1985;152:176.
31. Bashore RA, Phillips WN Jr, Brinkman CR III. A comparison of the morbidity of mid-forceps and cesarean delivery. Am J Obstet Gynecol 1990;163:1428.
32. Ullery JC, Teteris N, Botschner AW, et al. Traction and compression forces exerted by obstetric forceps and their effect on fetal heart rate. Am J Obstet Gynecol 1963;85:1066.
33. Wylie B. Forceps traction: An index of birth difficulty. Am J Obstet Gynecol 1963;86:38.
34. Mishell D, Kelly JV. The obstetrical forceps and the vacuum extractor: An assessment of their compressive force. Obstet Gynecol 1962;19:204.
35. Duchon M, DeMund M, Brown R. Laboratory comparison of modern vacuum extractors. Obstet Gynecol 1988;71:155.
36. Yeomans ER, Gilstrap LC. The role of forceps in modern obstetrics. Clin Obstet Gynecol 1994;37:785.

37. Wesley B, Van den Berg B, Reece EA. The effect of operative vaginal delivery on cognitive development. Am J Obstet Gynecol 1992;166:288.
38. Carmody F, Grant A, Mutch L, et al. Follow up of babies delivered in a randomized controlled comparison of vacuum extraction and forceps delivery. Acta Obstet Gynecol Scand 1986;65:763.
39. Niswander K, Henson G, Elborne D, et al. Adverse outcome of pregnancy and the quality of obstetric care. Lancet 1984;ii:827.
40. Mann LI. Pregnancy events and brain damage. Am J Obstet Gynecol 1986;155:6.
41. Nelson KB. Obstetric complications as risk factors for cerebral palsy or seizure disorders. JAMA 1994;251:1843.
42. Illingworth RS. Why blame the obstetrician? A review. Br Med J 1979;1:797.

Chapter 17

Episiotomy: Repair, Complications, and Follow-Up

◆◆◆

Ronald T. Burkman, M.D.

Introduction

The use of episiotomy during a vaginal delivery is a commonplace obstetric practice in the United States. At the time of their extensive review of the English language literature regarding episiotomy in 1983, Thacker and Banta[1] indicated that episiotomy was performed in about 60% of all deliveries in the United States. Further, they suggested that between 50%-90% of primigravidas undergo the procedure. Although episiotomy was first developed in the 18th and 19th centuries, it was only after 1900 that the practice was widely advocated in the United States. As suggested by Thacker and Banta,[1] the major reason for this transition to frequent use of the procedure was the belief among prominent obstetricians that labor and delivery was not a physiologic process, but rather a process that required active intervention by qualified birth attendants (e.g., physicians) in order to reduce morbidity and mortality. Even though there is a current resurgence toward less interventional obstetrics, it is unclear whether this change in attitude has significantly affected the incidence of episiotomy. This chapter will briefly highlight the situations related to episiotomy likely to result in malpractice claims, critically review the indications for episiotomy, examine the principles of initial repair and the management of both immediate and delayed complications, and suggest steps that might reduce practitioners' exposure to malpractice claims.

From: Donn SM, Fisher CW (eds.): *Risk Management Techniques in Perinatal and Neonatal Practice*. © Futura Publishing Co., Inc., Armonk, NY, 1996.

Situations Likely to Result in Malpractice Claims

Problems related to episiotomy are far less frequently a reason for mal-practice action in comparison to other causes, such as alleged fetal injury. In general, most claims result from complications of the procedure that occur within a year or so of the original procedure. Although late complications such as anal incontinence may not be diagnosed for many years after the original episiotomy, malpractice actions against the original practitioner in such circumstances are quite uncommon.

The most frequent immediate problems cited are painful intercourse (dyspareunia), fistula formation, and incontinence of stool. In such instances, plaintiffs will allege that the defendant practitioner failed to diagnose the problem leading to the complication, and/or failed to properly perform a repair, and/or failed to follow-up the patient appropriately. Plaintiffs may allege malpractice in instances of episiotomy breakdown on the basis of faulty initial repair, failure to diagnose and treat a breakdown early, or failure to provide appropriate instructions to the plaintiff such as avoidance of practices that might disrupt repairs (i.e., intercourse, enemas). As is true of many malpractice actions, scant documentation in the chart concerning diagnostic examinations or procedures used, type of repair performed, and details of follow-up hamper the ability to mount an appropriate defense.

Indications for Episiotomy

The three indications for the performance of an episiotomy are: 1. to prevent maternal laceration, particularly of the perineum; 2. to prevent de-layed maternal problems such as pelvic relaxation and anal incontinence; and 3. to shorten the second stage of labor in order to improve the health of the infant. Each of these indications will be discussed in detail. However, in reviewing the literature involving the risks and benefits of episiotomy, it is important to recognize that most of the data reported are derived from case series or retrospective cohorts rather than well-controlled clinical trials or carefully designed prospective cohort studies. Therefore, it is difficult to draw definitive conclusions, in many instances, because of the limitations of the available data.

Prevention of Laceration

Although use of episiotomy may reduce the risk of lacerations involving the periurethral tissue and vaginal walls, the major intent of the procedure is to reduce laceration of the anal sphincter (third degree perineal laceration) or lacerations that involve both the sphincter and rectal mucosa (fourth degree perineal laceration).

Figure 1 is a simplified drawing of the musculature pertaining to the rectum and anal canal. The external anal sphincter, which consists of skeletal muscle, surrounds the anal canal and is closely approximated to the puborectalis muscle, also known as the pubococcygeus muscle. This latter muscle is a relatively thick U-shaped muscle that originates from the pubic bones and attaches to the lateral walls of the vagina and rectum. The internal sphincter, which is smooth muscle, lies within the external sphincter. The external anal sphincter is innervated by branches of the pudendal nerve, which are derived from the second to fourth sacral segments (S2-4). The puborectalis is innervated by direct branches of the third and fourth sacral segments as well as collaterals from the pudendal nerve, and the internal sphincter from the supralevator branches of pelvic nerves originating from the S2-4 ventral roots. The internal sphincter is under autonomic control and accounts for 80% of the resting sphincter pressure, while the voluntary control is through the external sphincter and puborectalis muscle.[2] In general, the nerve bundles

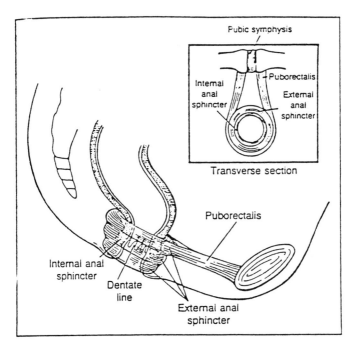

Figure 1. Diagram of the rectum, anal canal, and surrounding muscles. (Reproduced with permission from Madoff RD, Williams JG, Caushaj PF. Current concepts: Fecal incontinence. N Engl J Med 1992;326:1002.)

run from lateral to medial. For more extensive information on the anatomy and pathophysiology of the pelvic floor, interested readers are referred to several recent review articles.[2-5]

The literature relative to the association of episiotomy with either third or fourth degree perineal laceration is confusing primarily because of the presence of other potential risk factors. Table 1 reviews some of the reported rates of either third or fourth degree laceration relative to whether or not an episiotomy was performed and by type of episiotomy.[1,6-11] Except for the series of Combs and co-workers,[9] which involves only women delivered by forceps or vacuum extraction, the other data in the table do not fully correct for other potential risk factors. However, the data do suggest that there is no approach to the management of the perineum during vaginal delivery that can totally prevent these types of lacerations. Further, the data also suggest that both no episiotomy and mediolateral episiotomy offer less risk of severe perineal laceration than does the performance of a midline episiotomy.

Table 2 summarizes data from several studies that examined other potential risk factors for perineal laceration.[7-11] Although there was significant variation among the studies since some adjusted their relative risks for other risk factors, the data suggest that forceps deliveries, nulliparity, Asian ethnicity, and large infants probably increase the risk of third or fourth degree perineal laceration. Use of local anesthesia compared to regional anesthesia (usually epidural) and occiput posterior position may be less significant risk factors for this type of injury.

In summary, the data suggest that episiotomy does not protect against perineal laceration. Midline episiotomy compared to no episiotomy or mediolateral episiotomy may increase the risk of this complication. The performance of a midline episiotomy with a predictably large infant that extends to a fourth degree laceration may very well increase the physician's exposure to litigation.

Other risk factors such as operative vaginal delivery, nulliparity, Asian ethnicity, and infant size all appear to be risk factors often independent of the performance of episiotomy. However, one should not construe the data to indicate that the use of episiotomy is inappropriate. For example, with large infants, attempting to avoid episiotomy may lead to either lacerations that are more difficult to repair or greater risk of pelvic nerve damage from increased distension of the lower vagina.

Prevention of Pelvic Relaxation

Determining whether episiotomy affects the risk of subsequent pelvic floor dysfunction (e.g., cystocele, rectocele, uterine prolapse, stress urinary incontinence) is difficult. In the studies reviewed by Thacker and Banta,[1] the majority did not include pre-delivery assessment, most did not adjust for other potential confounders such as parity, type of delivery or infant size,

Table 1
Percentage of Women Experiencing a Third or Fourth Degree Perineal
Laceration During Vaginal Delivery by Type of Episiotomy

Study	Percentage with Laceration
Thacker and Banta 1983	
Midline (over 74,000 deliveries)	0.2–22.9
Mediolateral (over 10,000 deliveries)	0.0–9.0
Thorp 1989 (deliveries not stated)	
None	1.4
Midline	6.5
Green 1989 (3,065 deliveries)	
None	2.2
Midline	28.4
Shiono 1990 (24,114 deliveries)	
None	0.2
Midline	9.7
Mediolateral	1.8
Combs 1990 (2,832 deliveries)*	
None	14.3
Midline	39.8
Mediolateral	9.6
Walker 1991 (9,493 deliveries)	
None	1.0
Midline	3.0
Mediolateral	4.0
Helwig 1993 (448 deliveries)	
None	13.4
Midline	36.7

*Evaluated only forceps and vacuum extraction deliveries.

and follow-up was quite short. Overall, the studies reviewed suggested perhaps a modest benefit associated with episiotomy.

The study of Gainey[12] has the advantage of large study groups (1000 women in each of two study groups) and longer follow-up (2 months to 10 years). He studied women undergoing an "early" mediolateral episiotomy

Table 2
Risk Factors for Third and Fourth Degree Perineal Laceration
Other than Episiotomy*

Comparison	Range of Relative Risks
Forceps vs. spontaneous delivery	2.3–8.0
Nulliparous vs. multiparous	1.3–5.8
"Macrosomic" vs. "normal" weight	2.4–4.7
Asian vs. Caucasian ethnicity	2.3–3.7
Forceps vs. vacuum extraction	1.9
Local vs. regional anesthesia	1.0–2.4
Occiput posterior vs. occiput anterior	1.0–1.6

*Based on data presented in the following papers:
Combs CA, Robertson PA, Carey JC. Am J Obstet Gynecol 1990;163:100.
Green JR, Soohoo SL. Obstet Gynecol 1989;73:732.
Helwig JT, Thorp JM, Bowes WA. Obstet Gynecol 1994;82:276.
Shionio P, Klebanoff MA, Carey JC. Obstet Gynecol 1990;75:765.
Walker MPR, et al. Obstet Gynecol 1991;77:668.

plus outlet forceps delivery versus women undergoing a spontaneous delivery with an episiotomy performed only if laceration seemed likely. He concluded that episiotomy reduced the likelihood of any type of subsequent damage. Multiple deliveries increased the risk of injury; however, there was no difference in the risk of uterine prolapse or stress urinary incontinence between the two study groups. However, as pointed out by Thorp and Bowes,[6] this study introduced a potential confounder (forceps delivery) and may have had a detection bias since the evaluator was not blinded. In a more recent study, Gordon and Logue[13] evaluated perineal function 1 year after Cesarean section or vaginal delivery. They failed to demonstrate any difference in function when comparing Cesarean section to vaginal delivery, when evaluating vaginal delivery with or without forceps or episiotomy, and regardless of parity. In the West Berkshire Perineal Management Trial, patients were randomized into two groups: a restrictive group in which mediolateral episiotomy was reserved only for fetal indications; and a liberal group in which mediolateral episiotomy was used to prevent perineal laceration.[14] At both 3 months and 3 years after delivery, there was no evidence the episiotomy prevented stress urinary incontinence.[14,15] In summary, older literature has suggested some benefit to episiotomy in protecting against future pelvic relaxation. More recent studies present less convincing evidence of such protection. However, because of the paucity of well-controlled data, it is difficult to draw any definitive conclusions.

Shortening the Second Stage of Labor to Improve Fetal Outcome

Thacker and Banta[1] extensively reviewed the literature relative to reducing the duration of labor in an effort to improve fetal outcome. In the absence of high-risk situations, there was no evidence in the available literature that shortening the second stage of labor improved fetal outcome. Although the few studies that evaluated the role of episiotomy in labor suggested that the procedure shortened the second stage, most of the data was not well controlled. Further, there was no evidence that the length of the second stage correlated with immediate fetal outcome, such as Apgar scores, in healthy pregnancies. In summary, there are no data to suggest that routinely shortening the second stage of labor with or without an episiotomy improves fetal outcome in normal pregnancies. However, it also seems reasonable that the procedure is quite appropriate to help shorten the second stage of labor in instances of non-reassuring fetal heart rate tracings or for other indications for expedited delivery.

Episiotomy: Incision and Repair

Episiotomy is usually performed with scissors. Although debatable, the incision should be made as the perineum is distending in order to reduce stretching of perineal tissues that could result in unrecognized pelvic muscle and nerve damage. A midline episiotomy extends down toward—but not through—the rectal musculature's capsule. In addition, the vaginal mucosa, in many instances, should be incised for 3-4 cm above the hymenal ring. With a mediolateral approach, the scissors are angled at about a 45° angle away from the rectum. A two-step approach using an initial small midline incision followed by the mediolateral incision has been advocated by some.[16] As with the midline episiotomy, the vaginal mucosa is usually incised for a few centimeters above the hymenal ring.

There are a variety of approaches to the repair of an episiotomy.[16-19] As with most surgical repairs, adequate exposure and lighting, good anesthesia, appropriate instruments, careful and accurate anatomic approximation of tissue, control of bleeding, and use of the proper type and strength of suture material are important. After delivery of the placenta and inspection for lacerations of the vagina and cervix, most operators close the vaginal mucosa with 3-0 absorbable suture. Although one can debate whether or not to use chromic catgut or synthetic absorbable suture for episiotomy and perineal laceration repair, chromic catgut may be preferable for the vaginal mucosa to avoid prolonged retention of suture and associated dyspareunia. Although the vaginal mucosa, subcutaneous tissue, and skin can be closed with continuous suture, with extensive episiotomy incisions interrupted sutures are indicated to reduce the risk of breakdown. Although figure-of-eight sutures may be used to control bleeding, routine use is associated with more tissue damage. As with all surgical repairs, avoidance of suture line tension is important. When repairing a fourth degree perineal laceration, one may wish to avoid closure of the vaginal mucosa until repair of the rectal mucosa and sphincter muscle has been accomplished in order to maintain adequate exposure. The rectal mucosa is usually closed with a 4-0 suture. Although there is debate over whether or not to use continuous or interrupted sutures and whether one should always imbricate the mucosa rather than traverse the mucosa, more importantly one should ensure that at the end of the entire episiotomy repair that the vaginal mucosa and rectal mucosa are as widely separated as possible to avoid development of a fistula. When repairing the external sphincter, one may elect to use Allis clamps to identify the cut ends of the musculature on each side. One then closes the capsule with several interrupted 2-0 or 3-0 sutures. Although the use of a "crown stitch" to approximate the bulbocavernosus muscle and skin just distal to the hymenal ring has been advocated in the past, one should avoid tenting the skin in order to reduce the likelihood of postpartum dyspareunia.[18] Similarly, the use of a subcuticular closure for the skin will also reduce postpartum perineal pain and dyspareunia. With mediolateral episiotomy, repair of the base prior to closure of the vaginal mucosa and skin often enhances accurate re-approximation of the incised tissue. In addition, careful inspection to ensure that there is not an occult tear of the external sphincter is important. Because of the increased vascularity with this incision, figure-of-eight stitches may be required more frequently for this repair. At the conclusion of all episiotomy repairs, a rectal examination should be performed to ensure that a "button hole" tear above the repaired episiotomy has not been missed.

In the immediate postpartum period, one can utilize ice packs for at least 24 hours to reduce edema and pain particularly with extensive repairs. Topical witch hazel or anesthetic sprays may also provide local pain relief. Sitz baths also provide relief for many women, although there is apparent debate over this issue.[18] In addition to local measures, oral analgesia can be prescribed. Prior to discharge, the repair should be inspected to ensure that there is no evidence of substantial hematoma formation, infection, or break-down. With third or fourth degree perineal lacerations, one should give instruction on measures to avoid constipation and also advise patients to avoid rectal examinations, enemas, and intercourse for at least 4 weeks following delivery. Patients should be instructed to call if they note any breakdown or if unusual pain or bleeding occurs following discharge.

Immediate Complications of Episiotomy

The immediate complications of episiotomy include laceration or extension, infection, blood loss and hematoma formation, and breakdown. Perineal laceration has been discussed previously; this section will discuss the occurrence and management of these other problems.

Infection

Infection in association with episiotomy has been reported at rates of 0.5%-3.0%.[1] Simple infections are usually localized and may present with edema and erythema. Superficial infections can be treated with local measures such as sitz baths; with deeper involvement, opening and debridement of the perineal wound may be indicated. Antibiotics should be considered with marked cellulitis or in the presence of streptococcal infections. If the episiotomy repair did not involve the sphincter muscles or rectal mucosa, the episiotomy can then heal by secondary intention or granulation. If a third or fourth degree perineal laceration repair becomes disrupted, one should delay repair for several weeks to ensure that there is no infection and to allow the normal processes associated with repair of tissue injury to subside. Rarely, particularly in compromised individuals such as women with diabetes mellitus or acquired immunodeficiency syndrome, one may see necrotizing fasciitis. One will see edema and erythema initially without clear boundaries, followed by rapid progression to demarcated lesions that are dark in color with occasional associated hypesthesia. Signs of systemic toxicity such as fever, tachycardia, and hemoconcentration in association with the just described physical findings should suggest the possibility of this complication. These infections are associated with group A streptococci as well as a variety of anaerobic organisms. Treatment requires extensive debridement with wide margins to ensure removal of all necrotic tissue, along with high dose antibiotic treatment. Unless prompt intervention including extensive debridement occurs, one risks further spread of infection and even maternal mortality.[1] Finally, one needs to recognize that the occurrence of infection including necrotizing fasciitis, is also possible when spontaneous lacerations of the perineum are sutured following vaginal delivery; there is no comparative information on the incidence of infection in such situations versus episiotomy.

Blood Loss and Hematoma Formation

It has been estimated that about 10% of women undergoing vaginal delivery with episiotomy will lose about 300 mL more blood than one would anticipate without episiotomy.[1] To reduce blood loss associated with extensive episiotomy, particularly mediolateral incisions, one should promptly deliver the placenta, inspect for any additional tears above the episiotomy site, then reduce bleeding from the episiotomy site. Direct ligation of vessels is appropriate; figure-of-eight stitches may be needed with more generalized bleeding. The latter can be a problem following a prolonged second stage or with measures such as "ironing the perineum" to stretch perineal tissue. Both may result in occult disruption of the sphincter muscles and edema and friability of tissue at the time of repair that leads to increased blood loss.

A complaint of severe pain in the vulvar or pelvic region early in the postpartum period should alert one to the possibility of a vulvar hematoma. Occasionally, because of the extent of bleeding into the hematoma, women will also present with associated tachycardia or even shock. It should be recognized that such hematomas can occur totally independent of an episiotomy or even distal to the incision site. However, as a result of the location and increased vasculature in the incision line, mediolateral episiotomies present greater concern for this complication. Further, since mediolateral episiotomies can extend to the ischiorectal fossa, bleeding can extend to above the cardinal ligaments. Management includes prevention; at the time of episiotomy repair all bleeding should be controlled. Once the hematoma occurs, unless it is small and not progressing, it should be evacuated and any bleeding vessels ligated. Often the bleeding is diffuse, such that one needs to use figure-of-eight stitches to obliterate the cavity. Vaginal packing, following evacuation and ligation of vessels, may assist in cavity obliteration and control of oozing. However, patients need to be monitored closely to ensure that the packing does not mask hematoma formation above the pack. Occasionally, with diffuse bleeding that is difficult to control, one may elect to pack the hematoma cavity and remove the packing a day or so later.

Episiotomy Breakdown

There is no reliable information available regarding the incidence of episiotomy breakdown. It is likely a rare complication that occurs in association with infection, failure to control bleeding in the incision site, or from trauma to the site, such as early resumption of intercourse or use of enemas in instances of extensive perineal lacerations. One may need to delay re-repair for several weeks when there is evidence of extensive infection, in order to avoid continued infection risk and to allow the normal reparative processes to complete their course. With clean wounds, there are recent reports of early closure of episiotomy dehiscence, including fourth degree perineal laceration breakdowns.[20,21] Although good results have been reported, not all repairs are successful. For example Hankins et al.,[21] in a series of 22 patients, two women developed small rectovaginal fistulas that were successfully repaired later. However, early repair does reduce the anxiety of patients and the associated social dysfunction. However, early repair does require irrigation and cleaning of the breakdown site multiple times a day for several days before attempting re-repair. Any approach to management requires careful communication with the patient regarding the pros and cons of the approach. With breakdown of the sphincter musculature and rectal mucosa, consultation with a gynecologic surgeon with special expertise or a colon-rectal surgeon may provide assistance directed toward approaches of subsequent evaluation and treatment if deemed necessary.

Delayed Complications of Episiotomy

The major delayed complications that are potentially associated with the use of episiotomy are anal incontinence, perineal pain, dyspareunia, and rectovaginal fistula.

Anal Incontinence: Relationship to Pelvic Nerve Damage, Perineal Laceration, and Episiotomy

Anal incontinence, when related to obstetrical delivery, is often not apparent immediately after delivery. In fact, the peak incidence of the disorder in reported series is in the fifth and sixth decades.[20] The various components of anal incontinence include incontinence of flatus, liquid stool, and solid stool.[2,20-22] Although there are no reliable estimates available, the overall frequency of this problem is probably significantly higher than is apparent from the numbers of women requesting assistance, since it is such an embarrassing complaint that many will not seek help.[2,22,23]

The development of anal incontinence related to obstetric delivery is a complex process. Nerve conduction, electromyographic, radiographic, and endosonographic studies of women suggest that vaginal delivery, regardless of whether episiotomy is used or if a third or fourth degree perineal laceration occurs, can be associated with damage to the anal sphincter mechanism including its innervation.[22,26-33] In the recent study by Sultan et al.,[22] women were evaluated 6 weeks before delivery as well as 6 weeks and 6 months after delivery. Among the 48 multipara women experiencing vaginal delivery, 19% had bowel symptoms before delivery; an additional 6% developed symptoms 6 weeks after delivery. Among the 79 primipara women undergoing vaginal delivery, none had bowel symptoms before delivery; 13% developed symptoms by 6 weeks postpartum. Among those women with bowel symptoms, about one-third were improved by the time of the 6 month evaluation. Among the primipara women, 3% had shown clinical evidence of a third or fourth degree perineal laceration with repair at delivery, yet 35% of all primipara women had evidence of sphincter damage when evaluated by endosonography 6-weeks postpartum. About one-third of those women with evidence of defects also had bowel symptoms. Sphincter damage was apparent even among some women with an apparently intact perineum. The investigators noted that vaginal delivery, particularly first delivery, was associated with increased pudendal nerve terminal motor latency, but there was no association between increased latency and bowel symptoms. Women undergoing Cesarean section had no evidence of sphincter or nerve damage. Eight of ten women undergoing forceps delivery demonstrated defects; none of the five women undergoing vacuum extraction had evidence of a defect. This study, which included a pre-delivery evaluation, suggests that disruption of the sphincter is an important cause of anal incontinence, although not all women with injury develop symptoms. Avoiding either episiotomy or an apparent perineal laceration does not protect against this injury. In their view, pudendal nerve damage manifested as increased latency of conduction was less important in the etiology. However, one should note that this was a relatively short-term study and that others suggest that denervation of the pudendal nerve is an important factor in developing bowel symptoms. Table 3 provides information on the frequency of various types of anal incontinence and perineal discomfort according to whether or not there was laceration of the sphincter.[28,33,34] The data presented represent relatively long-term follow-up; however, other women experience transient problems that tend to clear during the first 3 to 6 months postpartum. Data from these studies also suggest that large babies and operative vaginal deliveries predispose to anal incontinence; the studies of Sorenson and Haadem confirm that primiparity also predisposes to this problem. In summary, disruption of the anal sphincter is clearly a risk factor for the development of symptoms of anal incontinence.

A number of investigators have also studied the role of pudendal nerve denervation in the etiology of anal incontinence.[25,30-32,35] Among women with lacerations of the external sphincter, 47%-60% show evidence of pudendal nerve damage even many months and years after delivery.[32,35] More importantly, vaginal delivery, regardless of whether or not an episiotomy is done or a sphincter laceration occurs, predisposes to denervation and subsequent re-innervation of fibers of the pudendal nerve. For example, Allen et al.[25] studied 96 primipara women who had undergone delivery with concentric needle electromyography, pudendal nerve conduction, and with perineometry. They demonstrated that there was evidence of re-innervation of the pelvic floor muscles in about 80% of the women who had undergone vaginal delivery. Further, forceps delivery and laceration of the perineal muscles did not appear to adversely influence the process. Pudendal nerve conduction times varied little over a 2 month period. However, the investigators noted that a significant problem with their conduction data was lack of pre-delivery evaluations. In summary, such data suggest that some denervation/re-innervation is a process of most vaginal deliveries. As suggested by Wall[5] and DeLancey,[36] the fetal head may produce distension that leads to stretching and ultimately disruption of nerve fibers with subsequent neuropathy. Thus, it appears that obstetricians are frequently faced with a paradox: whether to shorten a second stage using episiotomy and perhaps instrumentation and risk a perineal tear, or whether to allow a prolonged second stage of labor and risk increased pelvic floor denervation. There appears to be a correlation between reduced resting and contraction anal pressures and evidence of increased pudendal nerve terminal motor latency and evidence of re-innervation in at least one study.[32] Further, several investigators have noted that the success of surgical correction of anal incontinence is adversely influenced by the presence of a pelvic nerve neuropathy.[30,35,37,38] For example, in Jacobs and co-workers[30] series, an 80% surgical repair success rate was achieved in patients with obstetrics-related anal incontinence without evidence of nerve damage, while only an 11% success rate was noted in women with concomitant nerve injury. One should also recognize that some spontaneous healing and improvement in symptoms occurs over time. Obviously, with third and fourth degree perineal lacerations, immediate repair at the time of delivery is warranted. As noted by Hadeem and co-workers,[28] repaired women will continue to demonstrate improvement in anal sphincter strength for about 3 months after repair. Therefore, many early symptoms may abate over this time period. However, if symptoms that develop in the early postpartum period persist and there is evidence of a sphincter defect, one may wish to delay re-repair for up to 6 months since in the study by Sultan et al.,[22] about one-third of women with symptoms at 6 weeks postpartum showed improvement at the time of the 6 month evaluation. In summary, it appears that sphincter disruption and pelvic nerve damage are etiologic factors in anal incontinence. Further, both can occur in the absence of an episiotomy and both may even be difficult to recognize postpartum. Finally, the presence of sphincter disruption and denervation reduces the chance of subsequent successful surgical repair.

The approaches to treatment of anal incontinence include conservative measures such as high-fiber diets and stool-bulking supplements, biofeedback training, and a variety of surgical repairs.[2,23,26,30,32,35,37] However, it should be stressed that preoperative evaluation to identify the extent of the defect and the presence or absence of nerve damage is important in order that the patient be properly counseled about the likelihood of success. Further, it also should be noted that aging tends to accentuate the defects associated with denervation, such that repairs delayed for years from the time of original injury may be less successful.[2,23]

Dyspareunia and Perineal Pain: Relationship to Episiotomy

As noted by Thacker and Banta,[1] very little data are available about the incidence and severity of postpartum perineal pain and dyspareunia following episiotomy. Certainly, early postpartum perineal pain is universal with episiotomy. Late dyspareunia and perineal pain can occur whether or not a third or fourth degree laceration occurs (Table 3).[29,33,34] Unfortunately, none of the listed series in Table 3 has enough information or is of significant sample size to provide adequate estimates of the incidence of these problems according to use of episiotomy. In one study of midwifery patients undergoing mediolateral episiotomy at 3 months postpartum, 23% reported dyspareunia.[40] A British study determined that at 3 months, women undegoing episiotomy (usually mediolateral) compared to spontaneous laceration had a frequency of dyspareunia of 19% versus 11%.[41] Finally, Reading and co-workers[42] reported on survey results of 69 primipara women at 3 months postpartum who had undergone mediolateral episiotomy. Sixty indicated they had dyspareunia, with 53 relating the pain to the episiotomy. Unfortunately, all of these studies are of limited sample size, are not well controlled, and did not directly

---

Table 3
Presence of Anal Incontinence, Dyspareunia, or Perineal Pain, Nine or
More Months After Vaginal Delivery

Study	Third or Fourth Degree Laceration	No Laceration Controls
Haadem 1988 (11–83 month follow-up)		
59 with laceration; 48 controls		
Gas incontinence	4 (7%)*	0
Fecal incontinence	5 (8%)*	0
Dyspareunia	4 (7%)*	0
Perineal pain	15 (25%)	0
Sorenson 1988 (52–123 month follow-up)		
24 with laceration; 18 controls		
Gas incontinence	6 (25%)*	0
Liquid stool incontinence	3 (13%)*	0
Formed stool incontinence	1 (4%)*	0
Dyspareunia	4 (17%)	4 (22%)
Crawford 1993 (9–12 month follow-up)		
35 with laceration; 35 controls**		
Gas incontinence	6 (17%)*	1 (3%)
Liquid stool incontinence	1 (3%)	1 (3%)
Formed stool incontinence	1 (3%)	0
Dyspareunia	3 (9%)	3 (9%)
Perineal pain	4 (11%)	3 (9%)

 * $P < 0.05$.
** all subjects were primiparas.

collect antepartum information. Further, although anecdotally it is commonly believed that midline episiotomy produces less pain than mediolateral episiotomy, there are no controlled trials that have examined this issue. In summary, dyspareunia and persistent perineal pain are reported following vaginal delivery. However, there is a paucity of data on the incidence, change from antepartum experience, severity of the problem, or incidence according to presence or absence of episiotomy or according to type of episiotomy.

Anovaginal and Rectovaginal Fistulas

Anovaginal fistulas are adjacent to the external sphincter while rectovaginal fistulas have their gastrointestinal tract opening 3 or more cm above the anal canal. In modern day obstetrics, it is felt that most fistulas result from failure to either recognize or successfully repair a fourth degree perineal laceration.[43] In former years in the United States and in less developed countries where long obstructed labors are more common, pressure necrosis from the fetal head being closely pressed against pelvic structures is likely an important cause. In any event, the occurrence is still relatively uncommon. In one early series examining consequences of midline episiotomy, Kaltreider and Dixon[44] reported a frequency of rectovaginal fistula of 1 per 948 deliveries. In general, the diagnosis is not made until at least 10 days to 2 weeks following delivery. Patients may complain of passage of gas or feces into the vagina. Many small fistulas are asymptomatic. Since most rectovaginal fistulas are recognized rather late in the reparative process following delivery, closure should be delayed for several weeks. During this interval, edema decreases and the rest of the episiotomy site will usually heal successfully. To reduce undesired symptoms, patients can opt to utilize a diet that produces some degree of constipation. There are a variety of techniques available for repair including simple closure in multiple layers to the use of various flaps.[45] In the absence of co-existing conditions such as Crohn's disease, a "bowel prep" a day or two before surgery followed by clear liquids for several days postoperatively and then a low residue diet for 3-4 weeks is all that is required relative to handling of the gastrointestinal system.

Measures to Reduce Legal Exposure

As with most medical interventions, the cornerstone measures used to reduce legal exposure associated with the performance of episiotomy include good communication between providers and the patient, informed consent, prompt recognition and appropriate treatment of complications, and good documentation. As part of routine prenatal care, patients should be provided with information about various aspects of their care including use of episiotomy. Patients should be aware that non-performance of episiotomy carries potential risks. When patients express particular concerns or requests, these should be recorded in the chart. Including episiotomy as an item of the written informed consent may result in further discussion and understanding of the risks and benefits of the procedure at the time a patient presents for delivery. With extensive episiotomies and perineal lacerations, the medical record should provide adequate documentation of the technique of repair. Documentation should indicate that the repair site was inspected prior to discharge and that postpartum instructions were given. Follow-up of unusual complaints is important in order that complications are recognized promptly. When complex complications such as incontinence or fistula occur, one should liberally use consultation before embarking on a surgical repair. In short, attention to detail in patient management, maintenance of good communication pathways, and careful documentation reduce one's concern that a problem related to episiotomy will result in an adverse legal outcome. Finally, given the potential problems associated with midline episiotomy, obstetricians in the United States may need to re-evaluate the role of this type of incision versus mediolateral incisions in current obstetric practice.

> **Commentary by Mr. Bloch:** In my experience I have encountered or heard of very few cases except those that pertain to rectal vaginal fistula resulting from obstetrical trauma. Certainly, if the erosion through the rectal vaginal septum is as a result of a foreign body such as a pessary or sponge left after surgery, it is an easy case.
>
> From a medico-legal standpoint, the investigation is directed at *why* there was obstetric trauma if that was the cause of the fistula. Other causes of rectal vaginal fistula that have to be explored are those that come from suture penetration during episiotomy repair.

> **Commentary by Mr. Fisher:** Claims involving an alleged failure to repair the sphincter muscle properly, leading to inadequate sphincter control, carry with them a greater degree of damages than other problems usually associated with episiotomy repair/breakdown/re-repair.
>
> The failure of the sphincter muscle can lead to claims of permanent incontinence, wage loss, and other damages that can be "black-boarded" with some claimed objectivity at trial. For this reason, particular emphasis should be placed upon the methodology of repair of a fourth degree extension.
>
> Ordinarily, episiotomy repair is not described specifically in the medical records, nor does this attorney suggest that it should be. However, if a claim arises that the primary repair of a fourth degree extension was negligently performed, one can generally sus-

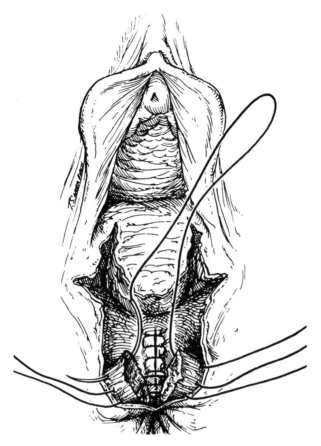

Figure 2. One suggested method of episiotomy repair. (Reproduced with permission from Pritchard JA, MacDonald PC. *Williams Obstetrics*, Sixteenth Edition. New York, Appleton-Century-Crofts, 1980, p. 433.)

pect that the plaintiff will be searching for something during *the deposition* of the doctor in order to create a medico-legal basis for a claim of inadequate primary repair of the sphincter.

The usual claim involves the re-approximation and suturing of the sphincter muscle. In that regard, there are plaintiff experts that claim "deep bites" of the sphincter muscle should be taken when suturing the muscle together. This claim is generally based upon the example in the *Williams Obstetrics* textbook (Sixteenth Edition, page 433), in which apparently the author depicts suturing deeply into the muscle in order to tie it together (Figure 2).

On the other hand, an alternative procedure involves suturing *only* the capsule of the sphincter muscle, and pulling the muscle together with the rationale that the muscle is much more friable than the capsule, and the sutures would pull through the muscle tissue (Figure 3).

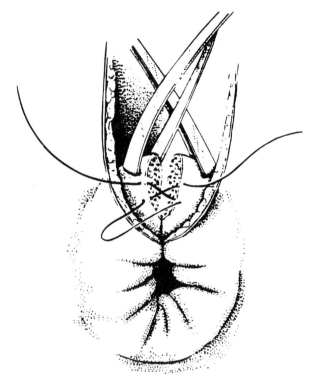

Figure 3. Another suggested method of episiotomy repair. (Reproduced with permission from Petterson RM. Episiotomy. In Pauerstein CJ [ed]. *Clinical Obstetrics*. New York, John Wiley & Sons, 1987, p. 847.)

This writer has been involved in at least two such cases where the plaintiff's expert refused to acknowledge the second method as an appropriate alternative and simply found negligence because there was a failure to take deep bites of the muscle.

Unfortunately, in a court of law, often textbooks and treatises are not admitted because they are considered "hearsay" evidence. In order for them to be admitted, generally it requires a finding of a particular textbook as being "authoritative" as to the subject matter indicated, or testimony from the defendant that they "relied" on the textbook or the particular method in the textbook for their suturing method.

It is, therefore, important for the defendant witness to acknowledge his particular method in a particular book, cited either as authoritative or one upon which he relied, as this testimony may provide an evidentiary basis for submission to the jury.

Without these pieces of information from the medical textbooks and the treatises coming before the jury, the lawsuit is simply in the posture of a "battle of the experts." A jury may find against a defendant even though there is an approved acceptable method in a textbook.

It should be noted that Figure 2 has existed "through the ages," and one wonders if the authors intended that the repair should be done as suggested in the drawing, or whether the repair is now being performed in much the same manner as Figure 3 suggests.

During a deposition the defendant doctor should be able to discuss both methods, show awareness of the alternative procedures, be able to cite them and essentially indicate the pros and cons of both, and why either method is an acceptable way to repair a fourth degree extension.

References

1. Thacker SB, Banta HD. Benefits and risks of episiotomy: An interpretative review of the English language literature, 1860-1980. Obstet Gynecol Surg 1983;38:322.
2. Madoff RD, Williams JG, Caushaj PF. Fecal incontinence. N Engl J Med 1992;326:1002.
3. DeLancey JOL. Anatomy and biomechanics of genital prolapse. Clin Obstet Gynecol 1993;36:897.
4. Norton PA. Pelvic floor disorders: The role of fascia and ligaments. Clin Obstet Gynecol 1993;36:926.
5. Wall LL. The muscles of the pelvic floor. Clin Obstet Gynecol 1993;36:910.
6. Thorp JM, Bowes WA. Episiotomy: Can its routine use be defended? Am J Obstet Gynecol 1989;160:1027.
7. Green JR, Soohoo SL. Factors associated with rectal injury in spontaneous deliveries. Obstet Gynecol 1989;73:732.
8. Shiono P, Klebanoff MA, Carey JC. Midline episiotomies: More harm than good? Obstet Gynecol 1990;75:765.
9. Combs CA, Robertson PA, Laros RK. Risk factors for third-degree and fourth-degree perineal lacerations in forceps and vacuum deliveries. Am J Obstet Gynecol 1990;163:100.
10. Walker MPR, Farine D, Rolbin SH, et al. Epidural anesthesia, episiotomy, and obstetric laceration. Obstet Gynecol 1991;77:668.
11. Helwig JT, Thorp JM, Bowes WA. Does midline episiotomy increase the risk of third- and fourth-degree lacerations in operative vaginal deliveries? Obstet Gynecol 1994;82:276.

12. Gainey NL. Postpartum observation of pelvic tissues damage: Further studies. Am J Obstet Gynecol 1995;70:800.
13. Gordon H, Logue M. Perineal muscle function after childbirth. Lancet 1985;2:123.
14. Sleep J, Grant A, Garcia J, et al. West Berkshire perineal management trial. Br Med J 1984;289:587.
15. Sleep J, Grant A. West Berkshire perineal management trial: Three year followup. Br Med J 1987;295:749.
16. Douglas RG, Stromme WB. Episiotomy: Repair and management of obstetric trauma. In: Douglas RG, Stromme WB (eds). *Operative Obstetrics*, Third Edition. New York, Appleton-Century-Crofts, 1976, p. 716.
17. Cunningham FG, MacDonald PC, Gant NF. Conduct of normal labor and delivery. In: Cunningham FG, MacDonald PC, Gant NF (eds). *Williams Obstetrics*, Eighteenth Edition. Norwalk, CT, Appleton & Lange, 1989, p. 307.
18. Varner MW. Episiotomy: Techniques and indications. Clin Obstet Gynecol 1986;29:309.
19. Patterson RM. Episiotomy. In: Pauerstein CJ (ed). *Clinical Obstetrics*. New York, John Wiley & Sons, Inc., 1987, p. 843.
20. Monberg J, Hammen S. Ruptured episiotomy resutured primarily. Acta Obstet Gynecol Scand 1987;66:163.
21. Hankins GDV, Hauth JVC, Gilstrap LC, et al. Early repair of episiotomy dehiscence. Obstet Gynecol 1990;75:48.
22. Sultan AH, Kamm MA, Hudson CN, et al. Anal-sphincter disruption during vaginal delivery. N Engl J Med 1993;329:1905.
23. Abrams AV. Anal incontinence. In: Cameron JL (ed). *Current Surgical Therapy*, Fourth Edition. Philadelphia, B.C. Decker, 1992, p. 239.
24. DeLancey JOL. Childbirth, continence and the pelvic floor. N Engl J Med 1993;329:1956.
25. Allen RE, Hosker GL, Smith ARB, et al. Pelvic floor damage and childbirth: A neurophysiological study. Br J Obstet Gynaecol 1990;97:770.
26. Ctercteko GC, Fazio VW, Jagelman DG, et al. Anal sphincter repair: A report of 60 cases and review of the literature. Aust NZ J Surg 1988;58:703.
27. Haadem K, Dahlstrom JA, Ling L, et al. Anal sphincter function after delivery rupture. Obstet Gynecol 1987;70:53.
28. Haadem K, Dahlstrom JA, Lingman G. Anal sphincter function after delivery: A prospective study in women with sphincter rupture and controls. Eur J Obstet Gynecol Reprod Biol 1990;35:7.
29. Haadem K, Ohrlander S, Lingman G. Long-term ailments due to anal sphincter rupture caused by delivery—a hidden problem. Eur J Obstet Gynecol Reprod Biol 1988;27:27.
30. Jacobs PPM, Scheur M, Kuipers JHC, et al. Obstetric fecal incontinence—role of pelvic floor denervation and results of delayed sphincter repair. Dis Colon Rectum 1990;33:494.
31. Smith ARB, Hosker GL, Warrell DW. The role of partial denervation of the pelvic floor in the aetiology of genitourinary prolapse and stress incontinence of urine. A neurophysiological study. Br J Obstet Gynaecol 1989;96:24.
32. Snooks SJ, Henry MM, Swash M. Faecal incontinence due to external anal sphincter division in childbirth is associated with damage to the innervation of the pelvic musculature: A double pathology. Br J Obstet Gynaecol 1985;92:824.

33. Sorensen SM, Bondesen H, Istre O, et al. Perineal rupture following vaginal delivery—long-term consequences. Acta Obstet Gynecol Scand 1988;67:315.
34. Crawford LA, Quint EH, Pearl ML, et al. Incontinence following rupture of the anal sphincter during delivery. Obstet Gynecol 1993;82:527.
35. Laurberg S, Swash M, Henry MM. Delayed external sphincter repair for obstetric tear. Br J Surg 1988;75:786.
36. DeLancey JOL. Pelvic floor dysfunction: Causes and prevention. Cont OB-GYN 1993;38:68.
37. Browning GGP, Motson RW. Anal sphincter injury—management and results of Parks sphincter repair. Ann Surg 1984;199:351.
38. Yoshioka K, Keighley MRB. Sphincter repair for fecal incontinence. Dis Colon Rectum 1989;32:39.
39. Fang DT, Nivatvongs S, Vermeulen FD, et al. Overlapping sphincteroplasty for acquired anal incontinence. Dis Colon Rectum 1984;27:720.
40. Buchan PC, Nicholls JAJ. Pain after episiotomy—a comparison of two methods of repair. J R Col Gen Pract 1980;30:297.
41. Kitzinger S, Walters R (eds). *Some Women's Experience of Episiotomy*. London, National Childbirth Trust, 1981.
42. Reading AE, Sledmere CM, Cox DN, et al. How women view post-episiotomy pain. Br Med J 1982;284:243.
43. Frisoli G. Maternal birth injuries. In: *Principles and Practice of Obstetrics and Perinatology*. New York, John Wiley & Sons, 1981, p. 975.
44. Kaltreider DF, Dixon DM. A study of 710 complete lacerations following central episiotomy. South Med J 1948;41:814.
45. Thompson JD. Relaxed vaginal outlet, rectocele, fecal incontinence, and rectovaginal fistula. In: Thompson JD, Rock JA (eds). *Te Linde's Operative Gynecology*, Seventh Edition. Philadelphia, J.B. Lippincott Company, 1992, p. 941.

Chapter 18

Shoulder Dystocia

◆◆◆

Robert B. Hilty, M.D.

Introduction

A newborn with some degree of residual neurologic damage, no prenatal history of risk factors noted, no record of a patient being counseled about the possibility of shoulder dystocia and the option for Cesarean section, no adequate intrapartum progress notes related to a "prolonged second stage of labor," and a delivery note with a brief but conclusionary, non-descriptive note regarding the methods used for delivery would present a case that few plaintiff's attorneys could refuse. When the above scenario occurs, the plaintiff almost has a guarantee of at least a pretrial settlement for a substantial amount, as well as a high likelihood of a verdict from a jury involving significant monetary awards for mental anguish, loss of use of the arm, denial of social pleasures, and perhaps more importantly, the loss of earning capacity, and in some states, punitive damages.

When the occurrence of an injury leads to an investigation by a plaintiff's attorney, two basic questions are asked: 1. Could the injury have been avoided?; and 2. Was the care provided consistent with *reasonable* treatment offered by other competent physicians in similar situations? The malpractice claim is based on one or both of two issues: 1. Although risk factors for shoulder dystocia are noted in the obstetrical literature, risk of injury was not recognized; and 2. The physician failed to perform appropriate maneuvers to reduce the risk of injury.[1]

The plaintiff's attorney will generally take the position that the standard of care requires the obstetrician to be able to: 1. "predict shoulder dystocia" because of risk factors apparent during the antenatal or intrapartum periods;

From: Donn SM, Fisher CW (eds.): *Risk Management Techniques in Perinatal and Neonatal Practice.* © Futura Publishing Co., Inc., Armonk, NY, 1996.

2. "diagnose shoulder dystocia" when it occurs; 3. "treat shoulder dystocia" in an appropriate manner; and 4. "document" (accurately) all procedures performed to resolve the shoulder dystocia. If these points are not retrievable from the medical record and/or the physician cannot verify the facts, the case is very difficult, if not impossible, to defend.

Medical Analysis

Although shoulder dystocia occurs in < 1% of deliveries, it remains an unpredictable emergency. The literature often cites factors "associated" with shoulder dystocia, but also points out that such factors cannot be used to diagnose which baby is at risk for the actual, rare occurrence (which is a major distinction that is often lost in the milieu of a legal confrontation). The literature clearly reflects that even the combination of historical facts, estimated fetal weight, and sequence of intrapartum events is ineffective in prospectively identifying infants whose births are complicated by shoulder dystocia. An even more distant relationship exists between these "associations" and the baby who not only endures shoulder dystocia but who also sustains permanent injury. Therefore, it is not medically feasible to prevent brachial plexus injury prospectively by providing "prophylactic" Cesarean delivery of those pregnancies with "associated" risk factors for shoulder dystocia.[2]

Commonly cited risk factors associated with, *but not predictive of* shoulder dystocia are listed in Table 1. Fetal and neonatal complications of shoulder dystocia are listed in Table 2.

> **Commentary by Mr. Volk:** A review of 85 cases of shoulder dystocia from the medico-legal literature reveals an interesting pattern in the recurrence of certain risk factors (Figure 1). For cases *tried* that resulted in a verdict for the injured child, the risk factors, in order

---

Table 1
Risk Factors Associated with Shoulder Dystocia

Antepartum
  Macrosomia (fetal weight > 4000 g)
  Diabetes mellitus
  Postdatism (gestational age > 42 weeks)
  Material obesity or excessive weight gain during pregnancy
  Previous large infant

Intrapartum
  Protracted labor
  Prolonged second stage of labor
  Operative midforceps delivery

Table 2
Fetal and Neonatal Complications Associated with Shoulder Dystocia

Intrapartum asphyxia
Traumatic birth injuries
  Fractured clavicle
  Fractured humerus
  Spinal cord injury
  Brachial plexus injury

of frequency, were the following: use of forceps; fetus > 8.8 pounds; maternal obesity prior to pregnancy; use of excessive traction; maternal diabetes (either familial, gestational, or pre-pregnancy); use of oxytocin; arrest of labor or prolonged second stage; mid-pelvic vacuum extraction; previous large baby; use of fundal pressure; postdate pregnancy; previous shoulder dystocia; excessive maternal weight gain during pregnancy; delivery maneuvers; labor induction; fetal heart rate monitor abnormalities; and the presence of meconium-stained amniotic fluid.

Since it is generally accepted that shoulder dystocia is an unpredictable event (even though all the required studies and evaluations to determine the risks prenatally have been done, and the awareness and response to the forewarning intrapartum abnormalities have been accomplished), the obstetrician must be prepared to face this unexpected emergency with an acceptable therapeutic approach. Some basic principles of both the antepartum and intrapartum aspects need to be stressed. These areas will be covered with special emphasis on the medico-legal implications.

Simply stated, the most cogent description of shoulder dystocia is that patients do present with "associated" risk factors for this rare event. Although this does not prognosticate shoulder dystocia or brachial plexus injury, the presence of these risk factors must heighten the awareness of the obstetrician to make preparations for the appropriate therapeutic maneuvers in the event that shoulder dystocia does occur.

Medical Management

Antepartum Problems

Anticipation of shoulder dystocia can be made on the basis of the presence of a risk factor. Documentation of the risk factors is mandatory, and additionally, a plan and reasons for a "trial of labor" with the knowledge and agreement of the patient is required. It should be noted that although the American

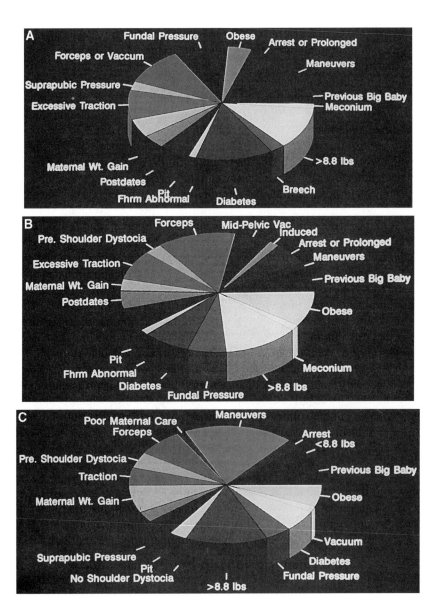

Figure 1. Factor analysis in shoulder dystocia litigation. **A.** Distribution of factors in cases that settled. **B.** Distribution in plaintiff verdicts. **C.** Distribution in defense verdicts.

College of Obstetricians and Gynecologists Technical Bulletin (Number 159) states, "consideration should be given to Cesarean delivery when the clinically estimated fetal weight exceeds 4,500 grams," not all physicians agree, especially when the patient is a multigravida who has delivered previously large babies. Furthermore, the bulletin does not define what it means by "consideration" as it applies to a specific case. However, the health care provider should be on notice that a plaintiff's expert will probably take the position that in such instances a Cesarean section should be performed, or more important, informed consent should be obtained and documented in the record if a trial of labor is to be attempted.

During prenatal care, sonographic evaluation of a suspected macrosomic fetus is an appropriate management technique. However, it is also known that sonography may be misleading. The current sonographic estimates of fetal weight are not sufficiently accurate to diagnose macrosomia defined by weight criteria. Many investigators describe an accuracy of only 47%-64% for the sonographic predictability of a large-for-gestational age fetus.[3,4]

Even if macrosomia is correctly predicted, most patients will not encounter shoulder dystocia. In fact, most patients with suspected macrosomic fetuses are appropriate candidates for a trial of labor. The advantage of performing sonography in cases of suspected macrosomia is two-fold. First, it provides further medical information as to whether a trial of labor should be undertaken, or whether an informed discussion (with consent) regarding a trial of labor versus Cesarean delivery should be undertaken with the patient. Second, the performance of a sonographically determined fetal weight estimate leaves one less avenue to challenge the care giver on the issue of the benefit of a trial of labor.

Most instances of shoulder dystocia actually occur in cases where the fetus weighs < 4000 g. Even where the fetus exceeds this weight, most are delivered without shoulder dystocia and permanent brachial plexus injury is a rare occurrence.

In terms of medical management, however, once risk factors arise during the prenatal course that suggest the potential for a large baby (i.e., gestational diabetes, unduly large fundal height, etc.), the physician needs to undertake certain evaluations for the proper medical management, including: 1. documentation of the awareness of the problem and the identification of the risk factor(s); 2. careful clinical evaluation of fetal size; 3. sonographic determination of fetal weight at the time of delivery; and 4. determination at the onset of labor as to whether or not a discussion and informed consent from the patient is warranted.

Intrapartum Problems

It is vital to observe the Friedman labor curve very closely (especially if a risk factor for a large baby is present). If there is a protracted active phase or a prolonged second stage, the physician *must* record reasons why labor slowed, an analysis of contraction activity, and the physical findings in detail. The nursing documentation alone is not adequate. The physician must document his/her personal evaluation of the patient, especially when there is an active phase arrest of labor. A complete note should include the suspected reason for the arrest, the position of the fetus, the adequacy of the pelvis, and the plan for the remainder of the labor and delivery process. The physician must be present and take total charge of the patient at this juncture and continue through to the delivery. Thorough, accurate, and repeated documentation is essential.

A vital component in many of the lawsuits filed because of shoulder dystocia and neurologic injury is a claim that the physician failed to appropriately evaluate a protracted labor and allowed a continued trial of labor when the baby was clearly macrosomic and unable to deliver vaginally. The classic situation that often presents is a protraction of labor, no documentation of the suspected reason, the application of oxytocin for augmentation, a continued prolongation of the labor, and then a difficult delivery complicated by shoulder dystocia.

Generally, a protracted labor is defined as 2 hours at the same cervical dilation in the active phase, or a second stage of labor which exceeds 2 hours. Either usually leads to expert testimony that a Cesarean section should have been performed. If either of these conditions occur, *it is critical that the attending physician clearly evaluate and document the reasons for the protraction, the methodology and plan, and the reasons why it is believed that the patient can deliver vaginally.*

Delivery

From the moment the shoulder dystocia occurs and is diagnosed, the delivering physician must have a *pre-set plan*, which is followed in approaching and resolving this emergency. There must be a standard and logical strategy (with justification and description of all reasons and steps) to confront the problem. There are many maneuvers and different sequences in which the maneuvers are attempted. None of these maneuvers is perfect, and all have failures and complications. A generally acceptable plan (as a guide rather than as a rule) is as follows: 1. shoulder dystocia is diagnosed ("turtle sign" and/or the inability to deliver the infant by routine maneuvers); 2. the presence of an anesthesiologist and pediatrician, as well as a qualified assistant (experienced nurse or obstetrician) is immediately requested; 3. the bladder is drained if it is distended; 4. *if* more space is needed for maneuvering, an episiotomy is performed or extended; and 5. the appropriate maneuvers are performed. These include: a. suprapubic pressure exerted by an assistant while downward traction is applied to the fetal head (remember, however, that *fundal pressure is an inappropriate way to reduce shoulder dystocia*); b. the McRoberts maneuver involves flexing the mother's legs against her abdomen; c. the Woods-screw maneuver rotates the posterior shoulder 180° in a corkscrew fashion; d. delivery of the posterior shoulder is sometimes accomplished by sweeping the posterior arm of the fetus across the chest and then delivering it; and e. the Zavanelli maneuver replaces the fetal head into the pelvis and is followed by Cesarean section.

Degree of Impaction/Description of Force

Severe shoulder dystocia often requires a series of maneuvers, significant difficulty in delivery, and in the end possible trauma, including injury to the baby's peripheral nervous system. The physician should not downplay the severity of the impaction. If the shoulder is severely impacted and there is significant wedging, the physician should state this clearly in the medical record. Describing the delivery as "'easily accomplished;qR but with a resultant child who has a severe brachial plexus palsy and a dysfunctional arm does not necessarily provide a defense (as some physicians may perceive). In other words, the physician should not be afraid to describe a severe and significant impaction. The more the severity of the impaction, the more reasonable it is to understand why a baby eventually suffered a neurologic impairment.

One must document a very clear and detailed description of whatever maneuvers are used (in chronologic order), including the *degree of difficulty* and the *time frame required*. Notation of "force used" is necessary to defend against the claim of "excessive force and/or lateral traction of the head and neck." The most important aspect of the delivery process is what *not* to do. Most lawsuits contend that excessive lateral traction was applied to the fetal head and neck, and that this was the cause of the damage. This maneuver may ultimately become necessary as a last resort because of the severity of the situation (failure of all previous maneuvers plus potential fetal asphyxia), and again very complete documentation is required to explain reasons for the use of force and/or lateral traction. Unfortunately, "excessive force" is often interpreted to mean "medical negligence." Although this is an obviously inaccurate correlation and assumption, it is a very real legal theory, often testified to by experts in obstetrics. The obstetrician, therefore, should make the medical record as clear as possible that gentle force was used in the initial maneuvers used to free the shoulder. However, as these maneuvers failed to reduce the shoulder, greater force became necessary to deliver the baby, albeit at a greater risk for nerve injury.

Injury

It is not always possible to deliver an undamaged infant after shoulder dystocia has been encountered. Even when the shoulder dystocia is managed optimally, brachial plexus injuries occur. Some of these injuries may be associated with the process of impaction at the pubic symphysis or during descent of the shoulders into the pelvis. This hypothesis is supported by a number of reported cases of brachial plexus injuries in infants in the vertex presentation delivered by Cesarean section, and to infants delivered vaginally when no shoulder dystocia was present.[5] In such cases, injury may be unavoidable.

> **Commentary by Mr. Volk:** The resulting disability to these children can be tragic. The largest shoulder dystocia verdict was $5 million in New York City and the smallest was $150,000 in Amarillo, Texas. The largest settlement was $2 million in the state of New York and the smallest was $75,000 in Ohio. In my review of the 85 published cases, the defense prevailed in only 4.6% of the cases where excessive traction or fundal pressure was a factor.

Documentation

As is obvious and expected in all medical management, thorough and complete documentation in the medical record is vital. The prenatal obstetrical history and physical examination form should have all the required questions answered so that no oversight of risk factors can occur. The same is true for the inpatient hospital record. Physicians must do a better job of documenting findings and events. More lawsuits are won because of good record keeping than because of the actual events.

> **Commentary by Mr. Volk:** Dr. Hilty echoes the advice of Dr. Diggman in an attempt to avoid complications, in what I refer to as "Diggman's rules": 1. prior consideration; 2. accurate knowledge; 3. a well-conceived plan of action; and 4. rapidity of execution. (Diggman WJ. Difficulties in delivery, including shoulder dystocia and malpresentation of fetus. Clin Obstet Gynecol 1976;19:3-12.)

Antepartum Documentation

The gestational diabetic, and the excessively large fundal height (often coupled with obesity and large maternal weight gain) are probably the two most recurrent themes in medico-legal situations. Because of this, the physician needs to document his/her *awareness and continuing vigil* for the possibly macrosomic fetus. A specific note regarding the recognition of these risk factors, as well as for the monitoring of the large baby is important in the prenatal records. It is the recognition of the potentially macrosomic baby that impacts upon the labor management as to whether a trial of labor or a Cesarean section or an informed discussion/consent should be done.

Clinical estimation of fetal weight on admission for labor and delivery, even though not very accurate, does substantiate a rationale for a trial of labor if it is believed that the baby is not macrosomic. Alternatively, sonographic evaluation provides correlation with the clinical evidence to help substantiate a reason for a trial of labor.

It is important to document the estimated fetal weight, for without it, when shoulder dystocia results in an infant weighing 10 pounds, the physician will have a most difficult defense in proving a basis for a trial of labor when this risk factor could have been identified.

Intrapartum Documentation: Protracted Labor

If an apparent protraction of labor occurs as a result of inadequate contractions, the physician must specifically document his/her evaluations of the contractions and his/her rationale for continuing to deliver from below. Documentation should include: 1. the physician's awareness of risk factors; 2. evaluation of the contraction pattern from both the electronic monitor and from physical palpation of the maternal abdomen; 3. evaluation of the pelvis, fetal size, fetal position, and adequacy in general for a vaginal delivery; and 4. a plan for management to be followed through the delivery.

It is important to remember that closer evaluation of the progress of the labor is mandated after a potential protraction disorder has been recognized, especially in the face of risk factors associated with shoulder dystocia. This may mean more frequent vaginal examinations, which include documentation of the progress of cervical dilatation, and most importantly, documentation of the progress of descent in the second stage of labor, assessed at regular intervals by pelvic examination.

Delivery Note

When the obstetrician has a shoulder dystocia case (irrespective of outcome), a detailed chronology should be written immediately to document the pertinent events of the pregnancy with special attention to the labor and delivery. Include *all* necessary events and also document reasons for decisions and actions. The entire summary of events, with detailed descriptions of the times and maneuvers used, should be carefully and thoroughly transcribed. Immediately after the delivery, the physician should review with the nurses and other medical personnel active in the patient's care, the events of labor and delivery, to ensure that their notes are also consistent with the events that transpired.

Lawsuits are often filed several years after the event. For the most part, fact witnesses do not recollect the exact events of the management of the delivery and are only refreshed by the review of their recorded notes. Therefore, accurately written notes regarding the delivery in detailed form by both the physician and the nurses who observe the delivery is an appropriate corroboration of the event. It should also be kept in mind, however, that the primary responsibility for making certain that the delivery note is complete and accurate rests with the attending physician. This duty should not be left to the house officer or the nurse.

Comments

If a lawsuit is filed, the physician should immediately organize the medical records and begin to prepare a defense. In many cases, the plaintiff's attorney and the defense attorney are more informed of the facts and details of a particular case than is the defendant doctor. Review of the medical facts should not be a cavalier undertaking, but must be thorough, in depth, and decisive. The physician should remember that for the most part, the delivery will not be well recalled, and therefore, detailed knowledge of all the facts as to the involvement of each individual is necessary.

The physician must also mentally review certain basics in obstetrics in order to be able to "verbalize" and communicate his/her knowledge. Examples of this include: 1. the difference between associated risk factors, and whether or not shoulder dystocia can be predicted; 2. the various associated risk factors and their impact upon management decisions, if any; 3. the parameters of the Friedman labor curve, protracted labor, and protraction management; 4. the cardinal events of passage of the fetus through the pelvis; 5. pelvic anatomy; and 6. the various maneuvers and approaches, and how they may be described verbally in explaining a delivery complicated by shoulder dystocia.

It is incredible to observe how many physicians appear wholly unprepared to verbalize a response to defend themselves during a deposition or trial. In a deposition, the physician must calmly and thoroughly answer questions regarding the subject (including details of the case in question), without losing self-control. The physician must be knowledgeable about the subject, must be practical regarding the handling of the case, must not dwell on subject areas not pertinent to the case or outside his/her speciality, and above all else must have emotional control and not allow the plaintiff's attorney to unravel him/her. Remember that arrogance wins nothing, but humility with assuredness wins most things.

The best defense against a malpractice claim is the ability to articulate a reasonable basis for one's clinical judgment based on documentation in the medical record. From a medico-legal viewpoint, the perception of what the physician does is almost always as important as what is actually done. Thus, good documentation of how shoulder dystocia was managed can be of enormous benefit if questions are raised years after the event.

> **Commentary by Mr. Volk:** I certainly agree that it is unbelievable that so many physicians are unprepared during litigation, but it is also unbelievable how poorly they: 1. document; 2. communicate with patients and other health care providers; 3. attempt to cover up; 4. send bad outcome patients to a collection agency or sue them for their fees; 5. refuse to provide a copy of the medical records to the patient; and 6. generally behave suspiciously. Litigation is a fact of life in this country, and it is not going to go away. The best defense against litigation is a well-trained physician who meets the standard of care and documents properly the patient's care and progress.

References

1. Nocon JJ. Shoulder dystocia-managing risks to avoid negligence. Contempt OB/GYN 1991;36:15.
2. Morrison JC, Sander JR, Magann EF, et al. The diagnosis and management of dystocia of the shoulder. Surg Gynecol Obstet 1992;175:515.
3. Sandmire HF. Whither ultrasonic prediction of fetal macrosomia? Obstet Gynecol 1993;82:860.
4. Fetal macrosomia. American College of Obstetrics and Gynecology Technical Bulletin Number 159, September 1991.
5. Cullins V, Johnson T, Repke JT. Shoulder dystocia—an organized approach. The Female Patient 1991;16.

Section IV

Pathologic and Laboratory Evaluation

Chapter 19

The Use of the Placenta in the Understanding of Perinatal Injury

◆◆◆

Kurt Benirschke, M.D.

Introduction

The placenta is the most important organ of the fetus. It supplies all nutrients and gases of fetal development and, simultaneously, it removes from the fetus all the waste products to be excreted by the mother. This fetal organ expresses the fetal genome and, in order not to be rejected by the mother immunologically, the placental cell markers contain certain specific genetic information that prevents them from being recognized as "foreign." Moreover, the placenta modifies the maternal system in many ways. For instance, placental trophoblastic cells invade the uterus with the aid of collagenase and stream up inside the maternal arteries to render them pharmacologically nonreactive. Placental hormone secretion alters maternal bodily functions in such a way as to maximize fetal development, and so on. It is indeed a remarkable, if transitory, organ.

The placental structure and function undergo many changes during development. An examiner must be cognizant of these changes and know how to interpret them to his/her benefit. During development of the placenta, certain alterations of its structure may reflect a significantly normal or abnormal fetal performance. Pathologic changes may indicate the time of a given trauma, or growth failure, and a variety of other insults, such as infections. The placenta, in fact, often provides an excellent means of interpreting prenatal events; however, this presupposes that one is familiar with the normal placenta. In this way the placenta also becomes an important organ in the assessment of the causes of perinatal death and injury. There are some placen-

From: Donn SM, Fisher CW (eds.): *Risk Management Techniques in Perinatal and Neonatal Practice*. © Futura Publishing Co., Inc., Armonk, NY, 1996.

tal findings that may be absolutely decisive in explaining fetal injury. That is to say, without a placental examination the injury may not be understood. This is true for situations such as knots in the umbilical cord, and when placental surface vessel thrombosis exists. They are so abnormal that if not recognized or recorded at birth, the understanding of the etiology of such problems as cerebral palsy might not be possible. Thus, the detailed examination of the placenta may be important in making decisions about possible "faults" in the delivery of obstetric or neonatal services. Its routine study should be undertaken so as to more fairly adjudicate such problematic cases. Experience suggests that plaintiff attorneys often agree that placental disease may have existed but then also usually insist that the important fetal injury was really caused by the enhanced susceptibility for hypoxia during labor. Clairvoyance is common *after* the fact; more important is to learn what really happens. It is the pathologist's duty to understand as fully as possible the time of abnormal development and the capacity for sequelae of all lesions we identify, recognizing that biologic life is one of gradual transition, not one of black and white events as theory may wish it to be.

This chapter provides some direction for the examination of the placenta and addresses the most frequent pathologic features that may be helpful in adjudicating "bad baby cases." It should be stated at the outset, however, that a single and precise etiology of the common entity, "cerebral palsy," does not exist. It is a spectrum of insults or deficiencies of the central nervous system that often manifest only in later childhood. The etiology of these deficiencies is very varied, and it is certainly much oversimplified to suggest that it is usually the result of perinatal "hypoxia," however appealing such simple interpretation may be. Perinatal hypoxia is but one such cause. The review by Kuban and Leviton[1] provides insight into this complexity, and others[2] have shown convincingly that Cesarean section, as opposed to vaginal delivery does not decrease the incidence of cerebral palsy.

> **Commentary by Mr. Volk:** I agree that the question of Cesarean section and its relationship to cerebral palsy is complex. However, when reviewing a medico-legal claim alleging that the failure to section caused or contributed to the dysfunction of the child, the focus is on whether or not a section would probably have reduced or eliminated that dysfunction. The analysis is not based on statistical data but the application of the facts to the delivery under review. Experienced attorneys who deal in medico-legal claims understand that simple interpretations may not be the correct ones. The problem occurs when attorneys inexperienced in the area attempt to litigate. Any attorney, skilled or not in the medico-legal area, understands the ethical obligation to not press non-meritorious claims.

However, sometimes these inexperienced attorneys adopt a view of a claim that is not based on scientific facts. I have never met an attorney reviewing a potential claim who does not want to know the facts. The solution is simple: Physicians should be readily available, for a reasonable fee for their time, in all specialities to honestly consult with attorneys so there is a free exchange of information between the legal and medical professions.

Examination

Most pathologists do not find the routine examination of the placenta to be very interesting. This is so primarily because most deliveries and most babies are normal and little need for a placental examination is perceived. Such placentas are thus also inferred to be normal. As a consequence, many colleagues have little appreciation of what a normal placenta should look like, and how it is best described, and what important lesions one should seek when perinatal problems arise. Ideally, the pathologist should first examine a minimum of 100 consecutive placentas in order to become familiar with the varied structure of this organ. The assistance of obstetricians and pediatricians should be sought to properly correlate the pathologic findings. Given this exposure, pathologists would be in a much better position to describe the organ for meaningful interpretation and sampling.

Certain items of this examination *must* be recorded in order to be useful for future interpretation:

1. weight (minus cord and membranes);
2. diameters and thickness;
3. color of the fetal surface;
4. color of the villous tissue (anemia makes it pale); and
5. condition of surface vessels, especially whether they show evidence of thrombosis.

The maternal surface must be studied, especially regarding the possible presence of clots. It is equally important to record the presence and percentage of infarcts and other lesions identified by palpation and sectioning. Twin placentas pose additional needs for the examination: in fused twin placentas, the nature of the "dividing membranes" must be assessed grossly or microscopically, and the nature of vascular anastomoses must be adjudicated correctly in monochorionic twins, something that requires knowledge and practice. This may require the injection with water, colored fluids, or milk for the recognition of smaller anastomoses. Finally, sufficient samples must be taken for histologic examination. These must include at least one section of cord, one of rolled membranes (the "jelly rolls"), one from a margin, and at least one from the center of normal placental tissue. Ideally, three of four such sections are fixed. Additionally, any areas of disease, such as tumors or infarcts must be preserved. Of course, all of these segments of placental tissue will be fixed first before they are trimmed for histologic study, usually in formalin solution. It is often helpful to prepare color photographs of abnormal placentas. This may provide much insight for future inquiries and is inexpensive to perform. Several texts are available to aid in the interpretation of pathologic findings and they provide access to the literature.[3-5]

Criteria for selection of which placentas should be examined have been proposed by committee agreement.[6] In addition, Altshuler[7,8] reviewed this topic in detail and provided tabular direction for sample selection. All placentas of multiple births, premature infants, perinatal deaths, and all abnormal deliveries should be studied. This is not a large number, perhaps 10% of routine populations. Inasmuch as little autolytic change affects the future placental examination, it is recommended that *all* placentas be stored in a refrigerator for several days, at least until the apparent normalcy of a given baby is assured. Placentas can then be discarded with little fear that their study results would be needed in the future. Others have given cogent evidence that a routine examination of *all* placentas is desirable and have also provided numbers that suggest this practice is cost effective.[9]

Color

One of the most common allegations in perinatal damage cases is that meconium-staining of the placenta indicates an asphyxial insult to have occurred during the process of delivery. It is then also suggested that earlier delivery, for instance by Cesarean section, would have prevented the fetal or neonatal damage. Let us examine this proposition in some detail.

Meconium is the bowel content of the fetus. It is sterile and consists mostly of debris, cells that have been ingested or are shed in the gastrointestinal tract. It also contains bile pigments, mucus, and enzymes. Normally, meconium moves gradually in a distal direction, to be discharged around the time of term delivery. Its propulsion is handled by the gastrointestinal hormone motilin. The concentration of this fetal hormone gradually increases during gestation and the development of this endocrine axis is so timed that a sufficient amount of motilin is "on board" to assure neonatal defecation at term. When the fetus is born beyond 40-weeks gestation, meconium is often discharged before birth, merely because of the status of developmental parameters. It is for this reason that meconium-staining of the placenta occurs in a majority of cases after 40-weeks gestation. Meconium discharge is quite uncommonly recognized before 35 weeks of gestation. If it is discharged at the early gestational age, the quality of the meconium differs much. It has less mucus, and that, among other features, makes it perhaps more difficult to recognize as meconium. The mere green staining of fluid or placentas, especially prematurely delivered ones, needs to be examined with the view that it could also be hemosiderin that causes the discoloration. In one of my own experiences with *consecutive* deliveries, 17% of placentas were meconium-stained, but virtually all infants fared well, at least neonatally. Only a minute fraction of these babies required intensive care, and virtually all were discharged with the mother. It is thus important to study the regression analysis of Altshuler and Herman.[10] In their sample, meconium staining was found to be "significant," as was the presence of nucleated red blood cells (NRBCs), chronic villous ischemia, intimal "cushions" in fetal vessels, and intervillous fibrin excess. Kallkury and colleagues[11] also found that 19% of consecutive placentas were meconium-stained, the majority without sequelae, but also, that hemosiderin in macrophages must be differentiated from the green discoloration of meconium. Naeye[12] stated that in the National Collaborative Perinatal Project, 64% of the cases of meconium in the amniotic fluid were associated with the presence of acute chorioamnionitis, 6% with post-term birth, and 6% with disorders that cause low blood flow from the uterus to the placenta. Only 0.2% appeared attributable to birth asphyxial disorders.[12]

It is often stated that fetal hypoxia leads to meconium discharge. This may be true at times, but certainly it is not usually, let alone always, the case. Thus, it is important to appreciate that most fetal deaths, occurring as the result of complete asphyxia, are not accompanied by meconium discharge. Meconium-staining of fetus and placenta is therefore not a reliable indicator of perinatal hypoxia. Some students of the placenta have attempted to assign different color descriptors (green-brown, yellowish-green, etc.) to meconium-stained placentas without agreeing on a standardization of impressions. Such designations are generally not capable of being interpreted by other observers, nor are they very helpful.

If one insists in believing that meconium discharge is a useful indicator of prenatal hypoxia, then some additional findings need to be taken into consideration. Meconium discharge may occur once, or it may happen repeatedly; indeed, fetal diarrhea has been observed sonographically. Bile-staining of amniotic fluid has also been observed from fetal vomiting in cases of fetal intestinal obstruction, confusing the issue of green amniotic fluid even further. A single meconium discharge may stain some or all of the amniotic fluid; this depends principally on the fetal movements and the quantity discharged. Thus, measuring its amount by a "meconium-crit" has not been found useful. Once discharged, meconium may be passed with amniotic fluid or it may remain in the intact sac. It may even be swallowed and thereby it could be removed from the amniotic fluid.

After it has been dispersed in the amnionic sac, meconium causes degenerative changes in the tissues with which it comes in contact, for it has toxic properties of an as yet unknown nature (Figure 1). The first result of this visible toxicity is the degeneration of the amnionic epithelium. This loses its organization and becomes "heaped," the nuclear staining disappears, and yellow pigment can be detected in the normally present macrophages of the amnionic connective tissue. The latter change takes approximately 1 hour as judged by experimental studies of the process.[13] In 3 hours or so, the meconium pigment reaches the macrophages of the underlying chorionic connective tissue, and later still it dissipates into the decidua capsularis of the membranes. It may ultimately disappear completely. Knowledge is difficult to obtain concerning the temporal aspects of meconium-staining of placenta and fetus, as the fetus is not usually "allowed" to remain for long after the discovery of meconium; delivery is rapidly accomplished to avoid the meconium aspiration by the fetus. If meconium is inhaled by the fetus, this has other complications, principally the development of the neonatal meconium aspiration syndrome. In legal proceedings it is also often alleged that meconium, after all, *can* penetrate deeper into the membranes if the placenta is left standing before being studied. Since usually nobody knows just how long a placenta sits before examination, the deeper staining of membranes could theoretically occur

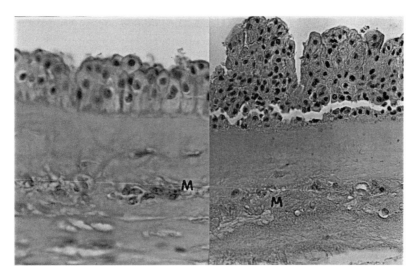

Figure 1. Degeneration of amnion epithelium in meconium injury. At left is an earlier phase with slight discoloration of the normally single-layered epithelium; meconium-laden macrophages are found in the amnionic connective tissue (M). At right is more advanced degeneration with "heaping" of the epithelium and detachment from the basement membrane.

after birth. To obviate such spurious objections, quick examination/fixation of the placenta is desirable; even better, a notation of the depth of staining made at the time of birth by peeling the amnion off the chorion can be decisive. If the underlying chorion is green at delivery, then discharge surely has taken place 3 hours or more before delivery. A good histopathologist will detect associated autolytic changes if the assertion of post-delivery staining holds true.

More interesting than the effect on placental membranes is the lesion of umbilical vessels that clearly results from prolonged meconium exposure. When one sections the meconium-stained umbilical cord, its Wharton's jelly is often stained green through and through. Yet, only few yellow macrophages may be seen histologicly because of the relative paucity of these cells in the umbilical cord. When meconium exposure to the cord has been prolonged, Altshuler and Hyde[14] recorded not only acute constriction of vessels in an experimental vascular perfusion set-up, but also that there is necrosis of the cord's vascular muscle walls. These are highly characteristic and impressive lesions that are not easily confused with any other insult, and are now recorded by many observers (Figure 2). Meconium's devastating cellular insult is very

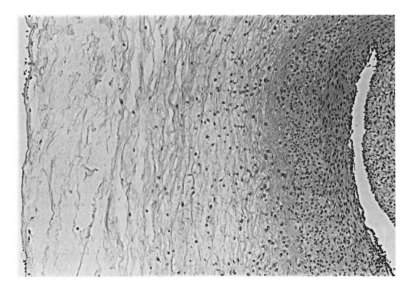

Figure 2. Portion of the umbilical cord with degeneration of peripheral portion of the umbilical arterial wall from meconium toxicity. At left is the necrotic amnionic surface of the umbilical cord adjacent to the edematous, degenerating Wharton's jelly. At the right is the lumen of one umbilical artery. The scattered round cells in the middle represent dead muscle fibers as a result of meconium injury. This child subsequently developed cerebral palsy.

obvious and its impact on fetal vascular perfusion of the placenta must be significant. Just how long it takes to stain the cord and then to cause this vascular degeneration is presently unknown, but it must take many, many hours to come about, probably days. Altshuler[8] reports that this vascular lesion may be observed after 16 hours or more of meconium exposure. Interestingly, meconium is not itself a cause of inflammation, as many very severely and deeply-stained placentas verify. It may lead to an increased susceptibility to infection, but it does not attract leukocytes as infection does, contrary to some older suggestions.

Infection and the Placenta

Listeriosis, a systemic bacterial infection, is not very common. It occurs most often in small, periodic epidemics and usually results from the ingestion of contaminated foods. The gram-positive bacillus not only has a great affinity to infect pregnant women, it also causes abscesses in the placenta and fetus. The disease that is produced in infected newborns has been referred to as "Granulomatosis Infantiseptica," actually consisting of disseminated abscesses. The administration of penicillin, ampicillin, and some other common antibiotics rapidly kills the organisms, and these antibiotics also rapidly traverse the placenta. Many cases have been observed in which treatment was successful and prolonged fetal growth in utero took place after therapy. After delivery, it has occasionally been possible to show that the placenta had healing abscesses with remnants of destroyed villi, easily recognized by gross placental examination. One may well expect that cases exist in which the fetal abscesses have been cured by the prenatal antibiotic therapy and in which scars of various organs may have resulted. Perhaps they are symptomatic in neonatal life or later childhood; it is not yet known.

Villitis of unknown etiology (VUE) is a relatively common placental disease and its extent varies greatly. It is exemplified by massive infiltration of the placental villi with chronic inflammatory cells. In fact, when one sees the severest forms of VUE, one wonders how the baby can possibly have lived in utero for so long. Often the fetus is stillborn, and even worse, the condition may recur in subsequent pregnancies. The etiology of VUE is unknown, and the recent suggestion that the infiltrating cells are of maternal origin and that they may represent a maternal rejection reaction is yet unconfirmed.[20] It may be instrumental in causing growth retardation and fetal death. If it can kill one fetus, it stands to reason that it may sub-lethally injure another. VUE differs from the characteristic chronic infectious villitis. VUE is not usually associated with the plasma cell infiltration of cytomegalovirus infection or the irregularly hypercellular villi of syphilis, but one must consider these in the differential diagnosis. If VUE does contain plasma cells, this is not typical. One may be able to identify the agent that caused the immunologic B-cell response, but that does not confirm the diagnosis of VUE. It is possible that several types of VUE will eventually be recognized.

Ascending chorioamnionitis is clearly the commonest infection of pregnancy and may occur after a long labor. Generally, its existence is of little consequence to the mature infant, but the same is not true for immature gestations. Good evidence exists that the organisms that cause chorioamnionitis ascend from the vaginal-endocervical tract. Chorioamnionitis begins as a peripheral deciduitis of the membranes, at the internal os of the uterus. This deciduitis may then go on to allow the organisms access into the amniotic cavity where they first cause chorioamnionitis and eventually funisitis (inflammation of cord vessels). This infection of amniotic fluid can happen with or without the rupture of the membranes. Most investigators now agree that the inflammation of the membranes is a frequent cause of rupture, especially around mid-gestation. In other words, infection of membranes may long antedate the rupture of membranes. A wide variety of organisms, which may be difficult to culture, can lead to chorioamnionitis, and some organisms (i.e., fusobacteria, group B streptococci) are clearly more important or aggressive in causing disease than are others. The primary problem with this ascending infection is that it is so difficult to diagnose early in its course. Importantly though, it induces premature labor by producing the enzymes for prostaglandin synthesis. Once this process has commenced, it may be extremely difficult to stop labor with antibiotics or tocolytic agents. The result of this infection can be a significantly preterm delivery with all the consequences of prematurity, such as brain hemorrhage, periventricular leukomalacia, and lung problems.[22] A majority of spontaneous pregnancy terminations between 20- and 30-weeks gestation are the result of this disease. Hankins et al.[23] found that umbilical cord blood gas values of normal premature infants were similar to term infants; when chorioamnionitis was present, however, this was significantly correlated with lower Apgar scores but had no influence on gas values. Once the infectious organisms have reached the amniotic sac, their protein products elicit the emigration of fetal and maternal polymorphonuclear leukocytes from their respective vascular compartments (i.e., pathologically identifiable chorioamnionitis and funisitis result). Once this process begins and pus reaches the amniotic fluid, it may be swallowed and aspirated, and the fetus may sustain aspiration pneumonia; alternatively, the fetus may become septic, an uncommon initial event. In addition to the premature delivery that is a common sequel of this infection, the deciduitis may lead to bleeding and what, to the clinician, appears to be abruptio placentae. Large clots may be delivered with the placenta, but real retroplacental bleeding does not commonly occur (it is retromembranous and marginal hemorrhage from deciduitis), and thus it does not represent true abruptio placentae.

Some authors have suggested that one can meaningfully subdivide chorioamnionitis into "stages" or "grades" and that these perhaps relate to differing fetal consequences. This is not particularly useful. The response to an infection by fetal and maternal leukocytes is very variable and it depends mostly on the nature of the organism, rather than the length of time of exposure to them. Thus, notoriously, group B streptococcal infection is not only difficult to diagnose, it may be a chronic infection of the maternal genital tract. It can have severe fetal and neonatal consequences, but the degree of leukocyte exudation in response to even large numbers of organisms is frequently minimal.

Routine neonatal neurosonographic study of premature infants has shown that *fetal* leukomalacia, prenatal brain cyst formation, and ultimately cerebral palsy relate primarily to two conditions: 1. chorioamnionitis; and 2. monozygotic (MZ) twinning.[24,25] It is not clear whether this degeneration from infection presupposes the existence of sepsis in utero, or whether the degenerative changes result from endotoxins, or possibly other proteins elaborated by the infectious process, such as tumor necrosis factor. Still, prenatal degeneration of brain tissue can occur in such apparently banal infections. Therefore, the study of the placenta of premature infants is especially important if one wishes to understand the reason for possible future defects. Finally, chorioamnionitis with the associated vasculitis of placental surface vessels may induce the formation of mural and occasionally occlusive thrombi in these vessels. They may further aggravate fetal problems. Thrombi occur, of course, only after a long existence of the infectious process and are thus occasionally useful in supporting the chronic nature of the insult. In the umbilical cord, chronic exudation of leukocytes occurs only in a peripheral direction, it does not happen centripetally. Thus, rings of exudate tend to form around the fetal blood vessels. The leukocytes that have thus emigrated from the fetal vessels have a limited lifespan (a few hours) and they die there. Ultimately, this exudate may calcify, the best indication of a really chronic prenatal infection. While this type of chronic funisitis is occasionally the result of a syphilitic infection, this is not invariably so.[26] Indeed, at times the microbial cause of the infection may remain obscure, as the inflammatory process and any possible therapy that was given may have cured the infection. Nevertheless, the chronicity of the infection does not then remain in doubt.

Multiple Pregnancy

There is a much higher incidence of cerebral palsy in twins. One possible reason is the greater frequency of premature birth of twins, with all the attendant problems of prematurity. Cerebral palsy can also be associated with chorioamnionitis because premature cervical dilatation is more common in multiple pregnancy. It is, however, striking to find that cerebral palsy is particularly more common in one of MZ ("identical") twins than it is in fraternal twins. This observation has suggested that especially deleterious circumstances exist in the prenatal environment of MZ twins.[25] Closer scrutiny indicates that the principal underlying cause leading to fetal problems of MZ twins relates to inter-twin placental vascular anastomoses in the placenta. These blood vessel communications exist in almost all MZ twins, because it is these twins who have a monochorionic placenta in about 60% of cases, a type not found in fraternal twins. Virtually all monochorionic placentas have some kind of anastomosis between the two fetal circulations, while practically none of dichorionic twin placentas possess them. Good evidence exists that blood flows often from one twin to the other through these vessels, and that this partitioning of fetal blood takes irregular courses in prenatal life. Thus, when only an artery-to-vein anastomosis exists between the circulations of twins, the typical fetal twin-to-twin transfusion syndrome develops. In this condition, one fetus becomes anemic (the donor), while the other (the recipient) becomes plethoric and develops hydramnios. The hydramnios, with overdistension of the uterus, may cause early premature delivery in such twins. A new laser vascular obliteration technique may prevent the continuation of the syndrome, thus proving the accuracy of the interpretation of the underlying mechanism.[27] It has been further observed that cerebral palsy is much more common when one MZ twin dies prenatally and the survivor thus becomes associated with a so-called fetus papyraceous, a flattened mass of skin and bones. Intensive study of this phenomenon and the similarity with the death of the original "'Siamese twins" (exsanguination of Eng, after the death of Chang, into the body of Chang with whom he was vascularly connected) now shows that in these cases of prenatal death of a monochorionic twin, sudden hypotension results in the survivor through the acute loss of blood into the dead fetus.[28] In fact, prenatally sustained brain degeneration has been sonographically recorded in such cases. Depending upon the time relationship of fetal death to the birth of the survivor, one may find a variety of signs of recovery; for instance, there may be a degree of anemia, a significant number of NRBCs, thrombocytopenia, an already normalizing pH, etc. It is hypothesized that the degree of this cerebral insult depends largely upon the size of the inter-twin vascular anastomosis and the time of gestation, as the degree of cardiac activity (blood pressure) is the important aspect of the hypotensive episode. It has been deduced that the insult to the surviving twin is sudden and massive, so that intervention by possible Cesarean delivery (if one happened to make the diagnosis of impending fetal death clinically) would invariably come too late. Moreover, it is currently impossible to make the diagnosis of inter-twin anastomoses prenatally. It has already been shown by Doppler methodology that reversal of blood flow does indeed take place after the death of one twin.[29] Most interestingly, brain damage to *both* twins has even been documented in stillborn MZ twin fetuses.[30] Apparently, complex vascular relationships exist in the monochorionic placentas of twins, through which blood exchange takes place, an aspect that is currently not fully comprehended. One problem in understanding this system better is that usually only an incomplete examination of placental vessels is made, and blood pressure relationships of the fetuses are never known. Another deficiency of current methodology is the inability to demonstrate flow in placental surface blood vessels.

Nucleated Red Blood Cells

NRBCs should not exist in any numbers in the neonatal circulation; the presence of even a few NRBCs is abnormal. The presence of these red blood cell precursors in the neonatal circulation has given rise to the name of the disease "erythroblastosis fetalis" (hemolytic disease secondary to Rh isoimmunization) in which many immature red blood cells circulate. They do so because of the fetal response to hemolytic anemia. When the pathologist identifies NRBCs in the fetal blood (during placental examination or in neonatal blood smears) it is his/her challenge to find an explanation for their existence. For instance, a common fetal cause of anemia, transplacental bleeding, may need to be excluded by Kleihauer-Betke stains of maternal blood.[31] This study is routinely advocated for unexplained stillbirths. When no hemolytic or hemorrhagic anemia exists in the neonatal examination, and NRBCs are abundant, another explanation has to be found for their presence. Commonly, the explanation is perinatal hypoxia, a relationship first described by Fox.[32] The release of NRBCs into the fetal circulation is regulated through a complex mechanism of hormones in response to tissue hypoxia. Anemia is but one such stimulus; others may be obstruction to umbilical cord blood flow, fetal growth retardation, infections, abruptio placentae, and a multitude of other prenatal causes of hypoxia. Nicolini et al.[33] found that fetal intrauterine growth retardation was strongly related to the presence of NRBCs and that the only rational conclusion was that chronic hypoxia is a strong stimulus for the presence of these abnormal cells. Placental findings in growth retarded newborns include infarction, chronic villitis, and thromboses.[34] The problem hampering a better understanding of the relationship of NRBCs to fetal problems is that there is no clear cut knowledge of the temporal relationship between the onset of the hypoxic event and the occurrence of NRBCs in the peripheral circulation. How long does it take for a given degree of hypoxia to result in a given number of NRBCs? This relation is only superficially understood, and it is also unknown if all stimuli (acute anemia vs chronic hypoxia) produce the same result. Ruth et al.[35] found that fetal erythropoietin (EPO) levels were markedly elevated in asphyxiated infants who ultimately suffered brain damage. There was, however, no correlation between the frequent elevation of EPO in pre-eclamptics and the outcome of their offspring.

NRBCs are enumerated in blood smears and their number is commonly expressed as NRBCs/100 white blood cells (WBCs). In cases of severe hypoxia or in profound fetal anemia there may be more NRBCs than WBCs, but in cases of moderate perinatal hypoxia (as in umbilical cord compression) the number may be 20-50 NRBCs/100 WBCs, occasionally more. The number of NRBCs falls quickly after birth, as the cells mature and no new ones are released from the precursor stores, unless anemia persists. Occasional traumatic hemorrhages can be timed and outcome studied. From two such cases it can be deduced that it takes at least one-half a day for significant numbers of NRBCs to be released. At the same time, the hematocrit falls to one-half its normal value. Much more information is needed in order to use this important feature of placental and neonatal blood study in properly understanding and adjudicating perinatal injury cases. It is important, how-ever, to know that NRBCs are abnormal in newborns. A very detailed discus-sion of the relation of NRBCs to hypoxia and what can be deduced from relevant animal models may be found in Altshuler's reviews.[7,8]

Abruptio Placentae

(See Chapter 13 on abruptio placentae.) The normal placenta remains attached to the endometrium until after delivery of the fetus. It detaches by uterine muscle contraction through shearing within the decidua basalis. Placenta accreta (lacking a decidual base) therefore cannot occur simultane-ously with abruptio placentae because it is stuck to the myometrium. Prema-ture detachment can occur because of spontaneous hemorrhage behind the placenta. If it is "concealed" (not bleeding from the cervix), then it may be painful because of uterine serosal pain, and the fetus may die suddenly; if at least > 50% of the placenta detaches there is insufficient perfusion for fetal survival. Abruptio placentae occurs most often as a complication of maternal hypertensive conditions. Decidual vascular occlusion causes decidual necrosis and vascular disruption. When the pregnancy continues for hours or days after this retroplacental hemorrhage, infarction of the overlying villous tissue commences and can be diagnosed by proper placental examination. Gradually, the retroplacental clot also changes color and texture; at first it becomes dry, compacted and "fibrous" in appearance, then it turns brown, then green, and eventually the clot resorbs. That takes weeks. The frequency of such old retroplacental hematomas detected only by placental examination is much greater than anticipated from clinical symptoms.[36] Abruptio placentae can also be the result of motor vehicle accidents and other trauma; it can result from uterine anomalies, uterine tumors, and perhaps even from fetal kicking.

This assumption was strengthened when Eden[37] reported two cases of maternal vaginal bleeding during pregnancy that were associated with severe pain, and in which the pain was caused by fetal movements. Upon sonographic study, it became apparent that the fetus was "punching" the area of the placenta (marginal) from which bleeding occurred.

Obstetricians occasionally observe that a placenta appears as though it had been detached at the time of Cesarean section, that it was "floating free in blood," or that it "came immediately" after the birth of the child. These observations often assume abruptio placentae to have occurred. When the abruptive process occurs so quickly, it cannot be diagnosed by placental examination. To make the pathologic diagnosis of abruptio placentae requires that at least some degree of compression of placental tissue is identified with the presence of a clot. For legal purposes, this may be difficult with the hyperacute event. Its verification might be enhanced if a photograph was available. Alternatively, good histologic sections and a detailed description are minimally needed. Nevertheless, it may be impossible to *prove* to everyone's satisfaction that an acute abruption took place and that it was the cause of any fetal problems or death. To *prove* a "chronic" (long existing) abruptio placentae is more readily possible. It is invariably associated with compression and death of villous tissue. In addition, discoloration of the clot and of the adjacent issues is the usual finding.

Even more complicated is the question of cocaine-induced abruption. Acker et al.[38] reported that cocaine and other substance abuse may be the cause of abruptio placentae. Doubtless, many substances cause uterine vascular constriction and some may even cause abruption, but this must be uncommon, as there has been no remarkable increase in abruptions despite the rapidly expanding use of illicit drugs.

Chorangiosis

The presence of an excessive number of capillaries in terminal villi has been termed chorangiosis or, less aptly, chorangiomatosis. Altshuler[39] has written the only definitive article on this uncommon but important condition, and pathologists have since learned to recognize the entity. This abnormality of vascularization of villi is clearly a condition that takes days or even weeks to develop before one can recognize it by pathologic study. It is characteristic of the placenta delivered at high altitude and is always considered to be a response to severe chronic hypoxia. Thus, when chorangiosis is observed in a delivered placenta it denotes a response by the fetus and the placenta to chronic hypoxia. The etiology underlying this structural placental response is varied and it cannot necessarily be deduced from the lesion alone, but it is safe to state that chorangiosis is a serious pathologic feature of the placenta.

To be sure, chorangiosis is more common in maternal diabetes, in cord entanglement, and in a few other conditions.[39] It results from many different adverse circumstances; they need to be sought in order to properly explain the lesion that so commonly accompanies fetal demise. Altshuler[39] found it in only 5% of placentas of infants admitted to his special care nursery. He listed a variety of associated conditions and has brought the thinking about chorangiosis up to date in his recent reviews.[7,8] Most puzzling is the observation that chorangiosis does not *always* exist when long-standing hypoxia resulting from conditions such as cord entanglement (i.e., in monoamniotic placentas) can be inferred from other pathology. Conversely, when it is found, it is a significant pathologic feature denoting chronic hypoxia, presumably primarily the result of deficient intervillous perfusion.

Umbilical Cord Problems

Many cases of fetal demise can only be explained by the examination of placenta and, especially, from understanding the umbilical cord biology. Cord signs are even discussed in fetal monitor patterns, and the identification of a tight knot in the umbilical cord with proximal congestion, more than any other event, may prove to even the most unbelieving observer that it can be the reason for fetal demise. It is thus disappointing that so few observations are made about the condition of the umbilical cord at birth, especially its length. The normal length is 55 cm, and the ultimate length of the umbilical cord is largely decided by early gestation; it depends primarily upon the degree of fetal movements. When neurologic deficits limit the fetal motions, or when the fetus is attached by bands to the placenta, then the cord remains short. When the fetus moves a lot, the cord may be excessively long and will entangle more readily with the fetus (neck and extremities). Long cords also lead more often to knots and prolapse of the cord. All of these factors need to be considered in evaluating fetal life. Excessive spiraling is a frequent cause of fetal demise (Figure 3). It is most common in abortuses, with the severely constricted segment near the fetal surface. Term babies also may suffer from excessive twisting and consequently reduced venous return from the placenta, and thus inferred reduced oxygen delivery. That a long time transpired in this reduced venous return is often reflected by thrombosis of surface blood vessels in the placenta, usually in the veins (veins are recognized because they lie below the superficial arterial branches). The age of thrombi can often be evaluated histologically. Thrombi are frequent; they are usually only mural in nature, and they may be associated with necrosis and/or calcification of the vessel wall, denoting even longer existence. When thrombi become occlusive, the peripheral villous tissue atrophies and is set out from any further functional performance. Not only is this related to intrauterine growth retar-

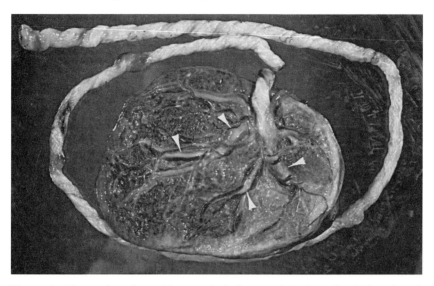

Figure 3. Placental surface with excessively long umbilical cord, which is heavily twisted, and extensive thrombosis of surface veins (arrows). The veins lie beneath arteries that cross over them. Thromboses appear as white bands. There had been recent intrauterine fetal demise.

dation, it can be lethal to the fetus. Occasional placental thrombi may embolize to the fetus, especially when the placenta is injured (perhaps kicked by the fetus). This is not unlike the pulmonary embolism in postoperative leg vein thrombi of adults, except that such emboli would likely arrive in other fetal organ systems. The difficulty is, of course, in proving embolism to have occurred in utero. In occasional cases this is possible.[40] Usually such an event is not even considered as a possibility. It should be cautioned, however, that even in fatal knots of the cord, thrombosis of vessels in the cord is not commonly found. When thrombi are present, most often they are mural and recent. Perhaps there is too much flow in the vessels normally to prevent much thrombosis. Conversely, damage to the vascular wall is not infrequent. The commonest form of necrosis seen is that associated with prolonged meconium-staining. Necrosis may also occur secondary to compression, to cord entanglement, and from other injuries. It does not necessarily involve the entire circumference of the vessel. Here again, arteries are more frequently affected than the umbilical vein.

Thrombosis of placental surface veins is perhaps the most obvious and important macroscopic observation on the placenta that can be made at the time of delivery. Therefore, it is surprising how rarely it is recognized by obstetricians and also by pathologists, even though it is a common finding.

Because of the importance of these features, it is strongly recommended that as a minimum, the length of the umbilical cord be measured at birth. Later, after some segment of cord has been taken for pH measurement, the actual length is difficult to reconstruct. Since truly short cords (< 30 cm) are uncommon (but often lethal), this requirement of measurement at the time of delivery should be taken more seriously. A previous recommendation, to record the number of umbilical vessels, is now being followed widely. Most physicians now recognize that the absence of one artery may have significance. Nearly 50% of the associated fetuses are either malformed or die. How significant a single umbilical artery is to the normal survivors is unknown, except that it may be associated with growth retardation, or even some chromosomal errors.[41] Excessive constriction is also often found in aborted fetuses and associated with excessively long cords.[42]

Diabetes

The placenta of a diabetic pregnancy exhibits no absolutely diagnostic feature. When the maternal diabetes is not treated or when it is poorly controlled, the placenta is large, congested, very friable, and it may exhibit chorangiosis. The only way a pathologist can arrive at the diagnosis of maternal diabetes is if he or she has available the fetal pancreas from autopsy. The identification of hyperplasia of Islets of Langerhans, or their nuclear polymorphism and excess proportion of beta cells in the Islets are highly diagnostic. The newborn may also be macrosomic. Surface vessels of the placenta may be thrombosed because of the common fetal hypervolemia. This constellation of findings then may lead to the study of glycosylated hemoglobin, the only other means of verifying maternal diabetes. Long-standing maternal diabetes often leads to maternal vascular and renal disease. When these are present, the findings in the placenta and fetus may be very different from those of gestational diabetes. The fetus may be growth-retarded, and the placenta may be small and have infarcts that are otherwise uncommon in gestational diabetes. In summary, it is difficult to use the placenta for the absolute diagnosis of maternal diabetes by the pathologist.

Conclusion

Careful and systematic examination of the placenta, as well as the umbilical cord and membranes, by an experienced investigator may reveal significant information that helps to define the etiology of fetal injury. This may be extremely useful in refuting allegations of malpractice.

Those undertaking placental examination, however, must be well trained and should appreciate normal and abnormal placental structure and histopathology. Placentas and placental tissues should be preserved until the newborn appears normal, or alternatively in the presence of neonatal abnormalities, a thorough examination should be performed and documented, and materials should be kept for future retrieval.

> **Commentary by Mr. Volk:** Placental pathologists can be consulted to deal with a causation issue, but are not consulted to deal with whether or not an obstetrician met the standard of care. Technically, they are not consulted to refute allegations of malpractice (whether or not the standard of care was met), but to give an opinion as to whether or not the alleged breach of conduct on the part of the obstetrician caused or contributed to the dysfunction of the child. We see placental pathologists consulted by a defendant physician to give opinions as to whether or not, for instance, the failure to timely perform a section proximately caused the cerebral dysfunction that exists in the child. If the alleged delay was, for instance, 1-2 hours, and the placental evaluation showed abnormalities that, in the opinion of the reviewer were of a chronic nature and were consistent with severe, chronic hypoxia or an event of a disasterous nature in the first trimester, the opinion would support the proposition that the delay did not proximately cause the cerebral dysfunction. The problem is that there may be evidence of chronic and acute events that could both contribute to the dysfunction. The child's attorney can, therefore, produce evidence that is persuasive that acute events at least contributed to the dysfunction. It is very difficult, if not imppossible, to rule out this theory, if there are facts to support acute and chronic events, because it makes perfect sense. The testimony is often that the longer the hypoxia occurs, the more injury occurs—while it is difficult to quantify, it is real.
>
> The second viable theory that makes perfect sense is that the fetus may have had some chronic happenings that, while abnormal, did not significantly damage the fetus, and these set up the fetus, for massive injury during significant delivery events. In other words, the fetus was in a jeopardized state, but was maintaining, when severe, acute hypoxia occurred that proved to be the "last straw."
>
> It is clear that placental pathologists are sometimes not able to determine the significance of a certain finding. We all know that placentas of completely normal newborns often have some "abnormal" findings. The opinion of the placental pathologist can, in many cases, be valuable. A problem occurs when a placental pathologist is asked to, or volunteers to, stretch the scientific aspects to assist a party in litigation.

It is also my experience that many placentas are not adequately evaluated, an accurate description of the findings is not reported, and appropriate and representative specimens are not retained. Some of the time, the placenta will not answer the questions presented. Four reasons for this come to mind (there are probably more):

1. The pathologist is not trained or skilled in placental evaluation.

2. The pathologist is busy and no one requested detailed placental analysis. The lab may also not have submitted all specimens that are needed.

3. The pathologist is not interested. (This does not seem to be a likely cause.)

4. Science does not exist to adequately correlate placental findings, injury to the child, and timing of injury.

References

1. Kuban KCK, Leviton A. Cerebral palsy. N Engl J Med 1994;330:188.
2. Scheller JM, Nelson KB. Does cesarean delivery prevent cerebral palsy or other neurologic problems of childhood? Obstet Gynecol 1994;83:624.
3. Benirschke K, Kaufmann P. *The Pathology of the Human Placenta*, Second Edition. New York, Springer-Verlag, 1990.
4. Baldwin VJ. *Pathology of Multiple Pregnancy*. New York, Springer-Verlag, 1994.
5. Kaplan CG. *Color Atlas of Gross Placental Pathology*. New York-Tokyo, Igaku-Shoin, 1994.
6. Travers H, Schmidt WA. College of American Pathologists Conference XIX on the examination of the placenta. Arch Pathol Lab Med 1991;115:660.
7. Altshuler G. A conceptual approach to placental pathology and pregnancy outcomes. Sem Diagn Pathol 1993;10:204.
8. Altshuler G. Some placental considerations related to neurodevelopmental and other disorders. J Child Neurol 1993;8:78.
9. Salafia CM, Vintzileos AM. Why all placentas should be examined by a pathologist in 1990. Am J Obstet Gynecol 1990;163:1282.
10. Altshuler G, Herman AA. The medicolegal imperative: Placental pathology and epidemiology. In: Stevenson DK, Sunshine P (eds). *Fetal and Neonatal Brain Injury: Mechanisms, Management, and the Risks of Practice*. Philadelphia, Decker, 1989, p. 250.
11. Kallakury B, Kelty R, Ross JS, et al. Prevalence, histologic characteristics and clinical significance of meconium in placentas. (abstract 26) Modern Pathol (Pediatr Pathol) 1993;6:5.
12. Naeye RL. *Disorders of the Placenta, Fetus, and Neonate. Diagnosis and Clinical Significance*. St. Louis, Mosby-Year Book, 1992.
13. Miller PW, Coen RW, Benirschke K. Dating the time interval from meconium passage to birth. Obstet Gynecol 1985;66:459.
14. Altshuler G, Hyde S. Meconium induced vasoconstriction: A potential cause of cerebral and other fetal hypoperfusion and of poor pregnancy outcome. J Child Neurol 1989;4:137.

15. Dominguez R, Segal AJ, O'Sullivan JA. Leukocytic infiltration of the umbilical cord. Manifestation of fetal hypoxia due to reduction of blood flow in the cord. JAMA 1960;173:346.
16. Herzen JL, Benirschke K. Unexpected disseminated herpes simplex infection in a newborn. Obstet Gynecol 1977;50:728.
17. Schwartz DA, Caldwell E. Herpes simplex virus infection of the placenta. The role of molecular pathology in the diagnosis of viral infection of placental-associated tissues. Arch Pathol Lab Med 1991;115:1141.
18. Robb JA, Benirschke K, Barmeyer R. Intrauterine latent herpes simplex virus infection. I. Spontaneous abortion. Hum Pathol 1986;17:1196.
19. Robb JA, Benirschke K, Mannino F, et al. Intrauterine latent herpes simplex virus infection. II. Latent neonatal infection. Hum Pathol 1986;17:1210.
20. Redline RW, Patterson P. Villitis of unknown etiology is associated with major infiltration of fetal tissues by maternal inflammatory cells. Am J Pathol 1993;143:473.
21. Benirschke K. Diseases of the placenta. Contemp Obstet Gynecol 1975;6:17.
22. Verma U, Tejani N, Klein S, et al. Obstetrical antecedents of neonatal periventricular leukomalacia (PVL). Am J Obstet Gynecol 1994;170:264.
23. Hankins GDV, Snyder RR, Yeomans ER. Umbilical arterial and venous acid-base and blood gas values and the effect of chorioamnionitis on those values in a cohort of preterm infants. Am J Obstet Gynecol 1991;164:1261.
24. Bejar R, Wozniak P, Allard M, et al. Antenatal origin of neurologic damage in newborn infants. I. Preterm infants. Am J Obstet Gynecol 1988;159:357.
25. Bejar R, Vigliocco G, Gramajo H, et al. Antenatal origin of neurologic damage in newborn infants. II. Multiple gestations. Am J Obstet Gynecol 1990;162:1230.
26. Fojaco RM, Hensley GT, Moskowitz L. Congenital syphilis and necrotizing funisitis. JAMA 1989;261:1788.
27. De Lia JE, Kuhlmann RS, Cruikshank DP, et al. Current topic: Placental surgery: A new frontier. Placenta 1993;14:477.
28. Liu S, Benirschke K, Schioscia AL, et al. Intrauterine death in multiple gestation. Acta Genet Med Gemellol 1992;41:5.
29. Jou HJ, Ng KY, Tneg RJ, et al. Doppler sonographic detection of reverse twin-twin transfusion after intrauterine death of the donor. J Ultrasound Med 1993;5:307.
30. Grafe MR. Antenatal cerebral necrosis in monochorionic twins. Pediatr Pathol 1993;13:15.
31. Zak LK, Donn SM. Feto-maternal hemorrhage. In: Donn SM, Faix RG (eds). *Neonatal Emergencies*. Mt. Kisco, NY, Futura Publishing Co., 1991, p. 423.
32. Fox H. The incidence and significance of nucleated erythrocytes in the foetal vessels of the mature human placenta. J Obstet Gynaecol Br Commonw 1967;74:40.
33. Nicolini U, Nicolaidis P, Fisk NM, et al. Limited role of fetal blood sampling in fetuses with growth retardation. Lancet 1990;i:768.
34. Salafia CM, Vintzileos AM, Silberman L, et al. Placental pathology of idiopathic intrauterine growth retardation at term. Am J Perinatol 1992;9:179.
35. Ruth V, Autti-Ramo I, Granstrom MJ, et al. Prediction of perinatal brain damage by cord plasma vasopressin, erythropoietin, and hypoxanthine values. J Pediatr 1988;113:880.

36. Benirschke K, Gille J. Placental pathology and asphyxia. In: Gluck L (ed). *Intrauterine Asphyxia and the Developing Fetal Brain*. Chicago, Year Book Medical Publishers, Inc., 1975, p. 117.
37. Eden JA. Fetal-induced trauma as a cause of antepartum hemorrhage. Am J Obstet Gynecol 1987;157:830.
38. Acker D, Sachs BP, Tracey KJ, et al. Abruptio placentae associated with cocaine use. Am J Obstet Gynecol 1983;146:220.
39. Altshuler G. Chorangiosis: An important placental sign of neonatal morbidity and mortality. Arch Pathol Lab Med 1984;108:71.
40. Wolf PL, Jones KL, Longway SR, et al. Prenatal death from acute myocardial infarction and cardiac tamponade due to embolus from the placenta. Am Heart J 1985;109:603.
41. Heifetz SA. Single umbilical artery. A statistical analysis of 237 autopsy cases and review of the literature. Perspectives Pediatr Pathol 1984;8:345.
42. Benirschke K. Obstetrically important lesions of the umbilical cord. J Reprod Med 1994;39:262-272.

Chapter 20

Umbilical Cord Blood Gas Analysis in the Assessment of Intrapartum Fetal and Neonatal Status

◆◆◆

Stanley M. Berry, M.D.

Introduction

The assessment of fetal intrapartum status and newborn condition, with regard to the presence or absence of asphyxia, continues to challenge perinatal care givers. Umbilical cord blood gas analysis at the time of birth provides objective information that is very useful in diagnosing whether or not perinatal asphyxia has occurred.

Much controversy exists over what constitutes "birth asphyxia." The American College of Obstetricians and Gynecologists (ACOG) defines *intrapartum asphyxia* by saying that this term "implies fetal hypercarbia and hypoxemia, which if prolonged, will result in metabolic acidemia. Because the intrapartum disruption of uterine or fetal blood flow is rarely, if ever, absolute, asphyxia is an imprecise, general term and should be reserved for the clinical context of damaging acidemia, hypoxia, and metabolic acidosis."[1]

Acidemia denotes an increase in the concentration of hydrogen ions in the blood. The term acidosis denotes an increase in the hydrogen ion concentration in tissues. It must be recognized that these two terms are often used interchangeably. Central to the definition of asphyxia is the presence of fetal hypoxia and hypercarbia leading to metabolic acidosis.[2] Prolonged asphyxia can cause neurologic damage. However, in the majority of newborns who demonstrate clear signs of acidemia, no neurologic damage occurs. In

From: Donn SM, Fisher CW (eds.): *Risk Management Techniques in Perinatal and Neonatal Practice.* © Futura Publishing Co., Inc., Armonk, NY, 1996.

other words, the majority of patients who have biochemical and clinical evidence of asphyxia never suffer neurologic damage.[3-8]

A lack of oxygen at the time of birth was first proposed as the major cause of cerebral palsy by an orthopedic surgeon named Little[9] in the late 19th century. In subsequent communications Little[10] acknowledged that a "large proportion of children who were deprived of oxygen at birth did not have cerebral palsy." However, his original observation on the significant causal relationship between hypoxia at birth and neurologic damage continued to propagate despite the lack of scientific evidence. At the present time, many medical and non-medical people believe that perinatal asphyxia is by far the most common cause of neurologic damage.[11,12] This belief, though not supported scientifically, contributes greatly to the high number of obstetrical malpractice claims in the United States today.

Apgar Scores and the Prediction of Acidemia

Many attempts have been made to accurately identify perinatal asphyxia. When Virginia Apgar[13] introduced her system for evaluating newborns she observed, "Resuscitation of infants at birth has been the subject of many articles. Seldom have there been such imaginative ideas, such enthusiasms, and dislikes, and such unscientific observations and study about one clinical picture." Apgar's method of newborn assessment is highly subjective. She introduced this system for the, "...reestablishment of simple clear classification of 'grading' of newborn infants, which can be used as a basis for discussion and comparison of the results of obstetric practices, types of maternal pain relief and the effects of resuscitation."[13]

The Apgar score, as it has come to be known, was used from the outset to arrive at a prognosis for the newborn based on physical signs that were thought to reflect the presence or absence of asphyxia. As numerous later studies showed,[14-18] the ability of Apgar scores as they are generally used (i.e., scores given at 1 and 5 minutes of life) are not predictive of asphyxia or subsequent neurologic outcome. Despite the well documented shortcomings of the Apgar score in the diagnosis of acidemia, it continues to be the predominant method used to assess the presence or absence of perinatal asphyxia.

Both the 1- and 5-minute Apgar score correlate poorly with acidemia.[5,19-21] In a study of the umbilical artery gases and Apgar scores of 1210 newborns, Sykes et al.[22] found that 21% of those babies with a 1-minute Apgar score of < 7 and 19% with a 5-minute Apgar score < 7 had severe acidemia. They defined severe acidemia as an umbilical artery pH of ≤ 7.1 and a base excess of ≥ −13. Conversely, these workers found that 73% and 86% of newborns with severe acidosis had Apgar scores of ≥ 7 at 1 and 5 minutes, respectively. These studies clearly demonstrate that Apgar scores do not reliably detect acidosis when it is present, and that normal Apgar scores commonly occur in newborns who are severely acidemic.

Continuous Electronic Fetal Heart Rate Monitoring and the Prediction of Acidemia

Because of its ability to accurately suggest fetal hypoxia, continuous electronic fetal heart rate monitoring (CEFHRM) fostered much enthusiasm among obstetricians. Many believed that this technique would facilitate a decrease in congenital neurologic damage by allowing physicians to recognize intrapartum asphyxia in a timely fashion and affect delivery before the fetus was harmed. At least eight prospective randomized trials have failed to document a reduction in perinatal morbidity from the use of this technique.[23-30] CEFHRM has been in widespread use in this country for the last 20 years, and in this time, the 2.1/1000 rate of cerebral palsy has not changed significantly.[31]

CEFHRM is excellent for identifying fetuses that are in good condition. This characteristic of the technique was confirmed in early work by Wood et al.[32] and by Mendez-Bauer et al.[33] The randomized trials previously cited[23-30] also corroborate this finding. However, even though the confirmation of fetal well being has obvious clinical utility, the specificity of this methodology is poor. Several studies that examined the relationship between abnormal fetal heart rate tracings and the presence of newborn umbilical cord blood gas values consistent with acidemia, found a poor correlation.[2,34,35] The false positive rates ranged from 60%-88%. Conversely, other workers have shown that the vast majority of children that have neonatal seizures, which can be characteristic of severe intrapartum hypoxia, do not display intrapartum fetal heart rate patterns that are indicative of hypoxia.[36]

Unfortunately, fetal heart rate monitor interpretation, like Apgar score determination, is subjective. The lack of objectivity in these two methodologies, and the widespread impression that a significant casual relationship exists between perinatal asphyxia and neurologic damage enhances the need for objective measures of asphyxia.

Fetal Acid-Based Physiology

Biosystems, such as those that exist within the fetus, depend on a stable milieu with respect to the amount of acid that is allowed to accumulate. Acids in the body are able to give off positively charged hydrogen ions (H^+). These ions dissociate from negatively charged atoms or molecules that are called bases. The molecule HCO_3^- (bicarbonate) is a common base in the body, and it can accept an H^+ ion to become H_2CO_3 (carbonic acid). This acid can either donate an H^+ ion, or it can be transformed to H_2O (water) and CO_2 (carbon dioxide). These reactions are illustrted in Equation 1:

$$HCO_3^- + H^+ \rightarrow H_2CO_3 \rightarrow H_2O + CO_2.$$

The acidity or, conversely, the alkalinity of a system is quantitated by measurement of the pH. pH is a reflection of the amount of free H^+ ions in the system. The Henderson-Hasselbach equation (Equation 2) depicts the relationship between pH and the amount of acid and base present as follows:

$$pH = pK + \log [base]/[acid].$$

The pH is directly related to the amount of base present, and inversely related to the amount of acid present (the more acid there is in the system, the lower the pH is).

A buffer is a substance that allows the body to maintain a stable pH when acid or base are added to the system. The function of buffers such as HCO_3^- in such a system is to bind with free H^+ ions. This is the mechanism that keeps the pH in the normal range. If the pH gets too high (alkalosis) or too low (acidosis), the biochemical reactions that supply the cells with oxygen and nutrients cannot function properly. Though bicarbonate is the most important buffer in fetal blood, hemoglobin, erythrocyte bicarbonate, plasma proteins, and inorganic phosphates are also important sources of buffering capacity.

Buffering capacity is quantitated by measuring the *base deficit*. This parameter is also called *base excess*. This number is almost always a negative number. As the base deficit falls, it indicates that the fetus is producing acid at an increased rate, and the available buffers in the system are being consumed.

Metabolism and Oxygen Exchange

The term metabolism, in the context of acid-base physiology, refers primarily to those biochemical processes involved in the conversion of nutritional substances to energy. Respiration, at the metabolic level, refers to those energy transforming reactions that consume oxygen. Human beings are capable of using two types of metabolism. Aerobic metabolism occurs when oxygen is not a limiting factor. Anaerobic metabolism occurs in situations where oxygen is sparse. Aerobic metabolism is about 19 times more efficient at producing energy.[37] The principle by-products of aerobic metabolism are H_2O and carbon dioxide. The main by-product of anaerobic metabolism is lactic acid. This substance leads to acidosis much more readily than carbon dioxide, which is easily eliminated under normal circumstances.

The lungs and kidneys are the main organs of acid-base stability or homeostasis after birth. In utero, the placenta is the organ of primary importance in regulating acid-base status. The intervillous space is the area within the placenta where oxygen and nutrients are exchanged between the mother and the fetus. This exchange is essential for fetal aerobic metabolism. Except for miniscule numbers of fetal cells that normally cross into the maternal circulation, and vice versa, the two circulations are separate.

Several mechanisms exist that inhibit the placental exchange mechanism. The vessels that supply oxygenated blood to the placenta first course between the smooth muscle fibers of the uterus. Normal uterine contractions squeeze these vessels, which leads to a momentary decrease in the amount of oxygen that the fetus receives. This brief drop in oxygen is tolerated well by the fetus in the vast majority of cases because the normal fetus has an oxygen "reserve." As long as oxygen levels have been optimal prior to the onset of contractions, this brief diminution in oxygen does not cause fetal problems. If the blood supply to the uterus is decreased by maternal factors like vascular disease or poor maternal oxygenation, or if contractions occur too frequently or forcefully, acidosis can ensue, and the fetal condition can deteriorate.

Acidemia, Hypoxia, Asphyxia, and Low Apgar Scores

Acidemia, hypoxia, asphyxia, and low Apgar scores occur perinatally when respiration is not optimal and carbon dioxide accumulates, or when oxygen delivery has been compromised, and the fetus must resort to anaerobic metabolism. This type of metabolism generates lactic acid as a major by-product. The presence of lactic acid increases the amount of H^+ ion present in the fetal circulation. H^+ ions generated by this mechanism quickly exceed the buffering capacity of the fetus, and the fetal pH decreases, first in the blood, and eventually in the tissues.

Debate continues about what the normal umbilical artery pH is in a healthy term newborn infant. Several authors have defined umbilical artery acidemia as a pH of < 7.2.[2,38] Others have argued that this number is too high.[1,39] One reason for the lack of universal agreement on a specific pH value below which acidosis occurs is because many people have tried to use acidosis to define asphyxia.

Asphyxia, though poorly defined, is often used to describe infants who are not vigorous and in excellent condition at birth. This term implies that hypoxia is present, which resulted in metabolic acidosis with or without hypercarbia.[2] Though Apgar scores are often used to define asphyxia, this use of Apgar scoring is flawed for two reasons: first, Apgar scoring is subjective; and second, many factors that are unrelated to intrapartum or peripartum hypoxia may give rise to low Apgar scores. These factors include gestational age,[40] maternal anesthesia and analgesia,[41] congenital conditions such as neurologic or muscular disorders, or malformations. Furthermore, resuscitation efforts, which include intubation and oral, pharyngeal, or tracheal suctioning, can lead to decreases in the Apgar score, by stimulating the vagus nerve, which causes a decrease in heart rate. Suctioning and intubation also interfere with attempts at spontaneous breathing by the newborn infant.

The basis for disagreement over a specific pH to define acidosis, or a precise definition of the term asphyxia is the fact that it is difficult to relate low Apgar scores, low umbilical artery pH, or blood oxygen levels to clinical compromise in the newborn. The vast majority of surviving newborns with low Apgar scores, or umbilical artery acidemia or hypoxia do not suffer any physical or mental compromise.

Types of Acidemia

There are three commonly defined types of acidemia. They include respiratory, metabolic, and a mixed acidemia.

Respiratory Acidemia

Respiratory acidemia is defined as a blood gas profile that includes a pH in the acidotic range, with an elevated pCO_2, and a normal HCO_3^-. This condition results from an excessive accumulation of fetal carbon dioxide.

The placenta is the organ of respiration for the fetus, and it is responsible for the elimination of carbon dioxide. This function is carried out by the lungs and the kidneys in children and adults. Any condition that impedes blood flow from the fetus to the placenta has the potential to result in a build up of carbon dioxide in the fetus.

Compression of the umbilical cord is the most common cause of decreased blood flow from the fetus to the placenta.[38] This occurs when the umbilical cord is compressed between the fetal body and the wall of the uterus during a uterine contraction. Cord compression can also occur when the cord is wrapped around the fetal neck or other body part and is compressed during a fetal movement or uterine contraction.

As stated earlier, acidosis results from the presence of excess H^+. In the case of a respiratory acidemia, the excess pCO_2 leads to increased H^+ through the formation of carbonic acid (H_2CO_3), which then dissociates as shown in Equation 1 to form HCO_3^- and H^+. In respiratory acidemia, if base excess is also calculated, it is in the normal range.

Metabolic Acidemia

Metabolic acidemia is defined as a blood gas profile that includes a pH in the acidotic range with a normal to elevated pCO_2, a low HCO_3^-, and a base deficit of 8-9 or lower. This type of acidemia is not caused by a simple excess accumulation of carbon dioxide.

As mentioned earlier, aerobic metabolism is the most efficient method of energy conversion available to the fetus. This pathway of energy production has CO_2 and H_2O as breakdown products, and they are easily eliminated under normal conditions. In order for aerobic metabolism to proceed, the placenta must be capable of efficiently exchanging carbon dioxide, oxygen, and nutrients between mother and fetus. Any condition that impedes this exchange for more than a short time, and allows the amount of fetal oxygen to fall can result in metabolic acidemia.

Optimal perfusion of the intervillous space is critical to the exchange processes. An example of decreased perfusion can occur during the progression of labor. As contractions become more intense and more frequent, intervillous space perfusion is compromised because the vessels that traverse the myometrium to supply this space are squeezed by the contracting muscle. When this perfusion reaches levels low enough that the fetal oxygen reserve is exhausted, anaerobic metabolism with lactic acid build-up can begin. If the process is not reversed in a short time, the ability of the fetus to buffer lactic acid is overcome and there is an excess accumulation of H^+ ions, and a metabolic acidosis ensues.

Conditions that result in damage to the vessels either within the placenta or those that feed the placenta will decrease the amount of oxygen, carbon dioxide, and nutrient exchange that is possible. This situation can erode the oxygen reserve of the fetus and make the fetus more prone to shift to anaerobic metabolism under conditions of decreased oxygen supply. Conversely, a fetus without a damaged placenta is able to tolerate suboptimal placental exchange conditions for much longer periods without shifting to anaerobic metabolism.

As H^+ ions accumulate, they are at first buffered by HCO_3^- according to the principles of the Henderson-Hasselbach equation. This results in an increase in pCO_2, a decrease in HCO_3^-, a decrease in H^+, and a rise in pH. Hemoglobin and other substances also buffer excess H^+ ions. As hemoglobin and bicarbonate are used to buffer H^+, the availability of these substances decreases. This reduction in the availability of buffers accounts for the decrease in base excess that is characteristic of a metabolic acidemia.

Mixed Acidemia

A mixed acidemia is defined as a blood gas profile that includes a pH in the acidotic range, with a combination of values for pCO_2, HCO_3^-, and base excess which do not meet the criteria for either metabolic or respiratory acidosis.[2]

Most fetal acidotic states are neither purely respiratory nor purely metabolic.[38] Respiratory acidotic states are characterized by a high pCO_2 and a normal base excess. In most cases of metabolic acidosis, the base excess is

Table 1
Umbilical Venous Blood Acid-Base and Gas Measurements
in 146 Normal Term Infants Born After Uncomplicated Labor
and Vaginal Delivery

	Mean	1 SD*	Range
pH	7.35	0.05	7.24–7.49
PCO$_2$ (mmHg)	38.2	5.6	23.3–49.2
PCO$_2$ (mmHg)	29.2	5.9	15.4–48.2
HCO$_2^-$ (mEq/L)	20.4	2.1	15.0–24.7

*SD = standard deviation from the mean.
Adapted from Yeomans ER, Hauth JC, Gilstrap LC, Strickland DM. Umbilical cord pH, PCO$_2$, and bicarbonate following uncomplicated term vaginal deliveries. Am J Obstet Gynecol 1985;151:798.

decreased, and the pCO$_2$ is either normal or elevated. A respiratory acidosis may have a metabolic component if the blood supply to the fetus is compromised enough to decrease the supply of oxygen below the level needed to maintain aerobic metabolism. A metabolic acidosis may have a respiratory component if the placental exchange of pCO$_2$ is impaired.

In many cases, it may be important to make a correct diagnosis regarding the specific type of acidosis present. For instance, a small degree of respiratory acidosis is unlikely to be associated with any adverse or long-term effects in the newborn. For this reason, it is very important that all umbilical cord blood gas specimens be analyzed for more than pH alone. pCO$_2$, HCO$_3^-$, and base excess must also be tested and documented. Without this complete set of values, it is not possible to accurately determine the type of acidemia present. This point cannot be emphasized enough.

Criteria used to define the type of acidemia present in newborns are displayed in Table 1.[42]

Collection of Umbilical Cord Specimens for Blood Gas Determination

Collection of umbilical cord blood at birth for blood gas analysis is relatively simple. Immediately after the birth of the infant two clamps need to be placed across the umbilical cord close to the baby and very close together. Another set of clamps should be placed about 8-20 cm away from the first set. As with the prior set, these clamps should be placed very close to one another. A smaller segment may be used, but getting a large segment ensures that an adequate specimen can be obtained. The cord is then completely transected between the clamps of each set.

The sample needs to be aspirated into a heparinized syringe to prevent the blood from clotting. One mL syringes work well for this purpose. The syringe should be flushed with heparin. A minimal amount of heparin solution (0.1 mL or less) should remain in the chamber. It is preferable to flush the syringe with a heparin concentration of 1000 units/mL because higher amounts can significantly alter blood gas values.[43] A sample of 1.0 mL should be drawn, though most modern blood gas analyzers can give a full profile on a 300 µL specimen.

Once the umbilical cord segment has been isolated, the blood sample does not need to be obtained immediately. At room temperature, there is not a significant difference in blood gas values between specimens obtained immediately versus those obtained up to 60 minutes after the umbilical cord segment has been taken.[44,45] If blood gas analysis is performed on a specimen that is aspirated into a heparinized syringe at birth and placed on ice in a refrigerator, the original blood pH and base excess values can be calculated from the following formula[46]:

$$pH_o = 0.917 + 0.00165 \bullet \text{Time (hours)} + 0.8716 \bullet pH_r$$

Where Time is the time interval (hours) from delivery to umbilical arterial blood gas analysis, and pH_r is the pH value of the remote blood gas analysis; $R^2 = 0.91$, $P < 0.0001$ for all coefficients.

Base excess, in a similar situation, is calculated using the formula:

$$BD_o = 0.7442 - 0.0523 \bullet \text{Time (hours)} + 0.9500 \bullet BD_r$$

where BD_r is the absolute value of base excess from a remote umbilical arterial blood gas analysis. For this equation $R^2 = 0.82$, $P < 0.001$ for the coefficients.

It is always prudent to place the specimen syringe on ice after the blood has been drawn. This will minimize potential changes in blood gas values, even though this practice is not essential, particularly if the specimen is analyzed within 60 minutes of collection.

Umbilical Artery Versus Umbilical Vein

The umbilical cord normally contains two arteries and one vein. Rarely, two vessel cords are identified that have one artery and one vein. The umbilical artery carries blood from the fetus to the placenta. This is blood from which the fetus has extracted oxygen, and it is being pumped back to the placenta where its oxygen content is replenished. The umbilical vein carries freshly oxygenated blood from the placenta back to the fetus. The oxygen status of umbilical arteries (and veins) is the opposite of that which is found in the human body after birth. This arrangement means that umbilical artery blood

Table 2

Mean Umbilical Arterial Acid-Base and Gas Values in
Preterm and Term Infants

	pH	PCO_2 (mmHg)	PO_2 (mmHg)	HCO_3^- (mEq/L)	Base Deficit (mEq/L)
Preterm infants* (n = 77)	7.29 ± 0.07	49.2 ± 9.0	23.6 ± 8.9	23 ± 3.5	−3.3 ± 24.0
Term infants** (N = 1292)	7.28 ± 0.07	49.9 ± 4.2	23.7 ± 2.8	23.1 ± 2.8	−3.6 ± 2.8

*Gestational age ≤ 35 weeks and birth weight < 2500 g.
**Gestational age 37–42 weeks and birth weight > 2500 g.
Adapted from Ramin SM, Gilstrap LC III, Leveno KJ, et al. Umbilical artery acid-base status in the preterm infant. Obstet Gynecol 1989;74:256.

reflects fetal status more directly, and umbilical venous blood more closely reflects whether the oxygen exchange status of the uteroplacental unit is optimal.

Since umbilical arterial blood more closely reflects fetal and newborn status, it is preferable to obtain specimens from this vessel. However, because the umbilical arteries are considerably smaller, it is not always possible to obtain blood from these vessels. The umbilical vein should definitely be sampled if it is not possible to obtain arterial blood. Furthermore, when situations arise in which there are important questions regarding intrapartum management or immediate newborn status, it may be helpful to have blood gas values from both vessels. Also, in situations where the origin of a specimen may be in question, differences in values obtained from the two vessels can aid in confirming the origin of the specimen.

Normal Umbilical Cord Blood Gas Values

Normal blood gas values for umbilical cord specimens have been determined for healthy term newborns as well as premature newborns (Tables 1 and 2). The umbilical venous data for the term infants were derived from 146 infants delivered vaginally who had normal fetal heart rate tracings.[47] The normal umbilical arterial values for preterm infants were derived from 77 premature newborns[48]; these values were compared to values derived from 1292 term infants, and no significant differences were found. It is noteworthy that no differences in blood gas values were found between the two groups even though the premature infants were much more likely to have low Apgar scores. This study underlines the fact that premature infants are much more likely to have low Apgar scores in the *absence of acidemia*. To a great extent, this finding probably relates to the neurologic immaturity that premature infants are much more likely to have.

Who Should Be Tested

The question of whether every newborn should have umbilical cord blood gas analysis is often raised. At this time, ACOG does not recommend universal umbilical cord blood gas analysis.[1] One of the strongest arguments against universal testing is that given the infrequent rate of cerebral palsy in the United States (2/1000), and given that only about 10% of these cases are associated with perinatal asphyxia, the practice is not cost effective. However, given the large number of malpractice lawsuits that are filed and allege birth asphyxia as the cause of neurologic injury, and the potential that exists for huge dollar figure awards, there may, in fact, be an economic justification for universal screening. An alternative approach may be to obtain an umbilical cord segment at the birth of every baby and later order blood gas analysis only on those cases in which a question arises as to the condition of the baby.

Summary

The assessment of fetal intrapartum status with respect to the presence or absence of asphyxia continues to challenge perinatal care givers. The term *intrapartum asphyxia* is poorly defined, but it implies fetal hypercarbia and hypoxia, which if prolonged, can lead to metabolic acidemia. CEFHRM and the assignment of Apgar scores are good methods for confirming the absence of perinatal asphyxia; however, both methods are subjective, and they lack specificity. Umbilical cord blood gas analysis is an objective method for identifying acidemia. While the vast majority of surviving newborns who are acidemic do not have neurologic compromise, by definition asphyxia cannot exist without alterations in the blood gas profile.

Universal umbilical cord blood gas analysis is not, at present, the standard of care. However, it provides information that is very helpful in resolving questions regarding intrapartum fetal condition as well as newborn status, with respect to the presence or absence of asphyxia and perhaps the appropriateness of intrapartum care.

References

1. ACOG Committee Opinion. Utility of Umbilical Cord Blood Acid-Base Assessment. Number 138, April 1994.
2. Gilstrap LC, Hauth JC, Hankins GDV, et al. Second-stage fetal heart rate abnormalities and type of neonatal acidemia. Obstet Gynecol 1987;7:191.
3. Winkler CL, Hauth JC, Tucker JM, et al. Neonatal complications at term as related to the degree of umbilical artery acidemia. Am J Obstet Gynecol 1991;164:637.

4. Dijxhoorn MJ, Visser GHA, Fidler VJ, et al. Apgar score, meconium and acidemia in relation to neonatal neurological morbidity in term infants. Br J Obstet Gynaecol 1986;93:217.
5. Dennis J, Johnson A, et al. Acid-base status at birth and neurodevelopmental outcome at four and one-half years. Am J Obstet Gynecol 1989;161:213.
6. Paneth N, Stark RI. Cerebral palsy and mental retardation in relation to indicators of perinatal asphyxia. Am J Obstet Gynecol 1983;147:960.
7. Ruth VJ, Ravio KO. Perinatal brain damage: Predictive value of metabolic acidosis and the Apgar score. Br Med J 1988;297:23.
8. Freeman JM, Nelson KB. Intrapartum asphyxia and cerebral palsy. Pediatrics 1988;82:240.
9. Little WJ. On the influence of abnormal parturition, difficult labour, premature birth and asphyxia neonatorum on the mental and physical condition of the child, especially in relation to deformities. Lancet 1861;2:378.
10. Little WJ. Quoted by Colliers JS. The pathogenesis of cerebral diplegia. Proc Soc Med 1923;1:11.
11. Paneth N, Fox HE. The relationship of Apgar score to neurologic handicap: A survey of clinicians. Obstet Gynecol 1983;61:547.
12. Hey E. Fetal hypoxia and subsequent handicap: The problem of establishing a causal link. In: Chamberlain GVP, Ott CJB, Sharp F (eds). *Litigation and Obstetrics and Gynecology*. London, Royal College of Obstetricians and Gynecologists, 1985, pp. 233-242.
13. Apgar V: A proposal for a new method of evaluation of the newborn infant. Curr Res Anesth Analg, July-August, 1953, 260.
14. Nelson KB, Ellenberg JH. Apgar scores as predictors of chronic neurologic disability. Pediatrics 1981;68:36.
15. Marrin M, Paes BA. Birth asphyxia: Does the apgar score have diagnostic value? Obstet Gynecol 1988;72:120.
16. Silverman F, Suidan J, Wasserman J, et al. The apgar score: Is it enough? Obstet Gynecol 1985;66:331.
17. Ruth VJ, Raivio KO. Perinatal brain damage: Predictive value of metabolic acidosis and the apgar score. Br J Med 1988;297:24.
18. Dijxhoorn MJ, Visser GHA, Fidler VJ, et al. Apgar score, meconium and acidaemia at birth in relation to neonatal neurological morbidity in term infants. Br J Obstet Gynaecol 1986;93:217.
19. Page FO, Martin JN, Palmer SM, et al. Correlation of neonatal acid-base status with Apgar scores and fetal heart rate tracings. Am J Obstet Gynecol 1986;154:1306.
20. Goldaber KG, Gilstrap LC, Leveno KJ, et al. Pathologic fetal acidemia. Obstet Gynecol 1991;78:1103.
21. Gilstrap LC, Leveno KJ, Burris J, et al. Diagnosis of birth asphyxia on the basis of fetal pH, Apgar score, and newborn cerebral dysfunction. Am J Obstet Gynecol 1989;161:825.
22. Sykes GS, Molloy PM, Johnson P, et al. Do Apgar scores indicate asphyxia. Lancet 1982;1:494.
23. Neutra RR, Fienberg SE, Greenland S, et al. Effect of fetal monitoring on neonatal death rates. N Engl J Med 1978;299:324.
24. Haverkamp AD, Thompson HE, McFee JG, et al. The evaluation of continuous fetal heart rate monitoring in high-risk pregnancy. Am J Obstet Gynecol 1976;125:310.

25. Kelso IM, Parsons RJ, Lawrence GF, et al. An assessment of continuous fetal heart rate monitoring in labor: A randomized trial. Am J Obstet Gynecol 1978;131:536.
26. Haverkamp AD, Orleans M, Langendoerfer S, et al. A controlled trial of the differential effects of intrapartum fetal monitoring. Am J Obstet Gynecol 1979;134:399.
27. Wood C, Renou P, Oats J, et al. A controlled trial of fetal heart rate monitoring in a low-risk obstetric population. Am J Obstet Gynecol 1981;141:527.
28. MacDonand D, Grant A, Sheridan-Pereira M, et al. The Dublin randomized controlled trial of intrapartum fetal heart rate monitoring. Am J Obstet Gynecol 1985;152:524.
29. Leveno KJ, Cunningham FG, Nelson S, et al. A prospective comparison of selective and universal electronic fetal monitoring in 34,995 pregnancies. N Engl J Med 1986;315:615.
30. Shy KK, Luthy DA, Bennett FC, et al. Effects of electronic fetal-heart-rate monitoring, as compared with periodic auscultation, on the neurologic development of premature infants. N Engl J Med 1990;322:599.
31. ACOG Technical Bulletin. Fetal heart rate patterns: Monitoring, interpretation, and management. Number 207, 1995.
32. Wood C, Newman W, Lumley J, et al. Classification of fetal heart rate in relation to fetal scalp blood measurements and Apgar score. Am J Obstet Gynecol 1969;105:942.
33. Mendez-Bauer C, Arnt IC, Gulin L, et al. Relation between blood pH and heart rate in the human fetus during labor. Am J Obstet Gynecol 1967;97:530.
34. Katz M, Shani N, Meizner I, et al. Is end-stage deceleration of the fetal heart rate ominous? Br J Obstet Gynaecol 1982;89:186.
35. Gilstrap LC, Hauth JC, Toussaint S. Second stage fetal heart rate abnormalities and neonatal acidosis. Obstet Gynecol 1984;62:209.
36. Minchom P, Niswander K, Chalmers I, et al. Antecedents and outcome of very early neonatal seizures in infants born at or after term. Br J Obstet Gynaecol 1987;94:431.
37. Friedman PJ. Carbohydrate catabolism and biosynthesis. In: Friedman PJ (ed). *Biochemistry*, Fifth Edition. Boston, Little Brown and Company, 1995, pp. 69-85.
38. Wible JL, Petrie RH, Koons A, et al. The clinical use of umbilical cord acid-base determinations in perinatal surveillance and management. Clin Perinatol 1982;9:387.
39. Hankins GDV. Umbilical cord pH and blood gas analysis. Contemp OB/Gyn 1989;33:119.
40. Catlin EA, Carpenter MW, Brann BS IV, et al. The Apgar score revisited: Influence of gestational age. J Pediatr 1986;109:365.
41. Caritis SN, Abouleish E, Edelstone DI, et al. Fetal acid-base state following spinal or epidural anesthesia for cesarean section. Obstet Gynecol 1980;56:610.
42. Gilstrap LC, Cunningham FG. Umbilical cord blood acid-base analysis. In: *Williams Obstetrics*, Supplement No. 1. Stamford, CT, Appleton & Lange, 1989, pp. 1-12.
43. Kirshon B, Moise KJ. Effect of heparin on umbilical arterial blood gases. J Reprod Med 1989;34:267.
44. Hilger JS, Holzman IR, Brown DR. Sequential changes in placental blood gases and pH during the hour following delivery. J Reprod Med 1981;26:305.
45. Duerbeck NB, Chaffin DG, Seeds JW. A practical approach to umbilical artery pH and blood gas determinations. Obstet Gynecol 1992;79:959.

46. Chauhan SP, Cowan BD, Meydrech EF, et al. Determination of fetal acidemia at birth from a remote umbilical arterial blood gas analysis. Am J Obstet Gynecol 1994;170:1705.
47. Yeomans ER, Hauth JC, Gilstrap LC, et al. Umbilical cord pH, PCO_2, and bicarbonate following uncomplicated term vaginal deliveries. Am J Obstet Gynecol 1985;151:7980.
48. Ramin SM, Gilstrap LC III, Leveno KJ, et al. Umbilical artery acid-base status in the preterm infant. Obstet Gynecol 1989;74:256.

Chapter 21

The Perinatal Autopsy and Risk Management: The Value of a "Standardized" Approach

◆◆◆

Trevor Macpherson, M.B., Ch.B., FRCOG (London)

Introduction

Barson: "What is required of the perinatal postmortem is guidance in the management of the next case."[1]

Wigglesworth: "Fetal and perinatal pathology is largely a post-mortem (and placental) specialty concerned with causes and mechanisms of reproductive loss. Fetal and perinatal pathology represents a deviation from the normal at some time in development."[2]

Hill: "The autopsy is the preeminent tool we have for...self criticism....the autopsy is a professional obligation."[3]

Vance: "Autopsies remain the best way to learn whether or not clinical judgments are made correctly."[4]

The autopsy has and continues to contribute to clinical medicine. Its contribution includes: 1 understanding the pathophysiology of disease; 2. education of health care providers, the public, and policy makers; 3. research (including epidemiology); 4. quality assurance; and 5. a reminder of the inherent uncertainty that still exists in medicine.[5,6] Correlation of clinical and autopsy findings have enlightened our understanding of the *pathophysiology* of disease and the effect of intervention in individual cases and for populations as a whole. Communication of autopsy findings on individual cases via confer-

From: Donn SM, Fisher CW (eds.): *Risk Management Techniques in Perinatal and Neonatal Practice.* © Futura Publishing Co., Inc., Armonk, NY, 1996.

ences, attendance at the autopsy, and family counseling provide valuable *educational* opportunities for health care providers and consumers, while aggregate data can guide health care policy on a local, national, and international level. The availability of samples from autopsies provides access to unique resources for *research*, while its contribution to the accuracy of the assigned cause of death provides more accurate data for epidemiologic studies on the prevalence of specific diseases in a population. Finally, the autopsy is essential to *quality assurance* as a standard for assessment of diagnostic accuracy and therapeutic outcome including iatrogenic disease. This quality assurance feature is important, since there is continued evidence that the autopsy reveals unexpected findings not diagnosed premortem—an aspect of particular relevance to risk management issues and a reminder to clinicians, students, the public, and attorneys of the *inherent uncertainty* that still exists in medicine.[6] "Uncertainty remains a major presence in medicine. Clinical diagnostic methods are far from perfect, the course of disease often defies prediction, and the effectiveness of a given treatment varies unexpectantly from patient to patient."[6] This uncertainty emphasizes the value of a "standard" protocol in performing an autopsy since even an autopsy may not always dispel this uncertainty.[6]

While the above contributions of the autopsy apply to both the adult and perinatal autopsy, the latter includes additional aspects to that of the adult. This is because the evaluation of an adverse perinatal outcome requires that the triad of maternal, placental, and fetal/infant factors be considered. The assessment of perinatal mortality and morbidity is incomplete without full consideration of this triad, since many problems arise during the pregnancy. Positive and negative findings are equally important, for even when a cause of death cannot be pinpointed it does mean that a myriad of known causes have been excluded that might have implications for the management of the next pregnancy.[2] Thus, in the perinatal autopsy it is equally necessary to diagnose disease as it is to describe non-disease.

This chapter is restricted to the autopsy of a perinatal death. "Perinatal" is defined as the period of life from fetal viability (at least 25 weeks gestation) through the first 28 days after birth. In practice it includes any infant who dies before discharge from the hospital, since perinatal events are likely to have contributed to these deaths. An infant who dies before birth is a stillbirth, and a death after birth is designated a neonatal death.

The information presented here focuses on "what should be done" rather than on the interpretation of particular findings, since documentation and some degree of standardization are considered to be essential to obtaining complete information on which to base interpretations of association and cause and effect. This applies in particular to the observation, documentation, and sampling of gross (macroscopic) abnormal and normal findings since this source of information is no longer available once the body and organs have been disposed. To limit the risk of such inadequate data collection a "standardized" technique and protocol is emphasized that can be applied in any perinatal pathology service. It is also important to emphasize that the perinatal autopsy should be done by those with training and interest in perinatal pathology since much of the pathology present is unique to this perinatal population.[7,8]

General Issues to be Addressed by the Perinatal Autopsy

The issues that need to be addressed by the perinatal autopsy are presented in Table 1. Table 2 lists the questions to be asked to determine the "completeness" of the autopsy itself. The "standardized" approach presented here includes both autopsy technique[9,10] and a protocol format of diagrams, check lists, and data sheets to document what was examined and found and thereby reduce the risk of not recording necessary information.[11] It emphasizes the importance of accurate weights and measures, which are key to the assessment of development and growth, and which in turn help to distinguish acute (short-term of hours or days) from chronic (long-term of usually weeks or months) events. Such distinction is critical to the assessment of the time relationship between disease and outcome. Accurate and complete information on individual cases improves the reliability of population comparisons.

Development refers to the normal structure and function of an organ or organ system. The *structure* component is the normal morphologic development of organs, which is abnormal when there are congenital anomalies as shown in Table 3, a categorization of death.[12] Anomalies may result from an abnormal karyotype, a gene defect, a teratogen, or most commonly are multifactorial indicating a combined contribution of genetic and environmental factors. *Functional* development refers to the extent to which organs and

---

Table 1
Issues to be Addressed by the Perinatal Autopsy

1. Is development of the infant within normal limits?
2. Is growth of the infant within normal limits for estimated gestational age (intra- and post-partum)?
3. What disease processes (pathology) are present (including iatrogenic)?
4. Is there discordance of clinicopathological correlation?
5. What is the categorization of death, cause of death, and sequence of events leading to death?
6. What are the implications of this perinatal death to future reproductive risk in this family?

Table 2
Questions to be Asked to Determine the "Completeness" of the Autopsy

1. Is there adequate documentation of gross features by diagrams, photographs, or descriptions?
2. Were all necessary examinations and measures done to adequately assess growth and development?
3. Were measures done according to accepted standards?
4. Were sufficient tissue sections taken to address the clinicopathological circumstances of the case?
5. Were appropriate special studies done (i.e., microbiology, radiographs, genetics, molecular biology, etc.)?
6. Does the commentary address clinical and pathological correlation or lack thereof?
7. Are the effect of established or new treatments or intervention discussed?
8. Is there an adequate assessment of cause of death and appropriate categorization of death?
9. Was an appropriate "protocol" and dissection procedure used to do the autopsy and record findings?
10. Is the risk for future pregnancies addressed?
11. Was it performed under the supervision of a pathologist competent in perinatal pathology?
12. If a trainee performed the autopsy, was he/she adequately supervised?
13. Was the placenta examined, and if so was this adequate?
14. Were tissues or other samples stored if indicated?

---

organ systems have attained the expected degree of "maturity" for a particular gestational age. In the liveborn, this entails sophisticated clinical assessments such as neurologic "scores." Lung immaturity is a major contributor to perinatal mortality.

Growth refers to the "size" of the body as a whole and individual organs as compared with that expected for the estimated gestational age. The individual weights and measures made are indicated on an Autopsy Data Sheet. These are also plotted on percentile charts or compared with tables of normals for each weight or measure. The use of a check list reduces the risk of not measuring and recording important parameters. The use of accepted techniques are critical to the reliability of these measures within and among population groups. Growth is categorized as Appropriate for Gestational Age (AGA: 10th-90th percentile), Small for Gestational Age (SGA: below 10th percentile), or Large for Gestational Age (LGA: above 10th percentile). Abnormal growth is usually associated with chronic disorders.

Specific *pathologic findings* refers to the gross, microscopic, or special study identification of those disorders seen in the perinatal period. In particular, these include evidence of hypoxia, infection, thrombosis, iatrogenic "in-

Table 3
Categorization of Death[12]

Congenital Anomaly
  Karyotype
    Normal
    Abnormal
  Structural Anomaly
    Multiple anomalies—syndrome/sequence/association
    Multiple anomalies—nonsyndrome/sequence/association

CNS neural tube defects	Renal/urinary tract anomaly
CNS nonneural tube defects	GIT anomaly
CVS congenital heart disease	Genital anomaly
CVS noncongenital heart disease	Musculo-skeletal anomaly
Respiratory tract anomaly	Facial/neck anomaly
Respiratory tract/urinary tract anomaly	Anomaly other

  Inborn error of metabolism

Utero-Placental Circulation Disorder (UPCD)

Cause unknown	Maternal factor
Placental factor	UPCD other
Umbilical cord factor	

Consequence of Preterm Birth (COPB)

Extreme prematurity	Multiple organ failure
Hyaline membrane disease	Encephalopathy
Bronchopulmonary dysplasia	Necrotizing enterocolitis
Air leak syndrome	COPB other
Intraventricular hemorrhage	

Infection

Maternal	Fetus/Infant
Bacterial	Bacterial
Viral	Viral
Other	Other

Specific Fetal/Infant Disorder

Hydrops fetalis	Meconium aspiration
Isoimmune	Aspiration (other)
Non-isoimmune	Persistent pulmonary hypertension of newborn
Twin transfusion syndrome	Fetal alcohol syndrome
Donor	Intrauterine growth retardation
Recipient	Disseminated intravascular coagulation
Birth trauma	
SIDS	
Feto-maternal hemorrhage	Specific disorder other

Unknown/Unclassified

jury," trauma from delivery, immaturity of organs, growth defects of specific organs, etc. The pathology found differs by frequency of specific disorders for premature versus term infants. The full description of these disorders is well described in perinatal pathology texts.[13-15] The risk management concerns include the numerous iatrogenic events—many of which are difficult to prevent in the premature infant.

A key component of the autopsy is to make a *clinicopathologic correlation* and to specifically identify any discordance of clinical versus pathologic events, particularly the recognition of unsuspected complications of medical care. Done well, this is critical to the education of health care providers. The frequent use and diagnostic sensitivity of sonography demands that these findings be reviewed and that they guide the autopsy.[16,17] A complete clinical history of the mother, pregnancy, labor, delivery, and neonatal course is key to accurate clinicopathologic correlation. A Clinical History Sheet guides the prosector in recording necessary information. Discussion with the clinician and completion of an Autopsy Information Sheet facilitates the clinical history review by identifying clinical events that require pathologic correlation. Review of clinical tests prevents duplication of these at autopsy and identifies additional tests that need to be performed. The accurate identification of all pathology and its clinical correlation is part of the quality assurance aspect of the autopsy. It is useful to classify diagnostic errors according to cause and magnitude.[18]

The autopsy provides the opportunity to gather full information on all clinical and pathologic events and to determine the *cause of death*, describe the events leading to death, and categorize the death for institutional and population studies. The uniqueness of perinatal events requires a special system for categorizing deaths similar to that recommended by the Study Group for Complications of Perinatal Care as shown in Table 3.[12] It is not always possible to assign a cause of death. A categorization system also enables comparisons within and among populations on the frequency of different causes of death. As an example, when a high rate of deaths is unexplained the completeness of the autopsy and placental examination might be reviewed.

Finally, the impact of the current adverse perinatal outcome must be reviewed as part of the counseling to families on *future pregnancy* risk. Because certain events have a higher than random risk of recurrence it is essential to identify these and counsel patients appropriately. Not to do so puts the provider at risk if a recurrence occurs.

Who Should Perform the Autopsy?

Since the intent of the autopsy is to gather information toward the understanding of perinatal events, it is crucial that it be performed by a pathologist with training and an interest in perinatal pathology.[7,8] Just as regional perinatal centers have been established to provide expert clinical care, a similar argument can be made that perinatal autopsies should be performed by "experts" in the related field of perinatal pathology. Because much key information is gathered at gross examination and depends on appropriate tissue sampling, the risk of "missing" key information is high. Such information might contribute to establishing a cause of death, making the necessary clinicopathologic correlation, or recognizing iatrogenic events. In academic centers trainees need to be carefully supervised by the attending pathologist, since most trainees do not do sufficient perinatal autopsies to acquire the degree of expertise needed to perform an adequate autopsy.

Preparation for the Autopsy

The review of the clinical history and identification of special interests has been discussed above. An autopsy requires appropriate consent and this must be signed and any restrictions identified and respected. The pathologist is required to determine that the case does not come under the jurisdiction of a medical examiner (coroner) and the local requirements for this designation must be known and followed. When in doubt the medical examiner should be asked for a ruling, which might include denial, request that the pathologist perform the autopsy and inform the coroner who will issue the death certificate, or perform the autopsy and only involve the coroner if unusual findings are found. If death occurs unexpectedly the then samples of gastric contents, serum, and spinal fluid should be collected and stored. Finally, it is essential to maintain accurate identification of the body at all times before, during, and after the autopsy. The mortuary should also have a fail proof system for preventing the removal by funeral directors of bodies of infants who require an autopsy.

The External Examination

It is necessary for the pathologist to be as thorough in the autopsy external examination as the clinician is when examining a living infant.[1] The external examination includes weights and measures and observations of the external body surfaces and structures. Descriptions of the methodology and explanatory diagrams are provided in published texts and chapters.[9-11,19] An extensive appendix of autopsy forms and weight and measure charts is presented in the text by Stocker and Dehner.[15] The external examination contributes to the assessment of dysmorphology, dermatoglyphics, congenital anomalies, nutrition, development, growth, hydration, infection, hypoxia, and the location of various external tubes and catheters.

Since perinatal *weights* are small, scales used should be accurate to 5 g for body weight and to 0.1 g for organ weights, and permit easy zeroing of the scale without cleaning between individual weighings. The Mettler PE

3600 (Analytical Instruments Company, Hightstown, NJ, USA) digital scale is one that meets these criteria. Weights are compared with standard tables to determine if they are within the normal range (within two standard deviations of the mean) for gestational age.

The techniques for external measurements have been well described and are interpreted by plotting on percentile charts to categorize growth as AGA, SGA, or LGA.[9,20] The crown-rump and crown-heel length (to nearest 0.5 cm), and the occipitofrontal circumference (to the nearest 0.2 cm) are essential measurements to assess growth, while abdominal circumference, chest circumference, and foot length are useful contributors.[10] Inter-nipple distance and facial measurements are useful when there is dysmorphology or congenital anomalies are present. These measures have been described by Merlob et al.,[20] who also describes measures of hands and limbs.

External examination aims to detect abnormalities of surface and subcutaneous tissues, location of invasive procedures such as catheters and tubes, and to evaluate development of external organs such as eyes, ears, limbs, face, and orifices. Following an orderly approach from cranial to caudal will reduce the risk of missing important features. Because external findings will not be available for future confirmation, evaluation by an expert pathologist is key as is photographic documentation.

The external examination includes evaluation of maceration and development, and documentation of abnormalities of the general body, head/neck/face, eyes, ears, chest, abdomen, external genitalia, and upper and lower extremities. A comprehensive list (Table 4) can be checked to indicate what was done with narratives added to describe abnormalities. A list reduces the risk of missing important findings. Note the external features that contribute to the assessment of development and maturity in Table 4. In the post-term infant (> 42 weeks) the finger and toe nails often extend beyond the end of the digit. In certain syndromes dermatoglyphics of finger prints and occipital hair pattern are important.

Finally, radiology provides useful information in cases with congenital anomalies, skeletal dysplasia, and in instances where skeletal defects are increased, such as the infant with a karyotype abnormality or the infant of a diabetic mother. It is also an excellent method to detect air leaks such as pneumothorax and pneumopericardium, and injection studies provide documentation of developmental vascular defects.[21] If radiology is not done to detect pneumothorax, a sterile needle and syringe partly filled with sterile saline should be introduced laterally into the pleural cavity. If a pneumothorax is present, bubbles will rise within the barrel of the syringe.

Table 4
Examinations

External Examination

Evaluation of Maceration	Head/Neck/Face	External Exam (cont)
Skin slippage	Scalp	Breast
Blebs	Scalp hair	Nipple
Bullae	Neck	Chest
Peeling	Face	Umbilicus/umbilical cord
Discoloration of skin	Lips	Anus
Discoloration of viscera	Mouth	External genitalia
Effusions	Upper jaw	**Extremities: Upper**
Discoloration of serosa	Lower jaw	Position
Eyes	Hard palate	Hands
Joints	Soft palate	Digits
Cranial Bones	Philtrum	Nails
Desiccation	Tongue	Creases
	Nose	Long bones
General	Choanae	**Extremities: Lower**
Anterior body wall	**Eyes**	Position
Posterior body wall	Palpebral fissures	Digits
Nutritional status	Eye lids	Nails
Body hair	Pupils	Long Bones
Edema	Sclera	Patella
Icterus	Conjunctivas	
Cyanosis	**Ears**	
Rigor mortis	Position	
Liver mortis	Pinnae	
Meconium staining	External canals	

Evaluation of Development
Skin
Vernix
Lanugo
Hair
Eyebrows
Eyelashes
Eyelids
Mucus plugs, nose
Ears
Nipples
Breasts
Fingers and nails
Toes and nails
Sole-wrinkles
Genitalia

(Table 4 continues)

Table 4 *(continued)*
Internal Examination

Subcutaneous tissue

Situs of organs

Gastro-Intestinal System Liver, etc.
Position
Capsule
Parenchyma
Ductus venosus
Hepatic vessels
Gallbladder
Biliary tree

Pleural Cavity
Mediastinum
Tubes/lines
Pleural surface
Pleural cavity

Organs of the Neck
Submaxillary glands
Parathyroids
Parotid glands
Tubes/lines

Intestinal Tract
Pharynx
Epiglottis
Esophagus
Stomach
Small intestine
Ileo-cecal valve
Appendix
Large intestine
Mesenteric nodes
Mesenteric attachment

Pericardial Cavity
Pericardial cavity
Pericardium

Peritoneal Cavity
Diaphragm
Peritoneal cavity
Peritoneal surfaces
Retroperitoneum
Umbilical vein
Umbilical arteries
Other

Endocrine
Pancreas
Adrenals
Thyroid

Respiratory System/Lung
Situs
Lobation
Pleural surface
Larynx
Trachea
Endotracheal tube site
Vocal cords
Bronchi
Pulmonary vessels
Pulmonary parenchyma
Hilar lymph nodes
Other

Heart and Vessels
Situs
Epicardium
Jugular veins
Innominate veins
Superior vena cava

Inferior vena cava
Right atrium
Foramen ovale
Coronary sinus
Tricuspid valve/cordae
Tricuspid papillary muscle
Right ventricle
Infundibulum
Pulmonary valve
Pulmonary arteries
Ductus arterossus
Left atrium
Pulmonary veins
Mitral vein/cordae
Mitral papillary muscle
Left Ventricle
Intraventricular septum
Aortic valve
Ascending aorta
Aortic arch
Great vessels of arch
Descending aorta
Coronary arteries/valves
Azygous vein
Peripheral arteries
Peripheral veins
Other

Genito-Urinary System
Kidney/ureter
Renal artery
Renal vein
Capsule
Lobulation
Cortex
Medulla

Renal pyramids
Calyceal system
Renal pelvis
Ureter
Urethra

Bladder
Wall
Lumen
Trigone

Genitalia/Male
Scrotum
Testes
Epididymis/Vas Deferens
Prostate/seminal vesicles
Penis

Genitalia/Female
Labia/clitoris
Vagina
Cervix
Uterus
Fallopian tubes/ovaries

Hematopoietic System
Spleen
Lymph nodes
Bone marrow
Thymus
GIT lymphoid tissue

Skeletal
Ribs manubrium
Costo-chondral junction
Vertebral bodies
Spinal column
Other

(Table 4 continues)

Table 4 *(continued)*
Neuropathology Examination at Autopsy

Brain	**Distal Muscles**	Caudate	**Spinal Cord**
Scalp soft tissues	Upper limbs	Putamen	External
Skull externally	Lower limbs	Claustrum	Cut surface
Skull bones	Intercostals	Globus pallidus	**Mature Myelination Present at:**
Anterior fontanelle	Other muscles	**White Matter**	Internal capsule
Posterior fontanelle	**Cerebral Hemispheres**	Subcortical	Corona radiata
Cranial sutures	Lateral ventricles	Central	Superior cerebellar peduncle
Fossa (ant/mid/post)	3rd ventricle	Periventricular/corpus callosum	Cerebral peduncle
Foramen Magnum	4th ventricle	**Cerebellum Gray Matter**	Midial longitudinal fasciculus/midbrain
Middle ear	Foramen of Monroe	Cortex	Middle cerebellar peduncle
Pituitary	Germinal matrix	Dentate nucleus	Pontocerebellar fibers
Dura	Choroid plexus	Other roof nuclei	Medial longitudinal fasciculus/pons
Dural sinuses	**Cerebral Hemispheres**	Vermis	Corticospinal tracts
Falx cerebri	Lateral ventricles	**White Matter**	Hilum and amiculum of inferior olive
Tentorium	3rd ventricle	Subcortical	Medial lemniscus
Spinal Cord	4th ventricle	Central	Pyramids
Dura	Foramen of Monroe	Periventricular	Medial longitudinal fasciculus (medulla)
Epidural space	F of Magendie and Luschka	Hilum of dentate	Posterior columns of cord
Peripheral Nerve/Muscle	Germinal matrix	**Midbrain/Pons/Medulla**	Lateral corticospinal tracts
Phrenic nerve	Choroid plexus	Midbrain	
Obturator Nerve	**Telen–Dien–Cephalon**	Pons	
Other nerves		Medulla	
Proximal Muscles	**Gray Matter**		
Upper limbs	Neocortex		
Lower limbs	Thalamus		
	Hypothalamus		

Internal Examination

Following the external examination, the body cavities are exposed using a standard Y-incision. In this manner the internal organs are exposed to permit adequate in situ assessment prior to evisceration and dissection. Since this in situ evaluation is not available for future review, expert pathologic assessment and photography are necessary. Although the thoroughness and clarity of the description of findings are more important than the precise manner and order of dissection, a standard routine does reduce the risk of missing important findings.[1]

Information gathered at the in situ examination includes organ location, size and regional relationships, fluid in serous cavities, surface hemorrhage, location and possible trauma from invasive procedures such as tubes and catheters, and tissue sampling for microbiology and recognition of infectious sites that require culture before external contamination.

The *abdominal cavity* is generally opened first as part of the initial external body Y-incision. The features assessed include: peritonitis; hemorrhage; organ location, size, and shape; ascities; pneumoperitoneum; adhesions; trauma from invasive procedures; location of intravascular catheters, tubes, or drains; infarction; thrombosis of mesenteric vessels; necrotizing enterocolitis; height of diaphragm; distance of liver from lower costal margin in mid-auxiliary line; bowel constriction, atresia, or malrotation; bladder size and wall thickness; retroperitoneal organs such as kidney (agenesis, hydronephrosis, dysplasia), ureters (hydroureter), pancreas, and adrenal glands; and internal genital organs. In the case of bilateral organs, comparison between the two sides is important. Unusual features should be photographed in situ. The liver and spleen are usually cultured at this time.

The *thoracic cavity* is generally exposed next and includes examination of structures in the neck. When the plastron is removed, the thymus and neck structures are observed. Mediastinal emphysema indicates an air leak, usually a consequence of pneumothorax. The *thymus* usually fills the anterior mediastinum and may be atrophic (response to stress), while hemorrhage may be noted in hypoxia. Thymic atrophy in a stillborn indicates that intrauterine stress has been present for 12 hours or more. An absent thymus is part of the DiGeorge Syndrome. Documentation of thymic size and relations can be documented by photography.

The thoracic features assessed include lungs, pleural cavity, pericardial sac, heart, and great vessels of the thoracic cavity and neck. The *lungs and pleural cavity* are evaluated for lung size, shape, number of lobes, and possible trauma of chest tubes or catheters. The *pericardial sac* is examined for pericardial effusion, blood, or air, and petechial hemorrhages. The external surface of the *heart* is evaluated for petechial hemorrhages and adhesions, and cultures are taken from the right atrium before the heart is opened. The great vessels are examined for their relationship to cardiac chambers and atresia or coarctation. Again photographs provide useful documentation.

The *opening of the heart* in situ is performed following the natural flow of blood and may be guided by sonographic or clinical findings.[9] When there are documented or suspected congenital anomalies it is best not to open the heart in situ, but to remove it intact and to perfuse it overnight prior to opening.[9] This makes assessment, photography, and measurements (valves and cardiac chambers) more accurate. Cardiac features to be assessed include size, shape, and position of the atria; the distribution pattern of the coronary arteries; the size, position and form of each ventricle, and size, relationships, and position of all the major arteries and veins of the heart and lungs. During the opening of the heart the thickness and internal features of the atria and ventricles are assessed as are the size, structure, and number of valve rings, and leaflets or cusps. If there is a history of congenital heart block, the conduction system should be removed.

Evisceration of General Organs

The evisceration of the organ block is best achieved using the Rokitansky procedure, which maintains the relationships of the organs for individual dissection. The evisceration proceeds from the neck caudally with care being taken cranially not to damage the esophagus and large vessels attached to the posterior body wall of the thorax, and caudally the structures attached to the walls of the pelvis. The most difficult parts of the dissection are the removal of the tongue and pharynx and the organs in the pelvis. The entire airway can only be adequately examined if the tongue is removed. For congenital anomalies of the lower gastrointestinal or genitourinary system it is important to remove the anus, rectum, and lower genitourinary system intact. Care is also required to completely dissect free the leaves of the diaphragm.

Organ Dissection

A detailed description of the organ dissection has been previously described.[9,10,19] Dissection commences with the tongue, upper respiratory tract, and upper gastro-intestinal tract, including opening of the esophagus and trachea posteriorly. The aorta is then opened posteriorly and the location of catheter tips recorded and thrombus formation excluded. Renal arteries and mesenteric vessels are then examined and opened. The heart is then separated from the lungs with great vessels attached and the aorta is cut above the renal arteries. Next, the lungs are separated from the organ block with care taken to preserve the diaphragm. With the lung, neck, and pulmonary blocks removed, the inferior vena cava is opened posteriorly as are both renal veins.

Then, in sequence, the adrenal glands, spleen, stomach, and duodenum (with esophagus attached), liver, pancreas, and genito-urinary tract are dissected free. Finally the remaining gastro-intestinal tract is freed from its mesenteric attachments. Keeping the organs and organ block moist, facilitates dissection. Each organ is carefully dissected free. It is important to observe the location of intravascular catheters including any associated thrombi, and to keep the renal block intact with aorta, renal vessels, ureters, and bladder. Each separated organ is weighed and measured and observations are recorded on the Autopsy Data Sheet. Comparison with standard weights and measures is used to determine normal organ size.[22] Abnormalities are compared with whole body weights and measures to assess symmetrical versus asymmetrical growth disturbances. Symmetrical disturbances of all organs is more likely to result from early systemic causes such as genetic defects or early infections, whereas asymmetrical growth changes are more likely secondary to placental factors with reduced nutrition or oxygenation to the infant after the second trimester of pregnancy. The organ check list guides the prosector to undertake a complete assessment of all organs.

Each organ is examined for perinatal pathology including hemorrhage, congestion, atrophy, infection, anomalies, infarction, etc. After weighing and measuring, the organs are routinely sliced and examined for internal gross abnormalities. Tissue sections are taken and are recorded on the Tissue Trimming Sheet, which also provides a format for documenting microscopic descriptions and diagnoses. Special studies are recorded on the Autopsy Data Sheet. Sections are routinely fixed overnight in 10% formalin, processed, cut, and stained for microscopic examination. In neuromuscular, skeletal, or metabolic diseases, special protocols need to be followed for adequate tissue sampling of distal and proximal muscle and nerve groups, or special enzyme studies.[14] When there is doubt about a metabolic diagnosis it is useful to set up tissue for culture and then to store frozen for future diagnostic studies.

Evisceration of Brain and Spinal Cord

The brain and spinal cord require particular care in dissection since their coverings and substance are very friable in the perinatal period. In addition to identification of pathologic findings, the gross (gyral pattern) and microscopic (myelination) features contribute to the assessment of gestational age. Acceleration of gyral maturation is noted in conditions of prolonged intrauterine stress (i.e., pre-eclampsia in the mother), while delay and dysmaturity are common in association with congenital anomalies. Microscopic findings of necrosis, calcification, or neuronal migratory delays correlate with timing and duration of intrauterine events such as hypoxia. The correlation of clinico-pathologic events is key for the central nervous system examination, since many critically ill newborns will have disturbed brain function in the form of encephalopathy, seizures, etc. In a stillbirth, the brain autolyses rapidly and the ability to make any meaningful observations and interpretations is dependent on the duration of intrauterine death. In situ examination of the scalp, cranium, dura, meninges, and brain itself may reveal findings that are evidence of traumatic birth injury.

As indicated above, the examination of the central nervous system includes the external examination of the scalp, cranium, and dural attachments. Hematoma, bulging fontanel, contusion, and bruising may be found. Cephalhematoma may be seen following vacuum extraction, and molding of the head and suture overlap indicate pressure effects on the cranium during the birth process. The scalp is opened via an incision made as a straight line from just behind one pinna to the other crossing over the top of the head near the posterior fossa. The scalp is then reflected anteriorly and posteriorly to expose the suture lines of the cranium. The brain is exposed via incisions adjacent to suture lines and then bending down the two lateral flaps thus created.[9] (Care must be taken to avoid injury to the prosector from sharp calvarium edges.) It is important to inspect the tentorium bilaterally paying particular attention to the junction of the falx cerebri and tentorium cerebelli for tears, fraying, or hemorrhage from trauma. Tears or hemorrhage of the falx cerebri are also noted, after which the falx with sagittal sinus can be removed. The dural sinuses are inspected for hemorrhage or thrombus. To visualize the posterior aspect of the midbrain structures and upper cervical cord it is necessary to make an incision in the midline posteriorly through to the upper cervical spinous processes.

With the aid of gravity, which permits the brain to fall in the desired direction, the brain is freed of its attachments to the cranium. Proceeding from front to back, the cranial nerves and vessels are identified and transected. Attachments of the falx anteriorly and the tentorium postero-laterally are freed. The upper cervical cord comes into view in the posterior fossa and is severed as far caudally as is possible. The technique of Langley[23] is useful for removal of the brain by gravity from the cranium. After removal of the brain, the dural sinuses and Great Vein of Galen are opened and examined for thrombi, and the pituitary gland is removed from the sella. Additional procedures include removal of the inner ear and eye. The inner ear can be dissected routinely,[10] or for congenital defects the technique of Sando et al. is more appropriate.[24] The eyes can be removed either through the anterior fossa or from the facial side using an ophthalmologic retractor. Photographs should be taken of all important findings including any abnormalities of the base of the cranium after removal of the brain.

The brain is weighed and fixed in ten times its volume of 10% buffered formalin. Because the brain is so soft, it is best fixed in 10% formalin for 2 weeks, and then in 80% alcohol for 2 days before gross dissection. Cassettes are placed in 80% alcohol for 2 more days prior to processing. After fixation, the brain is washed, weighed, and photographed. The gyral pattern is used to assess gestational age and then the respective portions of brain are separated for dissection. The cerebellum is removed from the base of the brain, as is the pons and midbrain. The cerebellum, cerebral hemispheres, and brainstem are examined and sectioned.[9,10,19] The cerebrum is sectioned coronally and all slices placed sequentially on a flat surface for examination. The size of the ventricles and presence of any focal lesions are recorded. The cerebellum and brainstem are weighed separately and sliced routinely.[9,10,19] Sections are taken.

The spinal cord can be removed by either the anterior or the posterior approach. The anterior approach is simple and usually recommended for the perinatal autopsy unless congenital anomalies require exposure of the posterior fossa for in situ examination such as for Arnold-Chiari malformation. Initially two lower lumbar vertebrae are removed and placed in formalin for sectioning. The remaining spinal cord is exposed via two parallel cuts caudally and cranially through the pedicles of the vertebrae. In this manner, the vertebral bodies are removed. The spinal cord dura is now opened anteriorly and the spinal cord is now removed by transecting the spinal nerves and the filum terminale caudally. The upper cervical cord has been previously transected from the posterior fossa. Sections of spinal cord are taken.

Microscopic Examination

General organ and central nervous tissue sections are sampled for histology. Tissue slices should be no more than 3- to 4-mm thick and sections taken are recorded on the cut-down sheet. They are then processed, cut, stained, and mounted for microscopy.

In addition to the identification of pathology, organs are assessed for appropriate maturity. The lungs (alveolar development), kidney (nephroblastema zone), and liver (extramedullary hematopoiesis), correlate somewhat with gestational age and should be compared with other estimates previously made. Evidence of intrauterine stress includes thymic atrophy (lymphocyte depletion including starry sky appearance), aspiration of squamous epithelial cells into lung airways, meconium aspiration into the lungs, and hypoxic responses such as petechial hemorrhages, particularly of serous surfaces and the thymus. The pathologic features of inflammation, infection, necrosis, hemorrhage, congestion, infarction, etc., are also sought.

Final Autopsy Report

Once gross, microscopic, and special study investigation has been correlated with clinical events, the pathologist is in a position to put all aspects of

Table 5
Perinatal Mortality Review Committee[8]

Committee Representation
 Obstetrics, neonatology, pathology, anesthesia, nursing, and quality assurance

Criteria for Review of Deaths
 All deaths > 20 weeks gestation or > 500 g birth weight

Committee Functions
 Review appropriateness of care
 Identify preventable deaths
 Make recommendations to improve care
 Monitor autopsy rate
 Establish criteria for placental examination
 Categorize deaths using an appropriate categorization system
 Prepare an annual report on perinatal deaths
 Maintain confidentiality

the case together by listing all the findings, describing the course of events that led to death, categorizing the death, and where possible assigning a cause of death. Wigglesworth[10] has presented a useful algorithm for categorizing death. A Preliminary Report should be sent within 3 working days and a Final Report issued within 30 days of completion. The Preliminary Report indicates gross pathology findings and some clinical information, and a similar format to that of the Final Report can be used. The Final Report contains full clinical, gross, microscopic, and special study information, and the commentary if relevant. It is also of value to record all relevant pre- and postmortem laboratory or other diagnostic tests in the report. A review of recent literature relevant to the case should be cited and discussed.

Application of Autopsy Information

Information from the autopsy attains its full application when it is used to review individual deaths, to update the death certificate, and to accurately categorize deaths so that perinatal mortality information can be reliably incorporated into vital statistics data.[25] This is of particular importance for the very low birth weight infant, where the rate of iatrogenic complications is higher and often unpreventable.[22] Accurate data improve the comparison of outcomes among care providers and help to establish objective complication thresholds, a key element in risk management.

The most appropriate review process of individual deaths is a Perinatal Mortality Review Committee, the guidelines of which are presented in Table 5. An institution can maintain meaningful tracking of annual events via an

---

Table 6
Perinatal Mortality Annual Report[8]

Items to be included in an Annual Perinatal Mortality Report
  Summary of major conclusions and recommendations
  Identification of areas requiring clinical research
  Current vs previous years perinatal mortality rate (PMR)
  Presentation of PMR by:
    Birth weight and gestational age
    Maternal age, parity, presentation, and route of delivery
    Maternal diagnosis
    Category of death
    Race
  Summary of placental pathology including percent examined

Annual Perinatal Report that includes items presented in Table 6. Finally, an accurate death certificate is essential to the reliability of state, national, and international perinatal mortality statistics, a key to making state and national comparisons. This is even more critical when one recognizes that infant mortality is used as a measure of the effectiveness of health care services at state, national, and international levels.

The Perinatal Autopsy and Some Specific Perinatal Events

Is the Autopsy and Placental Examination and Documentation Complete?

The above description of the autopsy technique and protocol for documentation will permit assessment of the completeness of the autopsy. Table 2 details the issues to be addressed. The completeness of the placental examination is assessed in Chapter 19. When there is discordance between clinical and autopsy information it is important to assess the reliability of the information gathered from each source. As clinical training and experience are important in evaluating a clinician's expected performance, the same can apply for the information gathered at autopsy. It is critical in the perinatal autopsy that weights and measures are accurate since they are the basis on which a distinction is made between acute and chronic disorders—a key factor in timing perinatal events. The precise manner in which they are made determines their accuracy.

Is the Death Associated with or the Result of Acute, Chronic, or Acute-on-Chronic Events?

A key contribution of the perinatal autopsy is to assign disorders into acute, chronic, or acute-on-chronic events. In particular, are there any chronic

Table 7
Autopsy Findings Indicating Chronic Events[27,28]

Growth Disturbances

Gross Features of Growth Deviation
Intrauterine fetal growth retardation by weights and measures
Reduced subcutaneous fat thickness by measurement
Thymic involution by size in anterior mediastinum and weight
Decreased organ size by weight—particularly the liver
Spared brain size by weight

Microscopic Features of Growth Deviation
Fatty liver with glycogen depletion
Fat deposits in fetal zone of adrenal cortex
Loss of cortico-medullary junction in thymus (involution)
Proliferative zone of growth place of long bones reduced

Other
Pulmonary arteriolar muscularization
Scarring of myocardium
Parenchymal scarring of kidney

events that have been present for days, weeks, or even months that have contributed to the perinatal death? If any such events are present, could they have been detected before birth? If so, would intervention from the time of detection have prevented the adverse outcome? The clinical history of the mother and her pregnancy provide clues of events that might contribute to adverse perinatal outcome.

The pathologist's role is to distinguish between acute, chronic, and acute-on-chronic events. The examination of the placenta and findings at autopsy are sources of information in making this distinction. The placental findings are discussed in Chapter 19. The clinical evidence of chronic events such as growth deviation, and assessment of fetal well-being in utero are discussed elsewhere in the text.

The characteristics of chronic intrauterine events present before birth and noted at autopsy are well established and are presented in Table 7.[27,28] They are more easily applied to a stillbirth because after birth additional changes occur that hinder the interpretation of microscopic findings in several organs. In both stillborn and neonatal deaths, however, whole body growth findings are useful in distinguishing acute from chronic events. Commonly used parameters of chronic intrauterine stress include growth retardation, loss of subcutaneous fat, and thymic involution. Thymic involution is of particular interest, since microscopic evaluation can be used to time the duration of intrauterine stress. A "starry sky" appearance indicates stress has been present for at least 12 hours and when there is depletion of lymphocytes in the cortex resulting in blurring of the cortico-medullary junction, stress has been present for an even longer period.[29] Severe involution is noted on gross dissection when a small thymus is evident on removal of the sternum. A reduced thymic weight confirms severe involution.

In an acute intrauterine death, infant growth and weight are normal and the features of chronic stress indicated in Table 7 are absent. The numerous findings seen at autopsy have been well described by Gillan[28] and these are presented in Table 8. These findings are often noted when acute "asphyxia" is noted clinically, but in and of themselves do not point to any particular diagnosis but merely to the fact that death most likely occurred from acute events. These acute events need to be interpreted in light of placental findings, since evidence of "chronic" circumstances might be seen in the placenta in the absence of "chronic" features in the infant. The timing of these acute events is extremely difficult because there are so many variables. Estimates are possible for the thymus and some central nervous system findings, provided the infant has not been dead too long in utero or in the case of a neonatal death that the infant did not live too long.

The designation of acute-on-chronic is made when there are both acute and chronic findings. The independent and related contributions of each need to be assessed to determine those acute events that follow previous chronic ones and those that are independent events. Again placental pathology needs to be considered in making this distinction.

This designation of events as acute, chronic, or both is one of the most useful contributions of the perinatal autopsy in understanding and explaining the events associated with or contributing to perinatal death. In particular it helps to distinguish events present before the onset of labor and thereby assists in the assessment of the extent to which the management of labor contributed alone or in addition to those "chronic" events already present. The importance of recognizing chronic disorders at autopsy again emphasizes the need for a complete autopsy with accurate weights and measures, recognition and recording of important gross observations, and sampling of organs appropriately—all features related to the expertise of the prosector. This is particularly relevant since many adverse perinatal neurologic outcomes result from events that preceded labor and delivery.[30,31] "We have little knowledge of the degree and duration of hypoxia which the human fetus can tolerate in labor and each has a different level of tolerance which makes assessment and development of (strict) guidelines for practice extremely difficult."[32]

When did Intrauterine Death Occur?

In some intrauterine deaths the exact time of the death is important in the evaluation of detection of adverse events or the likelihood that any intervention

Table 8
Autopsy Findings Indicating Acute Events[27,28]

Apart from specific organ changes listed below petechial hemorrhage of thymus, pleura, pericardium, epicardium, great vessels, and leptomeninges are commonly seen in acute asphyxia. The findings listed below do not correlate with any specific diagnosis but are features noted in infants with acute distress. The exact timing and duration of each entity is difficult because of numerous variables. However, in some instances broad categorization over several hours or days is possible as indicated below. The time in parentheses indicates the minimum time taken for the lesion to be detected.

Organ	Gross	Microscopic
Liver	Subcapsular hematoma	Fatty change/glycogen depletion
Central Nervous System	Subependymal hemorrhage	Nuclear karyorrhexis (12–24 hrs)
	Cerebral edema *cerebellar tonsillar herniation *flattening of cerebral gyri *narrowing of ventricle	"Gitter cell" response (2–3 days) Astrogliosis (7 days) Neurons in pons and Purkinje cells of the cerebellum are particularly vulnerable
	Infarction	
Heart	Petechial hemorrhage *epicardium *pericardium Dilation of right ventricle infarction	Papillary muscle necrosis Myocytolysis Coagulation necrosis
Kidney	Hemorrhage	Interstitial cortico-medullary hemorrhage
	Renal vein thrombosis	Zonal necrosis
Adrenal	Hemorrhage	Pseudofollicular microcysts in "adult cortex"
Thymus		Starry-sky appearance (12 hours)
Gastro-intestinal tract	Necrotizing enterocolitis Dilation of stomach	Necrotizing enterocolitis
Lung	Petechial hemorrhages Meconium aspiration	Aspirated squames Meconium aspiration
Bladder	Dilation	

Table 9
Broad Criteria Timing of Intrauterine Death[33,35]

Early	Intermediate	Late
Skin slippage (6 hours)	Bullae and desquamation (24 hours)	Skin red to brown (7–10 days)
"Parboiled" skin (4–8 hours)	Red-purple viscera (48 hours–5 days) Red serous fluid in cavities (as above)	Olive colored skin (weeks)
	Overriding of skull bones (5 days) Laxity of joints Liquefaction of brain (5 days)	Mummification

would have been timely. Intrauterine death can be grouped into three rather broad categories presented in Table 9 as described by Genest,[33] and Singer and Macpherson.[34] These groupings are, however, fairly broad and in particular do not separate the cases of < 24 hours where there is often the most interest. Genest and Singer, using photographs of stillborn fetuses and clinical history, present *gross criteria* for further subgrouping length of death into after 6 hours, after 12 hours, after 18 hours, and after 24 hours.[35] Their criteria are presented in Table 10. In addition they provide *microscopic criteria* for timing death as < 4 hours, after 48 hours, after 4 days, and after 7 days. These gross and microscopic criteria provide shorter time frames by which to assess the duration of fetal death. They are likely to be of most benefit in further segregating those deaths that occur within 24 hours of delivery.

Is There any Iatrogenic Disorder, is it Preventable, and did it Contribute to Adverse Outcome?

Particularly in the preterm infant iatrogenic disease occurs and in many instances is not preventable. A detailed review of such lesions has been published and only a summary is provided.[26] These injuries occur as the result of assisted ventilation (oxygen and barotrauma), tubes and catheters, total parenteral nutrition, exchange transfusion, blood sampling, and drug administration among others. Lists of some of these complications are presented in Table 11. While particular preventative measures apply to each area of complications, there are six areas that apply across all of them. These include recognition, communication, supervision, documentation, long-term follow-up, and research.[36]

Table 10
Finer Criteria for Timing of Intrauterine Fetal Death[33,35]

More than 6 hours	Areas of desquamation at least 1 cm in diameter on extremities; Brown-red discoloration of umbilical cord stump
After 12 hours	Areas of desquamation of face, abdomen, or back
After 18 hours	Desquamation involving 5% or more of the body surface
After 24 hours	Moderate or severe extent of desquamation
More than 2 weeks	Mummification

Conclusion

This chapter contends that a standardized autopsy protocol is a critical part of promoting the completeness of the perinatal autopsy and its ability to fully attain its goal of identifying the events associated with and causing perinatal mortality. It does so by: 1. guiding pathologists in the performance of the autopsy; and 2. standardizing the format for gathering, recording, and presenting autopsy data and findings so that valid comparisons can be made within and between population groups. This is essential if the quality of care and risk of occurrence of adverse outcome is to be evaluated in a particular case. The fact that unexpected findings continue to be found at autopsy in 15%-20% of cases emphasizes that medicine is still a science and art of uncertainty and that the quality assurance and self-criticism role of the autopsy remains.[37-39] In this light it is important that a complete autopsy be performed to improve the reliability of its findings and conclusions. Since much gross information cannot be assessed once the autopsy has been completed, the active involvement of an expert perinatal pathologist is key at the critical evaluation stages of macroscopic observation and tissue sampling. Finally, experience is necessary to adequately recognize and interpret those features that represent a deviation from normal at some stage during intrauterine or perinatal life, with the distinction between acute and chronic events being of particular interest in the timing and duration of such events. These events are unique to perinatology and require the involvement of pathologists with training and special interest in perinatal pathology.

Table 11
Iatrogenic Disorders by Category[26]

Complications of Assisted Ventilation	Obstruction of tube—by mucus	Nasal and choanal stenosis	Improper position
Acute pulmonary interstitial emphysema	Accidental extubation	Subglottic stenosis	Hypernatremia
Chronic persistent interstitial emphysema	Kinking	Gingival grooves	Heparin overload
Pneumothorax	Swallowing endotracheal tube	Granulomas	Occlusion of lumen
Pneumomediastinum	Apnea	Tracheal necrosis	Breakage of line
Pneumopericardium	Hypoxia	Necrotizing tracheobronchitis	Thrombocytopenia
Pneumoperitoneum	Rise in blood pressure	Tracheomegaly	**Umbilical Arterial Lines**
Subcutaneous emphysema	Aspiration	**Complications of Tubes and Lines**	Insufficiency of major vessels
Retroperitoneal air	**Complications of Endotracheal Suctioning**	**Tubes in Thoracic Cavity**	Loss of extremity
Air embolism	Hemorrhage	Infection	Visceral infarcts
Bronchopulmonary dysplasia	Inadvertent extubation	Scarring	Renal artery thrombosis
Necrotizing tracheobronchitis	Perforation of lung or main stem bronchus	Visceral perforation—lung/liver/spleen/diaphragm/pericardium/vessels	Intestinal ischemia
Hyaline membrane disease	Bronchopulmonary fistula	Obstruction/compression—aorta/phrenic nerve	Total aortic thrombosis
Acute Complications of Endotracheal Intubation	Hypoxia	Hemorrhage	Hemoperitoneum
Perforation—nasopharynx/oro-hypo-pharynx	Bradycardia	Fistula	Retroperitoneal hemorrhage
Injury—hemorrhage/edema/phrenic nerve damage	Systemic hypertension	**Parenteral Lines**	Hypertension form renal vessel thrombus
Pneumopericardium/hemopericardium	Increased cerebral blood flow with increased intracranial pressure	Infection	Congestive heart failure
Malposition—in esophagus/in one bronchus/too high or too low	Granuloma	Hemorrhage	Hemiparesis and paraplegia
	Chronic Complications of Endotracheal Intubation	Thromboembolism	Mycotic aneurysms
	Defective primary dentition	Infiltration	Thrombocytopenia
	Palatal groves	Trauma to vessel wall	False and aortic aneurysm
	Acquired cleft palate		Aortic thromboatheroma
			Urinary ascites from bladder injury

Table 11 *continued*
Iatrogenic Disorders by Category[26]

Tubes in Gastro-Intestinal Tract	Peripheral Arterial Lines	Complications of Exchange Transfusion
Apnea	Peripheral nerve damage	Hypocalcemia
Bradycardia	Arterial spasm	Hypoglycemia
Reflux aspiration	**Central Venous Lines**	Acidosis
Hemorrhage	Malposition	Hyperkalemia
Perforation	Lymphatic obstruction	Air embolism
Misplacement in trachea	Cardiac arrhythmia	Thromboembolism
Peripheral Intravenous Line	Extravasation of fluid—pericardial effusion	Post-transfusion infection—hepatitis/CMV/AIDS
Infiltration	Cardiac tamponade	Septicemia
Edema	Hydrothorax/ascites	Hypothermia
Infection	**Umbilical Venous Line**	Hyperthermia
Tissue necrosis	Hepatic necrosis	Intraventricular hemorrhage
Scarring	Hepatic abscess	Transfusion reaction
Contracture	Bowel injury from exchange transfusion	Thrombocytopenia
Loss of function	Cardiac injury	Leukopenia
Perforation of adjacent artery	Pulmonary injury	Heparin overload
		Deficiency of coagulation factors V and VIII
		Mortality
		UVC complication/perforation
		Portal vein thrombosis
		Hyperviscosity
		Fluid overload
		Graft-vs-host disease
		Necrotizing enterocolitis with bowel perforation

References

1. Barson AJ. The perinatal postmortem. In: Barson AJ (ed). *Laboratory Investigation of Fetal Disease*. Bristol, John Wright & Sons, 1981, pp. 476-497.
2. Wigglesworth JS. Role of pathology in modern perinatal medicine. In: Wigglesworth JS, Singer DB (eds). *Textbook of Fetal and Perinatal Pathology*. Boston, Blackwell Scientific Publications, 1991, pp. 3-9.
3. Hill RB. The autopsy a professional obligation dissected. Hum Pathol 1990;21:127.
4. Vance RP. An unintentional irony: The autopsy in modern medicine and society. Hum Pathol 1990;21:136.
5. Landefeld CS, Goldman L. The autopsy in clinical medicine. Mayo Clin Proc 1989;64:1185.
6. Anderson RE, Fox RC, Hill RB. Medical uncertainty and the autopsy: Occult benefits for students. Hum Pathol 1990;21:128.
7. Macpherson TA. The role of the anatomical pathologist in perinatology. Semin Perinatol 1985;9:257.
8. Macpherson TA, Valdes-Dapena M, Kanbour A. Perinatal mortality and morbidity: The role of the anatomic pathologist. Semin Perinatol 1986;10:179.
9. Valdes-Dapena M, Huff D. *Perinatal Autopsy Manual*. Washington, DC, AFIP, 1983.
10. Macpherson TA, Valdes-Dapena M. The perinatal autopsy. In: Wigglesworth JS, Singer DB (eds). *Textbook of Fetal and Perinatal Pathology*. London, Blackwell Scientific Publications, 1991, pp. 43-122.
11. Macpherson TA, et al. A Model Perinatal Autopsy Protocol. Washington DC, AFIP, 1994.
12. Macpherson TA. Categorization of perinatal death—USA. Pediat Pathol 1990;10:5.
13. Wigglesworth JS, Singer DB. *Textbook of Fetal and Perinatal Pathology*. Boston, Blackwell Scientific Publications, 1991.
14. Reed GB, Claireaux AE, Cockburn F. *Diseases of the Fetus and Newborn. Pathology, Imaging, Genetics and Management*, Second Edition. New York, Chapman and Hall Medical, 1995.
15. Stocker JT, Dehner LP. *Pediatric Pathology*. Philadelphia, JB Lippincott, 1992.
16. Chambers SE. An overview of ultrasound in obstetrics. In: Reed GB, Chaireaux AE, Cockburn F (eds). *Disease of the Fetus and Newborn. Pathology, Imaging, Genetics and Management, Second Edition*. New York, Chapman and Hall Medical, 1995, pp. 887-882.
17. Shen-Schwarz S, Neish C, Hill LM. Antenatal ultrasound for fetal anomalies: Importance of perinatal autopsy. Pediatric Pathol 1989;9:1.
18. Anderson RE, Hill RB, Gorstein F. A model for the autopsy-based quality assessment of medical diagnostics. Hum Pathol 1990;21:174.
19. Macpherson TA, Stocker JT. The pediatric autopsy. In: Stocker JT, Dehner LP (eds). *Pediatric Pathology*. Philadelphia, JB Lippincott, 1992, pp. 3-14.
20. Merlob P, Sivan Y, Reisner SH. Anthrometric measurements of the newborn infant (27 to 41 gestational weeks). Birth Defects 1984;20:7.
21. Talamo TS, Macpherson TA, Dominquez R. Sirenomelia, angiographic demonstration of vascular anomalies. Arch Pathol Lab Med 1982;106:347.
22. Singer DB, Sung CJ, Wigglesworth JS. Fetal growth and maturation: With standards for body and organ development. In: Wigglesworth JS, Singer DB (eds).

Textbook of Fetal and Perinatal Pathology. Boston, Blackwell Scientific Publications, 1991, pp. 11-47.
23. Langles FA. The perinatal post mortem examination. J Clin Pathol 1971;24:159.
24. Sando I, Doyle WJ, Okuno H, et al. A method for the histopathologic analysis of the temporal bone and the eustachian tube and its accessory structures. Am J Otol Rhinol Laryngol 1986;95:267.
25. Kircher T. The autopsy and vital statistics. Hum Pathol 1990;21:166.
26. Macpherson TA, Shen-Schwarz S, Valdes-Dapena V. Prevention and reduction of iatrogenic disorders in the newborn. In: Guthrie RD (ed). *Neonatal Intensive Care, Clinics in Critical Care Medicine*. New York, Churchill Livingstone, 1988, pp. 271-312.
27. Robinson HB. Fetal autopsy. In: Reed GB, Claireaux AE, Cockburn F (eds). *Diseases of the Fetus and Newborn. Pathology, Imaging, Genetics and Management*, Second Edition. New York, Chapman and Hall Medical, 1995, pp. 381-388.
28. Gillan JE. Intrapartum events. In: Reed GB, Claireaux AE, Cockburn F (eds). *Diseases of the Fetus and Newborn. Pathology, Imaging, Genetics and Management*, Second Edition. New York, Chapman and Hall Medical, 1995, pp. 285-317.
29. Van Baarlen J, Schuurman HJ, Huber J. Acute thymus involution in infancy and childhood. A reliable marker for duration of acute illness. Hum Pathol 1988;19:1155.
30. Blair E, Stanley FJ. Intrapartum asphyxia: A rare cause of cerebral palsy. J Pediatr 1988;112:515.
31. Nelson KB. Relationship of intrapartum and delivery room events to long-term neurologic outcome. Clin Perinatol 1989;16:995.
32. Smith NC. Intrapartum fetal monitoring. In: Reed GB, Claireaux AE, Cockburn F (eds). *Diseases of the Fetus and Newborn. Pathology, Imaging, Genetics and Management*, Second Edition. New York, Chapman and Hall Medical, 1995, pp. 1351-1360.
33. Genest DR. Fetal death: Maceration, autolysis and retention. In: Reed GB, Claireaux AE, Cockburn F (eds). *Diseases of the Fetus and Newborn. Pathology, Imaging, Genetics and Management*, Second Edition. New York, Chapman and Hall Medical, 1995, pp. 269-273.
34. Singer DB, Macpherson TA. Fetal death and the macerated stillborn fetus. In: Wigglesworth JS, Singer DB (eds). *Textbook of Fetal and Perinatal Pathology*. Boston, Blackwell Scientific Publications, 1991, pp. 263-283.
35. Genest DR, Singer DB. Estimating the time of death in stillborn fetuses. III. External fetal examination: A study of 86 stillborns. Obstet Gynecol 1992;80:593.
36. Fletcher MA, Macpherson TA. Reducing complications of perinatal care. Semin Perinatol 1986;10:163.
37. Battle RM, Pathak D, Humble G, et al. Factors influencing discrepancies between premortem and postmortem diagnoses. JAMA 1987;258:339.
38. Anderson RE, Hill RB, Key CR. The sensitivity and specificity of clinical diagnostics over 5 decades. Toward an understanding of necessary fallability. JAMA 1989;261:1610.
39. Goldman L, Sayson R, Robbins S, et al. The value of the autopsy in three medical eras. N Engl J Med 1983;308:1000.

Section V

Neonatal Issues

Chapter 22

Neonatal Resuscitation

Steven M. Donn, M.D.

Introduction

It is indeed fortunate that the overwhelming majority of newborns are able to successfully make the transition from fetus to newborn following the process of birth. This event is an extraordinary example of physiologic adaptation, which requires multiple steps to accomplish. An airway must be established, the lungs must be cleared of fluid and inflated with air, and fetal circulation must give way to adult-type circulation in a matter of seconds. When one or more of these steps fails to occur for any reason, maladaptation can lead to lifelong consequences if not recognized and promptly treated. It is therefore incumbent upon health care professionals to possess the requisite skills and knowledge to assist the newborn who is unable to make a spontaneous transition.

It is not the intent of this chapter to extensively teach either the physiology of transition or the essentials of neonatal resuscitation. Although a brief overview will be provided, several recent reviews are available for this purpose.[1-3] From the standpoint of risk management, it is more crucial to discuss strategies for assuring that health care providers and institutions are able to respond to the newborn in need of resuscitation, whether this be in the delivery room, nursery, or neonatal intensive care unit. Claims arising from issues of neonatal resuscitation often focus on items such as delayed institution of resuscitation, unskilled or inexperienced participants, use of inappropriate equipment or drugs, incomplete documentation in the medical record, and inadequate follow-up care, particularly in the immediate neonatal period. It is too often alleged that long-term neurologic disabilities such as cerebral palsy

From: Donn SM, Fisher CW (eds.): *Risk Management Techniques in Perinatal and Neonatal Practice.* © Futura Publishing Co., Inc., Armonk, NY, 1996.

and mental retardation were the result of or were aggravated by negligently performed resuscitation. Hospitals and health care providers without a well-planned method for responding to a depressed newborn will have considerable liability exposure in the event of an untoward outcome.

Fetal and Transitional Physiology

Fetal physiology is considerably different from neonatal physiology. The fetal lungs are fluid-filled and do not participate in gas exchange and waste removal occurring at this site. Pulmonary blood flow is diverted by means of altered vascular resistances; the pulmonary circuit is a very high resistance circuit, whereas the placenta is a very low resistance circuit. Blood flow thus takes the path of least resistance. Additionally, because there is little pulmonary venous return to the left atrium, right atrial pressure exceeds left atrial pressure, allowing for shunting of oxygenated blood across the foramen ovale, a flap valve in the atrial septum. Another fetal conduit, the ductus arteriosus, allows for further right-to-left shunting from the pulmonary artery to the aorta. Thus, oxygenated blood returning from the placenta is further diverted from the lungs in order to bring oxygen to the systemic (non-pulmonary) side of the circulation. Blood is carried to the placenta by the umbilical arteries, it becomes oxygenated (along with the removal of carbon dioxide and metabolic wastes), and it is returned to the fetus by the umbilical vein. Some of this blood enters the liver, while the majority flows to the inferior vena cava and then the right atrium.

Under normal circumstances, birth initiates a number of changes in fetal physiology. First, clamping of the umbilical cord and removal of the placenta abolishes this low resistance circuit and leads to a rise in systemic arterial blood pressure. Second, inflation of the lungs following expulsion of pulmonary fluid results in a significant fall in pulmonary vascular resistance. This enables a significant rise in pulmonary blood flow and the establishment of the lung as the organ of respiration. Increased pulmonary blood flow causes an increase in pulmonary venous return to the left atrium. As soon as left atrial pressure exceeds right atrial pressure, the foramen ovale closes, preventing atrial shunting. Increases in arterial oxygen tension initiate the constriction and ultimately the closure of the ductus arteriosus, separating the systemic and pulmonary circulatory pathways, and within a very short period of time, adult-type circulation is established.

Maladaptation

Maladaptation occurs when the normal transitional physiology is incomplete or fails to occur. A myriad of conditions may interfere with normal transition. They may be of maternal origin, such as severe maternal illness (i.e., advanced diabetes mellitus, maternal heart disease, or drug induced), which interferes with maternal oxygenation or uterine blood flow; they may involve placental conditions (i.e., abruptio placentae or placental infection), where maternal-fetal gas or nutrient exchange is adversely impacted; they may involve inherent fetal conditions (i.e., congenital anomalies, blood loss, or infection), where fetal oxygen uptake or delivery is impaired; and they may involve neonatal conditions (i.e., respiratory distress, apnea, infection, or congenital anomalies), which interfere with establishment of adult-type circulation. Most of these conditions result in a situation in which there is a failure to achieve the necessary reduction in pulmonary vascular resistance to reverse right-to-left shunting of blood, which allows for the persistence of blood flow through fetal channels after removal of the placenta; unfortunately, unless pulmonary blood flow is established, there is no means for fetal oxygenation to occur. This may initiate a vicious circle, whereby hypoxemia leads to metabolic acidosis, causing further pulmonary vasoconstriction and elevations in pulmonary vascular resistance and pulmonary arterial pressure, further aggravating right-to-left shunting and hypoxemia. The major therapeutic goal of neonatal resuscitation is directed at interrupting this circle by establishing adequate gas exchange and blood flow to enable appropriate oxygen uptake in the lung and delivery of this oxygen to the tissues.

Neonatal Resuscitation

Health care providers have always been taught about the "ABCs" of resuscitation: airway; breathing; and circulation. To this mnemonic may also be added the letters "D" (for drugs) and "E" (environment) for the newborn.

Airway

Several features distinguish the neonatal airway. It is obviously much smaller than its adult counterpart. This can hamper gas flow, which is proportionate to the fourth power of the radius. Additionally, it is incompletely formed with inadequate cartilaginous support sometimes interfering with its patency. Most newborns will have a viscous liquid in the airway at birth, including mucus, blood, amniotic fluid, or meconium, which may also potentially interfere with gas exchange. The first steps in neonatal resuscitation involve the establishment of airway patency.

Breathing

Lung inflation and the establishment of regular spontaneous respirations follow. The initial inflation of the lungs may require significantly greater pressure than do subsequent breaths. Term newborns may need 20 to 40 cm

H_2O to initially expand the lungs, whereas the preterm newborn may require 40 to 80 cm H_2O because of surfactant deficiency and lower compliance. In the absence of an airway obstruction, this can be provided by properly performed bag and mask technique and does not necessarily require endotracheal intubation. Adequate precautions need to be taken to assure adequacy of gas exchange and prevention of over-distension of the stomach if this technique is utilized. If endotracheal intubation is chosen, the appropriate size tube and depth of insertion is important. Tube placement should be verified clinically (assessment of breath sounds, chest excursions, heart rate, and color) and confirmed radiographically. Failure of the patient to respond should initiate a thorough investigation, including mechanical problems (i.e., equipment, defective gas source, improper technique) and patient complications (i.e., pneumothorax, hypovolemia, anemia).

Circulation

Circulation in this context refers to maintenance of cardiac output and tissue perfusion. In the newborn, cardiac output is primarily a function of heart rate, since there is a limited ability of the infant to increase stroke volume. The normal heart rate range is 120-160 bpm. Thus, the potential for impaired cardiac output exists when bradycardia is sustained. External cardiac massage, performed by chest compression, should be initiated if appropriately performed pulmonary resuscitation fails to bring about the desired increase in heart rate.

Other factors that play a role in tissue perfusion include blood volume, hemoglobin concentration, acid-base balance, temperature, and peripheral vascular resistance. If after the heart rate has been normalized, the infant still shows signs of impaired perfusion, a fluid bolus may be given. Most newborns will safely tolerate 10-20 mL/kg, even if they are normovolemic.

Drugs

In recent years, the use of resuscitation drugs in the newborn has been de-emphasized. More attention has been paid to mechanical resuscitation, since the majority of infants respond to the establishment of an airway and effective ventilation. However, a few pharmacologic agents still play a role in the management of a depressed newborn.

Epinephrine is used to treat bradycardia. Care must be taken to use the correct concentration (1:10,000). It may be given directly into the endotracheal tube, or alternatively intravenously. It should not be given through an arterial catheter because it can induce severe vasospasm. In rare instances, intracardiac use may be appropriate.

Sodium bicarbonate is indicated to treat *metabolic* acidosis. Effective ventilation must be established in order to avoid the "closed flask phenomenon" and the exacerbation of hypercapnea and acidosis.[4] It must be remembered that sodium bicarbonate is extremely hyperosmolar; the 8.4% stock solution has an osmolality of 1440 mOsm/L. It is best to dilute this to 4.2% and to administer it slowly (1.0 mEq/min). Also, since bicarbonate is a sodium salt, each mEq of bicarbonate given to the infant is accompanied by a mEq of sodium, and hypernatremia may result.

Naloxone may be given to a newborn whose depression is believed to be the result of narcotics administered to the mother during labor. However, its use is contraindicated if the mother is addicted to narcotics or opiates, since it may initiate an immediate withdrawal syndrome in the baby. If there is any question of drug use or abuse by the mother, it is better to support the infant by mechanical means.

Environment

Hypothermia can severely affect the newborn with transitional difficulties. It results in cutaneous vasoconstriction (to decrease evaporative heat loss through the skin) and the generation of lactic acid, thus promoting the vicious circle alluded to earlier. In addition, the infant must increase basal metabolism and oxygen consumption in order to maintain homeostasis. Hypothermia may also decrease surfactant production, further interfering with pulmonary function and oxygen uptake.

The best treatment of hypothermia is its avoidance. Infants are delivered "wet" into a delivery room, which is "cooled" to somebody else's comfort level. They should be immediately dried with a warm towel to prevent evaporative heat loss. They should not be left in contact with wet towels. They should be placed in a warming device (either a heated incubator or open bed with overhead radiant warmer); care should be taken by health care providers to avoid blocking the heat from getting to the baby. Keep incubator windows closed; do not stand over a baby who is under a radiant warmer. Make sure all intravenous fluids and inspired gases are adequately warmed. Covering the head, which has a substantial surface area, will also help to decrease heat loss.

Conduct of Resuscitation

Although the basic principles of neonatal resuscitation enumerated above have been applied for decades, there has not, until recently, been a consistent approach among either individuals or institutions. This has hampered the development of standards, the analysis of outcomes, and the appropriate quality assurance measures to recognize and correct inadequacies.

In 1987, the American Academy of Pediatrics (AAP) and the American Heart Association (AHA) jointly published the *Textbook of Neonatal Resuscitation*, written by Bloom and Cropley.[5] In addition to organizing a consistent approach to neonatal resuscitation, this project formulated a system of training and testing of individuals seeking certification in neonatal resuscitation. The program consists of educational source materials in a programmed learning text format and demonstrations of techniques and methods, performed on mannequins by trained instructors. Certification requires the individual to pass both written and practical examinations, and recertification is required every 2 years. The course is taught by regional instructors, who have not only been certified in the basic resuscitation course, but who have also taken and passed a course in how to teach the basic program.

The benefits of this approach are numerous. First, a consistent approach to neonatal resuscitation is finally being taught. Major institutional differences should no longer exist, and individuals should be able to apply their skills from one hospital to the next. Second, there now exist standards for skill and knowledge that must be demonstrated for certification. Third, institutions caring for newborn infants can establish objective requirements for those who will be participating in delivery room or nursery care of the newborn and can mandate certification as one of the requirements. Fourth, quality assurance activities can be established, with indicators chosen from components of the resuscitation program.

The risk management issues related to the implementation of this program are far-reaching, indeed. Hospital guidelines or protocols should now incorporate the ideals and methods espoused in the textbook. If this work is recognized by experts as *the* standard of care relative to neonatal resuscitation, deviations from its content will represent deviations from the standard of care in such cases. Health care professionals should be thoroughly familiar with the content of the text and its clinical applications.

This is not to say that what is written in the text is the last word in all aspects of neonatal resuscitation, and there may need to be exceptions based on individual or institutional circumstances. For instance, an area of ongoing controversy is the management of the meconium-stained infant. While most agree that the infant found with thick, tenacious, particulate meconium should have the airway suctioned in the delivery room, there is disagreement over the need to suction the infant with thin, watery, non-particulate meconium. The authors of the *Textbook of Neonatal Resuscitation* recognize this and urge hospitals and personnel to formulate their own plans of management under these circumstances.

Neonatal Resuscitation and Risk Management Techniques

Delivery Room Attendance

It is frequently alleged that the failure to have a neonatologist, pediatrician, or other physician present in the delivery room constitutes a violation in the standard of care. This assumes, of course, that no one else is capable of adequately performing neonatal resuscitation. As far back as 1979, the AAP's Committee on the Fetus and Newborn addressed this issue and concluded that skill and experience were more important than a title.[6] What is required at a delivery is the presence of an *individual* with the requisite skills in neonatal resuscitation, including a thorough knowledge of the physiology and pathophysiology of transition, and the basics of mechanical and pharmacologic management of resuscitation. It is essential that there be an individual who is solely dedicated to the care of the newborn; optimally, an assistant should also be available. As long as the individual possesses the requisite skills, it does not matter that he/she is a physician (neonatologist, pediatrician, family practitioner, anesthesiologist), nurse (neonatal, pediatric, obstetric), or certified nurse-anesthetist. The infant probably does not care who puts in the endotracheal tube, provided it is done correctly!

If circumstances exist where a known high-risk delivery is to occur, it is intuitive that the most skilled care providers be present. For instance, it is probable that an infant with a congenital diaphragmatic hernia is going to be critically ill in the moments following birth and will most likely require endotracheal intubation and ventilation as well as placement of catheters for vascular access. This should be considered in deciding who is to attend to the infant at birth. In contrast, an elective repeat Cesarean section at term is likely to produce a normal baby with perhaps some transient tachypnea not requiring airway management beyond suctioning.

It would behoove a health care facility to devise "guidelines" for attendance at deliveries that are based upon the population it serves and its personnel. Situations may differ greatly; the teaching hospital with 24 hour availability of house officers and many high-risk referrals is vastly different from the community hospital with no "in house" 24 hour coverage and the rare obstetrical or neonatal complication. In the latter example, guidelines might specify those conditions for which a primary resuscitator should be summoned *prior* to delivery (i.e., known preterm delivery, multi-fetal gestation, thick meconium-stained amniotic fluid), and the method by which a resuscitator is summoned *after* delivery in the event of an unanticipated complication.

All health care providers assigned responsibility for attending the newborn in the delivery room should be certified in neonatal resuscitation. Hospitals must devise performance reviews to assure that skill levels remain acceptable, and it should be recognized that unless these skills are used sufficiently, they will need to be re-taught at regular intervals. Use of simulations, such as "mock arrests" may serve as an assessment tool but are not a substitute for actual resuscitation.

Site of Resuscitation

Traditionally, neonatal resuscitation has been performed in the delivery room, generally on an infant bed placed a few feet from the delivery table. Although this was the most expedient way to initiate care, it was not always the best situation. Low ambient temperatures increase the risk of neonatal hypothermia (see above). The resuscitation must be done in the presence of the mother and possibly the father; this may be intimidating to the health care professionals, and more importantly, it may be emotionally devastating for the parents.

The delivery room is usually well-equipped to handle resuscitation of a newborn who is depressed; however, it is hardly comparable to the equipment and personnel available in the neonatal intensive care unit. In recent years, many hospitals have developed stabilization/resuscitation rooms, specifically designed and built for this purpose. Newborns can be swiftly moved from the delivery suite to the stabilization room, where a complete team with all the necessary equipment is prepared and waiting. While initiation of resuscitative procedures may be delayed for a few seconds while the infant is in transit, the trade off seems acceptable, in that: 1. a more effective resuscitation can be performed; 2. the room has been optimally designed so that all necessary equipment and drugs can be immediately located; and 3. the infant can be more safely moved to the intensive care unit after placement of the endotracheal tube and any other invasive devices.

If resuscitation is not performed in the delivery room but in some other location, care must be taken in the manner in which this is documented. This is especially true if pre-printed forms are used. "No resuscitative procedures were performed in the delivery room" can be a potentially self-incriminating and damaging statement. It is far better to write that "the infant was taken directly to the stabilization area where resuscitation was immediately commenced." If this cannot be sufficiently explained on the printed form, a narrative note should be placed in the medical record.

When to Start

As the subspecialty of neonatology has advanced, the limits of viability have been pushed further and further. Survival of infants of only 24 weeks gestation is not only common, it is a frequent occurrence, and there are reports of an occasional survivor who is even more premature.

The issue of viability is extremely difficult to predict prior to birth. Much of the decision making cannot be accomplished without an observation of the baby and how he/she has responded to the first few seconds of extrauterine existence. The decision to support an infant on the cusp of viability is a clinical judgment and is based on an impression of the health care professional(s) that the infant, given the appropriate degree of support, will be able to withstand the demands of life outside the womb.

In an earlier era, the practice was indeed different. Infants who were extremely premature were given a "trial of life"; that is, they were left alone and were reassessed at a later time. Those who were still alive were then resuscitated and supported. Unfortunately, for many of these infants, significant *post-natal* hypoxic-ischemic injury had already transpired.

The most prudent approach today is one of full support in the moments following delivery, unless it is clear to the responsible individual(s) that there is no chance for survival. In this way, outcomes should be optimized by eliminating post-natal complications from non-intervention. Health care professionals, however, are not obligated to maintain an aggressive approach later if clinical circumstances suggest that to do so is not in the best interests of the patient or the family. These issues are best addressed prior to delivery (see Commentary in Chapter 34).

When to Stop

One of the most difficult decisions is when to terminate the resuscitation of the newborn who fails to respond. There are no hard data to suggest exactly when resuscitative efforts should be stopped. Again, this falls into the area of clinical judgment. The decision should be made by the most experienced individual available at the time (in this case preferably a physician with experience in neonatology or pediatrics) after careful assessment of the events of labor and delivery, the neonatal period, and the performance of the resuscitation. It may be helpful to obtain objective information, such as serial arterial blood gases to help guide this determination.

It is useful, however, to review the findings of the National Collaborative Perinatal Project regarding the prognostic significance of Agpar scores. Review of the data indicates that unless Agpar scores are significantly depressed for a prolonged period of time, the incidence of cerebral palsy in *surviving* infants is surprisingly low. In fact, even if the Agpar score is 0-3 at 15 minutes, although nearly half of infants > 2500 g will die, < 10% of the survivors will display handicap.[7]

Because there are as yet no standardized or firm criteria that define starting or stopping points for neonatal resuscitation, and because these decisions are made subjectively on the basis of clinical judgement, retrospective analysis is both difficult and often overly critical. This applies to both quality assurance reviews and medico-legal opinions. Participants in the resuscitation should be cognizant of this and make every effort to record the reasons for decisions in the medical record.

Documentation

Inadequate documentation of the events of a neonatal resuscitation may be the deciding factor in the mind of a juror hearing a medical malpractice case. Although "not documented, not done" is often untrue, the burden of proof will shift to the defendants when documentation fails to establish that an indicated procedure was performed, or that a drug was given in a timely fashion.

While the care of the patient during a resuscitation is always first and foremost in the minds of the health care providers, there needs to be a way to avoid losing sight of what is being done for the patient. The best possible scenario is to have a dedicated "scribe" whose sole responsibility is the documentation of the resuscitation. If circumstances preclude having enough individuals to do so, participants must make every effort to document as much as possible, especially times, drug dosages, and routes of administration, patient response to treatment, and any other procedures performed. Very often, especially if the need for resuscitation was unanticipated, the flurry of activity results in documentation in places other than the medical record, such as the infamous "paper towel." If this happens, the information should be transcribed into the patient's chart as soon as possible. It would not be inappropriate to place the original paper in the medical record, along with a brief note to explain its existence.

Documentation of the exact times that events occur is often imperfect for a variety of reasons, including asynchronous clocks or wristwatches. In the long run, it is far more important to be sure that the events are recorded *in the proper sequence in which they occurred*. For example, was the trachea suctioned of meconium *prior* to the application of positive pressure ventilation? Was external cardiac massage instituted in the appropriate sequence of resuscitation? If the proper order of events is recorded, small discrepancies in the times of events are much more easily explained.

"Late" entries are also acceptable, provided they are done correctly. First, they should be clearly labeled as such. A brief explanation as to the circumstances delaying the entry should also be given. The entry should be timed according to when it was written, but it should clearly indicate the time that it references. An example of such is as follows:

"4/25/95 1745. Late entry. Physician Progress Note: I attended the birth of this unexpectedly depressed baby at 0615 this morning.

The baby was covered with thick meconium, was apneic at birth, and he appeared to have diminished perfusion. He required a prolonged resuscitation. This included laryngoscopy and intubation with tracheal suctioning and positive pressure ventilation (done at 0616), placement of an umbilical venous catheter (0628), administration of saline to expand blood volume (0630), and transfer to the NICU under the care of the neonatologist (0646). Immediately after transfer, I was called to the Emergency Room to evaluate a child with suspected meningitis. I subsequently went directly to my office, where I have been seeing patients until 1715. I returned to the hospital thereafter. I have reviewed the notes of the nurses who assisted in the resuscitation and concur with the events and times as they are documented."

Another method of promoting good documentation is the use of a pre-printed form for resuscitation, which can be generic to all resuscitations or specific to neonatal resuscitation. The form can be either a narrative type, or one which requires only the checking of boxes and listing of times. One advantage of such a form is that it is consistent for each resuscitation, serves as a reminder to do things that might be overlooked during a hectic time, and can be easily retrieved for review and quality assurance activities.

Whatever type of documentation is chosen, an effort should be made to assure that there are no inconsistencies between the various disciplines making entries in the medical record. Common pitfalls include different times for the same event (which usually reflects the use of multiple, non-synchronized watches or clocks), sequencing of events, and patient responses. This may occur more frequently when the individual recording the events of the resuscitation is not in a position to make a direct observation or cannot keep up with the rapid sequence of resuscitation. Notes should be checked and signed by all individuals who rendered care, and if there are differences in opinions, the bases for these should be explained. It will be far better than having to do so years later, under oath, in a court of law.

Another issue with potential medico-legal significance is the infant who does not survive, and for whom no post-mortem examination is permitted. It should never be assumed that the family will automatically grant permission for an autopsy. Every effort should be made to document all available physical findings in the medical records. This includes a complete physical examination and the recording of the major parameters of growth-birthweight, length, and head circumference, and an assessment of the gestational age. Deviations from the normal should be indicated. Any abnormal physical findings should be thoroughly described. Consideration should be given to the performance of a post-mortem radiograph ("babygram"), and if a chromosomal anomaly is suspected, blood should be obtained for a karyotype. It may be extremely useful to photograph the baby (a simple Polaroid® photograph serves nicely), and place the picture in the medical record. This should have an accompanying note explaining the circumstances, and it should be witnessed (and signed) by one or more other individuals. This may be the only tangible evidence that the infant was anomalous or non-viable, and may have a significant bearing on future genetic counseling.

Follow-Up Care After Neonatal Resuscitation

Maladaptation requiring neonatal resuscitation represents a potential threat to infant well-being. Infants requiring resuscitation should be presumed to be at risk for complications of hypoxia-ischemia and require careful observation and conservative management until they have demonstrated normal physiologic responses (see Chapter 25).

Consideration should be given to evaluating the acid-base balance of an infant following resuscitation. Residual metabolic acidosis may be an indicator of tissue hypoxia and should alert the health care team that additional surveillance is necessary. Careful charting of fluid status, including quantification of urine output and urinalysis, may give the first clue of impending renal dysfunction. Similarly, tachypnea or other signs of respiratory distress may be indicative of pulmonary injury. Such infants should generally not be fed enterally to lessen the risk for the development of necrotizing enterocolitis. Additional evidence of systemic non-neurologic hypoxic-ischemic injury should be sought, as outlined in Chapter 25.

A thorough neurologic examination should be documented, including head circumference. The absence of the neonatal neurologic syndrome should be established by inclusion of pertinent negatives such as normal tone and reflexes, an appropriate level of consciousness, and no convulsive activity. The Sarnat staging system for encephalopathy can also be used and does not require special equipment.[8]

Finally, consideration may need to be given to transferring the infant to a neonatal intensive care unit if there is evidence of increasing dysfunction and the need for more intensive care. This will depend upon the capabilities of not only the health care team, but also the institution.

Quality Assurance Activities

Quality Assurance (QA) activities are mandated by the Joint Commission on the Accreditation of Healthcare Organizations (JCAHO). It seems prudent to include neonatal resuscitation in hospital or service QA projects, which might focus on any of the aspects of risk management listed above. A multidiscipline approach that includes all participants in neonatal resuscitation should help improve aspects of care deemed inadequate but should also reinforce those things done well. QA activities can also be directed at individuals, such as interval assessments of knowledge and skills.

Summary

The infant who encounters difficulty in transition following birth is in need of prompt and effective resuscitation to avoid further hypoxic-ischemic injury. A properly performed resuscitation can be of immeasurable benefit to such infants.

Many different situations may result in maladaptation. These include maternal, placental, fetal, and neonatal conditions. Anticipating the infant who will be in need of resuscitation enables effective preparation and a well-planned approach to the problem.

The basic components of neonatal resuscitation remain the tried and true "ABCs," airway, breathing, and circulation, and in addition, drugs and environment. How these are applied to the infant has in the past been variable and inconsistent. In recent years, a national program promulgated by the AAP and AHA has resolved most of the variability and offers a consistent approach that is transferable from one individual or institution to the next. Health care providers and hospitals are strongly encouraged to adopt this approach to both training and conducting neonatal resuscitation.

Issues that are frequently cited in medical malpractice litigation include the failure to have a physician present in the delivery room, inadequacies in documentation, and inappropriate follow-up care of the infant requiring neonatal resuscitation. Health care facilities can safeguard against these claims by assuring the skills and experience of the personnel responsible for newborn care, drafting guidelines for attendance at or following deliveries, and quality assurance reviews to critique both performance and documentation.

Commentary by Mr. Fisher: Most neonatal resuscitation claims involve the care and treatment rendered to a depressed newborn within the first 30 minutes to 1 hour of life. Allegations are predicated primarily on the failure to quickly reverse respiratory acidosis, metabolic acidosis, and perfusion problems.

The following is a brief list of the commonly encountered criticisms in neonatal resuscitation cases:

1. There was a failure to aspirate meconium at and below the vocal cords prior to providing positive pressure ventilation.

2. There was an inordinate delay between delivery and the intubation of the infant.

3. Because of poor perfusion (poor capillary refill) there was inadequate circulation that was not timely corrected by volume expansion.

4. Metabolic acidosis persisted, either because of a failure to test for it, or a failure to treat with the correct dosage of bicarbonate to reverse the tissue acidosis.

In addition to the above claims, assertions are occasionally made that seizure activity was not adequately or expediently treated. However, this author has found that in most of these situations, as an isolated event, there is no good evidence that additional damage occurs during minimal seizure activity without apnea or bradycardia. Rather, this claim is often thrown in to confound and exacerbate the other claims primarily directed toward the resuscitation.

Although, in most cases, whatever damage caused the child to be depressed at delivery is probably the primary insult; the significance of the "additive effect" of mismanagement during resuscitation should not be underestimated. In many cases, the resuscitation claims are targeted because of the fact that the hospital is the "deep pocket," and the personnel who resuscitate are usually employed by or are agents of the hospital. The health care provider who delivers the baby and manages labor and delivery often is not an employee or agent of the hospital, and that health care provider may not have significant insurance coverage. Thus, plaintiff's attorneys will target the resuscitation as a very important part of their case simply for economic considerations.

Correctly documenting the timing and sequence of events (as discussed by Dr. Donn) is very important in avoiding claims of alleged medical malpractice. Noting that meconium was suctioned *before* positive pressure was given is vital to documentation, especially if the child develops meconium aspiration syndrome after delivery.

Documenting the specific time that the infant is intubated as well is important. Often the time is not found in the medical record, or at some point later on in the care and treatment of the infant it is noted that the child is "intubated," which makes it appear as though the intubation took place later than actually occurred in the particular case.

With respect to correcting blood gases, this is probably the most critical part of the resuscitation issue. As long as one can prove that there was no metabolic acidosis, one has a very strong argument that no injury could have taken place during the resuscitation *regardless* of what methods of treatment were alleged to have been faulty. Therefore, liberal blood gas testing is highly recommended as soon as reasonably possible after establishing airway, breathing, and circulation. Once the blood gas results return, if they suggest metabolic acidosis, immediate correction should be used if it is appropriate to do so (based upon other possible parameters of respiratory acidosis). If the health care provider performing resuscitation is concerned about whether or not to give bicarbonate, a consultation with a pediatrician or neonatologist should be immediately obtained. This author cannot emphasize enough that the *most critical issue in resuscitation* is proving that the baby did not sustain or continue metabolic acidosis.

Unfortunately, the time sequences regarding sampling and testing blood, and providing bicarbonate to correct metabolic acidosis are often poorly documented in the chart. Frequently, the chart simply reflects a time on a laboratory requisition regarding blood gas results, which unfortunately does not necessarily equate to the actual time the sample was taken. Therefore, the time that the blood was obtained, the time that the results were received, and the time that any treatment was given for blood gas abnormalities should be clearly contained in the medical record.

In summary, resuscitation must include expeditious correction of any cardiorespiratory abnormalities, expeditious testing for— and correction of—acidosis, and expeditious fluid therapy to ensure adequate circulation.

References

1. Donn SM, Faix RG. Delivery room resuscitation. In: Spitzer AR (ed). *Intensive Care of the Fetus and Neonate*. St. Louis, Mosby-Year Book, 1996, pp. 326-336.
2. Faix RG. Neonatal resuscitation. In: Donn SM, Faix RG (eds). *Neonatal Emergencies*. Mt. Kisco, NY, Futura Publishing Co., 1991, pp. 15-30.
3. Bloom RS. Delivery room resuscitation of the newborn. In: Fanaroff AA, Martin RJ (eds). *Neonatal-Perinatal Medicine—Diseases of the Fetus and Infant*, Fifth Edition. St. Louis, Mosby-Year Book, 1992, pp. 301-304.
4. Ostrea EM Jr, Odell GB. The influence of bicarbonate administration on blood pH in a "closed system": Clinical implications. J Pediatr 1972;80:671.
5. Bloom RS, Cropley C. *Textbook of Neonatal Resuscitation*. Dallas, American Heart Association/American Academy of Pediatrics, 1987.
6. American Academy of Pediatrics, Committee on Fetus and Newborn. Care of the newborn in the delivery room. Pediatrics 1979;64:970.
7. Nelson KB, Ellenberg JH. Agpar scores as predictors of chronic neurologic disability. Pediatrics 1981;68:36.
8. Sarnat HB, Sarnat MS. Neonatal encephalopathy following fetal distress. Arch Neurol 1976;33:696.

Chapter 23

Neonatal Infection:
A Medico-Legal Perspective
◆◆◆
Roger G. Faix, M.D.

Introduction

Despite the introduction of a wide array of potent broad spectrum antimicrobial agents into clinical practice during the last 50 years, infection remains a leading cause of neonatal morbidity and mortality. Although this is partially attributable to nosocomial infection in smaller and sicker infants who once died shortly after birth but now survive, well-formed infants who are not at the edge of viability continue to comprise a major portion of those afflicted. Advances in the understanding of the limited host defenses of newborn infants and the pathophysiologic mechanisms by which infection causes host injury have offered insights for new potential diagnostic, therapeutic, and prophylactic strategies as well as the limitations of current standard interventions.

Life-threatening systemic infection during the first 30 days of life occurs in 1 to 8 of every 1000 liveborn infants in this country.[1] Chronic congenital infection occurs in an additional 5 to 25 of every 1000 liveborn infants, although many of these may be asymptomatic. Improvements in antimicrobial therapy, life support technology, and supportive care have decreased mortality from life-threatening early onset neonatal infection, with many centers now reporting rates of 10%-20%.[2,3] Despite this encouraging improvement, many survivors continue to suffer significant neurodevelopmental morbidity, including cerebral palsy, mental retardation, visual and hearing deficits, and a variety of more focal problems. The reported mortality rates may represent systematic underestimates, since several investigators have demonstrated that routine performance of blood and/or spinal fluid cultures within 1 hour of

From: Donn SM, Fisher CW (eds.): *Risk Management Techniques in Perinatal and Neonatal Practice*. © Futura Publishing Co., Inc., Armonk, NY, 1996.

death strongly suggests the presence of active infection in many infants whose deaths were initially attributed to noninfectious causes.[4,5] The incidence of infection among low birth weight (< 2500 g) and very low birth weight (< 1500) infants has been reported to be almost an order of magnitude higher than for term infants,[1,6,7] at least partially reflecting the fact that premature delivery may be incited by infectious processes.[8] Mortality and morbidity attributable to neonatal infection are even more frequent among these tiny babies than in term infants, and correlate inversely with birth weight and gestational age.[2,9] Recent investigators have highlighted, however, that the relative risk of mortality attributable to infection is much greater among full-term infants than very low birth weight infants, in whom background mortality is comparatively high.[2]

The spectrum of infectious agents responsible for neonatal infections is not static. The dominant pathogens causing early-onset infection have changed for unknown reasons over the years, from group A streptococcus in the 1920s and 1930s to *E. coli* in the 1940s and 1950s to the current primary agent, group B streptococcus.[1,10] The possibility of further shifts exists. Advances in diagnostic techniques continue to reveal the potential significance of organisms not previously appreciated as perinatal pathogens (such as *Ureaplasma urealyticum* and Parvovirus).[11,12] Likely pathogens vary with geography, clinical circumstances, and local patterns. An awareness of all these factors is essential for evaluation and management of potential infectious problems in newborn infants.

Although effective antimicrobial agents are available for most pathogens, adverse outcomes continue to occur despite the timely institution of state-of-the-art therapy. Exploring the limitations of current interventions will help to identify areas for future progress and facilitate more realistic prognostication.

> **Commentary by Dr. Donn:** This point is worth emphasizing. Some infants do poorly even with timely institution of appropriate antibiotic treatment. Just because the outcome is less than satisfactory does not connote medical negligence.

Medical Analysis

Clinical Presentation

Neonatal infections have been categorized according to age at presentation, acuity and rate of progression of clinical signs, and the nature of the responsible microorganism. Such classifications can be useful for identifying likely organisms, guiding diagnostic evaluation, assessing prognosis, and facilitating long-term follow-up for survivors.

Acute infections are those that progress rapidly, produce significant derangement of vital signs, and may result in death or serious permanent injury. Unfortunately, signs associated with acute infection are often nonspecific and also can be produced by a wide variety of other common maladies (Table 1). *This nonspecificity prompts serious consideration of infection in the differential diagnosis of a wide array of neonatal signs.*

Acute infections may be further categorized according to the age of the infant at presentation. The dividing point between early- and late-onset infection has varied in different publications,[13,14] but many authors have selected 5 days.[1,10] With that criterion, early-onset infections have a clinical onset at or before 4 days of age while those at or beyond 5 days are considered to be late. Early-onset infection typically has a maternal source, is more likely to result in death or severe morbidity, and is more likely to involve the respiratory system. Late-onset infection may originate from the mother but may also arise from nosocomial sources, abnormal colonization patterns induced by antimicrobial therapy, or other origins; is less likely to result in death; and has an increased probability of involving the central nervous system. The likely responsible microorganisms also differ according to the age at onset, although some overlap exists.

Table 1
Clinical Signs Frequently Observed in Neonatal Acute Infection

Respiratory distress
Unexplained requirement for increased respiratory support
Temperature instability
Lethargy
Poor feeding
Apnea
Irritability
Abdominal distention
Cyanosis
Hypoperfusion
Oliguria
Petechiae/purpura
Seizures
Emesis
Blood glucose instability
Metabolic acidosis
Unexplained jaundice
Asymmetry of normally symmetric structures
Focal areas of inflammation
Thick, whitish-yellow, or purulent secretions

Chronic infection and congenital infection are terms that are often used interchangeably. In the strict sense, congenital infections are those already present at birth. Although early-onset group B streptococcal sepsis can be considered to be a congenital infection, the term is usually used to refer to intrauterine chronic infection. In many such infections, the responsible organism is still present at birth and may persist for years. Such organisms include cytomegalovirus, *Toxoplasma gondii* and *Treponema pallidum*. In other congenital infections, the organism may no longer be recovered, but permanent injury with chronic neurodevelopmental consequences has been sustained in utero (e.g., varicella-zoster, rubella). Most clinicians are aware of the potential for significant symptomatic disease in infants with chronic congenital infection. An array of teratologic and destructive lesions may occur in a variety of vital organs with the potential for severe derangement in the quality of life among those whose survive. Asymptomatic chronic congenital infection, however, is much more common than the symptomatic variety. Most of these infants are undetected, but some are discovered by screening laboratory tests performed as part of research programs or because of maternal high-risk factors. Infants with aymptomatic human immunodeficiency virus (HIV) infection almost always progress to full-blown symptomatic disease. Although the bulk of infants with asymptomatic congenital infection caused by organisms other than HIV remain asymptomatic, a portion may go on later to develop significant neurodevelopmental, visual, or auditory problems that interfere with the day-to-day quality of life, although the abnormalities are usually less devastating than those seen with symptomatic congenital infection.[15-17] The frequency with which later disease develops, the organs most likely to be affected, and the potential for mortality vary according to the responsible organism. Accordingly, surveillance for late complications is influenced by the identity of the organism (Table 2).

Transmission Routes

Microorganisms may gain access to the bloodstream and the deep parenchymal organs by a variety of routes. Infants with chronic intrauterine infection are typically invaded in association with maternal hematogenous dissemination and a breach of the placental barrier. Acute early-onset infection may also be transmitted by the maternal hematogenous route but is probably more frequently associated with ascent of the responsible invader from an infected or heavily colonized birth canal and subsequent migration across the amniotic sac.[18-20] Membrane rupture facilitates such passage, but intact membranes do not preclude this process.[21,22] Neonatal infection may result from aspiration of infected amniotic fluid and subsequent invasion across the thin pulmonary

Table 2

Examples of Late Complications of Initially
Asymptomatic Chronic Congenital Infection

Cytomegalovirus	*Sensorineural hearing loss Structural tooth defects Seizure disorders Indirect inguinal hernia Learning disabilities Microcephaly Motor deficits Mental retardation Chorioretinitis
Toxoplasmosis	*Chorioretinitis Seizure disorders Microcephaly Hydrocephalus Mental retardation
Syphilis	*Sensorineural hearing loss Interstitial keratitis Structural tooth defects Saddle nose Periosteal reactions Arthropathy Motor deficits Neurosyphilis
Rubella	*Sensorineural hearing loss Diabetes mellitus Thyroid dysfunction Other endocrinopathies Glaucoma Retinopathy Mental retardation Autism Immunopathy Panencephalitis
HIV	*Immunopathy and opportunistic infections Failure to thrive Anemia Encephalopathy Interstitial lung disease Nephropathy Peripheral neuropathy Myopathy Malignancy
Hepatitis B	*Chronic hepatitis Hepatocellular carcinoma Immune complex disease

*Most common.

epithelial barriers or by dense colonization of mucoepithelial surfaces followed by superimposed mechanical or hypoxic-ischemic disruption.

Late-onset infection may also result from disruption of a colonized mucoepithelial or airway surface. Several in vivo reports suggest the possibility of invasion by persorption, a process in which sufficiently large numbers of colonizing organism may cross a mucoepithelial barrier even without mechanical or hypoxic-ischemic disruption.[23,24] The source of late-onset infection occasionally may be entirely exogenous, as with contaminated parenteral solutions or indwelling appliances.

Mechanisms of Injury

To facilitate the development of new strategies for improving outcome, an appreciation of the underlying mechanisms by which host injury is induced is useful.[25-29] Host cells may be lysed or rendered dysfunctional by the direct action of structural components of the invading microorganism (e.g., endotoxin) or toxic metabolic products elaborated by the invader. Such pathogen-produced mediators may also indirectly injure the host cells by triggering pathophysiologic cascades (e.g., prostanoid pathways, coagulation, kallikrein-bradykinin) that induce local changes in vasomotor tone and integrity, as well as the oxygen/nutrient delivery properties of the local circulation. A frequent cause of injury is the inflammatory response of the host, which is mobilized to eradicate the invader but is often targeted imperfectly and may consequently injure "innocent bystander" normal host tissue. Viruses and intracellular pathogens may subvert the normal host metabolic machinery by diversion to fulfillment of the metabolic requirements of the invader. A few organisms (e.g., *Candida*) are capable of producing a macroscopic accumulation of microorganisms with interspersed inflammatory cells and proteinaceous material that is capable of interference with the normal pathway of flow for such body fluids as urine and cerebrospinal fluid (CSF).[30,31] Incitement of an inflammatory exudate in an enclosed space such as a joint, the pericardium, or the pleural cavities may cause ischemic necrosis of the underlying tissue or severe impairment of the compressed organ.

Review of the mechanisms by which host injury is inflicted suggests that killing the invading microorganism is only part of the solution. Lysis of the pathogen may transiently aggravate host injury by increasing the concentration of toxic cell wall components and invader-related metabolites as well as transiently accelerating the pathophysiologic cascades (e.g., coagulation, complement, neutrophil activation and chemotaxis, kallikrein-bradykinin).[25-29] Modulation of these cascades and more precise focusing of the inflammatory response offer the theoretical potential for significant improvement in outcome, but therapies to accomplish these goals remain experimental and are fraught with difficulties.[32,33] Institution of antimicrobial therapy as soon as possible is often perceived to be a critical determinant of outcome, but recent reports of bacterial meningitis in older children question the influence of the duration of antecedent signs and symptoms before antimicrobial therapy is initiated.[34,35] These studies reported that adverse outcomes (death or persistent neurologic sequelae) were equally frequent whether signs of illness had been present for < 24 hours, 24-48 hours, or > 48 hours before therapy. These authors suggest that the duration of antecedent symptoms might reflect inoculum size, strain pathogenicity, or other factors that determine the clinical acuity and progression rate of clinical signs. Children with an insidious presentation, with non-specific signs for which meningitis was only one possible explanation, frequently do better than those with more fulminant, rapidly progressive signs. Data to address this issue in newborn infants have not been reported. It should also be appreciated that antimicrobial therapy may minimize further replication and invasion but will not necessarily reverse injury that has already occurred. Some injuries are irreversible or incompletely reversible (such as those involving the central nervous system).

> **Commentary by Dr. Donn:** Cases involving allegations of delayed diagnosis and treatment of neonatal sepsis are often predicated upon the belief that earlier administration of antibiotics would have decreased sequelae and improved the outcome. As Dr. Faix indicates, there is reason to suspect that this may not always be true.

Diagnosis

As with most clinical problems, a careful review of the history should be performed. Both maternal and neonatal factors merit historical review and will influence diagnostic evaluation and the selection and initiation of empiric antimicrobial therapy. Pertinent maternal factors include: underlying illness; medications; acute illnesses superimposed during pregnancy, the intrapartum period, or postpartum; antenatal laboratory results; and features of the delivery that may predispose to perinatal infection. Neonatal history should include (but is not limited to) a review of the severity and duration of the presenting signs that have prompted consideration of infection; gestational age; antecedent illnesses; congenital anomalies; current medications (including antibiotics and potentially immunosuppressive agents); and indwelling vascular catheters, appliances, and surgical wounds.

A number of historical antepartum and intrapartum factors have been reported to be associated with an increased risk of acute early-onset infection, including (but not limited to): preterm labor (<37 weeks gestation) with no plausible noninfectious cause; preterm and/or premature (i.e., prior to the onset of labor) rupture of amniotic membranes; prolonged rupture of membranes (defined by various investigators as 6, 12, 18, or 24 hours prior to delivery); maternal chorioamnionitis; and the presence of active maternal infection at or near the time of delivery. Unfortunately, these factors are imperfectly sensitive and frequently non-specific. The validity of these factors as predictors for risk of early-onset neonatal infection may vary by hospital. At the University of Michigan Medical Center, for example, a review of 23 years of experience found that in the absence of maternal clinical chorioamnionitis, full-term infants born after 24 hours of ruptured membranes and with no clinical signs of infection in the first 2 hours of life were at no greater risk for infection than full-term asymptomatic infants born following <24 hours of ruptured membranes. Maternal factors that were predictive of increased risk of early-onset infection in an initially asymptomatic infant were preterm labor without a plausible noninfectious cause, preterm rupture of membranes, and maternal chorioamnionitis.

The importance of a careful, systematic physical examination cannot be overemphasized. Features that may be overlooked or given only a cursory inspection but that often contribute to identification or strong suspicion of a specific pathogen include the skin and visible mucoepithelial surfaces (Figure 1), umbilical stump, entry sites of indwelling catheters and appliances, external

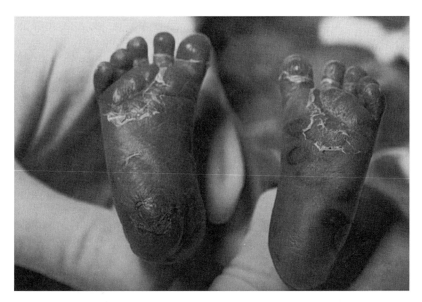

Figure 1. Hemorrhagic-appearing, but well-demarcated skin lesions on soles of feet of a premature infant with respiratory distress. Unusual skin lesions prompted evaluation for and subsequent confirmation of congenital syphilis.

wounds, sites of localized erythema or swelling, asymmetry of normally symmetric structures, changes in level of consciousness, and altered perfusion. Careful ophthalmologic evaluation may be particularly rewarding for suspected chronic infections. Examination may identify sites appropriate for local sampling or biopsy and may suggest the need for microbiologic or immunologic techniques to detect organisms not recovered by standard cultures. Although not technically part of the physical examination, it is worthwhile to review recent radiographs for suggestive abnormalities that may have been overlooked as the examiners focused on other portions of the radiograph (Figure 2).

Many clinicians use leukocyte counts with differential enumerations and indices derived from these data to assess the likelihood of infection and make decisions about further evaluation. Although a number of authors have published reference ranges for neonatal neutrophil counts,[36-38] those of Manroe et al.[39] are most widely used. Limiting the utility of neutrophil counts as a screen, however, is the observation by these authors and others that numerous noninfectious processes also give rise to systematic abnormalities; specificity is very low.[40-44] Since these standards change markedly over the first 24 hours of life, small errors in timing the specimen may significantly alter the interpretation of results. Predictable differences between simultaneous capillary, venous, and arterial samples have also been reported.[41] Another recent report noted that these reference ranges were frequently breached in a population of healthy full term infants with no perinatal risk factors for infection and opined that they should be broadened.[45] Even more troublesome are reports of infants with culture-proven systemic bacterial infection who had normal neutrophil counts and indices at the onset of infection. A neonatal rodent model of early-onset group B streptococcal infection demonstrated that it takes 4 hours after bacterial inoculation for neutropenia to appear.[46] More recently some of the co-authors of the original Manroe report have confirmed the suggestions of others that the reference ranges for neutrophil counts and indices for very low birth-weight infants are different than those for larger infants.[47] These revised reference standards encompass much broader ranges and may therefore be less sensitive for diagnosing infection. Clinicians should be aware of the limitations of neutrophil counts and indices as screening tests. Application of the Manroe standards to infants from the Holden Neonatal Intensive Care Unit at the University of Michigan Medical Center with proven acute infection and no infection is depicted in Table 3. Given the many vagaries of neutrophil counts and indices, two disparate approaches seem equally reasonable: 1. base decisions about obtaining cultures and starting therapy on clinical presentation and risk factors, using serial counts as one index of recovery or deterioration; or 2. use them as a screen in suspect infants, evaluating and initiating treatment in those who have abnormal re-

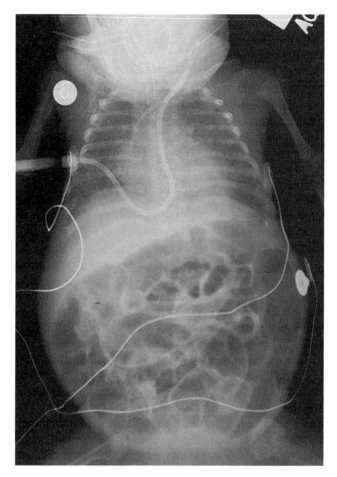

Figure 2. Abdominal and chest radiograph of an infant transferred for possible abdominal exploration because of persistent ileus and *Klebsiella* bacteremia. Note signigicant periosteal and bony changes, expecially in left hip and proximal femur and right humerus, consistent with septic arthritis and osteomyelitis. Drainage of hip joint and alteration in antimicrobial thereapy resulted in prompt resolution of bactermia and ileus and eventual normalization of bony changes.

sults, accepting that many uninfected infants will be treated and that a few who are infected will be missed. Prospective studies comparing these two strategies in large populations have not been reported.

Other investigators have used assays of single or multiple acute phase reactants (e.g., C-reactive protein, haptoglobin, erythrocyte sedimentation rate, interleukin-6) as screening tests in an attempt to enhance specificity and

Table 3

Classification of Neutrophil Counts and Indices Using the Manroe Criteria[39] in 860 Infants with Proven Acute Infection (1971–1994) and 560 with No Infection (1990–1993) from the Holden NICU at the University of Michigan Medical Center

	Proven Infection	
	Early (< 5 days) N = 346	Late (> 5 days) N = 514
Neutropenia	91 (26%)	24 (4%)
Neutrophilia	19 (6%)	118 (23%)
Increased immature count	80 (23%)	156 (30%)
Increased immature: total neutro- phils ratio	133 (38%)	173 (34%)
No abnormality in any of above	19 (6%)	33 (6%)
	No Infection	
	N = 280	N = 280
Neutropenia	28 (10%)	20 (7%)
Neutrophilia	42 (15%)	50 (18%)
Increased immature count	56 (20%)	28 (10%)
Increased immature: total neutro- phil ratio	83 (30%)	28 (10%)
No abnormality in any of above	126 (45%)	182 (65%)

predictive values.[48-51] Although these screens may yield fewer false positives than neutrophil indices alone, they still have significant limitations and are not always available. Although the use of these assays as screening tools for infection is fraught with difficulty, they may be useful in some settings as indicators of progression or resolution of inflammation in the infant with a proven or strongly suspected infection and may assist in making therapeutic decisions.

Chronic Infection

Laboratory evaluation of infants with suspected chronic congenital infection should be guided by clinical findings and epidemiologic considerations. Clinicians should be aware that there are many organisms that can produce chronic congenital infection other than those contained in the TORCH acronym (*To*xoplasma gondii, *R*ubella, *C*ytomegalovirus, *H*erpes simplex), and that at least one of the organisms (Herpes simplex) is typically a postnatal pathogen and rarely afflicts the fetus in utero. *Determining TORCH titers may be a misleading exercise.* Serologic tests for total antibody or IgG against the

TORCH organisms will more likely reflect maternal past history than ongoing neonatal or fetal infection, given the ability of maternal IgG to cross the placenta during the final trimester of pregnancy and the relatively high background rate of seropositivity for many of these organisms in the United States.[52] This may be particularly troublesome when assessing the presence of neonatal HIV infection, since transplacental maternal antibodies frequently persist for up to 15 months. IgM-specific titers against organisms causing chronic congenital infection may also be misleading, since such assays may be negative (depending on the technique used) in 30% or more of infants with culture-proven congenital infection caused by the tested organism.[53,54] Measurement of total IgM was once a popular test to screen for infection of all types in newborn infants, but has been more recently recognized to be non-specific and insensitive.[19]

Sensitive organism-specific tests are most likely to yield useful information. Such tests include qualitative and quantitative VDRL with confirmatory specific treponemal serologic tests; dark field microscopy of suspicious lesions on mother, infant, or placenta; viral cultures of urine, saliva, nasopharynx, conjunctiva, CSF, rectum, or other suggestive sites obtained within the first week of life; and careful histopathologic examination of the placenta. Biopsy of suspected sites of involvement with submission for organism-specific detection tests or culture may be very useful. Serial IgG-specific antibody assays may be useful if other microbiologic tests are not readily available. Antibody quantity that does not decline by 6 months of age is quite suspicious for active production by the infant. A two-dilution rise in titer or a newborn titer that is at least fourfold higher than in maternal serum at birth are strongly suggestive of the presence of infection in the infant. For serial testing to be truly interpretable, however, it is critical that the same laboratory simultaneously test all the sera at issue. Newer diagnostic tests using specific monoclonal antibodies, polymerase chain reaction, and other methods are available for some organisms and may offer distinct advantages in the future.

Acute Infection

Microbiologic testing to detect an invading microorganism is indicated if there is no strongly probable noninfectious explanation for the clinical presentation. Standard diagnostic tests are based on the recovery of actively multiplying organisms by culture, the observation of pathogens in normally sterile body fluids by direct microscopy with or without specific stains, or the detection of organism-specific antigens, metabolites, or nucleic acids.

Blood culture is the most common and frequently useful diagnostic test for acute infection. Although blood culture systems are generally formulated for recovery of bacteria, other organisms such as yeast may also be recovered.

At least 1.0 mL of blood should be obtained from a carefully prepared peripheral venous or arterial site or a freshly placed vascular catheter. Smaller amounts of blood may prevent the detection of organisms that are present in very low concentration early in infection. Larger volumes of blood may increase the yield, but may be problematic for the infant whose circulating blood volume is small. Cultures drawn through previously established indwelling vascular catheters may be useful for detecting infected catheters but should not replace the peripheral blood cultures. Quantitative cultures will facilitate determining if the catheter is the primary site or has been secondarily seeded by a bloodstream infection. One recent report indicated that obtaining multiple blood cultures will increase yield but also recognized that this is frequently impractical.[55] Many blood culture systems are now designed to permit concurrent aerobic and anaerobic processing, though this may require further division of an already small blood sample and a consequent reduction in the recovery of invading microorganisms. If one has to select either aerobic or anaerobic processing, the decision should be based on clinical circumstances and the likely pathogen. Anaerobic processing may be advantageous in the setting of a gastrointestinal malady in an infant more than 4 days old, since the involvement of strict anaerobes is not uncommon and other enteric bacteria are frequently microaerophilic and can still be recovered. In most other circumstances, aerobic processing may produce improved recovery of common microaerophilic neonatal pathogens and will facilitate the identification of such strictly aerobic organisms as Candida species.[56,57]

Indications for obtaining CSF for culture remain controversial. Lumbar puncture (spinal tap) will cause pain and may induce respiratory and hemodynamic compromise even with careful attention to proper positioning and airway patency.[58,59] Less common complications include spinal cord, nerve, or nerve root injury; intraspinal epidermoid tumor; and the theoretical possibility of introducing organisms into a previously sterile subarachnoid space.[60,61] Meningitis accompanies bacteremia in 25%-33% of cases[62-65]; knowledge that the central nervous system is involved may influence the choice, dose, and duration of antibiotic therapy. Occasionally, however, CSF may be the only source from which a microorganism can be recovered. Meningitis without concomitant bacteremia has been reported to account for 0%-15% of all cases of early-onset meningitis,[62-67] although one study has indicated a frequency of > 50%.[68] The incidence of meningitis among infants with late-onset infection is typically higher.[62,65,68] It has been recognized that isolation of organisms from the CSF alone is very unlikely in some settings, and it has been proposed accordingly that lumbar punctures may be safely forgone in such circumstances. Several authors have suggested that lumbar puncture may not be routinely necessary for preterm infants < 24 hours old who have pulmonary findings most consistent with respiratory distress syndrome and no historical risk factors suggestive of infection.[64,66] Others have opined that lumbar puncture may not be necessary for the well-appearing full term newborn infant who is undergoing evaluation primarily for historical or maternal risk factors, although published supporting data are limited.[67] A review of all infants with culture- or antigen-proven early-onset neonatal infection over a 23-year period at the University of Michigan was consistent with this opinion, revealing no full term, well-appearing newborns who had positive CSF but negative blood cultures. If a blood culture yields a pathogen in circumstances where a lumbar puncture was not performed, later examination of the CSF is indicated; a positive culture, antigen test, or evidence of ongoing inflammation should influence further therapeutic decisions. Age-specific rcfcrence ranges should be used for interpreting cytologic and biochemical studies of neonatal CSF, since they differ significantly from those in older children and adults.[69,70] It is appropriate for each health care facility to review local experience to determine guidelines regarding routine performance of lumbar puncture as part of the sepsis evaluation.

The method of urine collection strongly influences the validity and interpretation of culture results. "Bagged" urine specimens are frequently contaminated and uninterpretable, although negative results strongly support the absence of urinary tract infection. Specimens collected by sterile catheterization or percutaneous suprapubic bladder aspiration are much less likely to be contaminated. Several reports have indicated that urine culture in the first 3 days of life has very limited utility[71,72]; early urinary tract infections originate hematogenously and therefore almost always have accompanying positive blood cultures and little increased risk of an underlying genitourinary anomaly. Among older infants, however, isolated urinary tract infections are not uncommon and the risk of associated urinary drainage anomalies is increased. Culture and direct microscopy of appropriately collected urine should be routinely considered in older infants with suspected infection. Further evaluation of genitourinary anatomy should be performed in infants with proven urinary tract infection.

Sites of local inflammation may be aspirated or biopsied following sterile preparation for culture and/or microscopy and may yield recovery of an invading pathogen when other sampled body fluids are sterile. Identification of such localized foci is guided by careful physical examination and review of imaging studies.

The value of obtaining endotracheal aspirates as part of the evaluation for infection remains controversial. Tracheal colonization does not usually take place until 8 or more hours after birth, so that recovery of organisms from a sample obtained earlier than that probably represents invasion.[73] Organisms recovered from a tracheal aspirate after that time often represent colonizing organisms. Routine surveillance cultures of endotracheal aspirates have little predictive value and may be misleading.[74] Tracheal aspirate culture may occasionally be useful, however, in guiding antibiotic selection for the infant who has radiographic pneumonia and recovery of no organisms from normally sterile sites. *Cultures of gastric aspirates, external ear canal, or other superficial sites have very poor predictive value and are probably not worth the effort and expense unless done as part of an ongoing epidemiologic or research investigation.*[75,76]

> **Commentary by Dr. Donn:** Why anybody continues to do superficial cultures is a mystery. They are expensive and provide information that may force the clinician to act defensively, subjecting the baby to a sepsis work-up and antibiotic treatment that may not be clinically indicated. I would also encourage the abandonment of this archaic practice.

Viral cultures should be submitted in strongly suggestive clinical settings (e.g., an infant with a vesicular dermatitis), and seriously considered if an infant continues to manifest clinical signs strongly suggestive of infection despite 24-48 hours of broad-spectrum antibacterial therapy. Viral agents that may cause acute life-threatening neonatal disease include herpes simplex, adenovirus, respiratory syncytial virus, and a variety of enteroviruses. Viral agents may be specifically sought depending on the clinical signs in the infant, maternal symptoms, time of year, community outbreaks, and recent exposures of the infant, his/her visitors, and infant caretakers.

A number of microorganisms have recently been implicated as significant pathogens in infants requiring prolonged neonatal intensive care and may require special techniques for recovery. These organisms include (but are not limited to) *Ureaplasma urealyticum, Mycoplasma hominis, Mallasezia furfur, Aspergillus* species, *Mucor* species, and others. A knowledge of predisposing factors, associated clinical findings, and local recovery patterns will facilitate such diagnostic decisions.

Direct microscopy and staining of normally sterile body fluids may also reveal microorganisms long before culture results become positive and may greatly facilitate targeted selection of antimicrobial therapy. In the setting of antibiotic pre-treatment, acridine orange has been reported to be more sensitive than Gram stain for this purpose.[77,78] Some slow-growing microorganisms, such as *Candida* species, may be observed by direct microscopy long before cultures become positive.

It is not uncommon for standard microbiologic cultures to yield no organism despite the clinical appearance of sepsis. In some cases this may reflect the masking effect of antecedent antimicrobial therapy, but in others it may reflect the limitations of culture techniques and the inability to cultivate some microorganisms (e.g., *Treponema pallidum*, the agent responsible for syphilis). In the setting of antimicrobial pre-treatment, antigen testing of urine, CSF, or other appropriate body fluids may be useful and allow identification of a specific invading organism when cultures may not be revealing. Although specific antigen tests are available for a number of organisms, those targeted to group B streptococcus, *Streptococcus pneumoniae*, and *Escherichia coli* K1 are most likely to be helpful in neonatal settings. Urine specimens obtained by bag technique may be contaminated by groin or rectal flora, suggesting that specimens collected by sterile catheterization or percutaneous suprapubic bladder aspiration may be more reliable.[79] It has been demonstrated that infants who swallow group B streptococci into the gastrointestinal tract may have group B streptococcal antigen appear in their urine although invasive infection is not present.[80] The method of urinary sampling does not circumvent this difficulty. *Routine performance of antigen testing as part of all neonatal sepsis evaluations may produce a problematic number of positive antigen tests in settings where negative cultures should be reliable and may result in costly, dubious prolonged courses of antimicrobial therapy or increased laboratory expenses for tests that contributed little but confusion to clinical care.* This problem can be significantly reduced if antigen tests are requested only in circumstances where cultures may be uninterpretable because of antibiotic pre-treatment of the mother or infant.[81] Maternal intrapartum antibiotic therapy has been suggested to be an important cause of positive antigen tests when cultures are negative.[82] It should be recalled that negative antigen tests do not necessarily preclude the presence of infection because sensitivity is severely limited when there is only a small amount of organism/antigen present and because a large number of less common but real pathogens are not included in currently available antigen batteries.

> **Commentary by Dr. Donn:** Institutional guidelines for the use of antigen tests may help to eliminate some of the inconsistencies associated with their use.

New molecular biologic techniques have offered the theoretical possibility of increased sensitivity, specificity, and speed for identification of a variety of organisms. Nucleic acid techniques have recently been used to detect and classify the organisms responsible for cat scratch fever and Whipple's disease despite the inability to recover these organisms using culture techniques.[83,84] Similar approaches could be used for a wide array of other organisms that are not cultivatable with current techniques.[85,86] Monoclonal antibodies, polymerase chain reaction techniques, nucleic acid analysis, and the increasingly widespread availability of computerized genome libraries with well-defined organism-specific sequences offer many prospects for future diagnostic capability.

Treatment

If there is no strongly probable noninfectious explanation for acute clinical signs in an infant, one should seriously consider initiating empiric therapy as well as performing microbiologic testing. Many clinicians suggest that evaluation and therapy for infection should be entertained even if there is a probable alternative explanation, since concurrent sepsis may also be present. As indicated earlier, one should also seriously consider evaluation and therapy in an initially asymptomatic infant if the infant was delivered preterm (< 37 weeks gestation) without a plausible noninfectious cause, following preterm rupture of membranes, or in the presence of maternal chorioamnionitis. The selection of antimicrobial agents for initial empiric therapy will depend on the clinical circumstances of the infant, postnatal age, and the local recovery patterns of pathogens and corresponding antimicrobial susceptibilities.

The most commonly encountered organisms responsible for early-onset infection in this country include group B streptococcus, *Escherichia coli*, untypable *Hemophilus influenzae*, and *Listeria monocytogenes*. Organisms responsible for early-onset sepsis at the University of Michigan Medical Center over the past 3 decades are indicated in Table 4. Empiric therapy for early-onset infection should include agents that are effective against these most common isolates. For a symptomatic infant in a setting suggestive of viral disease (e.g., vesicular dermatitis, mother with herpetic lesions in or near the birth canal,

Table 4
Organisms Most Commonly Responsible for Early-Onset (< 5 Days of Age) of Acute Neonatal Infection Among Infants Admitted to Holden NICU at University of Michigan Medical Center (1971–1994)

Organism	Cases (Percent Mortality)		
	1971–1979	1980–1989	1990–1994
Group B Streptococcus	40 (40)	84 (14)	71 (6)
Escherichia coli	18 (50)	7 (43)	15 (7)
Enterococci	6 (17)	4 (0)	4 (0)
Pseudomonas aeruginosa	6 (83)	1 (0)	0 (NA)
Hemophilus influenzae, untypable	2 (50)	7 (0)	5 (20)
Listeria monocytogenes	3 (33)	2 (0)	1 (0)
Herpes simplex virus	1 (100)	3 (100)	5 (40)
Streptococcus pneumoniae	1 (0)	3 (100)	1 (100)
Other Gram-positives	11 (9)	26 (19)	13 (8)
Other Gram-negatives	12 (17)	5 (0)	5 (40)

failure to improve after 24-48 hours of broad spectrum antibacterial therapy), consideration of empiric antiviral therapy may also be warranted.

Organisms responsible for late-onset infection are more variable and more strongly influenced by the clinical setting. Isolates recovered from late-onset infections in infants who were healthy in the first days of life, discharged home, and readmitted with a new illness at < 1 month of age are different from those encountered in infants who have been continuously hospitalized since birth with significant underlying medical problems. Community-acquired late-onset infections are frequently caused by group B streptococcus, *Hemophilus influenza* type B, and *Streptococcus pneumoniae*. Late-onset nosocomial infections among infants continuously hospitalized since birth vary from center to center, but commonly include *Staphylococcus aureus*, coagulase-negative staphylococcus, gram-negative bacteria, and *Candida* species. Microorganisms responsible for late-onset nosocomial infections at the Holden Neonatal Intensive Care Unit at the University of Michigan Medical Center are indicated in Table 5. Selection of empiric antimicrobial agents should be guided again by the frequency and susceptibility pattern of isolates typical for the clinical setting. Despite the frequency of *Candida* recovery in late-onset infection, standard antifungal therapy with amphotericin B and/or flucytosine has enough potential for toxicity that inclusion is not recommended typically for initial empiric therapy. If reports in adults and older children of significantly less toxicity and almost equal efficacy with newer azole antifungal agents such as fluconazole compared to amphotericin can be confirmed in

Table 5

Organisms Most Commonly Responsible for Acute Late-Onset (≥ 5 Days of Age) Nosocomial Neonatal Infection Among Infants Admitted to Holden NICU at University of Michigan Medical Center (1971–1994)

Organism	Cases (Percent Mortality)		
	1971–1979	1980–1989	1990–1994
Staphylococcus aureus	22 (14)	34 (6)	21 (14)
Candida species	21 (29)	42 (14)	37 (11)
Escherichia coli	18 (39)	18 (6)	19 (10)
Enterococci	16 (25)	23 (17)	23 (0)
Klebsiella species	9 (22)	11 (0)	10 (0)
Group B Streptococci	3 (0)	1 (0)	5 (0)
Coagulase-negative staphylococci	30 (3)	83 (0)	87 (2)
Herpes simplex virus	3 (67)	1 (0)	5 (60)
Other Gram-positives	3 (33)	5 (0)	4 (50)
Other Gram-negatives	10 (30)	13 (31)	19 (32)

newborns, this recommendation may be reconsidered.[87,88] Barring such confirmatory evidence, heightened surveillance for fungi should be conducted and antifungal therapy initiated only if fungi are detected or the clinical picture of infection progresses despite broad-spectrum antibacterial therapy.

In our own NICU, ampicillin and gentamicin have been selected as the empiric antimicrobial agents for early-onset acute infection while vancomycin and gentamicin have been selected for late-onset acute infections. Alternative agents may be appropriate in other settings.

Antimicrobial therapy for chronic congenital infections is more problematic. Effective antimicrobial agents are available for *Treponema pallidum* and *Toxoplasma gondii* and should be used in an attempt to minimize adverse outcomes. Penicillin treatment of congenital syphilis is usually very effective at killing treponemes, but major sequelae may still happen if extensive injury has already occurred. Antitoxoplasma therapy is similarly limited, and also requires careful surveillance for drug toxicity. Although ganciclovir has significant activity against cytomegalovirus, therapeutic efficacy for reduction of neurodevelopmental morbidity in congenital infection has not been demonstrated. Additionally, the virus returns shortly after cessation of therapy and the drug frequently causes significant hematopoietic toxicity. Zidovudine is recommended for treatment of HIV infection, but is far from curative; other anti-HIV agents continue to undergo research and development. No agents with an acceptable risk:benefit ratio are available for rubella, enteroviruses, parvovirus, and many other causes of congenital infection.

In addition to antimicrobial therapy, life support should be used as needed, including respiratory, hemodynamic, and blood component interventions. Potential contributing factors should be eliminated if possible, including removal of indwelling vascular catheters or appliances that are not essential for therapy, replacement of those that are, and drainage of abscesses. The infant should undergo careful serial evaluation for the development of acute complications that might require additional interventions. The use of adjunctive therapy such as intravenous polyclonal immune globulin, hyperimmune or monoclonal antibody preparations, exchange transfusion, exogenous neutrophils, systemic cytokines, and other agents all remain experimental at this point.

If cultures of a normally sterile body fluid yield recovery of a pathogen, antimicrobial therapy can be tailored to that organism and body site. Such narrow-spectrum therapy may reduce the potential for antimicrobial toxicity and decrease selective pressures for resistant microorganisms. If initial cultures yield a probable pathogen, serious consideration should be given to obtaining follow-up cultures of the same body fluid 24-48 hours later to assess sterilization. If that site has not been sterilized, several possibilities should be considered. If very large quantities of bacteria are present, with most organisms in the stationary phase of the growth curve, penicillin-binding proteins (essential for the activity of most beta-lactam antibiotics) may be decreased or lost, with resultant resistance to these therapeutic agents.[89] The substitution of antimicrobial agents that work by a different mechanism may be beneficial, but recognition of this circumstance can be very difficult in the clinical arena and the comparative efficacy of such alternative agents has not been rigorously tested in a clinical setting. Slowly multiplying organisms may incorporate antimicrobial agents less rapidly, with the consequent expectation of longer survival for the invaders. Alternative explanations include the possibilities of microbial resistance to the selected agents; presence of infection in sites that the drugs may be less able or unable to reach in an active form (e.g., central nervous system, ocular aqueous humor, joint space, endocardial vegetations, abscess, intrathrombosis); administration of an inappropriately low dose(s) of antimicrobial agent; difficulties with drug delivery; or the presence of an infected intravascular catheter or indwelling appliance.

When available, antibiotic drug concentrations should be assessed to assure that therapeutic levels of antimicrobial agents have been attained and to reduce the potential for toxicity. In the absence of significant underlying renal disease or dysfunction of the eighth cranial nerve, it is probably unnecessary to measure drug concentrations before day three of therapy. By that time, it is usually apparent that antimicrobial therapy will either be discontinued, in which case drug levels are unnecessary, or will be administered for a longer course, in which case a steady state has probably been approximated and drug levels may be useful. Subsequent measurements of drug concentration may be indicated if there is a significant change in weight, renal or hepatic function, the addition of other drugs that may interfere with antibiotic disposition, or adjustments in dosing necessitated by previous levels outside of the target range. The need for peak and/or trough levels will vary depending on the antimicrobial agent and the clinical concern prompting measurement. The incidence of significant, irreversible toxicity appears to be low in the newborn.[90-93] Such toxicity is much more common with prolonged or multiple courses of therapy. In addition, the presence of superimposed or pre-existing conditions (including the infection that prompted antimicrobial therapy in the first place) makes it difficult to establish that later impairment is causally related to the drugs received. Organs known to be at risk for antimicrobial-related toxicity should undergo serial surveillance to facilitate dosing alterations, minimize injury, and maximize rehabilitative potential. It should be noted that antimicrobial-related nephrotoxicity occurs in the tubules earlier than in the glomeruli, with the result that glycosuria and urinary sediment abnormalities will be seen before elevations in serum creatinine; similarly, vestibular changes probably precede auditory changes, but there is no widely available method to assess vestibular function in ill newborns.

Duration of therapy has not been systematically evaluated in well-designed clinical trials. Recommendations vary by author, organism, anatomic site involved, the underlying health of the infant, and the rapidity of clinical response. Commonly used guidelines include continuation of therapy for 7-10 days with sepsis and minimal or no focal infection, and 21 days for meningitis caused by group B streptococcus or gram-negative enteric organisms.[1] In our own nursery, infants are typically treated for 7-14 days following sterilization of infected body sites. In most circumstances, true bacterial pathogens will be recovered from cultures within 48-72 hours.[94,95] Using contemporary blood culture systems, every infant in our own NICU with culture-proven early-onset infection since 1990 has had a positive blood culture by 24 hours after submission. Some organisms associated with late-onset infection, such as *Candida albicans* and some anaerobic organisms, may occasionally take longer than 3 days for recovery. The same is true for cultures of viruses and other non-bacterial microorganisms. If microbiologic tests are negative and the clinical course of the infant is inconsistent with infection, therapy can usually be discontinued by 48-72 hours. One recent report has attempted to define guidelines for discontinuing therapy after 24 hours.[96]

Failure to recover a microorganism from a normally sterile body fluid does not always exclude the presence of infection, and in such circumstances the clinician may opt to continue therapy based on the clinical presentation and the possibility that the culture results are unreliable (e.g., antibiotic pretreatment). In these circumstances, treatment is continued typically for 7-14 days, but reasonable clinicians may choose alternative courses with equal justification.

Completion of antimicrobial therapy does not mark the end of concern about infection. Since a number of organisms have been associated with relapse or recurrence (e.g., *Candida albicans*, *Staphylococcus aureus*), continued clinical surveillance for such complications should continue through the remainder of the hospitalization. *The infant should undergo longitudinal assessment of neurodevelopmental function, growth, and special sensory capabilities to facilitate timely diagnosis of difficulties and institution of appropriate rehabilitative efforts.*

Prophylaxis: Evolving Strategies

Although many advances in the treatment of neonatal infection have been made in past decades, prevention of infection would still be preferable to treatment. Most contemporary strategies for prevention fall into three broad categories: 1. augmentation of general immunocompetence; 2. maternal immunization; and 3. targeted chemoprophylaxis for specific organisms in high-risk settings.

Augmentation of neonatal immunocompetence has been limited to the administration of polyclonal immune globulin preparations or, in certain circumstances (e.g., hepatitis B), the administration of specific hyperimmune globulin and/or vaccine. Initially promising results with polyclonal intravenous immune globulin for prevention of nosocomial infection in very-low-birth-weight infants[97,98] have not been confirmed in subsequent large trials to date.[99,100]

Vaccines against some infectious diseases (e.g., tetanus, rubella) that are administered to the mother prior to pregnancy may result in significant transplacental delivery of protective antibody to the fetus after the 32nd week of gestation. Development of a highly immunogenic vaccine against all serotypes of group B streptococcus is ongoing, but is far from implementation.[101,102]

The American Academy of Pediatrics has issued guidelines for intrapartum chemoprophylaxis of early-onset group B streptococcal infection based on previous investigations that used maternal vaginal and/or rectal colonization and the presence of clinical risk factors, including rupture of membranes for > 18 hours prior to delivery, preterm gestation, and maternal fever, to identify those at highest risk for having an infected infant.[103] This strategy was devised so that potential benefit could be maximized while adverse effects of the antibiotic could be minimized. These guidelines have been highly controversial. Multiple concerns with implementation have been identified, including (but not limited to) extrapolation of culture results obtained at 24-28 weeks of gestation to the time of delivery, management of those with limited or no prenatal care, availability of laboratory results to the professional actually supervising the delivery, and whether the risk factors identified in the earlier studies are universally applicable.[104-107] Alternative strategies based on other techniques for identifying high-risk circumstances have been reported to be equally or more cost effective than the strategy proposed by the American Academy of Pediatrics.[108] A recent cost-benefit analysis compared 17 different strategies for chemoprophylaxis and suggested that universal intrapartum administration of ampicillin may be the most cost effective option.[109] Concerns about the potential for large-scale induction of ampicillin resistance among group B streptococci, increasing the incidence of infections by such ampicillin-resistant organisms as *Escherichia coli*,[110] the validity of some of the underlying assumptions in this analysis, and a desire for confirmatory empiric data have resulted in widespread reluctance to adopt such a program at this point. At present, there is no agreement regarding the best strategy for chemoprophylaxis of early-onset group B streptococcal infection and many reasonable clinicians offer good justification for not embracing the particular standards promulgated by the American Academy of Pediatrics. Several reports include cases in which intrapartum antibiotics failed to prevent early-onset neonatal group B streptococcal infection.[105,111,112] At present, intrapartum chemoprophylaxis for early onset group B streptococcal infection is best viewed as a strategy in evolution.

The Future

Further improvement in mortality and morbidity attributable to neonatal infection is most likely to derive from refined prophylactic strategies and the development of methods to ameloriate or better focus the inflammatory and other pathophysiologic cascades that accompany infection. For the present, effective therapy will continue to depend on an appropriate level of suspicion for the diagnosis and its complications, timely institution of antimicrobial therapy targeted to likely organisms, and the judicious application of life support therapy. Microorganisms often, however, manage to stay one step ahead of scientists and clinicians. It would not be surprising if successful strategies for prevention and treatment of early-onset group B streptococcal disease are developed and implemented, just as natural, poorly understood forces induce the emergence of an alternative, currently underrepresented perinatal pathogen. It is highly likely that microorganisms will continue to offer formidable challenges to perinatal clinicians despite ongoing advances in clinical science.

> **Commentary by Dr. Donn:** Clinicians today also face an additional challenge—early discharge of the infant—often at or before 24 hours of age. This may not always allow a sufficient period of observation for the development of early-onset infection. Two areas of risk management are therefore necessary. First, institutional guidelines should be developed to delineate conditions under which diagnostic evaluation and therapeutic intervention are indicated. Such indications have been addressed thoroughly by Dr. Faix. Guidelines should be inclusive rather than exclusive. Second, extensive education of the parents is necessary. Parents must be informed of the signs of infection and instructed to seek medical attention if any of the signs arise. Documentation that such a discussion was held should be placed in the medical record, and parental signatures acknowledging that they received and understood such instructions are also worthwhile endeavors.

References

1. Klein JO, Marcy SM. Bacterial sepsis and meningitis. In: Remington JS, Klein JO (eds). *Infectious Diseases of the Fetus and Newborn Infant*, Fourth Edition. Philadelphia, WB Saunders Co, 1995, p. 835.

2. Weisman LE, Stoll BJ, Cruess DF, et al. Early-onset group B streptococcal sepsis: A current assessment. J Pediatr 1992;121:428.
3. Gladstone IM, Ehrenkranz RA, Edberg SC, et al. A ten-year review of neonatal sepsis and comparison with the previous fifty-year experience. Pediatr Infect Dis J 1990;9:819.
4. Eisenfeld L, Ermocilla R, Wistschafter D, et al. Systemic bacterial infections in neonatal deaths. Am J Dis Child 1983;137:645.
5. Pierce JR, Merenstein GB, Stocker JT. Immediate postmortem cultures in an intensive care nursery. Pediatr Infect Dis 1984;3:510.
6. Schuchat A, Oxytoby M, Cochi S, et al. Population-based risk factors for neonatal group B streptococcal disease: Results of a cohort study in metropolitan Atlanta. J Infect Dis 1990;162:672.
7. Karpuch J, Goldberg M, Kohelet D. Neonatal bacteremia: A 4-year prospective study. Isr J Med Sci 1983;19:963.
8. Minkoff H. Prematurity: Infection as an etiologic factor. Obstet Gynecol 1983;62:137.
9. Vesikari R, Janas M, Gronroos P, et al. Neonatal septicemia. Arch Dis Child 1986;60:542.
10. Freedman RM, Ingram DL, Gross I, et al. A half century of neonatal sepsis at Yale, 1928-1978. Am J Dis Child 1981;135:140.
11. Waites KB, Rudd PT, Crouse DT. Chronic *Ureaplasma urealyticum* and *Mycoplasma hominis* infections of central nervous systems in preterm infants. Lancet 1988;2:17.
12. Morey AL, Keeling JW, Porter HJ, et al. Clinical and histopathological features of parvovirus B19 infection in the human fetus. Br J Obstet Gynaecol 1992;99:566.
13. Placzek MM, Whitelaw A. Early and late neonatal septicaemia. Arch Dis Child 1983;58:728.
14. Jeffery H, Mitchison R, Wigglesworth JS, et al. Early neonatal acteraemia. Comparison of group B streptococcal, other Gram-positive and Gram-negative infection. Arch Dis Child 1977;52:683.
15. Conboy TJ, Pass RF, Stagno S, et al. Intellectual development in school-aged children with asymptomatic congenital cytomegalovirus infection. Pediatrics 1986;77:801.
16. Saxon SA, Knight W, Reynolds DW, et al. Intellectual deficits in children born with subclinical congenital toxoplasmosis: A preliminary report. J Pediatr 1978;82:792.
17. Sever JL, South MA, Shaver KA. Delayed manifestations of congenital rubella. Rev Infect Dis 1985;7(Suppl 1):S164.
18. Gibbs RS, Castillo MS, Rodgers PJ. Management of acute chorioamnionitis. Am J Obstet Gynecol 1980;136:709.
19. Klein JO, Remington JS. Current concepts of infections of the fetus and newborn infant. In: Remington JS, Klein JO (eds). *Infectious Diseases of the Fetus and Newborn Infant, Fourth Edition*. Philadelphia, WB Saunders Co, 1995, p. 1.
20. Boyer KM, Gadzala CA, Burn LT, et al. Selective intrapartum chemoprophylaxis of neonatal group B streptococcal early-onset disease. I. Epidemiologic rationale. J Infect Dis 1983;148:795.
21. Boucher M, Yonekura ML. Perinatal listeriosis (early-onset): Correlation of antenatal manifestations and neonatal outcome. Obstet Gynecol 1986;68:593.
22. Miller JM Jr, Pupkin MJ, Hill GB. Bacterial colonization of amniotic fluid from intact fetal membranes. Am J Obstet Gynecol 1980;136:796.

23. Stone HH, Kolb LD, Currie CA, et al. Candida sepsis: Pathogenesis and principles of treatment. Ann Surg 1974;179:697.
24. Krause W, Matheis H, Wulf K. Fungaemia and funguria after oral administration of *Candida albicans*. Lancet 1969;1:598.
25. Saez-Lorens X, McCracken GH Jr. Sepsis syndrome and septic shock in pediatrics: Current concepts of terminology, pathophysiology and management. J Pediatr 1993;123:497.
26. Bone RC. The pathogenesis of sepsis. Ann Intern Med 1991;115:457.
27. Giroir BP: Mediators of septic shock: New approaches for interrupting the endogenous inflammatory cascade. Crit Care Med 1993;21:780.
28. Glauser MP, Zanetti G, Baumgartner J-D, et al. Septic shock: Pathogenesis. Lancet 1991;338:732.
29. Parrillo JE. Pathogenetic mechanisms of septic shock. N Engl J Med 1993;328:1471.
30. Patriquin H, Lebowitz R, Perreault G, et al. Neonatal candidiasis: Renal and pulmonary manifestations. Am J Roentgenol 1980;135:1205.
31. Mahboubi S, Kaugmann HJ, Schut L. Two instances of inflammatory aqueductal occlusion in prematures after neonatal Candida septicaemia. Clin Pediatr 1976;15:651.
32. Dinorello CA, Gelfand JA, Wolff SM. Anticytokine strategies in the treatment of the systemic inflammatory response syndrome. JAMA 1993;269:1829.
33. McCloskey RV, Straube RC, Sanders C, et al. Treatment of septic shock with human monoclonal antibody HA-1A. Ann Intern Med 1994;121:1.
34. Kilpi T, Anttila M, Kallio MJ, et al. Length of prediagnostic history related to the course and sequelae of childhood bacterial meningitis. Pediatr Infect Dis J 1993;12:184.
35. Radetsky M. Duration of symptoms and outcome in bacterial meningitis: An analysis of causation and the implications of a delay in diagnosis. Pediatr Infect Dis J 1992;11:694.
36. Akenzua GI, Hui YT, Milner R, et al. Neutrophil and band counts in the diagnosis of neonatal infections. Pediatrics 1974;54:38.
37. Gregory J, Hey E. Blood neutrophil response to bacterial infection in the first month of life. Arch Dis Child 1972;47:747.
38. Xanthou M. Leukocyte blood picture in healthy full-term and premature babies during neonatal period. Arch Dis Child 1970;45:242.
39. Manroe BL, Weinberg AG, Rosenfeld CR, et al. The neonatal blood count in health and disease. I. Reference values for neutrophilic cells. J Pediatr 1979;95:89.
40. Engle WD, Rosenfeld CR. Neutropenia in high-risk neonates. J Pediatr 1984;105:982.
41. Christensen RD, Rothstein G. Pitfalls in the interpretation of leukocyte counts in newborn infants. Am J Clin Pathol 1979;72:608.
42. Herson VC, Block C, Eisenfeld LI, et al. Effect of labor and delivery on neonatal polymorphonuclear leukocyte number and function. Am J Perinatol 1992;9:285.
43. Coulombel L, Dehan M, Tchernia G, et al. The number of polymorphonuclear leukocytes in relation to gestational age in the newborn. Acta Paediatr Scand 1979;68:709.
44. Baley JE, Stork CK, Warkentin PI, et al. Neonatal neutropenia. Clinical manifestations, cause, and outcome. Am J Dis Child 1988;142:1161.
45. Schelonka RL, Yoder BA, desJardins SE, et al. Peripheral leukocyte count and leukocyte indexes in healthy newborn term infants. J Pediatr 1994;125:603.

46. Christensen RD, Rothstein G, Hill HR, et al. Fatal early onset group B streptococcal sepsis with normal leukocyte counts. Pediatr Infect Dis 1985;4:242.
47. Mouzinho A, Rosenfeld CR, Sanchez PJ, et al. Revised reference ranges for circulating neutrophils in very-low-birth-weight neonates. Pediatrics 1994;94:76.
48. Philip AGS, Hewitt JR. Early diagnosis of neonatal sepsis. Pediatrics 1980;65:1036.
49. Pourcyrous M, Bada HS, Korones SB, et al. Significance of C-reactive protein responses in neonatal infection and other disorders. Pediatrics 193;92:431.
50. Harris MC, Costarino AT, Sullivan JS, et al. Cytokine elevations in critically ill infants with sepsis and necrotizing enterocolitis. J Pediatr 1994;124:105. 51. Buck C, Bundschu J, Gallati H, et al. Interleukin-6: A sensitive parameter for the early diagnosis of neonatal bacterial infection. Pediatrics 1994;93:54.
52. Alford CA, Pass RF. Epidemiology of chronic congenital and perinatal infections of man. Clin Perinatol 1981;8:397.
53. Stagno S, Pass RF, Reynolds DW, et al. Comparative study of diagnostic procedures for congenital cytomegalovirus infection. Pediatrics 1980;65:257.
54. Naot Y, Desmonts G, Remington JS. IgM-enzyme linked immunosorbent assay test for the diagnosis of congenital *Toxoplasma* infection. J Pediatr 1981;98:32.
55. Wiswell TE, Hachey WE. Multiple site blood cultures in the initial evaluation for neonatal sepsis during the first week of life. Pediatr Infect Dis J 1991;10:365.
56. Ilstrup DM, Washington JA. Effect of atmosphere of incubation on recovery of bacteria and yeasts in tryptic soy broth. Diagn Microbiol Infect Dis 1983;1:215.
57. Murray PR, Traynor P, Hopson D. Critical assessment of blood culture techniques: Analysis of recovery of obligate and facultative anaerobes, strict aerobic bacteria, and fungi in aerobic and anaerobic blood culture bottles. J Clin Microbiol 1992;30:1462.
58. Weisman LE, Merenstein GB, Steenbarger JR. The effect of lumbar puncture position in sick neonates. Am J Dis Child 1983;137:1077.
59. Gleason CA, Martin RJ, Anderson WJ, et al. Optimal position for a spinal tap in preterm infants. Pediatrics 1983;71:31.
60. Teele DW, Dashefsky B, Rakusan T, et al. Meningitis after lumbar puncture in children with bacteremia. N Engl J Med 1981;305:1079.
61. Shaywitz BA. Spinal taps and epidermoid tumors. Hosp Pract 1973;8:79.
62. Visser VE, Hall RT. Lumbar puncture in the evaluation of suspected neonatal sepsis. J Pediatr 1980;96:1063.
63. Hendricks-Munoz KD, Shapiro DL. The role of the lumbar puncture in the admission sepsis evaluation of the premature infant. J Perinatol 1990;10:60.
64. Weiss MG, Ionides SP, Anderson CL. Meningitis in premature infants with respiratory distress: Role of admission lumbar puncture. J Pediatr 1991;119:973.
65. Schwersenski J, McIntyre L, Bauer CR. Lumbar puncture frequency and cerebrospinal fluid analysis in the neonate. Am J Dis Child 1991;145:54.
66. Eldadah M, Frenkel LD, Hiatt IM, et al. Evaluation of routine lumbar punctures in newborn infants with respiratory distress syndrome. Pediatr Infect Dis J 1987;6:243.
67. Fielkow S, Reuter S, Gotoff SP. Cerebrospinal fluid examination in symptom-free infants with risk factors for infection. J Pediatr 1991;119:971.
68. Shattuck KE, Choinmatree T. The changing spectrum of neonatal meningitis over a fifteen-year period. Clin Pediatr 1992;31:30.

69. Sarff LD, Platt LH, McCracken GH Jr. Cerebrospinal fluid evaluation in neonates: Comparison of high-risk infants with and without meningitis. J Pediatr 1976;88:473.
70. Rodriguez AF, Kaplan SD, Mason EO Jr. Cerebrospinal fluid values in the very low birth weigth infant. J Pediatr 1990;116:971.
71. Visser VE, Hall RT. Urine culture in the evaluation of suspected neonatal sepsis. J Pediatr 1979;94:635.
72. DiGeronimo RJ. Lack of efficacy of the urine culture as part of the initial workup of suspected neonatal sepsis. Pediatr Infect Dis J 1992;11:764.
73. Sherman MP, Goetzmann BW, Ahlfors CE, et al. Tracheal aspiration and its clinical correlates in the diagnosis of congenital pneumonia. Pediatrics 1980;65:258.
74. Lau YL, Hey E. Sensitivity and specificity of daily tracheal aspirates in predicting organisms causing bacteremia in ventilated neonates. Pediatr Infect Dis J 1991;10:290.
75. Evans ME, Schaffner W, Federspiel CF, et al. Sensitivity, specificity, and predictive value of body surface cultures in a neonatal intensive care unit. JAMA 1988;259:248.
76. Finelli L, Livengood JR, Saiman L. Surveillance of pharyngeal colonization: Detection and control of serious bacterial illness in low birth weight infants. Pediatr Infect Dis J 1994;13:854.
77. Kleiman MB, Reynolds JK, Watts NH, et al. Superiority of acridine orange stain versus Gram stain in partially treated bacterial meningitis. J Pediatr 1984;104:401.
78. Mathur NB, Saxena LM, Sarkar R, et al. Superiority of acridine orange-stained buffy coat smears for diagnosis of partially treated neonatal septicemia. Acta Paediatr 1993;82:533.
79. Sanchez PJ, Siegel JD, Cushion NB, et al. Significance of a positive urine group B streptococcal latex antigen test in neonates. J Pediatr 1990;116:601.
80. Ascher DP, Wilson S, Mendiola J, et al. Group B streptococcal latex agglutination testing in neonates. J Pediatr 1991;119:458.
81. Maxson S, Lewno MJ, Schutze GE. Clinical usefulness of cerebrospinal fluid bacterial antigen studies. J Pediatr 1994;125:235.
82. Harris MC, Deuber C, Polin RA, et al. Investigation of apparent false-positive urine latex particle agglutination tests for the detection of group B streptococcus antigen. J Clin Microbiol 1989;27:2214.
83. Relman DA, Loutit JS, Schmidt TM, et al. The agent of bacillary angiomatosis: An approach to the identification of uncultured pathogens. N Engl J Med 1990;323:1573.
84. Relman DA, Schmidt TM, MacDermott RP, et al. Identification of the uncultured bacillus of Whipple's disease. N Engl J Med 1992;327:293.
85. Sanchez PJ, Wendel GD, Grimprel K, et al. Evaluation of molecular methodologies and rabbit infectivity testing for the diagnosis of congenital syphilis and neonatal central nervous system invasion by *Treponema pallidum*. J Infect Dis 1993;167:148.
86. Tompkins LS. The use of molecular methods in infectious diseases. N Engl J Med 1992;327:1290.
87. Robinson PA, Knirsch AK, Joseph JA. Fluconazole for life-threatening fungal infections in patients who cannot be treated with conventional antifungal agents. Rev Infect Dis 1990;12(Suppl 3):S349.

88. Saag MS, Powderly WG, Cloud GA, et al. Comparison of amphotericin B with fluconazole in the treatment of acute AIDS-associated cryptococcal meningitis. N Engl J Med 1992;326:83.
89. Stevens DL, Yan S, Bryant AE. Penicillin-binding protein expression at different growth stages determines penicillin efficacy in vitro and in vivo: An explanation for the inoculum effect. J Infect Dis 1993;167:1401.
90. Finitzo-Hieber T, McCracken GH Jr, Roeser RJ, et al. Ototoxicity in neonates treated with gentamicin and kanamycin: Results of a four-year controlled follow-up study. Pediatrics 1979;63:443.
91. Finitzo-Hieber T, McCracken GH Jr, Brown KC. Prospective controlled evaluation of auditory function in neonates given netilmicin or amikacin. J Pediatr 1985;106:129.
92. McCracken GH, Mize SG. A controlled study of intrathecal antibiotic therapy in gram-negative enteric meningitis of infancy: Report of the Neonatal Meningitis Cooperative Study Group. J Pediatr 1976;89:66.
93. Schaad UB, McCracken GH Jr, Nelson JD. Clinical pharmacology and clinical efficacy of vancomycin in pediatric patients. J Pediatr 1980;96:119.
94. Pichichero MD, Todd JK. Detection of neonatal bacteremia. J Pediatr 1979;95:958.
95. Rowley AH, Wald ER. Incubation period necessary to detect bacteremia in neonates. Pediatr Infect Dis J 1986;5:590.
96. Escobar GJ, Zukin T, Usatin MS, et al. Early discontinuation of antibiotic treatment in newborns admitted to rule out sepsis: A decision rule. Pediatr Infect Dis J 1994;13:860.
97. Chirico G, Rondini G, Plebani A, et al. Intravenous gammaglobulin therapy for prophylaxis of infection in high-risk neonates. J Pediatr 1987;110:437.
98. Baker CJ, Melish ME, Hall RT, et al. Intravenous immune globulin for the prevention of nosocomial infection in low-birth-weight neonates. N Engl J Med 1992;327:213.
99. Fanaroff AA, Korones SB, Wright LL, et al. A controlled trial of intravenous immune globulin to reduce nosocomial infections in very-low-birth-weight infants. N Engl J Med 1994;330:1107.
100. Weisman LE, Stoll BJ, Kueser TJ, et al. Intravenous immune globulin prophylaxis of late-onset sepsis in premature neonates. J Pediatr 1994;125:922.
101. Baker CJ, Rench MA, Edwards MS, et al. Immunization of pregnant women with a polysaccharide vaccine of group B streptococcus. N Engl J Med 1988;319:1180. 102. Baker CJ. Immunization to prevent group B streptococcal disease: Victories and vexations. J Infect Dis 1990;161:917.
103. Committee on Infectious Diseases and Committee on Fetus and Newborn: Guidelines for prevention of group B streptococcus (GBS) infection by chemoprophylaxis. Pediatrics 1992;90:775.
104. Larsen JW, Dooley SL. Group B streptococcal infections: An obstetrical viewpoint. Pediatrics 1993;91:148.
105. Gibbs RS, McDuffie RS Jr, McNabb F, et al. Neonatal group B streptococcal sepsis during two years of a universal screening program. Obstet Gynecol 1994;84:496.
106. American College of Obstetrics and Gynecology. Group B streptococcal infections in pregnancy. ACOG Technical Bulletin 1992;170:1.
107. Baker CJ. Group B streptococcal infection in newborns: Prevention at last? N Engl J Med 1986;314:1702.

108. Moule-Boetani JC, Schuchat A, Plikaytis BD, et al. Comparison of prevention strategies for neonatal group B streptococcus infection: A population-based economic analysis. JAMA 1993;270:1442.
109. Rouse DJ, Goldenberg RL, Cliver SP, et al. Strategies for the prevention of early-onset neonatal group B streptococcal sepsis: A decision analysis. Obstet Gynecol 1994;83:483.
110. McDuffie RS Jr, McGregor JA, Gibbs RS. Adverse perinatal outcome and resistant enterobacteriaceae after antibiotic usage for premature rupture of the membranes and group B streptococcus carriage. Obstet Gynecol 1993;82:487.
111. Pylipow M, Gaddis M, Kinney JS. Selective intrapartum prophylaxis for group B streptococcus colonization: Management and outcome of newborns. Pediatrics 1994;93:631.
112. Ascher DP, Becker JA, Yoder BA, et al. Failure of intrapartum antibiotics to prevent culture-proved neonatal group B streptococcal sepsis. J Perinatol 1993;13:212.

Chapter 24

Neonatal Hypoglycemia

◆◆◆

Marvin Cornblath, M.D.

Introduction

Between January 1, 1992 and June 30, 1994, a total of 110 medico-legal cases were reviewed by this author. Fifty-one (46%) concerned issues related to hypoglycemia. Forty-eight of these (95%) involved *neonatal* hypoglycemia, of which four had no glucose determinations done at any time during the neonatal period. Thirty-six (71%) were reviewed for defense attorneys and 15 (29%) were reviewed for plaintiff attorneys. Of the latter, three (20%) were considered to be valid claims.

Commentary by Mr. Volk: Twenty percent of all patients that inquire as to whether or not they have a valid complaint about medical treatment do not have a valid claim. The rate of accepted cases in my practice, which is primarily plaintiff's medico-legal work, is approximately 3%. The cases Dr. Cornblath had sent to him for review were obviously pre-screened by the attorney sending them. Attorneys have obviously sought Dr. Cornblath because of his work dealing with hypoglycemia, and this is as it should be. Attorneys must have access to well-qualified physicians to review the merit or non-merit of a case to prevent frivolous claims.

This experience can be contrasted with that during the decade between 1977 and 1987. Of 168 total reviews, 51 (30%) concerned hypoglycemia, with 42 (82%) involving neonatal hypoglycemia, 5 (10%) involving hypoglycemia in infants, and 4 (8%) involving hypoglycemia in children over a year in age. Thirty-nine (76%) were reviewed for defense attorneys and 12 (24%)

From: Donn SM, Fisher CW (eds.): *Risk Management Techniques in Perinatal and Neonatal Practice.* © Futura Publishing Co., Inc., Armonk, NY, 1996.

were reviewed for plaintiff attorneys. Of the latter, 5 (41%) were considered to be valid claims. It would appear that the number of claims involving hypoglycemia has increased in recent years (5.1/year from 1977-1987 vs 20.4/ year from 1992-1994).

> **Commentary by Mr. Volk:** I believe that this apparent increase in claims involving hypoglycemia is explained by the fact that Dr. Cornblath has been requested to review claims that are related to his field. Attorneys are more sophisticated now in seeking physicians that are well qualified to evaluate a claim, and because of his obvious expertise in this area, he has been frequently contacted.

Whether this is a unique or a general phenomenon is unknown, but it is quite clear that this increase in litigation has not been associated with an increase in medically significant neonatal hypoglycemia in either the term or preterm populations. Surveys of the glucose values in the John Hopkins Hospital Neonatal Intensive Care Unit and its term nursery, indicate a frequency significantly less than that of 4-150/1000 live births reported in the 1970s and 1980s.[1]

The typical claim usually included a variety of outcomes ranging from mild cerebral palsy, dyslexia, or mental retardation to a vegetative state or even sudden unexplained deaths. These outcomes are attributed to "hypoglycemia," particularly if there is no other obvious causation and the newborn fits into any "at-risk" category. This has occurred even when no glucose determinations were obtained at the time of the alleged mishap. It is even more common if either an infrequent low screening value by a glucose oxidase test strip method or an isolated low laboratory glucose determination were recorded, or when hypoglycemia has been listed as a discharge diagnosis.

> **Commentary by Mr. Volk:** Obviously, it is the physician's responsibility to determine what the diagnosis is. Attorneys have to function within the medical facts as they exist. Physicians are there at the time the events are occurring and have the opportunity to document the course of the patient. The review of a case by the attorney may be weeks, months, or years after the events, and the potential claim must be evaluated based on the data that exist. If the physician makes an incorrect diagnosis, it is very difficult, if not impossible, for that physician to testify in a case that the diagnosis was "mistaken."

In the vast majority, only one or two glucose values at most are in the "hypoglycemic" range. In fact, of the 102 previously cited claims, about 10% involved significant hypoglycemia resulting from known causes (hypopituitarism, hyperinsulinemia, etc.); another 15%-20% were well documented, but experienced relatively short transitional courses of hypoglycemia. The majority *would not fulfill any medical criteria for significant hypoglycemia*.[1] Unfortunately, if there is no other obvious explanation (or an alternative hypothesis) for the patient's outcome, it is a difficult message to deliver.

Another common allegation is that an isolated blood glucose determination of 0 mg/dL, either by screening methods or laboratory analysis, clearly produced the brain damage because of the "severe hypoglycemia." Most often, the result is erroneous because of mishandling of the blood sample.[1] Furthermore, neither glucose oxidase test strips nor most laboratory glucose analysis techniques can measure a zero glucose concentration with any degree of accuracy. It is striking that when appropriate repetitive glucose analyses have been carefully obtained and properly recorded, it has been relatively easy to determine the role, if any, that hypoglycemia had in any specific outcome.

> **Commentary by Mr. Volk:** Clearly, there are cases when a newborn or a child is injured by the failure to timely detect and correct hypoglycemia. To attempt to "prove" that the injury to the child is not a result of a remarkably low blood glucose level, the documentation of this would have to be extraordinary. From the legal standpoint, it is the physician's burden to prove that the patient was not injured by the episode. If the physician fails to "prove" during the episode that there was an erroneous lab result, that is his/her problem. Make no mistake about it, that is a serious problem. To attempt to retrospectively advance the proposition that the lab result was inaccurate, without facts that strongly support the position, would be next to impossible.

Furthermore, within the past 5 or 6 years, neonatal hypoglycemia has been redefined in Great Britain to include any plasma glucose concentration < 47 mg/dL.[2-6] This definition is based on a flawed retrospective analysis of data from a prospective controlled feeding study[2] and on minimal changes in the brainstem auditory evoked potential (BAER) of one of five hypoglycemic infants studied in the neonatal period.[3] This definition resulted in a frequency of hypoglycemia of 66% in the low birth weight infants studied.[2] The fallacy of these studies is detailed elsewhere.[7] The impact of these criteria applied to current medico-legal litigation has been significant.

Medical Analysis

A variety of definitions of significant neonatal hypoglycemia exist. In the past these have included: 1. the response of clinical manifestations to glucose treatment; 2. statistical norms; 3. theoretical norms; and 4. neurodevelopmental outcomes usually correlated with less than adequate neonatal data. None are totally relevant to current nursery or intensive care unit populations. New data show correlations between laboratory determinations of plasma glucose concentrations and changes in neurophysiologic function (brainstem auditory and visual evoked potentials), as well as increases in cerebral blood flow, blood volume, and glucose utilization.[8,9] Ongoing measurements of glucose transporters, hormones, and receptors, as well as alternative substrates should provide additional leads in redefining neonatal hypoglycemia. As in all biologic phenomena, specific neurophysiologic and metabolic responses occur over a wide range of low plasma glucose concentrations in groups of newborns. Deviations from this range of norms represent a continuum of abnormality in any one newborn infant.

Definitions

As first formulated in 1937 by Hartmann and Jaudon[10] and now based on clinical and experimental data from both animals and humans, neonatal hypoglycemia can be defined as:

Minimal Hypoglycemia: Plasma glucose concentrations between 35 and 45 mg/dL;

Moderate Hypoglycemia: Plasma glucose concentrations between 25 and 35 mg/dL;

Profound Hypoglycemia: Plasma glucose concentrations between 20 and 25 mg/dL.

The diagnosis of hypoglycemia requires a reliably significant low plasma or serum glucose value for a newborn that may be present without (asymptomatic) or with (symptomatic) clinical signs and symptoms. Whether or not plasma glucose concentrations between 25 and 35-45 mg/dL are of any significance or consequence remain to be seen. The evidence to date does not support the conclusion that these plasma values *alone* correlate with impaired neurologic or intellectual outcomes. Yet, a number of pediatric neurologists, neonatologists, and other medical "experts," some of whom are credible physician-scientists, believe that blood glucose values in the range of 38-45 mg/dL can cause serious central nervous system damage within as short a time as 30 minutes. One should demand reliable and recognized experimental proof for these conclusions.[11]

> **Commentary by Mr. Volk:** The test for giving an expert opinion is based upon a reasonable degree of medical probability coupled with the education, training, and experience of the physician testifying. An expert has the right to give an opinion in a medico-legal case based upon this standard. The standard does not require proof to a medical certainty (P < 0.05). The burden is "more probable than

not." The problem of bringing medicine into the courtroom is that the law requires the proof of a fact "more probably than not" (P < 0.5). This is the standard in all legal cases, not just medicolegal ones.

Clinical Management

Clinical management of neonatal hypoglycemia is based on four principles:

1. Screening of infants at high risk for hypoglycemia;
2. Confirming that low plasma glucose screening values are real;
3. Demonstrating that clinical manifestations resulted from the low glucose concentration, as evidenced by their prompt resolution after adequate therapy;
4. Carefully observing and appropriately documenting all of these events.

Screening

All glucose oxidase test strips, whether read by the eye or by a meter, are too unreliable and variable to initiate therapy in the asymptomatic newborn or to establish the diagnosis in the symptomatic newborn.

> **Commentary by Mr. Volk:** This brings up an interesting point: If the strips are so inaccurate, is it, or should it be, below the standard of care to utilize and/or rely on them? This physician would be interested in balancing the cost of blood glucose determinations versus the utility of screening newborns with them. Another way of evaluating this question is to balance the cost of blood glucose screening versus the cost of an impaired newborn from undiagnosed and untreated hypoglycemia. We all know, or should know, that the cost of caring for an injured newborn is tremendous, often involving hundreds of thousands of dollars.

Glucose screening is indicated in all infants at any age with the following clinical manifestations: tremors, cyanosis, seizures, apnea, hypotonia, irregular respirations, lethargy, difficulty in feeding, hypothermia or temperature instability, exaggerated Moro reflex, irritability, high pitched cry, change in mental status, and/or coma. Rarely, episodes of vomiting, tachypnea, bradycardia, and eye rolling also occur. It should be emphasized that these clinical manifestions, especially in the newborn, are usually the result of causes other than hypoglycemia.[12]

Infants at Risk

Screening of "at-risk" infants can anticipate hypoglycemia in infants who are:

1. Large for gestational age (weight > 90th percentile);
2. Small for gestational age (weight < 10th percentile);
3. Smaller of discordant twins (weight discrepancy > 20%);
4. Preterm (< 37 weeks) or post-term (> 42 weeks) infants;
5. Delivered to mothers with late, little, or no prenatal care;
6. Polycythemic (central hemoglobin > 22 g/dL or hematocrit > 65%);
7. Hypothermic (rectal temperature < 36.5° C);
8. Born to insulin dependent or gestational diabetic mothers or massively obese mothers;
9. Apgar score of 5 or less at 5 minutes or later;
10. Significant hypoxia or perinatal distress requiring major resuscitation.

Screening is also important in those infants with the following rare, but important problems:

1. Microphallus, anterior midline defect, and direct or persistent hyperbilirubinemia;
2. Exomphalos, macroglossia, and gigantism;
3. Severe erythroblastosis;
4. Isolated hepatomegaly.

A positive family history of neonatal hypoglycemia or an unexplained death in infancy are other important reasons for screening.

In some nurseries all newborns are screened. The major consideration here is to avoid leaving a low screening value unconfirmed or without a carefully documented follow-up, even in a normal healthy infant.

Timing

Routine screening is usually done shortly after admission to the nursery at 30 minutes to 2 hours of age and repeated before feedings over the first 24 hours of age. If the infant is not feeding well or has been "NPO" for any reason, glucose can be monitored at 4-6, 12, 18, and 24 hours of age or whenever clinical manifestations are present. For practical purposes, screening is commonly discontinued after three or more normoglycemic values have been achieved.

Confirmation

If the screening value is < 45 mg/dL, a blood sample should be obtained to confirm the low value by a reliable laboratory method. Careful handling of the blood sample is necessary to prevent glycolysis (e.g., keep on ice, collect in a tube with a glycolytic inhibitor, analyze promptly). If the laboratory value is also low, appropriate therapy and follow-up are indicated.

Establishing the Diagnosis

In *primary hypoglycemia*, the clinical manifestations subside within minutes to hours in response to adequate treatment with intravenous glucose if hypoglycemia alone is responsible. If not, the signs and symptoms may well be *secondary* to a variety of neonatal problems that occur with or without hypoglycemia.

Treatment

Treatment should be instituted once the diagnosis has been confirmed by a reliable laboratory method. The following guidelines usually are able to maintain glucose concentrations at or above the 40-50 mg/dL range. The method used depends on the concentration of the plasma glucose, the condition of the infant, and the results of follow-up monitoring.

During the first hours after birth, the asymptomatic infant or the infant manifesting only episodes of tremors, irregular respirations, tachypnea, or hypotonia should be given a feeding, nursed, or given glucose water, and another plasma glucose determination should be done 30-60 minutes later. To date, no instances of neurologic impairment or cerebral injury have been substantiated when this approach has been utilized. If the repeat blood glucose is still low, follow the guidelines presented in Table 1. Repeat "before feeds" screening should be done until three are clearly normoglycemic (> 40-45 mg/dL).

> **Commentary by Mr. Volk:** If I were defending a physician (I do some medico-legal defense) in a claim alleging injury from undiagnosed and inadequately treated hypoglycemia, I would be uncomfortable with this. There is clearly room for an attorney to allege that there was a failure to timely diagnose and treat. The inquiry from the attorney will be: "Knowing the tremendous risk to the child from this condition, why didn't you evaluate the child for hypoglycemia and prevent the cerebral injury?" The next inquiry will be "How did you know that the tremors, etc. were not signs and symptoms of neurologic insult that caused cerebral damage that was irrevers-

Table 1
Guidelines for the Treatment of Neonatal Hypoglycemia

Plasma Glucose (mg/dL)	Asymptomatic or Mildly Symptomatic	Symptomatic
35–45	Nurse or give formula or 5% glucose by nipple or gavage	Start intravenous glucose to provide 4–6 mg/kg/min
25–34	Start intravenous glucose at 6–8 mg/kg/min as 5%–15% glucose solution, depending upon fluid needs and baby's clinical condition	Increase to 6–8 mg/kg/min
< 25	Mini-bolus of 0.25 g/kg glucose as 2.5 mL/kg of 10% or 1.0 mL/kg of 25% glucose at a rate of 1–2 mL/min and continue at rate to provide 6–8 mg/kg/min	

ible, and why didn't you treat it?" The next inquiry will be the cost of obtaining a blood glucose determination.

If symptomatic with episodes of seizures, limpness, irritability, difficulty in feeding, or comatose, start intravenous glucose at 6-8 mg/kg/min, utilizing the concentration of glucose that provides the total daily fluid requirement for the infant's specific needs.

It should be emphasized that the medical diagnosis of hypoglycemia requires a significantly low laboratory plasma or serum glucose determination that has been collected, analyzed, and properly recorded.

Commentary by Mr. Volk: If the health care provides (physicians, nurses, and laboratory personnel) do not ensure that the specimen is properly drawn, analyzed, and recorded, great difficulty will be had defending. If the physician testifies that the result was not reliable for whatever reason, the next questions from the attorney will be: "Whose responsibility is it to ensure that the result is reliable, and where did you document that you did not rely on the result?"

Monitoring and Modifying Treatment

For infants receiving intravenous glucose therapy, blood glucose values can be monitored at 1- to 2-hour intervals to be sure that normoglycemia has been achieved. If hypoglycemia persists or recurs, increase the amount of parenteral glucose by no more than 2 mg/kg/min at 1 to 2 hour intervals.

After 12-24 hours, add sodium chloride (40 mEq/L) to provide 2-3 mEq/kg/day for maintenance requirements. After 24 hours, potassium should also be added to the infusion.

Once stable, glucose monitoring can be continued at 4 to 8 hour intervals until adequate feeds and normoglycemia have been present for approximately 24 hours. Then, decrease the rate of glucose infusion, again by no more than 2 mg/kg/min at 1 to 2 hour intervals until discontinuation of parenteral fluids. Do not stop hypertonic glucose infusions abruptly or reactive hypoglycemia may ensue.

In some infants to whom it may be difficult or impossible to give parenteral glucose, especially on an emergent basis, glucagon (300 mcg/kg, not to exceed 1.0 mg total dose) may be given subcutaneously or intramuscularly while vascular access is being attempted.

If hypoglycemia persists after infusions of 10-12 mg/kg/min or more, or for longer than 2-3 days, obtain a blood sample for glucose, insulin, growth hormone, cortisol, and thyroid hormone, as well as ketones, lactic acid, uric acid, and alanine measurements, in order to rule out pathologic or recurrent causes of hypoglycemia, such as hyperinsulinism, hypopituitarism, or glycogen storage disease. While awaiting a definitive diagnosis, administer prednisone (2 mg/kg/day orally) or hydrocortisone (5 mg/kg/day orally or parenterally), obtain a consultation from a neonatologist or endocrinologist, and consider transfer to a neonatal intensive care unit for definitive diagnosis and care. If the insulin:glucose ratio exceeds 0.3 and the low blood glucose persists or recurs with parenteral glucose and steroids, consider using diazoxide (5-15 mg/kg/day in three divided doses) until consultation or transfer occurs.

Hypoglycemia may be secondary to a large variety of neonatal problems. If the clinical manifestations have not subsided within minutes to hours in response to what should be adequate treatment, a systematic clinical and laboratory diagnostic evaluation is indicated to determine the primary etiology. For this reason, monitoring is indicated in infants with:

1. Central nervous system pathology, including intrauterine or perinatal infection, congenital defects, hemorrhage or infarction, seizures, and change in mental status;
2. Asphyxia or hypoxia-ischemia;
3. Sepsis, notably bacterial;
4. Congenital heart disease, especially hypoplastic left heart syndrome;
5. Multiple congenital anomalies;
6. Maternal drug use or abuse;
7. Hypothyroidism;
8. Neonatal tetany;
9. TORCH or other congenital non-bacterial infections.

While support of any low plasma glucose level is indicated, the primary disease is usually responsible for the morbidity or mortality in these infants.

Hypoglycemia requiring therapy may also occur following an exchange transfusion; post-operatively; with malposition of an umbilical artery catheter; and most commonly, following the abrupt cessation of hypertonic parenteral glucose. These should always be considered under the appropriate circumstances.

Documentation

It is essential to document in the medical record all of the blood glucose values, their time of drawing, source, and method of analysis, as well as all clinical manifestations that might possibly be related to the hypoglycemia. Finally (most importantly and all too often neglected), be sure to note the response of the clinical manifestations as well as that of the plasma glucose concentration to the therapy that has been initiated. This is critical in order to establish a diagnosis and to measure the effectiveness of therapy. It is also important that all relevant observations or notations be compatible with each other. The medical progress notes and the nursing notes should both accurately reflect the condition of the infant, the laboratory results, treatment, and responses.

Great deliberation must be taken before hypoglycemia is listed as one of the discharge diagnoses. Again, it should be established with reasonable certainty, based upon: 1. laboratory determination of significantly low plasma glucose concentration; 2. a description of compatible clinical manifestations; 3. treatment that restores a normal plasma glucose concentration; and 4. resolution of clinical manifestations after the establishment of normoglycemia.

Conclusion

The prognosis for infants with either hypoglycemia alone or in combination with other perinatal problems remains to be established. Hypoglycemia of short duration (12-18 hours), even if symptomatic, does not appear to have any proven or well-documented long-term sequelae. Thus, the diagnosis and treatment of neonatal hypoglycemia should be carried out expediently, but should not be considered a medical emergency.

If the hypoglycemia is profound, persistent, or recurrent, there may be long-term consequences. More often than not, the hypoglycemia is associated with, or secondary to, a multiplicity of problems ranging from central nervous system anomalies to intrauterine infections, and the outcome may be more directly related to the primary problem than the secondary hypoglycemia.

Commentary by Mr. Volk: The allegations that an attorney may make involving this type of case could be some, or all, of the following:
1. Failure to timely screen the patient for hypoglycemia.
2. Failure to timely order a stat blood glucose determination.
3. Failure to follow blood glucose determinations serially.
4. Failure to timely institute proper treatment.
5. Failure to consult with a specialist.
6. Failure to transfer the patient.

Rebuttal by Dr. Cornblath: As usual, the approaches by the physicians and attorneys continue to differ. While we, as physicians, look for solutions, the attorneys look for negligence or willful neglect.

Short single episodes of hypoglycemia, even those lasting hours, have never been shown to be harmful or to damage the central nervous system in the neonate. Yet, our analysis of the consequences of this entity continues to be the source of multiple litigations.

In part, there is a matter of definitions. With three terms used by Mr. Volk, i.e., "timely," "laboratory or blood sampling errors," and "proof by the physician," I will try to illustrate our difficulties in this area.

"Timely." Some 20-30 years ago, "timely" was defined as "immediately" or "within the hour." Now, the data clearly show that hours of a single episode of hypoglycemia do not produce discernible central nervous system damage or developmental delays. So, "timely" now for parenteral therapy may be within 2, 4, or 6 hours— the sooner the better, but not as a medical emergency. The diagnostic blood test should be a reliable laboratory analysis, even if it takes 30-60 minutes to get. In contrast, the attorney and his "experts" consider "timely" to be a matter of minutes.

"Laboratory or blood sampling error" is rarely the fault of the treating physician. The Division of Laboratory Medicine is responsible for the quality assurance of the glucose analysis and for training laboratory personnel to adapt to the particular needs of the newborn infant and his blood sample.

"Proof by the physician," at the time of an event, is often impossible. In looking after a neonate or any other patient for that matter, we have an impression and work with that *hypothesis* until a *diagnosis* becomes apparent. Only time and further studies will elucidate what actually had occurred at a specific time in the neonatal course! The attorney treats the *impression*, which is only a working hypothesis, as a firm diagnosis or if incomplete, as a missed diagnosis.

These issues must continue to be discussed and resolved if we are to improve the quality of care and reduce the need for litigation.

References

1. Cornblath M, Schwartz R. *Disorders of Carbohydrate Metabolism in Infancy*, Third Edition. Boston, Blackwell Scientific Publications, 1991.
2. Lucas A, Morley R, Cole TJ. Adverse neurodevelopmental outcome of moderate neonatal hypoglycemia. Br Med J 1988;297:1304.
3. Koh THHG, Aynsley-Green A, Tarbit M, et al. Neural dysfunction during hypoglycaemia. Arch Dis Child 1988;63:1353.
4. Hawdon JM, Ward Platt MP. Metabolic adaptation in small for gestational age infants. Arch Dis Child 1993;68:262.
5. Hawdon JM, Weddell A, Aynsley-Green A, et al. Hormonal and metabolic responses to hypoglycaemia in small for gestational age infants. Arch Dis Child 1993;68:269.
6. Hawdon JM, Ward Platt MP, Aynsley-Green A. Prevention and management of neonatal hypoglycaemia. Arch Dis Child 1994;70:60.
7. Cornblath M, Schwartz R, Aynsley-Green A, et al. Hypoglycemia in infancy—the need for a rational definition. Pediatrics 1990;85:834.
8. Pryds O, Griesen G, Friis-Hansen B. Compensatory increase of CBF supports cerebral metabolism in preterm infants during hypoglycemia. Acta Paediat Scand 1988;77:632.
9. Pryds O, Christiansen NJ, Friis-Hansen B. Increased cerebral flow and plasma epinephrine in hypoglycemic, preterm neonates. Pediatrics 1990;85:172.
10. Hartmann AF, Jaudon JC. Hypoglycemia. J Pediatr 1937;11:1.
11. Brent RL. The irresponsible expert witness: A failure of biomedical graduate education and professional accountability. Pediatrics 1982;70:754.
12. Pildes R, Forbes AE, O'Connor SM, et al. The incidence of neonatal hypoglycemia—a completed survey. J Pediatr 1967;70:76.

Chapter 25

Hypoxic-Ischemic Encephalopathy and Traumatic Intracranial Injuries

◆◆◆

Michael V. Johnston, M.D., Steven M. Donn, M.D.

Introduction

A significant proportion of obstetrical and neonatal malpractice litigation concerns allegations that permanent brain injury and subsequent neurologic disability (i.e., cerebral palsy, epilepsy, and mental retardation) arose from negligence by health care providers during the pregnancy, labor, delivery, and immediate neonatal period. While there is little question that some fetuses and infants do sustain permanent brain injury as a consequence of hypoxia and ischemia during this time frame, they represent a very small percentage of the total number of neurologically impaired infants.[1] Many of the events occur at a time when the fetus is not accessible to medical intervention. Many writers have repeated Little's[2] conclusion in 1862 that brain injury during the birth process is responsible for many cases of spastic cerebral palsy. However, careful experimental and epidemiologic research over the last two decades indicates that Sigmund Freud's[3] analysis of the cause and effect is more often correct. He concluded from his pioneering research on cerebral palsy that babies with pre-existing brain abnormalities tend to have abnormal labors and deliveries. Recent evidence indicates that babies with established cerebral palsy originating early in gestation are often carried to term and exhibit signs of "distress," such as abnormal fetal heart rate tracings and low Apgar scores because their abnormal nervous systems are poorly equipped to withstand the normal stresses of labor.[4,5] The signs of distress are then incorrectly assumed to be related to an acute disorder at term, such as asphyxia. This fundamental change in thinking about the causes and timing

From: Donn SM, Fisher CW (eds.): *Risk Management Techniques in Perinatal and Neonatal Practice.* © Futura Publishing Co., Inc., Armonk, NY, 1996.

of many childhood brain disorders is germane to arguments that are typically central to "bad baby" cases. In the medico-legal climate, the matter is further complicated by the frequent use of imprecise terminology or the inaccurate application of descriptors, which can later serve to undermine the successful defense of a malpractice claim (see Chapter 34).

Definitions and Diagnoses

Diagnoses and medical terms written about infants in the contemporaneous medical record are powerful evidence that is difficult to overcome even when, in hindsight, they have been clearly misapplied. Accordingly, the importance of choosing appropriate terminology for describing the physiologic events of the pregnancy, labor, delivery, and the neonatal period cannot be overemphasized. Diagnoses recorded in the neonatal record are often carried forward uncritically by subsequent health care professionals. One of the most overused diagnoses applied to infants with a variety of neonatal disorders is "birth asphyxia." When applied inappropriately, the term can imply negligence when none existed and also can inhibit the search for other causes of cerebral palsy, such as metabolic, infectious, and genetic disorders.

Understanding basic definitions is key to comprehending the mechanisms of brain injury in this setting. The term *hypoxia* refers to a reduction in the amount of oxygen that reaches the lungs and is technically called *alveolar hypoxia*. If this is sufficient to result in a decrease in oxygen in the blood, the term *hypoxemia* is used. From a practical standpoint, it has become common to use the two terms interchangeably. However, it is noteworthy that these terms do not imply anything about brain levels of oxygen and the brain's response thereto, which differs markedly according to the age of the fetus and other circumstances, such as the affinity of hemoglobin at different ages to release oxygen into the tissues. The percentage of available binding sites to which oxygen is bound is referred to as the *saturation. Oxygen levels in the blood are most accurately measured using blood gas analysis of the partial pressure of oxygen (also referred to as the oxygen tension)*, PaO_2. Two other terms, *hypercapnea* and *hypercarbia* refer to an elevation of carbon dioxide in the blood and indicate suboptimal lung ventilation and/or reduced blood flow to the lungs. Hypercapnea is associated with an elevated partial pressure of carbon dioxide in the blood, the $PaCO_2$. *Acidosis* refers to a condition characterized by lowering of the pH of the blood because of an excess in the hydrogen ion concentration. *Metabolic acidosis* results from the production of excess acids, such as lactic acid, and is generally a consequence of inadequate provision of oxygen to tissues or a metabolic block in the oxidation of energy substrates. *Respiratory acidosis* results from hypercapnea (hypercarbia) because carbon dioxide is inadequately removed from the blood and functions as a weak acid, lowering blood pH. *Mixed acidosis* occurs when both metabolic and respiratory components are involved. *Asphyxia* is a condition in which there is a failure of the organ of respiration. For the fetus, the organ of respiration is the placenta, whereas for the newborn it is the lung. Asphyxia should always include hypoxemia, hypercapnea, and acidosis. Unless all three conditions are present, an asphyxial state cannot be said to exist. From a neurologic standpoint, definition of the term is imprecise because there is no clear cut index of blood gas abnormalities that are known to cause brain damage. A recent National Institutes of Health consensus meeting on the definition of "acute perinatal asphyxia" generally agreed that an umbilical cord blood pH < 7.0, a 5 minute Apgar score of < 3, and hypercarbia and hypoxemia are important characteristics of asphyxia.[6] Asphyxia severe enough to damage the brain or other organs is also associated with *ischemia* or a reduction in regional blood flow.[7] Without ischemia, compensatory changes in regional blood flow and other physiologic variables, such as changes in oxyhemoglobin dissociation, can often deliver enough oxygen to remain below the threshold for tissue injury. The word ischemia is frequently coupled with hypoxia in the fetus and newborn giving rise to *hypoxic-ischemic* conditions. Brain hypoxia-ischemia severe enough to produce injury over the long term always produces brain dysfunction in the hours or days after the insult. This is referred to as *encephalopathy*, describing a condition in which many of the brain's functions are disrupted, including consciousness, body tone, swallowing, and breathing.[8,9]

Encephalopathy from hypoxia-ischemia is usually also associated with seizures beginning 8-24 hours after the insult.[8,10,11] It is generally accepted that hypoxemia in a baby does not damage the brain unless there is an acute clearly demonstrable period of encephalopathy.[9,12] The encephalopathy associated with asphyxia is called *hypoxic-ischemic encephalopathy* (HIE), because both conditions are necessary to produce damage under experimental circumstances. However, it is important to approach the differential diagnosis of encephalopathy in an infant with an open mind. Brain dysfunction severe enough to disrupt consciousness and other vital functions can be produced by many disorders, including pre-existing brain injury, trauma, inborn errors of metabolism, and sepsis. Pre-existing brain injury can often cause some signs of HIE such as seizures.[13] For example, several babies have been reported with cystic brain lesions diagnosed on antenatal sonographic examination. They then went on to display a brief period of neonatal seizures following delivery. These infants lacked the fully developed syndrome of HIE as described by Sarnat and Sarnat[8] and demonstrate the confusion that is possible when trying to make a specific diagnosis. It is often useful to assign the term "encephalopathy" to an infant without specifying that the encephalopathy resulted from asphyxia unless the circumstances are well founded.[14]

Words used to describe timing related to labor and delivery are also subject to confusion and careful selection of terms is again crucial. *Intrauterine* refers to the period of time the fetus remains in the womb, and it is often used synonymously with the term *prenatal*. *Intrapartum* refers to the period of time from the onset of labor until the delivery of the fetus, while *neonatal* refers to the first 28 days of the infant's life. *Postnatal* refers to events which occur after birth and generally relate to the infant, whereas *postpartum* refers to events after birth that relate to the mother. The term *perinatal* is rather imprecise; it refers to the period of time "around birth" but is non-specific. Various uses of perinatal define it anywhere from the twentieth week of gestation through the neonatal period. We prefer not to use it in the context of describing hypoxic-ischemic events for this reason. Timing of a harmful event is often critically important when assessing a health care provider's liability. Since it is the brain's response to the stressful labor and delivery that is important for long-term outcome, timing of an injury should be based on the assessment of the brain's function. However, good indicators of brain function are not available until birth, and even then it would be hard to assess. While intrauterine fetal monitoring provides a measurement of fetal stress, it is primarily a cardiovascular measurement and has been shown to be inadequate for assessing the impact of this stress on the infant's brain.[4] Currently, the most reliable evidence for the timing of a damaging hypoxic-ischemic event comes from the behavior and diagnostic testing of the newborn infant. To interpret this evidence, it is important to understand some of the important features of the pathophysiology of asphyxia.

Pathophysiology of Asphyxia

Asphyxia can result from numerous conditions that interfere with oxygen delivery and carbon dioxide removal. For the fetus, this may involve maternal problems (such as diabetes mellitus or severe hypertension), utero-placental problems (such as placenta previa or abruptio placentae), or fetal problems (such as severe anemia or congenital malformations).[15] For the newborn, it may involve infection, apnea, congenital malformations (such as heart defects or pulmonary hypoplasia), or a host of other conditions. Not all asphyxial states result in serious injuries. In fact, the vast majority of asphyxial insults are well tolerated and do not cause brain damage because of inherent protective mechanisms present in the fetus and newborn.[7,12] These protective mechanisms contribute to what is known as "fetal reserves" and they resemble the "diving seal reflex" that protects the vital organs of air-breathing aquatic mammals who undertake a prolonged dive in an environment devoid of oxygen.[16] These adaptive mechanisms work to preserve the total amount of

Table 1

Effects of Hypoxia-Ischemia on Various Organs/Systems and Its Evaluation

Organ/System	Major Effect(s)	Evaluation
Kidney	Acute tubular necrosis	Urine output Urinalysis BUN, creatinine
Lung	Shock lung Pulmonary hypertension	Radiograph Blood gases
Liver	Hepatocellular injury	Liver enzymes Bilirubin
Gut	Necrotizing enterocolitis	Stool blood Radiograph
Parathyroid	Hypocalcemia	Calcium
Pancreas	Hypo/hyperglycemia	Glucose
Muscle	Rhabdomyolysis	Urine myoglobin Muscle enzymes
Skin	Subcutaneous fat necrosis	Physical examination
Hematologic	Coagulopathy	Coagulation profile Red blood cell smear
Bladder	Asphyxiated bladder syn- drome	Bladder drainage
Hypothalamic	Syndrome of Inappropriate Antidiuretic Hormone (SIADH)	Serum osmolality Urine osmolality
Heart	Tricuspid regurgitation Myocardial dysfunction	Echocardiography
Adrenal	Hemorrhage	Sonography
Brain	Encephalopathy	Imaging EEG

oxygen delivered to the brain by increasing cerebral blood flow and other means at a time when available oxygen is limited.

When a fetus is faced with a hypoxic threat, the first goal is the preservation of oxygen delivery to the organs, which are essential to maintain life-the brain, heart, and adrenal glands (Table 1). The first two are for obvious reasons. The adrenal glands regulate intermediary metabolism and are responsible for elaborating the catecholamine hormones that maintain blood pressure and increase glucose in response to stress. In order to provide these organs with available oxygenated blood flow, a redistribution takes place, such that there is a marked reduction in blood flow to other organs not essential for immediate survival, such as the kidneys, lungs, liver, spleen, gastro-intestinal tract, muscle, and skin. For some period of time, this allows adequate delivery of oxygen to the brain. Oxygen delivery is the mathematical product of blood oxygen content times regional blood flow. If the oxygen content were to drop by 50% causing significant hypoxia, oxygen delivery remains the same if blood flow doubles. As long as this relationship allows adequate oxygen delivery to proceed and brain oxygen requirements are met, injury is avoided. If, on the other hand, compensatory mechanisms become exhausted, inadequate oxygen delivery can cause brain injury. Experimental models indicate that it is difficult or impossible to damage the brain through a hypoxic mechanism without a concurrent reduction in regional cerebral blood flow or ischemia.[7] This is why potentially damaging insults to the brain are referred to as "hypoxic-ischemic." It is noteworthy that the normal fetus is adapted to a relative state of hypoxemia in utero compared to extrauterine life. The immature brain's oxygen requirements are far below the oxygen requirements for older children and adults, another adaptation to the hypoxemic stress of birth.[17]

Because of the redistribution of blood flow, hypoxic-ischemic conditions severe enough to produce brain injury almost always cause hypoxic-ischemic injuries to multiple other organs as well.[18] Therefore, allegations that brain injury resulted from hypoxia and ischemia in the intrapartum period must be accompanied by evidence of hypoxic-ischemic injury to the other organs and systems. The interruption of oxygenated blood flow to these organs and systems results in measurable and predictable derangements of function (Table 1). Evidence of dysfunction is usually clinically discernible but should be verified by laboratory and radiographic studies (see below).

The Neurotoxic Cascade

Physiologic studies of asphyxia in fetal and neonatal sheep and primates have provided several insights into the pathophysiology of asphyxia that correspond to the clinical disorder in humans. Studies of infant monkeys demonstrated that prolonged partial occlusion of the umbilical cord is more likely to produce long-term brain damage than acute total asphyxia at birth.[16] This is consistent with observations in several other animal models showing that severe acute hypoxia or anoxia (total lack of oxygen) causes cardiac asystole before enough time has passed for permanent brain injury to occur. The newborn can withstand only brief periods of total asphyxia and if resuscitation is rapid, little or no brain damage results. Although this profound level of asphyxia is damaging if prolonged, long-term neurologic deficits are often prevented because complete asphyxia severe enough to damage the brain is often incompatible with resuscitation—that is, it is fatal. On the other hand, prolonged partial asphyxia allows long periods of brain damaging ischemia to take place without a lethal insult to the heart. This study in monkeys is compatible with clinical observations of the large National Collaborative Perinatal Project.[19] This enormous study indicated that prolonged periods of severely depressed Apgar scores (< 3) for > 15 minutes were required to see any significant increase in the incidence of cerebral palsy in survivors. Similar studies of the asphyxial periods needed to produce brain injury have been reproduced in sheep.[20]

Another concept that has become generally acceptable in both the experimental literature and in clinical practice is the idea of delayed neuronal necrosis and dysfunction following a hypoxic-ischemic insult.[21] From a clinical standpoint this means that a substantial delay occurs between the time that a hypoxic-ischemic injury is triggered or reaches threshold and the time that clinical and histologic manifestations appear. Clinically, a delay of 8-12 hours or longer typically occurs following a substantial hypoxic-ischemic insult and the subsequent appearance of encephalopathy and neonatal seizures.[11,16] The experimental animal literature has validated this concept in several ways. When brains of animals subjected to hypoxia-ischemia are examined microscopically, at intervals following the insult, no cellular changes can be seen for hours. Typically, an experimental animal or infant dying acutely from an asphyxial event has no abnormalities in the brain. Recent experimental study with investigational pharmaceuticals that can protect the brain from hypoxic-ischemic injury indicate that there is a variable but definite "therapeutic window" in which the drugs can be given following the insult to reduce brain injury.[21] All of these observations support the notion of a neurotoxic cascade or biochemical event triggered by hypoxia-ischemia to cause neuronal death.[21-23] Two key features of this cascade are the release of toxic levels of the neurotransmitter amino acid, glutamate, and generation of free radicals of oxygen that tear apart neuronal membranes. Although the details of this series of events are not germane to this discussion, the theory provides a conceptual framework that is indeed clinically applicable. These observations indicate that brain injury is not complete and irrevocable at the time of the asphyxial insult but requires hours to days to fully develop. The neurotoxic cascade can be manipulated with drugs and also with temperature with a trend towards enhanced injury and glutamate release with high temperatures and reduced glutamate release with low temperatures. The theory explains why partial prolonged ischemia can be worse than total asphyxia, since low levels of oxygen delivered to the brain during partial ischemia can promote generation of toxic oxygen free radicals.[7,24]

This information is also consistent with observations that an infant who has sustained an acute neurologic insult during labor and delivery sufficient to cause brain damage will display an acute neonatal neurologic syndrome, referred to as HIE, over many hours. Four features characterize this syndrome: 1. an alteration in the level of consciousness, ranging from irritability to coma; 2. a diminution or loss of neurologic reflexes; 3. an alteration in neuromuscular tone, with a predominance of hypotonia and persistence of weakness, particularly of the proximal limbs; and 4. convulsions (seizures), which occur in 30%-69% of cases, and which generally have their onset 8-12 hours after brain injury.[8-11,16] Additional features with a variable presentation include cerebral edema, which typically peaks at 2-3 days, increased intracranial pressure, which results in a tense, bulging anterior fontanel, and widening of the sutures.

From a clinical standpoint, two of the most important pieces of information relate to the characteristics of a seizure: the child's overall tone and mobility. Although the baby may have brief periods of stiffening with generalized muscle jerking during an acute severe asphyxial event, restoration of oxygenation generally causes flaccidity and low tone within minutes. Usually the terms "flaccidity" and "low tone" are used to describe the infant who is relaxed without neck stretching or outstretched limbs, and whose limbs are easily mobile when examined with joint motions. Prolonged periods of neck extension with high tone in the extensor muscles of the back or extensor spasm with rigidity of the limbs following an asphyxial event generally indicates that the infant's nervous system has been abnormal for weeks to months. Such infants are literally "born with cerebral palsy" and respond to the stress of labor and delivery with enhanced tone. Interpretation of involuntary movement in newborn infants requires experienced observers. Video-EEG observation may be necessary for careful observations.[25] There is debate about whether certain kinds of movements such as episodic arching actually represents seizure activity or are a "release." Therefore, careful analysis of "spells" in infants is important. However, based on our current knowledge, observation of "early seizures" places the actual hypoxic-ischemic insult at least 6 or more hours earlier. Not all neonatal encephalopathy is the result of hypoxic-ischemic brain injury. Many factors other than asphyxia can cause an infant to appear encephalopathic, including central nervous system malformations, infections, chromosomal anomalies, drugs and toxins, inborn errors of metabolism, and trauma.[14] Additionally, hypoxic-ischemic insults remote and unrelated to labor and delivery can result in an encephalopathic newborn. The proportion of encephalopathy related to intrapartum hypoxic-ischemic events is not known but has been estimated by some to be extremely small.[26] Infants with encephalopathy should be carefully evaluated for the presence of genetic or metabolic disease. Occurrence of minor congenital anomalies increases the chance that the encephalopathy is secondary to a congenital brain malformation.[1] Hypoplasia of the enamel of the primary teeth has been reported to occur frequently in infants with congenital cerebral palsy.[27] This may time the disorder that produced the cerebral palsy to mid-gestation when the enamel of primary teeth is forming.

Imaging studies of the brain can be helpful to detect evidence of early gestational malformations or insults that caused cerebral palsy in the fetus prior to delivery. For example, dysgenesis of the anterior genu of the corpus callosum originates at approximately 8 weeks of gestation, while dysgenesis of the posterior segment of the corpus callosum originates later in mid-gestation.[28] Malformations of the posterior fossa, including the Chiari malformations, the Dandy-Walker Syndrome, and its variant, the mega cisterna magna, originate at 4 to 18 weeks gestation.[29,30] Evidence of periventricular leukomalacia (see Chapter 26) in the term infant is also strong evidence for an earlier intrauterine event, since this picture of damage to the cerebral white matter seldom occurs beyond 34 weeks of gestation.[31] The diagnosis of periventricular leukomalacia (PVL) in a term infant suggests that the child's cerebral palsy resulted from a brain disorder usually between 24 and 34 weeks gestation.

Recent observations on cerebral palsy occurring in identical twins and in infants born to mothers with iodide-deficient hypothyroidism have enhanced our understanding of mechanisms for cerebral palsy produced in the second trimester of pregnancy.[32-34] In 15% of monozygotic twin pregnancies there may be an imbalance in blood flow, such that one twin suffers from hypovolemia from blood loss and hypoxia from utero-placental insufficiency during the second trimester.[35] There is a high rate of cerebral palsy related to PVL in survivors of these pregnancies. Cerebral palsy is also common in twins who survive the intrauterine death of the other twin.[32] This example clearly demonstrates the pathophysiologic mechanism that could damage the brain of a fetus in the second trimester followed by retention in utero for a number of weeks. Another example of an in utero mechanism of cerebral palsy is the incidence of rigid spastic cerebral palsy in Chinese patients with endemic thyroid goiter related to dietary iodine insufficiency.[34] Recent studies indicate that dietary supplementation through the end of the second trimester is successful at preventing cerebral palsy through this mechanism. Strangely, later supplementation does not. These studies indicate that brain development during the second trimester and early third trimester is critically important in organizing the motor systems that are abnormal in cerebral palsy. These examples illustrate how it is that infants can be "born with cerebral palsy."

Hypoxia-ischemia damages the developing brain's motor systems more easily than regions that will be used for learning and memory. This may be related to the active state of development of these systems in the fetus. In the preterm infant or fetus, the central white matter carrying motor nerve fibers to the limb muscles is selectively vulnerable to injury (see Chapter 26).

Gray matter structures, such as the basal ganglia, can also be damaged in the preterm infant or fetus along with the white matter pattern of PVL.[36] This can cause the motor disorder, spastic diplegia, or quadriplegia, sometimes associated with "extrapyramidal" cerebral palsy. In the term infant or fetus, the gray matter containing regions, such as the motor cortex and basal ganglia, become more vulnerable to hypoxic-ischemic damage and the white matter becomes less vulnerable.[37] During this period, damage to gray matter is much more prominent than is white matter injury. At term, some infants exhibit a parasagittal "watershed" pattern of cortical damage, which is associated with proximal limb weakness in the shoulders and thighs.[38] Damage to the basal ganglia, sometimes called "status marmoratus" can result in extrapyramidal cerebral palsy. Cases of relatively selective damage to the putamen and thalamus without other imaging abnormalities have been reported following severe asphyxia at term.[31] In infants born at term, PVL-type changes in white matter that are more prominent than damage to cerebral cortex and/or basal ganglia strongly suggest that injury occurred during fetal life prior to 34 weeks gestation. An important corollary of the special vulnerability of motor systems to hypoxic-ischemic damage is that mental retardation, with or without seizures, is very unlikely to be caused in a child by hypoxia-ischemia if the motor signs of cerebral palsy are absent.[12,21]

Another long-term sequela is acquired microcephaly. The head circumference, an indirect but predictive measure of brain size, falls within the normal range at birth, but because of the loss of cortical neurons, it never achieves its genetically programmed potential and eventually falls below the third percentile. It is noteworthy that a similar pattern can be seen after a second trimester brain insult.

Traumatic Intracranial Injuries

The modern obstetrical era has seen a dramatic fall in the incidence of infant deaths attributable to birth trauma. In 1993, traumatic birth injury accounted for only 3.7 infant deaths per 100,000 live births.[39] Many factors probably account for this improved outcome, including the development of sonography, the more liberal use of operative and assisted delivery, and better fetal surveillance.

The vast majority of traumatic injuries are fortunately benign. Serious traumatic injuries may occur in rare instances, even under the best of circumstances and without medical negligence. From a risk management standpoint, when traumatic injury does occur, clinical management should be directed to thorough diagnosis of associated problems and prompt treatment to minimize long-term complications. Risk management techniques include careful documentation of both obstetrical and neonatal events, recognized risk factors, the planned course of action, complications that were encountered and how they were handled, and all communications with the family. Any potentially serious problem should have a well-orchestrated plan of follow-up and appropriate consultation should be sought for those problems that require subspecialty expertise.

Etiology

Traumatic birth injuries result from the disruption of tissues by mechanical forces that place undue torsion, traction, or pressure on these structures. While this is clearly a different mechanism from injury caused by hypoxia and ischemia, the two may exist concomitantly and share an interrelationship.[40] For example, the fetus who sustains a significant hypoxic-ischemic insult in utero may become hypotonic resulting in the inability to withstand the normal forces of parturition.[41] Similarly, fetal macrosomia may prolong labor resulting in protracted fetal head compression, and if shoulder dystocia develops, it may cause stress on the fetal neck and shoulder girdle. Traumatic injury may occur to the fetus in an abnormal presentation as the result of the misapplication of the forces of labor and delivery.

Traumatic intracranial injuries (see below) require a significant degree of force. The brain of a fetus, even if preterm, has a very high water content (an excellent cushioning medium) and is surrounded by a bony skull. The forces necessary to disrupt the intracranial contents will almost always produce external evidence of trauma, such as bruising, abrasions, lacerations, or skull fractures. Although acceleration-deceleration injuries do occur, such as when a pregnant woman is involved in a high velocity motor vehicle accident, the rate of fetal descent and movement through the birth canal is but a fraction of that believed to be necessary to result in such injuries, even if the delivery is precipitous.

Obstetric Factors and Traumatic Birth Injury

A number of obstetric factors have been identified that may predispose the fetus to traumatic birth injuries. These include prematurity, malpresentation, assisted delivery, prolonged labor, shoulder dystocia, cephalopelvic disproportion, macrosomia, version and extraction, and maternal trauma.[42] However, the presence of one or more of these factors is not sufficient evidence that a poor neurologic outcome is the result of birth trauma. For instance, a fetus may be malpresented because of a pre-existing brain injury or anomaly that hindered fetal movement in utero. Nevertheless, it behooves the obstetrician to carefully document their occurrence and the resultant plan of action. Likewise, the pediatrician or neonatologist must thoroughly examine the infant to rule out even subtle injuries that could be of consequence.

The list of potential traumatic injuries is lengthy, but fortunately, the majority of these has a favorable long-term prognosis.[40] It is beyond the scope of this chapter to summarize each of these, and several reviews are available for this purpose.[40,42] In the context of working-up the encephalopathic newborn, traumatic intracranial and extracranial hemorrhages will be considered.

Traumatic Intracranial Hemorrhage

The clinical manifestations of traumatic intracranial hemorrhage depend upon the degree of blood loss, anatomic site, and associated injuries, including hypoxia-ischemia if present. Bleeding may occur within the subdural, epidural, or subarachnoid spaces, or it may occur within the brain parenchyma or the ventricular system. Combinations are also possible. When blood loss is significant, hypovolemia may lead to signs of hypoperfusion and shock. Neurologic findings may range from asymptomatic to profound coma or evidence of brainstem compression with respiratory arrest and cardiovascular collapse.

Subdural Hemorrhage

Three different circumstances may result in subdural hemorrhage (SDH).[43] In the first, the tentorium is lacerated and there is rupture of the vein of Galen and straight and lateral sinuses. In the second, the falx is lacerated and there is rupture of the inferior sagittal sinus. In the third, SDH results from rupture of the superficial cerebral veins. Newborns with infratentorial hemorrhage show evidence of compression of the midbrain and pons-stupor or coma, abnormal pupillary responses, skew eye deviation, and nuchal rigidity. If the falx is lacerated, cerebral signs are usually present-seizures and evidence of upper motor neuron dysfunction.[44] Rupture of superficial cerebral veins, the most common etiology, may produce no neurologic findings or cerebral signs.

The diagnosis of SDH is best made by computed tomography. Neurosurgical consultation is recommended, since symptomatic infants may require drainage or exploration in severe cases.

Epidural Hemorrhage

This rare form of intracranial hemorrhage may present diagnostic difficulties. Sixty to seventy percent will have an associated skull fracture. Neonatal epidural hemorrhage is venous, resulting from rupture of the dural emissary veins when the dura detaches from the internal cranial periosteum.[45] Symptoms may be delayed for up to several days and may evolve from a falling hematocrit and full fontanel to a tense, bulging fontanel with increasing head circumference and evidence of brainstem compression.[46]

Computed tomography is the imaging modality of choice. Treatment involves blood replacement and neurosurgical intervention for decompression, so prompt consultation is mandatory.

Subarachnoid Hemorrhage

Primary subarachnoid hemorrhage (SAH) may be multi-factorial, involving hypoxia, trauma, or both. The cause is frequently indeterminate. Traumatic SAH results from rupture of the dural bridging veins with bleeding into the subarachnoid space. The most common clinical presentation is neonatal seizure, followed by apnea and bradycardia. Many infants remain asymptomatic.[47]

The diagnosis should be based on neuroimaging evidence (computed tomography or magnetic resonance imaging) because the lumbar puncture is not reliable. Treatment is usually symptomatic and supportive. However, a significant number of affected infants will develop post-hemorrhagic hydrocephalus, sometimes delayed by several months, mandating close follow-up.[47]

Intracerebral/Intraventricular Hemorrhage

These are unusual traumatic lesions and are generally accompanied by other forms of intracranial hemorrhage and external signs of trauma. Neuroimaging will assist in defining the extent of involvement. It is important to distinguish primary hemorrhage from that which is secondary to hemorrhagic infarction, since the latter may be an hypoxic-ischemic lesion that antedated the events of labor and delivery. Other reasons for bleeding, such as a coagulopathy, platelet disorder, or arterio-venous malformation should be sought. In the event that platelet isoimmunization is diagnosed, this information must be given to the mother's obstetrician because of its implication for future pregnancies.

Subgaleal Hemorrhage

This uncommon form of extracranial hemorrhage is important because of its potentially life-threatening nature.[48] Very large quantities of blood may accumulate in the potential space between the galea aponeurotica of the scalp and the periosteum. Although it accumulates slowly, hypovolemic shock may eventuate. The presence of a taut, swollen scalp and a falling hematocrit should alert care providers, especially if delivery was instrument assisted. Coagulopathy is a frequent complication[49] and mortality rates exceeding 20% have been reported.[48]

Risk Management and "Traumatic Birth"

There are several points to be made in both the evaluation and documentation of traumatic birth injuries. The most obvious is that the mere entry of the word "trauma" into the medical record will be inferred by many to mean a negligently performed delivery (see Chapter 34).

Second, there are numerous clinical presentations that are usually attributable to other causes but which may actually be of traumatic origin.[41] These are shown in Table 2. Once trauma has been established as a significant factor, a careful and complete evaluation must be done, looking for evidence of other potential injuries.

Third, infants who have sustained birth trauma can develop injuries that are easily overlooked but which may have significant long-term sequelae.[41]

Table 2
Clinical Presentations Usually Attributable to Other Causes but Which May Result from Mechanical Birth Trauma

Sign	Possible Traumatic Causes
Primary apnea	Spinal cord injury (high) Subdural, epidural hemorrhage
Respiratory distress	Spinal cord injury Subdural, epidural, or (rarely) subarachnoid hemorrhage Nasal fracture of septum
Dislocation	Phrenic nerve injury Vocal cord abductor paralysis
Shock, hypoperfusion	Subdural or epidural hemorrhage Subgaleal hemorrhage Visceral injury (liver, spleen, kidney, rarely adrenal or intramural enteric hemorrhage) Spinal cord injury
Dystonia	Spinal cord injury Subdural, epidural, or subarachnoid hemorrhage Cerebral contusion Vertebrobasilar artery occlusion
Feeding problems	Mandibular, maxillary injury
Gastrointestinal obstruction	Intramural enteric hematoma
Seizures	Subdural or subarachnoid hemorrhage Skull fracture Cerebral contusion

Reproduced with permission from W.B. Saunders in Faix RG, Donn SM. Immediate management of the traumatized infant. Clin Perinatol 1983;10:503.

Table 3
Easily-Overlooked Injuries That May Have Significant Sequelae

Injury	Possible Sequelae
Subgaleal hemorrhage	Shock
Fracture involving optic foramen	Optic atrophy Blindness
Inner ear hemorrhage	Hearing loss Vestibular dysfunction
Facial bone fracture	Deformity Respiratory distress Feeding difficulty
Intramural bowel hematoma	Bowel obstruction Feeding difficulty
Ruptured Descemet's membrane	Astigmatism Amblyopia Myopia Strabismus
Hepatic hematoma	Shock

Reproduced with permission from W.B. Saunders in Faix RG, Donn SM. Immediate management of the traumatized infant. Clin Perinatol 1983;10:503.

Table 4
Clues to Other Causes of Neonatal Encephalopathy

Malpresentation
Abnormal amniotic fluid volume
    Oligohydramnios
    Polyhydramnios
Abnormal umbilical cord
Intrauterine growth retardation
Microcephaly
    True microcephaly
    Disproportionate "microcephaly"
Neuromuscular hypertonia/arthrogryposis
Dysmorphic features
    Cranio-facial
    Limb
    Midline
    Other anomalies

These are shown in Table 3. It is again incumbent upon health care providers to do a thorough assessment of any infant suspected to have had a traumatic delivery. Because of the devastating outcomes of some of these injuries, prompt consultation or referral to experienced specialists may minimize the medical complications and legal exposure.

Finally, it cannot be overemphasized that the majority of neonatal encephalopathy does not result from intrapartum hypoxia and ischemia. There are often clues that may suggest an alternative etiology, such as a congenital anomaly or lesion acquired well before the events of labor and delivery (Table 4). When one of these findings is present, a diagnostic evaluation is indicated.

Malpresentation

There is a statistical association between abnormalities of the central nervous system and abnormal presentations of the fetus, particularly the breech presentation.[1,50-53] The working hypothesis is that the abnormality of the brain results in abnormalities of fetal movement in utero, which leads to an abnormal presentation. In addition, as noted above, the abnormal presentation may contribute to intrapartum difficulties by prolonging labor, or by resulting in a maldistribution of the normal physical forces of labor and delivery.

Amniotic Fluid Volume

The volume of amniotic fluid is determined by differences in its rate of formation and its rate of absorption. This may be affected by neurologic dysfunction.

The primary determinants of amniotic fluid production are fetal urinary output and the placental contribution. A deficit of amniotic fluid, oligohydramnios, may be an indicator that one or both of these has been diminished. Utero-placental insufficiency is one such condition, indicating a chronic process. Fetal renal injury as a consequence of hypoxic-ischemic events prior to the intrapartum period is another.

Most of the amniotic fluid absorption occurs from fetal swallowing. Neurologic abnormalities may interfere with the fetal ability to swallow, resulting in an accumulation of amniotic fluid, polyhydramnios. There are, of course, other causes of polyhydramnios, such as maternal diabetes and fetal bowel obstruction, but its presence in a child with otherwise unexplained encephalopathy should be thoroughly investigated.

Abnormal Umbilical Cord

Abnormalities of the umbilical cord (see Chapter 19) may reflect abnormalities of intrauterine existence. Long umbilical cords are at a higher risk for compression and knotting; short umbilical cords may result from deficient fetal movements, which may be the result of neurologic impairment. Chronic utero-placental insufficiency may cause the cord to appear thready, with loss of Wharton's jelly, and there may be deep meconium staining. The presence of a single umbilical artery has been associated with other congenital anomalies.

Intrauterine Growth Retardation

Disturbance in fetal growth may result from numerous processes, including infection, utero-placental dysfunction, severe maternal illness, and fetal genetic disorders. Intrauterine growth retardation (IUGR) should never be dismissed without consideration. This is particularly true if there is symmetrical growth retardation, which affects not only body size, but brain size as well. Careful documentation of the head circumference at birth, determination of the proper gestational age, brain imaging (searching for calcifications, anomalies, infarcts, or hydrocephalus), and an appropriate work-up for infection are essential. Thorough communication with the family and the primary care physician, in which concerns for future development are discussed, seems appropriate, and this should be documented in the medical record.

Microcephaly

Although it seems intuitive that microcephaly is an indicator of an abnormally developed brain, the major error in its diagnosis is the failure to measure the head circumference at birth. This should never occur; part of the routine admission assessment of any newborn includes documentation of the occipito-frontal circumference. This not only provides immediate information on a major disturbance of growth, it also provides a reference point to which all subsequent measurements will be compared.

True microcephaly, like IUGR, always requires investigation. It is often accompanied by other anthropometric abnormalities, but it may also exist in isolation or as part of other syndromes. Another important clue to an earlier acquired brain injury is a head circumference that is disproportionately smaller than weight or length. For example, when it is observed that weight and length are plotted at the 75th percentile for gestational age, but the head circumference is only at the 20th percentile, concern should be raised that an event or events may have occurred that precluded the head (brain) from reaching its genetically programmed size. Although the head is not microcephalic, and thus might escape evaluation if only the percentile was considered, the discrepancy itself should initiate an investigation.

Neuromuscular Hypertonia/Arthrogryposis

In the acute phase following hypoxic-ischemic brain injury, there is initially hypotonia and depression of reflex status. Over time, tone normalizes, then increases (spasticity), and deep tendon reflexes are accentuated, indicating an upper motor neuron lesion. An infant exhibiting early hypertonia may be evidencing a well-established and not a recent injury.

Arthrogryposis refers to a condition in which the joints appear "frozen." It is a sign of a serious neuromuscular disorder characterized by severely limited or absent movement in utero. It merits a complete neurologic evaluation.

Dysmorphic Features

The infant with dysmorphic features bears close scrutiny. Cranio-facial, midline, and limb abnormalities are often associated with central nervous system anomalies. If IUGR is also present, consideration must be given to a chromosomal disorder. Appropriate consultation with a geneticist or dysmorphologist is essential for proper diagnosis, prognosis, documentation, and when necessary, genetic counseling.

A few precautionary statements need to be made regarding chromosomal analysis (karyotype). While it is not mandatory to determine the karyotype in the immediate neonatal period (after all, the chromosomes are not going to change with time), it may be useful if it will impact treatment decisions. If a karyotype is going to be performed, it should be obtained prior to transfusion in order not to obfuscate the results. Second, a normal karyotype does not rule out the presence of all genetic disorders, only those that are large enough to be within resolution limits of the test.

Summary

While it is clear that some children with cerebral palsy are indeed injured during the events of labor and delivery, the vast majority of infants undergoing some degree of hypoxia-ischemia in the intrapartum period are perfectly normal, and the majority of children with cerebral palsy have an etiology that is either unknown or unrelated to birth. The present understanding of intrapartum hypoxia-ischemia sufficient to produce permanent brain injury is that it also produces hypoxic-ischemic injury in other organs or systems, results in marked depression at birth and a predictable neonatal neurologic syndrome, and causes specific patterns of neurologic damage based on the gestational age of the fetus and the nature and severity of the insult.

Risk management techniques must be applied prospectively. Recognition of the encephalopathic infant is the first step. Abnormalities of neurologic function should be thoroughly investigated and documented. After information has been gathered and assimilated, it should be carefully and accurately communicated to the family.

For the infant who has undergone "fetal distress," careful prospective evaluation is also critical. Management should be directed at observing for any abnormalities of systemic (non-neurologic) organs and systems, and the documentation—not only of their occurrence—but also of their absence. Documentation of urine output and feeding are two examples of normal newborn activities that may be of crucial importance in subsequent years, once litigation ensues.

Finally, the importance of appropriate communication cannot be over-emphasized (see Chapters 34, 36, and 37). Care providers are encouraged to be descriptive rather than diagnostic. As an example, a description of a jittery or tremulous movement as such is far better than a description of the same movement as "seizure-like." All "depression" or "encephalopathy" is not "asphyxia" or "hypoxia-ischemia." Parents of a neurologically impaired newborn are understandably grief-stricken. They may have little ability to comprehend or even hear what is being told to them. This underscores the need for careful and complete documentation that is retrievable at a later date.

> **Commentary by Mr. Bloch:** It is troubling to see the extent to which the science of epidemiology is misused in obstetrical medical negligence cases. To say that a "very small percentage" of the total number of brain injured children are that way as a result of an hypoxic-ischemic event is meaningless if the total population referred to includes all neurologically impaired children. The population should only include those where there is a probable hypoxic-ischemic event and where both the neonatal course and the type of injury are consistent with the event. That excludes the great majority of neurologically impaired children who suffer from known genetic or metabolic injuries. That is, however, an appropriate exclusion because those children are not the subject matter of medico-legal investigations.
>
> In the recently released third edition of his textbook, "*Neurology of the Newborn*," Volpe[54] comments that the true incidence of cerebral palsy arising from intrapartum hypoxic ischemic events is somewhere between 12% and 23%.
>
> It is remarkable the extent to which partisan advocates have been able to publish in the obstetric and pediatric neurologic literature with an eye to having their publications used as evidence to preclude the causal link between negligence and injury. It is part of what Hill and Volpe refer to as the "currently fashionable attempt

to deny this causal relationship" when "an overwhelming clinical experience" makes it clear that a significant relationship does exist.[55] What is more frightening is that if these suggestions that perinatal events do not cause injury are concepts of modern day obstetric training, there may be an epidemic of preventable hypoxic-ischemic injuries because those obstetricians in training will have been led to believe that their intervention or non-intervention is statistically irrelevant to outcome.

There is no question but that inadequate oxygenation of the fetal brain can occur when the oxygen content of the blood is reduced below normal levels, or when cerebral blood flow is reduced. Likewise, there is no question but that events occurring during labor and in the immediate neonatal period can cause these consequences. In the modern era of medico-legal litigation, the trend is not that a case that should be successfully defended is not, but that defenses are successful when they should not be. Attempts to always suggest that the outcome is as a result of metabolic, infectious, or genetic disorders are unfair and misleading.

The same pediatric neurologists who may be nay sayers in terms of medico-legal cases do, in their clinical experience, take care of infants who are asphyxiated as a result of labor and immediate neonatal events. The diagnosis of these children is not based on any one thing but must be derived from the constellation of findings, symptoms, and outcomes.

To say that a child could not have sustained a hypoxic-ischemic event resulting in permanent neurologic injury because the umbilical cord blood pH was never < 7.05 is totally without merit. It is equally ridiculous to suggest that a severe acute hypoxic-ischemic event can never be the cause of neurologic injury unless there is other measurable organ damage, or if seizures are present within the first hour or two after birth. Many authors make these statements as parochial principles, disregarding the uniqueness of each physiologic event on a unique organism.

In a recent study, Dr. Jeffrey Phelan et al.[56] give an example of 14 cases of acute hypoxic-ischemic injury where the injury to vulnerable portions of the brain took place before other organ system damage could occur.

The advent of exquisite imaging by magnetic resonance imaging and even more advanced techniques will in many cases leave no doubt as to the exact nature of the injury. The differential for bilateral symmetrical lesions of the basal ganglia is very small and once progressive disease has been ruled out there should be no doubt about the impact of a severe hypoxic-ischemic event if the neonatal course is consistent.

The pendulum in obstetric malpractice cases has, unfortunately, been at both extremes. However, the process of going from neurologic injury being always caused by medical negligence to never being caused by medical negligence has served no valid purpose. What is necessary is a close examination of the facts of every case without being bound to epidemiologic statements that are overly broad and, for the most part, ignored by those involved in clinical care whose concern is for their patient rather than the creation of evidence that either supports or refutes legal cause.

The authors of this chapter place too much emphasis on rigid criteria, using somewhat outdated references in their discussion about the use of Apgar scores and the timing of seizures. If Nelson and Ellenberg[19] in 1981 said that there has to be an Apgar of < 3 for > 15 minutes to see any significant increase in the incidence of cerebral palsy in survivors, that flies in the face of much more current literature and common sense. Even ACOG, both in 1986 and in its famous Technical Bulletin 163, written in 1992, acknowledged that an Apgar score of 3 for > 5 minutes is a marker linking cerebral palsy and asphyxia. There is too much subjectivity in Apgar scoring to create artificial thresholds. One person's Apgar score of 4 is another person's Apgar 2.

Likewise, to suggest that seizures prior to 8 hours of birth are indicative of pre-existing injury ignores the many variations reported by clinicians with respect to the timing of the onset of seizures. Those involved in the care of children who sustain identifiable acute events such as abruption or prolapse often see seizures within the first 2-3 hours of birth. It is time that clinical experience becomes the focal point of these causal links.

The defense will always manage to locate experts who will either testify that the brain damage was not caused by asphyxia or that the brain injury could not have been prevented by earlier delivery. What is important is not the automatic application of unreasonable rigid criteria, but a thorough analysis of the events that occur antepartum, intrapartum, and postpartum. The newborn neurologic findings and newborn imaging studies are critical to this analysis. Intrapartum asphyxia remains a potentially avoidable cause of cerebral palsy.

No one contends that most cases of neurologic injury should result in medico-legal action. However, there are many cases involving infants who were exposed to hypoxic-ischemic events, both in the intrapartum and immediate neonatal period, and sustained brain damage that could have been prevented by earlier intervention and delivery. These are the cases that should give rise to medico-legal actions and should be evaluated in a fair and objective manner.

Rebuttal by Drs. Johnston and Donn: The issues raised by Mr. Bloch are frequently encountered during the course of malpractice litigation. We are all hampered to some extent by not having a true human model of HIE. Thus, the present level of information must be extrapolated from animal experimentation and confirmed by human clinical observation and epidemiologic investigation.

In responding to Mr. Bloch's first point, we have both seen numerous cases in which litigation was instituted even though the most likely source of the child's disability was metabolic or genetic. We do certainly agree that not all neonatal encephalopathy is "hypoxic-ischemic" in origin, and we hope that a careful search for alternative explanations would be a pre-requisite of any contemplated litigation. If the percentages cited are correct, 67%-88% of cerebral palsy (which is still a considerable majority) has some cause other than intrapartum hypoxia-ischemia.

By no means do we wish to "deny this causal relationship." However, what we are trying to emphasize is that there is a reasonable tolerance of the fetus to hypoxic-ischemic injury, and that prolonged partial asphyxia is a continuum that involves redistribution of blood flow with variable prolongation of cerebral oxygen delivery. Occasionally, the compensatory mechanisms are inadequate or become exhausted and brain injury occurs. In the overwhelming majority of such cases, recognizable neonatal clinical and laboratory evidence of hypoxic-ischemic complications are observed.

The significance of fetal acid-base balance and subsequent neurologic outcome was recently reviewed by Low in the same treatise cited by Mr. Bloch. This chapter and the accompanying commentary by Drs. Hill and Volpe affirm the validity and significance of fetal acidosis. Mr. Bloch is correct in suggesting the uniqueness of each case. Again, we are dealing with a biological system and not a machine; nevertheless, we do need a reference point if we are to deal with "probability."

Phelan's observation (not a true study) has thus far been published as an abstract only and has not undergone peer review. Based on the limited information provided, it appears that he is describing 14 cases of total or near-total asphyxia. Based on the animal models of Meyers and others, we would not expect to see other organ damage. Indeed, in our own clinical experiences, total asphyxia usually does not cause systemic organ damage. Yet, total asphyxia is a *rare* clinical event.

There is no question that brain imaging techniques have revolutionized our understanding of hypoxic-ischemic injuries. We must acknowledge some limitations of technique, however. Imaging tells us about structural brain injury, not functional. Imaging is also imprecise in determining the exact time of injury. Imaging is subjective and is dependent upon the expertise and experience of the interpreter.

Apgar scores were never intended to be a prognostic neurologic indicator. While our reference to the National Collaborative Perinatal Project may seem outdated, it is the largest data set available. It clearly indicates that the vast majority of infants who survive a 20 minute Apgar score of 0-3 do so *without* subsequent cerebral palsy. While Apgar scoring is somewhat subjective, it is our feeling that this applies more to higher scores than lower. An infant without a heartbeat and no spontaneous respiratory effort is not likely to be "overscored." We should also emphasize that intrapartum hypoxia-ischemia is not the only reason for depressed Apgar scores. An infant may be depressed from maternal medication, a congenital brain malformation, or a more remote asphyxial injury.

Finally, the timing of the first seizure is a useful observation. Granted, this does deserve more study, but based on both experimental animal models and observed human experience, there is a significant "window" between injury and seizures. Again, these are based on the prolonged partial asphyxia model. Mr. Bloch describes "earlier" seizures that follow a total or near-total asphyxia model. In the human newborn, we do not have sufficient information to address this; in the animal model, total asphyxia does not produce seizures.

Commentary by Mr. Fisher: Scientific validity or reliability should be based upon the experimental method that can re-create and re-produce an event using the same forces and criteria. The same holds true of diagnosis criteria, which lead to a "more probably than not" assumption that a disease or condition exists because of *repetitive signs and symptoms*. Absent guidelines and criteria, no one should be allowed to take the stand in a court of law and state that something "more probably than not" did occur.

In reviewing Mr. Bloch's commentary on HIE, one comes away with the following impression:

1. Mr. Bloch probably—and responsibly—takes only those cases that may very well represent HIE.

2. Mr. Bloch does not do defense work, and therefore does not see the other side of the coin; that is, that the majority of the cases filed do not represent HIE, but experts can be easily found to bend scientific principles for the plaintiff.

3. Mr. Bloch may have misinterpreted the intent of Dr. Phelan's studies, as well as the *Fetal Neurology* textbook.

4. Mr. Bloch, in essence, establishes *no criteria*, nor does he suggest that there are any legitimate criteria that ought to be used to determine whether or not a child has suffered an intrapartum hypoxic-ischemic event.

What I have experienced from the defense side includes the following:

1. Attempts to relate a clearly dysmorphic and genetically affected baby's cerebral palsy to hypoxia during labor.

2. Attempts to claim an exacerbation of even the fragile X genetic condition by events in labor and delivery.

3. Attempts to relate a normal newborn nursery course to an HIE during labor in a child with isolated autism.

4. Attempts to relate isolated learning disabilities to an otherwise benign nursery course.

5. Attempts to relate peripheral neurologic impairments, without central nervous impairments, to labor and delivery events.

6. Attempts to relate a Dandy-Walker malformation to hypoxia during labor and delivery.

7. Attempts to relate isolated frontal lobe atrophy to a labor and delivery hypoxic event.

8. Attempts to relate spastic quadriplegia to labor and delivery hypoxia, although a brain magnetic resonance imaging was normal.

9. Attempts to relate hypoxia to cerebral palsy, even though it never produced acidosis or any recognizable post-asphyxial sequelae.

Mr. Bloch echoes the commentary often encountered by those experts who find hypoxic-ischemic damage whenever they want to in any particular case. Those experts are often found criticizing the published criteria for determining the causal relationship with HIE, *and yet they provide no proof that their criticism is legitimate, nor do they provide any proof that they have other, more reliable, criteria.*

In essence, a system, whether medical or legal, that simply derives its conclusions from whomever is the best "testifier," not who has the best scientific evidence, is doomed to wallowing in a sea of words with no substance.

Every year, millions of dollars are spent on the litigation of hypoxic-ischemic baby cases. This money comes from *both* the plaintiff and the defense side in terms of costs, expenditures, etc. If would seem that those legitimate attorneys, whether they are plaintiff or defendant, would have a great interest in proving and establishing actual criteria to be used in these cases for legitimately identifying hypoxic-ischemic insult during labor and delivery. A consensus on these issues would have a major effect in the following:

1. Reducing litigation costs in the meritorious case and removal of the non-meritorious case.

2. Establishing professional integrity and credibility in both the legal and medical fields on these issues.

3. Ensuring that those individuals who are rightly entitled to a recovery receive it as quickly as possible.

4. Preventing the fabricated case from ever reaching litigation, which unfortunately, significantly raises the cost of insurance and social programs for those who are paying taxes into the system.

At present, the best and most positive criteria have been experimentally and scientifically proven within the limitations of our scientific method. Until better research can be done, and different criteria are developed, those suggested by the authors should be used. Anyone who wishes to differ from those criteria is certainly free to prove his/her point by the scientific method, but until this is done, the opinion is without a scientific basis.

Various cases have arisen in recent years regarding scientific methods, the most notable being Daubert vs Merrill-Dow at the Supreme Court level. There is a very good reason for the development of these cases. The legal system has had enough of the "charlatan witness," the false scientific theory, and the manufactured case. Even the legal system has recognized the problems inherent in the expert witness system and is demanding scientific credibility, one of the hallmarks of which is the experimental model that can be recreated using the same and similar criteria to produce the same and similar results.

Presently, ignorance is not just bliss, ignorance means dollars, since everyone knows that the common juror can be easily fooled by a "professional expert witness."

Commentary by Dr. Donn: The interchange presented above represents a microcosm of what transpires in the legal arena in many cases of alleged hypoxic-ischemic injury.

References

1. Nelson KB, Ellenberg JH. Antecedents of cerebral palsy: Multivariate risk analysis. N Engl J Med 1986;315:81.

2. Little WJ. On the influence of abnormal parturition, difficult labour, premature birth, and asphyxia neonatorum on the mental and physical condition of the child, especially in relationship to deformities. Lancet 1861;2:378.

3. Freud S. *Infantile Cerebral Paralysis*. Translated by L.A. Russim. Coral Gables, FL, University of Miami Press, 1968.

4. Painter MJ. Fetal heart rate patterns, perinatal asphyxia and brain injury. Pediatr Neurol 1989;5:137.

5. Kuban KCK, Leviton A. Cerebral palsy. N Engl J Med 1994;330:188.

6. Wright LL, Merenstein G, Hirtz D (eds). *Report on the Workshop on Acute Perinatal Asphyxia in Term Infants*. National Institutes of Health. Washington, D.C., U.S. Government Printing Office, 1995.

7. Vannucci RC. Experimental biology of cerebral hypoxia-ischemia: Relationship to perinatal brain damage. Pediatr Res 1990;27:317.

8. Sarnat HB, Sarnat MS. Neonatal encephalopathy following fetal distress. Arch Neurol 1976;33:696.

9. Levene MI, Grindulis H, Sands C, et al. Comparison of two methods of predicting outcome in perinatal asphyxia. Lancet 1986;1:67.

10. Finer NN, Robertson CM, Richards RT, et al. Hypoxic-ischemic encephalopathy in term neonates: Perinatal factors and outcome. J Pediatr 1981;98:112.

11. Hill A, Volpe J. Seizures, hypoxic-ischemic brain injury and intraventricular hemorrhage in the newborn. Ann Neurol 1981;10:109.

12. Paneth N, Stark RI. Cerebral palsy and mental retardation in relation to indicators of perinatal asphyxia. Am J Obstet Gynecol 1983;147:960.

13. Scher MS, Belfar H, Martin J, et al. Destructive brain lesions of presumed fetal onset: Antepartum causes of cerebral palsy. Pediatrics 1991;88:898.

14. Leviton A, Nelson KB. Problems with definitions and classifications of newborn encephalopathy. Pediatr Neurol 1992;8:85.

15. Peliowski A, Finer NN. Birth asphyxia in the term infant. In: Sinclair JC, Bracken MB (eds). *Effective Care of the Newborn*. Oxford, Oxford University Press, 1992, pp. 249-279.

16. Brann AW Jr. Hypoxic-ischemic encephalopathy (asphyxia) in the newborn, II. Pediatr Clin North Am 1986;33:451.

17. Altman DI, Perlman JM, Volpe JJ, et al. Cerebral oxygen metabolism in newborns. Pediatrics 1993;92:99.

18. Banagale RC, Donn SM. Asphyxia neonatorum. J Fam Pract 1986;22:539.

19. Nelson KB, Ellenberg JH. Apgar scores as predictors of chronic neurologic disability. Pediatrics 1981;68:36.

20. Williams CE, Gunn AJ, Mallard C, et al. Outcome after ischemia in the developing sheep brain: An electroencephalographic and histological study. Ann Neurol 1992;31:14.

21. Johnston MV, Trescher WH, Taylor GA. Hypoxic and ischemic central nervous system disorders in infants and children. Advances Pediatr, in press.

22. Rothman JM, Olney JW. Glutamate and the pathophysiology of hypoxic-ischemic brain damage. Ann Neurol 1986;19:105.

23. McDonald JW, Johnston MV. Physiological and pathophysiological roles of excitatory amino acids during central nervous system development. Brain Res Rev 1990;15:41.
24. Thordstein M, Bagenholm R, Thiringer K, et al. Scavengers of oxygen free radicals in combination with magnesium ameliorate perinatal hypoxic-ischemic brain damage in the rat. Pediatr Res 1993;34:23.
25. Mizrahi EM. Electroencephalographic/polygraphic/video monitoring in clinical management of neonatal seizures. In: Nelson NM (ed). *Current Therapy in Neonatal-Perinatal Medicine—2*. Philadelphia, B.C. Decker, 1990, p. 420.
26. Nelson KB. Timing the onset of cerebral palsy and other developmental disabilities: The epidemiologic evidence. In: Lou HC, Greisen G, Larsen JF (eds). *Brain Lesions in the Newborn*. Copenhagen, Munksgaard, 1994, pp. 136-144.
27. Bhat M, Nelson KB, Cummins SK, et al. Prevalance of developmental enamel defects in children with cerebral palsy. J Oral Pathol Med 1992;21:241.
28. Barkovich AJ. Apparent atypical collosal dysgenesis: Analysis of MR findings in six cases and its relationship to holoprosencephaly. Am J Neuroradiol 1990;11:333.
29. Barkovich AJ, Kjos BO, Norman D, et al. Revised classification of posterior fossa cysts and cystlike malformation based on results of multiplanar MR imaging. Am J Neuroradiol 1989;10:977.
30. Candy EJ, Hoon AH. Neuroradiology. In: Capute AJ, Accardo PJ (eds). *Developmental Disabilities in Infancy and Childhood*. Baltimore, Paul H. Brookes, in press.
31. Menkes JH, Curran J. Clinical and MR correlates in children with extrapyramidal cerebral palsy. Cerebral Palsy 1994;15:451.
32. Scheller JM, Nelson KB. Twinning and neurologic morbidity. Am J Dis Child 1992;146:1110.
33. Ville Y, Hyett J, Hecher K, et al. Preliminary experience with endoscopic laser surgery for severe twin-twin transfusion syndrome. N Engl J Med 1995;332:224.
34. Xue-Yi C, Xin-Min J, Zhi-Hone D, et al. Timing of vulnerability of the brain to iodine deficiency in endemic cretinism. N Engl J Med 1994;331:1739.
35. Patten RM, Mack LA, Harvey D, et al. Disparity of amniotic fluid volume and fetal size: Problem of the stuck twin-U.S. studies. Radiology 1989;172:153.
36. Cohen M, Roessmann U. In utero brain damage: Relationship to pathological consequences. Dev Med Child Neurol 1994;36:263.
37. Barkovich AJ. MR and CT evaluation of profound neonatal and infantile asphyxia. Am J Neuroradiol 1992;13:959.
38. Volpe JJ, Pasternak JF. Parasagittal cerebral injury in neonatal hypoxic-ischemic encephalopathy: Clinical and neuroradiologic features. J Pediatr 1977;91:472.
39. Wegman ME. Annual summary of vital statistics—1993. Pediatrics 1994;94:792.
40. Donn SM, Faix RG. Traumatic birth injury. In: Donn SM, Faix RG (eds). *Neonatal Emergencies*. Mt. Kisco, NY, Futura Publishing Co. Inc., 1991, pp. 51-62.
41. Faix RG, Donn SM. Immediate management of the traumatized infant. Clin Perinatol 1983;10:487.
42. Curran JS. Birth-associated injury. Clin Perinatol 1981;8:111.
43. Volpe JJ, Koenigsberger R. Neurologic disorders. In: Avery GB (ed). *Neonatology: Pathophysiology and Management of the Newborn*, Second Edition. Philadelphia, J.B. Lippincott, 1981, pp. 910-963.
44. Painter MJ, Bergman I. Obstetrical trauma to the neonatal central and peripheral nervous system. Semin Perinatol 1982;6:89.

45. Wigglesworth JS, Husemeyer RP. Intracranial birth trauma in vaginal breech delivery: the continued importance of injury to the occipital bone. Br J Obstet Gynaecol 1977;84:684.
46. Milhorat TH. *Pediatric Neurosurgery*. Philadelphia, F.A. Davis, 1978.
47. Palmer TW, Donn SM. Symptomatic subarachnoid in the term newborn. J Perinatol 1991;11:112.
48. Lehman D, Anderson H, Hausson G, et al. Postnatal subgaleal hematomas. Acta Obstet Gynecol Scand 1968;42:358.
49. Plauche WC. Subgaleal hematoma: A complication of instrumental delivery. JAMA 1980;244:1597.
50. Mazor M, Hagay ZJ, Leiberman JR, et al. Fetal malformations associated with breech delivery. Implications for obstetric management. J Reprod Med 1985;30:884.
51. Schutte MF, vanHemel OJ, VandeBerg C, et al. Perinatal mortality in breech presentations as compared to vertex presentations in singleton pregnancies: An analysis based upon 57819 computer-registered pregnancies in the Netherlands. Eur J Obstet Gynecol Reprod Biol 1985;19:391.
52. Braun FH, Jones KL, Smith DW. Breech presentation as an indicator of fetal abnormality. J Pediatr 1975;86:419.
53. Takahashi Y, Ukita M, Nakada E, et al. A clinic study on the prognosis of infants born by breech delivery. Acta Obstetrica et Gynaecologica Japonica 1985;37:531.
54. Volpe JJ. *Neurology of the Newborn*, Third Edition. Philadelphia, W.B. Saunders Co., 1995, p. 266.
55. Hill A, Volpe JJ (eds). *Fetal Neurology*. New York, Raven Press, 1989.
56. Phelan J, et al. Proceedings of the Society of Perinatal Obstetricians. Am J Obstet Gynecol 1995;172:364.

Chapter 26

Periventricular Leukomalacia

Steven M. Donn, M.D., Michael V. Johnston, M.D.

Introduction

Periventricular leukomalacia (PVL) is a condition that refers to softening or cavitation of the deep white matter at the external angles of the lateral ventricles. The myelinated fibers that make up the white matter carry information from the cerebral cortex to the trunk and extremities. PVL was first described by Virchow[1] in 1867, but it was not until the classic publication of Banker and Larroche[2] in 1962 that the pathologic significance and etiologic considerations were appreciated.

PVL is an important clinico-pathologic correlate of cerebral palsy in the preterm infant and thus commands a great deal of attention in medico-legal circles. Since the advent of sophisticated ultrasonographic (US) neuroimaging, much has been learned about this lesion, and clinicians are now usually able to make the diagnosis in the neonatal period.[3-8] In addition, newer techniques such as magnetic resonance imaging (MRI) have allowed the retrospective diagnosis of PVL in older children.[9-11] This can have a significant impact on the timing of a central nervous system insult and can provide valuable assistance in the defense of some medical negligence cases.

Medical Analysis

Definitions

The periventricular region refers to the anatomic area of white matter that surrounds the lateral ventricles, particularly at the posterior portions (external angles). White matter contains myelin-covered axons that originate

From: Donn SM, Fisher CW (eds.): *Risk Management Techniques in Perinatal and Neonatal Practice.* © Futura Publishing Co., Inc., Armonk, NY, 1996.

in cortical neurons and other neuronal cell bodies. This area is distinct from the periventricular germinal matrix region, from which subependymal or periventricular hemorrhage emanates. The germinal matrix is adjacent to the caudate nucleus, and it is the source of dividing neurons and glia during the first two trimesters of gestation. In contradistinction to periventricular hemorrhage, PVL is a hypoxic-ischemic lesion, brought about by a reduction in blood flow and oxygen delivery to the tissues of this region. Based on animal models that closely mimic human neonatal PVL, it appears that both hypoxia and ischemia must be present for PVL to develop. The primary aftermath of PVL is spastic cerebral palsy, a condition that results in a static motor encephalopathy, characterized by hypertonia of the extremities (particularly the legs), truncal hypotonia, hyperreflexia, and developmental delays. Additional impairments such as epilepsy, mental retardation, and deficits of hearing and vision may or may not accompany PVL. Cases in which only the legs are involved are referred to as spastic diplegia; cases in which all four limbs are involved are referred to as spastic quadriplegia. Anatomic sequelae of PVL include cyst or cavity formation in the area of the infarction; ventriculomegaly (enlargement of the ventricles), which occurs because of the loss of periventricular brain substance; and acquired microcephaly (head circumference more than two standard deviations below the expected mean), which is also the result of the loss of brain tissue (cortical atrophy).

Etiology and Pathogenesis

PVL is a lesion of the fetus and premature infant that originates from the special vulnerability of white matter during gestation, with the vast majority occurring between 24 and 34 weeks gestation. To date, there are no reported cases originating in infants beyond 36 weeks gestation. Some cases may originate as far back as 15 weeks gestation when the fetus first develops the ability to create a glial scar.[12] Typical PVL lesions have been observed in otherwise normal full term infants, indicating that they were injured in utero remote to delivery and continued to term.[13]

Hypoxia-ischemia superimposed on the relative immaturity of the cerebrovascular and anatomic architecture of the preterm brain has been emphasized as the primary pathogenetic factors in the development of PVL.[14] The unique susceptibility of the preterm infant to PVL has been explained by the watershed infarction hypothesis and the age-dependent vulnerability of the immature glial cells that manufacture myelin, the developing oligodendroglia. The periventricular white matter resides in an anatomic locus whose blood supply is derived from branches of the anterior, middle, and posterior cerebral arteries. However, as a result of inadequately developed collateral circulation prior to term, vascular border zones exist between these major arteries that are highly vulnerable to hypoxic and ischemic insults that reduce regional cerebral blood flow. Sufficient hypoxia-ischemia can result in infarction of this tissue with damage or death of tissue and subsequent sequelae, which depend on the severity and the extent of involvement. Hypoxia-ischemia also results in the release of glutamate in the periventricular region, and it has been demonstrated that toxic amounts of this neurotransmitter can damage immature oligodendroglia through an oxidative stress mechanism.[15]

This anatomic locus of injury in PVL also differs from the major areas of involvement of hypoxic-ischemic injury in the term infant, the parasagittal cerebral cortex and the basal ganglia (see Chapter 25). Parasagittal cerebral injury in the term infant affects the cortical gray matter in a semi-circular distribution that begins over the motor cortex. As a consequence, damage or loss of upper motor neurons at term can also result in the development of spastic cerebral palsy, but the distribution of neurologic involvement is generally different from that of PVL. Mild to moderate unilateral cases may result in spastic hemiplegia, with deficits confined to the side of the body contralateral to the lesion. Severe cases, as with PVL, may be bilateral and may also result in spastic quadriplegia. However, spastic quadriplegia resulting from extensive cortical damage generally produces more severe cognitive and behavioral deficits than does the damage from PVL. On a clinical basis, spastic diplegia with involvement of the legs greater than the arms is likely to represent PVL from preterm injury, whereas spastic hemiplegia from unilateral parasagittal injury is more likely to represent an injury sustained at term. However, it is also noteworthy that there is a prenatal etiology in more than half of full term infants who later develop hemiparetic cerebral palsy.[16] Brain imaging may assist timing of injury by distinguishing extensive cortical and basal ganglia damage caused at term from PVL originating prior to term.

Multiple factors may cause PVL. Fetal conditions that produce hypoxia-ischemia include cardiac arrhythmias, infection, severe anemia, thromboembolic events, twin-to-twin transfusion, death of a twin in utero, and impairment of oxygen delivery (i.e., abruptio placentae, umbilical cord compression, severe maternal hypoxia). Neonatal conditions include sepsis, hypotension, anemia, respiratory distress, asphyxia, and cardiac failure.[17-20] PVL can also result from primary infectious, inflammatory, and metabolic etiologies that may have little to do with hypoxia-ischemia.[3,22-24] Epidemiologic evidence suggests that there is a strong link between maternal febrile urinary tract infections during pregnancy and subsequent PVL. Toxic bacterial constituents can produce PVL-like lesions in experimental models. Inflammation of the umbilical cord or amniotic membranes is associated with PVL, and amnionitis has also been implicated in the initiation of premature labor.[23] Cytokines or chemicals produced by cells in response to infection or inflammation have been suggested as mediators of both preterm labor and PVL.

Factors that stimulate preterm labor may cause PVL through a cytokine-mediated mechanism. Free radical-mediated cell death has also been implicated in PVL.[15] Ischemic and non-ischemic mechanisms that produce PVL can activate a common set of biochemical mechanisms. Some cases that occur in utero may be caused by an associated obstetrical problem, but more commonly there are no obvious events recalled by the mother.

Sequelae

The most prominent neurologic sequelae of PVL are the result of its propensity to occur in specific loci. Within the periventricular white matter lie the lateral corticospinal (pyramidal) tracts, which link the motor cortex to the spinal cord. Damage to these tracts results in neurologic dysfunction manifest as spastic cerebral palsy. The tracts that are most medial and carry fibers to the feet and legs are most vulnerable to damage. Further laterally are the tracts that descend to the arms. They are often spared unless the insult is of a more severe nature. Thus, mild to moderate cases of PVL will usually result in spastic diplegia, and moderate to severe cases will result in spastic quadriplegia. PVL is almost always bilateral, although the degree of involvement can be asymmetrical. The location and size of PVL lesions in the white matter visualized by US in the neonatal period have been shown to correlate with the severity and distribution of portions of the body later affected by cerebral palsy.[25]

In addition to motoric impairment, PVL may also extend to include the acoustic and/or optic radiations, resulting in auditory and/or visual impairments. Cognitive deficits have been variably described, but many children affected with PVL are intellectually intact. Similarly, a convulsive disorder may be present or absent.

Medical Management

Neonatal Considerations

Since PVL may result from hypoxic-ischemic insults that occur prior to, during, or after the intrapartum period, the clinical presentation of the newborn is extremely variable. Prenatal insults may be undetectable; the infant may appear normal at birth or may exhibit other complications of prematurity, such as respiratory distress syndrome. Depending on how far removed the insult was from birth, there may be neurologic abnormalities that include disturbances of tone (especially early hypertonia) and relative microcephaly (the head may be disproportionately smaller than the other growth parameters as a consequence of early cerebral atrophy). Intrapartum insults will generally result in the constellation of findings described for the term infant (see Chapter 25). Multi-system dysfunction can be demonstrated, but because of the lesser development of the central nervous system, the neonatal neurologic syndrome may be more subtle. Postnatal insults may also produce a variable neurologic picture. Unfortunately, there are no pathognomonic features of PVL, and the neonatal diagnosis rests on neuroimaging techniques.

Diagnostic Evaluation

Neuroimaging often enables the diagnosis of PVL in the early neonatal period and has been shown to be highly predictive of subsequent neurologic impairment. This will be discussed in detail in Chapter 27.

In the neonatal period, cranial ultrasonography is the screening technique of choice. Serial scanning reveals a consistent pattern of injury. The earliest changes, occurring from 5 to 18 days post-insult, is described as echogenic, in which the involved areas appear as nearly homogeneous bright (white) echoes. This progresses to cystic or cavitary PVL over a period of weeks, in which the area of previous echogenicity contains discrete or coalescent echolucencies (holes). Thinning of white matter produces enlargement of the ventricles. Loss of brain substance may also lead to an enlargement of the ventricles and an increase in the extra-axial fluid spaces, referred to as echolucencies (holes). Loss of brain substance may also lead to an enlargement of the ventricles and an increase in the extra-axial fluid spaces, referred to as hydrocephalus ex vacuo.[18]

Because of the time lag between injury and the first appearance of sonographic imaging abnormalities, it is generally recommended that screening for PVL not be done before 7 days of age. However, this schedule would not enable the diagnosis of pre-existing PVL that antedated the occurrence of labor and delivery. Since most preterm infants, especially those < 35 weeks gestation, are also at risk for periventricular-intraventricular hemorrhage, and since most hemorrhages occur by 72 hours of age, a better screening policy involves an initial cranial sonogram by 3 days of age, with a follow-up study performed between 7 and 10 days of age. Additional studies should be performed as clinically indicated. Sonography is preferred because it is non-invasive, does not require ionizing radiation, is relatively inexpensive, and can be brought to the bedside.

Commentary by Mr. Bloch: This seems to be an appropriate screening policy to include or exclude PVL.

Computed tomography and magnetic resonance imaging of the brain can also be used to diagnose PVL. The latter has become an important assessment tool in the evaluation of the neurologically impaired child and can enable the retrospective diagnosis of PVL. Numerous studies of premature infants by sonography, including a recent large prospective study, indicate that ventricular enlargement is an important correlate of PVL and a strong prognostic indicator of later cerebral palsy. Ventricular enlargement often reflects loss of periventricular white matter volume as a result of shrinkage of PVL cystic lesions.[3] Ventriculomegaly is a far more powerful predictor of cerebral palsy than germinal matrix or intraventricular hemorrhage grades I-III.[4]

Neurologic Follow-Up

The primary sequel of PVL is spastic cerebral palsy. Infants or children who later manifest neurologic findings of truncal hypotonia and limb hypertonia, hyperreflexia, and developmental delays should be evaluated for the presence of PVL, particularly if spastic diplegia is present or if there is asymmetrical involvement in which the spasticity is worse in the legs than in the arms. In addition to a carefully performed and documented neurologic examination, neuroimaging confirmation is mandatory. Sonography may be used while the anterior fontanel is patent. Thereafter, MRI is probably the modality of choice. Further work-up depends on the constellation of findings (i.e., seizures), but because of the risk of associated problems, screening of visual, auditory, and cognitive function is recommended.

Summary

PVL is a lesion of the preterm infant characterized by damage to the periventricular white matter and the descending lateral corticospinal tracts. This primarily produces motoric impairment recognized as spastic diplegia and less frequently spastic quadriplegia. This locus of injury is different from that produced by hypoxia-ischemia sustained at term, where the parasagittal cerebral region and the basal ganglia are more vulnerable.

PVL may result from a number of conditions that lead to hypoxia and ischemia. These occur both in utero prior to the 37th week of gestation, and in the neonatal period in infants delivered prematurely. Recent evidence also indicates that PVL may be caused by additional problems that result in infectious, inflammatory, or biochemical injury to the periventricular white matter.

Newborns with PVL have a variable clinical presentation depending on the time, severity, and locus of injury. Preterm infants should receive routine sonographic screening, consisting of both an early (within the first 3 days) and a later (7-10 days) scan. Suspected cases should be closely followed, especially if there is cavitation or ventricular enlargement, and additional neurologic evaluations such as hearing and vision assessments are indicated.

Children who develop cerebral palsy beyond the neonatal period require a thorough neurologic assessment. From a risk management standpoint, this is especially true in three instances: 1. the term infant who has spastic diplegia or greater involvement in the legs than in the arms; 2. the child with spastic quadriplegia who had an unremarkable neonatal course; and 3. the child with spastic cerebral palsy who has no or minimal cognitive impairment. The evaluation must include neuroimaging.

> **Commentary by Mr. Bloch:** From a medico-legal standpoint, the existence of PVL becomes very much a defense issue, i.e., if it is PVL, then it was probably an event that occurred under non-negligent circumstances. The exception pertains to those cases where gestation might have been prolonged to term (this in itself is a very controversial area).

References

1. Virchow R. Zur pathologischen Anatomie des Gehirns I. Congenitale Encephalitis und Myelitis. Virchow Arch Pathol Anat 1867;38:129.
2. Banker BQ, Larroche JC. Periventricular leukomalacia of infancy. Arch Neurol 1962;7:386.
3. Paneth R, Rudelli R, Kazam E, et al. Brain damage in the preterm infant. Clin Dev Med 1994;131:209.
4. Pinto-Martin JA, Riolo S, Cnaan A, et al. Cranial ultrasound prediction of disabling and non-disabling cerebral palsy at age two in a low birth weight population. Pediatrics 1995;95:249.
5. Rogers B, Msall M, Owens T, et al. Cystic periventricular leukomalacia and type of cerebral palsy in preterm infants. J Pediatr 1994;125:S1.
6. Graziani LJ, Past M, Stanley C, et al. Neonatal neurosonographic correlates of cerebral palsy in preterm infants. Pediatrics 1986;78:88.
7. Appleton RE, Lee REJ, Hey EN. Neurodevelopmental outcome of transient neonatal intracerebral echodensities. Arch Dis Child 1990;65:27.
8. Monset-Couchard M, de Bethmann O, Radvanyi-Bouvet M-F, et al. Neurodevelopmental outcome in cystic periventricular leukomalacia (CVPL) (30 cases). Neuropediatrics 1988;19:124.
9. Truwit CL, Barkovich AJ, Koch TK, et al. Cerebral palsy: MR findings in 40 patients. Am J Neuroradiol 1992;13:67.
10. Volpe JJ. Commentary: Value of MR in definition of the neuropathology of cerebral palsy in vivo. Am J Neuroradiol 1992;13:79.
11. Feldman HM, Scher MS, Kemp SS. Neurodevelopmental outcome of children with evidence of periventricular leukomalacia on late MRI. Pediatr Neurol 1990;6:296.
12. Cohen M, Roesmann U. In utero brain damage: relationship of gestational age to pathological consequences. Dev Med Child Neurol 1994;36:263.
13. Menkes JH, Curran J. Clinical and MR correlates in children with extrapyramidal cerebral palsy. Am J Neuroradiol 1994;15:451.
14. Volpe JJ. Current concepts of brain injury in the premature infant. Am J Neuroradiol 1989;153:243.

15. Oka A, Belliveau MT, Rosenberg PA, et al. Vulnerability of oligodendroglia to glutamate: Pharmacology, mechanisms and prevention. J Neurosci 1993;13:441.
16. Nelson KB. Prenatal origin of hemiparetic cerebral palsy: How often and why? Pediatrics 1991;88:1059.
17. Donn SM, Bowerman RA. Association of paroxysmal supraventricular tachycardia and periventricular leukomalacia. Am J Perinatol 1986;3:50.
18. Bowerman RA, Donn SM, DiPietro MA, et al. Periventricular leukomalacia in the pre-term infant: Sonographic and clinical features. Radiology 1984;151:383.
19. Faix RG, Donn SM. Association of septic shock caused by early-onset group B streptococcal sepsis and periventricular leukomalacia in the preterm infant. Pediatrics 1985;76:415.
20. Sheller JM, Nelson KB. Twinning and neurologic morbidity. Am J Dis Child 1992;146:1110.
21. Ville Y, Hyett J, Hecher K, et al. Preliminary experience with endoscopic laser surgery for severe twin-twin transfusion syndrome. N Engl J Med 1995;332:224.
22. Kuban KCK, Leviton A. Cerebral palsy. N Engl J Med 1994;330:188.
23. Leviton A. Preterm birth and cerebral palsy: Is tumor necrosis factor the missing link? Dev Med Child Neurol 1993;35:549.
24. Leviton A, Paneth N. White matter damage in preterm newborns—an epidemiological perspective. Early Hum Dev 1990;24:1.
25. Bozynski MEA, Nelson MN, Genaze D, et al. Cranial ultrasonography and the prediction of cerebral palsy in infants weighing less than or equal to 1200 grams at birth. Dev Med Child Neurol 1988;30:342.

Chapter 27

Neuroimaging in High-Risk Perinatal and Neonatal Medicine

◆◆◆

James A. Brunberg, M.D.

Introduction

The imaging evaluation of perinatal neurologic dysfunction has been conspicuously altered over the past decade by advances in sonographic (US), magnetic resonance (MR), and computerized tomographic (CT) techniques. US, with markedly improved resolution and with capability for blood flow characterization, is often the initial and definitive procedure, replacing CT imaging for the characterization of germinal matrix or intraventricular hemorrhage (IVH). A potentially more substantive alteration has been the implementation of MR techniques for imaging of the brain and spinal cord, and for the routine characterization of arterial, venous, and cerebrospinal fluid (CSF) flow. In addition to these imaging functions, MR techniques also allow brain water diffusion to be quickly quantified, both in regions of normal developing white matter and in regions of pathologic alteration.

Despite the diagnostic and management techniques outlined in other chapters of this textbook, prenatally or perinatally acquired abnormalities of the brain and spinal cord continue to be major causes of neonatal death and long-term disability. While these abnormalities can result from diverse metabolic or physical mechanisms, the major neuropathologic manifestations of such damage are most conveniently categorized under broad clinico-pathologic headings of hemorrhage, hypoxia-ischemia, trauma, infection, metabolic dysfunction, and genetic or developmental alteration. The purpose of this chapter is to discuss the clinical utilization and timing of US, CT, and MR imaging in newborns with disorders of central nervous system (CNS) function

From: Donn SM, Fisher CW (eds.): *Risk Management Techniques in Perinatal and Neonatal Practice*. © Futura Publishing Co., Inc., Armonk, NY, 1996.

in the context of this broad general classification of neonatal brain dysfunction. Before doing so, the strengths and weakness of the three common neonatal neuroimaging modalities will be individually discussed.

Imaging Techniques

US is the most commonly used tool for imaging the neonatal brain. Its advantages are that it is widely available, portable, free of harmful sequelae, and relatively low in cost. Resolution is excellent for the purposes described below. US imaging does not require patient transportation or sedation and it is accomplished with minimal patient disturbance. Although often used as a "'screening" tool, its major definitive indications are for the identification of germinal matrix or IVH, for the identification of periventricular leukomalacia (PVL), for the estimation of gestational age based on gyral pattern, and for the characterization of the size of the lateral and third ventricles. Major congenital structural malformations can be identified with US, and Doppler technique can be used to characterize arterial and venous flow. US can also be used to localize cysts or other lesions in association with interventional procedures. Disadvantages of US are that its images are lower in resolution than are CT and MR, that it does not differentiate between gray matter and white matter, and that, for many purposes, it does not adequately demonstrate structural alteration involving the contents of the posterior fossa. Because of limitations imposed by the size of the anterior fontanel and by the shape of the ultrasound probe head, the cerebral cortex and extra-axial spaces at the superior convexities are generally not well visualized. US also does not demonstrate subarachnoid hemorrhage (SAH) unless massive, and it cannot be used to demonstrate anomalies of gray matter migration.

CT generally provides better characterization of brain parenchymal alteration than does US, with the exceptions noted below. This advantage relates to the ability of CT to readily distinguish between normal gray and white matter, and relative lack of interference by the skull with CT imaging of the cerebral hemispheres. It also allows for the characterization of the entire cerebral contour and for differentiation of cerebral cortex from the overlying subarachnoid and potential subdural spaces. Calcification, always a marker of cerebral parenchymal abnormality in the newborn, is better defined with CT than with US or MR. CT is also, by far, the best method for characterizing fractures or displacement of the skull or facial bones, and it is also the most sensitive method for detecting the presence of hemorrhage, especially in the subarachnoid space. Disadvantages of CT are that it requires transportation of the infant to the CT suite and that it involves ionizing radiation. In premature infants, CT may not distinguish areas of white matter infarction from surrounding normal white matter, which may be of similar attenuation at this age. In this situation, US is more definitive in identifying small foci of white matter necrosis. CT, however, remains more sensitive than US for establishing the presence of foci of cortical infarction at the convexities. In comparison with MR, CT is less capable of defining the process of normal myelination, and it is less sensitive for the identification of anomalies of neuronal migration.

MR imaging is the best technique for characterizing the development of normal myelination[1] and for diagnosing the presence of gray matter heterotopias or anomalies or cortical organization.[2] Posterior fossa anatomy and structure of the corpus callosum are readily identified. Regions of hemorrhage or infarction can often be dated, and the utilization of contrast enhancement allows for the detection of regions of disruption of the blood-brain barrier. With MR angiography, arterial or venous thrombosis can be diagnosed or excluded. MR imaging can be accomplished in any anatomic plane. There are no known sequelae to MR imaging. Disadvantages of MR are that it requires patient transportation to the imaging suite and that imaging generally cannot be done if there are central venous catheters that traverse the heart. Although heart rate, EKG, respiratory rate, blood pressure, oxygen saturation, and end tidal CO_2 can be monitored while the baby is in the magnet, special effort is initially required to ensure that all systems utilized for such monitoring are appropriate for the MR imaging environment. Mechanical respiratory support can be maintained with commercially available MR compatible respirators. An MR study generally requires 20-45 minutes, depending on the sequences utilized. During this period of time, relative immobility is necessary for periods of 2-5 minutes while individual pulse sequences are being completed. Sedation is uncommonly needed for neonatal MR imaging. Since MR imaging relies for its image contrast on relative tissue concentrations of water protons, and on the interaction of these protons with their immediate submicroscopic environment, small areas of calcification, which are readily seen with CT, may be missed. Despite these drawbacks, MR is increasingly recognized as the definitive imaging procedure for newborns with CNS dysfunction.

Imaging Utilization: Timing and Choice of Technique

In selecting the use and timing of one or more of the neonatal neuroimaging procedures, the clinician is forced to make choices based on the expected ability of each technique to define and document suspected structural alteration. The choice between imaging techniques may in part be based on equipment availability, cost, and on professional expertise with the use and interpretation of each technique. The decision hinges, however, both on the likelihood that the procedure will be able to document structural alterations associated with the expected underlying pathologic process and on the ability of the baby to tolerate the imaging procedure. Since there is no true "screening" imaging procedure that can satisfactorily evaluate changes associated with each of the clinico-pathologic processes responsible for neonatal neurologic dysfunction, an expected pathologic process must first be identified based on the patient's clinical presentation and conceptual age, and on the basis of results of other laboratory or imaging studies. A decision must also be made by the clinician as to whether the timing or type of imaging study should be chosen to define the potential presence of structural change that may reflect that neonatal neurologic symptomatology related to earlier, perhaps antenatal insults. Cystic lesions within brain parenchyma require a considerable period of time, probably weeks, to develop. The presence of a cavitary lesion in gray or white matter, when imaged at an appropriate time, can be indicative of an antenatal rather than intrapartum insult.[3]

The remaining portion of this chapter will focus on the development of a rationale for the selection of appropriate neuroimaging procedures in newborns with neurologic dysfunction relating to hypoxia-ischemia, trauma, infection, and congenital or developmental anomaly. The relationship of imaging decisions to maturation of neonatal brain vasculature, to neuronal and glial migration, and to the pattern of developing myelination will also be discussed. A more comprehensive discussion of specific imaging findings is available in recent textbooks.[4-7]

Hypoxic-Ischemic Encephalopathy

Pathologic alteration relating to hypoxia and ischemia in full term and premature infants is the major acquired perinatal cause of morbidity. Manifestations of this insult relate to conceptual age and to the type and duration of the insult. The pathogenesis of neuronal injury is complex, but at the cellular level is related to deprivation of oxygen and glucose and to the subsequent development of a sequence of cytotoxic alterations.[8] Cytotoxic changes are most prominent in anatomic locations where there is a release of glutamate or other excitotoxic amino acids, and where there are high concentrations of N-methyl, D-aspartate glutamate receptors. In these locations, there is a resultant intracellular calcium accumulation and free radical formation, both of which result in neuronal necrosis with subsequent glial reaction. Factors of neuronal and glial maturation, myelination development, and altering patterns of blood supply are also responsible for patterns of neuronal injury among infants of varying gestational age. Ischemia and compromised cerebral autoregulation are cardiovascular factors relating to the pathogenesis of hypoxic-ischemic encephalopathy.

Among newborns with suspected hypoxic-ischemic CNS insults, there are six clinico-pathologic patterns to be considered. These patterns include focal or multifocal cerebral infarction, selective neuronal necrosis, watershed infarction in the parasagittal regions, PVL, status marmoratus, and cerebral hemorrhage. Cerebral hemorrhage may occur both as a secondary phenomena in association with hypoxia-ischemia, but also independently in association with trauma. These six patterns represent the major forms of tissue alteration occurring in response to hypoxic-ischemic insult. Prior to imaging a newborn with suspected perinatal asphyxia, the child should be placed into one of these six groups. Grouping can be based on gestational age, clinical findings, and expected site of predominant neuronal dysfunction. Separation into these groups is important because of the differing sensitivities of the three imaging modalities for tissue alteration occurring at cortical and subcortical locations characteristic of each.

Focal or Multifocal Cerebral Infarction

Focal and multifocal cerebral infarction are terms used to describe a pattern of neonatal cerebral or brainstem infarction occurring within the distribution of one or several major cerebral arteries, veins, or venous sinuses. Tissue alteration occurs in the pattern of distribution of a specific vessel, not between vessels as occurs with watershed infarction (described below). Lesions are most frequently unilateral, and the most common pattern is within the distribution of the left middle cerebral artery. Vascular embolus and thrombosis are among the many processes associated with the occurrence of perinatal cerebral infarction. Focal cerebral infarction in the newborn is often accompanied by the early occurrence of seizures, usually on the first day of life.

Focal or multifocal cerebral infarction is eventually associated with tissue loss, the distribution of which is dependent upon the vessels involved. The distribution of volume loss with vascular causes usually allows distinction from tissue loss secondary to trauma and infection. Hydranencephaly with marked thinning or absence of the cerebral mantle most commonly results from antenatal bilateral infarction in the distribution of both internal carotid arteries, often combined with the basilar system.

Imaging by MR or CT (Figures 1 and 2) is the preferred means of demonstration of focal or multifocal cerebral infarction. Depending on conceptual age and on the size and severity of the lesion, CT alterations as regions of low attenuation and possible mass effect with effacement of regional sulci may not be detectable for 2-5 days. If an initial CT study is normal, but a study done 1 week later demonstrates a focal area of low attenuation

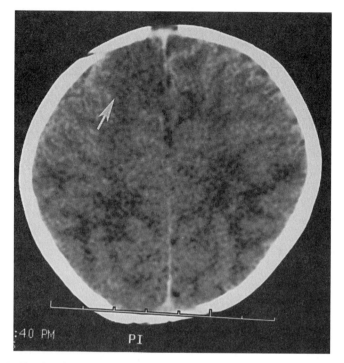

Figure 1. Focal infarct in term infant with congenital heart disease, recurrent left focal seizures, and suspected cerebral embolic event. CT demonstrates a right frontal focal region of low attenuation involving cortex and underlying white matter consistent with infarction.

consistent with infarction, the imaging results may suggest that the insult arose in close proximity to the clinical symptomatology. Imaging by CT done at the time of initial symptomatology may, however, be useful in defining whether the lesion is entirely perinatal in timing. An established arterial distribution region of low attenuation in a patient with physical symptoms and signs of < 12 to 24 hours duration may indicate that the insult was antenatal rather than intrapartum or postnatal in origin. Foci of calcification or the pattern of alteration may also suggest etiologic events that are more likely remote in duration.

US demonstrates increased echogenicity in the distribution of a cerebral infarct, whether diffuse or focal. The presence of such alteration may not be demonstrable for several days. Cortex and subcortical white matter are involved, and there may be effacement of regional sulci as well as a diffuse increase in echogenicity. This pattern persists for up to several weeks, and then evolves into an area or areas of echolucency, volume loss, and occasional

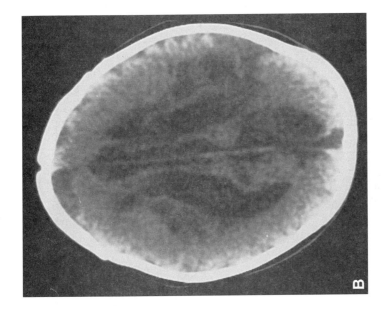

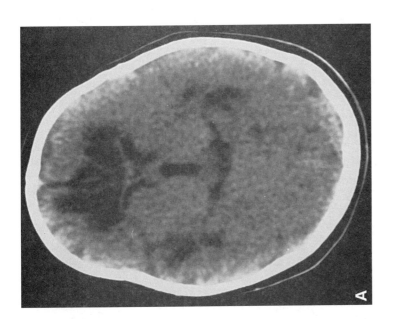

Figure 2. Intrauterine infarction in 34 week twin pregnancy with death of twin in utero. Head circumference was decreased at birth and there was no intrapartum or postpartum asphyxia. A and B. CT imaging at age 6 weeks demonstrates low attenuation in periventricular white matter consistent with extensive antenatal periventricular infarction.

echogenic calcification. The alterations seen initially with US may antedate the development of low attenuation on CT scanning. The latter will, however, generally provide a more accurate indication of the extent of cerebral injury after the acute phase (2-5 days) than does US. CT is also more sensitive to focal areas of cortical infarction, which may be missed with US of lower resolution and because portions of the cerebral convexities are not accessible to US imaging through the anterior or posterior fontanels.

MR imaging is increasingly utilized to characterize the nature and extent of parenchymal infarction in the newborn (Figure 3). Regions of high signal intensity of cerebral cortex on T2 weighted images and of low signal intensity on T1 weighted images appear to be more sensitive to the extent of parenchymal alteration than does CT or US imaging in this pattern of hypoxic-ischemic injury. Gadopentetate dimeglumide administered as a contrast agent appears to further increase the sensitivity and specificity of MR techniques. MR imaging may prove to be the preferred imaging modality for accurately defining the nature and extent of neonatal parenchymal injury.

Venous thrombosis most commonly involves the superior sagittal sinus but may involve the other major dural sinuses and/or the deep venous system. Imaging by CT may demonstrate increased attenuation in the thrombosed venous system but is less sensitive to alteration than are MR techniques. With MR imaging, (Figure 4) venous thrombosis may be demonstrated as the absence of a flow void or as regions of increased signal intensity on T1 weighted images because of hemoglobin metabolism to methemoglobin (Figure 5). MR angiographic sequences using phase contrast techniques demonstrate absence of normal flow in the involved vessels. There may be focal or multifocal cerebral edema or occasionally the presence of hemorrhagic infarction (Figure 6). Infarction with or without hemorrhage may be demonstrated in the thalamus and striatum in association with thrombosis of the deep venous system.

Selective Neuronal Necrosis

Selective neuronal necrosis is a pattern of cerebral or spinal cord injury that results from neuronal infarction with relative sparing of less vulnerable histologic components. Selective neuronal necrosis is the most common pattern of injury observed in term or preterm newborns with hypoxic-ischemic injury. Areas of greatest neuronal vulnerability include the cerebral cortex, especially Somers sector of the hippocampus in the term infant, and the subiculum in premature infants. Cortical neurons at the cerebral convexities may either be involved diffusely or may show a predilection for involvement in the deeper cortical layers. The depths of sulci, especially vulnerable because

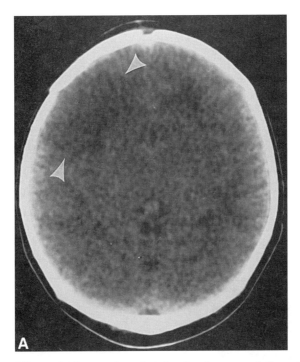

Figure 3. Middle cerebral artery branch infarction in a term infant with recurring seizures at age 7 hours. A. CT at age 2 days demonstrates a poorly defined region of low attenuation involving the right frontal cortex and subcortical white matter (arrow). B. At age 7 days T1 weighted MR image without contrast demonstrates a wedge shaped area outlined by increased signal intensity most likely from methemoglobin formation in a region of associated hemorrhage. There is a central region of low signal intensity in comparison with adjacent brain parenchyma. C. Following contrast administration there is dense enhancement of the region of infarction. D. Coronal T2 weighted images demonstrate the cortical infarction to be low in signal intensity, most likely from persisting deoxyhemoglobin in regions of petechial hemorrhage. Edema is associated with increased signal intensity in adjacent white matter. E. A CT study 6 months later demonstrates a region of persisting encephalomalacia involving cortex and underlying white matter.

(Figure continues on following pages.)

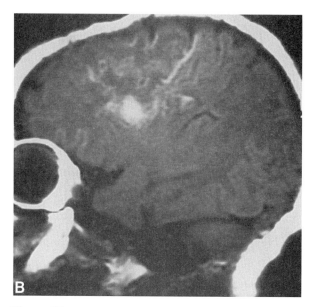

Figure 3B.

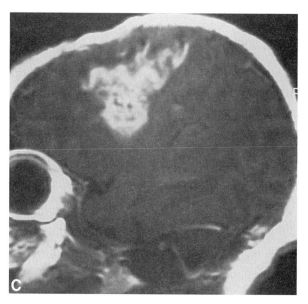

Figure 3C.

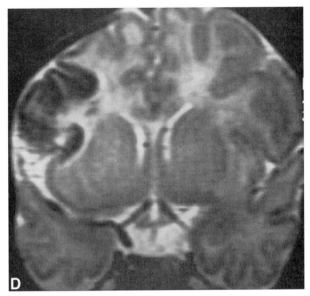

Figure 3D.

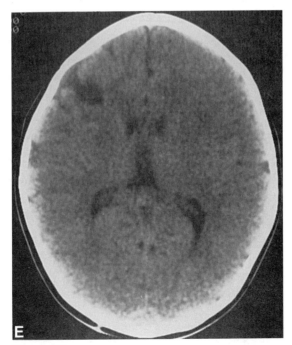

Figure 3E.

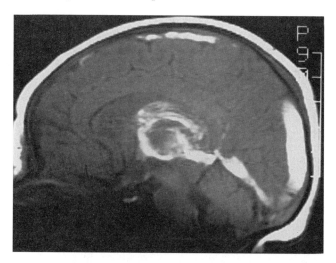

Figure 4. Sagittal and straight sinus thrombosis in an infant of 38 weeks gestation with tremors, cyanotic episodes, and suspected seizures on day 3. IVH and intraparenchymal hemorrhage were diagnosed with US. Subsequent T1 weighted MR imaging demonstrates increased signal intensity in the superior sagittal sinus, straight sinus, vein of Galen, internal cerebral veins, and in the subependymal venous system consistent with venous thrombosis. The high signal intensity results from metabolism of hemoglobin to methemoglobin, a process that generally is demonstrable within 24-72 hours. Identification of venous sinus thrombosis can also be accomplished with MR angiogaphy rather than static MR imaging.

of a relative paucity of regional vessels, may demonstrate regions of enhancement with MR imaging. Parasagittal watershed zones are similarly more vulnerable. Neuronal injury may also occur in the thalamus and/or basal ganglia as a component of selective neuronal necrosis in the term or preterm infant. Histologic studies have also demonstrated the common presence of selective neuronal necrosis involving multiple brainstem motor nuclear regions. Similar cell loss can be demonstrated histologically to involve the anterior horn cells of the spinal cord. In the cerebellum, the neurons most vulnerable to hypoxia and ischemia are the internal granule cells of the premature and the Purkinje cells of the term infant.

US is of limited use in the evaluation of the newborn with suspected laminar necrosis because cerebral cortex at the convexities cannot be well imaged as a result of problems with angulation of the transducer. Additionally, nuclear brainstem lesions are beyond the resolution of sonography, as they are with CT. Regions of neuronal alteration in the basal ganglia may, however, be visualized as increased echogenicity, similar to the pattern seen with petechial or small hemorrhage, but are not associated with significant mass effect.

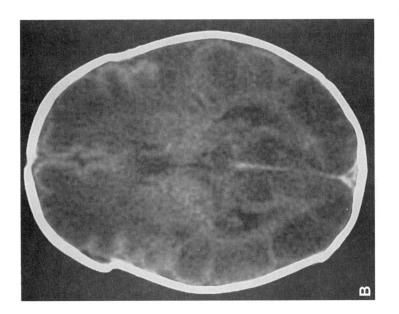

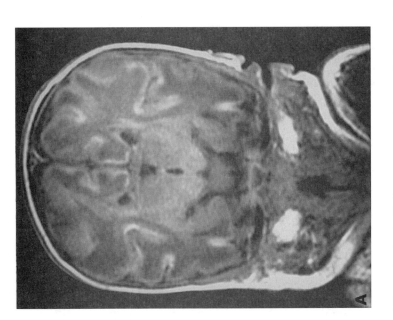

Figure 5. Cortical infarct, most prominent at the base of sulci, is demonstrated in an infant of 36 weeks gestation who was delivered by emergency Cesarean-section for abruptio placentae. Apgar scores were 0 at 1 minute and 6 at 5 minutes. A. T1 weighted MR at age 7 days, without contrast administration, demonstrates increased signal intensity at the bases of multiple sulci consistent with petechial hemorrhage into sites of cortical infarction. Also demonstrated is low signal intensity in subcortical and deep white matter consistent with edema and/or infarction. B. CT imaging at 18 days demonstrates persisting cortical and subcortical low attenuation that subsequently evolved into a pattern of mulicysic encephalomalacia.

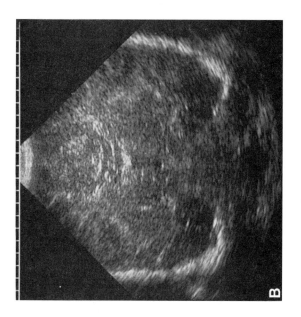

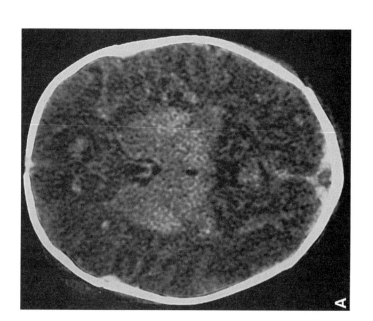

Figure 6. Diffuse cortical and subcortical edema in a term infant with delivery by emergency Cesarean section for abruptio placentae. Apgar scores were 0 at 1, 5, and 10 minutes and 4 at 20 minutes. Seizures began on the second day. A. CT imaging at day 8 demonstrates low attenuation of cortex and of white matter over both cerebral hemispheres with normal attenuation of the cerebellum and of gray matter within the basal ganglia. A small focus of high attenuation within the right frontal lobe is consistent with a region of hemorrhage. B. US on the same day demonstrates increased echogenicity throughout the white matter of both cerebral hemispheres.

When the process is diffuse, cortex and white matter are extensively involved and there will be a widespread increase in echogenicity, which may persist for up to 2 weeks. There will then be a diffuse pattern of low echogenicity with prominence of sulci, ventriculomegaly, and possible associated calcification.

Alterations on CT associated with severe cortical selective neuronal necrosis may be evident within 2-3 days of the insult as decreased cortical and subcortical attenuation. The decreased attenuation and loss of normal gray and white matter differentiation relates to neuronal necrosis and to associated surrounding edema. Thin or discontinuous regions of laminar necrosis may not, however, be evident, and changes in the hippocampus are not demonstrable in the acute phase, despite the histologic prominence of involvement at this location. A pattern of cortical volume loss manifest by large sulci is generally identified in 3-6 weeks following the suspected insult. The pattern of enlarged sulci over the cerebral convexities needs, however, to be distinguished from the enlarged CSF spaces, which can occur in association with communicating hydrocephalus or as a benign process in an otherwise normal child. Diminished CSF absorption at the arachnoid villi from prior SAH, meningitis, or elevated venous pressure in the superior sagittal sinus may also be associated with a pattern of CSF space prominence similar to that seen following selective neuronal necrosis. The distinction between such cerebral atrophy and the sulcal enlargement seen with communicating hydrocephalus often requires the correlation of serial head circumference measurements with the imaging data. Patients with a pattern of cerebral atrophy will not demonstrate normal head growth, while children with communicating hydrocephalus will demonstrate normal or rapid growth in head circumference with age.

The only imaging technique that can detect laminar necrosis is MR. With MR techniques, extensive neuronal necrosis limited to cortex or involving gray matter in the basal ganglia is readily appreciated. MR imaging correlates of brainstem nuclear dysfunction in the newborn have not yet been reported.

Watershed Infarction in the Parasagittal Regions

Watershed infarction in the parasagittal regions is a common pattern of cortical and subcortical injury resulting from ischemia and occurring in the term infant. The alterations involve the cortex and subcortical white matter and result from a fall in cerebral perfusion pressure, the residua of which are most prominent in the border zones at the periphery of the primary perfusion fields of the anterior, middle, and posterior cerebral arteries. This pattern of injury does not generally occur in the preterm infant. The insult can result from any cause of systemic hypotension, but is accentuated by the compromise in cerebral autoregulation, which is believed to occur in the newborn following prolonged hypoxemia or hypercarbia.

US imaging is less than optimal for the characterization of watershed infarction because the areas of involved cortex are not well visualized. CT imaging may demonstrate parasagittal decreased attenuation in the full term child within 2-3 days of the insult. Findings are often obscured, however, by the relatively low attenuation of white matter in the normal newborn. When the region of infarction is large, low attenuation of the cortex may be readily demonstrated. Over several months, the decreased attenuation of regional white matter and loss of white matter volume will be evident. The involved cerebral cortex may demonstrate gyral alteration limited to watershed zones.

MR imaging is optimal for the detection of watershed infarction, whether in its acute or chronic phase. Cortex and white matter alterations in signal intensity and abnormal enhancement following contrast administration can clearly identify areas of acute infarction. The ability of MR imaging to be obtained in any plane further improves the utility of this technique. Areas of cortical volume loss, gyral abnormality, white matter volume loss, and regional gliosis characteristic of the chronic state are easily identified.

Periventricular Leukomalacia

PVL is a pattern of white matter infarction that occurs in the premature infant. Regions of white matter infarction are most commonly symmetrically positioned around the lateral ventricles, especially at the trigones and anterior horns. White matter susceptibility to infarction in these regions relates to the pattern of arterial development in the premature infant. Between 22 and 30 weeks of gestation, the deep white matter is supplied by superficial perforating branches of the anterior and middle cerebral arteries, which arise from the cortical surface, and by deep perforators that arise from lenticulostriate vessels, choroidal arteries, and from thalamo-perforating vessels. The white matter of the premature infant that is susceptible to periventricular infarction is in the watershed zone between these two (superficial and deep) sources of perfusion. As with parasagittal watershed infarction occurring in the term infant, PVL occurs in association with diminished cerebral perfusion pressure. It is accentuated in situations that compromise cerebral autoregulation. White matter in the preterm infant may also be especially vulnerable to ischemia during a period of rapid differentiation of the oligodendroglia.

PVL is pathologically characterized by tissue necrosis with subsequent proliferation of macrophages and astrocytes. Within 2 weeks, there is cavity formation with continued gliosis and myelin loss. In comparison with the parasagittal pattern of watershed infarction found in the term newborn, preterm infants with PVL have relative sparing of cerebral cortex and immedi-

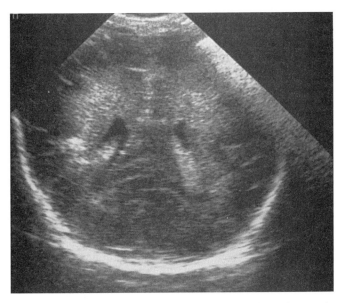

Figure 7. PVL in an infant of 34 weeks gestation with birthweight 1.92 kg and mild respiratory distress syndrome. US demonstrates prominent echogenicity in the white matter surrounding the trigones of both lateral ventricles. A focal region of high echogenicity on the right may represent a region of more extensive infarction or an area of hemorrhage. Note the normal high echogenicity of the choroid plexus within both lateral ventricles. CT imaging 1 day earlier had been normal.

ately underlying white matter. Patterns of white matter alteration identical to PVL have been demonstrated in newborns with antenatal rather than postnatal insults and may represent a response to the exposure of white matter to endotoxins. A more diffuse pattern of astrocytic response termed perinatal telencephalic leukoencephalopathy has also been described.

US is the preferred modality for the initial demonstration of PVL (Figure 7).[9,10] By 2 weeks following the insult, US demonstrates increased echogenicity of the periventricular white matter. These findings relate to tissue necrosis, gliosis, and macrophage proliferation. US does not distinguish reliably between hemorrhagic and non-hemorrhagic PVL. Within 1-3 weeks, thick walled echolucent cysts can then be demonstrated to develop within the area of infarction. They may or may not communicate with the lateral ventricles. Over additional weeks to months, these cysts generally resolve with resultant enlargement of the adjacent ventricular trigone and thinning of the remaining but gliotic white matter. It is this evolution of US alterations and not the initial echogenic appearance that firmly establishes the US diagnosis of PVL. It must be recognized that echogenicities in the peritrigonal region are not specific for PVL and may also be seen not only with hemorrhage but also in entirely normal premature infants.[11] US is insensitive to the detection of subtle ischemic lesions. When correlated with autopsy material, the sensitivity of US for the detection of hypoxic-ischemic injury associated with marked bleeding is as low as 28%.[12]

Imaging of PVL by CT in the acute phase is often unremarkable because the peritrigonal white matter of the premature infant is normally low in attenuation. The diagnosis can be made acutely if alterations are marked and if there is associated petechial hemorrhage. With time, CT will demonstrate decreased volume of white matter adjacent to enlarged trigones of the lateral ventricles. Regional sulci may be enlarged in keeping with volume loss.

MR imaging is less sensitive than US for the characterization of cerebral parenchymal alterations associated with PVL in its acute form but is especially useful in defining chronic parenchymal changes.[13] In the chronic stage, small cysts may still be demonstrable and there is irregularity in contour of the ependymal surface. Regional white matter is thinned and demonstrates increased signal intensity on T2 images because of delayed myelination and gliosis. Similar alterations can also be demonstrated in term infants who have sustained perinatal hypoxic-ischemic events.[14-16]

Status Marmoratus

Status marmoratus is a pattern of histologic alteration involving the basal ganglia that occurs following neonatal hypoxic-ischemic injury. It occurs more frequently in term than premature infants but can involve either group. In addition to early neuronal loss and gliosis, there is the late development of hypermyelination, especially in the putamen, globus pallidus, and ventral aspect of the thalamus. The acute lesion is histologically characterized by excessive capillary proliferation. The exaggerated regional response to ischemia is thought to relate to a transient dense glutaminergic innervation of these nuclear regions in the neonatal period, to the sequela of glutamate release, and to relative sparing of NADPH-diaphorase, and of dopaminergic neurons by the hypoxic-ischemic insult.

US imaging demonstrates increased echogenicity in the basal ganglia in the presence of acute infarction or hemorrhage. It often demonstrates increased echogenicity in the basal ganglia before alterations are detectable with CT.

Neuronal necrosis involving the basal ganglia and thalamus may be demonstrated by CT in the newborn as a diffuse area of low or high attenuation, depending on whether there is simply neuronal reaction or whether there is associated petechial or gross hemorrhage. Enhancement following contrast administration may reflect disruption of the blood-brain barrier or hypervascularity. With time there will be decreased volume of nuclear structures and low attenuation. Calcification of parenchyma occasionally occurs.

MR imaging readily demonstrates alterations involving the basal ganglia in the newborn with hypoxia-ischemia. T1 images without contrast administration may demonstrate increased signal intensity in the thalamus, globus pallidus, and putamen. This pattern of alteration may be secondary to petechial hemorrhage or to the presence of microcalcification. It is not yet clear whether such alteration reflects tissue injury occurring in the antenatal period of time, or whether such alteration can develop within 1-2 days of a postnatal insult.

Cerebral Hemorrhage

Intracranial hemorrhage can occur in the term or preterm infant and may involve one or a combination of intracranial compartments. Hemorrhage may be intraventricular, intracerebral, intracerebellar, subarachnoid, or subdural in location, and may be related to a number of etiologic factors. Choice of the imaging modality to utilize and of the timing of the study relates to gestational age and to clinical history.

Germinal Matrix/Intraventricular Hemorrhage

IVH occurs in newborns of all gestational ages but is much more common in the premature, where it occurs in approximately 40% of infants weighing < 1500 g.[17] IVH or germinal matrix hemorrhage is most likely to occur on the first or second day of life, and by the sixth day of life, 90% have occurred. It most commonly arises as bleeding within the germinal matrix at the head of the caudate nucleus or from within the choroid plexus with subsequent extension through the ependymal surface. Germinal matrix and IVH are classified as follows:

Grade I: Hemorrhage confined to germinal matrix.
Grade II: Intraventricular extension of germinal matrix hemorrhage with normal ventricular volume.
Grade III: Intraventricular extension with increased ventricular volume.
Grade IV: IVH with associated periventricular hemorrhagic infarction.

A frequent accompaniment of IVH is the presence of parenchymal hemorrhagic infarction involving white matter dorsal and lateral to the body of the ventricle. This area of hemorrhagic infarction is usually asymmetric and is usually most evident on the side of largest germinal matrix hemorrhage. Pathologic studies suggest that this parenchymal component most likely represents venous infarction and not true "extension" of hemorrhage from the germinal matrix. Periventricular hemorrhagic infarction is a phenomenon separate from hemorrhage that may occur into a region of PVL.[18] PVL itself is, however, a frequent co-existing process in the premature infant with IVH, as is selective neuronal necrosis involving brainstem nuclei.[19,20] Acute and chronic hydrocephalus are frequent sequelae of IVH. The pathogenesis of IVH has recently been reviewed.[4]

In term infants IVH most commonly arises from the choroid plexus but can arise from persisting germinal matrix in the region of the thalamo-caudate groove. There may be associated hemorrhage or hemorrhagic infarction in the thalamus.[21] In all neonatal age groups, IVH unassociated with germinal matrix hemorrhage most commonly arises from the choroid plexus.

US is the imaging procedure of choice for the identification of IVH and for diagnosis of hemorrhage into the germinal matrix. Imaging can be quickly accomplished at the bedside with minimal disturbance of the patient or of necessary support and monitoring equipment. Hemorrhage into the germinal matrix and the intraventricular component of hemorrhage are identified as areas of increased echogenicity. Over days or weeks, the area of hemorrhage will decrease in size and develop central echolucency. The intraventricular component will also decrease in echogenicity and may fragment. Within 1 week of the initial intraventricular bleed there will be increased echogenicity of the ependymal surface that will persist for several weeks. The presence of periventricular hemorrhagic infarction and PVL are also identified as intraparenchymal regions of increased echogenicity. US technique also allows for the identification of ventricular enlargement, a complication that may require intervention to prevent further parenchymal injury. The bedside capability of US equipment has been essential for the early and accurate diagnosis of IVH. Up to 40% of infants who develop IVH and are < 2000 g at birth will demonstrate the IVH by 5 hours of life. Approximately 90% of IVH occurs by the fourth day of life.[4] Hemorrhage grade established with US correlates well with long-term neurologic outcome. Repeat imaging after 5 days has been suggested to define the maximal extent of hemorrhage, since 20%-40% of infants with IVH will develop further bleeding with extension of the lesion.[4] The differentiation between associated cerebral parenchymal infarction and hemorrhage cannot be made with certainty using US technique, since both are associated with increased echogenicity and irregular margins, though hemorrhage is more likely to be associated with mass effect. Both may also result in cyst formation over 1-2 weeks. Imaging with CT or MR is therefore utilized when the differentiation of these types of parenchymal injuries is necessary. Increased ependymal echogenicity can be noted as hematoma within the ventricular system evolves, with the hematoma becoming less echogenic with time. Similar ependymal echogenicity can be seen in association with reactive changes in the ependymal surface that occur with

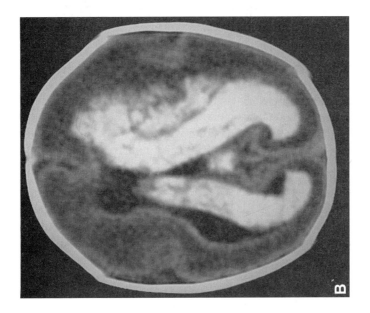

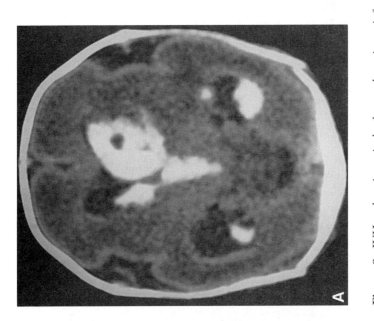

Figure 8. IVH and periventricular hemorrhage in an infant of 26 weeks gestation with neonatal respiratory distress syndrome. A and B. CT at 4 days demonstrates IVH and intraparenchymal hemorrhage as areas of high attenuation. There is associated ventriculomegaly and the immature pattern of gyral formation and of myelination is evident. C. US on the same day demonstrates echogenic IVH and intraparenchymal hemorrhage but also demonstrates an area of similar echogenicity that extends further laterally than the hemorrhage seen with CT. This more lateral component of echogenicity, consistent with a region of non-hemorrhagic infarction, is more evident on US than is a similarly located region of low attenuation of the CT study.

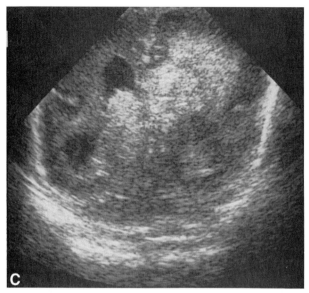

Figure 8C.

ventriculitis. US is subsequently used to exclude the development of progressive ventriculomegaly, a frequent accompaniment of IVH.

Imaging with CT is as useful as US for the characterization of IVH in the term and preterm infant but requires transportation of the infant to the CT suite (Figure 8). CT techniques are even more sensitive than US for the demonstration of small amounts of blood within normal size ventricles or for demonstrating small areas of hemorrhage within the choroid plexus. While US accurately defines the size and extent of IVH and germinal matrix hemorrhage and defines the presence of periventricular hemorrhagic infarction, CT is better able to define the presence of additional simultaneous lesions, including subdural hematoma and posterior fossa lesions.

MR imaging is sensitive to the presence of both hemorrhage and infarction but, like CT, requires transportation of the infant to the scanner. The role of routine MR imaging for defining the extent of cerebral parenchymal alteration following stabilization of the child's medical status has not yet been established.

Intracerebral Hemorrhage

Hemorrhage into the cerebral hemispheres occurs in both the term and preterm newborn (Figure 9). Etiologic factors include hemorrhagic infarction, trauma, coagulation disturbance, hypertension, and vascular anomalies such as vascular malformation (Figure 10) and aneurysm.[22] Although US will dem-

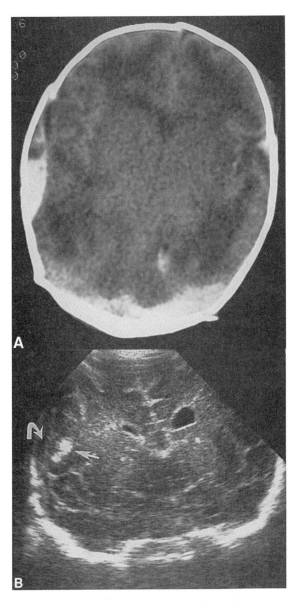

Figure 9. Thirty-two week gestation infant with subdural hematoma and temporal cortex contusion associated with a difficult vaginal breech delivery. Apgar scores were 1 at 1 minute and 7 at 5 minutes. A. CT at 2 days demonstrates a crescent shaped extra-axial hematoma with higher attenuation in the posterior aspect of the clot because of settling of red blood cells. There is minimally increased and decreased attenuation in the adjacent right temporal lobe. B. US at age 3 days demonstrates the extra-axial hematoma as a region of moderate echogenicity (curved arrow). The region of temporal lobe contusion is echogenic (arrow).

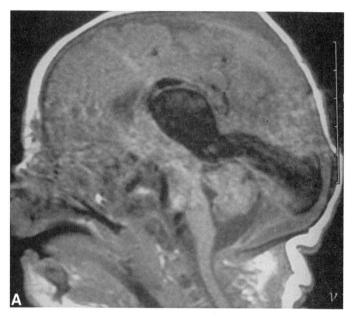

Figure 10. Vein of Galen malformation in a term infant with seizures, diminished responsiveness, and a loud cranial bruit. A. T1 weighted MR image demonstrates low signal intensity because of rapid blood flow within an enlarged vein of Galen and straight sinus. B and C. A three-dimensional phase contrast MR angiogram, viewed as if from below the cranial vault, demonstrates an enlarged vein of Galen and straight sinus (open arrow). Direct arterial fistulas are seen to arise from the right posterior cerebral artery (arrow) and left posterior cerebral artery (curved arrow). The right posterior cerebral artery originates from the basilar artery (arrowhead) and the right posterior communicating artery (wavy arrow). The left posterior cerebral artery originates almost entirely from the left internal carotid artery. The two images can be viewed as a stereoscopic pair by crossing your eyes until three images are seen. Focus on the middle image.

onstrate the presence of hemorrhage involving the cerebral hemispheres as an echogenic mass, an additional study, especially MR, is usually utilized to exclude underlying vascular anomalies, mass lesions, or major arterial or venous thrombosis.

Intracerebellar Hemorrhage

Intracerebellar hemorrhage is more common in the premature than in the full term newborn. It may arise from extension of IVH, from venous infarction, or in the full term infant may arise from traumatic injury to the dura or venous structures. As with hemorrhage involving the cerebral hemispheres, cerebellar hemorrhage may also relate to coagulopathy, or to increased arterial pressure or increased venous resistance in a newborn with impaired autoregulation. In the infant with hypoxia or ischemia there may be hemorrhage into the developing external granular layer of the cerebellum. Hemorrhage may also occur in subependymal regions where the germinal matrix is supplied by tenuous vessels with limited supporting tissue.

Imaging by MR offers the most precise diagnosis of hemorrhage into the posterior fossa, whether parenchymal or extra-axial in location. Sagittal images clearly define the margins of the tentorium. Flow within the major dural sinuses is easily verified, either with routine imaging or with MR angiography.

Images obtained by CT as 3-mm thick axial slices may also define the presence and location of hemorrhage within the cerebellar parenchyma, especially when combined with reformatting in the sagittal plane. Early diagnosis is essential for prompt appropriate management.

US may demonstrate asymmetrically increased echogenicity within one cerebellar hemisphere. For patients with suspected posterior fossa subdural or intraparenchymal hematomas, urgent CT or MR imaging is generally necessary to definitively establish or exclude the diagnosis.

Subarachnoid Hemorrhage

Blood may be demonstrated in the subarachnoid space in association with the presence of subdural, intracerebral, or intracerebellar hemorrhage. It may also occur as the result of rupture of an aneurysm or vascular malformation, or may occur in association with an infarction, tumor, or bleeding disorder. In these situations, SAH is considered to be present from an extension of the primary site of hemorrhage. Primary SAH, unassociated with the above processes, is relatively common in the newborn. It is usually not extensive and is associated with a generally favorable prognosis for subsequent neurologic development. Primary SAH is usually asymptomatic or is associated with seizures that begin on the second day. Extensive primary SAH is

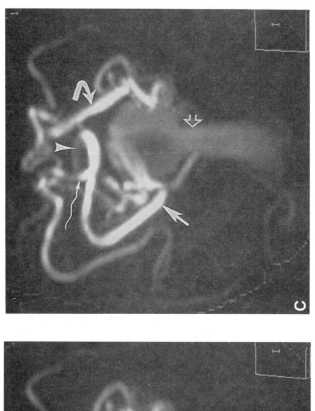

Figure 10C.

Figure 10B.

uncommon and is usually associated with other clinical and imaging manifestations of severe perinatal asphyxia.

The only imaging method that reliably detects SAH is CT. It will also demonstrate parenchymal alterations which may be responsible for secondary SAH. Since the subarachnoid space at the surface of the brain is normally echogenic, US does not reliably differentiate this pattern from similar alterations that occur in association with subarachnoid blood.

Subdural Hematoma

Subdural hemorrhage (SDH) is more common in the full term than in the preterm infant. SDH commonly results from the combination of a rapid passage of a relatively large infant through a relatively small, rigid birth canal, often with abnormal presentation and/or difficult forceps or vacuum extraction. The sites of bleeding include tentorial or falx laceration, rupture of superficial cerebral veins, and posterior fossa hemorrhage secondary to occipital osteodiastasis. Tentorial or falx laceration is especially likely to occur at the junction of these two dural structures, and the resultant SDH may arise either from the dura, from the encased venous sinuses, or from the vein of Galen. Hemorrhage may be entirely subdural, in the supratentorial or infratentorial compartments, or may also be subarachnoid in location. Superficial vein rupture is usually associated with subdural hematoma location over the convexities but may also be associated with cerebral contusion. Occipital osteodiastasis is another mechanism for the occurrence of subdural hematoma. In breech delivery, hyperextension of the head places pressure on the occiput and the occipital bone is displaced anteriorly lacerating the inferior sagittal sinus and dura. Subdural hematoma has also been identified as an intrauterine process, prior to the normal forces of delivery.[23-25]

Imaging by CT is the most commonly used method for demonstration of supratentorial or infratentorial SDH (Figure 11). Reformatted images allow localization of the hematoma to the posterior fossa or to infratentorial compartments, and allows characterization of the convexity of the occipital bone and its relationship to the foramen magnum. The scout image or a reformatted sagittal image may confirm the presence of occipital osteodiastasis.

MR imaging allows definitive identification of the relationship of the tentorium to SDH suspected to be within the posterior fossa. Small subdural hematomas over the cerebral convexities may be missed with MR technique.

US may detect an area of suspected hemorrhage within the posterior fossa but is less definitive in establishing the relationship of the hematoma to surrounding dural membranes and adjacent cerebellar parenchyma. SDHs over the cerebral convexities are echogenic when acute and hypo-echogenic

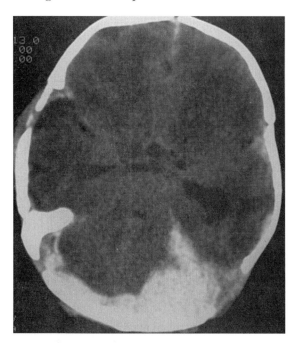

Figure 11. Posterior fossa subdural hematoma in an infant of 38 weeks gestation delivered by vacuum extraction. Apgar scores were 9 at both 1 and 5 minutes. At age 4 hours, there were episodes of apnea and bradycardia. CT imaging demonstrates a large subdural hematoma within the posterior fossa. There is mass effect manifest by displacement of the fourth ventricle and by effacement of the subarachnoid space in the posterior fossa. The lateral and third ventricles were enlarged on other images. The posterior fossa subdural hematoma was not demonstrable with US.

when chronic. Small hematomas at the convexities may be missed if the acoustic window at the anterior fontanel is not optimally large in size.

Except for the initial detection of IVH, which can readily be accomplished with US in the neonatal intensive care unit, CT imaging is the optimal technique for the detection and localization of hemorrhage within the cranial vault. It readily identifies the intraparenchymal, intraventricular, subarachnoid, or subdural location of hemorrhage and, with bone algorithms, defines the presence of possible associated cranial fractures. Areas of cerebral parenchymal abnormality are also easily identified.

Traumatic Encephalopathy

As indicated above, CT is the best single imaging procedure when perinatal trauma is suspected. It is important to add that for the infant with suspected child abuse CT imaging is also the study of choice. While US may be utilized to exclude large lesions, US and MR are both unable to detect small amounts of SAH, and may miss small subdural fluid or blood collections. In patients with a prior history of trauma, MR studies obtained weeks to months later are the most useful imaging procedure for characterizing residual gliosis, volume loss, or extra-axial fluid collection.

Intracranial Infection and Post-Infectious Encephalopathy

Infections involving the brain or meninges may be antenatal or perinatal in origin. Since CT demonstrates cerebral parenchymal calcifications better than does US, CT is generally utilized when a search is being made for cortical, basal ganglia, or periventricular markers of infection acquired in utero. These regions of calcification may also demonstrate focal of increased echogenicity with US examination.

Perinatal acquired viral or bacterial infection of the brain or meninges is best diagnosed on the basis of CSF and blood studies. Imaging findings are variable but supportive of the diagnosis. Imaging becomes of greatest use in the characterization of sequelae, including focal areas of cerebritis or abscess formation, the localization of arterial or venous infarction, the development of subdural effusion, or the occurrence of ventriculitis, hydrocephalus, or cerebral hemorrhage. US may be utilized to screen for the anatomic changes associated with these sequelae, as defined above. Definitive diagnosis or exclusion of many of these alterations, however, requires CT or MR imaging.

US is superior to CT for the characterization of ventricular septations that may occur in association with ventriculomegaly following intracranial infection of any cause. Septations represent glial or fibrotic responses to either IVH or to congenital or acquired infectious processes. Identification of such septae is important for the appropriate placement of shunting devices. With long TR, short TE MR sequences, septae are perhaps less well demonstrated than with US. They may be seen with MR either as anatomic structures and/or as barriers between fluid collections that have differing signal intensities because of differing protein content or flow/pulsation characteristics.

In infants with ventriculitis, US imaging demonstrates increased echogenicity of the ependymal surface. Regions of cerebritis appear as areas of echogenicity within the cerebral parenchyma that may not be distinguishable from areas of infarction. Contrast enhanced CT or MR imaging is the preferred imaging modality for the identification of an area of cerebritis or abscess, though subsequent US may be utilized to follow abscess size in response to treatment. MR imaging with contrast enhancement is more sensitive to meningeal inflammation occurring in association with meningitis than is US or CT imaging.

Congenital Structural Abnormalities

Migration Anomalies

MR imaging is the preferred technique for the demonstration of congenital structural and migration anomalies. Such alteration can frequently be demonstrated during the neonatal period of time, explaining recurring seizure activity or other neurologic dysfunction that may otherwise be attributed to a perinatal insult. Posterior fossa structural anomalies and abnormalities within the spinal canal are also best characterized with MR technique.

Hydrocephalus

Imaging by CT and US are similar in their utility for the demonstration of lateral and third ventricular size in the newborn, and for the characterization of ventricular size over time. At some point in the evaluation of ventriculomegaly, however, a CT or MR study must be accomplished to characterize patency of the aqueduct of Sylvius and to look for other congenital or acquired structural anomalies that may occur in association with or may be responsible for ventricular enlargement. An exception to this rule may be the initial management of a newborn with ventriculomegaly secondary to intraventricular extension of subependymal germinal matrix hemorrhage.

Conclusions

No current imaging procedure can be considered an effective "'screening" technique for the imaging evaluation of the newborn with symptomatology related to CNS dysfunction. The material in this chapter has been presented to emphasize the need for the correlation of gestational age, symptomatology, and suspected clinico-pathologic mechanism of injury in the selection of the most appropriate imaging study. For the preterm or term infant with seizures unrelated to the usual metabolic alterations, the choice of US as an imaging tool may be inappropriate since cerebral cortical structures are a prime potential location for structural alteration. In this group of infants, it may also be important to obtain early imaging to exclude the presence of a lesion that arose entirely in the antepartum period. Imaging by MR or CT is best utilized as the initial modality. For a premature infant with suspected PVL or IVH, US be the only imaging modality required during the newborn period of time. It must be recognized, however, that many of the patterns of neuropathologic alteration described above do not occur in isolation. Additionally, primary CNS developmental alterations or acquired antepartum CNS damage may predispose to intrapartum or postnatal hypoxic-ischemic events.

References

1. Barkovich AJ, Kjos BO, Jackson DE Jr, et al. Normal maturation of the neonatal and infant brain: MR imaging at 1.5 T[1]. Radiology 1988;166:173.
2. Barkovich AJ, Gressens P, Evrard P. Formation, maturation, and disorders of brain neocortex. Am J Neuroradiol 1992;13:423.
3. Scher MS, Belfar H, Martin J, et al. Destructive brain lesions of presumed fetal onset: Antepartum causes of cerebral palsy. Pediatrics 1991;88:898.
4. Volpe JJ. *Neurology of the Newborn*, Third Edition. Philadelphia, W.B. Saunders Company, 1995.
5. Barkovich AJ. *Pediatric Neuroimaging*, Second Edition. New York, Raven Press, 1995.
6. Siegel MJ. *Pediatric Sonography*. New York, Raven Press, 1995.
7. Wolpert SM, Barnes PD. *MRI in Pediatric Neuroradiology*. St. Louis, Mosby-Year Book, 1992.
8. Barks JD, Silverstein FS. Excitatory amino acids contribute to the pathogenesis of perinatal hypoxic-ischemic brain injury. Brain Pathol 1992;2:235.
9. Bowerman RA, Donn SM, DiPietro MA, et al. Periventricular leukomalacia in the pre-term newborn infant: Sonographic and clinical features. Radiology 1984;151:383.
10. Rodriguez J, Claus D, Verellen G, et al. Periventricular leukomalacia: Ultrasonic and neuropathological correlations. Dev Med Child Neurol 1990;32:347.
11. Laub MC, Ingrisch H. Increased periventricular echogenicity (periventricular halos) in neonatal brain: A sonographic study. Neuropediatrics 1986;17:39.
12. Hope PL, Gould SJ, Howard S, et al. Precision of ultrasound diagnosis of pathologically verified lesions in the brains of very preterm infants. Dev Med Child Neurol 1988;30:457.
13. Flodmark O, Lupton B, Li D, et al. MR imaging of periventricular leukomalacia in childhood. Am J Roentgenol 1989;152:583.
14. Krägeloh-Mann I, Hagberg B, Petersen D, et al. Bilateral spastic cerebral palsy— pathogenetic aspects from MRI. Neuropediatrics 1992;23:46.
15. Truwit CL, Barkovich AJ, Koch TK, et al. Cerebral palsy: MR findings in 40 patients. Am J Neuroradiol 1992;13:67.
16. van Bogaert P, Baleriaux D, Christophe C, et al. MRI of patients with cerebral palsy and normal CT scan. Neuroradiology 1992;34:52.
17. Papile L, Burstein J, Burstein R, et al. Incidence and evolution of subependymal and intraventricular hemorrhage: A study of infants with birth weights less than 1,500 gm. J Pediatr 1978;92:529.
18. Gould SJ, Howard S, Hope PL, et al. Periventricular intraparenchymal cerebral haemorrhage in preterm infants: The role of venous infarction. J Pathol 1987;151:197.
19. Armstrong DL, Sauls CD, Goddard-Finegold J. Neuropathologic findings in short-term survivors of intraventricular hemorrhage. Am J Dis Child 1987;141:617.
20. Skullerud K, Westre B. Frequency and prognostic significance of germinal matrix hemorrhage, periventricular leukomalacia, and pontosubicular necrosis in preterm neonates. Acta Neuropathol 1986;70:257.

21. Roland EH, Flodmark O, Hill A. Thalamic hemorrhage with intraventricular hemorrhage in the full-term newborn. Pediatrics 1990;85:737.
22. Schellinger D, Grant EG, Manz HJ, et al. Intraparenchymal hemorrhage in preterm neonates: A broadening spectrum. Am J Roentgenol 1988;150:1109.
23. Hanigan WC, Ali MB, Cusack TJ, et al. Diagnosis of subdural hemorrhage in utero. J Neurosurg 1985;63:977.
24. Atluru VL, Kumar IR. Intrauterine chronic subdural hematoma with postoperative tension pneumocephalus. Pediatr Neurol 1987;3:306.
25. Rotmensch S Grannum PA, Nores JA, et al. In utero diagnosis and management of fetal subdural hematoma. Am J Obstet Gynecol 1991;164:1246.

Chapter 28

The Postdates/Postmature Infant

◆◆◆

Robert E. Schumacher, M.D.

Introduction

It is clear that the clinician caring for an infant who is born "postdates" or appears "postmature" is dealing with an infant who is "at risk." The answers to the questions "at risk for what?" and "why?" are not nearly as clear. The perinatal mortality rate increases significantly when gestation becomes prolonged. Most of this mortality is attributable to stillbirth; however, the cause of any excessive neonatal morbidity/mortality is debatable. Some invoke neonatal gigantism (macrosomia) as causative, others blame Clifford's malnourished appearing dysmature infant as the major contributor to the problem.[1] Moreover, studies examining the epidemiology of the problem often come to apparently opposing views.

Definitions

Clinicians' confusing use of terms is not helpful. The terms "postdates," or "post-term pregnancy" usually refer to a pregnancy that has gone 2 weeks past its due date, thus beginning at 42 weeks gestation. Some begin using the same terms when pregnancy exceeds 41 weeks, a few at > 40 weeks.

The terms postmaturity and dysmaturity are thought of by most to be descriptive of the newborn and can be assigned to infants only after they have been examined. However, in his classic work describing the postmature infant, Clifford states that "postmaturity should be defined as pregnancies prolonged 300 days or more . . .".[1] In this paper, Clifford described the "Postmaturity Syndrome," which is ascribed to placental dysfunction. These infants were divided into three groups depending upon the degree of placental dys-

From: Donn SM, Fisher CW (eds.): *Risk Management Techniques in Perinatal and Neonatal Practice.* © Futura Publishing Co., Inc., Armonk, NY, 1996.

function encountered. The most severely affected infants were described as having little or no vernix, parchment-like skin, and showing evidence of having recently lost weight in utero. The skin, nails, and umbilical cord are stained yellow from having been in prolonged contact with meconium-stained amniotic fluid (MSAF). The group of infants so described ranged in gestational age from 284-324 days from the first day of the mother's last menstrual period (40 4/7 to 46 2/7 weeks gestational age). Thus, Clifford suggested the use of the term "the placental dysfunction syndrome" as applicable to infants who, irrespective of gestational age, fulfilled his physical criteria. Despite Clifford's clear definition of terms, many clinicians reserve the term "postmature" for infants who fulfill Clifford's physical criteria for the placental dysfunction syndrome and are "postdates." The term "dysmature" is used interchangeably with postmature/placental dysfunction syndrome when an infant is postdates. It is also used by many to describe an infant who is not necessarily postdates but fulfills Clifford's criteria for the placental dysfunction syndrome. The distinction between such infants and infants who are small-for-gestational age is based upon the nature of the growth failure present in the infant. Infants who are symmetrically growth retarded (proportionately small for length, weight, and head circumference) and do not show evidence of "wasting" are not dysmature. Infants can appear dysmature when not small-for-gestational age. They do, however, show the appearance of having lost weight in utero. The distinction between a true postdate/postmature infant and an asymmetrically growth retarded infant at (for example) 37-38 weeks gestational age is not appreciated by this author.

Given the confusion surrounding the nomenclature, any clinician caring for such infants is obliged to describe any and all of the physical characteristics of dysmaturity present in a patient. This includes an accurate measurement of weight, length, and head circumference. It is intuitive that in addition to detailed physical descriptions of dysmature newborns, clinicians must make efforts to assign a gestational age using widely accepted means (e.g., Ballard or Dubowitz assessment). Although rarely possible in the "real world," such an assessment should be made independent of knowledge of the gestational age assigned by obstetrical means.

Postdatism/Dysmaturity

Associations and Risks

By using such phrases as, "We have become convinced that there is a very striking clinical picture associated with intrauterine existence beyond the normal time," Clifford implied a cause-and-effect relationship between postdatism and dysmaturity.[1] It is interesting to note that, despite the insinuation, the relative risk of the postmaturity syndrome with increasing gestational age was not calculated by Clifford. Today many clinicians continue to assume that the relative risk of dysmaturity increases with increasing gestational age. There is little evidence in support of this idea. Sjostedt and co-workers[2] coined the phrase dysmaturity when, in their study of over 1000 infants, they pointed out that infants with signs of malnutrition were not the exclusive domain of post-date pregnancies.

McLean and co-workers[3] sought to define the relative risk of dysmaturity with gestational age. These authors noted that characteristically, fetal growth curves (including one published at their own institution) show a decreased rate of growth starting at about 37 weeks gestation. They speculated that many of these curves may be in error because of incorrect gestational age assignment in post-term pregnancies. In support of this, McLean cited some previous work, Kramer et al.,[4] showing that when using only last menstrual period dating, just 12% of infants thought to be postdates were so. Then, using dates confirmed by early ultrasound examinations in over 7000 pregnancies, McLean and coworkers[3] showed that no evidence for postterm weight loss or increased relative risk for dysmaturity could be found. These investigators concluded that "macrosomia, not intrauterine growth retardation, appears to be the valid concern in post-term pregnancies."

The "ponderal index" (PI) has been used by investigators as a means of identifying and/or quantifying the degree of wasting present in a dysmature newborn. The equation used is weight/length[3]. Although theoretically sound, unless a very accurate measurement of length is taken, this parameter is subject to magnification of measurement error. To minimize error in length measurement, some investigators advocate making use of the tonic neck reflex to overcome the natural tendency of the newborn to keep the hips and knees flexed.[5] In an often cited study, Miller[5] used the PI to characterize in utero growth in over 800 Kansas-born infants. This investigator published a figure of the distribution of PIs by percentile groups according to gestational age. He made the observation that after 38 weeks percentile values for PI did not change. That is a PI value of 2.20 represents the third percentile at all gestational ages > 38 weeks. He reported little variation in PI by sex or race. Although specifics were not given, the author did not find that mortality appeared higher in malnourished (PI < 2.20) infants.

It is conceivable to reconcile the observations: 1. that the relative risk of dysmaturity does not increase with increasing gestational age; and 2. the apparent increased mortality seen in post-date dysmature infants, if one hypothesizes an effect of gestational age on the sequelae of dysmaturity. That is, post-date dysmature infants are at increased risk for morbidity versus their term dysmature counterparts. Authors have addressed this hypothesis in several studies.

Sachs and Friedman[6] published an epidemiologic study of postdates pregnancy and found an overall nonsignificant rise in perinatal mortality in pregnancies lasting greater than or equal to 42 weeks versus deliveries occurring at 38-41 weeks. Perinatal mortality did rise significantly when infants were delivered beyond 42 weeks. The overall perinatal mortality rate was six times greater for small infants (< 2500 g) compared to larger infants, but there were too few small/post-date infants to test for an interaction between size and gestational age. Whether the lack of small post-date infants represented continued growth or expeditious delivery of growth retarded infants prior to 43 weeks was not addressed. Morbidity consisting of an increase in fetal "distress" in labor, MSAF, respiratory distress, meconium aspiration, and persistence of the fetal circulation was seen more often in post-date infants.

Callenbach and Hall[7] reviewed the courses of 53 postterm infants admitted to their neonatal intensive care unit (NICU). Infants who resembled Clifford's postmature infants and had PIs < 2.20 were compared with normally grown postterm infants. The authors reported that all deaths occurred in the normally grown group and that morbidity was equally distributed between the two groups. They conclude that the "postterm" infant should be considered at risk, even if normally grown.

Schumacher et al.[8] reviewed the history of 403 infants admitted to the University of Michigan at > 38 weeks gestation. Linear and logistic regression analyses were used to test the hypotheses that the presence or absence of the independent variables gestational age > 42 weeks or fetal malnutrition (PI < 2.20) were associated with a number of obstetrical and/or neonatal variables. The presence of significant interactions between gestational age and PI was sought for all outcomes. A significant interaction between advanced gestational age and low PI did *not* occur for any outcome variable. Thus, postdatism and dysmaturity appeared to contribute independent risks to infants admitted to an NICU. Primigravidas, MSAF, Cesarean section, birth trauma, and neonatal death were associated with postdatism but not dysmaturity. Preeclampsia, maternal smoking, neurologic abnormalities, and a need for extracorporeal membrane oxygenation were associated with dysmaturity but not postdatism.

Thus, with respect to certain common beliefs regarding infants born after prolonged pregnancy, the literature does not offer strong cause-and-effect type arguments in support of the concept of an increased risk of fetal malnutrition with post-term pregnancies. Neither does it support a role for advanced gestational age altering the consequences of fetal malnutrition.

Lastly, Naeye[9] reported on the causes of perinatal mortality excess in prolonged gestations. Twenty-six percent of the mortality excess resulted from congenital malformations.

In summary, the clinician faced with the prospect of caring for a postdates infant must be prepared for the consequences of continued good fetal growth (macrosomia), the appearance of malnutrition (the dysmature infant), or the infant with congenital anomalies. Effective communication with obstetrical colleagues should help the clinician in preparatory efforts. As discussed elsewhere (see Chapter 9) it is often difficult to accurately date a pregnancy, so communication with the obstetrical care taker regarding certainty of dates will also be important. Maternal risk factors for dysmaturity should be identified and communicated. In labor, obstetrical concerns for the well being of the fetus should be forwarded to the person(s) responsible for neonatal resuscitation.

Macrosomia

Obstetrical Risk Factors

Given McLean's et al.[3] observations concerning growth in post-date pregnancy, it would seem logical that as pregnancy continues past term the incidence of macrosomia and its complications will increase. As noted in Chapter 9, it is not always possible to identify fetal macrosomia; however, some authors have described epidemiologic risk factors for infant macrosomia and its complications. Spellacy and co-workers[10] in a study of 33,545 infants, described maternal characteristics and infant complications seen in 574 macrosomic (> 4500 g) infants. The overall frequency of macrosomia was 1.7%. Prolonged gestation, maternal obesity, and maternal diabetes were conditions that occurred with higher frequency in mothers who delivered macrosomic infants. These mothers were also older and had a higher parity score. However, the frequency of occurrence of high-risk maternal factors in the macrosomic infants was < 50% for each of the above factors, hence the positive predictive value of any individual maternal factor was low. (Maternal obesity did occur with 44% of the macrosomic infants.) Infant outcomes associated with macrosomia were shoulder dystocia, any "birth injury" as described by the pediatrician, and fetal death. Delivery by Cesarean section was associated with fewer birth injuries for the macrosomic infants. There was no increase in the frequency of congenital anomalies associated with the macrosomic group. Lazer et al.[11] described obstetrical associations and complications of macrosomia in 525 macrosomic infants (> 4500 g); this number represented 0.72% of the 73,030 infants delivered. Using a case-control retrospective study technique, macrosomia was associated with greater gravidity, diabetes mellitus, older maternal age, weight gain > 15 kg, a previous macrosomic infant, pregnancy-induced hypertension, and placenta previa. Cesarean section, especially for cephalopelvic disproportion was more common in the macrosomic infants; vacuum extraction deliveries were similarly increased in macrosomic group. The perinatal mortality rate was higher in the macrosomic group. The authors opined that the reasons for high mortality was "mechanical difficulty during passage of the macrosomic fetus through the birth canal." The macrosomic group had a higher incidence of Erb's palsy and fractured clavicle.

Management of the Macrosomic Infant

The implications of the above studies for the clinician who will be caring for a post-date infant are straightforward. Anticipate having to care for a macrosomic infant, especially if additional risk factors for macrosomia are present. Birth trauma, such as clavicular fracture and/or brachial plexus injury, is a problem to be anticipated.

Clavicular fracture can be silent, detectable only via crepitus or discontinuity to palpation. Care of the infant with a clavicular fracture is supportive. Care in the handling of the infant should be taught to the parents; they should be reassured that such a fracture is usually not a complicated or serious injury and that healing should occur without complications. Orthopedic consultation is usually not necessary. If a clavicular fracture is found, a careful search for other injuries such as brachial plexus injury should be undertaken.

Brachial plexus injury occurs in about 2.6 infants per 1000 live full term births.[12] This traction injury occurs when nerve fibers of the brachial plexus are stretched or avulsed and, as noted above, is associated with the delivery of large infants. Injury occurring to the fifth and sixth cervical segments results in Erb's palsy and is characterized by more proximal arm muscle weakness. When the lower cervical segments are involved Klumpke's palsy, which involves the hand muscles, can be seen. Care of the infant with signs of a brachial plexus injury is directed towards prevention of contractures. The extent of the injury should be documented. The limb should be immobilized gently; splinting is not recommended. Occupational/physical therapists may be consulted with therapy usually beginning 7-10 days after birth. Recovery may take many months. The parents should be made aware of the nature of the injury and the nature and timing of recovery.

A small percentage of brachial plexus injuries are accompanied by phrenic nerve injury and diaphragmatic paralysis.[13] Infants with signs of brachial plexus injury and respiratory distress should be investigated. Failure of diaphragmatic motion may be suspected by chest radiography and confirmed by fluoroscopic or ultrasonographic examination. Reports of respiratory distress of an insidious nature have been noted such that any respiratory distress in the first few weeks of life should make the clinician wary. Decreased diaphragmatic motion may predispose an infant to atelectasis and pneumonia. Parents should be made aware of this risk. The majority of infants with unilateral diaphragmatic paralysis recover but recovery can take months.

Brachial plexus injury may also be accompanied by ptosis, anhidrosis, miosis, and endopthalmus (Horner's syndrome). The physician must remember to look for this complication; ophthalmologic consultation may be required. In Eng's[14] series of infants with brachial plexus injuries, other traumatic lesions (fractured humerus, subluxation of the shoulder or spine, and facial palsy) were noted. Thus, infants with a brachial plexus injury should be examined carefully for evidence of associated trauma.

Shoulder dystocia may predispose to spinal cord injury in the newborn. This injury is said to be caused by excessive traction applied to the spinal cord/canal during birth.[15,16] A "pop" or snapping noise has been heard at the time of delivery of infants sustaining a spinal cord injury. Signs of this injury vary with the level of the injury, ranging from irreversible brainstem injury to mild injury that is recoverable. Both the early and late sequelae and management of this injury have been reviewed.[15,16]

The need for vacuum extraction and macrosomia are statistically related. Accordingly, such an infant may be at increased risk from adverse sequelae from the use of a vacuum extractor. The presence of the so-called "chignon," which represents a localized scalp tissue response to suction forces, should be anticipated. Such swelling may be of little consequence to the infant, but the parents should be made aware of this fact. Similarly, a cephalhematoma resulting from the disruption of vessels passing from the skull to the periosteum is usually of little consequence to the infant. Since these hematomas may contain significant amounts of blood, infants should be watched for signs of hyperbilirubinemia. Again, because such soft tissue injuries are often obvious, parents should be educated as to the clinicians' expectations and plans for such injuries (usually expectant management).

Finally because of the increased risk of prolonged entrapment, the clinician caring for a potentially macrosomic infant should be prepared to resuscitate the infant. Great care must be taken in the manipulation of the head and neck during resuscitation.

Dysmaturity

Obstetrical Associations

Even though questions exist as to whether dysmature infants are more commonly seen with increasing gestational age, the clinician expected to care for such an infant should be prepared. Clifford[17] stated that clues to possible placental dysfunction included shrinkage in the size of the uterus because of the resorption of amniotic fluid, maternal weight loss, and prolonged labor. As reported by Schumacher et al.,[8] ill dysmature infants admitted to an NICU are more common in pregnancies complicated by mothers who smoke, pregnancy-induced hypertension, fetal distress, and oligohydramnios. Ting et al.[18] were unable to find any statistically significant association with a number of maternal factors. Some investigators[19] have successfully used a "fetal PI" as a predictor of intrauterine growth retardation. Rayburn and colleagues[20] found that subnormal urinary estrogen:creatinine ratios and sonographic evidence of oligohydramnios were the most reliable predictors of dysmaturity; the former test is seldom used.

The presence of oligohydramnios seems an important maternal factor that should alert a pediatrician that an infant may be dysmature. Communication with obstetrical colleagues is therefore emphasized.

Neonatal Risks

As noted above, the neonatal risks of dysmaturity, as distinct from postdatism are not always clear. Elevated hematocrit values secondary to chronic placental insufficiency and consequent hyperviscosity syndrome are usually cited as consequences of dysmaturity.[21] Callenbach and Hall[7] and Ting et al.[18] report an increased hematocrit value in dysmature versus normally grown infants. Patterson and co-workers[22] found a similar association but they opined that this elevation in hematocrit was not related to fetal oxygenation but instead to differences in hydration. Using conductometric investigations of subcutaneous tissue, Bielecka-Winnicka[23] found evidence of dehydration in dysmature infants. This investigator noted that a lack of postnatal weight loss (usually ascribed to loss of extracellular water) gave credence to this idea of in utero weight loss. It seems prudent to obtain a hematocrit value in any dysmature infant.

Disturbances of coagulation have been reported in association with dysmature infants. Perlman and Dvilansky[21] prospectively studied the blood coagulation status of postmature infants, finding abnormalities in the postmature versus normal controls. Inspection of their data suggests that, although statistical differences in various measures of coagulation status existed, the values were usually not out of the normal range. Nonetheless, the care taker for a dysmature infant should be alerted to the possibility of a bleeding diathesis and document the presence or absence of bruising or other findings on physical examination.

Others[7,8] have found a low PI (vs normal) to be associated with acidosis at birth, the diagnosis of persistent pulmonary hypertension, central nervous system dysfunction, and need for extracorporeal membrane oxygenation. These latter findings were descriptive of infants in an ICU and relative risks for the non-ICU infant have not yet been ascertained.

The association of persistent pulmonary hypertension and dysmaturity may be present for several different reasons. Whether any of the causes of PPHN are associated with dysmaturity remains speculative. Increased pulmonary vascular resistance may be present by virtue of concomitant asphyxia. In this scenario, hypoxia, hypercarbia, and acidosis presumably lead to elevated pulmonary vascular resistance. Cardiac dysfunction may lead to relatively low systemic vascular resistance and favor right-to-left shunting. Chronic intrauterine hypoxia may lead to excessive pulmonary artery smooth muscle thickness and/or precocious extension of pulmonary artery smooth muscle to the acinar level. Research in this area is scant.

The association of meconium aspiration syndrome and dysmaturity, as opposed to postdatism, is not always clear. Clifford's[1] classic description of the stage 2 and 3 postmature infant included meconium staining of the infant as "definitional." If only this classic definition of dysmaturity is used, it is easy to see that there will be an increased incidence of meconium aspiration syndrome in such infants. If instead one uses a low PI as a marker of dysmaturity, the association of dysmaturity and meconium aspiration is not as solid. Callenbach and Hall[7] found that the incidence of meconium aspiration syndrome was similar in post-date infants whether normally grown or not. When gestational age and dysmaturity were treated as independent variables, Schumacher et al.[8] found meconium staining of the amniotic fluid associated with advanced gestational age but not dysmaturity. In this group of infants hospitalized in an NICU, neither postdatism nor a low PI was statistically associated with meconium aspiration. Rayburn and colleagues[20] found the incidence of MSAF to be similar in dysmature and post-date infants.

Infants with evidence of wasting are at risk for hypoglycemia presumably because of decreased glycogen stores (see Chapter 24). Hypoglycemia is also associated with polycythemia.[21]

Management of the Dysmature Infant

Caring for the dysmature infant starts with recognition of obstetrical risk factors. A clinician capable of resuscitating an infant should be present at every delivery (see Chapter 22). Careful attention must be paid to providing a stress-free environment to allow for a successful transition to an adult circulation pattern. Simple steps such as providing a neutral thermal environment are important. The liberal use of supplemental oxygen has little "downside risk" in term infants.

Once delivered, careful observation and documentation of the presence or absence of the physical characteristics associated with dysmaturity is needed. A complete blood count with platelet count will help to identify infants at risk for sequelae of polycythemia and/or coagulation disturbances. Controversy exists over the management of infants with polycythemia. Many clinicians simply observe polycythemic infants for signs and intervene only when an infant appears compromised. Others suggest routine screening and treatment (partial exchange transfusion) for polycythemia. Regardless of the treatment strategy chosen, all the evidence used for making decisions and the rational for the course of action chosen must be succinctly stated in the infant's record.

Bielecka-Winnicka's[23] observations on the fluid status of dysmature infants suggests that the clinician pay careful attention to fluid balance and assure adequate hydration in infants who appear dysmature. Dysmature infants should have their blood glucose status monitored. Early feedings, if not contraindicated, may prevent hypoglycemia. If hypoglycemia is suspected by using screening methods, its presence should confirmed by the hospital laboratory and its more accurate methodology (see Chapter 24).

Meconium Aspiration

A lengthy discussion concerning the significance of MSAF and early treatment is found in Chapter 9. Salient points are that although the presence of MSAF may be a sensitive indicator of distress, the positive predictive value of meconium-stained fluid for clinically meaningful fetal compromise is low. Most infants with MSAF do well. Other concomitant findings such as the presence of a worrisome fetal heart rate pattern or oligohydramnios should further alert the newborn care taker towards the need for resuscitation of a distressed infant. The *Guidelines for Perinatal Care*, a joint publication of the American Academy of Pediatrics and the American College of Obstetrics and Gynecology, states that someone capable of initiating resuscitation should be present at every delivery.[24] In the case of a fetus with meconium-stained fluid this means someone capable of clearing the newborn airway of meconium. When meconium is noted, the mother's care taker should identify and notify a newborn "resuscitator." Not only will this person have adequate time to prepare for a resuscitation, there may often be time to explain plans for management of the baby to the parents. Informed parents will be less likely to be surprised/upset when the need for resuscitation interferes with preconceived ideas of the delivery.

The finding of meconium in the airways of stillborn infants suggests that meconium can be aspirated in utero. Hooper and Harding[25] found that in an animal model of utero-placental insufficiency net fetal pulmonary fluid production slowed to the point that in some instances with normal fetal breathing movements net fluid flow was from amniotic sac into the lungs. Thus, meconium could theoretically be aspirated in utero even without fetal gasping. One can now envision a pregnancy with meconium-stained fluid producing either a normal infant, a non-asphyxiated infant with "incidental" meconium aspiration, an asphyxiated infant with no aspiration, or an asphyxiated infant with aspiration of meconium. Thibeault and co-workers[26] described such scenarios in a series of sick newborns with meconium aspiration syndrome with or without concomitant asphyxia. Meconium aspiration may occur concomitantly with other stress-provoking conditions such as sepsis, fetal anemia, or pre-existent fetal neurologic injury. Clinicians must resist the temptation to reflexively ascribe meconium aspiration syndrome to "birth asphyxia" and should perform a vigilant search for underlying causes of stress. Similarly, an infant born through meconium-stained fluid who develops respiratory distress may or may not have aspirated meconium. Additional information such as whether meconium was retrieved from the airway and/or whether chest radiographic findings are compatible with aspiration must be considered. Attempts to time the duration of meconium staining (and thus time an underlying "insult") have been attempted by several investigators.[27]

Meconium aspiration syndrome is often characterized by an initial obstructive phase followed by a pneumonitis or inflammatory type illness that typically worsens over a period of hours. Acute deterioration early in the course of illness should alert the clinician to the possibility of pneumothorax. Confirmatory transillumination of the chest and/or a chest radiograph should be obtained. Clinicians should be wary of the well-appearing infant from whom meconium was suctioned from the trachea. Infants who have aspirated but do not manifest initial signs of obstructive respiratory illness may, after some period of time, develop a severe chemical pneumonitis.

The clinician caring for a newborn with meconium aspiration should look for and record the presence or absence of additional organ system failure and/or signs of the syndrome of persistent pulmonary hypertension.

Congenital Anomalies

Naeye[9] described causes of perinatal mortality excess in prolonged gestations. In one paper, 26% of the mortality excess was ascribed to congenital malformations. Naeye[9] stated that this excess appeared to be in infants who had hypoplastic adrenal glands. Eden et al's.[28] review of perinatal deaths in post-date pregnancy found congenital malformations to be associated with perinatal death; the perinatal mortality rate for patients with a congenital malformation was 31.7 per 1000 live births. Lazer and co-workers[11] found no association between macrosomia and an increased incidence of malformations. Schumacher et al.[8] noted 8% of post-date NICU patients had major congenital anomalies. Anencephaly is an anomaly commonly cited as being associated with a post-date pregnancy.

Because of the association of anomalies and post-datism a careful physical examination and documentation of the same is warranted in all infants born "postdates." If a post-date infant should die, a post-mortem exam looking for internal anomalies is essential.

Summary

The case of an infant born postdates poses special concerns for clinicians. These infants are at risk for the consequences of macrosomia; they may or may not be at increased risk for the consequences of dysmaturity. Mortality excess in these infants is contributed to by the presence of congenital anomalies. Because of confusion surrounding definitions the clinician must accurately describe objective findings and resist the temptation to assign cause-and-effect relationships to what may be simple associations and epiphenomena. Communication with obstetrical colleagues and anticipatory behavior will provide the best care for these infants. Communication with and education of parents before and after delivery remain essential risk management tools.

> **Commentary by Mr. Peters:** Dr. Schumacher's medical analysis of "The Postdates/Postmature Infant" is thorough and consistent with the great weight of medical evidence. The purpose of this commentary is to amplify some of Dr. Schumacher's points and to explore several issues not explicitly addressed.
>
> The expectations of the pregnant woman and her participation in the decision-making options confronting the post-date pregnancy should be further explored. The role of third party payers as well as state and federal regulators must also be considered.
>
> Patient education is a pre-condition of informed consent. The increased fetal/neonatal morbidity and mortality associated with post-date pregnancy should be communicated to the patient in as calm and reassuring fashion as possible. The elusive bogeyman of "maternal stress" must be considered in this process. This of course, presents a delicate balancing act. The options of Cesarean section versus induction and the relative complications of each should be explained to the patient before a decision has to be made. An issue of recurring inquiry to plaintiff's attorneys for example, is the induced patient's surprise at a fourth degree tear despite episiotomy and the associated complication of recto-vaginal fistula. These complications are, of course, foreseeable as result of the larger fetus frequently associated with post-date pregnancy.
>
> As the screws of cost containment are tightened, the comparative costs of Cesarean section versus induction and the associated complications should be weighed and discussed with the patient. Obstetricians will be increasingly called upon to act as patient advocates as regulators and third-party payers continue in their attempts to substitute their judgment for that of the health care providers. It is probable that state legislatures will intervene in obstetrical practice

more than they intervene in any other medical specialty practice. Lengths of stay after delivery, screening tests, and the application or non-application of obstetrical services are expected to receive more public scrutiny—or interference—depending on one's point of view, than any other area of medical practice.

The education of the patient and her spouse or significant other as to the available courses of medical treatment and complications associated with post-date pregnancy is the best protection against medical malpractice suits and legislative intervention.

References

1. Clifford SH. Postmaturity-with placental dysfunction: Clinical syndrome and pathologic findings. J Pediatr 1954;44:1.
2. Sjostedt S, Engleson G, Rooth G. Dysmaturity. Arch Dis Child 1958;33:123.
3. McLean FH, Boyd ME, Usher RH, et al. Postterm infants: Too big or too small? Am J Obstet Gynecol 1991;164:619.
4. Kramer MS, McLean FH, Boyd ME, et al. The validity of gestational age estimation by menstrual dating in term, preterm, and postterm gestations. JAMA 1988;260:3306.
5. Miller HC. Fetal growth and neonatal mortality. Pediatrics 1972;49:392.
6. Sachs BP, Friedman EA. Results of an epidemiologic study of postdate pregnancy. J Reprod Med 1986;31:162.
7. Callenbach JC, Hall RT. Morbidity and mortality of advanced gestational age: Post-term or postmature. Obstet Gynecol 1979;53:721.
8. Schumacher RE, Donn SM, Kovarik SM, et al. The impact of gestational age on dysmaturity/postmaturity. J Perinatol 1989;9:401.
9. Naeye RL. Causes of perinatal mortality excess in prolonged gestations. Am J Epidemiol 1978;108:429.
10. Spellacy WN, Miller MS, Winegar A, et al. Macrosomia-maternal characteristics and infant complications. Obstet Gynecol 1985;66:158.
11. Lazer S, Biale Y, Mazor M, et al. Complications associated with the macrosomic fetus. J Reprod Med 1986;31:501.
12. Levine MS, Holroyde J, Woods JR, et al. Birth trauma: Incidence and predisposing factors. Obstet Gynecol 1984;63:792.
13. Gordan M, Rich H, Deutschberger J, et al. The immediate and long term outcome of obstetrical birth trauma I. Brachial plexus paralysis. Am J Obstet Gynecol 1973;117:515.
14. Eng GD. Brachial plexus palsy in newborn infants. Pediatrics 1971;48:18.
15. Donn SM, Faix RG. Long term prognosis for the infant with severe birth trauma. Clin Perinatol 1983;10:507.
16. Faix RG, Donn SM. Immediate management of the traumatized infant. Clin Perinatol 1983;10:487.
17. Clifford SH. Postmaturity. Adv Pediatr 1957;9:13.
18. Ting RY, Wang MH, McNair-Scott TF. The dysmature infant: Associated factors and outcome at 7 years of age. J Pediatr 1977;90:943.

19. Vilbergson G, Wennergren M. Fetal ponderal index as an instrument for further classification of intra-uterine growth retardation. Acta Obstet Gynecol Scand 1992;71:186.
20. Rayburn WF, Motley ME, Stempel LE, et al. Antepartum prediction of the postmature infant. Obstet Gynecol 1982;60:148.
21. Perlman M, Dvilansky A. Blood coagulation status of small-for-dates and postmature infants. Arch Dis Child 1975;50:424.
22. Patterson PJ, Dunstan MK, Trickey NRA, et al. A biochemical comparison of the mature and postmature fetus and newborn infant. J Obstet Gynecol Br Comm 1970;77:390.
23. Bielecka-Winnicka A. Conductometric investigations in subcutaneous and muscular tissue of postmature newborns with syndrome of skin dehydration. Biol Neonate 1965;8:321.
24. Freeman RK, Poland RL (eds). *Guidelines for Perinatal Care*, Third Edition. Elk Grove Village, IL, American Academy of Pediatrics and the American College of Obstetrics and Gynecology, 1992.
25. Hooper SB, Harding R. Changes in lung liquid dynamics induced by prolonged fetal hypoxemia. J Appl Physiol 1990;69:127.
26. Thibeault DW, Hall FK, Sheehan MB, et al. Postasphyxial lung disease in newborn infants with severe perinatal acidosis. Am J Obstet Gynecol 1984;150:393.
27. Miller PW, Coen RW, Benirschke K. Dating the time interval from meconium passage to birth. Obstet Gynecol 1985;66:459.
28. Eden RD, Seifert LS, Winegar A, et al. Postdate pregnancies: A review of 46 perinatal deaths. Am J Perinatol 1987;4:284.

Chapter 29

Intravascular Catheters

◆◆◆

Elizabeth L. Workman, R.N.C.,
Steven M. Donn, M.D.

Introduction

Catheterization of the vascular system provides access to the blood-stream, enabling the administration of medications, nutrients, and fluids, and the sampling of blood for the performance of various laboratory evaluations. There is no need to underscore the importance of intravascular catheters in the management of the sick newborn, especially one who is unable to tolerate feeding or enterically administered drugs. As neonatal care has evolved, technologic advances have greatly improved the range of equipment available to the clinician for providing access to the neonatal vascular compartment. Similarly, there has been an enormous improvement in the ability to monitor intravascular infusions. Nevertheless, complications still occur, including infection, tissue ischemia, thromboembolic events, and direct damage to underlying structures. These complications may arise subsequent to circumstances surrounding procurement of access, such as urgent resuscitative efforts. The skill level of clinicians attaining and utilizing vascular access may range from inexperienced house officers and nursing staff orientees to highly skilled medical and nursing personnel. Detection of complications and prompt initiation of appropriate interventions can have a significant impact on lessening the severity and even avoiding some of the sequelae of those complications.[1]

It is not the objective of this chapter to teach the techniques of vascular access. An excellent review is available for such purpose.[2] However, suggestions will be offered to minimize some of the complications associated with insertion techniques. The major purpose is to renew the awareness of the

From: Donn SM, Fisher CW (eds.): *Risk Management Techniques in Perinatal and Neonatal Practice.* © Futura Publishing Co., Inc., Armonk, NY, 1996.

potential for serious complications that exist from this activity and that must be foremost on the minds of those responsible for the care of newborns.

Venous Access

Umbilical Venous Catheters

The umbilical venous catheter (UVC) is often the first "line" placed during resuscitation and stabilization of the newborn infant. A properly positioned UVC permits central infusion of fluids, medications, and blood products. Measurement of central venous pressure enables assessment of blood volume and cardiac performance. In the very low birth weight infant, use of a UVC may avoid the need for repetitive peripheral venous catheters and reduce stress to the infant.

Available Equipment

Standard umbilical venous catheters are available in sizes 3.5, 5.0, and 8.0 Fr. Disposable vascular catheters specifically designed for use in the umbilical vessels are available either as an individually packaged product, or as part of a completely assembled disposable instrument set. If the catheter is to be left in place, one should be chosen that has a radiographically opaque marker so that its anatomic position can be accurately ascertained. The standard catheter has a single end hole. This differs from the commercially available catheter used solely for exchange transfusions, which has side holes in addition to the end hole. It is preferable to avoid using the "exchange" catheter on a continuous basis because of the potential for damage to the vessel lining from the side holes.

In addition to the single lumen catheter used for both venous and arterial access, the umbilical vein may also be cannulated with a double lumen silicon catheter. This allows the infusion of multiple pharmacologic agents that might otherwise be incompatible.

Infant feeding tubes have been used on occasion to secure umbilical vascular access, particularly in the delivery room setting. Use of these tubes should be restricted to emergency situations. They are stiffer than most UVCs, are not radiographically marked, and do not offer a connecting system that is as safe.

Accessory devices that may be used with UVCs include interlocking multi-directional stopcocks, invasive pressure transducers, infusion tubing, and administration pumps. A thorough understanding of all components by each potential care taker is necessary.

Insertion Techniques

Various methods have been described for umbilical vascular access, including a lateral approach through the side of the umbilical cord, and a direct cut-down technique in which the vessel is entered after transection and dilation. As with most procedures, the highest success rate occurs with the individual preference of the operator. In either case, careful sterile technique will help to minimize the risk of infection. This is especially important in the delivery room setting, where circumstances may seem to preclude adequate site preparation.

Estimating the depth of insertion *before* placing the catheter is helpful. For use as a central line, the tip should be advanced beyond the diaphragm. This distance is approximately equal to the distance from the umbilicus to the shoulder.[3] If the UVC is to be used only for resuscitative purposes, advancing the catheter until a good blood return is achieved (usually 3-5 cm) is sufficient.

Blood loss can be minimized by placing an umbilical tape around the base of the cord (which can be used as a ligature, should bleeding occur after the vein is dilated or after the catheter is inserted). All connections should be firmly secured. The catheter should be firmly taped in position using the "goal post" method[2]; suturing is optional, but if used, care must be taken to avoid placing sutures through the skin or through the umbilical arteries.

Complications

Unfortunately, malpositioning of the UVC can be a persistent problem and a source of complications.[4-6] The catheter can fail to pass through the ductus venosus and terminate in the inferior vena cava. Incorrect positioning of the catheter in the portal venous system ("UVC in the liver") and infusion of hypertonic solutions through the catheter can result in thrombosis of the hepatic veins and subsequent liver tissue necrosis.[6,7] Radiographic confirmation of catheter placement is essential. Malpositioned UVCs should generally be removed. If vascular access cannot be otherwise obtained, a low positioned UVC may be left in place temporarily, provided great care is taken to avoid the infusion of hypertonic or potentially sclerosing agents. Usually, only saline or blood products are utilized in this circumstance. Even well-positioned UVCs can be a source of complications, such as the formation of thrombi and emboli, as well as acquired infection. UVCs that terminate within the heart have produced cardiac arrhythmias and atrial perforations.[8]

Nursing Care

Nursing care of the infant at the time of umbilical vein cannulation should be directed at facilitation of the placement of the catheter while maintaining sterility of the equipment and the field. The infant should be closely monitored for stability of vital signs, since direct visualization may be impaired by the sterile drapes. These same drapes may also interfere with radiant warming devices, and therefore, nursing care must be directed to maintaining thermoneutrality by alternative methods, such as a warming mattress. Following radiographic confirmation of successful UVC placement and securing of the catheter, aseptic care and use of the line, whether administering fluids and medications or withdrawing blood for sampling, is an essential defense against acquired sepsis.

Documentation relevant to the use of a UVC should begin at the time of insertion and should include notation of the indications for use, site preparation and insertion technique, the size of the catheter and the length (in cm) of catheter inserted, the time of the follow-up radiograph, and the result of the radiograph. Satisfactory location of the catheter tip should be noted. If the catheter needs to be removed or repositioned, this must be documented. Secure anchoring of the catheter to maintain correct position must also be described. Ongoing nursing documentation must include *hourly* assessment of the integrity of devices (i.e., tape or sutures) used to maintain proper position. Displacement of the catheter should result in repositioning, if possible, or removal and replacement of the UVC if it is still medically necessary. Surveillance of the umbilicus for evidence of oozing or infection (omphalitis) is mandatory, and any changes should be immediately reported.

An additional feature of UVC therapy is central venous pressure monitoring using an invasive monitoring device. Careful inspection of the system for leaks and/or back-up of blood is critical. Care must be taken to avoid the entry of air into the system, and attention must be paid to waveforms (watching for evidence of dampening). Pressures should be recorded as ordered.

Peripheral Intravenous Catheters

Peripheral intravenous catheters are utilized for the provision of intravenous fluid, medications, and parenteral nutrition. In some situations (such as prior to a transport), a peripheral intravenous catheter may be placed as a "safety" port in order to have immediate vascular access in the event of an acute deterioration of the patient. Multiple sites can be cannulated, including the extremities (particularly the hands and feet) and the scalp.[2]

Historically, one of the most widely used devices for peripheral intravenous fluid administration was the "butterfly" needle. Today, the stainless steel "winged" needle has been largely replaced by the more flexible "over-the-needle" peripheral catheter, which is available in a variety of synthetic compositions (such as Teflon®), gauges, and lengths. Accessory pieces of equipment are integral to the use of peripheral intravenous catheters and include devices for securing the catheter, linking the catheter with infusing solutions, and automatically pumping these solutions.

Available Equipment

A wide range of catheters and infusion devices is available. These include the scalp vein needle and several types of over-the-needle cannulas. Sizes also vary, and typically range from 22-27 gauge for this purpose.

Peripheral intravenous solutions may be administered by gravity drip, although it is more difficult to control the rate of infusion using this method. Most neonatal intensive care units utilize some sort of pump device to accurately deliver the small fluid volumes generally required by this population. Most infusion devices enable the delivery of fluids in tenths of a milliliter per hour. Some will also measure venous pressure and will alarm if an increase is detected, enabling the clinician to evaluate for the presence of an infiltration.

Insertion Techniques

Peripheral intravenous catheters are introduced into peripheral veins after thorough preparation of the skin with a disinfectant such as povidone-iodine solution. It is useful to restrain limbs by using an armboard. If a scalp vein is chosen, shaving the hair will help in locating a vein and will make securing the catheter easier. Several techniques may be utilized to aid in the location of a suitable vein, including the use of a warm compress or soak for the hands or feet, use of a transillumination device for the extremities, and the use of a tourniquet. For the limbs, a rubber band can be placed around the arm or leg; for the scalp, a rubber band can be place around the head. Alternatively, an assistant can apply direct pressure proximal to the site of insertion.

Once the vein is located, the site is suitably prepared, the patient is restrained, and venipuncture is accomplished. The technique has several variations according to personal preference. One is to attempt to directly cannulate the vein, another is to advance the needle in the subcutaneous space followed by venipuncture. Usually there is a flashback of blood to indicate entry into the vessel, although this may not occur in states of vascular insufficiency. Care must be taken at this point to avoid through-and-through puncture or laceration of the vein while the catheter is gently threaded into place. The catheter should then be flushed to assure both patency and position and then secured to the skin with adhesive tape. The entry site and the skin over the catheter should not be obscured by the tape. The distal extremity and digits should be checked for adequacy of perfuson, and finally, the limb should be restrained. It may be helpful to attach a label indicating the time and date that the catheter was inserted.

Complications

Infiltration of intravenous fluids into the subcutaneous space is the most common complication.[1] In fact, virtually every catheter will eventually infiltrate if left in long enough. Care must be taken to avoid complications of infiltration, which include swelling, blistering of the superficial skin, and sloughing of the skin, which can be full-thickness.[1]

Tissue injury, including necrosis, is more frequently seen with some intravenous solutions than with others; calcium-containing solutions are especially sclerosing. Infection is another potential problem. Phlebitis should be suspected if there is a red streaking that follows the path of the vein.[9,10] Peripheral nerve palsies and pressure necrosis can result from inadequate perfusion secondary to restraint or padding that is too tight.[11] Blood loss from disconnected or cracked tubing can occur. Direct injury to underlying structures can also happen.[1-3] Scalp vein use has been reported to result in invasion of the subarachnoid space with subsequent deposition of intravenous infusion causing significant neurologic injury.[12]

Nursing Care

A large percentage of peripheral intravascular venous catheters used in the care of sick infants is placed by the nursing staff.[1] Standards of care for the use of peripheral intravenous catheters must include proper site selection, aseptic technique, accurate determination of intravascular placement, correct securing of the catheter, and immobilization of the extremities to prevent dislodgment. Further, peripheral intravenous catheter placement should be done in the context of maintaining the thermal stability of the infant and minimizing stress and discomfort.

Peripheral intravenous access sites can be found in the scalp or the extremities. The insertion site chosen should be as distal as possible on the vein to permit further use of the vein if the venipuncture attempt is unsuccessful. The site should avoid areas of inflammation or tissue breakdown as well as any area of circulatory impairment. Patient identification bands must be removed from an extremity prior to the insertion of an intravenous catheter, as they may impede perfusion to the area, interfere with visualization of the site, or exacerbate complications of an infiltration.[2] (However, if an identification band is removed, it should be immediately replaced on a different extremity.)

Preparation of the skin for venipuncture is done to render the insertion site free of pathogenic organisms. When a scalp vein is selected, hair should be removed by carefully shaving the area around the insertion site.[13] Povidone-iodine solution should be used to prepare the site. It should be applied briskly, then removed with alcohol after 60 seconds. Correct placement of the catheter within a vein is demonstrated by blood return into the catheter hub and unrestricted flow of flush solution into the vein when the catheter is flushed. Flushing should produce no discoloration or swelling at the insertion site. A tourniquet may help to locate a suitable vein, but it should be promptly released before attempting to flush the catheter.

Proper securing of the intravenous catheter has a great impact on the longevity of the catheter life as well as the adequate assessment of the site for possible complications. The peripheral intravenous catheter must be taped in place and the extremity immobilized using materials that permit adequate visualization of the site and adjacent area. For this reason, opaque tape such as cloth adhesive or "silk" tape is contraindicated for securing both the catheter to the skin and the extremity to a board. Many transparent taping materials are now available that provide adequate immobilization while allowing visualization. Clothing should not be permitted on an extremity being used as a peripheral intravenous site. Sleeves of shirts or gowns can obscure visualization and can cause compression and compromise in the event of an intravenous solution infiltration.

Appropriate use of the catheter lessens the risk of complications. Peripheral catheters can give access for many types of infusion solutions, but care must be taken not to exceed the tolerance of the vessel intima and the capacity for volume flow. Hypertonic solutions can produce damage to the vein as well as tissue breakdown and sloughing in surrounding areas. Hypertonic glucose, calcium, and potassium-containing solutions can cause tissue necrosis. This may result in impaired cell function and ischemia from increased pressure within a relatively closed tissue compartment.[14] Infiltration of vasoactive agents such as dopamine produces tissue ischemia that may lead to sloughing.

A basic component of nursing care of the infant requiring intravenous fluid therapy is the vigilant monitoring of fluid administration. Complications involving peripheral intravascular catheters can occur at any time. Therefore, the insertion site must be visible at all times and must be assessed at least hourly to enable discontinuation of any infusion at the earliest sign of infiltration.[15] When administering bolus volumes or potentially irritating medications, continuous site observation may be necessary.

Documentation in the medical record begins at the time of the insertion of the peripheral intravenous catheter. A note should be written that completely describes: 1. the insertion site; 2. the catheter device used, including its size and length; 3. the ability to infuse the catheter without restriction, redness, or swelling; and 4. the clinician's signature, time, and date. Thereafter, hourly documentation of the intravenous fluid solution, rate, and site assessment should be recorded. If a complication or problem is observed, this should be recorded as a change in assessment. Further documentation should then note discontinuation of the infusion, notification of the physician, and initiation of appropriate medical or surgical measures to deal with an infiltration or other complication.

Management of Complications

After discontinuing a peripheral intravenous catheter, attention must be paid to possible complications at the site. Significant fluid infiltration may result in edema and swelling severe enough to hinder perfusion. Cellulitis or phlebitis may develop at the site. Skin necrosis and sloughing, with damage to underlying structures such as nerves or tendons, may occur.[1] Aggressive surveillance and prompt response to any signs of complications are mandatory if risks are to be minimized.

Local therapy of infiltration consists of mechanical measures, such as elevation of the affected extremity and the application of cool dressings, and the use of pharmacologic agents, such as hyaluronidase, to prevent or ameliorate local tissue damage. Compresses or dressings should always be cool and never warm. Warmth causes an increase in the metabolic rate of the tissues, resulting in a greater oxygen demand, and hence, higher blood flow. Blood flow may already be compromised by the infiltration, and thereby increase the risk of worsening ischemic injury. Tissues are also at a greater risk for being burned, since blood flow is needed to help dissipate the heat. Prompt administration of "antidotal" agents, such as hyaluronidase or phentolamine (when a vasoconstrictive agent such as dopamine infiltrates) can greatly limit local injury, so it is imperative that medical attention be sought as soon as a significant infiltration is observed.

When infiltration occurs in an anatomically vital area, such as the dorsum of the hand, it is highly advisable to seek surgical consultation. Similarly, if it appears that significant skin damage has occurred, it is recommended that a surgeon, particularly a plastic surgeon, be involved in the subsequent management. Depending on the extent of injury, additional consultants may be necessary, including a neurologist and physical or occupational therapist if rehabilitation is needed.

Percutaneous Central Venous Catheters

The percutaneous central venous catheter (PCVC) is a specialized intravenous device that enables access to large central veins by way of the peripheral venous system. A very small cannula (generally sizes 22-28 gauge are used) is inserted into a superficial vein and is carefully advanced until its tip comes to rest within the right atrium. Veins that are usually chosen for cannulation include the antecubital, external jugular, postauricular, saphenous, and dorsal veins of the hand or foot.

Indications for using a PCVC include limited venous access, or the need for long-term venous access, such as an anticipated long course of parenteral nutrition or antibiotics. Because a central vein is used, higher concentrations of parenteral nutrition solution may be used to provide a caloric intake greater than that of peripheral intravenous nutrition.

Available Equipment

PCVCs are comprised of a synthetic (polyurethane or silicone) venous catheter introduced into the vascular space through a "break-away" butterfly needle or a "peel-away" introducer. Pre-assembled commercially-prepared kits are available that contain all the accessory supplies needed for catheter placement, such as cleansing solution, measuring tapes, flush solutions and syringes, and securing devices such as tape and occlusive film dressing.

Insertion Techniques

The placement of a PCVC is a procedure that requires a great deal of skill, patience, and experience and should not be undertaken by someone who has not been adequately trained to do so. It must be performed under the strictest aseptic technique possible, which includes the use of a standard surgical scrub, gown, and drape. The operator must be trained for the proper site selection, passage of the catheter through the removable introducer to a central location, and determination of an acceptable anatomic location. The position of the catheter tip must be confirmed radiographically. Adjustment in the final position may be necessary.

Fluids that are infused through the PCVC should be mixed with heparin (1.0 unit/mL) to reduce the risk of clotting. A minimal flow rate of 2.0 mL/hr is also recommended because of the small size of the catheter and its tendency to clot at a low flow state. Blood should not be aspirated through the catheter either.

Securing the catheter is another key to its success. It should be anchored at the insertion site by a transparent adhesive dressing to allow complete visualization. A loop of catheter external to the insertion should be made, and this loop is then taped to the patient. This will prevent dislodgment of the catheter tip if tension is placed proximal to the insertion site. Adequate, but not excessive, restraint of the patient is also exercised to prevent inadvertent removal of the catheter. The catheter should be removed at the first detection of complications or when it is no longer medically necessary.

Complications

The most common complication of the PCVC is clotting, which necessitates its removal. The catheters are also very delicate and may break, particularly at the juncture of the catheter and its hub or at the covered introducer.

Medical complications include: infection, which can be minimized by careful aseptic insertion technique and aggressive surveillance; edema of the cannulated limb, which can result from excessive restraint, decreased mobility, or occlusion of the vein; and blood loss from accidental disconnection of components. A transient problem that has been reported is the finding of erythema at sites where the catheter crosses bony prominences; if other signs of infection are absent, this is considered benign and the catheter may be left in place.[16-18]

Radiographic confirmation of the catheter placement is mandatory. Reports of arrhythmias, intracardiac migration, and atrial wall perforation with subsequent pericardial effusion suggest that termination of the catheter tip within the right atrium may be more hazardous than leaving the tip in a central vein.[19]

Nursing Care

The standards of nursing care during the placement of a PCVC include maintenance of thermal stability through the use of radiant warmers (or alternative devices), the maintenance of patient comfort through the use of analgesics and/or sedatives as needed to prevent procedure-related stress, and strict maintenance of sterile techniques both during placement of the line and in all interventions that involve the line. Safety considerations during placement of a PCVC begin with the precautionary warning against inadvertent withdrawal of the catheter following its passage beyond the needle tip. Adherence to this procedure may also minimize the risk of the inadvertent shearing of any portion of the catheter by the tip of the needle.

Occlusive transparent dressing securely stabilizes the PCVC, while at the same time provides easy visualization of the insertion site. Surveillance of the catheter should include assessment of the insertion site for drainage or inflammation. The incidence of phlebitis can be reduced by the removal of all powder from the sterile gloves used during placement of the line. The small size of the neonatal PCVC increases the risk of breakage of the line, especially in long-term use in the active infant; therefore, close observation for breakage is important in the prevention of ascending infection, air embolus, blood loss, or retraction of the catheter from the vascular space.

The clinician performing PCVC placement must document the procedure in the medical record. The complete note includes a description of the site selection and preparation, the catheter gauge and total length, the length of catheter actually inserted, the final tip location (as assessed radiographically), and the patient's tolerance of the procedure. The ability to achieve a blood return upon aspiration of the catheter and its ability to flush easily should also be noted. A description of the application of sterile occlusive dressing is recommended; replacement of this dressing is usually limited to the circumstance of the loss of occlusive coverage. Ongoing documentation of the use of the PCVC is the same as that for any vascular catheter. Nursing notes should document on an hourly basis the volume and type of intravenous solution infusing and the patency, security, and the appearance of the insertion site. The occurrence of any complication should be recorded immediately along with a full description of physical findings, interventions, any consultations requested, and the efficacy of treatments.

Arterial Access

Umbilical Arterial Catheters

The umbilical arterial catheter (UAC) has been an important aspect of neonatal care for decades. Catheterization of the umbilical arteries allows placement of a catheter within the aorta, enabling both the administration of fluids and medications and sampling of blood without poking or disturbing the baby. In addition, invasive blood pressure monitoring on a continuous basis is also possible.

The indications for UAC placement are generally the need to frequently monitor arterial blood gases, or the need for invasive blood pressure monitoring. In the former case, infants who require > 0.4 F_iO_2 to maintain adequate oxygenation are felt to need a UAC.[2,3]

Available Equipment

Standard commercially available UACs are 3.5 or 5.0 Fr size and are impregnated with a radio-opaque marker for radiographic localization. An 8.0 Fr catheter is also available, but is seldom, if ever, used in the neonatal setting. Commercially pre-assembled disposable trays are available from a number of medical equipment vendors and offer the advantages of decreased procedural set-up time, reduced risk of cross-contamination from re-use of instruments, and cost savings. There is variability in the connector end of the catheter; some devices have a tapered opening, while others have a threaded locking hub. Infant feeding tubes are not an acceptable substitute. The catheters provided in a standard exchange transfusion set should also not be used because the side holes may provoke damage to the intimal lining of the aorta.

Insertion Technique

Placement of a UAC is usually an elective procedure done under controlled circumstances. It can be a relatively difficult task and should be left to an adequately trained and experienced individual who is thoroughly familiar with the equipment, anatomy, and technique.

Insertion of the catheter is done under strict aseptic conditions after a full "surgical" preparation of both the operator and the periumbilical region. All equipment requires full sterilization. A gowned and gloved assistant should also be available to lend help if it is needed.

After the catheter has been placed it must be adequately secured. This is best done by the tape bridge[2]; although some prefer to suture the catheter in place, this may preclude the opportunity to re-position the catheter after radiographic assessment of its position. If suturing is done, care must be taken to avoid occluding the catheter and damaging the other umbilical artery or the umbilical vein.

Placement of the UAC must be checked radiographically. Acceptable positions for the UAC tip are "high" (between the sixth and tenth thoracic vertebrae) or "low" (between the third and fourth lumbar vertebrae). Each position has its proponents, and there is probably no consensus as to which is better, except in the circumstances of an infant of a diabetic mother (low position is preferred to avoid infusion of glucose into the pancreatic artery) or an infant with congenital heart disease (high position preferred). In any case, the placement of the UAC outside of these positions can result in serious, even life-threatening complications.[2] The catheter must be re-positioned or removed.

A precautionary comment is also necessary regarding removal of the UAC. Proper technique is necessary to avoid significant blood loss. Unlike venous catheters, which may be acutely withdrawn, the UAC must be slowly withdrawn to induce vasospasm. If pulled immediately, the artery will continue to pulsate, and large volumes of blood can be lost before hemostasis is achieved. The correct way to discontinue a UAC involves withdrawal to the 5.0-cm mark. The catheter is then withdrawn at a rate of 1.0 cm/min, more slowly if pulsations are still visible.[2,3] It would seem prudent that hospitals that utilize UAC therapy have a policy that delineates who may remove a UAC, assuring that proper training and instruction is done to avoid this specific complication.

Complications

The list of potential complications of UAC use is rather long. Fortunately, the most serious complications are generally quite rare. Anticipation of problems and a low threshold for discontinuation are key to minimizing serious sequelae.

Perhaps the most frequently encountered problem is transient vasospasm, which is clinically manifest as blanching. This is treated by attempting to induce reflex vasodilation through warming of the contralateral extremity for 10-15 minutes. If there is no response, the UAC must be removed. Loss of digits, or even the entire extremity, can occur if vasospasm is prolonged or if it results in thrombosis.[20,21]

Blood loss is another potential problem. It has several sources, including disconnection of stopcocks or connectors, inadvertent dislodgment of the UAC, or improper removal technique. Internal bleeding from arterial damage during insertion can occur, and both pelvic exsanguination[22] and hemoperitoneum[21] have been reported.

Renovascular hypertension is a recognized complication, presumably resulting from thromboembolization of the renal arteries.[23] Hematuria may also be present. Bladder injury has also been described.[24]

Infarction of various organs, particularly the bowel and kidneys may occur.[21] Paraplegia has also been seen; thrombosis of the artery of Adamkiewicz is believed to cause infarction of the spinal cord.[25-27] The combination of sepsis and a UAC has been reported to cause an aortic aneurysm.[28]

Great care must be taken when infusing or withdrawing fluids or blood through a UAC. Introduction of infectious agents or air (resulting in air embolism) can have devastating consequences. Controversy still exists as to what fluids should or should not be infused through the UAC. Present recommendations are to avoid hypertonic solutions and vasopressors whenever possible.

Nursing Care

Nursing care of the infant encompasses three phases involving the UAC. In the first phase, the nurse assists in the placement of the UAC by providing safe restraint of the infant, observation and monitoring of vital signs throughout the procedure, maintenance of the sterility of the equipment and field, and protection of the infant from thermal stress and discomfort. When proper tip position has been confirmed radiographically, the nurse will assist in securely immobilizing the catheter.

The second phase in nursing care is the proper utilization of the UAC. This begins with scrupulous maintenance of sterility of the line through aseptic technique in all interventions, such as withdrawing blood samples or infusing fluids or medications. Threaded, locking connections must be used on any device used with a UAC to prevent inadvertent disconnection and hemorrhagic blood loss. Great care must be taken to avoid infusing tiny clots or air bubbles into the catheter. A thorough knowledge of what may or may not be infused through a UAC is mandatory. Some agents, such as vasoconstrictors, may be subject to individual institution-specific guidelines.

Finally, nursing care must maintain ongoing, constant surveillance for evidence of developing complications. Because of the potential for arterial occlusive disease, which can result from thrombus, embolus, or vasospasm, all areas of the infant's body distal to the tip of the catheter must be visible and assessed at all times.[8] Therefore, diapers, socks, booties, clothing, bunting, and blankets are all contraindicated. The ambient environment must be adequately illuminated to provide suitable visualization for the detection of complications. Part of the nursing physical assessment should be a comparison of all four extremities for pulses and perfusion. In the event that blanching or ischemia of an extremity is detected, immediate interventions include placement of a warm dressing on the *contralateral* extremity *and* notification of the responsible physician. If there is no response after 10–15 minutes of warming, the UAC should be removed. Ongoing assessment of renal function should include accurate measurement of urinary output and testing of the urine for blood; positive findings should be brought to medical attention. Similarly, episodes of hypertension may be causally related and should be reported to a physician. Careful observation of the arterial pressure waveform (if it is being monitored) for signs of a dampened signal may indicate ensuing occlusion of the catheter.

Documentation begins with the date and time of insertion of the UAC. The medical record should contain: 1. the indication(s) for placement; 2. a statement of aseptic preparation of the site and sterile insertion technique; 3. the size of the catheter; 4. the depth of insertion of the catheter in cm; 5. the ability of the catheter to draw/flush; and 6. radiographic confirmation of satisfactory positioning (including the time of the radiograph). This note should be written or co-signed by the individual who actually placed the catheter. If subsequent re-positioning of the UAC is necessary, this should also be noted. Ongoing documentation must include each nurse's physical assessment, with notation of pulses, perfusion, and the appearance of the umbilical insertion site. An hourly record should be kept of the rate and volume of the fluids and medications infused through the UAC, its patency, and its security.

A description of evidence of complications should be made immediately upon observation, with appropriate documentation done of all diagnostic and therapeutic interventions that followed. Ongoing assessment of these interventions must also be noted until resolution of the complication.

Peripheral Arterial Catheters

The peripheral arterial catheter has had a recent resurgence in use in the neonatal intensive care unit, probably as a result of the improvement in the quality of the small (22 and 24 gauge) over-the-needle cannulas. The medical indications for the peripheral arterial catheter are similar to those for the UAC, with the exception that medications and high volumes of fluids cannot be infused through it.

Available Equipment

Percutaneous placement of arterial catheters may be accomplished using equipment and techniques similar to those used for peripheral venous catheters. However, the stainless steel needle should be avoided in this setting. Connecting "T-pieces," multi-directional stopcocks, infusion tubing, and pumps are generally used. All connections should be made using a threaded, locking device to minimize the risk of disconnection and significant blood loss. The peripheral arterial catheter can be used for blood pressure monitoring using the same transducer set-up that is utilized for a UAC.

Insertion Technique

The most common sites for placement include the radial and posterior tibial arteries. The superficial temporal and brachial arteries should not be used, and the femoral artery should only be considered as a last resort.[2]

Insertion can be facilitated by the use of transillumination.[29] This technique enables visualization of the artery and augments tactile localization. If the radial artery is selected, adequate collateral circulation must be demonstrated by performing a modified Allen Test and observing for ulnar blood flow when the radial artery is temporarily occluded by external pressure.

After successful cannulation of the vessel, the catheter should be gently flushed with heparinized saline and assessed for patency and backflow. It may then be taped securely in place, leaving the site visible. The extremity should be restrained, but great care must be given to avoid impairment of distal perfusion. The fluid infusing through the peripheral arterial catheter should contain heparin (0.5-1.0 unit/mL) to decrease the risk of clotting. It is generally run at the lowest rate possible (1.0-2.0 mL/hr). It is also recommended that dextrose be eliminated from the solution (it tends to promote clotting in the connectors), and normal or half-normal saline be used instead.

Complications

The major complications of the peripheral arterial catheter are thrombosis and thromboembolic events, leading to necrosis of fingers and toes.[30]

Vasospasm may also occur and may be associated with damage to underlying structures, especially nerves.[31] As is the case with other catheters, infection and blood loss are also possible but can be minimized by adhering to good technique.

Nursing Care

The tenuous nature of the peripheral arterial catheter directs the nursing care of the infant. That care is focused on careful handling and correct use of the catheter.

Stabilization of the peripheral arterial catheter prolongs the functioning of the line and reduces the incidence of some complications. As in the care of peripheral venous lines, taping and securing must be done with materials that contribute to ease of visualization of the site. At the time of site selection, circulation to surrounding areas must be demonstrated to ascertain that ischemia will not be induced should arterial flow be interrupted. This will also establish a baseline to which subsequent perfusion will be compared. Ongoing assessment of the extremity for evidence of blanching or discoloration of the digits is best achieved when immobilization of the extremity avoids obstruction of the site.[11] Ambient lighting must be sufficient to detect subtle disruption of arterial flow with blanching and ischemia of the tissues. Gentle manipulation is especially important when blood is withdrawn or the line is flushed, since arterial spasm is easily induced. Patency of the arterial catheter is maintained by a continuous infusion of an isotonic solution that is slightly heparinized to prevent clotting. The arterial line's function is to provide a source of arterial blood and to enable continuous invasive monitoring of arterial blood pressure. The line should not be used as an access site for the administration of glucose, electrolytes, or medications; severe arterial spasm with resultant ischemia and tissue necrosis can occur.

The clinician performing the peripheral arterial cannulation should document the procedure with a statement of the need for arterial access (indication), and that collateral circulation has been satisfactorily demonstrated. This note should also include: a description of site preparation; type and size of catheter used; success of cannulation; return of blood; ease of flushing; and attainment of an arterial blood pressure waveform, if monitoring is done. The patient's tolerance of the procedure should also be stated. Ongoing documentation includes hourly recording of type and volume of infusing solution, the patency of the line, and the quality of perfusion to the surrounding area. Early detection of signs of developing complications should be noted with a full description of findings and a record of all interventions. The interventions should be assessed further with follow-up documentation of their effectiveness until the complication resolves.

Conclusion

Vascular access, whether arterial or venous, provides the newborn with an extra-uterine "umbilicus," through which life-saving medications may be given and blood may be sampled. Complications associated with these devices do occur, some of which may be unavoidable.

The use of these invasive devices carries with it an added responsibility for health care providers in safeguarding the welfare of the patient. The best risk management techniques involve: 1. the placement of intravascular catheters under appropriate medical indications; 2. the use of proper insertion techniques that minimize the risks of blood loss, infection, or trauma to tissues; 3. adequate security of the catheter without obscuring the insertion site; 4. ongoing diligent assessment of the proper functioning of the line and scrutiny for the early detection of complications; 6. discontinuation of the line when it is no longer necessary, or at the first sign of a significant complication; 7. prompt notification of a physician if a problem is suspected or detected; and 8. careful and thorough documentation on a regular basis.

Commentary by Mr. Bloch: When presented with a case involving severe complications to a child occurring during the neonatal period from intravascular catheters, the first inquiry must be directed to the question of whether the catheter's presence was justified. Justification can usually be found in the neonatal setting, but appropriate documentation will take the question out of the realm of conjecture. If there is any reasonable basis for justification, a claimant's attorney will have a difficult time pursuing a claim where the injury occurs in a life-saving or life-stabilizing situation.

The second inquiry is usually directed toward the skill and technique involved in the insertion and whether appropriate monitoring of the catheter and catheter site took place. Again, the adequacy of appropriate documention is crucial.

Iatrogenically induced injuries, whether cosmetic or functional, may or may not be avoidable in any given case. Inquiry must be made as to who performed the procedure and the skill level of that person compared to others who were available. Nursing procedures and physician protocols should be universally present for the insertion and care of all indwelling intravascular catheters, whether umbilical, peripheral, or central. They should deal with selection criteria, aseptic technique for insertion, radiologic confirmation of appropriate position, and regularity of monitoring. If these procedures and protocols have been followed by competent personnel, bad outcomes will seldom give rise to legal action.

Because of the serious nature of the newborn's condition, injuries occurring from intravascular catheters may sometimes go unnoticed for periods of time. It is of utmost importance that care takers keep parents informed of possible complications, why they resulted, and what is being done.

Calcium containing intravenous fluid extravasation can cause devastating cosmetic injury. When the 1-year-old child has escaped the neonatal crisis and now presents with extensive sloughing on the scalp and forehead, or with ugly, disfiguring scar tissue and contractures in the extremities, it will be crucial to show that these complications were unavoidable, and were recognized early enough to minimize a bad outcome. It is also of critical importance that the care takers communicate the awareness of the problem and be certain that appropriate consultants are brought into the case early enough to be given the opportunity to minimize any damage.

For the most part, health care providers working in this arena should be able to function with great confidence as long as they are appropriately trained and careful. Plaintiffs' attorneys recognize the stressful and emergency conditions in existence at the time these activities are taking place. Lay personnel (whether judges or jurors) who are shown photographs of 1000 g infants are going to be very reluctant to find negligence in the treatment of such a fragile, tiny patient.

Their initial instinct will be amazement that treatment could have been rendered in the first instance that saved a life and resulted in a good outcome.

References

1. Johnson RV, Donn SM. Life span of intravenous cannulas in a neonatal intensive care unit. Am J Dis Child 1988;142:968.
2. Feick HJ, Donn SM. Vascular access and blood sampling. In: Donn SM, Faix RG (eds). *Neonatal Emergencies*. Mount Kisco, NY, Futura Publishing Company, 1991, pp. 31-50.
3. Donn SM (ed). *The Michigan Manual. A Guide to Neonatal Intensive Care*. Mount Kisco, NY, Futura Publishing Company, 1992, pp. 19-23.
4. Symchych PS, Crauss AN, Winchester P. Endocarditis following intracardiac placement of umbilical venous catheter. J Pediatr 1977;90:287.
5. Kulkaini PB, Dorand RD. Hydrothorax: A complication of intracardiac placement of umbilical venous catheter. J Pediatr 1979;94:813.
6. Scott JM. Iatrogenic lesions in babies following umbilical vein catheterization. Arch Dis Child 1965;40:426.
7. Morgan BC. Complications from intravenous catheters. Am J Dis Child 1984;138:425.

8. Mohan Rao HK, Elhassani SB. Iatrogenic complications of procedures performed on the newborn. Perinatology-Neonatology 1980; Sept/Oct:25.
9. Peter G, Loyd-Still JD, Lovejoy FH. Local infection and bacteremia from scalp vein needles and polyethylene catheters in children. J Pediatr 1972:80:78.
10. McNain TJ, Dudley HAF. The local complications of intravenous therapy. Lancet 1959;i:365.
11. Fletcher MA, MacDonald MG, Avery GB. *Atlas of Procedures in Neonatology.* Philadelphia, J.B. Lippincott Co, 1983.
12. Black VD, Little GA, Marin-Padilla M. Failure of inflammatory response to accidental intracranial lipid infusion. Pediatrics 1978;62:839.
13. Batton DG, Maesels MJ, Appelbaum P. Use of perpheral intravenous cannulas in premature infants. A controlled study. Pediatrics 1982;70:487.
14. Yosowitz P, Ekland DA, Shaw RC, et al. Peripheral intravenous infiltration necrosis. Ann Surg 1975;182:553.
15. Wehbe MA, Moore JH Jr. Digital ischemia in the neonate following intravenous therapy. Pediatrics 1985;76:99.
16. Dolcourt JL, Bose CL. Percutaneous insertion of silastic central venous catheters in newborn infants. Pediatrics 1982;70:484.
17. Durand M, Ramanathan R, Martinelli B, et al. Prospective evaluation of percutaneous central venous silastic catheters in newborn infants with birth weights 510 to 3,920 grams. Pediatrics 1986;78:245.
18. Chathas MK. Percutaneous central venous catheters in neonates. J Obstet Gynecol Nurs 1986;July/August:324.
19. Franciosi RA, Ellefson RD, Uden D, et al. Sudden unexpected death during central hyperalimentation. Pediatrics 1982;69:305.
20. Wesstrom G, Finnstrom O, Stenport G. Umbilical artery catheterization in newborns. I. Thrombosis in relation to catheter type and position. Acta Paediatr Scand 1979;68:575.
21. Marsh JL, King W, Barrett C, et al. Serious complications after umbilical artery catheterization for neonatal monitoring. Arch Surg 1975;110:1203.
22. Miller D, Kirkpatrick BV, Kodroff M, et al. Pelvic exsanguination following umbilical artery catheterization in neonates. J Pediatr Surg 1979;14:264.
23. Plumer LB, Kaplan GW, Mendoza SA. Hypertension in infants—a complication of umbilical arterial catheterization. J Pediatr 1976;89:802.
24. Dmochowski RR, Crandell SS, Corrieri JN. Bladder injury and uroascites from umbilical artery catheterization. Pediatrics 1986;77:421.
25. Aziz EM, Robertson AF. Paraplegia: A complication of umbilical artery catheterization. J Pediatr 1973;82:1051.
26. Krishnamoorthy KS, Fernandez RJ, Todres ID, et al. Paraplegia associated with umbilical artery catheterization in the newborn. Pediatrics 1976;58:433.
27. Haldeman S, Fowler GW, Ashwal S, et al. Acute flaccid neonatal paraplegia: A case report. Neurology 1983;33:93.
28. Bull PW, Winchester P, Levin AR, et al. Aortic aneurysm secondary to umbilical artery catheterization. Pediat Radio 1985;15:199.
29. Donn SM, Kuhns LR. *Pediatric Transillumination.* Chicago, Year Book Medical Publishers, 1983.
30. Cartwright GW, Schreiner RL. Major complications secondary to percutaneous radial artery catheterization in the neonate. Pediatrics 1980;65:139.
31. Koenigsberger MR, Moessinger AC. Iatrogenic carpal tunnel syndrom in the newborn infant. J Pediatr 1977;91:443.

Section VI

Maternal and Neonatal Transport

_____ Chapter 30 _____

Maternal Transport

◆◆◆

Clark E. Nugent, M.D.,
Barbara A. Colwell, R.N., M.P.H.

Introduction

Transport of the pregnant patient presents a time of significant risk for all involved. The challenges of any transport situation are further compounded by the need to optimize the care of two patients simultaneously. Whenever feasible, maternal-fetal transport is preferable to neonatal transport. Significant improvements in outcome have been described for babies born in tertiary centers versus babies who are outborn and subsequently transported to neonatal intensive care units.[1] Early assessment of risk and timely decision making is key in initiating maternal transport.

Decisions to transport are fraught with hazards if the patient is not adequately triaged and stabilized prior to leaving the referring institution. Minimum standards of care must be maintained during the actual transport despite the absence of ancillary resources and the logistical difficulties posed by travel.[2] Finally, all aspects of the consultation, decision to transport, transport itself, care at the tertiary institution, and outcome must be adequately documented. Complete and timely communication is essential for the safe and efficient transfer of care.

Given the complexity of this process, the potential for a less than optimal outcome is ever present. Delivery of a preterm fetus while en route, decompensation of a hypertensive patient, or fetal death during transport are all undesirable yet possible situations. This chapter will discuss risk management strategies pertaining to maternal transport.

From: Donn SM, Fisher CW (eds.): *Risk Management Techniques in Perinatal and Neonatal Practice.* © Futura Publishing Co., Inc., Armonk, NY, 1996.

The Decision to Transport

The decision to transport a pregnant patient is usually prompted by a perceived need for specialized care that is not available at the referring hospital.

> **Commentary by Mr. Goldman:** As discussed later, consent must be obtained for transport and shift of providers. You should begin to build rapport and discuss risk vs. benefit as early as possible including any time when there is discussion about need for transport.

A judgment must be made as to whether the risks associated with transport are warranted based on the severity and stability of the maternal and fetal condition. Implicit is the availability and direct evaluation by personnel familiar with the special needs associated with the pregnant patient. A thorough evaluation must occur to determine whether or not it is both clinically necessary *and* safe to transfer the patient. Transport solely on the basis of financial status is never warranted and places the referring institution at risk secondary to violation of federal statutes (see Chapter 33).[3] The decision to transfer a maternal patient may be made based on maternal condition, anticipated neonatal needs, or both. Other members of the perinatal team need to be consulted when considering the appropriateness of continuing to care for or transferring a high-risk mother or a potentially high-risk newborn. Pediatricians and nurses play an important role in assessing the home institution's resources and capabilities to provide care for mothers and infants requiring specialized services. In some cases a referring hospital may be very capable of caring for an unstable maternal patient but unable to care for the baby should delivery occur. In that instance, transport of the mother will provide specialized care for the newborn.

Consultation

In most geographic areas, regionalization of perinatal services has defined the usual referral pathway to a specific tertiary center (Level III) for the area's primary (Level I) and secondary (Level II) hospitals.[4] Recent changes in health care delivery (i.e., the emergence of large heath maintenance organizations for economic reasons) have begun to modify these regional alliances. The continuing development of managed care has the potential to further alter these relationships.

Formal regional referral relationships, geographic proximity, and the existence of required specialized services in the tertiary center are all factors that must be taken into account when selecting the center appropriate for a specific transport. In some instances, anticipated neonatal need may be the primary factor used in making the selection of the appropriate tertiary center. An example is a mother carrying a fetus in need of the services provided by pediatric surgeons or cardiologists. Transporting the mother to the appropriate center will ensure the most rapid access to specialized neonatal services.

After identifying the need to transfer a maternal patient, initial contact with the tertiary center staff should be made without delay. Referring physicians are in the best position to initiate the contact since they are most likely to be able to provide complete, accurate, and timely information about the patient's condition. In situations where the primary physician is unable to leave the patient because of her unstable status, a second physician or nurse may make the call.

The staff in the tertiary hospital should be able to provide rapid feedback to the referring physician's inquiry. Is there a bed available? Is there agreement as to appropriateness of transport? Is the transport accepted? Are there suggestions for stabilization, treatment, or precautions necessary prior to transport? Documentation of the telephone call is essential, as it provides an important record should it be necessary to reconstruct the event at a later date.

The person who takes the call at the receiving hospital and accepts the transport should be the person in the best position to respond both knowledgeably and quickly. Referring physicians would prefer to interact directly with the attending maternal-fetal medicine specialist. In some settings the perinatologist may not be the person who can most easily assess the current activity and status of necessary hospital resources and most readily respond to the request for transfer. If a fellow or chief resident is the responding physician, it is critical to have immediate access to the attending specialist for back-up and assistance in decision making. The perinatologist can make contact with the referring physician at a later time. Direct contact by the specialist fosters the relationship with the referring physician and facilitates the communication of sensitive feedback. If a thoughtful critique is in order, it is usually easier for the referring physician to receive input from the specialist than from a less experienced house officer.

Commentary by Mr. Goldman: Use of language is critical. Information should be provided without guilt or blame. The exchange should be documented including the medical information received and provided.

The initial phone consultation may result in a patient transfer, planning for a future outpatient referral at the tertiary center, or obtaining advice for the continued management of the patient at the primary hospital. Early consultation and transfer of care is preferable to emergency transport.

Assessment and Stabilization Prior to Transport

Several different scenarios may lead to a maternal transport. A previously stable patient may have a change in status that makes transport necessary. Alternatively, a patient may present for care on an emergency basis that requires a timely decision regarding whether or not specialized care is necessary. These are the patients who present the greatest risks and challenges to the health care team.

Although an exhaustive review of indications for transfer is beyond the scope of this chapter, there are several key issues to consider. First, what is the gestational age? Each institution should have criteria established for what gestational age limits they have the resources to manage. To electively continue to manage a patient at less than this gestational age poses a significant risk for all involved. However, there may be circumstances where transport is contraindicated because of other overriding maternal or fetal factors. It had once been a practice at many institutions not to transport a pregnancy that was "pre-viable." This philosophy has largely been abandoned, since the pregnancy may ultimately reach a gestational age where neonatal survival is possible, leading to a situation where the transport takes on a sense of urgency that otherwise could have been avoided.

Second, what is the patient's labor status? If it is determined that there is a high probability of delivery during transport because of active labor, then mother and fetus will be better off remaining at the referring institution. There are many more resources available in the referring hospital to support and stabilize a vulnerable mother and/or infant than in any type of transport vehicle.

Third, what is the fetal status? The transferring institution must be confident that transport will not place the fetus at high-risk of either demise or suffering an asphyxial event during the transport. On-line transmittal of fetal monitoring data is becoming more available. If this technology is not available, a worrisome fetal heart rate tracing can be transmitted by telecopier to the receiving institution to mutually arrive at a decision whether the fetus will tolerate transport.

Finally, is the maternal status stable enough that transport will not place her health in jeopardy? The evaluation should document that any urgent situations have been optimally stabilized for transport. Examples of such conditions would include volume resuscitation for bleeding from a placenta previa, control of hypertension, or stabilization and initiating appropriate anticonvulsant therapy following an eclamptic seizure.

Commentary by Mr. Goldman: In some of these cases, needs of the mother and the fetus may conflict and the physician is faced with the question of who is the patient. Of course, whenever possible both mother and child are the patient but in the rare case where needs conflict the law is coming to the view that mother's decisions control. See for example the In re: A.C. case from Washington, D.C.

The pregnant trauma patient presents a special challenge for assessment and stabilization. The evaluating service must be aware of the impact of maternal physiology on response to injury. Given the young, healthy status of most women during pregnancy, they are amazingly resistant to acute volume loss and one should not be lulled into complacency because of "stable" vital signs. It is not unusual to have an acute volume loss of 15% without any change in maternal vital signs. However, the expense of maintaining perfusion of the vital maternal organs is paid by the fetus as blood will be preferentially shunted away from the uterus. Indeed, an abnormal fetal heart rate tracing may be the initial indicator of ongoing maternal blood loss. If this is recognized in a timely manner, appropriate maternal volume resuscitation will often lead to correction of the abnormal fetal heart rate tracing.

Blunt abdominal trauma is especially risky to the fetus. Although it is rare to have significant direct fetal trauma in the absence of a major maternal injury, these fetuses remain at risk for abruptio placentae. Focal uterine tenderness, uterine contractions, or increased baseline tonus, and an abnormal fetal heart rate tracing in either the presence or absence of vaginal bleeding should alert the clinician to the possibility of placental abruption. Failure to appreciate the symptoms of abruption or transporting when an abruption is evolving, places the fetus at risk of suffering either a significant asphyxial insult or even death during transport.

Who is Responsible for the Patient?

Mishaps can occur if it is not clearly established who is responsible for the patient's management. This responsibility will vary depending on whether transport is "one way" or "two way." With one way transport, the referring institution is responsible for the patient until she arrives at the receiving hospital and has been accepted by tertiary personnel. With two way transport, the receiving hospital sends a transport team to the referring hospital to assess and potentially transport the patient. The receiving transport team usually assumes responsibility for care once they begin their initial assessment.

Commentary by Mr. Goldman: On transport and prior to that time, they are consultants only. This is an area that should be carefully considered and included in any transfer agreements that can specifically state when the receiving transport team assumes responsibility for care.

In the situation where the patient is found to be unsuitable for transport, the referring institution usually retains responsibility unless prior arrangements have been made for emergency privileges for the transport team.

The availability of one way versus two way transport systems vary by tertiary center and area. In some settings, centers responsible for a large geographic area find it both necessary and economically feasible to maintain a transport team and vehicles for two way transports. A dedicated maternal transport team with a highly skilled staff is very effective in picking up a patient and providing supportive care to the patient en route. The volume of patients, the distance, and the terrain that needs to be traveled may warrant the expense.

In other settings, the most efficient method of transport to a tertiary center is by one way transport. The patient is usually accompanied by a staff member (the physician, or more often, an experienced nurse) from the referring hospital. Once the decision to transport is made and the patient is determined to be stable, the transport can be initiated without waiting for the tertiary center's transport team to arrive.

Method of Transport

Method of transport (choice of vehicle) is dependent upon distance, terrain, weather, availability, and clinical status of the patient. In very low-risk situations, such as stable patients sent from nearby physician's offices, transport by private family car may be appropriate. Very high-risk patients coming a great distance over mountainous terrain may need to come by fixed wing aircraft. Rapid transport over a medium distance can be accomplished by helicopter. Weather conditions and availability of vehicle may modify the method of transport. Air travel may be grounded by inclement weather, or a center's resources could be tied up by multiple, simultaneous transport requests. In many situations, ground ambulance provides the safest and most expedient mode of transportation. It is important for each service to identify the safest, quickest, and most cost effective transport method for its area, for the specific patient, and for the clinical conditions necessitating the transport.

Placing a pregnant patient in any vehicle with limited space highlights the risk inherent in transport and the importance of stabilization prior to transport. It is very difficult to safely manage a delivery in a moving vehicle. Cesarean section for fetal indications is not an option. There is no extra room for infant equipment. The noise of a vehicle makes it very difficult to monitor patients during transport. A stable patient requires little or no intervention during transport but must still be continuously observed. The same standards of care related to observation and monitoring expected for the patient in the hospital are required during transport. Monitoring of vital signs, fetal heart tones, uterine contractions, intravenous infusions, and medications must be maintained with the same frequency. The maternal patient needs to maintain adequate lateral uterine displacement to avoid supine hypotension.

Communication and Documentation

Appropriate communication and documentation not only optimizes co-ordination of patient care between the two institutions, but it is also an effective risk reduction strategy. The referring institution will usually initiate the transport process by telephone. The rationale behind the decision to transport and timing of this decision should be documented in the medical record. Likewise, the individual accepting the transport should document that he/she has received sufficient information to adequately determine that transport is the best option. In addition, any recommendations for management prior to or during transport should be documented.

Prenatal and hospital records, including relevant electronic fetal monitoring tracings, should accompany the patient. With the ready availability of photocopy and facsimile equipment, there should rarely be a situation where the receiving hospital has to work with an incomplete data base.

A standard transport or referral form used by all hospitals in a region can be a useful tool to communicate information on transport. It provides immediate access to a summary of patient information for the receiving staff, and it documents care given to the patient during travel to the tertiary center. It should be short, easy to read and use, and include specific instructions for those who transport infrequently. The information contained on the form allows for ongoing data collection. Assessment of the data to identify trends can contribute to a thoughtful, tactful critique and facilitate periodic quality assurance reviews.

Perhaps the most important communication process is the direct exchange of information between the transport and receiving team. Unfortunately, in the haste to get the patient "plugged-in" on arrival, the transport team can be inadvertently ignored. This presents a less than optimal circumstance, since the transport team's insight into the patient status during transport may be of crucial importance. There should always be time for free exchange of information to avoid surprises that could have been anticipated and prevented. Respect paid to the referring hospital's transport team by the receiving hospital staff fosters good working relationships between institutions. This contributes to continuous efforts to improve the process of maternal-fetal transfer resulting in the best possible care for the transferred patient.

Finally, the follow-up communication provided by the tertiary center staff to the referring staff is critically important. The referring physician needs to know the patient's status to resume caring for the patient. Community physicians who do not receive feedback about their transferred patients may, if the option exists, choose to send their patients elsewhere. At the minimum, telephone calls should be made to the referring physician after stabilization, delivery (if it occurs), and at discharge. If the patient is hospitalized at the tertiary center for a long time, periodic calls should be made to keep the referring physician informed of the patient's status. After discharge, a letter and/or the hospital discharge summary can serve as the final communication, returning the patient to her primary physician.

> **Commentary by Mr. Goldman:** Receiving hospitals can also do presentations at outside hospitals on a periodic basis. These presentations can discuss procedures and can review transfers from the sending hospital. It is simply a way to keep good communications with the sending facilities.

Consent Issues

A crucial aspect of risk management for maternal transport is making sure that the patient and her family are fully informed as to the reason for and potential benefits of the transport.

> **Commentary by Mr. Goldman:** Families must be fully informed and must, where time allows, consent to the transport. For a discussion of consent, refer to Chapter 33.

Failure to do so can result in a frustrated and angry patient and family in a stressful setting potentially far from home and its usual support. A frank discussion should be held outlining the potential consequences for the patient if the transport is not accomplished. Although it is useful to try to prepare the patient for what will be done once she arrives at the receiving hospital, this cannot always be predicted with accuracy given the potential uncertainties that may be clarified by additional evaluation. The receiving hospital can lessen the stress of the situation by tending to simple logistical needs such as family lodging, psychosocial support, and facilitating return to the home community.

Avoiding "Us Against Them" Situations

Another vital component of risk management entails mutual respect between health care personnel at the referring and receiving hospitals. This is certainly facilitated by perinatal outreach programs aimed at establishing ongoing education and feedback between the institutions. Respect is enhanced when the various care providers have had the opportunity to interact on a face to face basis as opposed to being a strange voice at the other end of the telephone.

Tertiary center personnel, through an outreach program, can assist referring physicians and hospital staff by identifying specialized services available, clearly defining the referral process, and participating in problem solving efforts when necessary. Identification of appropriate patients for transfer, timing, stabilization and preparation of patients prior to transport, and communication of necessary information must be managed well by the referring staff. The occasional coaching of referring staff regarding specific difficult situations is more easily accomplished and accepted in the context of an ongoing working relationship. When there is open and frequent communication between the referring hospital and the tertiary center, feedback promoting positive change at the tertiary center is also facilitated.

Care should be taken in discussing the patient's previous management with her. Despite the attempt to be fully aware of the patient's care at the referring hospital, there can be nuances regarding the particular situation that are not appreciated. Offhand critical remarks can sow the seeds of distrust, undermining the relationships between patient and referring physician and between referring and receiving physicians. Additionally, this behavior has the potential to be the genesis of unwarranted legal action.

Summary

Improved perinatal outcome is the desired goal when the decision is made to proceed with maternal transport. The expectations of all parties involved need to be plainly stated. Defined objectives and attention to detail will significantly reduce the risk of adverse outcome for the patient, her unborn child, and the health care providers. Ultimately, effective communication between the various members of the health care team, both between themselves and the patient, will facilitate meeting this objective.

References

1. Bolan JC. Indications for maternal transport. In: MacDonald MG, Miller MK (eds). *Emergency Transport of the Perinatal Patient*. Boston, Little, Brown and Co., 1989, pp. 260-274.
2. American Academy of Pediatrics, American College of Obstetricians and Gynecologists. *Guidelines for Perinatal Care*, Third Edition. Elk Grove Village, IL, American Academy of Pediatrics, 1992, pp. 43-44.
3. Consolidated Omnibus Budget Reconciliation Act of 1985 (COBRA) (P.L.99-272), Title IX-Medicare, Medicaid and Maternal and Child Health Programs, Section 1867, Examination and Treatment for Emergency Medical Conditions and Women in Active Labor.
4. Bose CL. An overview of the organization and administration of a perinatal transport service. In: MacDonald MG, Miller MK (eds). *Emergency Transport of the Perinatal Patient*. Boston, Little, Brown and Co., 1989, pp. 34-43.

Chapter 31

Neonatal Transport

◆◆◆

Molly R. Gates, M.S., R.N.C.,
Sandra Geller, R.N., M.S.N.,
Steven M. Donn, M.D.

Introduction

One of the cornerstones of modern neonatal intensive care has been the regionalization of neonatal services within specific geographic areas. Regional neonatal care may be conceptually thought of as a hub, represented by the tertiary (Level III) neonatal intensive care unit (NICU), serving a larger periphery, represented by community (Level I) hospitals and secondary (Level II) facilities. Neonatal transport serves as the link between these various health care facilities; it is an extension of neonatal intensive care, which enables the movement of a critically-ill infant from one hospital to another. Although back transfer from a tertiary facility is a component of neonatal transport, it involves the relocation of a stable, convalescing infant and will not be considered in this chapter since it does not represent a major threat of litigation.

Regionalization of Neonatal Care

The factors that designate the status of a hospital are generally under the jurisdiction of a state's Department of Public Health. The American Academy of Pediatrics and the American College of Obstetricians and Gynecologists have attempted to define the various levels of neonatal care in *Guidelines for Perinatal Care*.[1] Level I centers are those providing routine newborn care. Level III centers are those providing all facets of neonatal intensive care, including mechanical ventilation and surgery. Level II centers

From: Donn SM, Fisher CW (eds.): *Risk Management Techniques in Perinatal and Neonatal Practice*. © Futura Publishing Co., Inc., Armonk, NY, 1996.

are intermediary. From a practical standpoint, Level II centers bridge the gap between Levels I and III; some provide mechanical ventilation, others do not.

The Decision to Transport

Health care professionals within an institution must determine the limits of care that they are able to provide without jeopardizing the well-being of a patient. This includes a thorough assessment of capabilities for assisted mechanical ventilation; the skills and experience of physicians, nurses, and paramedical personnel for handling sick infants; the availability of necessary monitoring equipment; and the level of vital support services, such as laboratory, radiology, and pharmacy. In addition, meticulous anticipatory management is necessary to predict when the seriousness of the patient's condition will exceed the capabilities of the health care providers or the institution. Neonatal transport must be considered prior to this to minimize the risk of patient decompensation en route to the tertiary center.

Although maternal transport (see Chapter 30) seems preferable to neonatal transport under most circumstances, there will be occasions in which it is not feasible or safe to transfer the mother (see Chapter 33). For instance, imminent delivery or maternal instability may preclude the possibility of transferring the mother. Additionally, some infants may appear entirely normal at birth only to subsequently develop manifestations of a congenital anomaly, infection, or inborn error of metabolism. When these conditions occur, neonatal transport becomes a necessary event. As such, it becomes an extension of neonatal intensive care and not a substitute for it. Accordingly, a neonatal transport service must be fully equipped and prepared to handle the myriad of medical emergencies that might arise during transfer.

Where to Transport?

Traditionally, Level I and Level II hospitals referred infants to a designated Level III Center in reasonably close geographic proximity. This led to the development of numerous "regional" interactions, including transfer and back transfer, consultation, outreach education, quality assurance, and shared protocols for patient stabilization and care. Over the past several years, these traditional referral patterns have been modified by a number of factors. First, the development of large provider networks and health maintenance organizations has fostered alliances that are organized along economic lines. Second, the emergence of large numbers of Level II centers capable of providing a number of previously exclusive Level III activities (particularly mechanical ventilation) has intercepted a significant percentage of infants previously sent to Level III centers. Many Level III centers have witnessed an erosion of their referral bases, and physicians practicing in Level I centers have seen decision-making taken out of their hands by third party payers. This in itself is a potentially hazardous situation, unless the appropriate steps are taken to assure that neonatal transport agreements include the ancillary services noted above.

Hospitals engaged in either the sending or receiving of newborns should consider the use of a transport agreement or contract. Issues to be addressed by such a document might include the specification of acceptable response times by the transporting service, delineation of clinical responsibilities around the time of transfer, means to effectively communicate (before, during, and after the transport), elaboration of conditions under which back transport could occur, determination of an outreach education program, and the performance of quality assurance activities on a regional basis. If such an agreement is used, it becomes the responsibilities of administrative personnel in each institution to periodically review performances and adherence to the agreed parameters.

Plans must also be made to handle unexpected contingencies that lie beyond the limits of a transport agreement, such as no available beds in the tertiary facility, a problem requiring a more specialized plan of intervention (such as extracorporeal membrane oxygenation or organ transplantation), or situations where transport is unsafe or infeasible (such as inclement weather or mechanical problems with equipment). Each institution should have familiarity with alternatives that can be utilized under such circumstances.

Who Should Transport?

Under most circumstances, transfer of a newborn from a Level I center should be done by a skilled neonatal transport team from the receiving Level II or III center. The team should be knowledgeable and experienced in all areas of neonatal transport medicine and critical care. Team members must be able to respond to unexpected problems in a timely manner and must possess superb resuscitative skills.[2,3] Occasionally, some situations arise that require transport but are not of a critical nature. For example, a stable newborn with significant hyperbilirubinemia potentially requiring an exchange transfusion could be safely transported by a non-neonatal transport service, provided that this was acceptable to both the sending and receiving institutions.

Transports involving patients sent from a Level II to a Level III center, or transports between Level III centers are not as straightforward. These transports should be evaluated on an individual basis. A number of factors have to be addressed to determine who is in the best position to transport the patient. These include: 1. patient stability; 2. actual time involved in moving the patient—it is quicker for the sending hospital to transport the patient one way than to have the receiving hospital send its team on a round trip; 3. choice of transport vehicle; 4. familiarity with ongoing treatments; and 5. experience in moving a critically ill baby. The critically ill infant poses a number of problems that must be addressed. The sicker the infant, the greater the time it will take to transfer the care from one group of individuals to the other. Complex therapies also require a great deal of time and attention, especially infusions of vasoactive drugs. When multiple factors are considered in reaching a decision about who will actually transport the patient, they should be recorded in either the medical record or transport log with the rationale used to reach the conclusion.

> **Commentary by Mr. Goldman:** This is an evolving area and the standard of care can change over time.

The composition of a neonatal transport team remains an open issue. There are no hard and fast rules that mandate the members of a team. Many different configurations are presently in use, including physician-nurse-respiratory therapist, nurse-nurse, and nurse-respiratory therapist models. Rather than specify a title for a transport team member, hospitals providing this service should specify requisite skills and experience. It is obligatory for transport team members to possess the ability to handle virtually any emergency that might arise during a neonatal transport, including cardiopulmonary arrest, tension pneumothorax, shock, hypoglycemia, and respiratory failure. It is incumbent upon each institution to be familiar with the types of problems encountered by its transport population, and further, to assure that personnel assigned to neonatal transport be fully trained and approved to deal with the full scope of these problems. Periodic performance review, continuing education, and quality assurance activities must take this into account.[4]

Arranging a Transport

Communication

Once a decision has been made to transfer an infant from one facility to another, prompt communication is the initiating event. Both the sending and receiving hospitals must carefully document that a telephone call was made to request transfer. This is important for the sending hospital because it indicates the decision to transfer and its time of occurrence, and it is important for the receiving hospital because it serves as a reference point from which to judge the timeliness of its response. Appropriate forms can be used for this purpose.[3]

The initial communication must include all relevant data, including the status of the baby, diagnostic studies and therapeutic interventions, and whatever historical information that is available. The receiving hospital personnel responding to the telephone call should document the content of the discussion, especially any recommendations made regarding management prior to the arrival of the transport team. Contemporaneously, arrangements for assembling and dispatching the transport team should be commenced. This is one of the most important elements of neonatal transport in institutions that do not have a free-standing transport team, particularly if personnel must be called into the hospital. The sending hospital personnel should be encouraged to maintain a communication link with the receiving hospital and to inform it of any changes in the patient's condition, especially if additional personnel or equipment become necessary, or if the patient expires and the transport is canceled. It is also important for the receiving hospital to give an estimated time of arrival, and if an unexpected delay ensues, to update this promptly.

Whether or not the referring physician remains with the baby until the transport team arrives is situation-specific and depends to a large extent on the condition of the infant and the capability of hospital staff to care for the infant. At times it may be necessary for reasons other than medical, such as providing support for the family. The physician must be cognizant of the mother's vulnerability at this time, and his/her presence can create a lasting impression of caring and goodwill. On the other hand, his/her absence at the time of transfer, coupled with a poor outcome, can also create a sense of abandonment that may ultimately lead to litigation.

Interim Management

The request to transfer the infant does not abrogate the referring hospital or physician from continued involvement until the arrival of the transport team. All necessary medical and nursing procedures must continue, including the documentation of such. If problems arise, frequent communication with the receiving hospital is strongly recommended.

The referring physician (or designated individual) can expedite the transfer by completing a number of tasks before the arrival of the transport team. Careful discussion with the family and obtaining informed consent for transfer can alleviate the transport team from having to do this task. Duplication of medical records should be accomplished at this time, and copies of radiographs or other pertinent studies should be made to avoid a delayed departure.

> **Commentary by Mr. Goldman:** The transfer agreement can specify exactly what materials should accompany the patient. There is an open question about whether the receiving facility should rely on outside tests or repeat the test. There are some cases where a receiving hospital relies on test results from an outside hospital and those results turn out to be inaccurate. In those cases, plaintiffs' attorneys argue that the receiving hospital, being a specialized tertiary care

hospital, should have repeated test results. For example, a patient is referred with a diagnosis of meningitis. Tests are not repeated and the patient is incorrectly treated for meningitis and a bowel malrotation is missed. In a managed care era there will be pressure to not repeat tests, but a hospital ought to have an index of suspicion about when tests are reliable and when they should be redone.

All vascular lines should be carefully labeled. The receiving hospital and/or transport team should be informed of any changes in status or management so that they may further prepare for the patient, even while underway.

Preparations should also be undertaken at the receiving hospital. Notification of consultants or arrangement for emergency tests, setting up a ventilator, and preparing intravenous infusions are examples of activities that can be initiated before the admission of the patient if suitable information is provided.

Vehicle Selection

The choice of the transport vehicle should always rest with the transport team. Although air transport by helicopter or fixed wing aircraft is glamorous and has a high profile, it may not be medically indicated or available. The referring hospital personnel should describe the patient's condition and stability only; the decision regarding the best mode of transportation is to be made by the accepting physician or his/her designate.

There are advantages and disadvantages to each type of transport vehicle. Ground ambulances provide the most stable in-transport environment, with good access to the patient and enough room for the crew and accessory equipment. They can be driven right to the hospital entrance and provide appropriate temperature control. They are subject to traffic constraints, can have a fair amount of noise and vibration, and exhaust fumes and a bumpy ride may lead to motion sickness in some individuals. Helicopters avoid traffic congestion, can bypass roads made impassable by snow, and are relatively fast vehicles. Disadvantages include limited cabin space and patient accessibility, noise and vibration, and the need for transportation between the landing site (or helipad) and hospital entrance. They are subject to weather constraints and require additional crew training and certification. Fixed wing aircraft appear best suited for transports > 150 miles in length. Some fixed wing aircraft are reconfigured for medical use, making them ideal for long distance transfer. However, transportation to and from the airports must be arranged, not all crafts are pressurized, leading to the need for the team to be aware of the problems created by altitude, and weather may also preclude their use. In general, ground ambulance is the least expensive mode of transport, while fixed wing aircraft is the most expensive.[2-4]

Not all insurance carriers will reimburse the cost of a neonatal transport. Some will pay for a ground transport but not one done by air. If patient safety and rapidity of transfer is not an issue, this must be carefully explained to the family. An unexpected medical bill of several thousand dollars can easily create hostility and increase the vulnerability to a future lawsuit.

Transfer of Care

The change of care provider, the switch to other equipment, and the actual physical movement required to enact neonatal transport carry inherent risks for omission, miscommunication, and disruption of clinical support. The degree of stress present in the situation increases the potential for human error. In order to reduce these risks, the personnel at the referring hospital and the transport team must be aware of them and work together to ensure a smooth, orderly transfer of care that promotes continuity of patient and family support.

Arrival of the Transport Team

Upon arrival at the referring hospital, the clinical members of the transport team remain together to hear a report of the patient's history, status, and current therapy. Preferably this is done at the bedside. This enables all members of the team to proceed from the same information base and provides an opportunity for verbal and visual double-checking with those who have been providing the care. For example, the referring hospital personnel can point out specific clinical findings as well as identification of infusion sites and solutions or tube placement markings. Laboratory and radiographic studies are reviewed. Actual radiographs rather than reports should be utilized.

The transport team enjoys a unique role in the referring hospital—that of welcome "guest."

> **Commentary by Mr. Goldman:** It is important to think about the "guest" role and to be careful not to badmouth the sending hospital to patients or to parents. If anything is to be said it is better to compliment the sending hospital, not to badmouth them. If it is appropriate, the transport team can say things like "the physicians at the sending hospital did an excellent job of stabilizing the patient and contacted us in a timely fashion."

The attitude communicated by the team through verbal and non-verbal messages can either foster or impair the collegiality necessary for a successful transport program. Clinical problem solving and changes in patient management may need to occur; however, a condescending or critical approach will only create tension. An adversarial relationship between care givers is not in the best interest of the patient and family, nor is it responsible practice for the referring personnel to "disappear" once the transport team arrives. At this time, the baby is a shared patient. It is imperative that both sets of care providers work together to complement the resources of each.[5]

The team conducts a brief but careful physical examination of the baby and initiates, with assistance from the transferring facility, any needed interventions.

> **Commentary by Mr. Goldman:** Until the baby is accepted for transport, care should be co-managed by both institutions.

Only those procedures required for adequate assessment or enhancement of the baby's stability should be performed. All others can be deferred until arrival at the NICU. For example, a baby being transferred for surgical repair of a birth defect might eventually need an arterial catheter for surgery, but if there is no current respiratory or cardiovascular compromise, catheterization should be deferred. Invasive procedures take time, risk further stress to the infant, and have the potential for complications or unwanted side effects. These "costs" must be weighed against the projected benefit to the infant's condition, particularly in view of the transport context.

Distance and mode of transport are other factors for consideration. Based on clinical judgment, is it likely that the tachypneic baby grunting in hood oxygen will tire sufficiently to require intubation before the probable arrival time at the NICU? Conditions are not optimal to intubate in a cramped ambulance on the shoulder of a busy expressway. Helicopters must land to perform such procedures. An elective procedure may be appropriate under these circumstances.

In principle, clinical care of the newborn to be transported is no different than that provided in the NICU. The same patient needs must be addressed in regard to thermoregulation, positioning, airway management, ventilation, circulatory support, skin integrity, patency of vascular catheter sites, etc. Whether in the NICU or elsewhere, failure to do so creates compromise. The challenge of transport care is to meet these patient needs without interruption while using portable equipment and limited personnel resources in a cramped space with limited lighting and supplies and potentially great fluctuation of environmental temperature while moving! The successful team anticipates these situational hazards and uses methods to circumvent their effects, thus reducing risk. For example, those transporting in frigid weather need to bring added devices to guard the patient against heat loss, such as warming mattresses or insulated aerospace type blankets. When possible, the team may elect to use the referring hospital's supplies in order to preserve the limited transport stock for emergency use en route to the NICU.

Special care must be taken to guard against drug administration errors, especially if supplies from the referring hospital are used. These medications may be in packaging or concentrations unfamiliar to the transport team. Having a second individual check the accuracy before the drug is given to the patient greatly assists in reducing these types of errors.

Preparation for Departure

When the transport team has achieved its initial goals of patient assessment and maximizing clinical stability, one team member usually goes to meet with the family, while others begin preparation for actual movement of the baby. A major task is transference of patient support equipment from that of the referral hospital to portable devices for transport with minimal disruption to the patient. The staff must be vigilant to guard against dislodgment or kinking of lines and tubes as well as to ensure proper positioning of stopcocks, on/off switches, and flow regulators. During this loading process, careful monitoring must occur for any signs that the baby is not tolerating the changes and requires supportive intervention. Such clinical signs may also signal equipment malfunction.

The time spent "fine-tuning" the baby's physical stability prior to actual movement is a worthwhile investment. Premature and/or sick newborns typically have minimal tolerance for any kind of external stressors. Attention paid to stabilization may help build some degree of fortification for the inevitable stress of physical movement into the transport incubator and vehicle, thus averting ill-timed deterioration.

The emphasis on stabilization prior to departure in neonatal transport is based on the premise that the skills and the equipment of the NICU are being brought to the baby, so there is no reason to unduly rush the return.[3] An exception to this approach is the patient who requires emergency care to achieve stabilization, for example the baby with congenital diaphragmatic hernia. Obviously, the more the referring hospital personnel can contribute to this stabilization effort while the transport team is en route to them, the less compromise to the infant and the more rapid the return to the NICU.

Likewise, the time invested by both the referring hospital staff and the transport team in preparing the family for the transfer of their baby will reap the benefits of more informed consent and goodwill at an emotionally fragile point in time. Introduction of the team to the family by the referring hospital physician fosters the concept of the shared patient and eases the transition to new care providers. Also, the continued presence of a supportive referring hospital staff member while the transport team is there provides a familiar person to reinforce what the team has told the family at a time when the family's stress level may not permit them to retain this needed information.

It is imperative that the family have an opportunity to see and touch their baby, no matter how critically ill.[6] An explanation of what has been done and some anticipatory guidance are needed. Without accurate, supportive communication and an opportunity to see the baby, parental fear and imagination can create totally unrealistic scenarios that are difficult to revoke later. Transport team members and hospital personnel need to choose their words carefully, however, so as to avoid misinterpretation that sets up future conflict.

Management En Route

Although limited by the environment, patient assessment and care continues in the moving vehicle back to the NICU. Team members must be positioned to observe the baby's color, chest excursion, and vascular access sites. Flashlights may be necessary to supplement interior lighting. Electronic monitoring may be used, but it is often rendered unreliable by environmental interference. Noise and vibration generally make it difficult to auscultate the chest. If this assessment is deemed necessary to verify well-being, the vehicle should be stopped. Longer transports may require temperature and blood glucose checks. In general, the observation and frequency of monitoring of the neonatal transport patient should be no less than what would be provided in the stationary NICU, though the methods used may differ.

Upon return to the NICU, activity and responsibility of the transport team is similar to that described on arrival at the referring hospital. The receiving care givers need to know what has happened and the baby's response to transport in order to continue planning care. Unloading to admit to the NICU is fraught with the same risks identified when moving the baby into the transport vehicle. Disruption in care can be minimized by communication between the team and the NICU personnel prior to return, so advance preparation for arrival can be made, such as preparation of infusions.

Documentation

The records collected during the transport are organized and maintained as part of the baby's hospital chart. These should include copies of both mother and baby charts from the referring hospital. Significant data needed to plan future care are found in these records. Failure to review them could create an error of omission. Certainly, these records must be legible, complete, and adequately photocopied to be readable.

Commentary by Mr. Goldman: As mentioned above, the receiving hospital has to decide whether they can rely on the outside records or whether there is a need to repeat certain tests. If the receiving hospital relies on outside records and the outside records turn out to be inaccurate, a plaintiff can claim that the receiving hospital had an independent duty to verify test results.

Maintenance of the integrity of the patient's medical record is a critical responsibility of the transport team, as the link between providers of care. The Joint Commission on Accreditation of Healthcare Organizations cites the medical record as the basis for planning patient care and evaluation of condition and treatment. It is the lasting source of communication between health care providers and serves to protect the legal interest of the patient, hospital, and professionals.[7]

The referring hospital personnel are responsible for documenting assessments, interventions, and infant reaction until the transport team begins charting. The referring hospital should consider maintaining documentation of care rendered in their setting regardless of who is providing it, so subsequent laboratory data, etc., will make sense in their hospital record. At the same time, the transport team needs to thoroughly describe its initial assessment of the patient and all subsequent interventions preparatory to and during transport. Creative form development and/or photocopying may be a way to avoid duplication of effort yet ensure adequate records for both groups of providers.

The goal is continuation of the infant's record of care without any gaps in the story.

> **Commentary by Mr. Goldman:** The charts should reflect facts, thought processes, and decision-making. The chart should be thought of as an audit trail that will be used after the fact to determine whether malpractice occurred. A useful exercise is to review past charts to see if you, as a clinician, can follow the thought process of the staff, i.e., you should look at charts every once in a while as if you have been retained by a plaintiff's attorney to review the care. Charts are not in place for name-calling, guilt, blaming, jousting, or incident reporting. These are highly inflammatory and should take place outside the medical record and under a quality assurance guideline.

The reader of the chart should be able to find documentation of the infant's clinical status from before birth throughout the NICU hospitalization. All procedures done during the conduct of neonatal transport must be carefully noted in the patient record. A description of what was done, a brief explanation of why it was done, and the report of how the patient responded should be included. Such details are useful to those assuming the continuation of care for the patient as well as invaluable if reconstruction of the events is ever required.

Decision-making and consultation discussions require sufficient description so rationale for intervention is identifiable. Again, careful choice of words is imperative. Properly signed consent forms covering transport, admission to the tertiary center, treatment, and exchange of information among health care providers are essential elements of transport documentation and become part of the medical record.[4] Medical orders must be written and signed. Non-physician teams may utilize pre-approved medical orders. Documentation for quality assurance purposes is recorded separately from the patient's chart.

Commentary by Mr. Goldman: Hospital protocols on quality assurance must be carefully authored to protect documents from discovery. There should be no mention in the medical record of incident reports or quality assurance documentation.

Special Circumstances

On rare occasions, the transport team is confronted with the patient who is so severely compromised it is considered unlikely that any benefit can be derived from transport to the NICU. Such a decision warrants considerable discussion with the referring physician and the neonatologist at the NICU, particularly if there is no physician on the transport team. Family members also need timely information about such a discussion. If the decision is made to withdraw support prior to transport, a detailed note must be written in the patient's record. Documentation should also be retained by the transport team. (Since admission to the NICU is nullified, there will likely be no patient record at the tertiary center.) Consideration must be given to requesting permission for autopsy, and if it is given, deliberation over where that study could best be done should be accomplished. Additional special documentation may be needed to permit legal transport of a deceased infant back to the tertiary center.

Staff Stress as a Risk Factor

Caring for critically ill newborns is stressful work. Neonatal transport imposes additional concerns. The physical and psychological burdens such stress places on care givers has the potential to jeopardize patient care if the stress levels escalate beyond team members' ability to cope sufficiently.[8] Consequences include a decrease in functional expertise, judgment, and communication skills of the team. The source of stress must be identified and appropriate strategies established to reduce stress levels.[9] All team members should be involved in this process, as each will be susceptible to different stress triggers.

Several sources of stress become immediately apparent. Maintaining a constant state of readiness for the unknown creates stress. Requests for neonatal transport often occur in response to an emergency situation where immediate assistance is needed. Physical distance and time constraints versus clinical urgency may create enormous conflict.

The practice setting and composition of the team is variable, requiring flexibility and rapid adaptation of members. The team must function independently of the familiar and extensive supports found in the NICU. The greater the distance away, the more dependent the team is on itself and the limited resources of transport.

Role stress may be experienced by nurse-led transport teams.[10] The specialized skills and knowledge of the tertiary care transport nurse(s) may exceed those of the referring physician, yet the referring hospital nursery is no place for a power struggle to occur over medical management of the sick newborn. Communication skills and sensitivity are needed to foster cooperation.[11]

The cramped physical environment of the vehicle, the potential for vehicular accident, uncertainty for the infant's outcome, emotional family members in crisis, and missing or malfunctioning equipment all contribute to escalating stress levels during neonatal transport.

Extreme care in the selection and training of the transport team members will serve to reduce stress. Ongoing staff education programs and quality assurance activities should include identification of stressors and management/reduction strategies.

Quality Assurance for Neonatal Transport

Transport programs and personnel benefit from periodic evaluation. Needed improvements and potential risks can be identified. Quality improvement programs need to address the organization, implementation, and utilization components of the transport service. Cost effectiveness is also a factor.

Quality improvement monitoring parameters include response time and equipment function. A review of clinical procedures initiated yields data about patient acuity and stabilization prior to transport. A variety of scoring systems have been proposed to create an objective, consistent picture of clinical status.[12] Simple review of the reasons for referral may identify a trend needing investigation. For example, a higher number of referrals for meconium aspiration syndrome may warrant discussion of labor and delivery practices. Collection and computerization of transport data provide useful resources for development of quality improvement and risk management programs.[13]

Case reviews are an effective quality improvement tool.[14] They educate by example as well as promote problem-solving dialogue. Surveys can be used to obtain satisfaction data. These can be given to parents as well as professionals. They are particularly useful in identifying risk areas with a cause rooted in differences between perception and reality.

Transport Team Continuing Education

Transport team training should utilize national standards and guide-lines.[4,15] Team members need an adequate number of transports to maintain necessary skills. If the number of transports declines, other mechanisms must be developed to simulate transport team function.

Continuing education should reflect regular evaluations of team members' competency and needs assessment data. Clinical topics are derived from an understanding of the types of patients being referred. In addition to didactic methods, skills workshops can be used to enhance ability and confidence in specific areas. Role playing may assist team members in developing communication strategies for difficult situations. Chart audits reinforce effective documentation. Special attention must be paid to safety training, vehicle orientation, and use of transport equipment. Team members must know how to troubleshoot equipment problems, repairing or substituting as needed. Transport team training and evaluation should be documented in appropriate personnel files.

Outreach Education

Outreach education brings the transport process full circle. The goal of the outreach program is to ensure education for the referring hospital personnel to promptly recognize conditions warranting transport, to know how to access the transport system for consultation and/or service, and to implement stabilization measures for interim patient care until the arrival of the transport team.[4] The ability to provide appropriate clinical support for neonatal stabilization coupled with timely access to regionalized transport services are believed to yield improved neonatal outcome.[16] Thus, participation in outreach education is a worthwhile investment for both community hospital and tertiary center personnel.

Outreach education programs often provide feedback on individual patient outcomes as well as quality assurance support. Case reviews similar to those conducted at the NICU can be offered to the referring hospital. These provide mutual educational and quality improvement opportunities for both the referring hospital and the transport team. Educational activities utilize a variety of formats to meet differing needs. The transport team itself has a golden opportunity to incorporate both formal and informal educational sharing at the bedside of the baby to be transported.

As a liaison between the referring hospital and the NICU, the outreach program can provide the transport team with knowledge about the referring hospital resources and the skill levels of its personnel, which will assist in planning transport services. This information is particularly useful in considering the use of return transfer of the convalescent infant.

Other Issues

Hospital Privileges

It remains unclear as to when patient care responsibilities shift from the referring institution and physician to the transport team and its institution.

> **Commentary by Mr. Goldman:** Patient care responsibilities ought to shift only after the infant is accepted for transfer and has been moved into the transferring vehicle. Language should be included in the transfer agreement specifically stating that the infant is the responsibility of the receiving hospital only after the infant has been accepted for transfer and placed in the transferring vehicle.

If arrival of the transport team in the referring facility heralds this transfer of responsibility, should transport team members have full privileges in the referring institution? After all, part of stabilization and treatment may entail prescribing drugs, performing procedures, and ordering tests. These are all delineated privileges. Alternatively, perhaps there should be an arrangement that designates the transport team members as limited active members of the hospital staff, with privileges restricted to those necessary for pre-transport stabilization and care.

In the case of institutions that do not utilize a physician for their transport team, the situation is even more confusing. Transport team members may have to perform interventions such as endotracheal intubation or thoracentesis, privileges that may be designated "physician-only" in the referring hospital. How does this impact the referring physician? Should he/she be compelled to remain at the bedside until the transport team departs?

At present, it seems that the best safeguard for a transport team member is good documentation. A carefully written note, which explains the basis for diagnostic impressions, the thought process behind therapeutic interventions, the procedure in detail (including indication, methodology, and patient response), and continued dialogue with the responsible physician can go a long way to protect oneself from claims of negligence.

Reimbursements

In the age of medical cost containment, neonatal transport seems to be a likely target for reductions in reimbursements. In fact, the concept of managed competition is antithetical to that of neonatal regionalization and has the propensity to dramatically alter this aspect of neonatal intensive care. Although the development of large subscriber-group networks may ultimately reduce the need and number of neonatal transports, it is not likely to do away with the need entirely. Neonatal health care providers must maintain an adequate level of funding to assure that the high quality of care provided during the transfer of a critically ill baby can continue.

Personnel performing neonatal transports are subject to the same risks as those who operate vehicles for any other reason. Cutting costs means cutting corners; this may decrease vehicle safety and imperil the passenger and crew. Similarly, it must be remembered that neonatal transport is a package. It includes not only the transfer of a patient, but also health care provider education, regional quality assurance, and more effective health care through the use of back transfer.

References

1. American Academy of Pediatrics and American College of Obstetricians and Gynecologists. *Guidelines for Perinatal Care*. Elk Grove Village, IL and Washington, D.C., 1992.
2. Donn SM, Faix RG, Gates MR. Neonatal transport. Curr Prob Pediatr 1985;15:1.
3. Donn SM, Faix RG, Gates MR. Emergency transport of the critically ill newborn. In: Donn SM, Faix RG (eds). *Neonatal Emergencies*. Mt. Kisco, NY, Futura Publishing Co., 1991, pp. 75-86.
4. Task Force on Interhospital Transport. Guidelines for Air and Ground Transport of Neonatal and Pediatric Patients. Elk Grove Village, IL, American Academy of Pediatrics, 1993.
5. Dunn N. Fostering good interhospital relationship through neonatal transport. Neonatal Network, Dec. 1982:20.
6. Siefert KA. Crisis intervention: Helping parents cope. In: Donn SM, Faix RG (eds). *Neonatal Emergencies*. Mt. Kisco, NY, Futura Publishing Co., 1991, pp. 627-634.
7. Joint Commission on Accreditation of Healthcare Organizations. Accreditation Manual for Hospitals, Chicago, JCAHO, 1991.
8. Marshall RE, Kasman C. Burnout in the neonatal intensive care unit. Pediatrics 1980;65:1161.
9. Weeks H. Dealing with the stress. Mat Child Nurs 1978;3:151.
10. Rapson MF. Role stress of nurse practitioners. Nurse Practitioner 1982;7:48.
11. Pinelli J, Ferguson MK. Transporting high risk newborns: The importance of communication. Neonatal Network, June 1985:23.
12. Hermansen MC, Hasan S, Hoppin J, et al. A validation of a scoring system to evaluate the condition of a transported very low birthweight neonate. Am J Perinatol 1988;5:74.
13. Donn SM, Gates MR, Kiska D. User-friendly computerized quality assurance program for regionalized neonatal care. J Perinatol 1993;13:190.

14. Philip AGS, Little GA, Lucey JF. The transport conference as a teaching strategy: Evaluation in the Vermont/New Hampshire regional perinatal program. Perinatol Neonatol 1984;8:63.
15. National Association of Neonatal Nurses. Neonatal Transport Standards and Guidelines, Second Edition, 1994.
16. Shenai JP. Neonatal transport: Outreach education program. Pediatr Clin North Am 1993;40:275.

Chapter 32

Emergency Vehicles and Crews: Maintenance and Safety Issues

◆◆◆

Peter L. Forster, B.A., M.B.A.,
Denise Landis, B.S.N., M.S.A.

Introduction

Risk management as a discipline has its origins in the health care setting in the malpractice "crisis" of the early 1970s. As the number of malpractice suits mounted, hospitals and other health care providers sought ways to manage their risks, hence risk management was born.

There are a wide array of activities that come under the general heading of risk management; this chapter will be confined to a discussion of those tasks pertinent to critical care transport. Generally speaking, all risk management activities are concerned with the general principle of assessing where things can go wrong, and putting in place procedures and/or protocols to eliminate or minimize the risk exposure to patients, transport staff, and institutions.

Risk management programs for critical care transport must use the expertise of the hospital's risk management office to be effective. Many, if not most of the major issues confronting a transport medical director already will have been addressed, in some fashion, by the risk management office.[1] Issues pertaining to patient transport that a hospital risk management office typically addresses include:

1. Incident reporting procedure.
2. Patient complaint resolution procedure.
3. Attorney contract procedure.
4. Patient confidentiality/release of information procedures.

From: Donn SM, Fisher CW (eds.): *Risk Management Techniques in Perinatal and Neonatal Practice*. © Futura Publishing Co., Inc., Armonk, NY, 1996.

5. Employee injury procedure.
6. Body mechanics procedure.
7. Sharps safety and disposition procedures.
8. Preventive maintenance procedures.
9. Loaner equipment procedures.
10. Defective equipment procedure.
11. Product recall procedure.
12. Fire, safety, and disaster procedures.
13. Post-accident/incident (media) plan.
14. Conservative response procedures (i.e., refusal to fly/drive).
15. Regulatory compliance (i.e., OSHA, infection control).

Quality Assurance

The hospital quality assurance (QA) program, in addition to the risk management program, is a necessary resource for assessing and managing the risks in a critical care transport program. In order for the critical care transport program to function optimally, it is important that there be consistency between the hospital, the transport program's risk management effort, and QA programs. QA is a systematic program by which care rendered to patients is measured against established criteria. Potential problems in patient care are identified, activities to address these problems are designed, thresholds of performance are established, and performance is measured against the standard. The risk of patient injury prior to and during transport is the major focus of both risk management and QA programs applied to critical care transport programs.

The critical care transport program should seek, whenever possible, to integrate QA and risk management activities. This can include staff education and training programs, intervention strategies, problem resolution policies, monitoring systems, and continuous quality improvement efforts. The basis of the QA and risk management efforts should be patient-focused and oriented to team performance. Examples of QA/risk management activities in critical care transport include:

1. Clinical performance standards (e.g., the percentage of time an activity or procedure is performed according to a prescribed protocol-airway management, pharmaceutical intervention, ventilator settings, etc.).
2. Case presentation/review/rounds.
3. Standard operating procedures/protocol performance.
4. Retrospective documentation review/audit.
5. Transport performance standards (e.g., response time of emergency vehicle or transport crew, or both).
6. Transport program's compliance with external standards.

Comparing a transport program's operation against an industry or national standard is an effective tool for assessing risk. Although the transport industry is relatively new, recent accreditation activities by national and federal agencies should be referenced by transport programs.

Accreditation and Standards

In October 1993 the Commission on Accreditation of Ambulance Services of the American Ambulance Association developed standards that are reported to be incorporated into the 1995 Joint Commission for the Accreditation of Health Care Organizations standards to assess the pre-hospital portion for emergency vehicles.[2] Therefore, the prudent critical care transport provider will incorporate these standards into his/her own operation.

The Commission on Accreditation of Air Medical Services of the Association of Air Medical Services (AAMS) also has developed a voluntary process (1991) for both rotor and fixed wing transport systems.[3] Both commissions have recognized the changes in the industry and will continue to review and revise the standards as developments occur.

The Federal Aviation Administration (FAA) issues Federal Aviation Regulations (FARs) that regulate and mandate the operation of aircraft in the national airspace system in the 48 contiguous states, Hawaii and Alaska. FAR Part 91 governs all general operations and flight rules and FAR Part 135 contains flight rules for air taxi and commercial operations that are pertinent for all air-medical operations. The safe operation of the aircraft is the ultimate responsibility of the pilot, and crew members must function under his/her direction. The FAA also publishes recommendations for the construction and operation of helipads. (Helipad Design Guide—Advisory Circular 150/5390-2A.)

Each state has separate licensure requirements for ground or air ambulances that are administered by the state health or transportation departments.

Elements of a Safe and Well-Maintained Transport Program

The transport of a patient between two facilities indicates effective communication between the referring and receiving institutions. Ideally, an established communications network with an efficient and around-the-clock central communications center should be accessible to facilitate the transport of a patient. A hospital-based transport system should have a transport team readily available for requests and a minimal mobilization time. Many critical care transport programs have the luxury of choosing between ground, helicopter, or airplane vehicles. This allows the transport service maximum flexibility in choosing the appropriate vehicle to meet the patient's medical condition and distance to be transported.

Emergency Vehicles

Ground Ambulances

There are several vehicles that could be available for the transport of patients to and from facilities that include ground, rotor wing (helicopter), and fixed wing (airplane or jet). Many of the conventional ground ambulances have been modified to accommodate the pediatric and neonatal patient. In addition to the standard equipment in an ambulance, the vehicle must have capabilities to transport and secure an incubator (or two), ventilator support (which includes the ability to blend air and oxygen), and an electrical inverter to support the equipment. If an institution contracts with a local ambulance company for transports, then these items need to be included in the ambulance. A reasonable and feasible response time for a transport should be agreed upon by both parties. The advantages of ground transport are numerous and include cost, safety, availability, and adequate space for patient management. However, speed, range, and time can inhibit the quick response that a critically ill patient frequently requires.

Rotor Wing

Air medical transport has become the recognized standard for the transport of critically ill and injured patients since its civilian application began in the early 1970s. Particularly during the 1980s transfer of patients by air became an accepted choice for transport. Rotor wing or helicopter vehicles have the capability of flying a distance of 100-200 miles or further without refueling and can land at pre-determined sites or helipads at the referring institutions. Helicopters have become very sophisticated in their interior design, and can be large enough to accommodate two incubators and provide the space to treat a patient adequately. However, helicopters can be susceptible to turbulence, noise, and vibration, and are dependent on weather conditions for safe operation. Much has been written about the relative safety of single versus twin engine helicopters.

Fixed Wing

Fixed wing or airplane vehicles have the capability of performing long distance transports but have the complication of requiring additional ground transports for the transport crews and patient to and from the airport. Fixed wing transports are generally most cost effectively utilized for transports > 150-200 miles. Clinically, an understanding of the working of pressurized and non-pressurized aircraft should be incorporated into the decision about whether a jet or propeller-driven airplane is required. The science of flight physiology is defined as the relationships between the interdependent variables of temperature, pressure, volume, and mass of gases.[4] Understanding these physical laws will assist the flight crew with the changes brought on by altitude, which become particularly important on ascent and descent, particularly if the patient has respiratory compromise.[5]

Airplanes may or may not be pressurized. Non-pressurized aircraft are generally propellor airplanes and include the Navajo®, Cessna 404 Titan®, or Seneca®, and could be disadvantageous as they will not allow flight altitudes that could avoid adverse weather conditions or high altitude winds. This could impair patient care and cause motion sickness for both patient and flight crews. Pressurized aircraft are generally jets or turbo-props and include the Citation®, Westwind®, Falcon®, and Lear® jets, which are advantageous in that they can be pressurized allowing altitudes of > 8000 feet. Cabin pressurization reduces the effect of high altitude by maintaining a preset barometric pressure within the cabin. Flight crews have the option of manipulating the cabin pressure, thus providing the optimum environment for patient care. Aircraft should be configured so that the patient's condition can be maintained during transport. Suction, oxygen, inverters, litter systems, and hooks for intravenous fluids are just some of the items that may be standard equipment in an aircraft. These aircrafts should have sufficient room to provide complete access to the patient in the event that a procedure must be performed during the flight.

Depending upon the patient's condition and need for transport, several vehicles may be required for one transport. The crew may be transported by ground one way and may find the urgency to return to the receiving institution as quickly as possible and choose to activate a helicopter. Some procedures, such as extracorporeal membrane oxygenation (ECMO), may require a similar type of arrangement if the ECMO unit and patient do not fit in the aircraft. The helicopter may be utilized to transport the ECMO team and surgeons to the referring facility; however, ground transport may be required for the return transport. State-of-the-art patient equipment has made air transport a viable option for this very specialized transport.

The importance of patient information and the critical nature of the patient's condition require that a well-managed transport program consider the benefits of a dedicated communications center. Staffed by a full-time communications specialist/dispatcher monitoring multiple telephone and radio frequencies, the communications center can provide an essential documentation and coordination function to the transport program. The ability to tape record conversations between referring, receiving, and transport staffs, with quick replay capabilities, can assist immeasurably in smoothing out transport difficulties. Additionally, a communications center can act as the data management center, utilizing computer assistance to maintain vital clinical and administrative information for QA and research activities.

> **Commentary by Mr. Goldman:** In order for data to be confidential, the data should be part of the hospital's QA system. Careful attention should be paid to state laws on protection of QA data. If careful attention is paid, then the data should be immune from discovery and use in malpractice cases. Clearly in some cases, the hospital will *want* data to be available because the data will show that the hospital promptly responded to a call, or that the patient's condition was misrepresented in some way by the sending hospital. Data should be kept in a factually accurate and retrievable manner.

Transport Team Composition

Transport team compositions vary around the country and around the world. A team should be able to provide quality critical care not only at the scene or referring institution but during the actual transport as well. Teams can include physicians, nurses, paramedics, respiratory therapists, or any combination of these. Vehicles may have restrictions that limit the size of the team. The medical director of the transport program, who has the medical responsibility for patient care, may have to determine crew configuration. The transport team should have specific training, management, and experience with critically ill infants or the high-risk pregnant woman.

Critical care teams should be available to respond emergently or have protocols in place that dictate response times. A dedicated team will promote shorter mobilization and response times because they are accustomed to doing transports and will have vehicles ready for immediate response. When there are options among the various transport vehicles (ground, helicopter, or airplane), the clinical requirements of the patient requiring a rapid response, combined with the cost of the transport, should dictate which mode is most efficient and effective.

> **Commentary by Mr. Goldman:** While cost is important, it should not be a primary factor—patient safety should be. It is not possible to defend a malpractice case alleging cost efficiencies.

All members of transport teams must be licensed to practice within the state where the base hospital is located.

> **Commentary by Mr. Goldman:** There are specific licensing and staff privilege issues when crews cross state lines and when crews do procedures in outside hospitals. State licensing and hospital privilege

requirements should be analyzed and discussed in advance with referring hospitals.

Hospital-based transport programs function under the premise that most patients will be admitted to that hospital; therefore, the transport team assumes patient care at the time of transfer.

Commentary by Mr. Goldman: Each transport team assumes patient care at the time of transfer. Patients must be initially assessed to determine need for transport and patient stability. Once the patient is removed from the referring hospital, and control is relinquished, then the transport team assumes responsibility for patient care.

The transfer team functions under the policies and procedures of its base institution and similarly is under its medical control and direction. Many states govern the minimum level of activity to maintain the licensure that is required for that state. Formal transfer policies outlining the responsibilities of both the referring and receiving hospitals are important considerations for the critical care transport team.

Vehicle and Crew Safety

Maintenance of vehicles can be scheduled or unscheduled. Routine maintenance can often be scheduled during "slow" or "down" times, which would cause the least amount of disruption to normal operations. Unscheduled maintenance is more difficult to deal with, as it can be of a nature that will ground the vehicle until the problem is fixed. Vendor contracts may include a back-up vehicle that could be utilized under certain conditions, such as maintenance requiring longer than 24 hours of service time. Performance standards should be incorporated into any contract where out-of-service time is clearly defined for all contract parties. Another consideration is the ability to take the vehicle to an appropriate service center, or alternatively, the vendor provides additional maintenance personnel.

Transport programs should have an internal safety committee that consists of various interdisciplinary team members. The safety committee should function under the direction of the program administrator and medical director and can provide safety programs for all staff, address concerns or issues by staff, and be an extension of the external state safety program (if one exists). Many states have formed trade associations closely linked to the AAMS. These state committees can address issues that involve all programs in the state or country, such as personal and protective gear, flight-following in the state, or the development of a survival course for the state programs. (As of this writing, no standards for personal protective clothing or headwear have been established.)

Insurance

While a comprehensive review of all insurance considerations is beyond the scope of this chapter, there are some practical insurance considerations that need to be addressed. First, a close examination of existing travel accident insurance coverage provided by the employing hospital should look for exclusions for staff using unscheduled, non-commercial aircraft, or staffing other emergency vehicles. Staff should also be advised to review all personal life insurance policies with their insurance agents for similar exclusions. Examining the insurance coverage provided or excluded for non-employees (students, observers, family members) should also be done. Where these insurance exclusions exist, a liability release form will inform non-employees of their uninsured status and provide some limited protection in the event of accident or injury (Figure 1).

```
          ASSUMPTION OF RISK AND WAIVER OF LIABILITY

   I, _____, (name), am an emergency medical technician
   _____, (insert professional status).  I am
   interested in obtaining more information about helicopter
   transport of injured patients.  On my own time and not part of
   any job responsibilities, I wish to go on an actual transport in
   a helicopter.

   I understand that the _____, (name of
   institution and program), is willing to allow me to go on a
   transport, but only at my own risk.  I understand that I will
   have to go through a safety orientation and will have to strictly
   follow all safety rules.  I further understand that I will not be
   a _____ (name of institution) employee or
   volunteer nor will I be acting on behalf of my employer.  Rather,
   I will simply be an interested citizen on the helicopter flight.
   I will not be taking part in patient care and will not provide
   any patient care.

   I understand and agree that the _____ (name of
   institution), its agents and employees will not be responsible
   for my safety or well being.  I understand and agree that the ____
   _____ (name of institution) does not provide any
   insurance for me.  If I am injured or killed, I will not have any
   coverage for the _____ (name of institution)
   and I agree that I am assuming any risks of injury up to and
   including death and neither I nor my estate will make any claim
   against the _____ (name of institution and
   program), or agents or employees of the _____
   (name of institution).

   I hereby assume the risk of any injury up to and including death
   from my participation in this activity.


   _____
   Signature
```

Figure 1. Example of form used to obtain liability waiver from non-employee participants in transport activities.

Emergency vehicle insurance requirements can be a significant financial burden and vary greatly by the degree of risk and the replacement cost of the vehicle. Professional insurance assistance is required on at least an annual basis to ensure the adequacy of coverage provided.

Conclusion

The transport of critically ill patients has evolved tremendously during the past 20 years from exclusive use of ground vehicles to the availability of a number of highly specialized, sophisticated critical care ambulances on the ground and in the air. Regardless of the transport mechanism, however, health care professionals must strive to provide the safest environment possible for the patient and crew and be guided by risk management principles.

References

1. Martin PB. Quality assurance. In: *Risk Management Handbook for Health Care Facilities*. American Hospital Association, American Hospital Publishing, Inc., 1990, p. 108.
2. Standards for the accreditation of ambulance services. Commission on Accreditation of Ambulance Services, 1993.
3. Accreditation Standards of the Commission on Accreditation of Air Medical Services, revised edition August, 1993.
4. Waggoner RR. Flight physiology. In: Lee G (ed.) *Flight Nursing: Principles and Practice*. St. Louis, Mosby-Year Book, p. 2.
5. Donn SM, Faix RG, Gates MR. Neonatal transport. Curr Prob Pediatr 1985;15:1.

_____ Chapter 33 _____

The COBRA Regulations: Obstetrical Implications

◆◆◆

Susan Healy Zitterman, J.D.

Introduction

Since its passage in 1986, the Emergency Medical Treatment and Active Labor Act,[1] more commonly referred to as "COBRA," has significantly impacted on hospital treatment of patients with emergent conditions in general, and of pregnant women in particular.

Commentary by Mr. Goldman: COBRA is the Congress Omnibus Budget Reconciliation Act. Congress always has a budget reconciliation and in 1986 as an addendum to that general law the Emergency Medical Treatment and Active Labor Act was included. Other such budget laws have included things like the patient self-determination law.

The obligations imposed by the Act are broad and pose particular liability risks in the case of pregnant patients (Table 1).

The Act initially imposes an obligation upon hospitals that have an emergency department to provide to *any* individual who comes to the hospital seeking examination or treatment for a medical condition, an "appropriate medical screening examination." The screening is to determine whether or not an "emergency medical condition" exists, and must be performed within the capability of the hospital's emergency department, "including ancillary services routinely available to the emergency department."[2]

From: Donn SM, Fisher CW (eds.): *Risk Management Techniques in Perinatal and Neonatal Practice.* © Futura Publishing Co., Inc., Armonk, NY, 1996.

Table 1
Summary and Procedural Checklist of Requirements Under COBRA*

I. Conduct Appropriate Medical Screening Examination
  A. Examine within capability of emergency room department and ancillary services
  B. Determine whether there is an "emergency medical condition"
    1. Acute severe symptoms, and health or any bodily part in serious jeopardy, *or*
    2. Pregnant women having contractions, *and*
      (a) inadequate time for safe transfer *or*
      (b) transfer *"may"* pose a threat to woman or child
  C. Err in favor of finding an emergency
II. If No Emergency Exists
  A. May discharge or transfer without further treatment
  B. Document no emergency
III. If Emergency Condition Exists
  A. Treat until stabilized
    1. Stabilized defined as
      a. No material deterioration likely during transfer within reasonable medical probability; or
      b. Pregnant woman with contractions has delivered
    2. Document stabilization before discharge or transfer
  B. Transfer upon informed written request, *or*
  C. Transfer on certification
    1. Prepare certificate
      a. Signed (or countersigned) by physician;
      b. Based on information at time of transfer;
      c. Lists risks and benefits; and
      d. Determines benefits outweigh risks
    2. Arrange for appropriate transfer
      a. Transferring hospital provides treatment within its capacity to minimize risk;
      b. Receiving facility has agreed to accept and treat, and has space and qualified personnel;
      c. Available medical records are sent; *and*
      d. Qualified personnel and transportation equipment used during transfer as required.

---

*This checklist addresses liability under COBRA, but does not purport to evaluate common law or state statutory law that might impose other obligations on hospitals regarding emergency room treatment.

Commentary by Mr. Goldman: The theory behind the law was to stop "patient dumping" where for economic reasons a hospital would take a Medicare or Medicaid or uninsured patient and send the patient to another hospital for treatment. The law attempted to stop this kind of dumping and ensure adequate, appropriate, and timely care for the Medicare and Medicaid and uninsured population.

COBRA imposes detailed requirements on physicians and hospitals with respect to the care, treatment, and transfer or discharge of individuals coming to a hospital who have an "emergency medical condition." The particularly encompassing definition of what constitutes an emergency medical condition, especially in the care of pregnant women, accounts for much of the broad responsibilities and liabilities imposed by the Act.

Emergency Defined

An "emergency medical condition" initially is defined such that it may apply to all patients, pregnant or not. This is a medical condition manifesting itself by "acute symptoms of sufficient severity (including severe pain)" such that the absence of immediate medical attention "could reasonably be expected" to place the health of the individual (or, if pregnant, that of the unborn child) in "serious jeopardy," or cause "serious impairment to bodily functions" or "serious dysfunction of any bodily organ or part."[3]

The Act *also* defines "emergency medical condition," in the case of "a pregnant woman who is having contractions" to mean that either:

1. there is inadequate time to effect a safe transfer to another hospital before delivery; *or*
2. transfer *"may"* pose a threat to the health or safety of the woman or the unborn child.[4]

The definition of emergency medical condition specific to pregnant women has been interpreted by the Fifth Circuit Court of Appeals in the seminal decision of *Burditt v. U.S. Department of Health & Human Services,*[5] to mean that the Act's treat or transfer limitations are not triggered simply on the basis of contractions alone, and to allow hospitals to "transfer at will, women in uncomplicated labor who, within reasonable medical probability, will arrive at another hospital before they deliver their babies." However, that same Court cautioned that a hospital that transfers a woman in labor when the timing call mandated by the Act is close "risks a battle of experts regarding anticipated delivery time, distance, and safe transport speed."[6]

Moreover, an emergency medical condition in a pregnant woman having contractions can also exist even if delivery is not imminent. This would occur where "transfer may pose a threat to the health or safety of the woman or the unborn child."[7] One appellate Court, again in *Burditt,* interpreted this provision to broadly provide protection to women in labor "who have any complication with their pregnancies regardless of delivery imminency." Because better medical care is available in a hospital than in an ambulance, observed the Court, whether a transfer "may pose a threat" and put the patient within the protections of the Act "depends on whether the woman in labor has any medical condition that could interfere with the normal, natural delivery of her healthy child."[8]

As further noted by the Court in *Burditt*, the Act's protections for pregnant women having contractions apply upon the showing of *possible threat*; it "does not require proof of a reasonable medical probability that any threat will come to fruition." In other words, Congress "required less of a showing of probability and severity of harm for women in labor than the general population under its definition of emergency medical condition."[9]

Stabilization

Once an emergency condition is identified upon appropriate screening, the Act usually requires treatment "within the staff and facilities available at the hospital until the patient is stabilized."[10]

"Stabilization" is defined by the Act, and does not occur until:

With respect to an emergency medical condition, that no material deterioration in the condition is likely, within reasonable medical probability, to result from or occur during the transfer of the individual from a facility or, with respect to an emergency medical condition described for a pregnant woman who is having contractions, that the woman has delivered (including the placenta).[11]

Thus, stabilization does not occur in a pregnant woman having contractions until delivery (including the placenta).

Commentary by Mr. Goldman: For example, in certain cases pregnant patients could still have an emergency medical condition such as pre-eclampsia or could have trauma from a fall or motor vehicle accident. In these cases necessary care must be delivered to diagnose and stabilize the patient.

Moreover, even if contractions have not begun or have stopped, a pregnant patient could still have an emergency medical condition for reasons other than those related to labor/contractions and then, generally, must be treated until stabilization occurs. Once the patient is stabilized, however, the limitations of the Act no longer apply, and the patient may be transferred to another facility or discharged without liability under the Act.

Commentary by Mr. Goldman: Patients may be transferred only in accordance with the Act, so that it is still necessary to notify the receiving facility to be sure that they have the ability to accept the patient.

Transfer Before Stabilization

Only under limited circumstances and after specific steps have been taken does the Act allow hospitals to transfer patients before they are stabilized. The term "transfer" is generally defined by the Act to mean movement of the patient outside of the hospital's facilities, and thus includes both discharge and transfer to another facility.[12] Transfer before stabilization may occur only where: 1. the individual, after being advised of the risks and the hospital's duties under the Act, requests the transfer in writing; or 2. a physician has signed a certification meeting the Act's requirements. The physician in the certification must specifically state that "based upon the information available at the time of transfer, the medical benefits reasonably expected from the provision of appropriate medical treatment at another medical facility out-weigh the increased risks to the individual and, in the case of labor, to the unborn child from effecting the transfer . . . ," and must summarize those risks and benefits.[13] Although not required by the Act, common law informed consent requirements would dictate that a consent to transfer also be obtained from the patient or the patient's legal representative even where the physician prepares the required certification in order to head off state law medical malpractice claims.

In addition, the transfer to another medical facility must be an "appropriate transfer." This means, first, that the transferring facility must provide medical treatment within its capacity that minimizes the risks to the individual and, if pregnant, to the unborn child. Second, the receiving facility must have agreed to accept the transfer. Third, the medical records must be forwarded. Finally, transfer must be effected through "qualified personnel and transportation equipment, as required, including the use of necessary and medically appropriate life support measures during transfer . . . ."[14]

Burditt's Facts and COBRA Violations

The facts in *Burditt* itself reveal both the encompassing nature of the Act's coverage and obligations, and rather flagrant violations of the Act by the treating physician in that case. In *Burditt*, Mrs. Rosa Rivera arrived at the emergency room of the hospital at or near term with her sixth child. She was experiencing 1 minute, moderate contractions every 3 minutes and her membranes had ruptured. She also had a dangerously high blood pressure of 210/130 mmHg.

The on-call physician, Dr. Burditt, who was also head of the hospital's obstetrics and gynecology department, was summoned. He examined the patient and arranged for her transfer by ambulance to a hospital approximately 3 hours away. However, Burditt refused to read the hospital's guidelines regarding the requirements of the Act, and only signed the certificate authorizing transfer when told he had to do so before transfer could occur. Burditt gave no reason in support of the conclusion on the preprinted form that the medical benefits from the transfer outweighed the risks, but stated to the nurse that the patient represented more risk than he was willing to accept from a malpractice standpoint.

Burditt never bothered to examine the patient again. About 1.5 hours later the patient left by ambulance without any medication or life support equipment having been ordered. The nurse who accompanied the patient delivered her healthy baby in the ambulance approximately 40 miles into the 170-mile trip to the second hospital.

In upholding the $20,000 civil penalty assessed against the physician by the Department of Health & Human Services, the Court in *Burditt* found that Mrs. Rivera had an emergency medical condition under both criteria that apply to women having contractions. That is, the Court concluded that Mrs. Rivera was in an emergency medical condition because there was inadequate time to safely transfer her to the second hospital before she delivered her baby.[15] This was based on expert testimony that, under facts revealed by Burditt's examination results at 5:00 p.m., Rivera would more likely than not deliver within 3 hours. (That examination had revealed that Rivera had carried several pregnancies to term, that she had ruptured membranes, contractions beginning at 7:00 a.m. and becoming regular before 4:00 p.m., a cervix dilated to 3 cm, and a smaller-than-usual fetus.)

The Court found that these circumstances also fell under the second test for an emergency medical condition in a woman having contractions by virtue of Rivera's hypertension. This, the Court noted, *could have* interfered with the normal, natural delivery of her healthy child and, therefore, possibly did "pose a threat to the health or safety of the woman or the unborn child."[16] Such a mere possibility triggered the Act's protections, and its sanctions for violation of those protections, even though the possible risk never materialized.

Once it was established that the patient had an emergency medical condition, the Court in *Burditt* turned to the issue of whether the procedure for transfer met the requirements of the Act for transfer prior to stabilization. Not surprisingly, the Court found that there had not been compliance. While there was a signed certification as required by the Act, the Court found that the signing physician had not actually deliberated and weighed the medical risks and benefits of transfer before executing the certification. Of some solace, however, is the fact that the Court in *Burditt* noted that "the signer need not be correct in making a certification decision; the statute only requires a signed statement attesting to an actual assessment and weighing of the medical risks and benefits of transfer."[17]

The transfer was *also* found inappropriate in *Burditt* because of the lack of qualified personnel and transportation equipment. This resulted from the absence of a physician and a fetal heart rate monitor. The Court agreed that the latter was necessary because of evidence that hypertensive women face increased risk of placental abruption, and without a fetal heart rate monitor in the ambulance, it would be almost impossible to perceive this condition during transport.[18]

Burditt thus dealt with a situation where the patient clearly fell within the protections of the Act (as having both contractions with delivery imminent and critically high blood pressure, which independently posed a possible threat to the mother and child). Further, the transfer was shown to be neither medically appropriate nor worth the risk, and improperly executed without appropriate personnel and equipment.

> **Commentary by Mr. Goldman:** Finally, the other hospital never agreed to accept nor did the patient ever request to be transferred.

While, at least in retrospect, the facts of *Burditt* make the analysis fairly simple, there are an infinite number of circumstances where what the Act requires may not seem so clear.

Some Hypothetical Cases and the Act

Consider a situation where a woman in preterm labor, at 30 weeks gestation, with blood pressure of 180/110 mmHg, dilated to 2 cm, with mild contractions, comes to the emergency room of a Level I hospital. This probably should be considered an "emergency medical condition" under the Act—a transfer *may* pose a threat to the health or safety of the woman or unborn child from a discharge.

> **Commentary by Mr. Goldman:** There should be clear discharge instructions with a copy to the patient in language understandable to the patient.

If there is any reasonable doubt or possibility of complication, the most prudent course to limit liability would be to proceed as if there was in fact an emergency medical condition.

Under these facts, this would mean taking steps within the facility's capabilities to stop the contractions so that the patient could then be transferred in relative safety to a higher level facility. The physician might begin intravenous tocolytic therapy to stop the contractions, and magnesium sulfate treatment to prevent seizures.

Should the contractions stop, the physician probably could conclude that the benefits of a transfer would outweigh the risks. To so proceed under the

Act then, would require written certification from the physician that, at the time of the transfer, the medical benefits from transfer to another facility outweigh the increased risks to the mother and child. This analysis must reflect the patient's condition at the time of transfer and not earlier, and the risks and benefits must be listed in the certification.

These documentation requirements will assist in confirming that (unlike the situation in *Burditt*) an analysis was in fact performed. Documentation will also provide concurrent justification for the decision, which, in retrospect and with complications, may appear ill advised.

In addition to certification by the physician, the receiving facility must be contacted and agree to accept the transfer. Finally, medical records must be forwarded, and the transfer must be effected through "qualified personnel and transportation equipment, as required . . . ." Under these hypothetical facts, this would include continued intravenous administration of magnesium sulfate during the transfer.

Complications may arise where the patient refuses to consent to treatment or refuses to consent to a transfer. Under the Act, this hospital will be deemed to have complied with the treat or transfer requirements if it offers the patient treatment or transfer, as applicable, and advises the patient (or "a person acting on the individual's behalf") of the risks to the patient of the refusal of such treatment or transfer. In either case, the hospital under the Act must take all reasonable steps to secure the patient's *written* "informed consent" to refuse such treatment or transfer.[19] All of this, of course, should be documented. Under new amendments effective in 1995 hospitals are required to report violations of this law to the Health Care Financing Administration.

Consider another situation where there is a presentation to the emergency room of a pregnant woman who is at or near term, is experiencing very irregular contractions, is only minimally dilated, and the required initial medical screening reveals that there is no reason to suspect that mother and child are anything other than healthy. Under such circumstances, it might be medically appropriate to determine that such a pregnant patient, although having contractions, does not meet the other requirements for an emergency medical condition to exist and does not need any hospitalization for the time being.

Care, however, should be taken to document that if the patient is sent home, there is plenty of time to safely return to that or another hospital before delivery, and that there is no apparent threat to the health or safety of the woman or the unborn child from the discharge.

In other words, if there is not yet an emergency medical condition, under the Act the hospital could lawfully discharge the patient, even for economic reasons. However, extreme caution must be taken under such circumstances because judicial scrutiny would be particularly close and likely hostile if the reason for discharge is economic.

Conclusion

COBRA unquestionably places broad and complex requirements on hospital emergency rooms and obstetricians to ensure the safety of pregnant patients and their unborn children. However, the penalties for failing to meet these requirements, and for "patient dumping," are severe. They range from civil fines on hospitals and physicians and tort liability for damages, to suspension or termination of the hospital's Medicare provider agreements.

As hospital emergency rooms and obstetricians have become familiar with the Act, and protocols have been (and certainly should be) in place at the hospitals to assist practitioners in following and meeting, step by step, the analyses required by the Act, compliance will continue to become less onerous. From a risk management and liability containment perspective, it is imperative that the requirements are met in good faith, and that all efforts in this regard are also well documented. This will enable hospital and physician alike to respond to administrative inquiries or those by a patient's attorney, and to meet or diffuse criticisms fueled by an adverse outcome.

References

1. 42 U.S.C. ® 1395dd *et seq.*
2. *Id.* ® 1395dd (a).
3. *Id.* ® 1395dd (e) (1) (A).
4. *Id.* ® 1395dd (e) (1) (B) (i) and (ii).
5. 934 F. 2d 1362, 1369 (5th Cir. 1991).
6. *Id.* at 1369.
7. 42 U.S.C. ® 1349 (e) (1) (B) (ii).
8. *Burditt, supra,* note 5, at 1370.
9. *Id.* at 1370.
10. 42 U.S.C. ® 1359dd (b).
11. *Id.* ® 1395dd (e) (3).
12. *Id.* ® 1395dd (e) (4).
13. *Id.* ® 1395dd (c) (1) and (2).
14. *Id.* ® 1395dd (c) (2).
15. *Burditt, supra,* note 5, at 1369-1370.
16. *Burditt, supra,* note 5, at 1368-1369.
17. *Burditt, supra,* note 5, at 1371.
18. *Burditt, supra,* note 5, at 1373.
19. 42 U.S.C. ® 1395dd (b) (2) and (3).

Section VII

Communication

Chapter 34

Inappropriate Word Choice in the Labor and Delivery and Newborn Medical Record

◆◆◆

Jeffrey H. Chilton, J.D., Thomas R. Shimmel, J.D.

Introduction to Medical Management Disputes

Medical malpractice litigation has increased dramatically during the last three decades. It is inconceivable that this rising number of lawsuits can be attributed to an increased incidence of negligence in light of the advances made in medical technology and practitioner training. Rather, society itself has become increasingly litigious, and patients are now compelled to sue when an untoward event occurs or an undesired result is obtained.

This is especially true in the fields of perinatal and neonatal medicine. Injuries sustained in the newborn period, such as brachial plexus palsy, seizure disorders, and cerebral palsy, are often long-term in nature. Such injuries attract plaintiff attorneys as they can yield substantial sums of money. Plaintiffs now utilize experts in neuropsychology, pediatric neurology, vocational rehabilitation, and physical therapy who testify that an injured child will never work and will need lifelong nursing care, and an economist then testifies that the cost will amount to millions of dollars.

In assisting with the defense of a malpractice lawsuit, a key physician role will be to explain complex medical principles to a jury comprised of lay persons with little, if any, prior exposure to such complex concepts, while remaining appropriately sympathetic and composed. When confronted with such a monumental task, some physicians blame the legal system. Despite its

From: Donn SM, Fisher CW (eds.): *Risk Management Techniques in Perinatal and Neonatal Practice.* © Futura Publishing Co., Inc., Armonk, NY, 1996.

flaws, however, the system remains, and the financial incentives ensure that attorneys will continue to pursue medical malpractice claims.

It is important to keep in perspective that, no matter how catastrophic the injury, a case cannot be brought before a jury without physician testimony that applicable obstetrical or neonatal standards of care were violated. A foremost historic role of defense counsel is to discredit such experts through research into each expert's prior sworn testimony and vigorous cross-examination concerning the underlying facts of a particular case. Forcing such an expert to reach conclusions that are illogical and inconsistent with established medical principles is also effective in discrediting the witness. Through such efforts, an expert may legitimately be characterized as a "professional witness" who should be afforded little credibility. A concomitant defense strategy is to develop expert opinions supportive of the care rendered, and defense counsel often use the leading physicians in a particular field who are extensively published and nationally recognized for their expertise and perspective on a particular issue. Often the chairperson of the department with which plaintiff's expert is affiliated is retained by the defendant to ascertain whether plaintiff's experts practice what they preach.

An important aspect of plaintiff's discovery plan is the detailed analysis of the medical records combined with thorough cross-examination of the fact witnesses involved in the patient's care and treatment. In concert with the cross-examination of physicians and supporting personnel, plaintiff's counsel will direct his/her experts to dissect the medical record in a retrospective fashion to buttress plaintiff's claims concerning key issues of negligence and causation. Thus, a medical record cannot be viewed by a physician as merely a method of providing documentation of the patient's health care. This is especially true in obstetrics, where subsequent treating physicians will rarely have a medical need to extensively review a patient's history.

A well-documented record made contemporaneous to the events that reflects an appreciation of possible medico-legal ramifications is of invaluable assistance in the successful defense of a medical malpractice case. Carelessly worded entries, on the other hand, can be of irreparable harm in medical management disputes.

Medical malpractice litigation is a civil action. Unlike a criminal proceeding, a physician questioned about charting issues has no rights against self-incrimination. Skilled plaintiff attorneys are well-versed in semantics. Thus, even where plaintiff's experts have been effectively neutralized, the best witness or "expert" for the plaintiff becomes the physician involved with the case at issue when asked to explain an inarticulately phrased record upon cross-examination.

This chapter seeks to assist physicians in establishing a record that is complete yet clear and concise so as not to negatively impact the ability to successfully defend should a less than ideal medical outcome occur. The examples provided in this article are derived from cases handled during our firm's 25-year history of defending physicians and hospitals in malpractice cases. Perhaps the most significant examples occur in documenting "fetal distress," "birth asphyxia," or similar terminology and in the inappropriate usage of superlative modifiers.

Fetal Distress and Fetal Heart Rate Monitoring

"Fetal distress" is the most damaging term in the English language relative to obstetrical malpractice cases. Although physicians and nurses have been instructed to avoid this usage, the term continues to appear quite regularly to the great detriment of the health care provider. Unfortunately, while the terminology is inartful, vague, and given to multiple medical interpretations, it is amazingly clear to a lay juror in a "birth trauma" lawsuit.

Health care providers should realize that a case is very difficult to defend when "fetal distress" appears in the record. The plaintiff's counsel and the plaintiff's expert can easily convince a jury that the fetus was suffering injury at the time that "fetal distress" was recorded and that a Cesarean section should have been performed to avoid such damage.

To a layman, the term "distress" has a very ominous meaning. *Webster's Ninth New Collegiate Dictionary* defines the term "distress" as: " . . . a painful situation, . . . the state of being in great trouble, great physical or mental strain and stress." Simply stated, *"fetal distress" should not be placed in a medical record to explain the fetal condition.* The difference between the medical concept and the layman's interpretation of "fetal distress" is so significant that, based on the legal implications alone, this term should be abandoned.

Since most diagnoses of "fetal distress" are derived from an interpretation of the fetal heart rate monitor strip, it would be appropriate to substitute an accurate description of the fetal heart rate pattern in place of the non-specific and often incorrect diagnosis of "fetal distress." The term "fetal distress" is often used to justify the need for a Cesarean section based on a monitor strip interpretation. Generally, most fetuses are delivered before they are in dire need or in actual "fetal distress," and this again illustrates how the medical definition differs from that understood by lay jurors.

Describing the *actual appearance* of the monitor strip to justify a Cesarean section or some other appropriate intervention (forceps, vacuum extraction, etc.) is a more accurate and less damaging method of documentation. Accurate documentation is key in describing fetal heart rate monitor patterns; without accurate documentation, consequences similar to those that arise in the "fetal distress" scenario ensue.

Good documentation of fetal heart rate patterns involves describing any abnormalities in a non-subjective way using acceptable terminology and methodology. For example, during the labor process, a nurse actually documented the following: ". . . gross decelerations on monitor strip." The particular monitor strip in question was never found; however, after the patient was taken to the delivery room, a second monitor strip revealed occasional variable decelerations with good beat-to-beat variability and reactivity. Nevertheless, the loss of the former monitor strip left the defense with only the conclusion of "gross decelerations." Webster's description of "gross" is almost as bad as "distress": ". . . glaringly noticeable, usually because of inexcusable badness."

The child in the above situation was born without any significant acidosis but later developed cerebral palsy. Plaintiff's experts were able to testify not only that there was significant "fetal distress" but also that the damage occurred during labor. From the defense standpoint, loss of the applicable monitor strips made it virtually impossible to explain why the nurse's interpretation was incorrect.

If the health care provider interprets a late or variable deceleration or some other abnormality, he/she is certainly compelled to document that in the chart. *However, any documentation of an abnormality in the medical record should be accompanied by the reassuring factors that reflect the overall interpretation of the monitor strip.* Since there are numerous aspects to consider in interpreting the monitor strip, most of which, even in the presence of abnormalities, establish fetal well-being, the health care provider must chart all of these factors to explain why an expeditious delivery was not necessary in the face of an abnormality.

In other words, reassuring factors (i.e., stable baseline, good return to baseline, adequate beat-to-beat variability, good long-term variability, accelerations, non-repetitive type decelerations, mild decelerations, and second stage pushing pattern) must be a part of the documentation accompanying an abnormality. In fact, the health care provider should *describe the reassuring factors prior to describing the abnormality.* In this way, a jury will be shown reassuring factors before addressing the abnormality. *Present the positives before the negative in an almost aggressive, adversarial charting style for the most beneficial effect in a medico-legal circumstance.*

The vast majority of the literature discussing the potential relationship between fetal heart rate monitoring and poor neurologic outcome has continually found very little correlation between the two (see Chapter 11). The literature is replete with references that most decelerations, as well as other fetal heart rate abnormalities, are rarely ominous or dangerous. This supports the hypothesis that, in most cases where decelerations occur, very reassuring factors concomitantly appear that must be charted.

Variable decelerations are frequently targeted by plaintiff attorneys despite a plethora of references in medical literature that the same are rarely ominous or dangerous. For example, Roger Freeman asserts in his text, *Fetal Heart Rate Monitoring*, Third Edition, that: ". . . variable decelerations are the most common periodic change observed in laboring patients, being present in over 50% of them at one time or another."

Medico-legal problems develop when physicians use excessive modifiers, such as "severe," "profound," "deep," or "gross" to describe these decelerations. If physicians or nurses use these terms inartfully or incorrectly, plaintiff's experts will find it easier to convince a jury that the fetus suffered brain damage at the time of the decelerations, thereby justifying a claim for an earlier Cesarean section.

It is important to remember that the modifier will be the focus of attention, leading to a sympathetic and empathic closing argument by a skillful plaintiff's attorney. Again, this is why reassuring factors must be documented in the chart to accompany abnormalities described.

Although various authors have attempted to classify variable decelerations as mild, moderate, significant, insignificant, severe, or non-severe, no universal agreement regarding the application of such modifiers exists. *ACOG Technical Bulletin No. 132* describes variable deceleration significance as follows: "Most such patterns are innocuous and are commonly encountered in normal labor. A variable deceleration becomes significant when it decreases to less than 70 beats per minute, persists at that level for at least 60 seconds, and is repetitive."

In the *Handbook of Fetal Heart Rate Monitoring*, Julian Parer, M.D. describes "severe" variable decelerations as those that decrease to below 60 bpm for 60 seconds from the beginning of the deceleration to its end (the 60-60 rule). These examples illustrate that not only do the definitions vary, but the descriptive modifiers used also differ (e.g., "significant" vs "severe").

Obviously, neither description is incorrect. While the use of modifiers is probably unnecessary from a medical standpoint, such modifiers can have a significant impact in the legal environment. In making a medical determination, it is probably more important to look at the other factors (i.e., baseline, beat-to-beat variability, accelerations, responses to conservative measures) than to decide whether or not a deceleration is severe.

Documentation of severe, profound, or significant variable decelerations has the same effect as the use of the terminology "fetal distress." It suggests not only that the fetus is in grave danger but, arguably, that one waited too long before undertaking appropriate interventions. In order to avoid damaging legal argument resulting from the charting of a particular pattern, simply charting the pattern's appearance, noting the type of deceleration and the depth to which it descends would be equally effective from a medical standpoint and less likely to lead to legal argumentation.

A few rules of thumb with respect to fetal heart rate monitoring documentation would include the following:

1. Document all reassuring factors first.
2. Describe abnormalities using numbers rather than graphic modifiers.
3. Document an actual subjective conclusion in the medical record regarding fetal well-being.
4. If unable to document reassuring factors in the face of a repetitive abnormality, expedited delivery may be warranted.

Finally, there are those patterns that defy description or, in some cases, patterns that nurses have difficulty describing in terms of the type of abnormality or deceleration. It is a mistake to attempt to classify in the medical record the type of abnormality at this point, since a documentation error can make the difference between a defensible or an indefensible lawsuit. For example, mistaking mild variable decelerations for late decelerations can devastate an otherwise defensible lawsuit. Thus, when the pattern is unclear or confusing, a simple numerical description of the strip is better than an interpretation of the pattern type.

Most lawsuits are premised on the notion that a pattern was overlooked, misinterpreted, or responded to inappropriately. When an abnormality persists on a monitor strip, the physician needs to establish fetal well-being or risk a very difficult lawsuit should a poor outcome occur. Use of "fetal distress" should be completely abandoned in favor of more accurate descriptions of the fetal monitor strip and the decision criteria for treatment or non-treatment, intervention or non-intervention, and conservative methods or expedited delivery.

Perinatal Asphyxia, Birth Asphyxia, and Hypoxic-Ischemic Encephalopathy

Neonatologists, pediatricians, and other attending physicians in the newborn period continue to indiscriminately utilize the phrases "perinatal asphyxia" and/or "birth asphyxia" in the chart. Persons charting during the newborn period should use caution in using these phrases, and physicians must discipline themselves to chart birth or perinatal asphyxia only after having definitively diagnosed the same, following the passage of an appropriate period of time and a thorough investigation of all possible causes.

A cautious approach to using "birth asphyxia" or "perinatal asphyxia" is necessary to successfully defend obstetrical management disputes. Experience has demonstrated that a physician charting these phrases will be subpoenaed by plaintiff's counsel to provide deposition and/or trial testimony. This physician will be used to provide expert support for plaintiff's claims that an alleged failure to expedite a delivery caused the neurologic sequelae observed during the newborn period. If defense counsel has successfully developed facts and expert opinions demonstrating that the neurologic sequelae did not result from an alleged failure to perform a cesarean section, plaintiff's counsel will counter by presenting the physician who initially charted "birth asphyxia" and/or "perinatal asphyxia."

Such terms make an obstetrical case very difficult to defend and place the physician in a most uncomfortable position during deposition or trial. Across the country, scenarios similar to the following occur at deposition and at trial:

Plaintiff's Counsel-Q: Doctor, is it true that you are a board-certified neonatologist who provided medical care to my client, the plaintiff-minor, under the auspices of the defendant Hospital?
Physician Witness-A: Yes.
Plaintiff's Counsel-Q: And as a physician who provided treatment to my client, you were under an obligation to appropriately care for and ascertain the cause or causes of my client's condition, correct?
Physician Witness-A: Yes.
Plaintiff's Counsel-Q: And your first note concerning my client, written by you approximately 6 hours after birth, indicates "birth asphyxia," correct?
Physician Witness-A: Yes, but . . .
Plaintiff's Counsel-Q: No, doctor, let me remind you again that you are only to answer the specific question posed to you. Understand?
Physician Witness-A: Yes.
Plaintiff's Counsel-Q: Doctor, wouldn't you agree that asphyxia is generally defined by the medical community as a condition due to lack of oxygen resulting in apparent or actual tissue acidosis?
Physician Witness-A: Yes, in a general sense.
Plaintiff's Counsel-Q: And generally, doctor, wouldn't you agree that a lack of oxygen can cause significant neurologic deficits exactly as those afflicting my client, the plaintiff-minor?
Physician Witness-A: Yes, it's possible.
Plaintiff's Counsel-Q: Doctor, you didn't chart "possible" when you referenced "birth asphyxia" did you?
Physician Witness-A: No, I did not.
Plaintiff's Counsel-Q: And wouldn't one reasonably assume that if a doctor places in the record the phrase "asphyxia," which we now know to mean a condition due to lack of oxygen, and puts as a modifier the phrase

"birth," wouldn't common sense indicate that you are saying as a physician that my client's neurologic deficit was caused by a lack of oxygen during the labor and delivery itself?

Physician Witness-A: Counsel, it is well-known that a child with a prenatal injury from an infection often will be asphyxiated at delivery, simply because the brain cannot function in the child independent of the mother's maternal fetal circulation. This does not mean that the timing of the delivery itself caused the asphyxial pattern that I observed.

Plaintiff's Counsel-Q: But at the time of your charting, made contemporaneously with the events described, you did not place any qualifier in your note suggesting that further investigation was required as to why the asphyxial picture existed, did you?

Physician Witness-A: Unfortunately, I did not.

Plaintiff's Counsel-Q: And, doctor, you have staff privileges and an employment relationship with the Defendant Hospital and also know professionally the Defendant obstetrician in this matter?

Physician Witness-A: Yes, I do.

Plaintiff's Counsel-Q: And you are now aware that the defendants are claiming that my clients' injuries were as a result of occurrences during the prenatal period, correct?

Physician Witness-A: Yes, I have that general understanding now.

Plaintiff's Counsel-Q: So isn't it convenient on your part now to elaborate upon, in an after-the-fact manner, your explanation as to what you meant by the phrase "birth asphyxia"?

Physician Witness-A: Well, one has to wait many, many days during the nursery course to develop facts to either support or refute my initial impression of "birth asphyxia."

Plaintiff's Counsel-Q: Well, doctor, did you note that the plaintiff-minor had a 21-day hospitalization?

Physician Witness-A: Yes.

Plaintiff's Counsel-Q: And, doctor, did you have an opportunity to review subsequent records made after your initial impression of "birth asphyxia"?

Physician Witness-A: Yes.

Plaintiff's Counsel-Q: And did you note that three resident physicians and one other staff physician also subsequently charted "birth asphyxia"?

Physician Witness-A: Yes, but I just assumed that they picked up on my initial impression in that regard and simply didn't change or modify it.

Plaintiff's Counsel-Q: Doctor, isn't it true that, even at the time of plaintiff-minor's discharge from the hospital, the diagnosis of "birth asphyxia" was not even changed then?

Physician Witness-A: Yes, but again I assume that they were merely picking up my initial impression.
Plaintiff's Counsel-Q: So once again you assumed .... Thank you, doctor, I have no further questions.

The above scenario is, or course, for illustrative purposes, and similar methods of cross-examination are used for all of the inappropriate language in labor and delivery/newborn records that are discussed in this chapter. For purposes of this chapter, the cross-examination set forth has been abridged; in actuality, cross-examination of a physician may be intense and of considerable length. The physician who charts in such a manner is often subjected to hours of similar questioning involving implicit innuendoes of some form of after-the-fact conspiracy by the health care professionals to mask the alleged malpractice.

It is a misfortune that such charting, which often makes a case completely indefensible, continues to appear in records, because it need not occur in order for a physician to appropriately perform his duty to the patient and to the community as a whole. If a physician is attuned to the medico-legal climate and the most current medical thinking on the issue of perinatal asphyxia, then charting can serve not only the patient but will provide a record to aid in successfully countering plaintiff's accusations when an untoward event occurs.

A conclusion of birth asphyxia, perinatal asphyxia, or hypoxic-ischemic encephalopathy (HIE) should only be noted in the chart where the medical facts absolutely warrant it. To act otherwise often places the physician in a difficult position when the defense to a lawsuit is proffered.

The absurdity of charting in such a manner until all available medical facts are analyzed can be seen from a recent case wherein the pediatrician noted on the second day of life that the plaintiff-minor had suffered "birth asphyxia with resultant hypoxic encephalopathy." When questioned concerning this note, the physician indicated that he based this assessment primarily on the low Apgar scores of 1 and 5, seizures, and an increased serum creatinine and blood urea nitrogen levels, which were indicative of kidney damage to the newborn. Although the physician witness had intended to perform a computed tomographic (CT) brain scan, none was conducted during the initial hospitalization, and the cranial sonogram performed suggested some congenital hydrocephalus. Unfortunately, however, the physician could not rule out birth asphyxia as a cause of this development.

Fortunately, a CT scan was performed at another medical institution, which indicated that the plaintiff-minor had a congenital brain anomaly and that approximately one-half of this newborn's brain was missing! Instead of waiting until such definitive testing was conducted, the initial attending physician had cavalierly written the initial diagnosis of "birth asphyxia." While the plaintiff-minor may in fact have been hypoxic and exhibited some evidence of encephalopathy at delivery, this was resolved, much as it is in many newborns presenting by breech, and therefore, had no bearing on the newborn's subsequent condition. Although charted as a definitive diagnosis, the "birth asphyxia" was related not to management in labor and delivery but to the fact that the newborn had a gross brain abnormality that prevented the infant from functioning properly at birth. Thus, the low Apgar scores in this case reflected a newborn without brain function rather than a newborn who had been damaged during labor and delivery. Consistent with the most current medical literature, physicians should no longer use the term "perinatal asphyxia" as a very broad phrase for any baby with low Apgar scores.

The *ACOG Technical Bulletin No. 163*, published in January 1992, points out that the phrase "perinatal asphyxia" is imprecise; unfortunately, the long history of its usage prevents abandonment. Moreover, *ACOG Technical Bulletin No. 163* directly states that:

> "In assessing a possible relationship between perinatal asphyxia and neurologic deficit in an individual patient, *all of the following criteria must be present before a plausible link can be made* (emphasis added):
> 1. profound umbilical artery metabolic or mixed acidemia (pH $\leq$ 7.00);
> 2. persistence of an Apgar score of 0-3 for longer than 5 minutes;
> 3. neonatal neurologic sequelae, e.g., seizures, coma, hypotonia; and
> 4. multi-organ system dysfunction, e.g., cardiovascular, gastrointestinal, hematologic, pulmonary, or renal."

Volpe's *Neurology of the Newborn*, thoroughly demonstrates that the clinical features evaluated in diagnosing intrapartum hypoxic-ischemic injury continue to evolve from birth to > 72 hours of life. Physicians should use the most current medical literature to support their medical decisions. It is our recommendation, based upon decades of defending medical management disputes, that the physician note in the newborn record that the infant was "*depressed*" at delivery and chart thereafter only the objective results of laboratory studies. Thereafter, subsequent physicians should describe and treat the conditions as they arise and should avoid making large, sweeping, and often unsubstantiated generalities such as "birth asphyxia," "perinatal asphyxia," or "HIE." Hopefully, this chapter and the discussion it generates will prompt physicians, through their departmental committees, to work together in charting in an appropriate and defense-oriented manner.

Superlative Modifiers

Our current legal climate makes it absolutely necessary for physicians and other health care professionals to remember the purpose of medical record charting. The goal is to state facts in a clear, concise, and objective manner to provide subsequent treating physicians with an adequate history.

Modifiers broaden or restrict a term's definition. While a modifier in the hands of a skilled writer makes reading more meaningful and pleasurable, medical records were never meant to be poetry! Attorneys skilled in semantics can use an inappropriately utilized modifier in the medical record to support a malpractice theory through vigorous cross-examination of the person charting in such a manner.

Medical records are generally replete with inappropriate superlative modifiers. Descriptive modifiers used to denote heart rate patterns, such as profound, severe, excessive, or prolonged, will be addressed in greater detail in the next section of this chapter. Frequently, one also encounters phraseology related to modalities of treatment, such as the ordering of a Cesarean section or the monitoring of vaginal bleeding.

When describing the modality of treatment, it is unfortunate that superlative modifiers are utilized at all. Thousands of interviews with prospective physician witnesses prior to their depositions or trial testimony have confirmed that the use of modifiers does not hasten the occurrence of the prescribed treatment. Thus, there is no medical justification for usage of modifiers such as "urgent," "stat," or "emergency" when an order is noted in the record. Such phraseology does not serve the patient but does benefit the plaintiff's counsel should an untoward event occur. Plaintiff attorneys are proficient at describing a medical scenario wherein the Cesarean section should be performed within seconds, and it is extremely difficult for a jury to understand that a 30-minute lapse between the time at which a Cesarean section is ordered and the time at which it is performed is common and well within the standard of care. Adjectives describing the urgency of the Cesarean section are absolutely unnecessary and do not by any means cause the Cesarean section to be performed in a more prompt manner. Such terms only bolster the "hysteria" of plaintiff's counsel in describing the extreme urgency of the situation.

Mothers with active vaginal bleeding also present situations wherein a physician believes that superlative modifiers must be utilized. Obviously, vaginal bleeding is of a medical concern to physicians, yet there is no compelling need to use phraseology such as "excessive" in charting the occurrence.

"Excessive" is ambiguous and subject to various interpretations. One can rest assured that the plaintiff's attorney will utilize the interpretations that is most damaging to the defense in a medical management dispute. Obviously, the physicians evaluate the loss based upon the maternal and fetal status, including an assessment of blood counts, fetal heart rates, and vital signs. When a physician utilizes inappropriate phraseology, it only creates an additional argument for the adversary in raising innuendoes by suggesting that the physician failed to respond to a severe situation.

Superlative modifiers serve little, if any, purpose in the provision of health care. They do, however, have considerable jury appeal in the hands of a skilled plaintiff's attorney. While the judge will instruct a jury that the questions posed by an attorney do not constitute evidence, jury behavior research strongly suggests that emphasis on provocative words in questioning witnesses serves to buttress the plaintiff's case on both a conscious and subconscious level. If physicians continue to chart superlative modifiers such as "severe," "massive," or "deep," they can anticipate those words will be uttered repeatedly during rigorous cross-examination. In a situation that is medically complex, it is difficult for a lay jury to separate the specific medical meaning of a superlative modifier from their general understanding of words such as "severe," "massive," or "deep." Your adversaries will do everything in their power to use your phraseology against you. Do not provide your opponent with such an unwarranted and unjustified opportunity.

Remarks and Observations

We hope this chapter will generate substantive discussions between health care professionals. We encourage all persons with charting responsibilities to write objectively, utilizing information gleaned from continued analysis of current medical literature.

While the responsibility of exonerating a hospital or physician from claims of medical malpractice remains with the defense attorney, the health care practitioner should chart carefully, always bearing in mind that chart entries will be strictly scrutinized by plaintiff attorneys and their experts in their quest to find malpractice in even the most benign of admissions.

Commentary by Dr. Donn: This chapter reminds me of the Liza Doolittle refrain in *My Fair Lady*, "Words, words, words, I'm so sick of words . . ." Yet, as the authors so elegantly emphasize, it is the written word that so often condemns or defends the writer when independent recollection of the events in question have long since faded.

Many of the principles espoused in this chapter are never taught in medical or nursing school. Much of "chartmanship" is instead passed from one generation of practitioners to the next (see Dr. Schreiner's comments on "Med Speak" in Chapter 1). We often write, "patient *denies* use of alcohol" rather than "patient does not use alcohol," suggesting that he/she is not to be believed. Is it any wonder that a patient contemplating litigation might be offended when reviewing his/her own medical record?

It may indeed be best to eliminate the use of the term "fetal distress," but like so many other medical terms, it has become almost a reflex to apply it to situations in which there is an irregularity or abnormality in the fetal heart rate. "Asphyxia" has a bit more objectivity because it applies to a specific biochemical or physiologic condition (see Chapter 25). It becomes confusing, however, when timing parameters are attached as descriptors. For instance, does "*birth*" asphyxia refer to the condition *developing* at birth or to the condition *being present* at birth? "Perinatal" is very imprecise and depending on the specific epidemiologic application could range from the 20th week of gestation through the first year of life.

I would like to offer a few additional caveats. First, health care providers must be aware of how medical record diagnoses are entered and coded in their own institutions. A commonly used system is the *International Classification of Diseases*, Ninth Revision (ICD-9). This reference defines asphyxia as an Apgar score of < 6, for example. An aggressive health records analyst may carefully search the hospital chart for as many diagnoses as possible for reimbursement purposes. Thus, a completely healthy newborn who has a 1-minute Apgar score of 5 is coded as having had "birth asphyxia" and the attending physician may unwittingly add a confirmatory signature to the face sheet or discharge summary. Second, the medical record is not the place to record speculation. Keep to the facts. Do not comment on what "might" have caused the condition if the data base is incomplete or requires other expertise. Third, refrain from entering second and third-hand information in the record. If, for some reason, this must be done, identify the source of information. Finally, the age-old cliche about the "doctor's handwriting" has more than a remote link to risk management. Be sure that all entries are legible and decipherable. Avoid the use of jargon and, importantly, abbreviations that no one will remember 10 years later. Keep in mind that the medical record may be used to recreate past events at a time when few of the actual participants are still available. What you said—and how you said it—will have an enormous impact on how others will interpret what was done.

Chapter 35

Risk Management in Medical Consultation

John V. Hartline, M.D., C. Giles Smith Jr, J.D.

Introduction

Consultation among physicians is essential to assure that high quality care is available to all patients. Success in the process of medical consultation requires a combination of events: recognition of the need for consultation; preparation for the consultation request (by the physician requesting the consultation); actual consultation by the consultant physician; communication with the referring physician and with the patient and/or family; and finalization or follow-up. This process is best accomplished with respect and friendliness among the participants. A detailed account of the process of consultation in general and for neonatology in particular has been recently published.[1]

Medical consultation is associated with hope, considerable anxiety, and some potential risks. The physician requesting the consultation feels a sense of vulnerability. He/she has recognized encountering a difficult or unusual patient or case and that some important things may have been missed or not done. He/she also needs to admit into the doctor-patient relationship another physician who may be more knowledgeable.

Commentary by Mr. Goldman: He/she also needs to admit into the doctor/patient relationship another physician who may be more knowledgeable, or the other physician may have different views or different approaches that are to be considered.

Sometimes the requesting physician wants or needs only advice or reassurance; other times, actual help in the patient's hands-on care is requested.

From: Donn SM, Fisher CW (eds.): *Risk Management Techniques in Perinatal and Neonatal Practice.* © Futura Publishing Co., Inc., Armonk, NY, 1996.

Most essentially, what is desired is the assistance of another physician to assure that the best care is offered to the patient. A consultation is requested.

Consultation physicians possess a high depth of knowledge and experience in a relatively narrow area of medicine. It is essential for consultants to recognize the primary care physician's difficult task in selecting the unusually sick patient or the unusual condition from among the myriad of patients with less complex problems. One of the luxuries of the consultant is having this distinction already made by the referring physician.

The consultation relationship is vulnerable to a number of difficulties that justify analysis from the perspective of risk management so as to meet the needs of patients for excellent care, of physicians for ongoing collegial cooperation to provide that care, and of all for continuing education. Risk management requires an understanding of these vulnerabilities and the use of techniques to eliminate or at least reduce the potentials for adverse patient outcome and for legal liability of the physicians involved. "The ultimate goal of any risk management system is to improve the quality of patient care and any risk management approach that focuses on the patient will be successful. Risk management is also the development of a system that protects the assets of an individual or institution, minimizes the risk of a lawsuit, and ultimately makes for more defensible medicine."[2]

The focus of this chapter is on the process of the relationship between the consultant and referring physician. It goes without saying that competence within one's primary care or specialty practice is essential to good care and to the ability to manage risk. But, competence alone may not serve to reduce risks to the minimum, especially when multiple physicians are involved, the patient is very ill, or when the outcome is less than optimal.

As is discussed in greater detail in other areas of this book, medical liability is based on the presence in a particular case of the four "Ds": Duty; Dereliction of the duty; Damage; and Direct relationship between the failed duty and the damage (proximate cause).

> **Commentary by Mr. Goldman:** Actually, there is a fifth element. The doctor-patient relationship must exist before the four "Ds" go into effect. This is important for consults since a "curbside" consult where there is no relationship creates no legally enforceable duty.

Of these, the duty element is the subject most specifically related to medical consultation. From the legal or risk management perspective, the issue is whether the consultant has, by virtue of something he has said or done or by virtue of what someone else expects of him, incurred a "duty" that he must then adequately discharge. Duty in this context is not the duty the consultant may have as a physician to act professionally or responsibly toward his colleagues, nor the duty to conform to the requirements of the hospital of which he is a member of staff, nor the responsibility to comply with the myriad requirements, practice pointers, technical bulletins, etc., of one's specialty college or society. Duty here refers to the legal obligations that the consulting physician owes to the patient. Once a legal duty has been established, however, the failure of the physician to comply with any of these sets of rules or requirements may constitute the second element of legal liability, dereliction of duty, but that is another subject.

Duty has been defined, simply but well, as the obligations imposed by law to conform to a particular standard of care.[2] For purposes of legal liability of the consultant, the issue is whether, or at what point, that obligation came into existence in favor of the particular patient who is now claiming that he was injured by the acts or inaction of one or more physicians who had some involvement in his care and treatment. The answer lies in the particulars, expressed or implied, of the relationship that the consultant establishes with that patient. If the understandings, expectations, agreements, or actions to which the consultant is a party amount to no physician-patient relationship at all, no legal duty to conform to a particular standard of care arises. Lacking a physician-patient relationship, the consultant cannot be held liable for malpractice no matter what the injury, the cause of the injury, or the quality of the consultant's advice or involvement.

On the other hand, the duty arises and applies when the particulars of the relationship—what was requested, what was offered, what was expected, what was undertaken, what was done—establish a professional relationship between the consultant and the patient.

> **Commentary by Mr. Goldman:** For example, a physician accepts a patient in transfer and agrees to see and assess the patient. Here a relationship is established. Equally, a relationship is established if a physician agrees to render specific treatment. However, if a consult is simply advice given to a physician by another physician where the consulting physician does not see the patient or agree to assume care there is no legally binding relationship or duty to the consulting physician.

Failure to comply with the standard of care that may be pertinent causes liability for injury, which that failure actually and/or foreseeably caused. The task is to anticipate what agreements between physician and patient or between primary care giver and consultant, what conversations between physicians, or what contributions or undertakings of the consultant to the care of the patient may be held subsequently in a court of law to have established a physician-patient relationship, and hence, a duty on the part of the consultant.

Consultants may serve a purely educational role to colleagues, which does not involve actual patient care but may serve to help the primary physician with a specific patient. The following hypothetical cases illustrate some of the "bright line" tests, few as they may be, to address the question regarding legal duty of the consultant to the patient.

Case 1: A family physician in a smaller hospital or community is presented with a patient who is 20 weeks pregnant and who is in preterm labor. It appears that the patient may deliver without being able to be transferred. The family physician calls a neonatologist at the Perinatal Center asking what the approach to care for the 20 week infant may be if the child is liveborn. The physician says, "We have nothing that we can do to change the outcome for infants delivered at 20 weeks. Comfort care and support of the family can help the mother and father best in the situation at 20 weeks." After delivery, the child is given comfort care only based on this advice. The child survives and ultimately is transferred to a neonatal unit. There he is diagnosed as a 24 week infant who potentially could have benefitted from aggressive care beginning in the delivery room.

Although the consultant physician gave educational advice to the family doctor, does this communication establish a relationship between the pregnant woman and/or her child and the consultant? In the situation above, there was no communication between the patient or the patient's family and the consultant. There communication between the physicians did not provide that the consultant had specific responsibilities to the infant or mother. The interaction was an educational exchange. The judgment as to whether or how the information exchanged applied to the specific patient was the responsibility of the primary physician. When the consultant does not see the patient's chart, does not see the patient, and does not even know the patient's name, giving advice of a general or even specific nature has been uniformly held by the courts as not establishing a relationship between the patient and the consultant. Thus, no legal duty exists on the part of the consultant. Even if the consultant's advice was argued later to have been incorrect, incomplete, and inappropriate and even to have caused injury to the patient, the consultant cannot be liable for malpractice.[3-5]

The key factor is whether the consultant agreed, explicitly or by his actions, to undertake to diagnose or treat the patient. If there is such an agreement or, of course, an actual undertaking of the process of diagnosis or treatment, the law imposes the duty on the consultant to provide appropriate care, with liability attaching for dereliction of the duty that results in injury to the patient.[6,7]

Commentary by Mr. Goldman: Generally, the consulting physician must have an actual review involving the patient rather than simply second-hand knowledge.

Factors that the practitioner may believe avoid the imposition of legal duty in a particular case are often viewed as insignificant by the legal system. For example, the fact that the patient is not paying for the consultant's services or that no one is paying for the services does not preclude the finding that care or treatment was undertaken by the consultant. Even though the services may be volunteered or gratuitous, the legal duty to conform to the applicable standard of care is imposed. As in all cases, once the duty is imposed, the physician is liable for failure to adequately discharge the duty if harm results.[8-10]

The fact that a series of physicians were involved in the care or the fact that the patient was not aware of who was treating her or of the involvement of a particular consultant are not dispositive on the issue of whether a particular physician undertook to diagnose or treat; the duty is imposed on each physician who agrees to undertake care of the patient.[11,12]

Case 2: A consultant physician receives a call from another physician about an infant delivered after prolonged rupture of membranes. From their discussion, the consultant feels that the appropriate evaluation has been done, the appropriate tests ordered, and the appropriate treatment has been rendered. The primary physician feels that the peripheral perfusion of the infant is normal although some acrocyanosis is present. He asks the consultant to affirm his findings. The consultant looks at the baby but does not perform a comprehensive examination and agrees with the finding. The primary care physician writes "perfusion evaluated with Dr. Consultant who agrees that it is normal" into the record. The primary care physician continues to manage the patient. Several hours later, the baby's condition precipitously deteriorates, and the child dies. To what degree is the consultant liable in this case?

Often consultants provide "curbside" advice without a formal request for evaluation or management. This may involve affirming the findings of the primary physician or may include discussion of laboratory results, radiographs, or treatments. This type of relationship among physicians is desirable for both education and patient care. It is also cost effective in that care remains with the primary physician rather than being transferred to the more expensive consultant. If the primary care physician writes "perfusion evaluated with Dr. Consultant" or "blood test results reviewed with Dr. Consultant," does this educational interaction establish the duty, or does it support the quality of care of the primary physician?

Cases with facts similar to this hypothetical one, have been held as not establishing a relationship between the patient and the consultant, with it axiomatically following that the consultant had no duty to the patient, and could not be held liable for harm to the patient, which arguably, flowed from his "consultant."[7]

Case 3: A pediatrician went with an attending family physician into the newborn's room, discussed the case, looked at the patient and agreed that the patient was improving. The pediatrician was offered the opportunity to assume care of the patient, but he declined to take over the care because the patient was improving. The following day, the child had seizures and a diagnosis of meningitis followed. The court held that there was no physician-patient relationship established and the consultant was not liable for the alleged negligent failure to suspect meningitis.[13] It is possible for the duty to be owed the patient to be held to be limited to a specific request.

Case 4: An emergency room physician was asked to review a radiograph regarding the placement of an orogastric feeding tube. On review of the film, the tube was determined to be in the trachea and the situation was appropriately rectified and so noted in the record by the emergency room physician. A pneumothorax present on the radiograph was missed, resulting in an action against the emergency room physician. The court held that the physician's duty to the patient was limited to the issue of the feeding tube in this case and he was not held liable for the failure to diagnose the pneumothorax.[14]

> **Commentary by Mr. Goldman:** Of course, the result may have been different if the radiologist responsible for interpretation of the radiograph missed the pneumothorax. Here a court would say that a relationship existed since the radiographer intended to render care for the patient and be reimbursed for the care.

Although the above case relieved the emergency room physician of liability, it is not certain that all courts would rule the same. It would have been preferable for him to have noticed the pneumothorax. It would seem reasonable for consultants in similar situations to be sure that evaluations of radiographs or laboratory data be thorough and any noted abnormalities outside of the range of the consultation request be documented and communicated to the primary physician.

In such situations, when a consultant with limited knowledge of the patient's history performs a limited hands-on examination of a patient and even when there is a clear understanding between the physicians that the consultant has not been asked to undertake any other role in continuing care, it is likely that an injured party would allege that the consultant had established a professional relationship. For this reason, it is particularly important for the documentation in the record to state the limits of the request. If a consultant who had not established a physician-patient relationship is sued on a theory that such a relationship existed, some states allow the filing of an affidavit of non-involvement, which provides for prompt and summary dismissal of an uninvolved physician unless the plaintiff specifically opposes the affidavit.

The cases lacking an actual contact with the patient (such as the telephone consult) where there is no "laying on of hands" on the consultant's part more reliably represent the proposition that a professional relationship is not established.[5] Limited contact as noted above requires special attention to limit liability risks. In that availability, for educational reasons, is an important role for consultants, consultants should be sure that appropriate documentation is completed.

If the primary physician requests a formal evaluation of the patient for a specific purpose, then a duty between the consultant and the patient is established if the consultant agrees to see the patient. When a consultant has agreed that she will see a patient, for the first time, whether later in the same day or 2 weeks later, the duty associated with the patient-physician relationship is held not to be established until the patient actually is seen. Exacerbation or deterioration of the patient prior to that personal contact has generally been held not to be the liability of the consultant.[15,16] This is not the case, however, if the consultant has a pre-existing contractual agreement with a hospital, health maintenance organization, or other managed care entity to which the patient is related to come when called. If harm occurs when such a consultant negligently fails to arrive in a timely manner, the court views the relationship as coming into existence when the patient presents and the consultant is called.[17]

> **Commentary by Mr. Goldman:** The theory here is that a relationship exists at the time the patient becomes a subscriber to the managed care entity so that all physicians who agree to participate and provide care have a contractual relationship with the subscriber.

Consultants may accept the request to participate in the care of a patient and then successfully finalize that role and return care to the requesting primary care physician. Delineation of the onset and end of the consultant's legal duty is essential to risk management in such scenarios.

Case 5: A neonatologist attends the Cesarean delivery of a term infant at the request of a pediatrician who is unable to break away from patients in the office. Review of the mother's history indicates a cervical culture positive for group B beta streptococcus (GBS) during pregnancy. The membranes ruptured 10 hours before arriving at the hospital. The baby is found to be in a transverse lie presentation and prompt Cesarean delivery is done with the neonatologist in attendance. The mother is afebrile, and the baby is term and normal appearing at birth. Because of the history of the GBS and in that delivery was effected without maternally administered antibiotics, the neonatologist examines the baby carefully and finds no abnormality. He also contacts the pediatrician and discusses all the above with him. The consultant note is written, ending with "history of GBS in mother discussed and pediatrician will assume care and follow the baby closely." The pediatrician assumes care, and the neonatologist leaves the hospital. Several hours later, the child is noted to be pale, tachypneic, irritable, and intermittently apneic. The pediatrician responds promptly to the nurses' call, but the child rapidly deteriorates and dies. A suit is brought. To what degree is the neonatologist liable?

Consultants may often assume limited care for the patient in lieu of the primary physician because of his/her absence or the patient's need for a specific evaluation or procedure. During that time there is unquestionably a relationship established between the consultant and the patient and a duty to conform to the pertinent standard of care. Certainly the neonatologist above would have the duty to perform competently in the delivery room and provide any needed ongoing care demanded by the baby's condition. He also has the responsibility to communicate the events of the delivery to the pediatrician and to recommend appropriate follow-up to the pediatrician. He also must affirm that the ongoing care will be assumed by the pediatrician and notify the family and nurses of the same. On the other hand, it would not be reasonable to assume that he has responsibility for all future evaluation or care of events occurring subsequent to his transfer of responsibility to the pediatrician.

The courts recognize the right of a physician, once having become involved in the care, to terminate his relationship with the case and with that, his legal duty to the patient. The consultant who renders service and effectively terminates his involvement has no exposure to liability for subsequent developments that are alleged to result from the care of the physician who took over or took back management of the case from the consultant. The physician remains liable for the consequences of his care, even if the consequence occurs or is recognized after the termination of his relationship with the patient.

How does the consultant know when his relationship with the patient and his liability exposure have been effectively terminated? Courts have defined the termination of the relationship in various ways. The physician-patient relationship continues to exist, of course, as long as the physician is taking part in the treatment of the patient.[18] To effectively terminate the legally recognized relationship and duty, more is required than the unilateral decision of the consultant that his assistance is no longer needed. Once the consultant becomes legally involved in the care, the physician-patient relationship is considered to exist until it is explicitly ended by mutual consent of the parties, dismissal of the physician by the patient, or until the physician determines that his services are no longer beneficial to the patient and reasonable arrangements or opportunity has been afforded for other medical care to be procured.[19]

Effective termination of the consultant's involvement is best accomplished by a verbal contact between the consultant, the patient, and the requesting physician, with concurrent or prompt documentation of the contact. The common method of simply "signing off" by mentioning in a progress note that further services do not appear necessary leads to no trouble in the routine case, but certainly such a method may be inadequate protection for the consultant in a case that becomes unexpectedly complicated or has a poor outcome. The consultant remains exposed to liability until the previous or next care giver sees the note and acquiesces in it by resuming the patient's care. Until then, legal review is likely to hold the consultant as responsible for tests that may have been previously ordered and are not reported, for requests from the nursing staff and, of course, for changes in the patient's condition that deserve the prompt attention of a physician.

Even after successful transition of the patient to another physician, liability exists, deriving from the consequences of the consultant's care. In addition to the direct sequelae attributable to the consultant's actions, there is potential liability associated with foreseeable future consequences resulting from events during the consultation period.

Case 6: A neonatologist attends a Cesarean delivery at the request of the obstetrician. The Cesarean is done because of a non-reassuring fetal heart rate pattern. The woman is at term, the pregnancy was uncomplicated. At delivery, the amniotic fluid was clear. The infant was initially depressed, with an Apgar score of 3 at 1 minute. After clearing the airway and assisting breathing using bag/mask for 30-45 seconds, the infant responded with gradually increasing vigor. At 5 minutes, the Apgar score was 6. By 10 minutes, the Apgar score was 8. Cord arterial blood pH was 7.21. Over the next 2 hours, the baby was observed and did well. Capillary blood gases and blood glucose levels were normal. The baby weighed 3.5 kg. She had a normal suck, but she did not take much by nipple. The neonatologist approved the transfer of the child to the regular nursery, and the child's pediatrician was called and assumed the care of the baby. The neonatologist placed a consultation note on the record documenting the above and the acceptance of the patient by the pediatrician. Later that day, the pediatrician examined the baby and recorded a normal examination. The nurses reported that the baby was not taking much at feedings. The pediatrician ordered tube feeding supplements of 40 mL of formula every 3 hours. The following day, the child's weight had increased to 3.6 kg and she was receiving most of her feedings by gastric tube, only nippling 10-15 mL per feeding attempt. Later in the day, a seizure was noted. The pediatrician's work-up revealed no abnormal physical or laboratory findings except for a serum sodium of 119 mEq/L. The neonatologist is contacted again. His recommended fluid restriction resulted in restoration of normal serum electrolytes and diuresis was noted the following day. Blood glucose values were normal throughout this episode. The diagnosis was seizures associated with hyponatremia secondary to the syndrome of inappropriate secretion of antidiuretic hormone (SIADH).

Could the consultant neonatologist be held responsible in any way for the "iatrogenic" hyponatremia associated with the fluid supplemented ordered by the pediatrician? The question here raises the issue of what situations could be reasonably foreseen based on the events in the delivery room. It is the responsibility of the consultant to convey concern regarding reasonably likely future consequences of the events that occurred during the time of the consultation. After a stressful delivery, fluid retention is not uncommon. Since water intoxication could have been anticipated and potentially avoided, one may argue that the neonatologist should have advised that the child's weight, urine output and specific gravity, and intake be closely monitored to assess for SIADH. The consultant must remember that he may be more aware of, or sensitive to, potential problems than the primary physician who does not consider these concerns day in and day out. On the other hand, it is not helpful to include a long list of rare and unlikely concerns simply to cover oneself. In situations like this, the consultant must foresee the reasonably likely risks, identify them to the primary physician, and agree who will follow the patient. This discussion should be documented in the consultant's note, including the willingness of the primary care physician to assume care and follow-up of the case.

Foreseeability has significance that extends beyond the consequences that might befall the patient seen by the consultant. Duty comes into existence when it is foreseeable that harm could come to another, even if the potential harm relates to a child later conceived. This scenario has resulted in liability for failing to give Rh immune globulin resulting in injury from hemolytic disease to a child conceived later.[20] Similar liability has arisen from failing to immunize the rubella antibody negative non-pregnant woman who thereafter develops rubella during pregnancy and delivers an affected infant.[21] The existence of the legal duty to a future individual is determined by balancing three factors: the relationship between the parties (i.e., the existence of a physician-patient relationship); the foreseeability of harm to the person ultimately injured; and, public policy concerns.[22] These cases establish the importance of an understanding of the future predictable consequences of the conditions seen and diagnosed by consultants. Many of the conditions seen in the perinatal period are associated with potential future consequences based on genetic inheritance, empiric data, or other factors. Consultants must document these to the patient and to the record.

Commentary by Mr. Goldman: The physician may need to determine the need for genetic testing and counseling. With the ongoing advances in this field it is important for the primary care physician to keep up and to know when to refer the patient for things like testing for cystic fibrosis.

Case 7: A pediatrician calls a neonatologist to evaluate a 2-day-old baby who appears well except for persistent tachypnea and asks for advice as to what to do next. After reviewing the history (negative) and examining the baby (tachypnea only), the neonatologist suggests that hematocrit and white count be checked, blood sugar measured, and that a chest radiograph be done. The pediatrician says, "Thanks for seeing the baby. I'll watch after him now." The neonatologist completes a written consultation that includes the above recommendation and the desire of the pediatrician to manage the baby. The pediatrician decides to continue observation without the added testing because of the limited symptoms and so notes on the chart. Later, the baby is noted to be cyanotic and a chest radiograph now reveals a huge heart. Severe congenital heart disease is eventually diagnosed and suit alleging failure to make a prompt diagnosis is brought against the pediatrician and the consultant.

This case illustrates three important issues in consultation. The first deals with the place of the consultant's advice to the primary physician. Is it necessary for the primary care physician to follow the advice of the consultant? It is not necessarily so. Certainly, following the consultant's advice is the usual consequence, but, the primary physician has the prerogative to use or not use the recommendations. Referring physicians should be sure to document deviations from the consultant's recommendations, including the rationale for taking a different approach.

The second question deals with the degree to which the consultant is responsible to assure that the patient ultimately gets care that is within the realm of acceptable practice. Again, consultants must be knowledgeable of not only their own approach to a problem, but also of the other ways to look at the situation. In some cases, the consultant may realize that there are several options that fall well within the standard of care. Some consultants are more conservative than others. If there is a range of acceptable responses, consultants should be sure that their written recommendations include the range of possibilities. Or, if in oral conversation with the primary care physician it is agreed that a particular course is acceptable, this should be supported in the note. Consultants who fail to acknowledge and accept approaches that fall within the standard of practice of similar consultants can undermine their referring physicians and may make referring physicians reluctant to call. Often, the primary care physician may have trained in an area where the approach used was an acceptable one but different than that of the local consultant. If the choice of the primary physician is consistent with such a standard, the consultant should be reluctant to intervene. On the other hand, should the referring physician fail to respond to significant or urgent needs identified by the consultant, it may be necessary to press the issue. Should contacting the primary physician not result in appropriate measures for the patient, the consultant may need to involve the unit director, chief of service, or whomever is identified in the hospital's medical staff bylaws to address standard of care issues.

> **Commentary by Mr. Goldman:** Always remember that the duty is to the patient and the analysis should always be what it is necessary to do to provide appropriate care for the patient.

A third related question deals with the degree to which the consultant should proceed with testing or procedures. Prospective planning and documentation regarding the relative roles of the referring and consulting physicians should be an integral part of the request for consultation. If the consultation is for evaluation and advice regarding further management, the consultant should not proceed unless the patient's condition demands an urgent intervention. Although many institutions' consultant request forms have places to indicate whether the consultant is called for "advice" or "management," nothing is as effective for both patient care and risk management as a verbal discussion between physicians that is confirmed in the medical record.

Sometimes the consultant is called because the primary physician feels that a certain procedure is needed and he/she is not qualified to do it. This issue illustrates the need for consultants and referring physicians to come to an understanding at the start of the consultation process. Consultants are placed in an unenviable position if the patient or family is expecting some specific procedure or test and the consultant does not feel it is indicated. In fact, some consultants may feel pressured to conform to such expectations for social or legal reasons. Consultants should be called to analyze problems rather than to do a particular test or procedure. Often the consultant's experience may resolve the issue without the expected testing.

Case 8: After transport of an infant to the neonatal intensive care unit (NICU), review of the referring hospital record reveals numerous reports by the nursing staff to the physician regarding duskiness and lethargy, to which the physician did not respond until the child experienced a respiratory arrest. Resuscitation was performed by the nurses with assistance of the anesthesiology staff. The pediatrician came in and referred the baby to the NICU. Sepsis was confirmed at the NICU. The consultant neonatologist wrote a letter to the referring physician expressing his concern that the child's presenting symptoms should have led to the child being seen, worked up, and transferred earlier.

In this case, there is concern that the primary physician failed to appropriately respond to the nurses' calls and to recognize a significant problem in a timely fashion. It could be tempting to consider these failures as causal should future problems be noted. The consultant has an obligation to discuss the case with the referring physician in an educational manner as part of quality assurance. For this reason, personal or phone discussion is preferable to letter writing when these cases present, in that such a letter could later be incriminating in cases where the perceived neglect was not found to be present when all facts are known. Perinatal centers should participate as invited consultants in the quality assurance activities at referring hospitals. These meetings are generally protected from discovery and in this setting, peer review can be done in an educational manner without producing potentially incriminating documents that are discoverable. Rarely do physicians purposely ignore significant observations. But, if significant findings were not appreciated, "honesty, as usual, appears to be the best policy, but the consultant first should discuss the situation with the referring physician before sitting down with the patient and the family and explaining the problem."[23] The degree to which the patient and/or family are contacted by the primary physician and concern and caring are demonstrated, the less likely that the patient/family will blame the physician.

Case 9: An NICU is contacted to transport an infant in respiratory failure. The primary physician is in attendance when the transport team arrives. The nurse on the transport team intubates the baby and asks the primary physician to order a radiograph. A pneumothorax is noted, and the transport nurse proceeds with the placement of a chest tube (consistent with protocols established at the NICU), which is then complicated by hemothorax. During transport, the child needs volume replacement, and a subsequent thoracotomy is needed following admission to the NICU. The child has a rocky course leading to death.

This case illustrates the difficulty in establishing responsibility when individuals from the NICU are working in an institution where they do not have privileges, but at the same time are proceeding per protocols of the NICU or in accordance with recommendations made by the neonatologist by telephone. In general, once the infant's care is assumed by personnel acting under the direction of the consultant physician there will be a duty established between the consultant and the patient. For this reason, it is key that such personnel are highly trained and that communication lines are open throughout the transport process. The protocols for procedures and the manner of certification of personnel should be carefully documented and reviewed by counsel familiar with the laws of the involved state.

Case 10: The neonatologist serves as medical director of the NICU. While on duty, she is made aware of the delivery of an infant who presents with significant symptoms, such as persistent cyanosis and tachypnea. The primary physician is notified and says, "I'll see the baby tomorrow. No, I don't want any tests or x-rays or consultations at this time." What are the responsibilities of the neonatologist?

Although being a medical director does not automatically make the physician directly responsible to monitor all care within the unit on a minute basis, each unit must have established means for questions of quality of care to be addressed in a timely manner, immediately if necessary. Since the director in the case above has been made aware of a significant concern, she has responsibility to act on behalf of the patient. If prompt contact with the primary physician does not result in his taking the appropriate action or if he cannot be reached, unit directors may assume care for the immediate problem while activating the appropriate measures within the medical staff.

> **Commentary by Mr. Goldman:** Here the duty is established by the role of the director to be responsible for patient care within the NICU.

Summary

The hypothetical case situations cited above are meant to emphasize the importance of planning and documentation in the consultation process as the foundations of risk management. It was suggested that this chapter could have been written in two words, "talk, write."

> **Commentary by Mr. Goldman:** Perhaps it could be four words, "clarify relationship, talk, write."

True, but expanded discussion of the relationship of the consultation process to the concept of duty owed the individual patient is needed for the primary physician and consultant to avoid pitfalls when more than one physician is involved in patient care.

Duty is established when the patient contacts (or is directly referred to) a physician and the consultant physician accepts and sees the patients. In addition to the issues relating to the standard of care, which of course must be met in order to avoid liability, the consultation process adds questions as to who has the responsibility, for what, and for how long.

Although it is common practice for physicians to indicate telephone or educational contacts with consultants in the record, in these cases, the responsibility (duty) rests with the primary physician. Such documentation may be done to reflect thoroughness on the primary physician's part, and to that end it is good. On the other hand, some may feel that these notes indicate involvement of the consultant and reduce the risk of the primary physician. Remember, duty is not established by educational conversations, but by mutual consent with actual undertaking of care by the consultant.

Commentary by Mr. Goldman: In general, "laying on of hands" with intent by the consultant to be involved in and responsible for a portion of the care is required to establish a relationship. "Laying on of hands" can also mean reading and interpreting a radiograph or a pathology slide.

Although a case may be real to the primary physician, the situation is hypothetical to the consultant unless he/she is actually involved with the patient. The degree to which hypothetical recommendations apply to the patient at hand is in the judgment of the primary physician unless formal consultation is requested and the consultant accepts and sees the patient.

When a consultant is contacted for a specific patient with a formal request for evaluation and/or management, both the primary physician and consultant should interact in such a way so as to limit unnecessary risks for both. The mechanics of involvement should include the following:

1. The reasons for the consultation should be communicated to the patient, the consultant, and the chart.
2. The primary physician should indicate whether the consultation is urgent, and if so, verbal contact is mandatory.
3. The initial contact with the consultant should address the scope of the request: evaluation and recommendation; consideration for specific testing or procedure; joint management; or transfer of care.
4. The primary physician should provide the consultant with up to date clinical information relating to the request.
5. The consultant should also document what information was made available to her at the time of the consultation.

    Commentary by Mr. Goldman: The consultant also needs to decide if added tests are required or if tests need to be repeated or specific procedures need to occur.

6. The primary physician should inform the patient and the nursing staff of the consultation (the former is part of the informed consent process, the latter is necessary to assure that clinical questions are addressed to the appropriate physician depending on the agreement between consultant and primary physician).

    Commentary by Mr. Goldman: Of course the patient should understand the reason for the consult and agree to it or request alternative approaches satisfactory to the primary physician.

7. The physicians should document their communications in the patient's medical record.

If action (order writing) is left with the primary physician, he should be sure that the consultant's recommendations are addressed either by the appropriate orders or by a note with rationale as to why specific recommendations were not followed. If the consultant dictates her report and that report will be associated with any delay in getting to the medical record, she should put a timed and dated succinct note in the chart as to the major findings and recommendations. Once the consultation process is completed, the consultant should sign off verbally with the primary physician and in the record and a finalization communication should be held with the patient and/or family. This conversation should include that the consultant will be available should concerns recur regarding the problem(s) addressed in the consultation.

> **Commentary by Mr. Goldman:** Care has to be taken to be sure that the consultant-patient relationship is not open-ended, and that it is defined for a certain purpose over a specified time span.

For consultants, potential liability is associated with timeliness of the response to the consultation, actions taken or not taken while performing the consultation, and reasonably foreseeable consequences related to the question addressed in the consultation. The last of these may be of most concern to the consultant. Documentation of recommendations in the consultation report and explicit indication of responsibility for follow-up can go a long way to define the duty (or lack thereof) of the consultant. "It is difficult, if not impossible, to convince a judge or jury that the care provided was any better than the record."[2]

Finally, diplomacy and tact in verbal and written communication are essential, and lack thereof is frequently associated with medical malpractice actions.[23] Differences of opinion should be resolved professionally and in private, not via shouting matches in the nursing station or hallways. Not only does a friendly approach and manner at all times foster business for the consultant, it establishes a relationship conducive to cooperation in patient care, education, and problem solving. All patient care is largely an art, and individual patient response to treatment is never assured. Remember, when in doubt, do the friendliest thing. It may also limit risk for all parties in the consultation process.

References

1. Hartline JV. Consultation: The art of conveying science and opinion. In: Pomerance J, Richardson CJ (eds). *Neonatology for the Clinician*. Norwalk, CT, Appleton and Lange, 1993, p. 37.
2. Cetrulo CL, Cetrulo LG. The legal liability of the medical consultant in pregnancy. Med Clin North Am 1989;73:557.
3. *Hill v. Kokosky*, 186 Mich App 300, 463 NW2d 265 (1990).

4. *Ingber v. Kandler*, 513 NYS2d 11, 128 AD2d 591 (1987).
5. *Cintron v. New York Medical College Flower and Fifth Ave.* Hospitals, 597 NYS2d 705 (NY A.D., 1993).
6. *Green v. Walker*, 910 F.2d 291 (CA 5, 1990).
7. *Flynn v. Bausch*, 238 Neb 61, 469, NW2d 125 (1991).
8. *Roth v. Tuckman*, 558NYS2d 264, 162 AD2d 941 (1990).
9. *Peterson v. Phelps*, 123 Minn 319, 143 NW 793 (1913).
10. *Young v. Crescente*, 132 NJL 223, 39 A2d 449 (1944).
11. *Nardone v. Reynolds*, 538 F2d 1131 (C.A. Fla, 1976).
12. *Stafford v. Shultz*, 42 Cal2d 767, 270 P2d 1 (1954).
13. *Sullanger v. Setco Northwest, Inc.*, 702 P2d 1139 (Or App, 1985).
14. *Minister v. Pohl*, 206 Ga App 617, 426 SE2d 204 (1992).
15. *Roberts v. Hunter*, 426 SE2d 797 (S.C., 1993).
16. *Weaver v. University of Michigan Regents*, 201 Mich App 239, 506 NW2d 264 (1993).
17. *Hand v. Tavera*, 864 SW 2d 678 (Tex App, 1993).
18. *Rule v. Chesseman*, 181 Kan 957, 317 P2d 472 (1957).
19. *Fortner v. Koch*, 272 Mich 273, 261 NW 762 (1935).
20. *Yeager v. Bloomington OB/GYN*, 585 NE 2d 696 (Ind App, 1992).
21. *Monusko v. Postle*, 175 Mich App 269, 437, NW 2d 367 (1989).
22. *Walker v. Rinck*, 604 NE 2d 591 (Ind 1992).
23. Tanner JR. Physicians' office liability exposure. In: Troyer GT, Salman SL (eds). *Handbook of Health Care Risk Management*. Rockville, MD, Aspen Publishers, Inc., 1989, p. 381.

Delivering Bad News

◆◆◆

Virginia Delaney-Black, M.D.

Introduction

Caring for intensively ill newborns and speaking with parents has been part of my responsibility for close to 20 years. I have had some excellent teachers along the way including George Little and Judy Frank who coached me through my first and very memorable parent meetings, Lu Lubchenco who taught me what long-term follow-up really meant, and Ron Poland who listened to the frustrations of learning to be an effective attending physician. In writing this chapter, I have relied heavily on all these mentors. Life as a neonatologist has always been predictably unpredictable, and we face many technological as well as societal changes. As Jerold Lucey, Editor of Pediatrics, has written, "In the brave new world we are facing, patients are often referred to as 'customers'. We are 'care providers'. It is obviously wise to listen to 'customer viewpoints'."[1] In keeping with Dr. Lucey's advice, I have also relied upon my conversations with parents as well as publications soliciting and reporting their opinions. In helping infants and families, we must also reflect on what we would expect for our own children or grandchildren.

Introduction

Delivering bad news to new parents is reminiscent of the not-so-humorous story that circulated several years ago. A woman, answering her door, is met by a telegraph company agent. Expecting a happy, singing telegram, she cajoles the very reluctant gentleman into singing it to her. "Your son is dead," he croaks miserably. While an example of poor humor, it is a good description of what often happens after unanticipated complications. The

From: Donn SM, Fisher CW (eds.): *Risk Management Techniques in Perinatal and Neonatal Practice.* © Futura Publishing Co., Inc., Armonk, NY, 1996.

parents, anticipating the joyous occasion of the birth of a healthy child receive instead the news of serious illness or imminent death from a stranger who is often as reluctant as the telegraph agent to be placed in the uncomfortable position of delivering the bad news.

Most of us who choose to be pediatricians have done so because we are gratified by working with children and their parents. My own career choice was made after the first several months of a university hospital internal medicine residency. The majority of my patients had had serious chronic diseases with poor prognoses. In just a few months, many had been readmitted to the hospital. To make matters worse, many of these conditions were induced at least, in part, by poor health choices including smoking, alcoholism, and obesity. In contrast, the postpartum floor and the newborn nursery where I spent an elective rotation were filled with families who were delighted to be in the hospital! It was not hard to convince me that I would much rather spend the next 35 years working with babies and parents. Even in those days, neonatal intensive care units (NICUs) had many more discharges than deaths. Today, with improvements in mortality rates, most of our conversations with parents can be happy occasions. When the news is not good, we, like the unhappy telegraph agent, must first deal with our own reluctance to be the messenger.

Loud Silences

Robert and Peggy Stinson in their book *The Long Dying of Baby Andrew* confront one of the most difficult communication problems: the conversation that does not occur.[2] It is not surprising that in the hectic and sometimes frantic pace of the NICU, communication is sometimes relegated to a later time or delegated to the intern, resident, or bedside nurse. Acute, life-threatening events require the team's intensive care and may not *immediately* provide a means of freeing one member of the team to contact the parents. Less obvious, but equally significant medical problems may await the results of an ultrasound study, the interpretation of an EEG, or the availability of a laboratory test from a clinical laboratory hundreds of miles away. Patience is easier to preach than to accept, and the ICU is not a place for patience. Stat blood work and radiographs, computerized reporting, and even crash carts all gear us to expect that diagnostic tests and drugs are immediately available. From the parent's perspective, communications should also be provided "stat." While acute life-threatening changes in the infant's clinical course require prompt telephone communication, other changes in the clinical course may be better communicated by timely scheduling of a family meeting.

To be an effective participant in their infant's care, the family must be informed of up-to-date data as well as their infant's clinical condition.

Commentary by Mr. Goldman: Providing information is an important way to establish rapport and avoid bad feelings that could lead to litigation. Remember that perceived rudeness and lack of communication by staff is the most frequent reason mentioned in predisposing patients to consult a lawyer.

If neonatal intensive care is to be a partnership between parent and professionals, then each partner must be able to determine when communication is needed. Letting the parents know how and when the attending is most easily reached returns at least an element of control back to the parents.

Seventy-Six Trombones or Too Many Horns?

Information provided to the NICU family comes from a variety of medical personnel including the anticipated sources: nursing; resident; and attending physicians. Other sources less obvious, but equally likely, include subspecialty consultants, technicians, the ward clerks, family members, other parents, and even family acquaintances.

Commentary by Mr. Goldman: Information also comes from television—"20/20" and "Dateline" type programs—and the rest of the news media. Miracle cures are reported in grocery store checkout counter newspapers daily, so patients may come in with unreasonable expectations.

With so many sources, the information may become distorted. Even when the same factual information is provided, the word choice and nonverbal communication may make communication ambiguous. According to Roderic Phibbs, "Despite the machines and technology . . . infant intensive care is essentially provided by people, a lot of people, who all care intensively. There is no more personal form of medicine than that which is practiced in the newborn ICU."[3]

With so many people communicating with the family, it is not surprising that confusion may occur. According to Harrison,[3] one infant in a newborn ICU had 483 different care givers during a 3-month hospital stay. It would be miraculous if all 483 care takers had the same opinion and communication style. They cannot and do not. Each professional, depending upon his/her area of expertise and personal characteristics, may focus on one aspect of care. An example of the mixed messages parents receive is reported by Nance.[4] A couple, separated by the glass partitions of the nursery, each spoke to a physician about their preterm infant. One care taker providing information about general clinical care stopped to speak optimistically to the father who nodded and smiled at his wife. Outside the window, the neurology subspecialist . . . "stopped to tell me that he feared Zachary was developing hydrocephalus and (he) described the shunt they would have to put in his head . . . The (nursery) glass between us prevented us from hearing what the other heard." Clearly, each physician was correctly describing a single aspect of care but neither, because of the brief communication, provided an appropriate encompassing view of the child's condition. It would have been far better if these two specialists had each provided his assessment in a planned group meeting that described both the daily care issues (feeding, growing) and the subspecialty concerns (hydrocephalus). Off-hand and incomplete statements do not give adequate attention to the child's full needs and give less credibility to the staff.

Variety May be the Spice of Life, But . . .

Medical treatment, particularly in the NICU, may also be a source of variability. The subspecialty consultants and the neonatologists when faced with a child requiring interventions need to provide information on alternative treatments. A unique article authored by parents, provides ten principles for family-centered neonatal care.[5] Among them is the availability to parents of information about the uncertainty of medical treatments including whether or not the therapy has undergone controlled clinical trials. A second principle states that when life-threatening decisions or those that entail "great suffering" or "significant ethical controversy" are discussed, the parents have the right to refuse aggressive treatment.

> **Commentary by Mr. Goldman:** These are difficult issues to discuss, including issues such as the futility of treatment. In some cases it may be useful to seek advice from an ethics committee.

While I am unaware of any physician choosing to overtly omit the discussion of important alternative treatments, we do make countless decisions based upon our experience and professional judgment that change from time to time as new treatments and research become available.

Families with a first premature child born in 1980 and a second in 1990 would be surprised at the difference in care choices in the 1990s. Even more rapid changes exist in the treatment of some problems such as pulmonary hypertension, where much controversy currently exists between centers and sometimes even within centers. Among the choices of the attending physicians are conservative ventilation versus hyperventilation, early extracorporeal membrane oxygenation (ECMO) versus no ECMO, nitric oxide, and analgesia or paralytics. The choices are staggering particularly for many parents who are already dealing with significant stresses including alteration of the parental role, and the sights and sounds of the NICU environment.[6,7]

To not provide some discussion of the viable alternative treatments leaves the physician open to criticism and later parental distress. "What are they not telling me?"

> **Commentary by Mr. Goldman:** The rules of informed choice require an open non-judgmental discussion of the procedure, its risks, benefits, and alternatives so that parents can choose with the physician an appropriate course of care. An appropriate course of care may be what the physician thinks is medically appropriate or may, in some cases, be what the parent feels is in the child's best interest for medical, moral, or religious grounds. In extreme cases a physician may be forced to disagree with a parent's assessment such as, for example, cases of abuse or neglect. However, typically, parents will be provided with the information and then make an informed choice. It is a physician's job to provide sufficient information so that the parents can understand the options. Physicians are not required to make parents into experts but are required to provide the level of information that a knowledgeable person would want to know in order to be able to make an informed choice.

How much information the physician provides is an unanswerable question. Does it include a discussion of fluid management, such as risks and benefits of low versus high infusion volumes for prematures? How about indomethacin versus surgical ligation of the patent ductus arteriosus (PDA), or early versus late PDA ligation? The list could be endless. Not all parents want, need, or are able to interpret the same amount of medical information. Balancing the child's urgent care needs, the physician's available time, and the parents' need to know is an acquired skill. Harrison's[5] point is still well taken. We can not afford to assume a paternalistic position of suggesting that only we can understand and manage the current problem. Taking on an excess of responsibility for the child's care may also suggest that we have magical powers and can assist every 23 week gestation infant to grow up to be a healthy, happy young man or woman. Conversely, when our lack of magical powers are altogether too obvious, we cannot expect the family who has had little participation in the care of their infant to suddenly feel comfortable making the ultimate decision about life support just because we have given them bad news.

> **Commentary by Mr. Goldman:** The goal is joint involvement in decision-making. Parents need to understand that there are medical choices that involved medical chances and need to feel that they are a part of the decision-making process.

Commentary by Dr. Donn: Neonatologists have always taken pride in the anticipatory way that problems are managed. There is no reason why this type of care should not be extended to the prenatal period. The anticipated birth of an infant who will be on the fringe of viability should engender a frank discusion with the parents regarding the prognosis for their child and what treatments might be necessary to achieve the best outcome. This requires a thorough knowledge of outcome statistics (which may differ from one institution to the next). It is not unreasonable—and is, in fact, preferable—to make a medical recommendation as to whether or not resuscitation should be offered in this situation. I concur with Gordon Avery's approach that "It is necessary . . . to take some stance and allow them (parents) to give agreement or disagreement rather than throwing the entire weight of decision in their laps . . . The moment of delivery is the *worst* time to attempt such a discussion (Avery GB. Ethical dilemmas in the treatment of the extremely low birth weight infant. Clin Perinatol 1987;14:361).

While the issue of medical versus parental rights remains controversial, involvement of parents in critical decision-making seems prudent. Using the process of informed consent as a paradigm, parents should be informed about each available option *and* its potential risks and benefits, a medical recommendation should be offered, and parents should be given the opportunity to accept or reject that recommendation. When an impasse arises, every effort should be made to resolve differences without having to seek legal intervention, which should only be utilized as a last resort.

Wishful Thinking

There is nothing more frustrating to any of us from child to adult than a broken promise. Even if inadvertent, the published reports of remarkable outcomes for critically ill or tiny prematures is a tacit promise of the magical powers of modern medicine. Gutheil, Bursztajn, and Brodsky[8] point out that in times of uncertain outcome, patients seek reassurance that all will go well. During this period of uncertainty, it is not surprising that the family wishing for omnipotence and yet facing their own powerlessness would want to transfer magically curative skills to the physician. "Even if I can't make my baby well, he/she will." The authors suggest that confronting the unrealistic expectations of the family directly is seldom effective. Telling them "I've done everything I can do" is, in a sense, abandoning them at a critical time. The confrontation also fails to eliminate their wishful thinking and provides no comfort.

Commentary by Mr. Goldman: Empathy followed by discussion is an important risk management tool, a good way to establish rapport, and a good way for us to behave as human beings.

They suggest that acknowledging the family's fantasies, "I wish I could . . ." and then providing a "rational" alliance of fallible individuals— the family and the physician—one can then, as mature adults, collaborate to provide the best realistic outcome. This collaboration can also provide the basis for the physician to further separate reality from fantasy. Simply stating common expectations may help the family recognize them as unrealistic. Many families would like us to anticipate all of the potential complications. When placed in this light, the family can agree with the physician that, while they too would like to anticipate the exact course of their child's illness, it is not a realistic expectation.

It is also important, at this juncture, to be sure that the family feels supported. If the attending responsibility is to be shared, the physician can indicate that "Dr. Jones or I will be available to care for Johnny throughout this critical time." This approach avoids promising either directly or by implication what cannot be promised: a happy outcome. It does not confront the family's wishes but rather acknowledges them, while at the same time it provides a therapeutic alliance and offers both empathy and an ongoing relationship.

As professionals, we anticipate that families will use denial in dealing with uncertain outcomes. We may be less aware of our own use of denial in caring for critically ill children. Siegler[9] and Waller et al.[10] suggest that the physician denies his/her feelings about death by "hanging crepe" or offering the bleakest of outcomes. If death is inevitable, the staff are freed from responsibility for the poor outcome. Validity of this hypothesis is provided by comparison of morbidity and mortality predictions by physicians and nurses in an NICU setting. In a study of professional attitudes toward very low birth weight infants, Lee et al.[11] confirmed that close to 50% of both nurses and physicians overestimated mortality and morbidity, while just 15% underestimated the risks. Comparison of physician, nursing, and family beliefs indicated that families of very low birthweight infants were less likely to believe that nursing staff or hospital ethics teams should be involved in treatment decisions to save an infant. Delegating decision making to courts of law and governmental health policies were rated lowest by all three groups.

Professional attitudes toward aggressive care of high-risk infants are not static. Todres et al.[12,13] compared physician attitudes between decades. While the majority of physicians (86%) identified Baby Doe regulations as being too intrusive, the physicians reported that patient care experiences (70%), legal pressure (24%), uncertain legislation (18%), and journal articles (13%)

had contributed to their changing opinions regarding life-saving therapies. Religious affiliation and younger physicians were more likely to choose aggressive intervention.

Having at hand recent mortality and morbidity statistics provides the physician with objective data that may serve as a background for making his/her clinical judgments. Clearly, mortality data have changed significantly in the last decade. Families need the most updated information to make viable choices.

> **Commentary by Mr. Goldman:** Mortality data are simply statistical data for a group and do not predict individual outcomes, so parents must understand uncertainty. Also, when "viable choices" are discussed you must look at the individual's point of view. If parents believe in faith healing, then that would be a "viable choice" for them. If parents are Jehovah's Witnesses, then avoidance of blood would be a "viable choice" for them. Parents' wishes should be respected whenever possible, but in difficult cases state law would require reporting to juvenile court so that the court can assess whether a guardian needs to be appointed for the child.

Can We Talk?

Unfortunately, in the first critical hours of a child's life, both parents may not even be physically available, particularly after general anesthesia or in the case of neonatal transport. During those difficult times, even when we do try our best to provide accurate and timely information, through no fault of our own we may not adequately communicate with the parents. On one such occasion, I had attended an emergency delivery of a small premature infant. After his stabilization and nursery admission, I spoke with his mother in the recovery area. She was alert and oriented and asked appropriate questions. Early the following morning, I received a telephone call from the irate covering obstetrician who indicated that no physician had spoken to his client. When I returned to the recovery area, now dressed in street clothes and a white coat, his client did recognize me. In her memory, I had been just one more set of green scrub clothes indistinguishable from the obstetrical nurses and residents, the fourth-year medical student, or even the cleaning staff. Now, although I do not necessarily expect her to remember me, I do leave a business card with the mother as one tangible connection to her child's doctor.

While fathers are not medicated, their concerns for both their partner and their child, the assumption of added responsibilities for the home, and the need to be in both the NICU and the postpartum unit may make them less than ideally available to carefully comprehend unfamiliar words.

Commentary by Mr. Goldman: Words must be carefully chosen and defined. For example, "cannula" for parents with a child on oxygen is not the same as "cannula" for a baby about to be placed on ECMO. Medical jargon should be avoided, and even if parents are using medical terms the physician must be careful to check and see if the parents really understand the meaning of the terms.

In the first hours after admission, there may also be inadequate time to provide as much background education as both parents and professionals would like. Despite these limitations, inclusion of family in more than a one-way discussion of the infant's care plan is essential.

In her excellent article, Nancy King[14] describes an observational study of NICU decision-making. Parent-physician contact peaked on days 1-2 with additional peaks prior to surgery, at times of crisis, and prior to discharge. While appropriate parental permission was obtained for all procedures, according to King, families were "informed but neither equipped for decision, nor viewed as having a significant role in most decisions, they were not told, or did not know how to ask what their child's condition meant." When consideration for withdrawal of support was later made, parents were unprepared.

To better prepare families for receiving later bad news and participating in the decision-making process, more information at the first parent-physician meeting is necessary. Perlman et al.[15] suggest that parents and physicians focus on different areas in this meeting. Audiotaped conferences and questions from 43 first meetings were reviewed. Physicians indicated that they had provided the parents with information on diagnosis (100%) and prognosis (100%) but little information regarding causes of illness(4%) or current management (6%). According to the physicians, the single most important information to provide to the parents was prognosis. Conversely, parents remembered current management more frequently than any other area (67%) and rated management as the single most important area to them. When information about the cause of illness was not recalled by the parents, they more frequently rated the meeting as not helpful. Interestingly, while the physician questionnaire indicated that only in 6% of conferences was management discussed, the audiotape revealed that some management information was actually provided by the physician in 94% of the meetings. Eighty-three percent of parents listed a detailed explanation of their child's condition as one of the primary factors that they considered as constituting a successful meeting. Clearly, families need information about the treatment plan. When provided in adequate breadth, it will permit them to become involved in treatment choices at a later time should the infant's condition not improve or complications of treatment occur.

Commentary by Mr. Goldman: All of us hear what we want to hear. Failure to communicate is a critical element in the underlying causes of malpractice cases. It may be helpful to ask targeted questions to parents (i.e., instead of asking whether parents have questions, ask whether they understand the proposed management or if they have questions about the cause of the child's illness).

When an infant's care in the NICU is expected to be prolonged, regular meetings with the multidisciplinary team may keep both the family and staff apprised of what each is feeling in regard to the care of the infant. This can be a useful time to review the family's needs (transportation, community referrals, breast feeding issues, insurance concerns, etc.) as well as the infant's ongoing and anticipated medical needs. Periodic group meetings can supplement the family's need for ongoing routine information, which may be provided at the bedside.

Pinch and Spielman[16] followed 28 families longitudinally after hospitalization of their infants in a tertiary unit. Four children died and the remaining children were approximately equally divided into three groups: no residual abnormalities; questionable outcomes; and serious medical problems. Most parents had at least a high school diploma and more than half were white collar. Twenty-three were married, 22 had hospital insurance, but only seven felt they were financially secure. While most felt that health professionals had made the best choices for their infants under the circumstances, most felt that they were excluded from the decision-making process because of the intricacies of the child's health status. Several months after the decision, they questioned what was the correct choice. Decision making by all the health care workers was now more likely to be viewed negatively. One of the families interviewed reported that "we were treated slightly dishonestly. They weren't really being dishonest—they just weren't telling us the whole story." Well-documented is the recurring parent need for the "whole truth."[15]

Commentary by Mr. Goldman: Patients and parents are stronger and more willing to hear and understand bad news than health care professionals tend to believe. It is generally more appropriate to provide information in an empathetic and factually accurate manner than it is to withhold information.

Several authors acknowledge that professionals may have inadequate opportunity to address all of the care choices available and suggest supplementary materials including videotapes and parent support groups as important aids in parental education.[3,5,16] Unfortunately, appropriate videotapes are not widely available and parent groups may not consistently meet the family's needs.

Commentary by Mr. Goldman: However, well-structured parent groups with social work involvement can be useful in getting parents to understand the course of treatment for their baby. It also allows them an opportunity to have support for grieving if they are away from family support.

D-Day: Approaching the Parents with Bad News

To the well-informed parent, the need for a family conference is often much anticipated. It may follow a period of fact-finding such as sonography, brain imaging interpretation, EEG report, and the awaited evaluation by the neonatal neurologist. It is extremely important to have up-to-date reports and, when possible, the final (not preliminary) report available and on the chart. Conferences are typically scheduled in advance at a time that takes into account the needs of both the parents and the staff. It is no favor to schedule a late evening conference working around parent's schedule if critical members of the team (primary nurse, social worker) are not available. The time choice should, when possible, give the family adequate time to make appropriate arrangements so that siblings may be left at home. While less than ideal, just about every member of our staff has at one time or another provided sibling care so that parents might be available to meet together. However, after a meeting, parents may often need to be alone and may not immediately feel up to parenting an older sibling. Children are well aware of their parents' distress and, when possible, should be spared the ordeal of coming to the NICU at meeting times.

Waiting patiently for a family conference to discuss a poor prognosis is more than one can humanly expect. Even without the anxiety provoked by the NICU setting, waiting for the physician is a common source of irritation. Foster and Lousia[17] in a letter to the New England Journal of Medicine report several small studies that relate patient waiting time as the major complaint "dwarfing all other (physician) criticisms combined." At this particular time, more than ever, as the physician seeks the parents' understanding and acceptance of a poor outcome, he/she needs for the parents to be receptive to a dialogue and not more anxious and angry at the disrespect implied by the physician's tardiness. When truly unpreventable circumstances delay a scheduled meeting, the parents are usually more comfortable visiting their infant than waiting in an office.

Who should be present at this meeting will vary depending upon the families' needs and wishes. Among the professionals, the primary nurse, a specific house officer, the chaplain, unit social worker, subspecialists, and the attending physician may each have a role to play. For example, some parents reported the importance of having the support of the unit social worker,[4] while others found her inclusion intrusive.[2] Even at a "teaching hospital," the parents' needs must be strongly considered in choosing how many house officers and students should be included in this very personal meeting. It is my belief that the house officer caring for the infant should, under most circumstances, be involved in the decision-making process even if only as a reporter and observer. Parents, however, should not feel that their child and they are minor constituents in this process. The urge to bring the "whole" medical team should be successfully fought. Hospitals and professionals are intimidating enough even in small numbers. The family need not be made aware of the number of team members for added intimidation.

While critically ill children may be cared for by multiple subspecialty teams, often the attending physician can act as the spokesperson for the other subspecialists. In particularly complicated cases, or when a long-term relationship with one subspecialty group is anticipated, as in the case of a child with complex heart disease, the presence of one of the subspecialists may be helpful to discuss specifics regarding his/her area of specialty. I have witnessed an entire subspecialty service (attending, two fellows, four residents, and a bevy of medical students) attempt to squeeze into a tiny family conference area to discuss with a bewildered set of parents their child's incurable inherited disease. The family conference is not a side show and such behavior is inexcusable. Families deserve privacy.

> **Commentary by Mr. Goldman:** It is important to be aware of items such as the size of the room, whether there is sufficient time for a full conference, whether there are intimidation factors (such as 12 doctors and one parent or such as health care professionals standing over parents or impatiently looking at their watches). Remember that body language can speak more than words.

Parents should also be encouraged to invite to the family conference other family members, friends, and community supporters who will enhance their experience. It is not always clear whom the parents will view as supports during this session. Some have chosen to include their own parents, aunts, uncles, siblings, in-laws, family friends, ministers, and even their older children. A family member who seem supportive to the care providers may be viewed by the parents as demeaning or controlling. On the other hand, a friend or more distant relative, particularly if he/she has some medical expertise, may be particularly helpful to the family. When the medical expertise of the relative or friend may be limited, this should be acknowledged. It is easy to indicate that our own medical expertise is broadest in our area of subspecialty and that should the family or the family's medical expert have questions particularly outside their area of expertise, we would be happy to answer any clarifying questions.

When the group is large, I usually start with family introductions identifying each family member and confirming their importance to the infant and this meeting. Misunderstandings and limited information hamper any family's ability to make decisions, so I usually ask one of the parents to summarize what they understand about their infant's condition. "When you have a baby in the NICU, a lot of people tell you things about what's going on. It would be really helpful to me if one of you can tell me what you understand about Sara's condition." Then I listen. Often the parents will provide me with an excellent chronological discussion of what has happened to their child. Sometimes I learn things I did not know about the medical history, the family, or their understanding. When the designated spokesperson has completed his/her story, I thank the spokesperson acknowledging what difficulty they have had. I then ask the other parent if this is what he/she understands. Jellinek and colleagues[18] suggest that the family be asked if anything similar has happened to them before and if so, what helped them to cope.

I use what information the parents have provided me as the starting point for my discussion of what I see as the current problems. "That's how I see Sara's current condition, too. There are a few tests that have come back since we last talked and . . . ." If the staff (including me) has done its work well, there may be little additional information that I need to provide. In that case, I can openly agree with the family's assessment confirming their understanding.

Once the factual information has been discussed, I usually ask an openended question about what the parents have been thinking. "I know this has been a difficult time for you. Have you been talking with each other about Sara's condition?" Recently in the process of discussing her concerns, one mother admitted she had been wondering how much longer her son could tolerate his present condition. This gave me the opportunity to agree with her concerns and initiate a discussion of resuscitation status.

It is important also, to provide the family an opportunity to verbalize their concerns about what may have contributed to their infant's condition. Legitimizing these concerns may be possible by indicating, "Some families are concerned that something they did during pregnancy may have contributed to their infant's condition." Usually these concerns are unrealistic, and one can be supportive in reassuring the family that this did not contribute.

Parents may feel more involved in their child's care if they can participate in day-to-day decision and care taking roles. At the family conference, one can confirm the importance of their participation by asking if they have specific questions, concerns, or changes in the day-to-day management that they would find helpful. This may include having the family bring in clothing, toys, or helping with the design of their child's name card.

> **Commentary by Mr. Goldman:** Assignments for parents are important but they must not be done to create make-work. If the parents perceive them as make-work they will not feel included as part of the team.

Grandparents have a unique position in family conferences. In addition to sharing the parents' concern about their grandchild, they also are distraught at the pain of their own "child." Acknowledging each participant's anxiety helps to legitimize their obvious suffering. I also remind parents that not everyone mourns in the same way. Fathers often need to not talk about how they are feeling as much as mothers usually need to talk. Discussing how each of the family members is handling his/her pain and common wish for the child's health may help them to cope with their partner's grieving style. No matter what the outcome of their child, the parents also need to know that the staff and attending physician are available to them for further questions or just a time to talk. This invitation should be open-ended. Often a family who has chosen not to return for a follow-up discussion after a death of a child will call me months or even years later. An anniversary of the child's death, the loss of another family member, or the beginning of a new pregnancy may be the impetus for asking more questions. The hospital staff members, particularly the nurses who cared for the infant, have often shared more time with the baby than even close family members. It is critical that the family not feel cut off from the hospital and staff. Support groups for perinatal loss and periodic memorial services at the hospital are all helpful to some parents.

> **Commentary by Mr. Goldman:** Of course, empathetic two-way communication is essential for reasons much more basic and important than risk management.

Summary

The admission of a newborn to the NICU is a critical and painful time for the family no matter how uncomplicated the child's anticipated course. When the child does not thrive, the family's resources may be stressed to their limit. Direct, frequent, and compassionate communication with the staff will not eliminate the stress but may help to provide accurate and realistic information. Together, the parents and staff can then make choices that optimize each infant's care. We, like the parents, would like to guarantee a normal outcome. However, the medical diploma and years of experience confer no magic cures and no crystal balls. We can acknowledge our shared wishes for a normal outcome, our limited vision, and our desire to provide the best possible care under the circumstances. When we forge a therapeutic alliance with the family, we are less likely to act defensively and arrogantly. Our behavior recognizes that children may have many physicians and nurses but only one set of parents. Even with the best communication and medical care, we cannot completely alleviate the family's loss of control. We can, in fact, only do our best.

References

1. Lucey JF. Parent dissatisfaction with neonatal intensive care unit care and suggestions for improvements. Pediatrics 1993;92:724.
2. Stinson R, Stinson P. *The Long Dying of Baby Andrew*. Boston, Little Brown and Co., 1979, p. 65.
3. Harrison H. *The Premature Baby Book*. New York, St. Martin's Press, 1983, p. 124.
4. Nance S. *Premature Babies: A Handbook for Parents*. New York, Arbor House, 1982, p. 96.
5. Harrison H. The principles for family-centered neonatal care. Pediatrics 1993;92:643.
6. Alfonso DD, Hurst I, Mayberry LJ, et al. Stressors reported by mothers of hospitalized premature infants. Neonatal Network 1992;11:63.
7. Miles MS, Fung SG, Kasper MA. The stress response of mothers and fathers of preterm infants. Res Nurs Health 1992;15:261.
8. Gutheil TG, Bursztajn H, Brodsky A. Malpractice prevention through the sharing of uncertainty. N Engl J Med 1984;311:49.
9. Siegler M. Pascal's wager and the hanging of crepe. N Engl J Med 1975;293:853.
10. Walper DA, Todres ID, Cassem NH, et al. Coping with poor prognosis in the pediatric intensive care unit. Am J Dis Child 1979;133:1121.
11. Lee SK, Penner PL, Cox M. Comparison of the attitudes of health care professionals and parents toward active treatment of very low birth weight infants. Pediatrics 1991;88:110.
12. Todres ID, Krare D, Howell MC, et al. Pediatricians' attitudes affecting decision-making in defective newborns. Pediatrics 1977;60:197.
13. Todres ID, Guilemin J, Grodin MA, et al. Life-saving therapy for newborns: A questionable survey in the state of Massachusetts. Pediatrics 1988;81:643.
14. King NP. Transparency in neonatal intensive care. Hastings Center Report 1992;22:18.
15. Perlman NB, Freeman JL, Abramovitch R, et al. Informational needs of parents of sick neonates. Pediatrics 1991;88:512.
16. Pinch WJ, Speilman ML. Parental perceptions of ethical issues post-NICU discharge. Western J Nurs Res 1993;15:422.
17. Foster JD, Lousia DB. Waiting times and public satisfaction with medical care. N Engl J Med 1979;301:1349.
18. Jellinek MS, Catlin EA, Todres ID, et al. Facing tragic decisions with parents in the neonatal intensive care unit: Clinical perspectives. Pediatrics 1992;89:119.

Section VIII

Documentation and Risk Management

Chapter 37

Obstetrical Forms: Nursing Documentation

◆◆◆

Charles W. Fisher, J.D., Michael P. Burke, B.A. Rosemary Cicala, R.N.

Introduction

Unfortunately, many, if not most, medico-legal controversies result from chart documentation. The medical record, which contains only a limited picture of the actual medical treatment, becomes the major focal point in a lawsuit. Its significance, in terms of the persuasive ability to win or lose a case from the medical records, should not be underestimated.

Most of the "first line of defense" arises from the nursing documentation that occurs during patient care. Nursing notations in three separate areas have been identified as important targets in litigation. These areas include documentation regarding antepartum testing and monitoring, labor and delivery triage, and labor and delivery documentation relative to fetal heart rates in the laboring patient. While impossible to address every situation that arises or exhibit every "possible form" that could be used for the various fact situations, this chapter addresses a limited number of pivotal medico-legal situations and the methods of documentation that the nurse can use to prepare not only a substantively adequate document, but one that is legally effective as well.

Antepartum Testing

Often, depending on the level of the hospital, the obstetrical nurse is called upon to evaluate and interpret non-stress tests. The patient arrives in

From: Donn SM, Fisher CW (eds.): *Risk Management Techniques in Perinatal and Neonatal Practice.* © Futura Publishing Co., Inc., Armonk, NY, 1996.

the antepartum testing unit where the nurse performs the tests and then reports the findings to the physician at his/her office. Although having a resident and/or the attending physician review the strip immediately after the test is performed constitutes a better practice, the test is often not seen by a physician for 24-48 hours or, in some cases, not at all. *This does not relieve the nurse of her potential liability for accurately interpreting and documenting the results of the non-stress test.* The importance of accurate interpretation and documentation becomes readily apparent when, often years later, a lawsuit is filed and whether or not a strip was reactive is in controversy. The mere documentation that the strip was "reactive" is probably not sufficient to convince a jury. The rationale behind the determination that a monitor strip is or is not reactive must be included in the record at the time of the interpretation. By describing the reasoning for the interpretation, a jury will be presented with a medical record that includes the criteria and findings that support the medical conclusion. If these things are not included in the medical record, the jury may believe that the witness is simply "making it up" in order to explain away a misdiagnosis.

The criteria and information needed to document a reactive non-stress test includes the following: 1. designating it as reactive; 2. indicating any interventions used during the test, such as position changes, juice/crackers, abdominal stimulation, and vibroacoustic stimulation; 3. describing the accelerations with the appropriately used rule (for instance, the 15-15 rule); 4. evaluating long-term variability; and 5. ruling out decelerations of any type.

Including the above criteria in the medical record will enhance the appearance of a reactive non-stress test. It should be noted and recognized that merely because there is decreased long-term variability or an occasional sporadic variable deceleration, a non-stress test may still be deemed reactive. However, the nurse should hesitate to designate such a strip reactive without receiving physician verification. Some Level III institutions require the nurse to define a non-stress test as "non-reactive" if there are *any* periodic decelerations whatsoever. In order to change that nursing designation a physician would have to intervene, review the strip, and express the specific reasons why it is reactive in spite of a periodic type of deceleration.

The important point to be made is that when there is a suspicious finding, the nurse should delay her documentation of whether it is reactive or non-reactive and simply contact the doctor. It is also very important for the nurse to document any telephone discussion with the physician regarding test findings. This is especially true where there is apparent activity but decreased long-term variability and/or periodic, but irregular, decelerations. The nurse should document the following: 1. the name of the physician and the time of the contact; 2. the specific information relayed to the physician, even if only a notation that "all of the above" was provided to the physician; and 3. the physician's instructions.

Finally, the nurse needs to make a specific note regarding any discharge instructions issued for the patient. Although these instructions come primarily from the physician, some hospitals issue standard follow-up instructions to patients after non-stress testing.

Triage Record

The areas of potential liability in triage include the failure to diagnose preterm labor, the failure to diagnose ruptured membranes, and the failure to diagnose abruptio placentae. Secondary areas, such as the sufficiency of physician contact, the question of repeating vital signs or vaginal exams prior to discharge, and the appropriateness of discharge instructions sometimes occur as isolated issues but usually are found in combination with the three primary issues listed above.

While physicians often make the final decisions, diagnosis, and instructions, in some instances the nurse performs examinations and relays information via telephone to an off-site physician. In either case, it is important to understand that the nursing documentation generally contains greater detail than a physician's single progress note regarding his/her impressions. Therefore, the nursing documentation is important even where the physician is present and making all of the clinical decisions.

Preterm Labor

If a patient is determined to be in false labor and is going to be discharged, two very important functions must be carried out and documented by the staff. First, the record should clearly indicate that the contractions have stopped or are so irregularly spaced that the patient is not in active labor. It is *not* sufficient to simply rely upon a monitor strip as evidence of insufficient contractile activity since plaintiffs can challenge the adequacy of transducer application and thus claim that faulty application caused a misdiagnosis of preterm labor. When contractions are present, they should be documented in terms of frequency, duration, and strength via palpation since there are occasions when, although contractions are present, the patient may still not be in preterm labor. To avoid arguments regarding the type and nature of contractions, palpation and documentation regarding the same again becomes very important. Therefore, a specific note indicating the absence of contractions per monitor *and* palpation is required to fully defend against such claims.

Secondly, unless one can clearly document no contractions whatsoever and an initial vaginal examination reveals a completely closed, long, and thick cervix, it is highly recommended that a complete vaginal examination be performed prior to the patient's discharge.

The performance of the above-mentioned items and the documentation of the negative findings establishes a very strong case against preterm labor. On the other hand, the failure to appropriately document negative findings with respect to both contraction activity and cervical dilatation makes a case difficult to defend, especially if the patient presents to another health care provider a few hours later, completely dilated.

Finally, discharge instructions should be provided to the patient in written form and should include a list of specific signs and symptoms of preterm labor (bleeding, pain, etc.). Most importantly, specific instructions regarding physician follow-up including a designation as to when the follow-up visit should occur must be included.

Premature Rupture of Membranes

To rule out ruptured membranes, the health care provider should initially prepare a detailed history of the specific complaint. Second, any time the issue of possible ruptured membranes occurs, nitrazine and ferning tests should be performed.

Simply documenting a history of possible preterm rupture of membranes does not describe the situation as observed or experienced by the patient. Obviously, there is a difference between constant leaking and leaking that occurs with coughing or sneezing, the latter of which could represent urinary incontinence in pregnancy. Histories such as these are especially important if the nitrazine and ferning tests are negative. The history can confirm or negate the belief of premature rupture of membranes.

Therefore, from an historical perspective, the nurse should document the following: 1. the date and time the alleged rupture occurred; 2. the manner in which the fluid is released; and 3. the consistency, color, and character of the fluid.

Once the issue of possible rupture of membranes has been raised, the patient should not be discharged without nitrazine or ferning tests. During the speculum examination, the discharge or pooling of the fluid should be documented in the chart.

A history more consistent with urinary loss than with amniotic fluid loss, a negative exam for leaking fluid or pooling, and a negative nitrazine or ferning test, make a strong case to support ruling out ruptured membranes. Infection is a significant medico-legal issue as it can be a primary cause of vaginal discharge or a secondary problem related to ruptured membranes. The nurse should document the evaluation for infection, any cultures performed, discussion with the patient, and follow-up instruction. Signs and symptoms of infection including increased temperature, malaise, chills, tender abdomen, and decreased fetal movement should be thoroughly explained to the patient and are important to note in the chart.

Discharge instructions should direct the patient to follow-up with her physician within a few days or at their next regularly scheduled appointment. Obviously, the shorter the time before follow-up, the better for confirmation.

Abruptio Placentae

Many claims arise not only from the failure to diagnose abruptio placentae (see Chapters 13 and 14) but from also the failure to treat an abnormal pattern in labor and delivery. Most difficulties in defending abruptio placentae cases arise from the retrospective interpretation of the medical record.

Many medico-legal lawsuits arise from the claim that the "bloody show" was actually evidence of an abruption and that the significance and volume of that bloody show was misinterpreted and not misunderstood by the nurse. In that respect, retrospectively reviewing a chart with multiple documentations of "bloody show" will not solve the issue as to the volume of the bloody show, whether it was continuous or intermittent, and whether it was related to cervical dilatation versus an abruption.

The first question to be raised is whether bloody show should be documented in triage or labor and delivery. Bloody show is essentially a normal consequence of labor, whether of a small, moderate, or large amount. Therefore, a bloody show arguably need not be documented in the medical record, since it is a normal condition of labor. Its relevance to labor is insignificant, since true labor is not diagnosed by bloody show but by progressive cervical dilatation. Bloody show is almost incidental to the diagnosis of labor. Therefore, when labor actually occurs, the bloody show would need not be documented as a normal consequence. The nurse could testify that routine bloody show would not be documented; therefore, if the record contains no such documentation, the amount of bloody show must clearly have been totally unrelated to anything indicative of an abruptio placentae.

Many institutions document bloody show, and this is not only acceptable but a common practice. The problem that arises concerns the ability to accurately determine the amount of bloody show. A designation of it as small, medium, or large does not specifically indicate the amount and it leaves the door open for the argument that the event really was actually an abruption as opposed to a "large bloody show."

Therefore, a better method of indicating the amount of bloody show should be used. Describing the size (i.e., dime size, quarter size) of the blood that appears on the peripad between patient evaluations more clearly illustrates the amount of blood present. If described as bloody show the size of a quarter on two separate evaluations an hour apart, it becomes obvious that such a laboring patient has not suffered an abruption that could be diagnosed by a significant amount of blood. On the other hand, describing that same bloody show as "moderate" on those two separate checks an hour apart does not clearly illustrate the clinical picture. Further, describing it as moderate on the two occasions, may suggest to some that the bleeding was continuous during that hour interval; describing it simply as a quarter-size collection on a peripad, however, indicates that it likely was not continuous, free-flowing, or active-flowing blood.

Thus, documentation of "bloody show" in triage and in labor and delivery should be accurately recorded on the medical record. Changes in bloody show, most importantly increases in significance of bloody show, not only need to be documented, but the chart should contain a clear indication that the physician has been notified of this event. Obviously, such changes, as well as complaints of pain and increased abdominal tenderness, increase the likelihood of placental abruption and warrant immediate physician notification.

In addition, triage documentation needs to rule out abruption where there is no labor but simply some "spotting" during the pregnancy. Generally, if the patient is not in labor, the source of the blood cannot ordinarily be ascribed to a dilating cervix. Where a patient is not in labor yet experiences spotting, the following clinical criteria should be applied to rule out abruptio placentae: 1. the specific amount of blood seen; 2. whether the blood is actively flowing or is evidence of old clots; 3. the condition of the uterus, including a description of tenderness, firmness, etc.; 4. a specific description of the patient's comfort level; 5. the results of any abdominal and/or rectal exam; and 6. any ultrasound scan results.

Recognizing that abruptio placentae can occur in many forms, including those that are completely occult that appear suddenly and without warning, and those that begin with only a slight amount of blood that suddenly advance to severe and significant, one should realize that a retrospective analysis readily identifies alleged "red flags" that preceded the sudden deteriorating event. Most of the time, the red-flag claim arises by identifying prior episodes of bleeding or uterine tenderness, or by claiming a failure to adequately and accurately describe the clinical situation and through the use of innuendo to claim an inappropriate evaluation.

Finally, if abruptio placentae has been ruled out, clear discharge instructions should be given to the patient regarding signs and symptoms and follow-up with the attending physician.

Labor and Delivery

Almost universally, the primary area of inadequate documentation in labor and delivery arises in the documentation of the fetal heart tones. Medicolegal claims usually challenge the frequency of documentation, the documented interpretation as it correlates to the monitor strip, and the documentation of physician contact when abnormal patterns present.

Documentation of nursing interventions for abnormal heart rates do comprise quite a few lawsuits, but this area of challenge does not reach the significance or severity of the prior three issues.

Frequency of Documentation

Frequency of documentation depends to some degree upon whether the patient is in the latent phase versus active phase of labor. Presently, the American College of Obstetricians and Gynecologists (ACOG) standards do not express any specific standard of care for the frequency of documentation in the latent phase, but they do set forth a standard for the active phase of labor. However, if the patient is in the labor and delivery area, it should be assumed that she will be treated as a laboring patient in a lawsuit; therefore, the parameters for the frequency of documenting fetal heart rates should be applied as though the patient were in active labor.

Essentially, the fetal heart rate should be documented every 30 minutes in the first stage and every 15 minutes in the second stage for low-risk patients, and every 15 minutes in the first stage and every 5 minutes in the second stage for high-risk patients.

This is not an ideal standard; however, it is the established standard of care. Documentation that occurs less frequently constitutes a violation of that standard of care.

Different forms exist for the documentation of fetal heart tones, from a graphic chart style to progress notes. Either style is acceptable.

Fetal Heart Rate Interpretation

In litigation, the major problem is the method by which decreased variability (either beat-to-beat or long-term), variable decelerations, and late decelerations are documented. Most forms seem to emphasize abnormal monitor strip findings to the extent that they obviate any reassuring signs that should also be documented. For instance, one may have decreased beat-to-beat variability and accelerations, the latter of which indicate fetal well-being. To the health care professional, the presence of accelerations supersedes the finding of decreased beat-to-beat variability. Often, however, a record noting a periodic change from normal variability to decreased variability stands out like a sore thumb to the plaintiff's attorney and the jury.

Thus, the medical form should initially provide categories that address reassuring factors before addressing periodic changes. In this manner, the appropriate emphasis on the positive, reassuring signs will be set forth in the medical record.

As an example, one should indicate the baseline rate, reactivity, and other reassuring findings before addressing abnormalities. It is difficult to maintain a defense claiming the absence of fetal distress if several pages of nursing notes indicate multiple and repetitive variable decelerations. In this illustration, significant variable decelerations were repetitively documented in the record, yet the significance of the reoccurring events was unappreciated by hospital personnel. As a result, no intervention occurred. Alternatively, if the record describes adequacy of beat-to-beat variability, reactivity with accelerations, rapidity of return to baseline, adequate fetal movement upon palpation, etc., then one is presented with a more accurate interpretation of the monitor strip in that particular instance.

Therefore, the simple rule of thumb is to document normal, reassuring, and positive findings prior to noting any suspicious or abnormal ones. The medical form should provide for this in a step-wise method if in graphic form, and nursing protocol and training should compel documentation in this way if documenting fetal heart rates in progress notes.

When describing abnormal findings, documentation should be as accurate as possible. This applies most importantly to decreased variability (both long-term and short-term), variable decelerations, and late decelerations.

With respect to decreased short-term variability, *ACOG Technical Bulletin #132* indicates three to six beats to constitute adequate beat-to-beat variability. Many times there is an "over call"; that is, too often decreases in beat-to-beat variability are documented when, in fact, there are still three to six beats per minute. Rather than risking potential mistakes in evaluating variability, the nurse would be better served to simply document the numerical range observed.

Presently, AWHONN is addressing the issue of nursing evaluations of short-term variability and long-term variability. AWHONN now suggests that long-term variability be simply described in its most basic elements, that is, "present" versus "absent." Likewise, short-term variability would be described in its most basic elements: "marked"; "present"; and "absent."

There is no agreement relative to the evaluation of these two elements of fetal monitoring and no universal agreement as to the significance of each. Until the time that some method of documentation is uniformly accepted, one can use either the numerical documentation system or the AWHONN system. More important than the system utilized is the nurse's ability to recognize a "problematic pattern" that warrants a physician evaluation.

With respect to variable decelerations, documentation by the nursing staff should not describe the decelerations as mild, moderate, or severe. Simply noting the occurrence of a variable deceleration existing and subsequent physician contact is sufficient for nursing practice from a medico-legal standpoint. Multiple definitions have been used to describe a significant or severe variable deceleration. Therefore, it serves no purpose to identify the variable in terms of such subjective terminology. If the physician is not present, the length and depth of the variable deceleration can be described to the physician over the phone. This allows for a more accurate portrayal and, more importantly, permits for the physician's interpretation rather than a subjective interpretation by the nurse.

Therefore, in documenting in the patient's chart, the periodic change of a variable deceleration should simply be designated as such without any further qualifying information regarding the nature of the deceleration.

Describing the variable deceleration components in greater detail in the record often becomes confusing because "return to baseline," and "poor return to baseline," have not been clearly differentiated. It is obvious a good return to baseline follows a variable deceleration, but the point at which it becomes a prolonged or poor return to baseline is not defined in any textbook. From a nursing documentation standpoint, it is probably appropriate to document a good return to baseline. However, the determination of a slow return to baseline, is more appropriately left to the subjective judgment of the physician.

Physician Contact

While it is clearly within the nurse's province to document the occurrence of a late deceleration, it is sometimes difficult to determine whether the deceleration is variable or whether it is late. Rather than guessing, simply designating a "deceleration" without any modifying term, is appropriate. More important is the question of whether decelerations are repetitive, and the nurse should request physician assistance to diagnose the deceleration. The appropriate documentation, therefore, simply notes the occurrence of decelerations and contact with the physician.

Two final important pieces of information should be noted in the medical record relative to decelerations. First, the deceleration and/or decelerations that are repetitive and persistent should immediately lead to contact with the physician. The specific time that the physician is contacted, the information relayed, and the instructions received should be placed in a progress-style note in the medical record. Presence of the physician in the room should be documented, noting the specific time, and the fact that the physician has reviewed or is reviewing the monitor strip.

Nursing interventions, such as increasing intravenous fluids, giving oxygen, or changing position of the patient, should be documented either on the monitor strip or on the medical record with a specific time designation. Actually, the medical record is of greater importance in preserving evidence since monitor strips are frequently lost. Depending on hospital protocol and the habit and routine in particular obstetrical departments, it is probably more advisable to document as much information in the medical record as possible, rather than noting the same on the monitor strip.

With respect to labor and delivery, perhaps the most important function of documentation is to reflect the rapidity of physician contact and/or response in the face of an abnormal fetal heart rate monitor strip or a persistent set of decelerations, *regardless of type*. The medical record should reflect that once the pattern is documented, almost instantaneous contact or attempts to contact the physician or physicians in charge occurred. The record should reflect no significant gap between the occurrence of the abnormality and the physician involvement.

Conclusion

Multiple forms have been devised for antepartum testing, triage records, and labor/delivery flow charts or progress notes, and no one particular form is better than another. This chapter identifies important events that need to be accurately documented in the medical chart, regardless of the form used. This accuracy is important, not only for medical purposes, but to defend against medico-legal actions.

Perhaps more than 90% of severe damage, high exposure cases arise from poor documentation of fetal heart rate patterns in labor and delivery and the subsequent immediate management of fetal heart rate abnormalities. Most of the information provided to those who review quality care and/or to juries who review standards of care come directly from the medical records. In most instances, witnesses do not accurately recall the detailed events of a particular set of circumstances, and especially in a court of law, a claim that a nurse or doctor remembers detailed events about one particular patient from several years earlier raises the issue of credibility, not only as to the witness' recollection of events, but also as to the veracity of the defendant's claims. This must be considered by every individual who makes entries in the medical record.

_____ Chapter 38 _____

Prospective Risk Management

◆◆◆

Margaret Copp Dawson, R.N.,
Rita W. Cikanek, B.S., HCA

Introduction

Goals of a Risk Management Program

The essential goal of a risk management system is conservation of resources: financial and human. The foundation of risk management is an adequate insurance program. The development of such a program is beyond the scope of this chapter, which focuses on a system for early notification, investigation, and resolution of claims within a facility or health care system.[1]

Early identification of potential claims and of areas of risk in care delivery provides opportunity for intervention to allow early resolution of claims and to adjust systems *before* an occurrence results in a claim. It is an axiom of risk management, supported by research, that the longer a claim remains open, the more costly it becomes. Clearly, the time and emotional cost of litigated claims are significant to health care providers, and conservation of these resources is aligned with fiscal goals.

No research is required to demonstrate the obvious fact that prevention is superior to reaction. Loss prevention activities, aligned with quality programs of clinical staff and facility, provide the greatest long-term payoff in risk management.

---

[1] Sources of information include physicians' and nurses' professional associations, state Medical Society, state-specific professionally-owned liability insurance companies, and the American Society for Healthcare Risk Management, American Hospital Association, One North Franklin, Chicago, Illinois 60606.

From: Donn SM, Fisher CW (eds.): *Risk Management Techniques in Perinatal and Neonatal Practice.* © Futura Publishing Co., Inc., Armonk, NY, 1996.

When early resolution of a potential claim is not possible, prompt risk management consultation can contribute to a more effective defense of the litigated claim through accurate documentation and preservation of key evidence.

The Risk Management Process

The risk management process begins with notification of a potential claim. An investigation, analysis of liability, and resolution of the claim follow. The process includes a review and improvement of systems that are found to have been causally related to the events leading to the claim. The risk management process concludes with analysis of the experience to evaluate the efforts of the risk management team in managing the claim.

Notification

Key to early intervention in claims management and in loss prevention is effective communication between providers and the risk manager. The risk manager must be known to providers and perceived as a team member with resources available to providers. All staff should share a clear understanding of criteria for reporting potential claims and the mechanism for reporting.

Notice to the risk manager that a potential claim has occurred or been discovered triggers the system. Providers and risk managers establish criteria for identifying claims and a mechanism for communication.

Criteria for identifying a potential claim are developed through collaboration of the risk manager and clinicians. The risk manager and clinical team may analyze past experience within the practice to determine which injuries have resulted in claims/litigation. Occurrence of these injuries or outcomes should then trigger notice to risk management (Table 1). Particular procedures or referrals may signal injuries and should elicit a report to risk management. For example, anytime a consultation to Neurology is initiated for a newborn, risk management should be informed. Similarly a consultation to Plastic Surgery for an infant who has had a problem with an intravenous catheter should trigger a report. Transfer of a term infant to intensive care is reportable as an indication of a potentially preventable injury/claim. Review of a case for presentation at a morbidity/complications conference may initiate a report. These systems will sometimes result in multiple reports of the same case; however, such dual reporting should be tolerated, even encouraged, since backup reports can prevent a case from becoming lost to risk management follow-up, otherwise known as "falling through the cracks."

Opportunities to collaborate in developing reporting criteria and to facilitate reporting abound. Attendance of the risk manager at departmental meetings (quality assurance, morbidity and mortality, staff meetings, rounds)

Table 1
Events or Findings That Should be Reported to Risk Management Regardless of When They Become Known to Providers

Ante/Prenatal

Fetal deaths during procedure (sonography, amniocentesis)
Intrauterine death in last trimester
Maternal morbidity with question of delay in diagnosis or preventability: maternal stroke, deep vein thrombosis, arterio-venous malformation
Maternal hospitalization for reasons other than early onset of labor
Hospitalization for previously undiagnosed eclampsia or pre-eclampsia
Hospitalization for uncontrolled diabetes
Noncompliance of high risk mothers
Positive toxicology screens
Anomalies associated with maternal drug use
Failure to administer Rh Immune Globulin
Prolonged rupture of membranes greater than 24 hours before clinic visit
Maternal death
Trauma in obstetric patient

Delivery

Infant death in the delivery room
Maternal death
Shoulder dystocia
Apgar scores < 6 at 5 minutes
Maternal uterine rupture
Positive toxicology screens (mother and baby)
Neonatal arterial blood pH < 7.2
"Crash" Cesarean sections with infant morbidity
Forceps injuries, significant bruising
High forceps delivery
Medication errors, blood administration errors
Meconium below the vocal cords
Blood transfusions
Active herpetic lesions with vaginal delivery
Complications during vaginal birth after prior Cesarean section
Equipment failure (monitors, vacuum extractor, infusion pumps)
Fetal monitoring irregularities
Injury to baby (hemorrhage, fractures, lacerations)
Rupture of membranes greater than 24 hours with infant injury
Prolonged fetal decelerations less than 90 bpm
Suspected asphyxia or hypoxic-ischemic injury
Vaginal delivery of baby greater than 4,500 g
Abruptio placentae
Negative outcome with family who questions quality of care
Transfer of term infants to a higher level of care (ICU, other)

Postpartum/Neonatal

Anomalies associated with maternal drug use
Intravenous complications (infiltration, etc.) requiring intervention or consultation

Table continues on next page

Table 1 *(continued)*
Events or Findings That Should be Reported to Risk Management
Regardless of When They Become Known to Providers

Postpartum/Neonatal

Incomplete discharges (failure to administer medications, tests to mother or baby)
Medication errors
Unexpected infant death
Complications of procedures (pneumothorax, multiple, or traumatic intubation; diagnostic procedure complications with injury to baby)
Negative outcomes with family who questions quality of care
Information from external clinicians that indicate potential liability, notice of bad outcome for mother or baby, or family allegations of malpractice even where none is believed to have occurred
Apneic spells in a term infant
Need for neurologic evaluation of newborn
Any infant requiring physical therapy in the nursery
Kidney dysfunction or syndrome of inappropriate antidiuretic hormone
Any record that documents "birth asphyxia" or "cerebral anoxia"
Maternal death
Transfer of mother or baby to ICU/higher level of care
Failure to administer Rh Immune Globulin
Deep venous thrombosis or pulmonary embolism in the mother
Requests to review or receive copies of the medical record of mother, baby or both for any reason other than continuing care

---

will facilitate both processes. A clinician who sees the risk manager on a regular basis will be reminded of cases he/she should report at a time and place where the report can be made directly.

> **Commentary by Mr. Goldman:** Departments can make risk management part of the job responsibility of a physician in the department so there will always be a contact person with knowledge about department activities.

Also, as the risk manager grows to understand the substance and subtleties of the practice better, he/she can better analyze which occurrences ought to be reported as having the potential for developing into an actual claim. The meeting can provide an opportunity for discussion of reportable events and about how a potential claim might be managed once reported.

The value of contact between clinicians and the risk manager cannot be over-emphasized. Not only can they develop clear systems for communication (how and under what conditions), but as both parties learn each other's styles and points of view, they can work better as a team with families/patients in managing individual claims and in controlling potential loss in the aggregate.

Other means of defining reportable events/injuries include the following: 1. data gathered by the risk manager regarding the past claims experience of the institution or the practice can be analyzed to identify sources of claims; 2. clinicians may be able to identify certain procedures that result in injuries that later develop into claims. For example, any injury that requires additional treatment either leading to increased expense to the patient/family or that significantly lengthens the episode of the case has the potential to develop into a claim; 3. litigation and claims experience within the state, region, and nation may point toward liability risks and reportable injuries/events within the specific practice setting; and 4. attention should be given also to clinicians' assessment of risks associated with emerging practices and practice patterns. There should be similar involvement of the risk manager with Nursing and Midwives in participation in defining reporting criteria, attendance at meetings and provision of in-services.

The risk manager should be a familiar face to clinicians, appearing as an invited guest to all departmental meetings where treatment issues are discussed. An annual presentation on risk management topics such as documentation, communication, reporting criteria, and local, state, and national trends in claims and litigation within the specialty may be expected from the risk manager.

The risk manager should prepare a presentation for the department or service chair annually of claims experienced historically and in the previous year (high frequency claims, high dollars for individual claims, high frequency of claims, or potential claims associated with a particular practitioner or team), potential claims, risk issues that have emerged over the past year, litigation in progress and recently concluded, claims that have been resolved, and claims that have first been reported as litigation.

Commentary by Mr. Goldman: Review of this material can help identify trends or correctable issues.

Annual review of the success of the collaborative risk management program affords an opportunity to improve the system. Unsuccessful early resolution of potential claims bears analysis. If service of a lawsuit precedes internal notification of risk management by clinicians, the case should be brought to the attention of the service chief or department chair. It is the responsibility of the service chief to communicate with the clinicians to determine where the reporting system failed and reinforce as necessary adherence to the system. Risk management will be an agenda item at all staff meetings in services with an aggressive risk management program, allowing frequent discussion of reportable events. The risk manager should provide to clinicians (physicians, midwives, nursing, and ancillary personnel) a written list of reporting criteria and in-service education/discussion of the criteria as well as management of claims and potential claims for all groups annually and as requested.

Any person who has knowledge of a potential claim should be encouraged, indeed expected, to report. Physicians, nurses, medical record analysts, and ancillary clinical staff (respiratory therapists, social workers, utilization management personnel) all may learn of a potential claim. Reporting to risk management should be viewed as a professional or institutional obligation, as a constructive action in the best interest of patient care. Never should it be viewed as punitive or "tattling." Physicians must take care not to give the impression that their "command" or control is violated by reporting by other disciplines.

Communication by telephone or in person is preferred to a formal paper report (incident or occurrence report), as it allows immediate discussion and consultation.

> **Commentary by Mr. Goldman:** It is also preferred because it is less likely to be discoverable by the plaintiff. The "work product" rule—items disclosed to the legal staff or their investigators in preparation for litigation are not discoverable—protects this information from discovery, whereas incident reports may be discoverable in certain states.

Initial information reported includes name and medical record number of the patient, date of occurrence, dates of admission, the alleged or actual injury, and names of clinical staff knowledgeable of the event.

Investigation

Investigation begins with a review of the medical record, including past records if available. Interviews of clinical staff involved in the event are conducted by the risk manager and may include written statements. All facts pertinent to the event, many of which may not be detailed in the medical record, are collected. Full disclosure of all details is essential, including personal factors that might have contributed to the event. Documentation of the investigation is protected either through quality assurance or attorney work product.

> **Commentary by Mr. Goldman:** Quality assurance rules vary from state to state and must be carefully followed to obtain this protection.

Staff should be cautioned not to keep any notes relevant to the event in their personal or work files, as such documents might be subject to subpoena should litigation result.

Protection of the investigation from subpoena in the event of litigation is an important consideration. In settings where the risk manager is an attorney, attorney-client privilege may protect the investigation. Where there is an in-house counsel who directs defense of professional liability claims, that person may "supervise" the investigation, and all documents may be directed toward him/her. Where there is no attorney available within the health care system or facility, early involvement of defense counsel following a catastrophic outcome is recommended. Memoranda can then be written to the defense attorney, thereby acquiring protection through attorney-client privilege and work product. Risk managers are encouraged to consult with their legal counsel to develop a system for protecting the results of the investigation. Defense counsel may wish to have early notification by the risk manager involvement even of those claims that are resolved prior to litigation in order to contribute to the investigation and to prevent inadvertent compromise of potential defense of the claim should early resolution fail.

> **Commentary by Mr. Goldman:** Attorneys may also need to be involved to draft releases or take cases involving minor children through Probate Court for settlement approval.

Additional protection for the investigation and ensuing loss prevention activities may be available through statutes relating to health care quality assurance activities. Legal counsel can consider this, also, in setting up a protected system for the individual facility.

Materials that document the facts of the event are gathered and secured by the risk manager. These include fetal monitor strips (originals or copies if the originals are routinely archived at the institution), raw data, notes and working documents for laboratory and other tests, as well as sonograms. Placentas are sent for analysis. Blood and stool samples are stored and/or sent for analysis, for example stool for cocaine screening.

Medical Record Review

During the medical record review, the risk manager will critically analyze the completeness and objectivity of the documentation. In a complex situation, the risk manager may advise a clinician on how to document in a factually complete manner, excluding potentially damaging speculations or premature conclusions. It has been said that in litigation the medical record "determines and incites the case." All effort expended in ensuring accurate and non-damaging documentation is worthwhile. For example, in a complex situation with a bad outcome, the clinician might ask the risk manager or an experienced and uninvolved clinician to review a draft entry. The reviewer assists in ensuring that the documentation *does not contain* the following: 1. the emotions of the writer; 2. speculation as to cause of the bad outcome; 3. references to systems problems in the record, as opposed to the care and treatment of the individual patient; and 4. finger-pointing or blaming, and inflammatory words such as accidental, careless, defective, error, faulty, inadequate, inadvertent, inappropriate, misadventure, negligent, sloppy, unrecognized, substandard, etc.

The risk manager will ensure that the medical record *does contain*: 1. all facts pertinent to the event; 2. a complete plan of care and rationale for this plan; 3. appropriate context for the event in question; 4. notes from all clinicians involved in the case, especially the senior physician leading a team of house staff, for example; and 5. all pertinent documents such as code sheets, labor and delivery sheets, consent forms, and anesthesia records.

Documentation of the event should be complete, but the amount of detail should not be such that it calls attention to the event should there be attorney review of the record at a later date. Explanations for why a mistake was made or for why a failure in communication occurred are potentially very harmful. Such explanations belong in the quality assurance/incident report system, not in an individual medical record. These insights can also be shared with the risk manager in the interviews that are part of the case investigation.

Concurrent review of the record as events unfold enables the risk manager to assist clinicians in correcting potentially damaging documentation. The following examples are illustrative:

1. Some entries show the evolution of damaging documentation that bear no causal relationship to the infant's problem, but could easily make defense of a claim extremely difficult. "Problem: Decreased responsiveness/lethargy due to maternal morphine versus sepsis versus congenital neurologic disorder" becomes "Problem: decreased responsiveness/lethargy due to maternal morphine" becomes "Problem: lethargy due to morphine." The next entry, following intervention by the risk manager, would say simply "Problem: Neuro" and proceed with the note.

2. If the plan of care is altered, it is important in the context of a bad outcome to be clear in the record that the plan was deliberately changed rather than give the impression that a part of the plan was simply forgotten. Being able to reconstruct the decision-making process in the care of an ill newborn can be critical to successful defense of a claim. As an outsider to the clinical events, the risk manager can recognize an omission and bring it to the attention of clinical staff.

3. Unfortunately, the medical record offers an opportunity for blaming, finger-pointing, and defensive exchanges between clinicians and/or

disciplines. Review by the risk manager can bring a swift end to such exchanges. No way exists to correct what has already been written, but the duration of the exchange can be shortened by a vigilant reviewer.

4. If it is necessary to add information to the record that relates to prior events, the risk manager can guide clinicians in doing so appropriately, e.g. *"November 4, 1995 in reference to events of November 2, 1995 . . ."* Never should documentation be altered or removed, nor should a previous note be added to a later date, as such action may give the appearance or cover-up or fraud and make courtroom defense of the claim impossible.

5. If the record contains damaging speculation, the risk manager can advise physicians or other disciplines on how to reduce the damage by placing the speculation in perspective of clarifying earlier entries.

6. In the event of a potential claim, the risk manager should always review a draft of the formal discharge summary before it is completed and placed in the medical record, as this is the first document a plaintiff's attorney generally examines if the claimant seeks counsel. The discharge summary draft is reviewed for considerations listed above.

Certain documents are of critical importance. Notes by the attending or senior physician on the team are not always present if much of the care has been done by house staff or midwives/nurse practitioners. The risk manager may advise a way to add notes, such as a summary of recent events. If the patient has been discharged or more than a week has passed since the event, it may be too late to make a medical record entry that would help defense of a claim. The advice of the risk manager should be given careful consideration in such a situation.

Interviews

All staff who had involvement with the event under investigation may be interviewed by the risk manager. Such interviews should take place one-on-one, as soon after the event as possible. The goals of the interview are to establish facts pertinent to the event, to learn facts that may have had a bearing on the outcome, but that do not appear in the record, and to elucidate the issues operative in the event for further follow-up.

During the interview all staff are asked how they think the bad outcome might have been prevented. This focuses attention on analysis of the care rendered for breaches in the standard of care as well as systems analysis to determine if some flaw in the present system contributed to the injury under discussion. For example, if a delay occurred in recognizing fetal stress because nurses were unable to contact the responsible physician, the paging system or the coverage roster might be at fault. Such problems are usually amenable to improvement, and full advantage ought to be taken of an opportunity to discover and repair deficiencies, thereby preventing future claims. One might learn that additional education is needed, that a particular piece of equipment is not user-friendly, that barriers exist to effective interdisciplinary communication, or that documentation practices or forms are not clinically useful. One might learn, also, of problems with an individual practitioner. Whatever is discovered, care must be taken: 1. to be sensitive to the dangers of disclosing from whom the information was obtained; and 2. that problems identified ("put on notice") are addressed.

The most useful method for conducting such an interview is one-on-one, to protect confidentiality in potentially sensitive subjects. Having the medical record available is essential, as the discussion should include the following:

1. Discussion of the purpose of the interview (to establish facts of what occurred, to expand upon the factual information available in the medical record and to begin the process of "loss prevention" or "what we can learn from this experience").
2. Discussion of confidentiality (every attempt will be made to keep sources of sensitive information confidential; an appeal may be made to the clinician's professional responsibility to the patient, as well as any state requirements attendant to the clinician's license).
3. Chronologic review of the events that directly involved the interviewee. Refer to the medical record for accuracy.
4. Analysis of how the injury or bad outcome might have been prevented.

A formal meeting ("sentinel event review," see below) with multiple participants to review the events and analyze systems problems that may have been causally related to the outcome should occur later. Information gained in individual interviews may guide the later discussion. The formal sentinel event review should occur as a Quality Assurance/Continuous Quality Improvement activity.

Additional information about the family and socio-demographic facts are gathered at this stage, also. Social workers and nurses are interviewed, and their documentation is also reviewed. Care is taken that allegations are not given substance, that family behavior is described in factual and not pejorative terms. Family constellation, past experiences with the health care system, employment and economic status, cultural, ethnic, and religious background are all important to the risk manager in determining how best to approach developing a collaborative relationship with the family.

During this stage, family meetings may occur to explain an event or to plan future care. The risk manager will review sensitive issues with clinical staff prior to the meeting. Approaches can be developed to avoid speculative, self-blaming, or inaccurate explanations of events. The risk manager may be present at the meeting itself, both as a witness to what is said for future reference in working with the family and to assist the clinical staff in correctly interpreting the family's understanding of the information presented.

Documentation

Great attention is paid to the accuracy and quality of medical record documentation, for it is the medical record that defines the case in litigation. It is far easier to explain events or play out the facts so that the "story is told" at the time care is occurring rather than later in a deposition when all explanations can be made to appear defensive and self-serving. Concurrent charting carries far greater credibility than testimony during litigation. Mistakes in charting are difficult at best to explain once litigation has begun and innocent additions to or corrections of the medical record if made improperly can render defense of a claim completely impossible.

The medical record forms both the factual and the subjective context for the case. A sloppy or illegible record colors in the minds of the jury the quality of the care rendered to the patient. If a physician is asked at a deposition or at trial to read his or her note in the record and is unable to do so, great damage has been done to the credibility of the witness, even as to his or her professional competence. If the record gives the appearance of a smoothly-functioning team, where the patient is monitored and assessed, a plan is developed, carried out and evaluated, and changed as necessary, then explanations for why something went wrong are potentially believable.

The outcome of the trial will often hinge on testimony of expert reviewers of the record. If the expert is to support the care of the patient, the story of that care and the episode must be clear and must be legible. Attentiveness by the medical and nursing staffs must be evident in the record. An absence of entries in the record may be explained later as the result of multiple emergencies or demands of other patients, but believability of such testimony after a suit has been initiated is not great, as it can so easily be made to appear self-serving. Undocumented attention paid to the patient is not available to a reviewer, and even a sympathetic reviewer cannot explain or overlook absences in the record. Every contact with the patient should be documented.

Concurrent review of the record by risk management as events unfold is ideal in developing a record that serves the patient's diagnosis and treatment and does no harm to professionals should a lawsuit be filed. Care must be taken, however, that the medical record contains *absolutely no references to contact with the risk manager or actions or involvement of the risk manager.* Such entries act as red flags to subsequent reviewing attorneys.

Analysis

In some cases, liability is obvious to clinicians at the time of the event or shortly thereafter. In these cases, additional review may be needed only for internal institutional reasons. More often, however, the presence or absence of liability is not clear. In these cases, the risk manager, with the help of clinicians, obtains an objective review from an internal expert, if available, or by an external expert who is paid for the review. Review by nurse experts may be warranted in cases where liability may lie with this discipline. Most commonly, however, it is physician review that is sought. The risk manager will engage the reviewer in a manner that protects the product from later subpoena or other disclosure.

Analysis of the claim and liability exposure will be undertaken by the risk manager in collaboration with the department chair, chief of the medical staff, and administrators. The composition of a review committee will vary with the organization. It should include, however, individuals who are clinically knowledgeable and individuals who are knowledgeable about medical practice, such as defense counsel. A review committee should consider all claims above the settlement authority of the risk manager. Following the review and analysis of the claim, the risk manager will report to the insurance carrier for hospital claims and/or will assist the physician clinical staff in reporting to the carrier, if different.

Billing Intervention

The risk management program will flourish in an atmosphere of collaboration with other departments within the health care entity, especially the accounts department. A risk management program must have a system in place for notification of the billing office(s) of a potential claim or "risk management case." Requests to hospital or clinic patient business office and to physician billing offices may be made to hold billing while analysis of liability is undertaken. This should include billing for consultation services. Patient balances after insurance may be written off. Balances may simply be held pending resolution of a claim. Such action is not an admission of guilt or liability, but may be presented as "a good will gesture to restore good patient relations."

Review of the patient's entire billing history should follow notification of a potential claim. Unpaid balances from past services should always be determined, then held and perhaps written off, also, if the seriousness of the potential claim warrants this. At times this will be a business decision, weighing cost of potential defense of a claim against the loss of not collecting a patient balance. This holds true also in cases where it is strongly believed that there is no liability, but a less than satisfactory outcome has resulted. In the case of a potential claim, all collection efforts should cease until the claim has been investigated and internal reviews completed. Only then and only through a deliberate decision should collection efforts be resumed. An attitude of forgiveness may swiftly convert to an attitude of blame upon receipt of a bill for services that resulted in a less-than-desirable outcome or that involved admitted error.

Developing a Relationship with the Family

In many circumstances, the risk manager will choose to visit the family while the patient remains in the hospital. This allows face-to-face discussion of the potential claim, planning for future care, an expression of concern on behalf of the hospital and clinical staff, and a willingness to work with the family toward an explanation of a bad outcome and/or resolution of a claim. The impact of human interaction concern should not be underestimated. The risk manager allows the family to ventilate difficult emotions and to make requests for assistance to minimize the impact of the event in question. Contact with the family affords the hospital, through the risk manager, an opportunity to correct misinformation and to provide information where it is lacking. Many families seek an attorney to "learn the truth"; much time, money, and grief may be saved if the risk manager can intervene to provide the "answers" families seek.

> **Commentary by Mr. Goldman:** Assistance to the family—including financial aid—is not an admission of liability and cannot be mentioned in court.

Resolving the Claim

The particular insurance structure will determine settlement process and authority of the risk manager. Typically, an institution has a Claims Committee that may grant authority to settle a claim prior to or during litigation. Physicians may assist the risk manager in presenting a case and its analysis and recommendations for resolution to the Claims Committee. Settlements are made in exchange for a formal agreement not to bring litigation in the matter. Legal counsel assists in cases that involve minors, as oversight by probate judges is generally required.

Physicians should not feel shy about sharing with families that they are aware of the family's involvement with risk management. The risk manager represents the hospital and its staff and should be acknowledged as a team member. Further, the efforts made are not adversarial, but are an attempt to avoid an adversarial relationship. Discussion of the financial detail of settlement negotiations is not appropriate for the physician, however, as this does have great potential for interfering in the treating relationship.

Loss Prevention: Sentinel Event Review

Following a serious, negative, and potentially avoidable outcome, a *sentinel event review* should be undertaken by the risk manager and/or the hospital's quality management program. This type of review differs from physicians' "morbidity and mortality" conferences.

A sentinel event review is scheduled within 30-60 days of the event. All participants in the event(s) leading to the bad outcome attend the review; supervisory or management staff may be present, also.

> **Commentary by Mr. Goldman:** In some cases, in order to obtain a complete understanding of the event, subsequent treaters or other staff (pathologists) may also be included.

The meeting is chaired by the quality assurance chair of the department, perhaps co-chaired by quality assurance representatives from two disciplines, for example Obstetrics and Nursing. Also present may be a "review panel" of senior clinicians who serve as internal experts and who were not directly involved in the events under review. A representative of the institutional quality assurance program attends, as well as the risk manager. The medical record is available, as are pertinent pieces of equipment if they were involved in the event.

The review begins with a statement of purpose for the process: to learn from the event by analyzing systems and processes that may have contributed to the injury, determining improvements that can be made so that future injuries might be prevented. In addition, quality monitors will be suggested to assure that the intention to correct systems problems is achieved. Monitors, however, may be developed at a different meeting of the departmental Quality Assurance Committee following the review.

All participants are introduced by name and the role they played in the events. The primary physician states the events chronologically as concisely as possible. A discussion follows as to what should have occurred if the injury was to be avoided. The chairs of the review direct what should have occurred if the injury was to be avoided. The chairs of the review direct discussion toward specific issues, some of which may have been identified earlier. Care is taken that the review does not become a blaming session or focus on criticism of individuals. Certainly individual responsibility for any injuries must in some cases be acknowledged and dealt with, but that is accomplished by management and supervisors, not in a group situation. The group is directed to propose solutions for issues or problems or to refer them to specific committees or groups for further study.

Accountability for development and implementation of solutions and study of remaining issues is assigned to specific individuals. These accountable persons are given the responsibility to report within a specific time frame to the quality improvement body of the institution.

A report on the review is sent to the Quality Improvement Committee of the institution. The focus of the report is the changes recommended or issues for further study, the names of the persons responsible for implementing changes or conducting further study, and the time frame for reporting. Quality monitors may also be recommended in the report. The risk management program will support this process and follow implementation of loss prevention actions recommended by the sentinel event review.

Quality Improvement Committee Interface

It is very important that a formal structure is established that can provide interface between the staff who have responsibility for quality improvement functions and those who are charged with prevention of financial loss. The goals of both of those disciplines is to assure delivery of the best possible patient care and to assure that established standards of care are recognized, documented, and practiced. This can be accomplished through education, development of practice guidelines and/or clinical pathways, and trending and analyzing patient care data. A proactive quality improvement program will identify systems problems and poor practice patterns that contribute to adverse outcomes. It should also meet the needs of external agency requirements.

The organizational structure of a program to improve quality and manage risk should require participation of all practitioners in the department. The chairman of the department has overall responsibility for the quality activities of the department. A system that works well in a large university setting may have a Department QA Liaison who will be responsible for reporting required or appropriate data to the Hospital Quality Improvement Committee. Each division within a department should have a QA coordinator who is responsible for developing indicators for monitoring and reporting. Each practitioner will be responsible for reporting cases that meet indicators to be reviewed on a weekly basis by the Department QA Administrator and Divisional QA Coordinator. The QA Coordinator will be responsible for making sure that appropriate cases are discussed in division meetings. The QA Administrator will be responsible for coordination and monitoring of QA activities and identifying clinical trends and problem areas. All cases identified as potential risk for litigation will be reported to the Hospital Risk Management representative. The Department Quality Improvement Committee will meet at least monthly to review appropriate cases for the purpose of looking at trends or practice patterns and at individual cases that may require further follow-up, corrective action, or loss prevention activities. If a Sentinel Event Review is requested by Risk Management, the Division QA Coordinator will participate in that review process.

Risk Management Case Study

Dr. Clark, Neonatologist, called Sally Smith, Risk Manager, to report that Baby Brown was admitted to the unit about 7:00 a.m. today following shoulder dystocia, one episode of seizure activity, and failure to urinate for the past 6 hours. Mr. Brown, father, and Ms. Rich, grandmother, have been in the unit several times and are visibly upset. They have stated that a nurse told them the baby should have been delivered by Cesarean section several days ago. The Risk Manager made a note to discuss proper relaying of information to patients/families at the next staff meeting of Labor and Delivery nurses. Dr. Clark indicated that the family was still on the unit and agreed to introduce Sally Smith, Risk Manager, to them. Risk Management learned that Ms. Rich was a primary care patient of Dr. Fox, who has been on staff for many years. Dr. Fox agreed to visit her on the unit, since Ms. Rich indicated it might be helpful to talk with someone she knows and trusts. Alice Kane from Social Work was called to counsel the family. Since the family had been with the patient for most of the night, Risk Management reserved a room in a motel within walking distance of the hospital so that they could remain nearby but have an opportunity to get much needed rest. She assured them she would cover the expenses for 3 days as a courtesy. They were very appreciative.

The Risk Manager paged Dr. J. Larsen, who had delivered the baby, and arranged an interview immediately. Dr. Larsen stated that Ms. Brown had received her prenatal care in the Obstetrics Clinic from Drs. Larsen and P. Phillips. Dr. Larsen stated Ms. Brown was a G2P1 diabetic who was seen in the Clinic on the day prior to delivery with a slightly elevated blood pressure and proteinuria. She was admitted for induction of labor. Her induction and early labor were managed by Dr. Phillips. Labor had progressed reasonably well over 14 hours. Dr. Larsen was paged about 6:00 A.M. to report to the labor room urgently because of failure to progress at the second stage of labor. The patient was fully dilated at 4:00 A.M. but had made very slow progress since. The fetus was experiencing some heart rate decelerations to 80-90. The head was crowning when she arrived in the delivery room, but

Ms. Brown's pushing was not effective. Dr. Larsen tried to rotate the anterior shoulder but was unsuccessful and asked the nurse to go for assistance. The episiotomy that was done earlier was made larger. Because of two other imminent deliveries, the help that was sought did not arrive for 6 minutes. The infant was then delivered and had Apgar scores of 2 and 4 at 1 and 5 minutes and was immediately handed to the pediatricians, who intubated her and took her to the intensive care unit.

Nancy Green, RN, indicated that she was the only one assisting with delivery of Baby Brown when Dr. Larsen asked her to go for help. She first paged the anesthesiologist on-call for assistance, but he misunderstood the urgency and continued his rounds on other patients instead of reporting to the labor room as she had requested. She then asked the circulating nurse to go for obstetrical help. In the meantime, the pediatricians awaiting delivery were attempting to apply suprapubic pressure (but were not knowledgeable enough to be effective). The patient's husband was present in the delivery room, so it was difficult to communicate the urgency without causing alarm and perhaps upsetting the patient. When help finally arrived, they were able to deliver the infant with the use of forceps and suprapubic pressure. The infant appeared floppy, but the pediatricians intubated her and took her to the ICU. Nurse Green also indicated that she felt there was not enough staff in the unit to take care of the number of deliveries that night. Three deliveries took place in less than an hour. Without complications they may have been able to manage, but faced with a difficult delivery they had to utilize staff who were rendering care to other patients. Nurse Green and Dr. Larsen were advised not to discuss the case with anyone other than immediate care providers and to send any personal documentation that they might have made to the legal file.

The Risk Manager paged Dr. Phillips and learned that he was not scheduled to be on duty for 2 days. She scheduled a meeting with him and arranged for the monitoring strips to be secured in a special file. She then located the medical record, and noting previous sonography reports, phoned the Radiology Department and requested that any films made during the patient's prenatal care be secured. A review of the medical record indicated that Ms. Brown had experienced slightly elevated blood pressure readings at her last three clinic visits. Her baseline pressure since her early prenatal visits was 108/70. Three weeks ago it was 130/80 and most recently it was recorded as 150/86. Blood glucose was slightly elevated, and the patient's home chart used to monitor daily glucose levels indicated it was not controlled as well as it had been during the previous visits. Obstetric records revealed a request for an urgent consult with Endocrinology, but the response from that consultation was not received in the obstetrics department for several days. The Endocrinologist indicated that glucose control was difficult at that time, and it may be wise to consider induction and early delivery. She noted at those two visits Ms. Brown was seen by Dr. Bleu, on-call resident, since neither Drs. Larsen nor Phillips were available. A sonogram performed 1 month earlier indicated that the fetus had been diagnosed as macrosomic. Baby Brown weighed 4564 g at birth. Review of Baby Brown's medical record revealed that an EEG and CT brain scan were ordered. The admitting note to NICU by Resident Jones listed *Impression: seizure activity, brachial plexus injury, anoxic injury secondary to birth asphyxia*. Demographic data show the family to be from a rural area, father works as a mechanic in a small machine shop that supplies automobile parts, mother is a daycare worker. They have a 2-year-old daughter.

After completing the record review, the Risk Manager paged Dr. Jones and asked him to check his documentation regarding potential birth asphyxia, since his early note does not reflect that this is simply a consideration rather than an established fact. Documentation in the medical record should reflect that the patient is being evaluated to determine the etiology of her problems, and while a working diagnosis may be established, it should be listed as rule-out or "suspected" rather than as a substantiated diagnosis.

The Risk Manager contacted the Obstetrics Department Quality Assurance Chairman and asked that the case be on the agenda for review at the next scheduled meeting. She asked the Risk Management Physician Liaison to review the case and be prepared to present at that time.

The Social Worker informed Risk Management that the family of Baby Brown was anticipating the worst and were overwhelmed with the prospect of taking care of a potentially handicapped child. Sally visited Mr. and Mrs. Brown on the patient unit. She assured them that the hospital would work with them to assess the care needs and to provide assistance in meeting those needs when possible. She informed them that she will be glad to assist them in finding answers to the many issues they have raised regarding her care and the outcome of her delivery. She agreed to arrange a meeting with experts who can provide answers.

The case was presented by Dr. Drew at the Obstetrics Quality Improvement Committee. He stated that he had reviewed the case and had a number of issues regarding the management of Ms. Brown both before and after her delivery. Lack of continuity of care in the clinic may have contributed to an adverse outcome. The record demonstrated that a sonogram 1 month earlier suggested the possibility of a Cesarean delivery. The American College of Obstetrics and Gynecology criteria specify that a fetus of a diabetic patient suspected of weighing > 4000 g should be delivered by Cesarean section. Later, the endocrinologist indicated that blood glucose was becoming difficult to control and an early delivery may be advisable. This information apparently was not made immediately available to the obstetrics staff treating the patient. He also noted that review of the monitoring strips indicated that the fetus had experienced some prolonged decelerations 2 hours before Dr. Larsen was paged, and those apparently were not reported. The Risk Manager stated she found there were other systems problems that had an impact on management of the case. She believed there was insufficient staffing in the Labor and Delivery Rooms. Laboratory results that should have been relayed to medical staff immediately were not made available for several hours. Documentation in the record may be a small problem also. The Committee recommended that sentinel event review be held with all of Ms. Brown's care providers.

After the investigation and all pertinent information had been assembled, the Risk Manager asked Dr. Drew, Obstetrician, to accompany her as she presented the findings to The Quality Liability Management Committee. Dr. Clark, Neonatologist, was invited to present information regarding potential outcome of Infant Brown. He projected that the infant would need Physical Therapy and Rehabilitation Services for several years, although she was expected to be weaned from the ventilator. She would need special schooling at least for several years and maybe longer. It was difficult to determine the extent of disability now. That may not be known until the child is 2 years of age or older. The Committee assisted the Risk Manager in establishing a reserve that was then reported to the insurance carrier for hospital and physician claims.

The Risk Manager informed the Billing Department that she was working with the Brown family and would like to be informed of any patient care balances outstanding after final collection from the patient's medical insurance. She was careful to follow-up with a memo listing the dates of service and asked for a report regarding the amounts of any outstanding balances. She also informed them that the family would be receiving future care and she will also want to be informed and make a decision if it is appropriate to write off patient balances from future accounts. She was informed by Ms. Jackson, Billing Representative, that there is also an outstanding balance for Ms. Brown for antenatal stress testing. The Risk Manager will write a memo to have those bills adjusted also.

When preparation plans for discharge of Baby Brown were under way, the Risk Manager was included in family meetings along with the Neonatologist, Rehabilitation staff, and discharge planning nurse. The baby would be discharged but would have a home care nurse visit each day for 2 weeks. Needs for continuation of that care would be reassessed at that time. A physical therapist visit would occur daily for a month with reassessment of those services periodically. The Risk Manager will receive copies of medical reports and care plans as visits and changes are made. She may assist with financial needs when services are not covered by insurance. The family was told that an investigation was under way and if the institution believed that a financial settlement was the appropriate way to resolve issues and restore good patient relations, the hospital would much prefer to do so through arbitration of the two parties rather than through court trials. The family was also informed that they may retain representative counsel to work with Risk Management if they felt more comfortable with having someone more knowledgeable about legal issues. The family was pleased with the arrangements since they had the help they required to take care of the immediate needs of Baby Brown and could avoid inconvenience and investment of a great deal of time. The Brown family elected to seek representation of a local attorney. It was agreed by both the attorney and Risk Management that any funds provided to take care of the current needs of Baby Brown would be considered part of a final settlement.

The Risk Manager contacted the Quality Improvement Administrator to share plans for the sentinel event review. She was careful to make a list of all staff who had participated in the care of Ms. Brown in the antenatal, delivery, and postpartum periods. The group included obstetricians, pediatricians, and nurses who assisted with labor and delivery, as well as radiologists who interpreted the original studies, and the endocrinologist who was consulted regarding diabetic control. Other members included in the review panel were the Risk Manager, the Physician Chairman of the Hospital Quality Improvement Committee, a Hospital Associate Administrator responsible for nursing, and a chairman, chosen at large to conduct the meeting. The Chairman of Obstetrics was chosen to chair this Sentinel Event Review Panel. The date for the review was established for approximately 1 month after the incident (delivery of Baby Brown). Dr. Larsen began the discussion by summarizing the case. Each member was asked to state his/her role in the patient's care and what obstacles/events he/she believed contributed to a less than satisfactory outcome. The group then made recommendations to prevent recurrence of the care/systems problems they identified. Those recommendations included: 1. assessing staffing needs for the night shift in Labor and Delivery; 2. pick-up and delivery of "stat" laboratory tests and consult reports; and 3. clinic scheduling for continuity.

Conclusion

Developing an effective system for prompt notification of potential claims, a method for working with families and patients toward the mutual goal of early resolution and restoration of good patient relations, and a system for pursuing meaningful loss prevention activities can positively influence professional liability claims for physicians and hospitals. Each system must be tailored to the specific facility and its personnel. An ideal system as described above can serve as a guide in efforts to reduce the cost, both human and financial, of professional liability litigation.

Index

Please note: t refers to tabular matter